First Edition	1970
Second Edition	1972
Third Edition	1977
Fourth Edition	1983
Fifth Edition	1993

Mellows:
The Law of Succession

Fifth Edition

Clive V Margrave-Jones, MA, LLM(Cantab)
Solicitor
Part-time Lecturer in the Faculty of Law, Aberystwyth

Butterworths
London, Dublin, Edinburgh
1993

United Kingdom	Butterworth & Co (Publishers) Ltd, 88 Kingsway, LONDON WC2B 6AB and 4 Hill Street, EDINBURGH EH2 3JZ
Australia	Butterworths, SYDNEY, MELBOURNE, BRISBANE, ADELAIDE, PERTH, CANBERRA and HOBART
Belgium	Butterworth & Co (Publishers) Ltd, BRUSSELS
Canada	Butterworths Canada Ltd, TORONTO and VANCOUVER
Ireland	Butterworth (Ireland) Ltd, DUBLIN
Malaysia	Malayan Law Journal Sdn Bhd, KUALA LUMPUR
New Zealand	Butterworths of New Zealand Ltd, WELLINGTON and AUCKLAND
Puerto Rico	Equity de Puerto Rico, Inc, HATO REY
Singapore	Butterworths Asia, SINGAPORE
USA	Butterworth Legal Publishers, AUSTIN, Texas; BOSTON, Massachusetts; CLEARWATER, Florida (D & S Publishers); ORFORD, New Hampshire (Equity Publishing); ST PAUL, Minnesota; and SEATTLE, Washington

A CIP Catalogue record for this book is available from the British Library.

ISBN 0 406 02438 3

Printed and bound in Great Britain by
Mackays of Chatham PLC, Chatham, Kent

Preface

The Law of Succession has occupied the whole of my professional life. It is a field in which I have specialised as a solicitor in a trust and probate orientated practice. It is also a subject which I have consistently taught to university law students. I therefore hope that this new edition will maintain the traditon of encapsulating the experience of teaching and practice.

I have always warmed to the lively style of the previous editions of this book, which is often more effective in stimulating students than a mere categorisation of rules. Accordingly, I have endeavoured to maintain the character of earlier editions, but in a new format designed to assist the reader to locate more readily the material he or she needs.

Over 10 years have elapsed since the publication of the last edition of this book. During that time there have been some substantial changes to the law, which have been incorporated throughout.

The enforceability of contracts to make a will relating to land has been cast into doubt following the Law of Property (Miscellanous Provisions) Act 1989. Nevertheless, in many cases the doctrine of proprietary estoppel may prove to be a substitute for the former doctrine of part performance.

The decision of *Wood v Smith* of 1992 has clarified the requirements of an operative signature on a will. *Re Finnemore* of the same year exhaustively reviewed the doctrine of dependant relative revocation. In 1993, the Court of Appeal's decision of *White v Jones* reinforced a solicitor's duty of care to disappointed beneficiaries.

Following the Falklands War, the Gulf War and, sadly, the continuing deaths of servicemen in Northern Ireland, privileged wills are still a relevant topic, although it still has to be determined whether under English law a quasi-soldier can take advantage of the privilege.

The chapter on intestacy has been substantially rewritten, in particular to incorporate the amendments effected by the Family Law Reform Act 1987 and the Human Fertilisation and Embryology Act 1990.

As always, there are a plethora of cases relating to family provision, although in a book such as this, there is naturally a limit to the cases that can be considered.

In the area of non-contentious probate, the text has been updated where appropriate in line with the Non-Contentious Probate Rules 1987, as amended in 1991.

The chapter on devolution of settled land has been retained in a shortened form in the hope that it will continue to provide a useful synopsis of the law in a form which may not be readily assimilated from the standard textbooks.

I have always taught *donatio mortis causa* in some detail in the belief that it would one day be reactivated. My confidence has been justified following the decision of the Court of Appeal in 1991 in *Sen v Headley* and the further decision in that year of *Woodwood v Woodwood*. It is felt that this area is due for further revival, and Chapter 34 has been expanded accordingly.

Taxation, especially inheritance tax, is inevitably entwined with the Law of Succession. I have therefore introduced a new taxation division. This division comprises an introduction to the law of inheritance tax, sufficient it is hoped to give the student a feel of the subject. This is followed by a brief conventional treatment of income tax and capital gains tax during the administration of the estate. Finally, in this division has been included a short chapter on estate planning which of necessity is limited, but hopefully provides a sufficient glimpse to stimulate the interest of the student.

I should like to thank my friend and colleague, Cherry Wright for her helpful comments on the balance of the contents of the book. I should also like to thank my colleague Alistair Brierly for reading the chapter on total intestacy.

I should like to express my appreciation to the Butterworths team for their assistance throughout in the preparation of this new edition. I attach particular importance to an index. I have been particularly fortunate that this task was undertaken by Elizabeth Ingham, who received her registration with the Society of Indexes as a result of indexing my *Inheritance Tax Guide*.

Of necessity, in view of the length of the text, as much of the statutory material is readily available elsewhere, the Appendices have been reduced to keep the book within manageable limits. However, I have included a family relationship chart (Appendix D) as I sometimes find that students are confused when describing remoter relatives.

I hope that the new edition of this book will continue to be of interest and use to students studying for degress, and subsequently while undergoing professional training. It is also hoped it is a book worth keeping by them after qualification. Above all I hope that, whoever the reader, he or she will find this subject alive and stimulating.

The law is stated as at 3 September 1993.

Clive V Margrave-Jones
Faculty of Law
Aberystwyth

Contents

Contents

Contents

PART V PROBATE

CHAPTER 16 Grants of representation 247

CHAPTER 17 The appointment of executors and administrators 252

Contents

Contents

Contents

Contents

Contents

Table of statutes

References in this Table to *Statutes* are to Halsbury's Statutes of England (Fourth Edition) showing the volume and page at which the annotated text of an Act may be found.
References in the right-hand column are to paragraph numbers.
Page references printed in **bold** type indicate where the Act is set out in part or in full in the Appendices.

List of cases

List of cases

PARA

Grover's Will Trusts, Re, National
Provincial Bank Ltd v Clarke
(1971) 13.11, 13.12
Grundt's Estate, Re (1915) 17.48
Guardian Trust and Executors Co of
New Zealand Ltd v Darroch
(1973) 8.14, 8.16
Gue, Re, Smith v Gue (1892); affd
(1892) 11.23
Gunnis-Wood, Re (1974) 31.12
Gunstan's (or Gunston) Goods, Re,
Blake v Blake (1882) 6.24
Gurney v Gurney (1855) 6.37
Guthrie v Walrond (1883) 30.7
Gyett v Williams (1862) 30.58
Gyles, Re, Gibbon v Chaytor (1907) . 31.37

H

Haas v Atlas Assurance Co Ltd
(1913) 25.9
Hadley, Re, Johnson v Hadley (1909) . 26.6
Hagger, Re, Freeman v Arscott
(1930) 4.14, 4.18, 4.20, 4.24
Haig, Re, Powers v Haig (1979) . 14.55
Hale's Goods, Re (1915) . . 7.19, 7.21
Hall, Re (1950) 17.49, 19.22
Hall v Hall (1868) 5.49
Hall v Hill (1841) 10.57
Hall v Warren (1861) 10.25
Hall's Estate, Re (1943) 18.17
Hall's Estate, Re, Hall v Knight and
Baxter (1914) 30.64
Hall's Goods, Re (1871) . . . 6.10
Halpin's Goods, Re (1873) . . . 2.11
Halston, Re, Ewen v Halston (1912) . 11.9
Hamer's Estate, Re (1943) 8.90
Hamilton, Re, Trench v Hamilton
(1895) 2.15
Hamilton v Buckmaster (1866) . . . 11.52
Hamilton v Ritchie (1894) . . . 10.14
Hamlet, Re, Stephen v Cunningham
(1888) 10.33
Hammersley v Baron de Biel (1845) . 3.2,
3.4, 3.5, 3.25
Hammond, Re, Hammond v Treharne
(1938) 10.30
Hammond's Estate, Re (1935) . . . 13.16
Hampshire's Estate, Re (1951) . . 8.57
Hampson v Guy (1891) 5.49
Hancock, Re, Hancock v Pawson
(1905) 30.121
Hancocke v Prowd (1670) 28.33
Handley v Stacey (1858) 5.24
Harden's Estate, Re, Clayton and
Hunt v Brown (1959) 5.48
Hardgrave, Re (1978) 31.34
Hardwicke (Earl) v Douglas (1840) . 10.31
Hardy v Shaw (1975) . . . 12.30, 12.32
Hardy's Goods, Re (1861) 8.84
Hardyman, Re, Teesdale v
McClintock (1925) . . . 9.3, 9.5, 11.5

PARA

Harker's Will Trusts, Re, Kean v
Harker (1969) 31.20
Harland Peck, Re, Hercy v
Mayglothing (1941) . . . 32.35, 32.61
Harley v Moon (1861) 30.54
Harman v Harman (1686) 26.39
Harmes v Hinkson (1946) 5.9
Harmood v Oglander (1803) . . . 32.46
Harmore v Brook (1674) 3.13
Harris, Re, Leacroft v Harris (1909) .
30.116
Harris v Fergusson (1848) 23.6
Harris v Knight (1890) . . . 18.43, 18.50
Harrison, Re, Public Trustee v Best
(1934) 34.22
Harrison, Re, Turner v Hellard
(1885) 10.33
Harrison v Jackson (1877) . . . 30.41
Harrison v Rhodes (1753) 31.41
Harrison v Rowan 5.5
Harrison v Rowley (1798) . . 17.30, 27.2
Hart v Tulk (1852) 5.3
Hart's Will Trusts, Re, Public Trustee
v Barclays Bank Ltd (1950) . . . 11.33
Harter v Harter (1873) 5.54
Harvell v Foster (1954); revsd (1954) . 19.34,
22.13, 22.16
Harvey, Re, Banister v Thirtle (1950) . 11.55
Harvey, Re, Public Trustee v Hoskin
(1947) 30.47, 30.49
Harwood v Baker (1840) 5.9
Havergal v Harrison (1843) . . 18.18A
Haves, Re, Haves v Haves (1951) . 30.90
Hawes v Leader (1610) 27.4
Hawkes, Re, Reeve v Hawkes (1912) . 32.7
Hawkesley v May (1956) 28.37
Hawkins, Re, Watts v Nash (1924) . 34.13
Hawkins v Day (1753) 26.48
Hawkins v Hawkins (1880) . . . 30.7
Hawksley's Settlements, Re, Black v
Tidy (1934) 8.26, 10.10
Haynes v Haynes (1853) 30.58
Haynes' Goods, Re (1842) 17.17
Hayward, Re, Kerrod v Hayward
(1957) 12.30, 30.97
Hayward v Kinsey (1701) 28.33
Head v Gould (1898) 28.45
Heath's Goods, Re (1892) 8.85
Heath's Will Trusts, Re, Hamilton v
Lloyds Bank Ltd (1949) 9.9
Heathcote's Estate, Re (1913) . . . 17.36
Heather, Re, Pumfrey v Fryer (1906) .
30.105
Hedges v Hedges (1708) 34.1
Heinke's Estate, Re (1959) 5.24
Helier v Casebert (1665) 28.23
Helliwell, Re, Pickles v Helliwell
(1916) 10.18
Hensman v Fryer (1867) 32.29
Henvell v Whitaker (1827) 32.18
Hepburn v Skirving (1858) 11.46
Hepworth v Hill (1862) 32.4

1

The law of wills

CHAPTER 1

The will in the context of estate planning

1.1 The law of succession in its narrow sense is concerned with the devolution of a person's estate on death. The distribution of the estate is determined by the terms of the deceased's will. To the extent that the disposal of a deceased's estate is not determined by his will, whether because there is no will or the will does not dispose of his entire estate, distribution is governed by the inflexible rules relating to intestacy.

1.2 While technically a testator has total testamentary freedom, in practice restrictions may be imposed on this freedom. Under the family provision legislation the court can override the terms of the will to make provision for dependants. Nevertheless, despite these often limited restrictions, there remains a wide power of disposition on death.

1.3 The law of succession, however, has a broader aspect as part of an ongoing process of giving throughout one's lifetime to plan for death. This aspect of estate planning is often not simply to determine the beneficiaries, but also to effect the transmission of assets from one generation to another, incurring the minimum of tax in the process. In its wider sense therefore, the law of succession is an integral part of estate planning. This process will often commence many years ahead of death by way of making lifetime gifts. Now that inheritance tax is avoided on most lifetime gifts made more than seven years before death, this may be considered a relatively easy exercise based on life expectancy. However, the decision to make a lifetime gift is often much more complex. There is the uncertainty of how much provision a donor should make to protect himself in his old age. There is the possibility that the donee will become a spendthrift, be made bankrupt or predecease the donor. Increasingly, the donor may find that much of what he has given away is dissipated in the donee's divorce settlement. Then there are the vagaries of politics: inheritance tax is a politically sensitive tax and what is planned under one political regime may be undone by another.

1.4 There may even be opposing taxation advantages and disadvantages in making lifetime gifts. Until the Finance Act 1992 the tendency was to make lifetime gifts and hope to survive seven years; in some cases that may not now be the most favourable route. With the effective removal of inheritance tax in many cases in respect of businesses and agricultural property,[1] it may

3

be more beneficial to give them by will than by a lifetime gift. On death such assets may be passed on free of all capital taxes. They do not attract inheritance tax and there is a capital gains tax-free uplift in their value at death[2] that may be passed on to the next generation, notwithstanding that the assets may be sold immediately following death. This is incidental to the more general benefit of enabling a testator to retain control of his assets until death.

1   After 9 March 1992; see below, para 35.26.
2   Taxation of Chargeable Gains Act 1992, s 62(1); see below, para 35.20.

1.5   Accordingly, there are always good reasons for a person to decide to retain the assets in his estate and dispose of them by his will rather than make lifetime gifts.

1.6   There is an increasing tendency to make wills. Even if someone has only a few thousand pounds or less to dispose of he or she may be anxious to appoint a testamentary guardian. It is probable that most people who own their own homes, albeit with the assistance of a mortgage, make a will: owning their own home, their assets are often transformed from being reckoned in only a few thousands to many thousands of pounds. With the dramatic growth in home ownership, the proportion of the population which dies testate steadily increases. Even those intent on making lifetime gifts will usually not give away all their wealth, and there is always a place for a will. More and more, then, a will is changing its nature – from an isolated transaction to but one instrument in several in overall wealth planning.

1.7   In planning any will the intending testator, with his professional advisers, will have regard to:
(a)   the persons to be benefited;
(b)   the circumstances in which they are to be benefited;
(c)   the amount of that benefit;
(d)   the type of that benefit; and
(e)   the means by which that benefit can be conferred with the greatest taxation advantage.
In most cases, the intending testator will have only a very general idea of what is to happen. His professional adviser must seek first to clarify his own thoughts; envisage circumstances which might arise, and ascertain whether account is to be taken of them; and then plan the way in which that result is best to be achieved. Perhaps the most common example is that of a married man with two children, who decides to make a will. He may have decided only that he wants all his property to go to his wife, and then to his children. Does he in fact want his wife to have only a life interest, and so no right to the capital? What is to happen if his wife remarries: is she (and her future husband) to continue to benefit, or are his children to benefit at that stage? If on the death of his wife one of his children is dead, but that child has children of his own, are those children to take the share of the deceased child? The professional adviser has rapidly considered eventualities which probably have not even entered the head of his client.

1.8   When the testator's intentions are ascertained in this way, the taxation implications are then considered. In general, inheritance tax is payable on all the property which a person owns or in which he has a life interest[1] and it is payable on each death. However, if the intending testator leaves all his property to his wife, and he dies first, that property will be free of tax on his death. This, then, may point to the desirability of giving the property to the wife. On the other hand, the more property the wife owns at the date of her death, the greater will be the amount of tax payable at that time and the total tax payable may be reduced if the testator gives part of his property to his wife and part to his children.[2]

1 To the extent that it exceeds the current (1993/94) threshold of £150,000. See below, paras 35.41–35.42.
2 When the combined relief can effectively be increased to, currently (1993/94), £300,000. See below, para 37.4.

1.9 If the property is not to be left to the wife and children in succession, but is to be split up in some other way, questions may arise as to the burden of the tax. Lifetime gifts will benefit first from the inheritance tax-free threshold, thereby throwing the burden of the tax on the estate.[1] The tax payable on the estate itself will, in the absence of a contrary provision in the will, be borne by the residue, not by the specific gifts.[2] A testator may well wish to vary this provision.

1 See below, paras 35.3, 35.18.
2 Inheritance Tax Act 1984, s 211. See below, para 35.58.

1.10 From these simple examples it will be seen that a professional adviser must himself be able to envisage what might happen: know what can be done; and know how best it can be done. The skill in envisaging what might happen is a combination of the logical consideration of possibilities, coupled with the ability to balance a desire on the one hand to make provision for such contingencies and, on the other hand, not to make the will too complicated. Logically, there is no end to the circumstances which might happen, and provision can only be made for some.

1.11 In the second phase, considering what can be done, a will can consist of simple gifts, or it can create a trust. A person can by will tie up wealth for the benefit of his family, either in fixed proportions or in proportions to be fixed later by the exercise of powers of appointment[1] or of selection. Provision can be made for persons outside the family to whom a moral obligation is owed, or even, to a limited extent, for animals and causes.[2] In fact, any type of express trust can be created by will. Even a provision which looks like a simple gift may lead to a trust if the beneficiary is not sui juris when the will comes into effect. Thus, if a testator leaves his estate to his two children at the age of 18 and either of them is under that age at the testator's death, their representative shares will be held in trust until the attainment of that age. A wide investment clause may be desirable, as may be powers of advancement, appropriation, insurance and other clauses designed to facilitate the administration of the estate.

1 A discretionary trust is one of the most flexible methods of providing for future contingencies. They are considered in more detail in paras 37.19, 37.24–37.29.
2 *Pettingall v Pettingall* (1842) 11 LJ Ch 176; *Re Dean* (1889) 41 Ch D 552.

1.12 The third general point, how best the testator's wishes can be brought into effect, will appear from the remainder of this book.

CHAPTER 2

The nature of a will

Definition of a will

Duality of meaning

2.1 The word 'will' has two distinct meanings. The first, and strict, meaning is metaphysical, and denotes the sum of what the testator wishes, or 'wills', to happen on his death. The second, and more common, meaning is physical, and denotes the document or documents in which that intention is expressed. Where there is more than one document which complies with the provisions of the Wills Act 1837, it is customary to refer to the main instrument as the will, and to subsidiary instruments as codicils. However, as the Privy Council observed in *Douglas-Menzies v Umphelby*,[1] all unrevoked testamentary instruments which a man may leave together constitute one will in the strict sense.[2]

1 [1908] AC 224 at 233.
2 See eg *Lemage v Goodban* (1865) LR 1 P & D 57 at 62; *Green v Tribe* (1878) 9 Ch D 231 at 234; *Re Elcom, Layborn v Grover Wright* [1894] 1 Ch 303 at 314, CA.

Characteristics of a will

2.2 A will in the physical sense may, then, be defined as a declaration in prescribed form of the intention of the person making it of the matters which he wishes to take effect on or after his death, until which time it is revocable.[1] This definition indicates the following characteristics of a will:
(a) the scope of a will is not confined to dispositions of property;
(b) a will operates only as a declaration of intention;
(c) it must, usually, be in prescribed form;
(d) it is always revocable;
(e) it takes effect on death; and
(f) it is ambulatory.
These characteristics must now be considered further.

1 This definition is based on that of Hanbury, namely, 'a declaration in prescribed manner of intention of the person making it with regard to matters which he wishes to take effect on his death'.

Scope not limited to property

2.3 Although the primary aim of a will is almost always to dispose of property, a will can also:
(a) appoint executors;
(b) appoint trustees where a trust will arise under the will. The trustees are usually the same persons as the executors, although their function is different,[1] but other persons may be appointed if the testator wishes;
(c) appoint special personal representatives of settled land;[2]
(d) appoint guardians of children who are minors;[3]
(e) revoke previous wills;
(f) confer special powers on executors and trustees, such as the power to invest outside the provisions of the Trustee Investments Act 1961, or the power to distribute the estate in specie, without requiring any consent;[4]
(g) exclude various equitable rules, such as the rules of apportionment known as the rules in *Howe v Earl of Dartmouth*[5] or the rule in *Re Earl of Chesterfield's Trusts*;[6]
(h) give directions as to burial or cremation; sanction the use of the body or eyes for purposes of transplant or other therapeutic or educational use. In many cases directions of this nature are merely declarations of desire, without legal effect, and it is for the executor to decide as to the disposal of the body;
(i) exercise a testamentary power of appointment, that is, a power which the testator has been given under a previous will or settlement and which is exercisable either by deed or will, or by will alone.
A document which effects one or more of the foregoing objects, without disposing of any property, is a will.[7]

1 See below, para 22.1; in essence, the function of an executor is to administer the estate and distribute the assets, whereas the function of a trustee is to retain assets, often for a long period of time.
2 See below, para 24.11; special personal representatives are the persons who are responsible for vesting settled land in the next tenant for life entitled under the settlement following the death of the previous tenant for life.
3 Under the Guardianship of Minors Act 1971, s 4(1), (2), either parent may appoint a testamentary guardian.
4 See below, para 33.1. Administration of Estates Act 1925, s 41, confers a power of appropriation which can in general be exercised only with the consent of the beneficiary.
5 (1802) 7 Ves 137.
6 (1883) 24 Ch D 643.
7 The fact that it is a will does not necessarily mean that it will be admitted to probate. See below, para 18.6.

Declaration of intention only

2.4 The courts have said repeatedly that a will operates only as a declaration of intention.[1] There are two aspects of this. In the first place, by making a will the testator does not in any way interfere with his power of disposition in his lifetime. Accordingly, if the testator makes a will leaving his house to Arthur, he may nevertheless sell or give away the house in his lifetime: in this case Arthur will generally receive nothing under the will even though this provision is not formally revoked.[2] In the second place, the executor has a supervening authority to sell property in the course of the administration of the estate, even if it is the subject of a specific gift in the will.[3] Further, the amount of the deceased's liabilities may be sufficiently large to absorb all of his assets, in which case the dispositive parts of his will will have no effect.[4]

1 *A-G v Jones and Bartlett* (1817) 3 Price 368 at 391; *Re Baroness Llanover* [1903] 2 Ch 330 at 335; *Re Thompson* [1906] 2 Ch 199 at 202; *Re Westminster's Deed of Appointment* [1959] Ch 265 at 271.
2 This is as a result of the doctrine of ademption; see below paras 30.36ff.
3 See below, para 26.28.
4 See below, para 26.30.

Prescribed form

2.5 With one exception, a will must be in writing, signed by the testator or by someone at his direction and in his presence, and it must be witnessed by two persons. These formalities are considered in detail in chapter 6. The exception enables military personnel when on actual military service and sailors at sea to make wills without formality. This type of will, known as a privileged will, is considered in chapter 7.

Revocable

2.6 A will can always be revoked, unless after making it the testator ceases to be of sound mind, and so loses his testamentary capacity. In *Vynior's Case*[1] the will contained a declaration that it was not revocable, but this declaration was held to be invalid. Even if there is a contract not to revoke the will, the will itself may be revoked although an action for damages for breach of contract may lie.[2]

1 (1609) 8 Co Rep 81b.
2 See eg *Synge v Synge* [1894] 1 QB 466.

Takes effect on death

2.7 A will takes effect only on death. Therefore, until death, the beneficiaries and executors have no interest whatever in the testator's property, and they do not acquire any interest until death. Accordingly, if a beneficiary dies between the time when the will is made and the testator's death, his estate will, generally, derive no benefit under the will.[1] On the other hand, as is explained below, it does not necessarily follow that a document which takes effect only on death is a will.

1 Subject to any provision against lapse: see below, para 30.15. See also *Re Currie's Settlement* [1910] 1 Ch 329 at 334.

Ambulatory

2.8 A will is said to be 'ambulatory', that is, as a will does not take effect until death, it is capable of dealing with property acquired after the date when it was made, provided, of course, that such property is still owned by the testator at his death. Thus, a gift by will made in 1993 of 'all my stocks and shares' will include any acquired subsequently and still held by the testator at the date of his death in 1995.[1]

1 In the absence of evidence of a contrary intention.

Wills distinguished from other transactions

Gift inter vivos

2.9 A will is distinguishable from a lifetime (inter vivos) gift as regards both the time when it takes effect and the formalities required. Generally, a gift inter vivos takes effect forthwith, whereas a gift by will takes effect only on death, although a future interest can be conferred by inter vivos gift. The formalities are also different. The only formal requirements of a will are those relating to writing, signature and attestation.[1] Various formalities are necessary for gifts inter vivos. Thus a gift of land must be by deed;[2] a gift of land where the title is registered at the Land Registry must be effected by an instrument of transfer which is registered;[3] a gift of shares in a company must be by transfer and registration;[4] and so on according to the type of property.

1 Above, and see ch 6 below.
2 Law of Property Act 1925, s 51.
3 Land Registration Act 1925, ss 19 to 23.
4 Stock Transfer Act 1963.

2.10 Usually, of course, there is no problem in deciding whether a document is intended to effect a gift inter vivos or to operate as a will. In some cases, however, this has caused difficulty. In *Milnes v Foden*[1] Sir James Hannen P laid down this test:

'The true principle appears to be that if there is proof, either in the paper itself or from clear evidence dehors, first that it was the intention of the writer of the paper to convey the benefits by the instrument which would be conveyed by it if considered as a will; secondly, that death was the event which was to give effect to it, then whatever may be its form it may be admitted to probate as testamentary. It is not necessary that the testator should intend to perform or be aware that he has performed a testamentary act.'

Thus, in *Re Morgan's Goods*[2] a settlor executed three deeds of gift under which property was given to trustees for the benefit of children, and the deeds provided that they were not to take effect before the settlor's death. These deeds were held to amount to wills, and probate was granted accordingly. In *Re Slinn's Goods*[3] a woman granted her savings to her niece by a deed which also complied with the formal requirements of the Wills Act 1837. The court admitted extrinsic evidence that she wished to settle her affairs, and held that this document could be admitted to probate.[4]

1 (1890) 15 PD 105.
2 (1866) LR 1 P & D 214.

3 (1890) 15 PD 156.
4 See also *Re Montgomery's Goods* (1846) 5 Notes of Cases 99; *Robertson v Smith* (1870) LR
   2 P & D 43; *Re Anziani* [1930] 1 Ch 407; *Fielding v Walshaw, Re Walshaw's Goods* (1879)
   48 LJP 27; *Green v Andrews* (1877) 41 JP 105.

2.11 If, however, an attempt has been made to create a gift inter vivos, but
the attempt has been ineffective, then the document by which that attempt
has been made will not be regarded as a will, even though it refers to the
person's death.[1] This is because a person must intend a document to take
effect on death if it is to be admitted as a will. The courts, therefore,
attempt to ascertain the intention of the donor, and then to examine
whether the formal requirements of the method of disposition which he
attempted to make have been satisfied.

1 *Dillon v Coppin* (1839) 4 My & Cr 647; *Re Halpin's Goods* (1873) 8 IR Eq 567.

Revocable settlement inter vivos

2.12 If Andrew wishes to leave his house to Benjamin, he may do so by
will in the usual way. He may also achieve a result which is similar in many
respects by conveying the house inter vivos to trustees to hold upon trust for
Andrew for life with remainder to Benjamin. Andrew may also include a
power of revocation in the deed to provide himself with the equivalent
power to revoking his will. If Benjamin survives Andrew, the result would
for many purposes be the same as if the gift had been made by will.[1] But
Benjamin has, on the making of the settlement, received an interest in
remainder. If, therefore, Benjamin predeceases Andrew, without Andrew
revoking the settlement, Benjamin's estate will take the interest which
Benjamin would have taken if he had survived.[2] Thus, a revocable
settlement creates a present interest in property, whereas a will confers an
interest only upon death.

1 There are differences. The property subject to a settlement, unless the settlement could be
   avoided as having been made in defraud of creditors (under Insolvency Act 1986, s 423 or
   Law of Property Act 1925, s 172) cannot be taken as assets for the payment of creditors (see
   below, para 26.13), nor would it abate on an insufficiency to pay legacies (see below, paras
   30.53ff).
2 As to the doctrine of lapse which applies where a similar position arises by will, see below
   para 30.15.

Donatio mortis causa

2.13 A donatio mortis causa is a revocable gift by a person made in
contemplation of his impending death, and conditional upon that death. It is
considered fully in chapter 34.

Nominations

2.14 A nomination is a direction to a person who holds funds on behalf of
another to pay those funds in the event of death to a nominated person. In

many cases, nominations operate by statute, and their effect is considered later.[1] However, there can also be non-statutory nominations, particularly in connection with pension schemes. The rules of many pension schemes provide, in essence, that if the employee dies during the course of his employment the amount of his contributions will be paid to a person nominated by the employee in writing, and in the absence of any nomination to the employee's personal representatives. Where a nomination is made, it does not operate as a will. While the document does affect the devolution of property on death, the property passes directly from the fund to the nominee, and at no time forms part of the estate. The nomination operates by virtue of the rules of the scheme, and not as a will, and it does not, therefore, have to satisfy the requirements of the Wills Act.[2]

1 See paras 25.6–25.8.
2 Chappenden [1972] JBL 20.

Precatory instruments

2.15 There are a number of decisions encountered in the law of trusts as to precatory words where, in essence, one person leaves property to another and expresses the hope that the recipient will apply that property to a particular purpose without imposing any trust or obligation to that effect.[1] If a person executes an instrument intending it to be a guide only, but without intending it to be binding on any person, it may be conveniently referred to as a precatory instrument. It will not be admitted to probate and will have no binding effect.[2] In *Re Littler*[3] the court was concerned with the estate, valued at over £1m, of Prince Littler, who was known as a 'king' of pantomime. At the same time as making what was accepted as a codicil to his will, he signed and had witnessed two documents setting out about 40 gifts of money and personal property to friends and employees. Evidence was given that the deceased wanted to indicate his wishes to his executors by those documents, but to leave it to them to decide whether to give effect to the gifts. The case was settled, and Walton J was not called upon to give a decision. If, however, he had accepted that evidence, the documents would have had no binding force, even though executed with the formalities of a will.

1 Eg *Lambe v Eames* (1871) 6 Ch App 597; *Re Adams and Kensington Vestry* (1884) 27 Ch D 394; *Re Diggles, Gregory v Edmondson* (1888) 39 Ch D 253; *Re Hamilton, Trench v Hamilton* [1895] 2 Ch 370; *Comiskey v Bowring–Hanbury* [1905] AC 84. The practice has received statutory recognition: see Inheritance Tax Act 1984, s 143.
2 *Griffin and Amos v Ferard* (1835) 1 Curt 97; *Re Blow* (1978) 82 DLR (3d) 721.
3 See the *Daily Telegraph* for 26 February 1975.

Dispositive effect of a will

2.16 The Wills Act 1837, s 3, provides that every person may dispose of his real and personal property, whether legal or equitable, by will. When a will became operative following the passing of that Act, therefore, the will itself operated to pass the legal estate in property where the testator himself had the legal estate vested in him. This was modified by Sch 9, Law of Property

(Amendment) Act 1924, which provides that 'the Wills Act 1837 takes effect to enable equitable interests to be disposed of subject and without prejudice to the estate and powers of a personal representative'. Although it could have been expressed more clearly, the result of this provision is that a will operates only to confer an equitable interest on the beneficiary.[1,2] The legal interest devolves on the executor, and if he does not require the property for the purposes of the administration of the estate, he transfers it to the beneficiary. In view of this, it is sometimes said that a will now takes effect only in equity.[3] Although this is true in so far as property is concerned, a will does have significance for the legal estate, because the legal estate will devolve upon the executors named in the will merely by virtue of their appointment as such.[4]

1 *Bennett v Slater* [1899] 1 QB 45; *Eccles Provident Industrial Co-operative Society Ltd v Griffiths* [1912] AC 483 at 490; *Re Danish Bacon Co Ltd Staff Pension Fund, Christensen v Arnett* [1971] 1 All ER 486.
2 Although even this 'equitable interest' is only of a limited type; see below, para 29.1.
3 Eg *Williams on Wills* (6th edn) p 7.
4 See below, para 23.3.

Terminology

It may be convenient at this stage to indicate the meaning of terms frequently used.

Codicil

2.17 Any document which complies with the formal requirements of the Wills Act, and is intended to operate on death, may be described as a will.[1] As has been said,[2] however, it is more usual to refer to the document which is the primary testamentary instrument as the will, and to any testamentary document which modifies or varies it as a codicil.

1 *Douglas-Menzies v Umphelby* [1908] AC 224 at 233.
2 Above, para 2.1.

Executors, administrators and personal representatives

2.18 In general terms, an executor is the person appointed by the will to administer the estate.[1] Where the deceased dies intestate, that is, without leaving a will which disposes of property,[2] or where he leaves a will without appointing executors, the person who administers the estate is known as the administrator. Their functions are the same, and their positions similar.[3] Executors and administrators are known collectively as personal representatives.

1 See below, para 17.2, for a more detailed definition.
2 Administration of Estates Act 1925, s 55(1)(vi).
3 See below, para 22.1.

Bequests and devises

2.19 A bequest is a gift by will of personalty, and a devise is a gift by will of realty. Although both terms are still met frequently, the word 'gift' itself is appropriate to cover both.

CHAPTER 3

Testamentary contracts and promises

3.1 Consider this situation. Albert, an elderly man, asks Beryl to move into his house and to look after him for the rest of his life. He tells her that if she does so, she will have the house on his death. Beryl moves into the house, and looks after Albert, but on his death it is found that he did not make a will leaving the house to her. Is she entitled to it? Or this situation: David makes a will leaving all his property to his niece, Nell. He then asks Nell to live in his house and look after him, and he promises that if she does so he will not alter his will. On his death it is found that David did alter the will, and made a new one leaving all his property to his brother, Eric. Is Nell entitled to his property? In these and any other cases where it is alleged that there was a contract to make a will, or a contract not to revoke a will, it is necessary to ask the following questions:

(a) Can the contract be valid?
(b) If so, what is the general nature of the alleged contract?
(c) Is there in fact a contract at all?
(d) Is the contract enforceable?
(e) What is the position if the contract is broken?
(f) To what extent, if at all, will the court vary the contract?
(g) What relief, if any, is available if there is no contract, or no enforceable contract?

Is the contract valid?

3.2 It was stated earlier in this book[1] that a will can always be revoked. How, therefore, can a contract not to revoke a will be valid? And how can a contract to make a will be valid if it is an express or implied term of that contract that the will, once made, will not be revoked? Does not such a contract conflict with the fundamental notion of freedom of testamentary disposition? The courts adopt two principles. First, a contract to make a will is capable of being valid.[2] So, in *Synge v Synge*[3] the court upheld a contract by the deceased to make a will leaving property to a woman whom he wished to marry. Likewise a contract that the intending testator will leave his house to a woman if she will act as his housekeeper can be valid.[4] The second principle is that while probate must be granted of the last valid will of the deceased, whether or not it accords with contractual obligations which he incurred, if the contractual obligations are still subsisting, but are inconsistent with the will, then the court will act outside the will to give effect to them. The rules as to freedom of testamentary disposition, and as to the revocability of wills do not, therefore, make any such contract automatically invalid.[5]

1 Above, para 2.6.
2 *Hammersley v De Biel* (1845) 12 Cl & Fin 45; *Laver v Fielder* (1862) 32 Beav 1; *Coverdale v Eastwood* (1872) LR 15 Eq 121; *Re Fickus, Farina v Fickus* [1900] 1 Ch 331; *Synge v Synge* [1894] 1 QB 466; *Re Edwards, Macadam v Wright* [1958] Ch 168, [1957] 2 All ER 495; *Parker v Clark* [1960] 1 All ER 93; *Schaefer v Schuhmann* [1972] AC 572, [1972] 1 All ER 621, PC.
3 [1894] 1 QB 466.
4 *Re Edwards, Macadam v Wright* [1958] Ch 168, [1957] 2 All ER 495; *Parker v Clark* [1960] 1 All ER 93.
5 See Lee 'Contracts to make Wills' (1971) 87 LQR 358.

The general nature of the alleged contract

Contracts to make a will

3.3 If there is a contract to make a will, it will fall into one of two broad categories:
(a) a contract merely to make the will; or
(b) a contract to ensure that specified property will pass to the promisee on death in any event.
If the contract comes within the first category, it is completely discharged by performance when the will is made; and if it is not made the promisee is entitled to be placed only in the same position as if it had been made. In the decision of the Privy Council in *Dillon v Public Trustee of New Zealand*[1] Henry Dillon was involved in litigation with his sons. Eventually this was settled on the basis that he would make a will leaving certain land to them. He made a will in accordance with the terms of settlement, leaving the land to the sons, and the remainder of his property to his wife. After his death, the widow applied to the New Zealand court for an order extending her benefit under the will. It will be seen[2] that in England and Wales, as well as in New Zealand and in most other Commonwealth jurisdictions, the court has the power to alter the effects of the will to make provisions, or greater provision, for spouses and certain other persons.[3] In this case, the Privy Council held that at least for the purposes of this legislation, Henry Dillon had completely discharged his obligations under the contract by making the will, and that his children were in the same position as any other devisee. Thus, it was held that the court had power to give the whole or part of the land to the widow, to exactly the same extent as it would have had this power if the will had not been made in pursuance of any contract.

1 [1941] AC 294, [1941] 2 All ER 284, PC.
2 Below, paras 14.1ff.
3 In *Dillon* the application was made under the Family Protection Act 1908 (New Zealand).

3.4 It follows, therefore, that if the contract is merely a contract to make a will, there is no assurance to the promisee that he will receive any property on the death of the deceased. A contract merely to make a will does not imply that the will, once made, will not be revoked. Even if the will is not revoked the assets may be required for the payment of the deceased's liabilities, so that they may not pass to the beneficiaries named in the will. But if there is in fact a contract, it is unlikely that the parties will have intended these results. Accordingly, where there is no clear arrangement to the contrary, the court gives effect to a contract to make a will, as if it is one to ensure that the property will pass to the promisee on the death of the deceased in any event.[1] In this case the contractual obligation is only discharged by performance when the property has actually passed to the promisee; and if it does not effectively do so under the deceased's will, the promisee has a claim against his estate. *Dillon v Public Trustee of New Zealand* must be contrasted with the later case of *Schaefer v Schuhmann*.[2] In a nice example of the combination of the old and new worlds, the testator lived at 124 Nuwarra Road, Chipping Norton. When he was in poor health, he engaged a housekeeper to look after him and his house at a salary of $12 a week. About two months later, he agreed with the housekeeper that she would cease to be paid, but would become entitled to the house on his death. The testator then executed a codicil to give effect to this agreement. Following his death, the testator's daughters made an application under the New South Wales family provision legislation[3] and the court was minded to increase their legacies. The question was whether any part of the value represented by the house could be taken for this purpose, and the Privy Council held that it could not. In this case the contract was construed as a contract to procure that the house would pass to the housekeeper in any event, so that it was not discharged when the testator executed the codicil.[4]

1 *Hammersley v De Biel* (1845) 12 Cl & Fin 45; *Synge v Synge* [1894] 1 QB 466.
2 [1972] AC 572, [1972] 1 All ER 621, PC.
3 Testator's Family Maintenance and Guardianship of Infants Act 1916–1954.
4 See Gordon 'The Contract between Limitations on Testamentary Power by Statute and Contract' (1941) 19 Can BR 603, (1942) 20 Can BR 72.

Contracts not to revoke a will

3.5 A similar point arises where there is a contract not to revoke an existing will, or a contract not to revoke a provision in an existing will. It is clear that such a contract is valid, notwithstanding the revocable nature of wills,[1] and although the court will not restrain the revocation of the will itself, it will recognise the contract by restraining the disposal of the property in contravention of the agreement,[2] or award damages.[3] The question here is whether the testator merely contracts that he will not revoke the will, or whether he contracts that the property will pass to the promisee in any event. Clearly, if the testator himself revokes the will he is in breach of his contract in either case. However, a will can also be revoked by operation of law. It will be seen that, in general, where a person who makes a will subsequently marries, the will is revoked automatically on that marriage;[4] and also that where a beneficiary dies before the testator the gift in the will for that beneficiary lapses.[5] If the contract is merely a contract not to revoke a will, the contract will not be regarded as being broken where the revocation occurs by operation of law,[6] but where the contract is to procure that the property will pass to the promisee in any event, the contractual obligations will remain outstanding until death.[7]

1 *Robinson v Ommanney* (1883) 23 Ch D 285; *Re Marsland, Lloyds Bank Ltd v Marsland* [1939] Ch 820, [1939] 3 All ER 148. As to the revocable nature of wills, see above, para 2.6.
2 *Synge v Synge* [1894] 1 QB 466.
3 *Hammersley v De Biel* (1845) 12 Cl & Fin 45. In *Staib v Powell* [1979] Qd R 151, the Queensland court gave effect to a contract by the testator not to revoke a will conferring a benefit on, inter alios, his daughter-in-law made in consideration of his daughter-in-law agreeing to look after him and his wife.
4 Below, para 8.61.
5 Below, para 30.15.
6 *Re Marsland, Lloyds Bank v Marsland*, above.
7 See *Robinson v Ommanney*, above.

3.6 When considering the remainder of this chapter, it is important in each case to be clear as to the nature of the contract or alleged contract which is being considered.

Is there a contract?

3.7 It is now necessary to consider whether there is in fact a contract. For there to be a valid contract to make a will, or a valid contract not to revoke a will, there must be the same basic elements as with any other ordinary contract. The elements are as follows.

Intention to enter into contractual relationship

3.8 The testator must intend, at the time of the alleged contract, thereby to enter into a binding obligation either to make a will or not to revoke a will. This test will not be satisfied if, for example, the testator announces his intention of making some testamentary provision, but nevertheless of retaining his freedom to change his mind.[1] Likewise, the test will not be satisfied if the testator merely describes an existing state of affairs, such as that he has made a will leaving his property equally among his children.[2] Rather less obviously, if the testator executes an instrument which he thinks will operate as an inter vivos gift, he cannot thereby intend to make a will, which will operate only on his death.[3] Where the testator intends to make a will, but it is not clear whether he intends to bind himself to do so, his relationship, if any, with the promisee may be taken into account. If the degree of relationship is very close, as in the case of a testator intending to make provision for his spouse, this fact may raise a presumption that there is no intention to enter into a binding obligation to do so.[4]

1 *Re Hudson, Creed v Henderson* (1885) 54 LJ Ch 811; *Sinnett v Herbert* (1871) LR 12 Eq 201 at 206; *Re Fickus, Farina v Fickus* [1900] 1 Ch 331.
2 *Re Allen, Hincks v Allen* (1880) 49 LJ Ch 553.
3 *Vincent v Vincent* (1887) 56 LT 243.
4 See, by analogy, *Shadwell v Shadwell* (1860) 9 CBNS 159; *Balfour v Balfour* [1919] 2 KB 571; *Jones v Padavatton* [1969] 2 All ER 616.

Offer and acceptance

3.9 The acceptance may take the form of making a reciprocal will[1] but it often takes the form of the doing of a non-testamentary act. Thus, if a man offers to make a will in favour of a woman if she will marry him, she may accept the offer by marrying.[2] And, as has been shown, a person may accept the offer by acting as a housekeeper.[3]

1 As in the case of mutual wills: see below, para 4.6.
2 *Re Broadwood, Edwards v Broadwood (No 2)* (1912) 56 Sol Jo 703.
3 *Schaefer v Schuhmann* [1972] AC 572, [1972] 1 All ER 621, PC.

Consideration

3.10 The contract may be for consideration, or made by deed. If it is not for consideration but by deed, it will be enforced by damages but not by specific performance.[1]

1 *Robinson v Ommanney* (1883) 23 Ch D 285; *Re Parkin, Hill v Schwarz* [1892] 3 Ch 510; *Beyfus v Lawley* [1903] AC 411.

Certainty of obligation

3.11 A testator may intend to enter into a contract, but the terms may not be sufficiently specific for a contract to be in existence. Thus, in one case[1] the House of Lords held that there was no contract where the testator agreed that he would not alter his will 'unless unforeseen events occur'.

1 *Maunsell v White* (1854) 4 HL Cas 1039.

Certainty of subject matter

3.12 The property which is to pass under the will must be specified with sufficient certainty, but where the other requisite elements are present, the courts will strive to hold that the subject matter has been sufficiently identified. Thus, in an old case[1] the court upheld a contract to make a will leaving a beneficiary a sufficient sum of money to enable him to purchase a property at £1,500 cheaper than the highest prospective purchaser would pay. But sometimes the subject matter is too vague. Thus, an alleged contract to make a will making 'ample provision' for a person is not capable of being enforced.[2] In some circumstances, the problem is to ascertain the time at which the property is to be identified. Suppose the testator promises to leave to the promisee 'all I have'. Is this everything which the testator owns when the promise is made? Or does it include property which is acquired afterwards? Or does it just mean such property as the testator has at the date of his death? The parties could validly enter into any of these arrangements but, in the absence of clear intention to the contrary, the court will construe a contract in these terms as covering only the property which the testator owns at the date of his death. On this basis, there is no implied promise that the testator will not reduce his estate during his lifetime[3] and it follows that the testator is at liberty to dispose in his lifetime of property which he acquires after the promise is made.[4]

1 *Bromly v Fettiplace* (1700) Freem Ch 245.
2 *MacPhail v Torrance* (1909) 25 TLR 810.
3 *Cochran v Graham* (1811) 19 Ves 63; *Needham v Smith* (1828) 4 Russ 318; *Palmer v Bank of New South Wales* [1973] 2 NSWLR 244.
4 *Needham v Kirkman* (1820) 3 B & Ald 531.

3.13 While in cases such as this the court will not restrict the testator's powers of outright disposition inter vivos, it will restrict attempts by the testator to make a disposition of his property in his lifetime which will nevertheless give him the use of property during his lifetime, and an effective power of disposal on his death. If, therefore, the testator promises to leave all his property to the promisee, the court will intervene if in his lifetime he disposes of property to trustees to hold upon trust for himself during the remainder of his life, and thereafter to such persons as he should appoint.[1] Likewise, it seems that where the promise relates to only part of the testator's property, while he can make a genuine outright disposal of the whole or part of that property, if he converts the form of that property into other property which he retains, the conversion will not be allowed to operate to the disadvantage of the promisee. There is little authority on this, but in *Lewis v Madocks*[2] the contract was to make a will leaving all the testator's personalty to the promisee. The testator sold some of his personalty, and used it for the purchase of land. The court held that the land stood charged with a sum equal to the purchase money in favour of the promisee.[3] It is by no means clear how far this principle extends. If the testator promises to leave his furniture to the promisee, and during his lifetime he sells a table and buys a motor car, it is unclear whether the promisee is entitled to a sum of money charged on the motor car.

1 *Harmore v Brook* (1674) Cas temp Finch 183; *Jones v Martin* (1798) 6 Bro Parl Cas 437.
2 (1803) 8 Ves 150.
3 See also *Cochran v Graham*, above.

Is the contract enforceable?

3.14 Where a contract to make a will involving the disposition of land was made before 28 September 1989, it falls within the scope of s 40, Law of Property Act 1925. If such a contract was made on or after that date, it falls within the provisions of s 2, Law of Property (Miscellaneous Provisions) Act 1989. As a contract may have been made long before the testator's death, it will therefore be necessary to consider both the old and the new law.

Contracts made before 28 September 1989

3.15 Where the contract to make a will involving the disposition of land was made before 28 September 1989, it is governed by s 40, Law of Property Act 1925. The section provides that the contract will be enforceable only if there is a note or memorandum in writing of the contract, signed by the deceased or by some other person authorised by him.[1] A will itself may constitute such a note or memorandum, so that where the deceased made a will reciting the contract, and subsequently revoked the will, that will, although revoked, was held to constitute a sufficient memorandum for the purposes of the provision.[2]

1 *Humphreys v Green* (1882) 10 QBD 148; *Maddison v Alderson* (1883) 8 App Cas 467.
2 *Johnson v Nova Scotia Trust Co* (1973) 43 DLR (3d) 222.

3.16 Where there is no note or memorandum in writing, the contract may nevertheless be enforceable under the equitable doctrine of part performance.[1] For this doctrine to apply, the plaintiff must establish:
(a) that he acted on the contract to his detriment;
(b) that the acts in question indicate, on the balance of probabilities, the existence of a contract;
(c) that the acts in question indicate that the contract relates to land;[2]
(d) that the acts in question establish a contract concerning the particular land;[3] and
(e) that the acts in question are consistent with the terms of the contract as alleged.

1 Preserved in Law of Property Act 1925, s 40(2).
2 *Steadman v Steadman* [1976] AC 536, [1974] 2 All ER 977, HL; *Nicholson v Lyle Estate* (1974) 10 NSR (2d) 78; *Re Gonin, Gonin v Garmeson* [1979] Ch 16, [1977] 2 All ER 720.
3 *Re Gonin*, above.

3.17 On the first of these requirements, nothing further need be said. On the second requirement, whether or not the acts in question indicate, on the balance of probabilities, the existence of a contract, is a question to be decided on the facts of each case, but in the classic case where a woman moves into a house to look after the deceased, two considerations are particularly important:
(a) What is the relationship between the testator and the plaintiff?
(b) What, if anything, did the plaintiff give up in order to move into the house?
On the first point, it has been seen[1] that where the relationship is close, that may suggest that there is no contract in existence. On the second point, it is much more likely that there is a contract if the promisee has given up something of value than if he has not.

1 Above, para 3.8.

3.18 In the well-known decision in *Maddison v Alderson*[1] the appellant alleged that she had served the deceased, a farmer, as his housekeeper in consideration of an oral promise which he made to her that he would leave a farmhouse to her. At first she received wages, but latterly continued in his service without wages. The deceased had signed a will in her favour, but the will was ineffective because it was not witnessed,[2] and as a result the deceased died intestate.[3] The House of Lords held that there was no sufficient act of part performance. The fact that the appellant continued in the service of the deceased without remuneration did not necessarily point to the existence of a contract: it was equally explicable on the basis that the appellant might have wanted a home; or hoped that the deceased would in due course provide her with some, as then unspecified, reward. As it has been subsequently interpreted,[4] the crucial fact in *Maddison v Alderson* was that the appellant did not dispose of a property or give up a tenancy in order to live with and look after the deceased. This decision is to be contrasted with *Wakeham v Mackenzie*.[5] The deceased orally agreed with the plaintiff that if she would move into his house and look after him for the rest of his life, she should have the house and contents when he died. The parties agreed that she should pay £2 a week for her board. At that time the plaintiff had a tenancy of a council flat, but she gave that up, moved into the deceased's house, looked after him, and paid the agreed weekly sum. All these facts, when taken together, were held to indicate the existence of a contract.[6]

1 (1883) 8 App Cas 467.
2 As to witnessing, see below, para 6.26.
3 The intestacy provisions are discussed in ch 12.
4 In *Wakeham v Mackenzie* [1968] 2 All ER 783.
5 Above.
6 See also *Thompson v Guaranty Trust Co of Canada* (1973) 39 DLR (3d) 408, where the appellant performed valuable and arduous services in the operation and management of a farm, on which the deceased relied, in pursuance of an oral contract by the deceased to leave the farm to the appellant. The Supreme Court of Canada held that there was sufficient act of part performance.

3.19 The need for the person seeking to establish the existence of a contract to show that his acts indicate the particular contract alleged is harshly illustrated by the Alberta decision in *Shillabeer v Diebel*.[1] In that case the testator's son claimed that the testator promised to leave his house to the son if the son paid him rent for ten years, and thereafter paid the taxes and insurance in respect of the property. The son paid the rent, taxes and insurance, and also maintained the property. The court held[2] that the acts of the son were not unequivocal evidence of the existence of the alleged contract, as they were equally consistent with the grant of a lease.

1 (1980) 100 DLR (3d) 279.
2 Following *Steadman v Steadman* [1976] AC 536, [1974] 2 All ER 977, HL.

Contracts made after 27 September 1989

3.20 Where the contract to make a will involving the disposition of land is made after 27 September 1989 it falls within the provisions of s 2, Law of Property (Miscellaneous Provisions) Act 1989. The section provides that such a contract must:
(a) be in writing and incorporate all the terms agreed in one document;[1]
(b) incorporate all the terms in a document, either by setting them out in the document or by reference to some other document; and
(c) be signed by or on behalf of each party to the contract.
As the contract itself must be in writing and signed by all the parties, a will, being signed by the testator only, cannot form the contract.[2] This is in contrast to the earlier position where the will itself could constitute a memorandum.[3] In practice therefore most attempts to enter into a contract

to make a will involving the disposition of land will now fail to comply with s 2.

1 There is also provision, not relevant in the case of a will, for exchange of two identical documents.
2 An interesting situation would arise if the other party were a witness to the will that incorporated the terms, either in it or by reference to another document. The witness could not benefit under the will but the testator would not be in breach of the contract as he would have made a valid will; it presumably could be argued that it was not an effective will to make a gift to the intended party; see above, para 3.5.
3 *Johnson v Nova Scotia Trust Co* (1973) 43 DLR (3d) 222.

Proprietary estoppel

3.21 It must be considered therefore whether the doctrine of proprietary estoppel is available to assist a party who has acted to his detriment having been encouraged to believe that he would inherit. This fell to be determined in *Re Basham*.[1] The deceased had married the plaintiff's mother in 1941 when the plaintiff was 15. From that time onwards until the deceased retired some 30 years later, the plaintiff had worked for the deceased without payment, initially helping him to run various public houses and subsequently a service station. On a number of occasions the plaintiff and her husband contemplated moving from the area, but were dissuaded from so doing in the belief, encouraged by the deceased, that he would leave his estate to the plaintiff on his death. The deceased subsequently died intestate, leaving two nieces as his statutory next of kin. It fell on Edward Nugee QC to determine whether the plaintiff could rely on the principle of proprietary estoppel, which he considered may in its broadest form be stated as follows:[2]

'Where one person (A) has acted to his detriment on the face of a belief, which was known to and encouraged by another person (B), that he either has or is going to be given a right in or over B's property, B cannot insist on his strict legal rights if to do so would be inconsistent with A's belief. The principle is commonly known as proprietary estoppel, and since the effect of it is that B is prevented from asserting his strict legal rights it has something in common with estoppel. But in my judgment, at all events where the belief is that A is going to be given a right in the future, it is properly to be regarded as giving rise to a species of constructive trust, which is the concept employed by a court of equity to prevent the person from relying on his legal rights where it would be unconscionable for him to do so. The rights to which proprietary estoppel gives rise, and the machinery by which effect is given to them, are similar in many respects to those involved in cases of secret trusts, mutual wills and other comparable cases in which property is vested in B on the faith of an understanding that it will be dealt with in a particular manner.'

1 [1987] 1 All ER 405.
2 Ibid at 410.

3.22 The judge then proceeded to set out the four criteria necessary to establish proprietary estoppel:

(a) the plaintiff must have a belief at all material times that she was going to receive the deceased's property on his death;
(b) that belief had been encouraged by the deceased;
(c) the plaintiff had acted to her detriment; and
(d) the acts done by the plaintiff were done in reliance on or as a result of her belief that she would become entitled to the deceased's property on his death.

The facts of the case satisfied these criteria and the plaintiff was entitled to the deceased's estate accordingly.

3.23 The doctrine of proprietary estoppel, although more restrictive than the former doctrine of part performance, may prove to be a useful alternative in appropriate cases in overcoming the rigidity of s 2 of the 1989 Act.

Breach of contract

When the breach occurs

3.24 Where there is a contract to make a will, it is normally broken at the date of death of the deceased. If, however, the contract is to leave a specific item of property which the deceased disposes of in his lifetime, the contract is broken at the time of the disposal.[1] If the contract is to make the will by a particular date, the contract is broken at that date. If the contract is not to revoke a will, it is broken at the time of revocation.

1 *Synge v Synge* [1894] 1 QB 466.

Damages

3.25 Where the contract is broken, the basic remedy is in damages.[1] However, the amount of the damages is not necessarily the value of the property itself. If the contract is broken during the lifetime of the deceased, the value of the property must be discounted. Suppose that the deceased agreed to leave to the plaintiff a house, and that he sells that house in his lifetime for its full market value of £100,000. The plaintiff has lost not £100,000, but the right to receive £100,000 upon the death of the deceased. Having regard to the age and health of the deceased at the time of breach, the actuarial value of the right to receive £100,000 on his death might be only, say, £50,000, and that sum will be the amount of damages. Secondly, if the contract was merely to make a will, rather than to procure that specific property would pass to the plaintiff in any event, the damages will be calculated on the basis that the property might be taken for debts, or might be subject to intervention by the court under the family provision legislation.[2]

1 *Hammersley v De Biel* (1845) 12 Cl & Fin 45; *Synge v Synge*, above.
2 *Dillon v Public Trustee of New Zealand* [1941] AC 294, [1941] 2 All ER 284, PC.

Specific performance; injunction

3.26 Where the contract was to procure the passing of property to the plaintiff in any event, an order for specific performance may be granted.[1] Further, if the plaintiff learns that the testator is planning to dispose of the property, he may obtain an injunction to restrain the disposal.[2]

1 *Goilmere v Baltison* (1682) 1 Vern 48; *Dufour v Pereira* (1769) 1 Dick 419; *Coverdale v Eastwood* (1872) LR 15 Eq 121.
2 *Synge v Synge*, above.

The order of the court

3.27 Where, following the death of the deceased, the court awards damages, or grants a decree of specific performance, on the ground that a contract has been broken, it will operate behind the will, but it will not alter the will itself. The will is a valid will, and must be admitted to probate. If the property is still in the hands of the personal representatives, the court will order the personal representatives to transfer the property to the plaintiff in the course of the administration of the estate. If the personal representatives have parted with the property, the court will order the beneficiary to transfer it.

Benefit under other title

3.28 The doctrine of satisfaction[1] may apply where the promisee is entitled to damages for breach of a contract to make, or not to revoke, a will in his favour, but where he is entitled to some benefit from the deceased's estate, as where he is entitled on intestacy. The amount of the entitlement on intestacy is deducted from the entitlement to damages, and if the entitlement on intestacy exceeds the damages, no damages are in fact recoverable.[2] It seems, however, that this doctrine will not apply:
(a)   where there is a contrary intention; or
(b)   where the obligation under the contract was to provide a benefit different in kind from the other entitlement. If, therefore, the contract was to provide income, such as an annuity[3] or a life interest under a trust fund,[4] this will not be satisfied by an entitlement under the intestacy rules.

1 For the general doctrine of satisfaction, see below, paras 30.86ff.
2 *Wilcocks v Wilcocks* (1706) 2 Vern 558; *Blandy v Widmore* (1715) 2 Vern 709; *Garthshore v Chalie* (1804) 10 Ves 1.
3 *Couch v Stratton* (1799) 4 Ves 391; *Salisbury v Salisbury* (1848) 6 Hare 526.
4 *James v Castle* (1875) 33 LT 665.

Events not giving rise to breach

3.29 Where the contract is merely to make a will, rather than to procure the transmission of some item of property in any event, the plaintiff is in the same position as if the will was in fact made.[1] Suppose that the deceased contracted merely to leave a legacy of £5,000 to David, and David died before the deceased. If a will had been made in those terms, the legacy would have lapsed[2] and, accordingly, David's estate will not be entitled to claim against the deceased's estate.[3] Where the contract is not to revoke an existing will, or not to revoke a provision in an existing will, the contract is not broken if the will or the provision is revoked by operation of law.[4] The plaintiff does, however, have a remedy if the contract was to procure the transmission of the property in any event.[5]

1 *Jervis v Wolferstan* (1874) LR 18 Eq 18.
2 See below, para 30.15.
3 *Needham v Smith* (1828) 4 Russ 318; *Jones v How* (1850) 9 CB 1; *Re Brookman's Trust* (1869) 5 Ch App 182.
4 *Re Marsland, Lloyds Bank Ltd v Marsland* [1939] Ch 820, [1939] 3 All ER 148.
5 *Robinson v Ommanney* (1883) 23 Ch D 285.

Intervention by the court

3.30 Where the contract was entered into after 31 March 1976 the court has a power in certain circumstances to modify or annul the contract.[1] This power is described in chapter 15.

1 Inheritance (Provision for Family and Dependants) Act 1975, s 11.

Position where no contract

3.31 Where the existence of a contract cannot be proved, or a contract is unenforceable, the courts, at least in some Commonwealth jurisdictions, are becoming increasingly willing to try to find some remedy for the plaintiff.

Quantum meruit

3.32 Where there has been a testamentary promise, but in terms too vague to be enforced as a contract, or where a contract is unenforceable, but, nevertheless, the circumstances indicate that the plaintiff was to be recompensed, the plaintiff is entitled to a reasonable sum from the deceased's estate. In *Reynolds v McGregor*[1] the plaintiff did errands for the deceased, a woman aged 90, and provided her with food. The deceased said that she would compensate the plaintiff well, or would leave her well provided for on her death. She did neither, and the plaintiff was held entitled to succeed on a quantum meruit claim. And in *Hink v Lhenen*[2] the deceased made an oral promise to leave his house to his daughter in consideration of services to be rendered. The court in Alberta held that the contract was not capable of specific performance, but that the daughter was entitled to claim in quantum meruit for the services rendered. She was, however, required to give credit for the benefit of rent-free accommodation which she had enjoyed in the deceased's house.

1 [1973] QL 314 (Queensland).
2 (1974) 52 DLR (3d) 301 (Alberta).

Unjust enrichment

3.33 If the deceased and the plaintiff both thought that a valid contract or a valid will had been made for the benefit of the plaintiff, but in fact the contract or will is not valid, the court might hold that the beneficiaries must nevertheless give effect to the purported arrangement. This might be the case, for example, if the deceased agreed to leave to the plaintiff his house, and thought that he had made a will to this effect, although the will was defective. There is no direct authority[1] but assistance may be derived by analogy from the decision of the Nova Scotia Supreme Court in *Re Spears and Levy*.[2] In that case, a man and a woman believed that they were validly married, although the marriage was in fact invalid. The woman, not being entitled under the intestacy provisions as a wife, claimed from the estate remuneration for her services to the deceased during the time when she thought she was married. The court held that the deceased and the woman expected that the woman would receive the widow's share on intestacy, and that the beneficiaries would be unjustly enriched if that expectation was defeated. The beneficiaries were, therefore, held to be bound by a constructive trust to pay to the woman the amount which she would have received as a widow. It remains to be seen how far the courts in England and Wales will follow the example of their more courageous Commonwealth counterparts.

1 But the reasoning in *Lawford v Billericay RDC* [1903] 1 KB 772 may be applied by analogy.
2 (1974) 52 DLR (3d) 146.

3.34 Where the plaintiff was being maintained by the deceased, he might have a right of application under the Family Provision legislation. This is considered in chapter 14.

CHAPTER 4

Joint and mutual wills

4.1 The usual will is one made by one person alone, and is intended to take effect independently of any other will. However, wills can be made jointly, or mutually, or jointly and mutually.

Joint wills

4.2 When two or more persons incorporate their testamentary wishes in one document, and if the formalities prescribed by the Wills Act are observed, they are said to have made joint wills. These must be clearly distinguished from mutual wills, which are discussed in the next section of this chapter.

4.3 A joint will does not take effect as one will, but as the separate wills of the parties who have made it. Thus, if a husband and wife make a joint will, and the husband dies first, the document can be admitted to probate first as the will of the husband on his death, and secondly as the will of the wife on her death.[1] A joint will which is not a mutual will can be revoked by either or both parties at any time, and without the consent of the other. A joint will which is also a mutual will can still be revoked without the consent of the other party, although adverse results ensue.[2] Apart from the mere fact that a joint will is written on the same piece of paper, it is for all purposes regarded as the separate wills of the parties who made it. Thus, one party can make a separate codicil to a joint will[3] and can republish[4] a joint will by a separate will.[5]

1 *Re Duddell* [1932] 1 Ch 585; see also *Re Stracey's Goods* (1855) Dea & Sw 6; *Re Lovegrove's Goods* (1862) 2 Sw & Tr 453; *Re Miskelly's Goods* (1869) 4 IR Eq 62; *Re Piazzi-Smyth's Goods* [1898] P 7; *Re Heys Estate* [1914] P 192.
2 Unilateral revocation can lead to actions for breach of contract or breach of trust. See below, para 4.17.
3 *Re Crofton's Goods* (1897) 13 TLR 374.
4 As to republication see below, p 104.
5 *Re Fletcher's Goods* (1883) 11 LR Ir 359.

4.4 A joint will is generally clumsy, and inconvenient, because on the death of the first person to die, the will itself is retained at the Probate Registry.[1] Its use can be recommended in only two circumstances. First, where a mutual will is made, it may be convenient for this to be made as a joint and mutual will. Secondly, a joint will may be convenient to exercise a joint power of appointment, in which case the power is deemed to have been exercised when the second person dies.[2] A joint will may, of course, also exercise a power of appointment given to one party alone.[3]

1 In the Registry of Wills of Living Persons, until the death of the surviving joint testator. This, however, does not prevent its revocation by the survivor.
2 *Re Duddell* [1932] 1 Ch 585; in this case it was confirmed by a testator's separate will, but this is not necessary.
3 *Re Stracey's Goods* (1855) Dea & Sw 6.

4.5 There is no merit in having a joint will where the parties own property jointly. In the case of a joint tenancy, on the death of one party the property passes automatically to the survivor, even if there is only scintilla temporis between the deaths of the parties.

Mutual wills

Types of mutual will

4.6 Mutual wills are wills made by two or more persons, usually in substantially the same terms and conferring reciprocal benefits, following an agreement between them to make such wills and not to revoke them without the consent of the other.[1] Mutual wills may be made either in the form of a joint will, or as separate wills. There are two basic types of mutual will:
(a) reciprocal life interests, with remainder over. Thus, husband and wife may make mutual wills giving a life interest to the survivor with remainder to their son;
(b) absolute gifts, with alternative provisions in the event of the predecease of the other person. Husband and wife may each make wills leaving the whole of their property to the survivor, but providing that if the spouse does not survive, then the whole of the property shall go to their son.
Although mutual wills are often made by husband and wife, they can be made by any two or more persons and are sometimes found made by other relatives, such as two sisters, who might, for example, wish to confer life interests on each other, with remainders to charity.

1 Burgess (1970) 34 Conv (NS) 230.

Revocation

4.7 Mutual wills involve a conflict of principle. Wills are mutual wills only if made in pursuance of a prior agreement not to revoke without the consent of the other. This is a contract and is enforceable.[1] On the other hand, it is a cardinal principle of the law of wills that a will may always be revoked.[2] The solution to the conflict which has been evolved is that the will itself may always be revoked, but such revocation may give rise to an action for breach of contract. Furthermore, it is established that on the death of the first person to die, a trust arises in favour of the beneficiaries, and if the survivor revokes his will proceedings may also be taken for breach of trust.

1 See below, paras 4.9–4.15.
2 Above, para 2.6; see also *Forse and Hembling's Case* (1588) 4 Co Rep 60 b.

4.8 Actions in respect of breach of contract or breach of trust relate only to the dispositive part of the will. The new will is fully effective to deal with non-dispositive matters, such as the appointment of executors or guardians. Suppose, therefore, that Harry and Wendy make a mutual will under which they leave a life interest to the other, with remainder to Andrew, and appoint Edward to be the executor. Suppose also that after the death of Harry, Wendy revokes her will and makes a new one leaving all her property to Roger, and appointing Thomas to be her executor. The revocation of the first will is effective, and Thomas will obtain probate of the second will. However, as a trust arose on the death of Harry, Thomas will hold Wendy's property upon the trusts declared by the mutual will.

Agreement not to revoke

4.9 In order for wills to be mutual wills, there must be prior agreement not to revoke without the consent of the other, and such agreement must be strictly proved.

The agreement
4.10 The agreement itself may relate to the whole will, or merely to part. Thus, in *Re Green*[1] a husband and wife made wills leaving their property to each other, with the proviso that the survivor was to leave half of that property to certain specified charities. The wife died first, and the husband remarried, making a second will practically wholly in favour of the second wife. Vaisey J held that the second will was effective to deal only with half of the husband's property, the other half being subject to the trusts of the mutual will.

1 [1951] Ch 148.

4.11 The essential nature of the agreement is not that identical wills should be made, but that there should not be any unilateral revocation. In *Re Oldham*,[1] for example, where a husband and wife made almost identical wills leaving their property to each other, with provision for various relatives if the other died first, it was held that an agreement to make the wills could be proved from the letters written to the solicitor who prepared the wills, but that there was no proof of an agreement not to revoke. Thus, when the husband died first, and the wife remarried, her new will in favour of her second husband was held to be effective.[2]

1 [1925] Ch 75.
2 For the effect of a subsequent marriage on a mutual will, see below para 4.30.

Proof of agreement

4.12 If there is an agreement not to revoke, that agreement may be oral or in writing,[1] and it may or may not be recited in the will itself. The most satisfactory way of recording the agreement is to recite it in the will itself,[2] for where the agreement is not recorded in the will it is easy for it to be overlooked on the death of the survivor. Consider again the example of Harry and Wendy given at para 4.8. If there is no mention of the agreement in the wills, then the remainderman would know that he was mentioned in Harry's will, but this would not give any indication that it was made in pursuance of a prior agreement. If Wendy made a new will, probate would be granted of that new will, without any reference to the previous will. There is no way which ensures that the remainderman in these circumstances will ever learn that he is a beneficiary under the mutual will. It may well be that the comparative dearth of reported cases on mutual wills is due to the fact that in many cases an unrecited agreement has gone unnoticed.

1 *Stone v Hoskins* [1905] P 194; *Re Heys Estate* [1914] P 192; *Re Oldham* [1925] Ch 75; *Gray v Perpetual Trustee Co Ltd* [1928] AC 391.
2 As in *Re Green* where the husband, in his will, provided that his wife 'will provide in her will for the carrying out of my wishes as expressed in this my will for the event that I shall survive her and in consideration of such promise by me she has agreed to leave me all her property on my undertaking to provide for the carrying out of the terms of the will as expressed in her will of even date herewith for the event that she shall survive me and for that purpose I have provided . . .'. See also *Re Hagger* where the will contained a recital of an agreement not to revoke unilaterally.

4.13 Where the agreement not to revoke a will unilaterally is not recited in the will the party who is seeking to establish the existence of the agreement must show that it does so on the balance of probabilities.[1] The fact that the wills are executed at the same time, and have the same or similar terms, is relevant but by no means conclusive.[2] Further, it seems that the court leans against findings that there was a definite agreement, in two circumstances. The first is where under the wills each party has an absolute interest in the event of his surviving. This was the position in *Re Oldham*,[3] where Astbury J drew a distinction between the situation where the survivor has only a life interest and where he has an absolute interest. The judge observed: 'If the spouses intended to do what the plaintiff suggests (ie create mutual wills) it is difficult to see why the mutual[4] wills give the survivor an absolute interest in the whole of the property of the one who does first.' The reason behind this statement appears to be the difficulty of determining the extent of the property subject to the trust. This is considered later.[5]

1 *Re Cleaver, Cleaver v Insley* [1981] 2 All ER 1018.
2 Ibid.
3 [1925] Ch 75.
4 The judge was using the expression 'mutual wills' in the wide sense of identical or reciprocal wills.
5 See below, para 4.23.

4.14 The other situation in which the court may lean against finding that there was an agreement is where the whole of the property of the parties is covered by the mutual provisions. This may, but does not necessarily, overlap with the position where absolute interests are conferred. In *Lord Walpole v Lord Orford*[1] the court rejected the contention that there were mutual wills because of lack of evidence of any agreement, but also said that such an arrangement would have been inequitable because it covered all the property of the parties. There is indeed difficulty as to the extent of the property covered[2] but it probably overstates the position to describe the arrangement as inequitable. If there is clear evidence of agreement to make mutual wills covering all the property of the parties, this will be binding.[3]

1 (1797) 3 Ves 402.
2 See below, para 4.23.
3 *Re Hagger* [1930] 2 Ch 190.

4.15 It has been said repeatedly that the requisite agreement not to revoke will not be implied from the fact that the wills are made in identical or largely identical terms.[1]

1 *Re Oldham* [1925] Ch 75 at 87; *Gray v Perpetual Trustee Co Ltd* [1928] AC 391 at 400.

Unilateral revocation during joint lifetimes

4.16 If there is an agreement not to revoke this can clearly be varied or cancelled by mutual agreement. The agreement will also be revoked if one party unilaterally alters his will in the joint lifetimes. Where this occurs, the other party is released from his obligation not to revoke his own will. Thus, in *Stone v Hoskins*[1] a husband and wife made mutual wills leaving most of their property to the survivor. The wife changed her mind, and secretly made a new will revoking the previous will. She died first. Her husband claimed that the first will was not revoked because he had no notice of revocation, but this contention was rejected. The revocation was effective. The court went on to say that where the revoker is the first to die, the survivor can alter his will.

1 [1905] P 194.

4.17 As well as being entitled to make a new will, the other party also has a right to sue the revoker, or his estate, for damages for breach of contract. But what does this amount to? The object of damages for breach of contract is to compensate for loss, but in this case it is very difficult to calculate the loss. Where one party revokes unilaterally, the other has lost the possibility[1] of receiving an unascertained amount[2] at an unspecified time.[3] In addition, the innocent party has been released from his obligations. The problem of calculating damages may be so difficult, and the likely amount of those damages so small, as to make the threat of an action for breach of contract no serious deterrent.

1 'Possibility' because he might survive.
2 Unless a fixed amount is specified in the will.
3 'Unspecified' because the date of the revoker's death is not known.

The trust

Commencement
4.18   Until the death of the first person to die, the relationship between the parties is solely contractual. Where the wills are unrevoked at the death of the first to die, a trust arises at that time. Accordingly, where the wills confer life interests, with remainders over, the remainderman acquires a vested interest on the death of the first to die. Thus, in *Re Hagger, Freeman v Arscott*[1] a husband and wife made a joint mutual will under which the whole of the property was to be held upon trust for the survivor for life, and thereafter upon trust for nine persons of whom one was Eleanor Palmer. The wife died in 1904, and the husband in 1928. Eleanor Palmer died in 1923. Clauson J held that although she did not survive the husband, her share became vested upon the death of the wife, and so her estate became entitled on the death of the husband to the share which she would have taken herself had she been alive at that time.

1   [1930] 2 Ch 190.

Basis of trust
4.19   Why should equity impose a trust upon the death of the first to die? In the old case of *Dufour v Pereira*[1] Lord Camden said: 'he, that dies first, does by his death carry the agreement on his part into execution. If the other then refuses, he is guilty of a fraud, can never unbind himself and becomes a trustee of course. For no man shall deceive another to his prejudice. By engaging to do something that is in his power, he is made a trustee for the performance, and transmits that trust to those that claim under him.'

1   (1769) 1 Dick 419.

4.20   *Dufour v Pereira* was also considered to be based on the ground that equity intervened solely because the survivor had taken the benefit of the agreement, and it would then be inequitable to allow him to revoke his own will. It now seems clear, however, that whether or not a benefit is actually taken is irrelevant to the question whether or not the trust exists.[1] On the one hand, the fact that a benefit is taken does not per se lead the court to declare the existence of a trust. In *Re Oldham, Hadwen v Myles*,[2] for example, the survivor took a benefit, but her property was not subject to a trust because the court was not satisfied that there was an agreement not to revoke. On the other hand, it seems that the survivor cannot be released from his obligation by refusing to take any benefit. In *Re Hagger, Freeman v Arscott*,[3] where the wife died first, Clauson J was rather hesitant. He said: 'Therefore I am bound to hold that from the death of the wife the husband held the property, according to the tenor of the will, subject to the trusts imposed upon it, at all events if he took advantage of the provisions of the will.'

1   *Re Dale* (1993) 137 Sol Jo LB 83, where as a preliminary issue it was decided that it was not necessary for the survivor to obtain any benefit under the will of the first to die.
2   [1925] Ch 75.
3   [1930] 2 Ch 190.

4.21 In *Gray v Perpetual Trustee Co Ltd*[1] it was said that in the absence of a definite agreement, it is irrelevant that the benefits under the will of the first to die have been accepted. This seems clearly in accord with principle. The survivor is only one of the beneficiaries under the trust; it would be surprising if renunciation of benefit by him could prejudice the position of the remainderman.

1 [1928] AC 391.

4.22 The basis for the trust is, therefore, the more general consideration that it would be inequitable for the survivor to allow the other to die in the belief that the arrangement was firm, if he could subsequently resile. It must be admitted, however, that a contrary view has been reached in some other jurisdictions, where a subsequent benefit is essential.[1]

1 See eg *Denyssen v Mostert* (1872) LR 4 PC 236; *Minakshi Ammal v Viswantha Aiyar* (1909) ILR 33, Mad 406.

Scope of trust property
4.23 The trust which arises under a mutual will on the death of the first to die is an implied trust. The scope of the implied trust depends on the type of interest conferred by the mutual will. Suppose, first, that husband and wife make mutual wills leaving a life interest to the survivor, with remainder to their son, and that the wife dies first. The wife's property will be subject not to an implied trust, but to the express trusts of her will. In this case, it is her husband's property only which becomes subject to the implied trust. If, however, the husband and wife made mutual wills leaving an absolute interest to the survivor, but with a proviso that if the other spouse dies first, the property goes to the son, and the wife dies first, the whole of the property, both what was his own, and what was derived from his wife, will be subject to the implied trust.

4.24 In the light of this, it is now appropriate to consider in greater detail the facts of *Re Hagger*.[1] It will be recalled that in this case husband and wife made a joint mutual will, leaving a life interest to each other, and thereafter upon trusts for various persons including Eleanor Palmer. The property concerned was situated at Wandsworth.[2] It was agreed that so far as the property could be shown to be the property of the wife, Eleanor Palmer obtained a vested interest at her death, but it was also argued that so far as the property could be shown to have belonged to her husband, Eleanor Palmer took no interest because as regards his part, the document became effective only on his death. Clauson J said: 'So far as the husband's interest in the property is concerned, the will operated as a trust from the date of the wife's death.' In reaching this decision he was influenced by what he considered to be the intention of the parties.

1 [1930] 2 Ch 190, para 4.18 above.
2 It was held on a joint tenancy.

4.25 In view of this, it is not difficult to see why the courts have leant against upholding wills as mutual where all the property is included. Consider further the example of the husband and wife making mutual wills leaving a life interest to the survivor with remainder over. If the wife dies first, all the property of the husband from the date of her death is, in principle, subject to the trust under which he is life tenant. In strict principle it appears that the surviving husband would be obliged to treat this as any other trust fund. He would, for example, be obliged to convert all the property into authorised investments, and thereafter enjoy merely the income. He would be obliged to sell his house, for a house for occupation is not an authorised investment.[1] He would even be forced to sell his clothes and invest the proceeds of those in trustee investments. Clearly the court would strive to find some way to avoid the absurdity. As so much depends on what the court considers was the intention of the parties, it may be that the husband would be deemed to have had implied authority to spend the money during his lifetime. This overcomes one difficulty, but only raises another in its place: is the husband to be entitled to defeat the whole arrangement by spending the whole trust fund, or at least the whole of his property? And if he can spend it, can he give it away, and so achieve by inter vivos disposition – perhaps by revocable settlement[2] – what he could not achieve by will. The answer is provided by *Re Cleaver*.[3] In that case, a husband and wife made mutual wills under which, apart from certain pecuniary legacies to their respective families, each of them left his residue to the other, or in the event of predecease of the other, to the husband's three children. The husband died first, and the wife received the whole of his estate under his will. The wife then revoked her own will, and made a new will leaving all her estate to one only of the children. Nourse J held that the constructive trust attached to the property of the wife, including that which she received from the husband, at the date of his death. However, the judge also held that the wife was implied to be at liberty (a) to make 'ordinary gifts of small value', but not to make larger voluntary dispositions, and (b) in all other respects to deal with the combined property for her own benefit. In *Re Cleaver* the court was able to reach a workable solution, but only by implying provisions into the agreement between the parties. The basic problems remain where these aspects are subject to express provisions which exclude the scope for such implications.

1   *Re Power* [1947] Ch 572.
2   See above, para 2.12.
3   [1981] 2 All ER 1018.

4.26 There is, however, a further difficulty. If the mutual wills cover the whole of the property, although the trust arises at the date of death of the first to die, it appears that after-acquired property will become subject to it. It could, perhaps, even be argued that income from the capital is after-acquired property in the hands of the survivor, and so ought also to be regarded as capital.

4.27 A somewhat similar approach to that in *Re Cleaver* was adopted by the court in *Ottaway v Norman*,[1] a case on secret trusts. In that case, the testator, Harry Ottaway, owned a bungalow where he and his housekeeper, Eva Hodges, lived as man and wife. He wanted the property to go to William, his son by his predeceased wife, and discussions took place between all three. Harry made a will leaving the bungalow to Eva, on the basis that Eva would hold it in trust for herself, and thereafter it would pass to William. The essence of the decision was that Eva took the property on the secret trust. However, it was also suggested that the secret trust governed Eva's money at the time of her death. There were two possibilities. It might include all money which Eva had at her death, including money which she had acquired before Harry's death, and money which she had acquired afterwards from all sources. There was not sufficient evidence, however, to show that that was intended. The second possibility was that Eva should be bound by a trust affecting only money derived from Harry's will. Brightman J said:[2]

> 'I am content to assume for present purposes but without so deciding that if property is given to the primary donee on the understanding that the primary donee will dispose by his will of such assets, if any, as he may have at his command at his death in favour of the secondary donee, a valid trust is created in favour of the secondary donee which is in suspense during the lifetime of the primary donee, but attaches to the estate of the primary donee at the moment of the latter's death.'

But this arrangement is meaningless and unworkable unless it includes the requirement that the primary donee should keep the money separate and distinct from his own money. On this point also there was no evidence, and the judge therefore decided that the trust did not attach to the money.

1   [1972] Ch 698, [1971] 3 All ER 1325.
2   [1971] 3 All ER 1325 at 1334.

4.28   If a mutual will is to be made, it is therefore most important that clauses to deal with these difficulties should be included. The law can imply a trust only where there is no express provision.

Other effect

4.29   It appears that where a joint tenant makes a mutual will, he thereby severs the joint tenancy in property subject to the will.[1]

1   *Re Heys Estate* [1914] P 192.

Marriage and mutual wills

4.30   The effect of subsequent marriage on a mutual will is open to some doubt. The Wills Act 1837, s 18, provides that a will is revoked by subsequent marriage unless that will is made in contemplation of that marriage. If, therefore, a person who had made a mutual will, not in contemplation of marriage, subsequently marries, does that revoke the will, and if so does the person who marries render himself liable to an action for damages?

4.31   In *Re Green*[1] it will be remembered that all the property of the first to die went to the survivor, who was obliged to leave half of it to certain charities. The husband survived and remarried, making a second will in favour of his new wife. It was held that the second will was effective only to deal with the other half of the husband's property. The trust had arisen previously on the death of the first wife, and the husband's subsequent marriage did not affect it. This seems correct in principle, although the possible effect of s 18 does not appear to have been mentioned in argument.

1   [1951] Ch 148.

4.32   The nearest case which illustrates the effect of the subsequent marriage on the contractual liability is *Re Marsland*.[1] In that case a husband in a deed of separation made with his wife covenanted not to revoke his will. After his first marriage came to an end, he remarried. The will was revoked and the Court of Appeal held that the contractual remedy did not lie. A distinction was drawn between intentional revocation, which did give rise to an action for damages, and revocation by operation of law, which did not.[2] These principles will probably apply to mutual wills.

1   [1939] Ch 820, CA.
2   See above, para 3.29.

CHAPTER 5

Making a will – the mental elements

5.1 A will is valid only if at the time when it was made the testator:
(a) had attained the age of 18;[1]
(b) had an animus testandi; and
(c) complied with the formal requirements laid down in the Wills Act 1837.[2]

The only exception to the rule that a person must be over 18 applies in the case of privileged wills, and the exception is considered in chapter 7. The requirements as to form are considered in the next chapter, and this chapter deals with the animus testandi. An animus testandi means in effect that:
(a) the testator had the mental capacity required to make a will;
(b) the testator had the intention of making a will; and
(c) the testator exercised his genuine free choice in the making of the will.

1 Wills Act 1837, s 7; Family Law Reform Act 1969, s 1.
2 Unless the will is a 'privileged will': see below, ch 7.

Testamentary capacity

The problem

5.2 There is no direct correlation between the mental capacity required to make a will, and mental disorder for the purposes of the Mental Health Act 1983.[1] As will be seen, a person who is competently detained under that Act can, in some circumstances, make a valid will, and a person who has never been near a mental hospital can have such unsoundness of mind as to vitiate any will he purports to make. Accordingly, each case is considered on its own facts. This flexibility is desirable, but it throws upon the court the need to hold a balance. On the one hand, if the court sets too high a standard, those who are dissatisfied with a will are encouraged to allege mental unsoundness on the part of the testator. On the other hand, if the court sets too low a standard, effect will be given to the most absurd wills. The balance between these two extremes has not, however, been constant. It is probably true that the degree of mental capacity now required is lower than was previously the case.

1 See Fridman (1963) 79 LQR 502.

5.3 As will be seen, sometimes the result of a case may depend largely on whether the will is rational on its face.[1] This, however, needs great care. It follows from the fundamental notion of testamentary freedom that a testator can make a will in such terms as he wishes. 'By the laws of this country, every testator, in disposing of his property, is at liberty to adopt his own nonsense.'[2] And whether or not the will contains nonsense, in principle the motive behind a provision is also irrelevant. 'Testators are not bound to have good or any reasons for what they do.'[3] This salutary principle is established because the testator may have made his will from a motive which is completely unknown to the court. The position was summarised by Wigram VC in *Bird v Luckie* in the following terms:[4]

'No man is bound to make a will in such a manner as to deserve approbation from the prudent, the wise, or the good. A testator is permitted to be capricious and improvident, and is moreover at liberty to conceal the circumstances and the motives by which he had been actuated in his dispositions. Many a testamentary provision may seem to the world arbitrary, capricious, and eccentric, for which the testator, if he could be heard, might be able to answer most satisfactorily.'

1 See particularly the rules as to the burden of proof: below, para 5.9.
2 *Vaughan v Marquis of Headfort* (1840) 10 Sim 639 at 641, per Shadwell VC; cf *Jeffries v Alexander* (1860) 8 HL Cas 594 at 648, per Lord Campbell.
3 *Hart v Tulk* (1852) 2 De GM & G 300 at 313 per Knight-Bruce LJ.
4 (1850) 8 Hare 301 at 306, 307.

5.4 Yet the fact remains that if the will is irrational on its face, it will be easier to set it aside. Sir Joseph Jekyll, a former Master of the Rolls, left his fortune to pay the National Debt. His will was set aside on an application by relatives, the judge observing that the bequest was 'a very foolish one. He might as well have attempted to stop the middle arch of Blackfriars bridge with his full bottomed wig.'[1] The cases are often difficult to distinguish, although the principle is clear. A testator may make an apparently irrational will, and such irrationality will affect the will if, and only if, it indicates unsoundness of mind. Yet, in practice, what apparent irrationality, which cannot be explained, would not indicate unsoundness of mind?

1 Quoted in Croake James *Curiosities of Law and Lawyers* p 491.

The test of mental capacity

5.5 In the *Marquess of Winchester's Case*[1] it was said 'It is not sufficient that the testator be of memory when he makes a will to answer familiar and usual questions, but he ought to have a disposing memory, so that he is able to make a disposition of his lands with understanding and reason.' This test was expanded by Cockburn CJ in *Banks v Goodfellow*,[2] where he said:

'As to the testator's capacity, he must, in the language of the law, have a sound and disposing mind and memory. In other words, he ought to be capable of making his will with an understanding of the nature of the business in which he is engaged, a recollection of the property he means to dispose of, of the persons who are the objects of his bounty, and the manner in which it is to be distributed between them. It is not necessary that he should view his will with the eye of a lawyer, and comprehend its provisions in their legal form. It is sufficient if he has such a mind and memory as will enable him to understand the elements of which it is composed, and the disposition of his property in its simple forms.'

1 (1598) 6 Co Rep 23a.
2 (1870) LR 5 QB 549 at 567, quoting from *Harrison v Rowan* 3 Washington at 595.

5.6 Accordingly, Cockburn CJ laid down three criteria to establish testamentary capacity.
(a) The testator must have 'an understanding of the nature of the business in which he is engaged'. He must therefore appreciate the nature of a will and its effect: that it is ambulatory and does not take effect until death and is revocable until death.
(b) The testator must have 'a recollection of the property he means to dispose of'. He must therefore realise the extent of the property of which he is disposing. This is likely to be a relative test and indicates that the testator ought to have in mind the extent of his assets appropriate to his level of wealth and not necessarily have to recall every item he owns. Indeed, when a testator makes his will, the assets he owns at that time may be radically different from those which he owns when he dies. However, the testator should be aware, for example, that when he disposes of the residue of his estate he is disposing of all assets which he owns at death other than those which have been otherwise disposed of in the will.
(c) The testator must be aware of 'the persons who are the objects of his bounty'. This indicates that the testator must be aware of persons who would normally have a moral claim on his bounty. There is nothing to prevent a testator disinheriting such persons,[1] but if he decides to do so he must at least be aware of their existence. If the testator is not conscious of the existence of the potential claim on his bounty, he will not have testamentary capacity. This is illustrated in *Battan Singh v Amirchand*.[2] In that case the testator had made several previous wills benefiting his four nephews. Then, shortly before he died, and when he was very ill with the last stage of consumption, he made a will stating that he had no relatives, and leaving all his property to two creditors. The Privy Council refused to uphold the will as, clearly, on the face of it he was not conscious of the existence of his nephews.[3]

1 Except to the extent such persons may make a claim under the family provision legislation: see below, ch 14.
2 [1948] AC 161. An appeal to the Privy Council from Fiji.
3 It was set aside on the ground of attendant suspicion and also because it was felt that the testator did not understand what he was doing.

5.7 *Banks v Goodfellow* is an attempt to formulate working rules in order to answer the more general question: is the testator's judgment impaired in so far as it relates to testamentary matters? As it was put in a Canadian decision:[1]

> 'Will making does not require a sound judgment . . . if it did, a great many wills might well be ruled invalid, although no question of insanity could arise. What must be shown is that the judgment, whatever its personal quality, is not affected by a disorder of the mind, so as to poison the affections, pervert the sense of right, or prevent the exercise of the natural faculties of the testatrix. It is the perverse influence of mental disorders affecting judgment that invalidates the will, not the use of judgment under the influence of "normal" perverseness, whimsy, or fantasy.'

1   *Re Gregory* (1979) 37 NSR (2d) 640 at 657, per O'Heam J. In this case, the court upheld the will of a testatrix who was acting in a senile and paranoid manner, but where judgment was not affected.

5.8   An interesting illustration of the degree of mental capacity required is provided by *Re Park's Estate*.[1] In that case, the testator was a rich old man who had been married for over 50 years. His wife died in January 1948, leaving him with no close relatives, his nearest relative being a nephew of the half-blood.[2] In March 1948 he executed a complicated will, leaving large benefits to his solicitors. The will also conferred substantial benefits on the step-nephew. In May 1948 he had a stroke and had another in May 1949, by which time he was incapable of looking after himself. He then became engaged to the cashier of his club. He settled shares worth £6,000 on her, and on 30 May 1949 he married her. The marriage operated to revoke the 1948 will.[3] The ceremony of marriage took place on the morning of 30 May: he celebrated in the afternoon by making a new and complicated will in favour of his new wife, under which she was left £1,000. He died shortly afterwards. There was then a contest between the second wife and the step-nephew. The second wife alleged that the second will was invalid, because the deceased was not capable of appreciating the complicated will he had made. If this was so, she would take the whole estate under the intestacy rules. The step-nephew retaliated by asserting that if there was insufficient mental capacity to make a will in the afternoon, there was also insufficient mental capacity to contract a valid marriage in the morning. Therefore there was no valid marriage, and the 1948 will remained effective. At first instance, Karminski J held that the testator understood the nature of the ceremony of marriage, which he held to be valid, and he therefore found in favour of the wife. The judge also said that a lesser degree of capacity was required for marriage than to make a will. While the Court of Appeal upheld the decision, it disapproved of this statement by the judge,[4] and drew a distinction between the capacity required to make a simple will and that required to make a complicated will, as in this case.[5]

1   [1954] P 89.
2   The expression 'half-blood' denotes step-relationship.
3   By virtue of s 18, Wills Act 1837; see below, para 8.61.
4   Per Hodson LJ at 135: 'In my opinion there is no sliding scale of soundness of mind by reference to which different matters on which the law is required to take cognisance may be measured.'
5   In cases such as this, even if the will in favour of the spouse is not upheld an application can be made to the court under the family provision legislation: see below, chapter 14.

The burden of proof

5.9 Where a question of possible mental incapacity arises, it is important to know where the burden of proof lies. The following rules may be deduced.

(a) In every case the person propounding a will must satisfy the court that the will is valid, that is, that it complies with the formal requirements of the Act and that the requisite mental element is present. This was expressed by Parke B in *Barry v Butlin*[1] as: 'the onus probandi lies in every case upon the party propounding a will; and he must satisfy the conscience of the court that the instrument so propounded is the last will of a free and capable testator'.

(b) Whenever possible, evidence must be adduced as to the testator's mental state at the time when the will was made. If that evidence is available, the question will be decided accordingly, but, if it is not available, certain presumptions will be made.

(c) If the will is rational on its face, it is presumed that the testator was sane at the time when it was made.[2] Accordingly, where a will, rational on its face, is being attacked on this ground, the person attacking may prove either that the testator did not have adequate mental capacity generally, or that he lacked that capacity at the particular time that the will was made.

(d) If the person attacking the will proves generally that the testator did not have mental capacity, the burden of proof shifts once again to the propounder to establish that, notwithstanding the general incapacity, there was adequate capacity at the time when the will was made.

(e) If the will is irrational on its face, there is a presumption that the testator did not have adequate mental capacity, so that those propounding it must satisfy the court of the testator's capacity at the time when the will was made.[3] This proposition itself causes difficulty because there is considerable authority that eccentricity or mere foolishness is not sufficient to show mental incapacity.[4] What is the distinction between an irrational will on the one hand, and eccentricity or foolishness on the other? In *Mudway v Croft*[5] it was said that what is eccentricity in one person may amount to mental incapacity in another, and that eccentricity must be tested against the whole life and habits of the testator.

(f) There is also a presumption of the continuance of a mental state. Therefore, where a court is satisfied that a testator had full mental capacity some time before making a will, it will presume, until evidence is shown to the contrary, that he continued to have that capacity until the will was made.[6] Likewise, where there was incapacity before the making of the will, that state, in the absence of contrary evidence, will be presumed to have continued to the time when the will was made.[7]

1 (1838) 2 Moo PCC 480; see also *Cleare and Forster v Cleare* (1869) LR 1 P & D 655; *Harmes v Hinkson* (1946) 62 TLR 445.
2 *Wellesley v Vere* (1841) 2 Curt 917; *Symes v Greene* (1859) 1 Sw & Tr 401.
3 *Harwood v Baker* (1840) 3 Moo PCC 282 at 291.
4 *Wellesley v Vere* (1841) 2 Curt 917; *Mudway v Croft* (1843) 3 Curt 671; *Frere v Peacocke* (1846) 1 Rob Eccl 442; *Pilkington v Gray* [1899] AC 401.
5 (1843) 3 Curt 671.
6 *Chambers and Yatman v Queen's Proctor* (1840) 2 Curt 415.

7   *Smee v Smee* (1879) 5 PD 84; *Groom v Thomas* (1829) 2 Hag Ecc 433; *Banks v Goodfellow* (1870) LR 5 QB 549 at 570.

Will made during lucid interval

5.10   It follows from paragraphs (d) and (f) above that where the testator was of unsound mind prior to the making of the will, it is for those propounding the will to show either that by the time the will was made the testator had recovered from that unsoundness, or that the will was made during a lucid interval. A lucid interval does indeed mean 'interval', so that it is not necessary to show final recovery.[1] In *Chambers and Yatman v Queen's Proctor*,[2] for example, the court admitted to probate a will made during a lucid interval on one day, even though the insanity had returned to the extent that the deceased killed himself on the following day.

1   *Ex p Holyland* (1805) 11 Ves 10 at 11; *Creagh v Blood* (1845) 8 I Eq R 434 at 439; *Prinsep and East India Co v Dyce Sombre* (1856) 10 Moo PCC 232.

5.11   The cases before the Mental Health Act 1959[1] are full of references to the old terms 'idiot' and 'lunatic'.[2] In future, cases of this nature are most likely to arise where an order for the control and management of the testator's property has been made under the provisions of the Mental Health Act 1983, s 95. An illustration of the general position derived from the old law is *Re Walker's Estate*.[3] In that case, a large amount of property had been settled on a young woman who had always had to be kept under supervision and who, when she was 21, was found lunatic by inquisition.[4] She had periods of delusion during which she was violent and dangerous, but apart from these delusions she took a general interest in affairs. While not affected by delusions, she made a will which three doctors certified she was capable of making, and the will was admitted to probate.

1   Now superseded by the Mental Health Act 1983.
2   At common law an idiot was a person of unsound mind from the time of his birth, and a lunatic was a person who became of unsound mind at some time during his life. However, as a result of the Mental Deficiency Act 1913, the common law definition of idiot was extended to any person who became unsound at any age up to 18.
3   (1912) 28 TLR 466.
4   One of the old procedures.

Delusions

5.12   In *Dew v Clark and Clark*[1] it was said that a delusion is a belief in the existence of something which no rational person could believe, and which could not be eradicated from the testator's mind by reasoned argument. It will be clear that delusion may or may not affect the person's mental capacity.

1   (1826) 3 Add 79.

5.13   Where the delusion does not affect either the testator's property or the objects of his bounty, it will not prevent him making a valid will.[1] Where the delusion does affect either of these matters, it is a question of degree whether the delusion is so strong that his powers of critical judgment are so overborne that he has lost his power of considering rationally the circumstances which he ought to consider in making the will.[2] On the one hand, therefore, a person may take a view of the objects of his bounty which is harsh, but can be said to be rational. On the other hand, the view may be so harsh and irrational that the will cannot be allowed to stand. In *Dew v Clark and Clark*[3] a daughter alleged that her father was not capable of making a valid will because of his attitude towards her. The will was rational on its face, and the burden of proof was therefore on the daughter.[4] She was able to discharge this by showing that the father refused even to see her for the first three years of her life; that he forced her to sleep with an insane woman; and that he himself was found lunatic by inquisition some time after he had made the will.

1 *Jenkins v Morris* (1880) 14 Ch D 674; *Frere v Peacocke* (1846) 1 Rob Eccl 442; *Smith v Tebbitt* (1867) LR 1 P & D 398; *Boughton v Knight* (1873) LR 3 P & D 64; *Smee v Smee* (1879) 5 PD 84; *Murfett v Smith* (1887) 12 PD 116.
2 *Banks v Goodfellow* (1870) LR 5 QB 549; *Hope v Campbell* [1899] AC 1; *Re Walker's Estate* (1912) 28 TLR 466; *Re Belliss* (1929) 141 LT 245.
3 (1826) 3 Add 79.
4 Above, para 5.9(c).

5.14 Probably the best statement of the position is again from the judgment of Cockburn CJ in *Banks v Goodfellow*:[1]

'Here, then, we have the measure of the degree of mental power which should be insisted on. If the human instincts and affections, or the moral sense, become perverted by mental disease; if insane suspicion, or aversion, take the place of natural affection; if reason and judgment are lost, and the mind becomes a prey to insane delusions calculated to interfere with and disturb its functions, and to lead to a testamentary disposition, due only to their baneful influence – in such a case it is obvious that the condition of the testamentary power fails, and that a will made under such circumstances ought not to stand.'

1 (1870) LR 5 QB 549 at 565.

5.15 A delusion which impairs testamentary capacity may affect only part of a will or codicil, in which case probate may be granted of the remainder. In *Re Bohrmann's Estate*,[1] for example, a man had made a will and three codicils in which he made substantial gifts to charity. Towards the end of his life, he began to suffer from a delusion that he was being persecuted by the London County Council.[2] Shortly before his death he made a fourth codicil, in one clause of which he said that all references to English charities were to be read as references to the corresponding American charities. Langton J omitted this clause from probate, but granted probate of the remainder.

1 [1938] 1 All ER 271.
2 The forerunner of the (now abolished) Greater London Council.

5.16 The existence of a delusion may, and usually will, be proved by extrinsic evidence, for there is often no indication on the face of the will that the testator is suffering from a delusion. For example, if a testator refuses to accept that his daughter exists, and leaves all his property to charity, there will be nothing in the will itself to cast doubt upon the testator's capacity. For this reason, the court has refused to grant probate of some wills which on their face appear rational.[1] In a Canadian decision[2] the testator made a will appointing his son to be his executor and making him the sole legatee. On its face, the will was entirely rational. However, the testator had committed suicide and had left an incoherent suicide note. The court admitted extrinsic evidence to show that the testator was in a disturbed state of mind, and this evidence was extended to show that the testator had had a delusion that those around him, particularly his wife, were trying to poison him, and in order to escape from them he would sometimes sleep in a tree. The will was not admitted to probate.

1 *Symes v Green* (1859) 1 Sw & Tr 401; *Smith v Tebbitt* (1867) LR 1 P & R 398.
2 *Re Onofrichuk* [1974] 2 WWR 469 (Saskatchewan).

5.17 It is not always possible to know whether the testator was mistaken or deluded in a particular respect. In *Re Nightingale*[1] the testator, who was a widower, made a will in July 1972 under which his son was the principal beneficiary. He was seriously ill, having had one lung removed, and in the following month he made a further will cutting out his son from any benefit. Between the dates when the first and second wills were made, on two occasions the testator had attempted to sit up while struggling for breath, and the son had gently pushed him back on the pillows. The testator made his will in August 1972 because, based on those two incidents, he thought that his son was attempting to shorten his life. The main possibilities were that the testator was right in his belief; or that the son's conduct was innocent and that the testator developed an irrational fear and suspicion of his son. There was no clinical evidence of any failure of reasoning or understanding. Goulding J held that it was for the propounders of the August will to establish that the testator was of sound mind, memory and understanding when he made it, and this involved them establishing that the son had attempted to murder the testator. They were not able to show that, and the son therefore succeeded in proving the July will.

1 *Re Nightingale, Green v Nightingale (No 2)* (1974) 119 Sol Jo 189.

5.18 In many ways it is unfortunate that the law developed for the most part in the nineteenth century, when the courts were convinced that there was a sharp distinction between those who were rational and those who were not, and were only too happy to pass judgment on what was rational and what was not. As a result, many pronouncements are unsatisfactory to modern ears, which recognise the many gradations between the extremes of rationality and irrationality. Accordingly, perhaps more importance should now be placed on the actual facts of a case than some statements of principle might suggest.

Insanity following will

5.19 To make a valid will it is only necessary for a person to have full mental capacity at the time when the will is made, so that if he becomes mentally ill after the will is made, the will will remain effective. Where the mental illness is such as to deprive him of animus testandi, he will also not have animus revocandi. Thus, mental illness following the will can make the will irrevocable.[1]

1 See below, para 8.5.

Will made by court

5.20 Section 96 of the Mental Health Act 1983 gives to the Court of Protection power to make a will on behalf of an adult[1] mental patient where it believes that the patient is incapable of making a valid will for himself. A will made under this provision can serve all or any of the purposes which the will of a sane person can serve. Thus, it may dispose of property; exercise a power of appointment; or appoint executors.[2] This power is considered later.[3]

1 Mental Health Act 1983, s 96(4).
2 Ibid, s 96(1)(e).
3 See below, para 6.44.

Time for testing testamentary capacity – the rule in *Parker v Felgate*

5.21 As it is only necessary for a person to have full mental capacity at the time when the will is executed, it might be thought that this is the only time which is relevant. In a lenient mood, however, the courts have evolved a rule, known as the rule in *Parker v Felgate*.[1] Under this rule, if a testator, when competent, has given instructions to another person, usually his solicitor, to prepare a will, and the will is in fact prepared in accordance with those instructions, then the will is valid even though, when he actually executes it, the testator is no longer competent to make a will. This rule is objectionable in principle, for in principle the requisite testamentary capacity should accompany the execution of the will, but it is a means of upholding wills in circumstances in which the courts favour them being saved.

1 (1883) 8 PD 171.

5.22 In *Parker v Felgate*[1] a testatrix, when ill, gave her solicitor instructions to prepare a will leaving legacies to her father and brother. The testatrix went into a coma, but she was brought out of it when the new will was ready. She was told that the document shown to her was her will, and she was asked whether she wanted someone to sign on her behalf. This was done. It was established that at the time when the will was signed, the testatrix did not remember the instructions which she had given to the solicitor, and it was also established that if each particular disposition had been put to her separately, she would not have been able to understand it. It was also established, however, and this is the basis of the decision, that when the will was executed, she did know that at some time previously she had given instructions for a will to her solicitor, and that she believed she was executing a will made in accordance with those instructions. On this finding, the will was held to be valid.

1 (1883) 8 PD 171.

5.23 While, as in *Parker v Felgate* itself, this doctrine saves wills in bona fide circumstances, the scope for abuse is manifest. Accordingly, it seems that the court will apply the rule only where there is no ground for suspicion.[1] In particular, the court will enquire into the circumstances very closely where instructions are given through third persons, or where the person drawing the will takes some significant benefit under it. In *Battan Singh v Amirchand*[2] instructions had been sent through an intermediary. The Privy Council refused to uphold the will, both on the ground of the attendant suspicion, and also because there was a suspicion that the testator did not understand what he was doing.

1 See below, paras 5.35–5.40.
2 [1948] AC 161. See above, para 5.6(c).

Other conditions affecting capacity

Drink and drugs

5.24 There is no presumption that even a habitual drunkard, or, presumably, a drug addict, has no testamentary capacity at the time when the will is made.[1] A person opposing the will may, however, prove that at the time when the will was made the testator was under the influence of drink or drugs,[2] and where this is done the court will require evidence that, notwithstanding the inebriation, the testator had the necessary capacity. So, in *Re Heinke's Estate*[3] the testator, a heavy drinker, had executed a codicil whilst in 'The Cobweb', the last in a round of public houses in which he habitually drank. The codicil, which was executed in suspicious circumstances, uncharacteristically revoked a gift in his will to his housekeeper and mistress of 16 years' standing. Sachs J held the codicil to be void on the grounds that the deceased was not of sound mind, memory and understanding and did not have knowledge and approval of the contents of the codicil when he executed it.

1 *Ayrey v Hill* (1824) 2 Add 206; *Handley v Stacey* (1858) 1 F & F 574.
2 *Ayrey v Hill*, above; *Handley v Stacey*, above; *Wheeler and Batsford v Alderson* (1831) 3 Hag Ecc 574; *Brunt v Brunt* (1873) LR 3 P & D 37.
3 [1959] CLY 3449, (1959) Times, 22 January.

Blindness and illiteracy

5.25 Where it is shown that the testator was blind or illiterate, the burden of proof is on the propounder to show that the testator had knowledge of the contents of the will at the time of its execution.[1] This requirement will be satisfied if the will, or at least a summary of it, is read over and explained to the testator prior to execution. In practice this requirement is best met by incorporating a suitable attestation clause reciting this fact, which provides prima facie evidence to the Probate Registry.

1 Non-Contentious Probate Rules 1987, r 13.

Old age and infirmity

5.26 Old age and infirmity do not generally give grounds for suspicion or enquiry of themselves, and are more usually used to strengthen suggestions that the testator had no knowledge of the contents, brought on some other grounds such as undue influence,[1] or that the will was prepared by a principal beneficiary.[2] Where, however, it is alleged that the testator did not have knowledge of the contents of the will by reason of old age or infirmity, the courts will require to be satisfied as to his mental state.[3] Where a testator is elderly and infirm it is highly desirable that his will should be witnessed by a medical practitioner who satisfies himself as to the testator's capacity and understanding.[4]

1 *Ashwell v Lomi* (1850) LR 2 P & D 477, see below, paras 5.46–5.48.
2 *Re Holtam* (1913) 108 LT 732.
3 See eg *Murphy v Lamphier* (1914) 32 OLR 19; *Lamb v Brown* (1923) 54 OLR 443.
4 *Re Simpson* [1977] LS Gaz R 187.

Testamentary intention

5.27 If the testator had the capacity to make a valid will, the next question to be considered is whether he had the intention to do so, that is, whether he had, in the strict sense, an animus testandi. The test is whether, by the act which he did, the testator intended to make a disposition of his property to take effect on his death,[1] or to do any of the other things which can be done by will.[2] It is not necessary for the testator to know that what he did in law constituted the making of a will.

1 See *Re Stable, Dalrymple v Campbell* [1919] P 7; below, para 7.26.
2 See above, para 2.3.

5.28 If a document appears on its face to be a will, and satisfies the formal requirements, there is a presumption that the testator intended to make a will. This presumption can be rebutted by evidence of a contrary intention[1] – that the will was intended as a joke,[2] for example. As it was said in *Lister v Smith*:[3]

'If the fact is plainly and conclusively made out that the paper which appears to be the record of a testamentary act was in reality the offspring of a jest, or the result of a contrivance to effect some collateral object, and never seriously intended as a disposition of property, it is not reasonable that the court should turn it into an effective instrument.'

47

1   *Trevelyan v Trevelyan* (1810) 1 Phillim 149; *Re English's Goods* (1864) 3 Sw & Tr 586; *Lister v Smith* (1868) 3 Sw & Tr 282; *Re Nosworthy's Goods* (1865) 4 Sw & Tr 44; *Cock v Cooke* (1866) LR 1 P & D 241; *Re Coles' Goods* (1871) LR 2 P & D 362.
2   *Nichols v Nichols* (1814) 2 Phillim 180.
3   (1868) 3 Sw & Tr 282 at 288.

Conditional intention

5.29   When it is established that the testator had the intention to make a will, it may be necessary to ask the further questions:
(a)   Was the intention to make a conditional, or an unconditional, will?
(b)   If the intention was to make a will which was itself unconditional, do one or more of its provisions come into operation only if a condition is fulfilled?

Conditional wills
5.30   A will may be made with the intention that it shall become operative only upon the happening of a specified event. For example, the will may provide that it is to come into force only if the testator survives his wife, or if he returns from a dangerous mission. If the condition is not fulfilled, the will is of no effect[1] so that if a conditional will is expressed to revoke a previous will, it is inoperative to revoke that previous will if the contingency does not happen.[2]

1   *Parsons v Lanoe* (1748) 1 Ves Sen 189; *Re Winn's Goods* (1861) 2 Sw & Tr 147; *Roberts v Roberts* (1862) 2 Sw & Tr 337; *Re Robinson's Goods* (1870) LR 2 P & D 171.
2   *Re Hugo's Goods* (1877) 2 PD 73.

5.31   The principle governing conditional wills is easy to state, but often difficult to apply in practice. Wills which may be conditional are often made in the face of unusual danger, but there is often difficulty in knowing whether in fact the testator intended the will to come into force only upon the happening of that event, or whether the prospect of death from that cause was merely the motive for making an unconditional will. The question arises for consideration where the deceased does not die as a result of the contemplated danger, but from some other cause.

5.32   A useful discussion of the cases[1] is contained in *Re Spratt's Goods*.[2] In *Re Spratt's Goods* itself the testator was an army officer serving in New Zealand at the time of the Maori war. During the course of the war, he wrote to his son saying that more English officers would be killed if they stayed in New Zealand much longer. He also said[3] that if anything happened to him, his son was to have everything. The testator was not killed in the war, but survived for 32 years, without having revoked his previous will and without having made a new one. The result depended on whether the testator intended his son to take his property only if he was killed in the war, or whether he was to take in any case. The court held the will to be unconditional, so that the son took.[4]

1   *Strauss v Schmidt* (1820) 3 Phillim 209; *Burton v Collingwood* (1832) 4 Hag Ecc 176; *Re Hobson's Goods* (1861) 7 Jur NS 1208; *Re Thorne's Goods* (1865) 4 Sw & Tr 36; *Re*

Dobson's Goods (1866) LR 1 P & D 88; *Re Martin's Goods* (1867) LR 1 P & D 380; *Re Mayd's Goods* (1880) 6 PD 17.

2 [1897] P 28.

3 As he was a soldier on actual military service, he could make a will informally; see below, chapter 7. His letter could, therefore, operate as a will.

4 See also *Re Vines's Estate, Vines v Vines* [1910] P 147.

5.33 In *Re Govier*,[1] on the other hand, a husband and wife made a joint will which commenced 'in the event of our two deaths'. The will was made in 1941, and evidence was forthcoming that they made the will at a time when they were living in an area which was subject to severe bombing attacks and would have had in mind being killed together by the same bomb. The will was held to be conditional upon them dying at the same time and therefore inoperative on the death of one of them some years later from natural causes.[2]

1 [1950] P 237.

2 See also *Re Rowland, Smith v Russell* [1963] Ch 1; and note at 79 LQR 1.

Conditional provisions

5.34 If the will itself is intended to be unconditional, it is then necessary to see whether any particular provision is conditional and, if so, whether the condition is satisfied.[1] This is a matter of construction, and does not affect the making of the will.

1 The position is the same if the will itself is conditional, but the condition is satisfied.

Suspicious circumstances

Will prepared by beneficiary

5.35 Whenever a person who prepares a will benefits under it, the court will require evidence that the testator knew and approved of its contents.[1] This is a separate question from whether the testator was subject to undue influence[2] and the approach is quite different. Where the beneficiary prepares the will, the court will itself require to be satisfied that the testator knew and approved its contents without, necessarily, the party opposing the will making any allegation of impropriety on the part of the beneficiary. In effect, therefore, the burden of proof is placed at the outset on the beneficiary. It will be seen, however, that the party opposing a will on the ground of undue influence must himself prove it.

1 *Wintle v Nye* [1959] 1 All ER 552, below.

2 See below, paras 5.46–5.48.

5.36 It had previously been thought that evidence that a will had been read over to the testator prior to signature would be sufficient. Indeed, Sir J. P. Wilde in *Atter v Atkinson*[1] had said: 'Once get the facts admitted or proved that a testator is capable, that there is no fraud, that the will was read over to him, and that he put his hand to it, and the question whether he knew and approved of its contents is answered.' While this may remain correct where the will is simple, when the will is more complicated, the propounder must now also show that the effect of the will was appreciated by the testator.[2]

1   (1869) LR 1 P & D 665.
2   This follows Lord Cairns LC in *Fulton v Andrew* (1875) LR 7 HL 448 who referred to the duty 'to bring home to the mind of the testator the effect of his testamentary act'.

5.37   In *Re Ticehurst*[1] the testatrix had made a will leaving three houses which she owned to their respective tenants. At the age of 82 she made a new will leaving the houses to relatives. She did not herself see a solicitor, but arranged for the will to be prepared by correspondence with a solicitor. Her own eyesight was bad, and she conducted the correspondence by an amanuensis, the wife of one of her nephews. There was evidence that the deceased was lively and alert for her age, and that the draft of the will had been read out to the testatrix before its execution. However, the suspicion of the court was aroused because the nephew who was the husband of the amanuensis would have received one of the houses under the new will. On the facts the suspicion was not dispelled, and the new will was not admitted to probate.

1   *Re Ticehurst, Midland Bank Executor and Trustee Co Ltd v Hankinson* (1973) Times, 6 March.

5.38   Perhaps the best example of the operation of the rule is *Wintle v Nye*.[1] In this case there was at no time any suggestion of fraud or undue influence, the case depending solely on whether the testatrix knew and approved the contents of her will. The testatrix made her will in 1937, shortly after the death of her brother. During her brother's lifetime, she had apparently had no experience of dealing with her own financial affairs, and naturally turned to Mr Nye, the family solicitor. At first she instructed him to prepare a will under which he and a bank were to be joint executors, and the residue of the estate was to go to certain named charities. She was not content with the draft will prepared by the solicitor, and had a long series of interviews with him, at the end of which a will was prepared under which the solicitor was appointed to be the sole executor. Certain annuities and charitable legacies were given, and the residue was given to the solicitor. When questioned about this, the solicitor said that the testatrix's first concern was for her sister Mildred, to whom she had left an annuity, that she did not wish Mildred to get control of more than that, but that if the testatrix left the residue to him, he could supply further sums for her maintenance. This explanation was, perhaps, less than convincing. Some time later, the testatrix executed a codicil revoking the charitable legacies contained in her will. Her motive in so doing was to ensure that adequate funds were available for the payment of the annuities, which might otherwise have abated.[2] In fact there were ample funds for the payment of the annuities, and the only effect of the codicil was to increase the size of the residuary estate, which went to the solicitor. When the testatrix died, her estate was valued for estate duty purposes at £115,000. There then enters upon the scene Colonel Alfred Daniel Wintle, a retired cavalry officer, who in no uncertain terms thought that the solicitor Nye had behaved shabbily. His first attack was a frontal charge – literally so, for it ended in him debagging Nye, and proceedings being taken against him. The second attack was against the will itself. Colonel Wintle purchased the interest of a beneficiary who had a small share in the estate, and three days later issued process against Nye. He admitted in court that he purchased this share with the sole object of getting Nye into court. He lost at first instance, and in the Court of Appeal, but was successful in the House of Lords. It is worth quoting part of the judgment of Viscount Simmonds in extenso.[3] He said:[4]

'It is not the law that in no circumstances can a solicitor or other person who has prepared a will for a testator take a benefit under it. But that fact creates a suspicion that must be removed by the person propounding the will. In all cases the court must be vigilant and jealous. The degree of suspicion will vary with the circumstances of the case. It may be slight and easily dispelled. It may, on the other hand, be so grave that it can hardly be removed. In the present case, the circumstances were such as to impose on the respondent as heavy a burden as can well be imagined. Here was an elderly lady who might well be called old, unversed in business, having no one on whom to rely except the solicitor who had acted for her and her family; a will made by him under which he takes the bulk of her large estate; a will made, it is true, after a number of interviews extending over a considerable time . . . but [having] a complexity which demanded for its comprehension no common understanding; on her part a wish disclosed in January 1937 to leave her residuary estate to charity which was by August superseded by a devise of it to him; and on his part an explanation of the change which was calculated as much to aggravate as to allay suspicion; the will retained by him and no copy of it given to her; no independent advice received by her and, even according to his own account, little pressure exercised by him to persuade her to get it; a codicil cutting out legacies to charities allegedly for the benefit of annuitants, but, in fact, as was reasonably foreseeable, for the benefit of the residuary beneficiary. All these facts and others that I do not presume to enumerate demanded a vigilant and jealous scrutiny by the judge . . .'

1 [1959] 1 All ER 552.
2 See below, paras 30.53ff, for the doctrine of abatement.
3 Because it brings home the caution which solicitors must exercise in the preparation of wills under which they benefit. Advocates will also see this as an example of the technique of releasing in rapid sequence a succession of charges, so that the opponent withers under the attack.
4 [1959] 1 All ER 552 at 557.

5.39 The same principle will apply if the benefit is for a close member of the family of the person who prepares the will. In *Thomas v Jones*[1] the testatrix executed a will appointing her solicitor to be the executor and leaving most of her property to the solicitor's daughter. The court held that the circumstances were so suspicious that the will was not to be upheld.

1 [1928] P 162.

5.40 Where a will prepared by a solicitor confers a substantial benefit on him or his family, he may be guilty of professional misconduct and liable to be struck off the roll.[1]

1   *Re A Solicitor* [1975] QB 475, [1974] 3 All ER 853, where the Court of Appeal upheld a
    ruling of the Disciplinary Committee of the Law Society that in such a case the solicitor has
    a duty, not merely to tell his client that he should take independent advice but, if the client
    refuses to do so, to refuse to act any further in the matter. The principle is now incorporated
    in paragraph 15.08 of *The Guide to the Professional Conduct of Solicitors*, published by the
    Law Society (6th edn, 1993).

Will prepared by others

5.41   The circumstances will usually be suspicious if instructions for the
making of the will are transmitted through an intermediary who will benefit,
even if that beneficiary takes no other part in the preparation of the
document. The decisions in *Battan Singh v Amirchand*[1] and *Re Ticehurst*,[2]
which have already been mentioned,[3] are examples of this.

1   [1948] AC 161.
2   (1973) Times, 6 March.
3   See above, paras 5.6(c) and 5.37 respectively.

Gifts of residue

5.42   The problem is particularly acute with regard to gifts of residue.
Where the person who prepares the will, or the intermediary who transmits
the instructions, is to take the whole or a substantial part of the residue of
the testator's estate, it seems that the court will require to be satisfied not
only that the testator intended that person to take a residuary gift, but also
that the testator was aware, broadly, of the anticipated quantum of benefit.
Wintle v Nye[1] is itself an example. In the British Columbia decision in
Russell v Fraser[2] a bank manager took down from the testatrix, aged 79,
instructions for a will, under which he was to be the residuary beneficiary.
He relayed the instructions to a solicitor who prepared the will. On a later
occasion, the solicitor went through the will with the testatrix while the bank
manager was not present. She agreed to its terms, but there was no specific
discussion as to the size of the residue, which amounted to about $C180,000.
The court held that as the bank manager had transmitted the original
instructions for the preparation of a will under which he benefited, the onus
was upon him to show that the testatrix knew and approved the contents of
the will, and as he could not show that the testatrix realised the approximate
amount of his benefit, the will could not stand.

1   [1959] 1 All ER 552; above, para 5.38.
2   (1980) 118 DLR (3d) 733 (British Columbia Court of Appeal).

5.43   This is to be contrasted with another Canadian decision, *Re Doiron*.[1]
The testator, a bachelor, had made a will giving his estate to his brothers.
He went into a home for the aged, and after he had lived there for about
three years, the woman who ran the home contacted a solicitor to draw up a
new will for the testator, under which he left all his property to her. The
solicitor visited the testator at the home, and privately discussed the
contents of the document with him. The court held that (a) the woman's

part in arranging for a will to be prepared under which she was the sole beneficiary caused the circumstances to be suspicious, but (b) she had discharged the burden on her by showing that the testator had read the will with the solicitor when she was not present, and that he could have altered it, or not signed it, if he so wished.

1   (1980) 27 Nfld & PEIR 211 (Prince Edward Island Supreme Court).

Suspicion without benefit

5.44   While in most cases the suspicion is aroused because a beneficiary is in some way connected with the making of the will, the rule is not restricted to such circumstances.[1] In *Eady v Waring*[2] the testator had made a will leaving, inter alia, a substantial legacy to his niece. Then, at the age of 78, he went to live with his married brother, and made a new will appointing the married brother's son to be one of the executors, and leaving most of his estate to the married brother. The son had been instrumental in arranging for the will to be made, although he did not benefit under it. The court held that the circumstances were suspicious, and refused to uphold the will.

1   *Barry v Butlin* (1838) 2 Moo PC 480; *Fulton v Andrew* (1875) LR 7 HL 448; *Low v Guthrie* [1909] AC 278; *Davis v Mayhew* [1927] P 264; *Re R* [1951] P 10.
2   (1974) 43 DLR (3d) 667 (Ontario).

Lack of free will

Coercion

5.45   Where a will is accompanied by force, fraud, fear or undue influence, that will, or the affected part which is produced in this way, is not regarded as the act of the testator, and so probate will be refused. There is little authority on force and fear – but little is needed to show that a will signed only because the testator is being banged on the head with a truncheon until he does sign will not be regarded as valid.[1]

1   See, however, *Mountain v Bennet* (1787) 1 Cox Eq Cas 353; *Nelson v Oldfield* (1688) 2 Vern 76.

Undue influence

Absence of presumption
5.46   By contrast with some other branches of the law[1] there is never a presumption that a will is made under undue influence because there is a relationship between the testator and beneficiary: it must always be proved. Thus, in *Parfitt v Lawless*[2] a testatrix left all her property to a Roman Catholic priest who had lived with the testatrix and her husband as their

chaplain, and who was her confessor. An attempt was made to raise a presumption of undue influence[3] although there was no positive evidence that he had exercised any influence at all over the testatrix. It was held that there was not even a case to go to the jury.[4]

1   Eg contract, and in particular gifts to a person in a fiduciary position.
2   (1872) LR 2 P & D 462.
3   Cf *Archer v Hudson* (1844) 7 Beav 551.
4   See also *Wheeler and Batsford v Alderson* (1831) 3 Hag Ecc 574; *Wyatt v Ingram* (1832) 3 Hag Ecc 466; *Walker v Smith* (1861) 20 Beav 394; *Croft v Day* (1838) 1 Curt 782; *Tuckwell v Cornick* (1844) 2 LTOS 336; *Greville v Tylee* (1851) 7 Moo PCC 320; *Ashwell v Lomi* (1850) LR 2 P & D 477.

5.47   The reason for this difference from the law of contract is that many of the usual relationships which in contract give rise to the presumption, such as parent and child, husband and wife, solicitor and client, are just those relationships which would naturally give rise to the testator's bounty. Furthermore, in the case of an inter vivos transaction, the parties can protect themselves by taking independent advice, whereas in the case of a gift by will, the beneficiary may well not know of the gift until after the testator has died. Although undue influence will not be presumed from the existence of a relationship between testator and beneficiary, the circumstances surrounding the making of the will can give rise to such a presumption.

5.48   Such circumstances arose in *Re Harden*.[1] Following the death of her husband, Mrs Harden took up an interest in spiritualism, holding meetings in her lounge, which she renamed the sanctuary. She was introduced to a well-spoken gentleman, Mr Hunt, as being a suitable person to attend her seances. After meeting Mrs Harden, Mr Hunt, seeing the potential, had embarked on an eight-guinea postal course, which was his sole instruction as a spiritualist medium. During subsequent seances, Mr Hunt transmitted to Mrs Harden, at dictation speed, messages 'from the other side' as to what she should do with her possessions. In consequence, Mrs Harden made two wills which were essentially in Mr Hunt's favour. Stevenson J had little hesitation in coming to the conclusion that Mr Hunt had used undue influence over Mrs Harden to procure the making of her wills. He had taken possession of her mind and subdued it to his purpose so that effectively she had written not the records of her own mind but those of Mr Hunt. This went beyond mere persuasion.

1   *Re Harden's Estate, Clayton and Hunt v Brown* [1959] CLYB 3448, (1959) Times, 30 June.

Difference from persuasion
5.49   Persuasion of a testator does not itself constitute undue influence unless the persuasion is so overpowering that it leaves the testator with no freedom of choice, and so amounts to coercion. As stated by Sir J. P. Wilde in *Hall v Hall*:[1]

'Persuasion appeals to the affections or ties of kindred, to a sentiment of gratitude for past services, or pity for future destination, or the like, – these are all legitimate and may be fairly pressed on a testator. On the other hand, pressure of whatever character . . . if so exerted as to overpower the volition without convincing the judgment . . . will constitute undue influence, though no force is either used or threatened. In a word, a testator may be led but not driven.'

While the testator retains his freedom of choice there will be no undue influence, but 'his will must be the offspring of his own volition, and not the record of someone else's'.[2] The court will therefore more readily find that undue influence has been exercised where the testator is of weak mental capacity or in a weak state of health.[3]

1 (1868) LR 1 P & D 481 at 482.
2 Ibid.
3 *Hampson v Guy* (1891) 64 LT 778.

Burden of proof

5.50 Although it is always for the person propounding a will to satisfy the court that it is valid[1] this does not extend to disproving undue influence. It is always for the person alleging undue influence to prove it.[2] In *Re Cutcliffe's Estate*[3] the Court of Appeal made it clear that an allegation of undue influence should be made only where there is strong evidence, and that if an allegation is made on insufficient evidence, the person making it will probably be condemned in the costs.

1 Above, para 5.9(a).
2 *Boyse v Rossborough* (1857) 6 HL Cas 2; *Low v Guthrie* [1909] AC 278; *Tyrrell v Painton* [1894] P 151; *Craig v Lamoureux* [1920] AC 349.
3 [1959] P 6.

Did the testator know and approve the contents of the will?

5.51 It is important to contrast the position where there is undue influence, and where the testator did not know and approve the contents of his will. As has been shown,[1] if undue influence is alleged it must be proved by the person making the allegation. If, however, a person opposing the will can satisfy the court that the circumstances surrounding its making are suspicious, the burden of proof shifts. It is for those opposing the will to show that the circumstances are suspicious. If they do so, in effect the burden is then shifted to those propounding the will to show that the testator knew and approved the contents. But the degree of proof is different in the two cases. A finding of undue influence involves at least a moral condemnation of the person using that influence. Strictly, a finding that the testator did not know and approve the contents of his will is morally neutral, although in the circumstances of a particular case moral guilt might be present. But because moral guilt is necessarily present in undue influence, the judge will require clear evidence of it, and where there is any doubt about the strength of the evidence it is, where appropriate, better to issue process requiring the executor to prove only that the testator knew and approved the contents of the will.[2]

1 Above, para 5.50.
2 As in *Wintle v Nye*, above, para 5.38. Under RSC Ord 76, r 9(3), an allegation can be made of want of knowledge and approval without making an allegation of undue influence; *Re Stott, Klouda v Lloyds Bank Ltd* [1980] 1 All ER 259. The courts so dislike allegations of undue influence which cannot be supported that they may order the legal advisers personally to meet the costs; see *Re Bisyk (No 2)* (1980) 32 OR (2d) 281 (Ont).

Mistake

5.52 The final aspect of the mental elements in the making of a will is that of mistake. There are three situations in which mistake may arise:
(a) the wrong document may be executed;
(b) there may be mistake going to the motive for a provision in a will;
(c) there may be mistake as to the effect of a will, or of one or more of its provisions.

Execution of wrong document

5.53 Where a document is executed by mistake, probate of it will be refused. Thus, in *Re Meyer's Estate*[1] two sisters executed similar codicils. Then by mistake they each executed the document intended for the other. The court refused to grant probate.[2] This is as far as the English courts will go, although in Canada on similar facts probate was granted of the correct document.[3]

1 [1908] P 353.
2 Following the decision on similar facts of *Re Hunt's Goods* (1875) LR 3 P & D 250 on the basis that the testatrix did not know and approve the contents of the will she had signed and that if she had known the contents she would not have signed it.
3 *Re Brander* [1952] 4 DLR 688. See Harding Law *The Law of Wills* (1977) p 64.

Mistake as to motive

5.54 If the testator intended certain words to be included in the will, and they are so included, then probate of the will is granted including those words, although the testator is mistaken as to their legal effect. In *Collins v Elstone*[1] the testatrix was given incorrect information as to the effect of a revocation clause, but as she intended those words to appear in the document, they were admitted to probate.[2] Likewise, if a testator uses technical language, even if he is mistaken as to its effect, such language is admitted to probate.[3]

1 [1893] P 1.
2 See also *Fulton v Andrew* (1875) LR 7 HL 448; *Harter v Harter* (1873) LR 3 P & D 11; *Rhodes v Rhodes* (1882) 7 App Cas 192; *Gregson v Taylor* [1917] P 256.
3 See below, para 5.58(b).

Mistake as to contents

5.55 Where a word or clause has been included in the will by mistake, and without the knowledge of the testator, probate will be granted of the will with these words omitted.[1] The court will not, however, omit part of the will from probate if the effect of the remainder of the will is altered. In *Re Horrocks*[2] a solicitor drew up for a testatrix a will which contained a gift of residue for such charitable or benevolent objects as her trustees might select. After her death, the solicitor, who was also the executor, said that this was a typing error, and he sought to omit the word 'or'. This would have the effect of making the words 'charitable' and 'benevolent' cumulative. The court refused to make the deletion, for it altered the effect of what remained.

1 *Re Oswald's Goods* (1874) LR 3 P & D 162; *Morrell v Morrell* (1882) 7 PD 68; *Re Moore's Goods* [1892] P 378; *Re Boehm's Goods* [1891] P 247; *Re Reade's Goods* [1902] P 75; *Vaughan v Clerk* (1902) 87 LT 144; *Marklew v Turner* (1900) 17 TLR 10.
2 [1939] P 198.

Rectification

5.56 In the case of the will of a testator dying before 1983, the court had no power to add words which the testator had intended to include. It had power only to omit from the will words of which the testator did not know and approve, so leaving a blank space in the probate copy of the will.

5.57 In respect of the will of a testator dying on or after 1 January 1983, however, if the court is satisfied that the will failed to carry out the testator's intention, it has power in two sets of circumstances to rectify the will in order to give effect to those intentions:[1]
(a) where there is a clerical error; or
(b) where the person who prepared the will failed to understand the testator's instructions.
In *Re Reynette-James*[2] a draft will had been approved by the testatrix, but the engrossment omitted 33 words dealing with the residue of the estate. This error was not discovered until after her death and the court was unable to include the words in the probate copy. If the same facts occurred after 1982 the court would now have power to rectify the will to incorporate the missing words.

1 Administration of Justice Act 1982, s 20.
2 *Re Reynette-James, Wightman v Reynette-James* [1976] 1 WLR 161.

Limitations
5.58 The court's power to rectify is limited to the two sets of circumstances envisaged by s 20.[1] If the will fails to carry out the testator's intentions for some other reason, however, the court has no power to add words but only its residual power as it existed prior to 1983, to omit words of which the testator did not know and approve. Rectification would not therefore be available where:
(a) a draftsman deliberately omitted words;
(b) the testator failed to appreciate the legal effect of the wording used in the will – say, a technical term the meaning of which he did not understand;
(c) there is uncertainty as to the intended meaning of the wording;
(d) there is a lacuna in the will as the testator did not apply his mind to the particular events that actually occurred.

1 Administration of Justice Act 1982, s 20.

Time limit

5.59 An application to rectify a will must be made within six months from the date on which a grant of representation to the deceased's estate is first taken out.[1] Although the court has discretion to extend this limit, the personal representatives are protected if they distribute the estate once the six-month period has expired without an application being made.[2]

1 Administration of Justice Act 1982, s 20(2).
2 Ibid, s 20(3).

1   For the formalities applying to wills of persons dying before 1983, see the 3rd edition of this book.

6.9   Some Commonwealth countries have attempted to deal with the problem by introducing the doctrine of 'substantial compliance' which is established in some United States jurisdictions.[1] Where this is done, formalities are prescribed, but the court is given power to grant probate of a will where the formal requirements are not complied with, but the court is satisfied that the deceased intended the document to be his will. An example is s 12(2) of the Wills Act of South Australia, which reads:

'(2)   A document purporting to embody the testamentary intentions of a deceased person shall, notwithstanding that it has not been executed with the formalities required by this Act, be deemed to be a will of the deceased person if the Supreme Court, upon application for admission of the document to probate as the last will of the deceased, is satisfied that there can be no reasonable doubt that the deceased intended the document to constitute his will.'

There is, however, no such doctrine in England and Wales[2] and it is now necessary to consider the requirements as to form prescribed by the Wills Act 1837, as amended.

1   See (1975) 88 Harvard Law Rev 489.
2   The Law Reform Committee, 22nd Report, pp 4–5, in 1980 recommended conferring such a dispensing power on the court. This particular proposal was not adopted in the Administration of Justice Act 1982, which only adopted the recommendation to relax the rules relating to formalities.

Writing

One document

6.10   The requirement that a will must be in writing does not mean that it must be in the testator's handwriting. Nor does it mean that it must necessarily be in anyone's handwriting. Probably any permanent form of visual representation will be sufficient. A will may, therefore, be handwritten, typed, printed, or be in any combination of these.[1] If it is handwritten, it may be in ink, or pencil, or partly one and partly the other.[2] There is no requirement as to the material on which the will must be written. Thus, a will may be written on the shell of an egg.[3] There is also no requirement as to the language in which the will is written. It may be written in a foreign language or, indeed, partly in code, provided this can be deciphered from extrinsic evidence.[4] It may also be written in indirect speech.[5] Suppose therefore that a person seeking to produce a modern rival to the Elgin Marbles chips out his will in the form of a strip cartoon over 176 blocks of marble and then signs it at the end. It may cause havoc with the Probate Registry's filing system – but will probably be valid nevertheless.

1   Interpretation Act 1889, s 20; see also *Re Moore's Goods* [1892] P 378; *Re Smithers* [1939] Ch 1015 at 120, [1939] 3 All ER 689 at 692.

2   *Re Lawson's Goods* (1842) 6 Jur 349; *Re Hall's Goods* (1871) LR 2 P & D 256; *Re Adams' Goods* (1872) LR 2 P & D 367; *Re Tonge's Goods* (1891) 66 LT 60.
3   *Re Barnes' Goods* (1926) 43 TLR 71.
4   *Kell v Charmer* (1856) 23 Beav 195.
5   In *Re Opuku, Goh v Donyinah* [1973] 1 GLR 273 (Ghana Court of Appeal).

More than one document

6.11   There is no requirement in the Wills Act 1837 that a will must be written on one sheet of paper only. The courts have, however, developed a requirement that, if the will is written on more than one piece of paper, all sheets on which it was written should be attached at the time of execution.[1] While this is a matter of common prudence, the rule was relaxed so that it then became sufficient for the sheets to be held together at the time of execution, for example by holding them with finger and thumb, even though there is no permanent means of attachment.[2] In *Sterling v Bruce*[3] the High Court of Northern Ireland went further and held that where a will is written on more than one piece of paper, it is not necessary for the pieces to be physically joined at all, and that it is sufficient if the pieces of paper are in the same room as that in which the execution is effected.[4] It is to be hoped that the sensible approach adopted in *Sterling v Bruce* will be followed in England.

1   *Cook v Lambert* (1863) 3 Sw & Tr 46; *Re West's Goods* (1863) 32 LJPM & A 182; *Re Horsford's Goods* (1874) LR 3 P & D 211; *Lewis v Lewis* [1908] P 1.
2   *Lewis v Lewis*, above; *Re Little, Foster v Cooper* [1960] 1 All ER 387.
3   [1973] NI 255.
4   In *Sterling v Bruce* itself, an attempt to show that certain sheets formed part of the will failed because there was no evidence that those sheets were in the room at the time when the will was executed.

6.12   The papers which comprise the will are those which the testator intended should comprise it. Where a sheet of paper is placed in an envelope, the paper and the envelope are together capable of constituting the will, although it will usually be difficult to show that the testator intended the envelope to be part of the will itself, rather than a container for the will.[1]

1   See eg *Re Mann's Goods* [1942] P 146; *Re Beadle, Mayes v Beadle* [1974] 1 All ER 493; below paras 6.19 and 6.20.

Signature of testator

Meaning of 'signature'

6.13   Although the Wills Act says that the will must be 'signed' by the testator, the courts have decided that this does not mean what it says.[1] This provision has been construed as meaning that the testator must put on the document some mark which he *intends* to be his signature. A 'signature' made by a rubber stamp is satisfactory.[2] A mark is acceptable as a signature,[3] even, it appears from a Canadian case, if the hand of the testator is guided when the mark is made.[4] In *Re Finn*[5] the testator, who was admittedly illiterate, went even further: he dipped his thumb in the ink pot, and made a blot on the will with his inky thumb. That was accepted as a valid signature.

1 See, generally, Sherrin (1970) 114 SJ 198.
2 *Re Jenkins* (1863) 3 Sw & Tr 93.
3 *Lemaine v Staneley* (1681) Freem KB 538; *Baker v Dening* (1838) 8 Ad & El 94; *Hindmarsh v Charlton* (1861) 8 HL Cas 160; *Re Kieran* [1933] IR 222.
4 *Re White* [1948] 1 DLR 572.
5 (1935) 105 LJP 36.

6.14 A testator may sign just his initials,[1] or part of his signature, provided in every case that the actual mark he did make was intended to be his signature. Thus, in *Re Chalcraft*[2] the testatrix was on the verge of death. Her normal signature was 'E Chalcraft'. She began to sign her name, and had got as far as 'E Chal' when she could not go on. On a liberal construction, the court held that this was all that she intended to put as her signature, and the will was admitted to probate. This decision must be contrasted with that in *Re Colling*.[3] While in hospital, the testator started to sign his will in the presence of a patient, and the ward sister, as witnesses. After he had started to sign his name, but before he had completed his signature, the sister was called away to attend to another patient, and the testator completed his signature in her absence. It was clear that the testator intended to sign the will with his full signature, and he had not, therefore, 'signed' in the presence of both witnesses.

1 *Re Savory's Goods* (1851) 18 LTOS 280; *Re Emerson's Goods* (1882) 9 LR Ir 443.
2 [1948] P 222.
3 [1972] 3 All ER 729.

6.15 If the testator intends to use a full name, apparently it need not be his own.[1] Thus, in *Re Glover's Goods*[2] a will was admitted to probate where it was signed by a woman in the name of her first husband after her second marriage, and in *Re Redding's Goods*[3] the will was held to be effectively signed where the testatrix had used an assumed name. Further, it seems that to be a 'signature' it is not necessary to use a name at all. In *Re Cook's Estate*[4] the court accepted as a valid signature the words 'your loving mother' and in *Rhodes v Peterson*[5] the word 'Mum'. The testator must, however, make some mark. Accordingly, it is not effective to pass a dry pen over a signature already on the paper, in the form of a mock signing,[6] though this might perhaps be valid as an acknowledgement.[7]

1 *Re Clarke's Goods* (1858) 1 Sw & Tr 22.
2 (1847) 5 Notes of Cases 553.
3 (1850) 2 Rob Eccl 339.
4 [1960] 1 All ER 689.
5 1972 SLT 98.
6 *Playne v Scriven* (1849) 1 Rob Eccl 772; *Kevil v Lynch* (1874) IR 9 Eq 249; *Re Maddock* (1847) LR 3 P & D 169.
7 See below, para 6.21.

6.16   The result of these decisions is that it is necessary for the testator to make a mark on the paper, but the courts will accept as a signature whatever mark was intended by him as a signature.

Signature by another

6.17   The testator need not sign the will himself. The will is valid in this respect if it is signed by someone else who signs in the presence of the testator, and by his direction. The concept of being in the 'presence' of the testator is considered later.[1]

1   Below, para 6.25.

Operative intention

6.18   It must appear that the testator by his signature intended to give effect to the will.[1] Under the original s 9 of the Wills Act 1837, it was necessary to show that, in some sense, the will was signed at the foot or end, but under the present provision the signature can be anywhere on the document provided that it is apparent that it is intended to give effect to it. An example is *Re Hornby*.[2] In that case the testator wrote out a will, and as he did so he left in the text towards the end a 'box' in which, when he had finished the whole text, he wrote his signature. The will was upheld on the basis that the signature was intended to validate the whole will.

1   Substituted s 9(b), Wills Act 1837.
2   [1946] P 171, [1946] 2 All ER 150.

6.19   The problem has arisen most commonly where the testator writes the text of a will on a piece of paper, places the piece of paper in an envelope, and signs the envelope. It has been seen[1] that the paper and the envelope are capable of together constituting the will. Is, then, the signature on the envelope intended to give effect to the will, or is it intended to identify the contents? In each case it is a question of fact. In *Re Mann's Goods*[2] the testatrix wrote on the envelope 'Last Will and Testament of J. C. Mann'. She signed this and her signature was witnessed. This envelope was then placed into a larger envelope and sealed. The court held that the signature was intended to give effect to the will, and probate was granted.

1   Above, para 6.12.
2   [1942] P 146.

6.20   In other cases[1] probate has been refused where it could not be shown that the signature was intended as the signature to the will. So, in *Re Beadle, Mayes v Beadle*[2] the testatrix asked two friends, Mr and Mrs Mayes, whom she knew as 'Charley' and 'Maisy', to help her make a will. The testatrix dictated her will, and Mrs Mayes wrote it down. The testatrix signed the paper in the top right-hand corner, and Mr Mayes also signed it, but Mrs Mayes did not. The paper itself was therefore not properly attested.[3] The testatrix then took an envelope and wrote on it 'My last will and testament, E. A. Beadle, to Charley and Maisy'. The paper was then put into the envelope, which was sealed. Mr Mayes wrote on the back: 'We certify that the contents of this letter was written in the presence of ourselves', and both he and Mrs Mayes signed it. The name of the testatrix therefore appeared on the front of the envelope, and those of the witnesses on the back. Goff J held that when the testatrix signed on the front of the envelope, she did not intend to give effect to her will (which she thought she had already effectively signed), but merely to identify the contents.

1   Eg, *Re Bean's Estate* [1944] P 83.
2   [1974] 1 All ER 493.
3   Because it was not itself attested.

6.21   At what stage, however, does the operative signature have to be made? Must the entire will have been completed before the testator can sign it? The answer was provided in *Wood v Smith*.[1] Shortly before his death the testator had made a holograph will commencing with the words 'My will by Percy Winterbone . . .'; he then proceeded to write out his wishes. When he had completed writing he had then asked the witnesses to sign the document as witnesses. It was pointed out to the deceased that he had not yet signed the document himself, to which he replied that he had already signed at the top of the document, referring to the opening words in the will where his name 'Percy Winterbone' appeared. The deceased also remarked that he could sign the document anywhere. Accordingly the witnesses than added their signatures to attest the document. The validity of the execution of the will was challenged as the signature had been written on the document before the dispositive contents had been written so that it could not have been intended 'to give effect to' those contents. This argument found favour with the deputy judge in the Chancery Division on the basis that when the testator signed the document it did not contain any disposition at all and therefore his signature could not give effect to a document which at that point of time did not exist. Scott LJ, delivering the judgment in the Court of Appeal, was unable to agree with this approach.[2] The test in the new s 9 is whether the signature of the testator was to give effect to the will and as, in the present case, the testator indicated in clear terms to the witnesses that he intended his name at the beginning of the document to give effect to the whole document, which was completed in one operation, it complied with the section's requirements.[3] The test formulated was therefore whether the document was completed and signed in one operation. Scott LJ refused to commit himself on whether such a will completed on different occasions would be valid, although he inclined against it.

1   *Wood v Smith* [1992] 3 All ER 556.
2   Ibid at p 562b.
3   Although in the event the Court of Appeal upheld the finding on the separate issue that the deceased did not have testamentary capacity at the time of the execution of his will.

Signing or acknowledging in the presence of witnesses

Acknowledgment of signature

6.22 The testator must either sign his will in the presence of two or more witnesses or acknowledge his signature in their presence.[1] If the will is signed by some other person by the direction of the testator,[2] that can be when the witnesses are present, so that there are present the testator, the signer, and the witnesses. Alternatively, the will can be signed in advance, and that signature acknowledged by the testator.

1 Substituted s 9(c), Wills Act 1837.
2 See above, para 6.17.

6.23 The testator acknowledges his signature by speaking any words, or doing any act, which shows that he adopts or recognises the signature as his own. In principle, the acknowledgment is of the signature, not of the will, but it is nevertheless sufficient for the testator to say words to the effect that 'this is my will' even though he does not say 'this is my signature'.[1] However, as the acknowledgment is of the signature, it is not necessary that the witness should know that the document is a will.[2] It is sufficient if the testator merely asks the witnesses to sign the document which he produces and they see his signature upon it.[3] Alternatively, the acknowledgment may be merely by gesture.[4] It was stated[5] that to draw a dry pen over a signature on a will did not constitute a signing of the will for the purposes of the Act. It may be, however, that such a gesture would amount to an acknowledgment of the signature.[6]

1 *Keigwin v Keigwin* (1843) 3 Curt 607; *Wright v Sanderson* (1884) 9 PD 149; *Re Balcom* (1975) 22 NSR (2d) 707 (Nova Scotia).
2 *Keigwin v Keigwin* (1843) 3 Curt 607.
3 *Gaze v Gaze* (1843) 3 Curt 451.
4 *Re Davies' Goods* (1850) 2 Rob Eccl 337; *Re Owston's Goods* (1862) 2 Sw & Tr 461.
5 Above, para 6.15.
6 *Lewis v Lewis* [1908] P 1.

6.24 A signature can be acknowledged only if the witnesses either see or have the opportunity of seeing the signature.[1] In *Re Groffman*[2] the deceased said to two friends at a coffee party, 'I should like you now to witness my will'; at the same time gesturing to his coat pocket where the folded will was, but not taking it out. The only table in the room was covered with coffee cups and cakes, so the deceased and one of the friends went into an adjoining room, where the deceased took the will out of his pocket, revealing the signature on it. As the friend was the only person present in that other room, the production of the will by the deceased was not a valid acknowledgment, and although there was no doubt that the deceased intended to make his will, it was rejected.[3]

1 *Re Gunstan's Goods* (1882) 7 PD 102.
2 [1969] 2 All ER 108.
3 See Baker (1969) 85 LQR 462.

The concept of presence

6.25 The substituted s 9 of the Wills Act 1837 refers three times to the concept of presence:

(a) someone other than the testator can sign the will on his behalf if he does so, inter alia, in his presence;

(b) the testator must sign the will or acknowledge the signature in the presence of the witnesses; and

(c) each witness must sign the will or acknowledge the signature in the presence of the testator.

It is clear that the witnesses need not actually see the testator sign, nor need he see them sign.[1] The test is whether the person in whose presence the signature is made could have seen the other signing had he wished to do so. Thus, if the testator is in one room and the witnesses in another, but there is a hole in the wall, then if the witnesses from where they were standing could have looked through the hole in the wall and seen the testator signing that is sufficient.[2] If, however, the witnesses would have needed to have moved in order to see through the hole in the wall, and there is no evidence that they did alter their position, the attestation is bad.[3] In *Casson v Dade*[4] in 1781 a testatrix drove to her solicitor's office to sign a will. She signed it but found the office hot and went outside to sit in her carriage. When she was in the carriage she could not in fact see the witnesses through the window of the office but at the very moment when the witnesses were signing the horses backed just so that there was a line of sight through the window of the carriage and the window of the office in such a way that had she so wished the testatrix could have seen the witnesses signing. The attestation was good. The test is therefore whether a testator was able to see the witnesses sign if he had cared to look. The test is the same for a blind testator, he being attributed with notional vision.[5]

1 *Tod v Earl Winchelsea* (1826) 2 C & P 488; *Jenner v Ffinch* (1879) 5 PD 106; *Carter v Seaton* (1901) 85 LT 76.
2 *Shires v Glascock* (1685) 2 Salk 688.
3 *Norton v Bazett* (1856) Dea & Sw 259.
4 (1781) 1 Bro CC 99.
5 *Re Piercy's Goods* (1845) 1 Rob Eccl 278. However, Pearce J in *Re Gibson* [1949] P 434, when considering the ability of a blind person to be a witness, inclined to the view that witnessing is essentially a visual act. If this view is correct, however, one person can be in another's 'presence' only if the latter can see; thus a blind person could not make a will – unless, which is unlikely, 'presence' has different meanings when applied to a testator and to a witness.

6.26 This and similar cases are clear examples of the extent to which the courts will go in order to save a will if possible. Indeed, in *Winchilsea v Wauchope*[1] it was stated that where a line of sight exists there is a presumption of good attestation if there is no evidence to the contrary. With modern technology, a straight line of sight should possibly be construed as including a visual but not physical presence: for example, signing or witnessing a will over closed-circuit television.[2] Presence presupposes not only a physical, or at least visual, presence, but also a mental presence on the part of the testator and the witnesses. If the testator loses consciousness before both witnesses have signed (or acknowledged their signatures), the will fails.[3]

1 (1827) 3 Russ 441.
2 In practical terms this is more likely to extend to a revocation of a will by destruction by another person in the presence and by the direction of the testator (see para 8.37). Suppose a solicitor destroys a will by direction of the testator who is viewing the act over a videophone. Is this a valid revocation?
3 *Right v Price* (1779) 1 Doug KB 241; *Re Chalcraft* [1948] P 222.

Attestation

Requirements

6.27 Each witness must either
(a) attest and sign the will; or
(b) acknowledge his signature in the presence of the testator.[1]
It is not necessary for the witnesses to sign the will or acknowledge the signature in the presence of the other witness or witnesses.[2]

1 Substituted s 9(d), Wills Act 1837.
2 Ibid.

Attest and sign

6.28 A witness who is to come within the first limb, that is, to attest and sign the will, must witness the signature of the testator and sign his name with the intention of attesting the signature. 'Sign' has the same meaning as that considered above in the context of the signature of the testator.[1]

1 Above, paras 6.13–6.16.

6.29 Section 14 of the Wills Act 1837 provides that if a person who witnesses a will is not at the time of such attestation, or at any time subsequently, competent to be called as a witness to prove the execution of the will then the will is not on that ground invalid. It is not clear whether this provision relates to the general credibility, or only to the mental capacity, of the witness. It probably means the former, so that, to this extent, it is not necessary for an intending testator to satisfy himself about the mental capacity of the witness.

6.30 It is established that the witnesses must sign the will with the intention of witnessing the testator's signature, and not with some other intention. So, in *Re Beadle, Mayes v Beadle*,[1] the facts of which have been mentioned earlier,[2] one of the reasons the will was formally invalid was that the witnesses signed the envelope, not with the intention of witnessing the signature, but as part of the process of identifying the contents.[3]

1 [1974] 1 All ER 493.
2 Above, para 6.20.
3 See also *Re Beauchamp Estate* [1974] 2 WWR 645 (Alberta). Before they married, a

husband and wife made wills, which would normally have been revoked on their marriage (see below, para 8.61). After the marriage they both signed a document to the effect that their wills made before marriage should continue in force as if there had been no marriage. The husband and wife both signed the document, together with one other person, and the question was whether the document was executed as a will. It was held that it was possible for a person to sign in two capacities, so that the husband and the other person could have signed as witnesses to the signature of the wife. It was held, however, that the husband and wife did not intend to sign in two capacities, and that they signed only to execute the document on their own behalf and not also to attest the signature of the other. The document was therefore not admitted to probate.

Acknowledgment

6.31 Instead of attesting and signing the will, a witness can acknowledge his signature. In this case it is, perhaps, surprising that he does not have to 'attest and acknowledge'. Accordingly, if the witness has already signed the document, it is permissible for him then to acknowledge his signature in the presence of the testator. The operation of this provision is illustrated by the facts of *Re Colling*.[1] It will be recalled[2] that the ward sister, one of the witnesses, was called away while the testator was actually signing his will. In the absence of the sister, the testator completed his signature, and the other witness, a patient, attested the document. When the sister returned, the testator and the other witness acknowledged their signatures and the sister then attested. Under the law as it then was[3] the formalities had not been complied with. If the same facts had occurred after 1982 the will would have been validly executed, as the patient would have acknowledged his signature on the same occasion as the sister signed. 'Acknowledgment' of a signature by a witness has the same meaning as in the case of acknowledgment of a signature by a testator.[4]

1   *Re Colling, Lawson v Von Winckler* [1972] 3 All ER 729.
2   Above, para 6.14.
3   The original s 9 did not permit a witness to acknowledge his signature. The substituted s 9 was incorporated by the Administration of Justice Act 1982, s 17, in respect of wills of testators dying on or after 1 January 1983.
4   Above, paras 6.13–6.16.

In the presence of the testator

6.32 It is likely that for the purposes of the requirement that the witnesses must either attest and sign the will, or acknowledge the signature, in the 'presence' of the testator, the expression 'presence' has the same meaning as that discussed above.[1]

1   Paras 6.25–6.26.

6.33 There is no requirement for the witnesses to sign the will, or acknowledge the signature, in the presence of each other. It is, therefore, sufficient if the testator signs his will or acknowledges his signature in the presence of two witnesses; one goes out of the room while the other signs; and then the other comes back and signs when the first has left the room.

The attestation clause

6.34 It is desirable although not essential that a will should conclude with an attestation clause. This clause, which may be adapted to the circumstances, is designed to provide prima facie evidence that in the particular circumstances of the case the requirements of the Act have been fulfilled.[1] Without such a clause, although the will will not be necessarily invalid, it will be necessary to prove in some other way that the statutory requirements have been fulfilled.[2] This will usually involve tracing one of the attesting witnesses, or someone else who was present at the time of execution, and obtaining from that person an affidavit confirming exactly what happened at the time of execution. If such evidence cannot be obtained because it is impossible to trace the witnesses the will may nevertheless be admitted to probate under the presumption considered later.[3]

1 Such a clause is contained in the specimen will in Appendix C. Most such clauses provide that the witnesses have also signed in the presence of each other. Although this is not an essential requirement to establish validity (see para 6.33) it strengthens the presumption of validity.
2 Non-Contentious Probate Rules 1987, r 12(1). If no such evidence is available, evidence of the deceased's handwriting may be accepted under r 12(2), or of any other matter that may raise a presumption in favour of due execution.
3 See below, paras 18.43–18.46.

Witnesses benefiting

Prohibition of benefit

6.35 Section 15 of the Wills Act 1837 provides that if a person who would derive a benefit under the will acts as a witness, then, although the attestation by that person is good, he cannot take any benefit under the will. A person who is a spouse of the witness at the time of execution of the will is also excluded from any benefit under the will, but the subsequent marriage of a beneficiary and a witness will not invalidate the gift.[1]

1 *Thorpe v Beswick* (1881) 6 QBD 311.

6.36 A further illustration of the way in which the courts have construed this provision of s 15 narrowly is provided by the fact that they will uphold a gift if it can be said to have arisen under any testamentary instrument which the witness did not attest. In several cases it has been decided that if a beneficiary attests the will and the will is confirmed by a codicil which he does not attest then he is entitled to take the gift as it can be said that he takes under that codicil.[1] In *Re Trotter*[2] it was even held that in these circumstances the beneficiary could take notwithstanding the fact that he witnessed a subsequent codicil as well as the will itself. Likewise, if a beneficiary takes a gift under a will and witnesses not the will but a codicil to it the gift remains effective.[3]

1 *Anderson v Anderson* (1872) LR 13 Eq 381; *Re Trotter, Trotter v Trotter* [1899] 1 Ch 764; *Re Elcom, Layborn v Grover* [1894] 1 Ch 303.

2 [1899] 1 Ch 764.
3 *Gaskin v Rogers* (1866) LR 2 Eq 284.

6.37 There is some inconsistency as to the position where a gift is altered. In *Gaskin v Rogers*[1] the will provided for a beneficiary to receive a contingent gift. He did not witness the will but witnessed a codicil where the nature of the gift was altered from a contingent to an absolute gift. On these facts he was held not entitled to take. By contrast, in *Gurney v Gurney*[2] the will provided for the payment of a legacy and for the residue to be divided equally between two named persons. The residuary beneficiaries did not witness the will but they did witness a codicil which revoked the legacy. This obviously had the result of increasing the residuary estate, and accordingly their benefit, but they were nevertheless held entitled to take the whole of the residuary estate as provided by the codicil.

1 (1866) LR 2 Eq 284.
2 (1855) 3 Drew 208.

6.38 For a gift to be avoided on the ground that a beneficiary attests the will it must be shown that the beneficiary is to take the gift beneficially and not as a trustee.[1] Thus, in *Re Ray's Will Trusts, Public Trustee v Barry*[2] the testatrix, who was a nun, left her property to the person who should be the abbess of her convent at the date of her death upon trust for the convent. The will was witnessed by two other nuns one of whom at the date of death of the testatrix was the abbess. In holding that the gift was effective the court gave two reasons: first, that the gift was not a beneficial legacy and, secondly, that the gift was to a person identified by a formula under which the testatrix could not know at the time the will was made who in fact would take the gift. It is uncertain whether in these circumstances the gift would have been effective had this formula been used but the gift had been intended to be beneficial.

1 *Cresswell v Cresswell* (1868) LR 6 Eq 69; *Re Ryder* (1843) 2 Notes of Cases 462; *Re Ray's Will Trusts, Public Trustee v Barry* [1936] Ch 520.
2 [1936] Ch 520.

6.39 The cases are not consistent where one of the witnesses is to take a benefit under the will under a secret trust. In *Re Fleetwood, Sidgreaves v Brewer*[1] it was held that the beneficiary under the secret trust could not take a gift under the will but this was not followed in the more recent case of *Re Young, Young v Young*.[2] The decision in *Re Young* is more in keeping with the general liberal construction of s 15.[3]

1 (1880) 15 Ch D 594.
2 [1951] Ch 344.
3 There is no provision in English law on the lines of the Wills (Interested Witnesses) Act 1977 of Victoria, Australia. Section 5 of that Act provides that 'where the Court . . . is satisfied that the entitlement of the applicant under the will was known to and approved by the testator and was not included in the will as the result of the exercise of any undue influence by any person the Court . . . may by order declare that [the general provision preventing a beneficiary from taking a benefit] does not apply to or in relation to the applicant in respect of the will' of the testator.

Supernumerary witnesses

6.40 Section 1 of the Wills Act 1968[1] provides that if the will is witnessed by more than two persons, and there are at least two witnesses who do not take any benefit under it, the other witness or witnesses may take any benefit conferred upon them. Accordingly, if a witness receives any benefit under the will, however slight, his signature must be disregarded when determining whether there are two other witnesses who do not benefit under the will. So, for example, if a testator gives his dog to his daughter and the residue of his estate of £1 million to his son, and the will is witnessed by the son and daughter and a third party, s 1 will not save either of the gifts.[2]

1 The 1968 Act was passed to reverse the rule in *Re Bravda's Estate* [1968] 2 All ER 217, in respect of persons dying on or after 30 May 1968, regardless of the date of the will.
2 It may then be necessary to look at the old law, which might still save a gift supernumerary witness whose signature was added not for the purpose of witnessing the will but merely to confirm approval of the contents: *Kitcat v King* [1930] P 266.

Professional charging clauses

6.41 Because of the rule which prevents a trustee deriving any benefit from his office in the absence of express provision,[1] a solicitor or other professional person who is appointed to be the executor of the will cannot make a charge for his services. It is therefore customary for a solicitor who is also appointed the executor of the will to include in the will a charging clause, which is a clause enabling him to make a proper professional charge in connection with the work done by him as executor. Such a charging clause is, however, regarded as conferring a benefit on him under the terms of the will so that notwithstanding the presence of such a clause he cannot in fact make a charge if he also witnesses the will.[2]

1 See *Robinson v Pett* (1734) 3 P Wms 249 at 251.
2 *Re Barber* (1886) 31 Ch D 665; *Re Pooley* (1888) 40 Ch D 1. See also *Re Orwell's Will Trusts, Dixon v Blair* [1982] 3 All ER 177, [1982] 1 WLR 1337. However, an appointment outside the will, such as the subsequent appointment as a trustee of a solicitor who witnessed the will, does not preclude him from relying on the charging clause: *Re Royce's Will Trusts* [1959] Ch 626.

Duty of a solicitor to a beneficiary witness

6.42 Where a testator wishes to confer a benefit on a particular person, a solicitor will be negligent if he does not point out to the testator that neither that person nor his spouse should witness the will, or if he does not take reasonable care to ensure that the person or his spouse does not act as a witness. If he fails in this duty, and, as a result, the person is precluded from taking a benefit, the solicitor will be liable in damages to that person. So, in *Ross v Caunters*[1] the testator instructed solicitors to draw up a will to include a share of residue for his sister-in-law. The solicitors sent the will in this form to the testator, so that he could execute it, but they did not warn him that the will should not be witnessed by a beneficiary or the spouse of a beneficiary. One of the witnesses was the husband of the sister-in-law, and, as a result, she was precluded from taking the benefit under the will. The sister-in-law successfully sued the solicitors, and recovered damages equivalent to the value of the share of residue.[2] The duty of care has been extended to ensuring that assets in a testator's estate will pass as intended.[3] The principle has also been extended to include a duty to ensure that instructions to make a will are carried out expeditiously if the circumstances demand.[4]

1 [1980] Ch 297, [1979] 3 All ER 580.
2 No duty of care is owed to those whom the testator did not wish to benefit: *Sutherland v Public Trustee* [1980] 2 NZLR 536.
3 *Kecskemeti v Rubens Rabin & Co* (1992) Times, 31 December, QBD: whether the testator held an interest in property as a beneficial joint tenant or tenant in common.
4 *White v Jones* [1993] 3 All ER 481, CA.

6.43 If the solicitors are negligent, the amount of damages will not necessarily be the value of the gift under the will. It seems that there must be taken into account any sum which the beneficiary receives under the intestacy rules, if that beneficiary is entitled on intestacy, and also any sum which that beneficiary might recover by making an application under the family provision legislation.[1]

1 In *Whittingham v Crease* [1978] 5 WWR 45, 88 DLR (3d) 353 the testator's solicitors requested the spouse of a beneficiary to witness a will. The spouse did so, so that the beneficiary could not take under the will. The beneficiary sued the solicitor. The Supreme Court of British Columbia held that although there was no contractual relationship between the solicitor and beneficiary the solicitors owed a duty to the beneficiary. In *Whittingham v Crease* the beneficiary was entitled to part of the estate under the intestacy rules. The court held that the measure of damages was not the difference between what the beneficiary received on intestacy and what he would have received under the will, but the difference between what he would have received on a successful application under the family provision legislation and what he received on intestacy.

Execution of will of mental patient

6.44 Section 96 of the Mental Health Act 1983 confers upon the Court of Protection power to make a will on behalf of a mental patient. Where the power is exercised, the Court directs or authorises a person, known as 'the authorised person',[1] to make the will on the patient's behalf. The will is executed by the authorised person, who signs the name of the patient and also his own name. The will must be attested in the usual way by two witnesses, who must sign in the presence of the authorised person. Thereafter the will is sealed with the official seal of the Court of Protection.[2] A will executed in this way takes effect as if it were executed by the patient, and he had the capacity to make a valid will,[3] except that it cannot govern immovable property outside England and Wales[4] and except also that it is of limited effect where the patient is domiciled outside England and Wales.[5]

1 Mental Health Act 1983, s 97(1).
2 Ibid, s 97(1)(c).
3 Ibid, s 97(4).
4 Ibid, s 97(4)(a).
5 Ibid, s 97(4)(b); see Hunt and Reed (1970) 34 Conv (NS) 150.

6.45 In *Re D (J)*[1] Megarry V-C stated the following principles which the Court of Protection would follow when exercising this power:
(1) the patient is to be regarded as having a brief lucid interval[2] when the will is made;

(2) in this notional lucid interval, the patient is taken to:
    (a) have a full knowledge of the past; and
    (b) realise that he will immediately relapse into his actual mental state;
(3) the actual (and not a hypothetical) patient is to be considered;
(4) during the notional lucid interval the patient is to be deemed to be advised by competent solicitors; and
(5) the patient is to be envisaged as taking a broad brush to the claims of his bounty, rather than an accountant's pen. Thus, although the will may properly contain gifts reflecting a general recognition of outstanding hospitality and kindness, such gifts 'in quantum may bear very little relation to the cost or value of those kindnesses'.

Point 3 is important. It shows that the court will adopt a deemed subjective and not an objective approach, and in this respect differs from the objective approach taken earlier in *Re Davey*.[3] In *Re D (J)* Sir Robert Megarry V-C stated:[4]

'Before losing testamentary capacity the patient may have been a person with strong antipathies or deep affections for particular persons or causes, or with vigorous religious or political views; and, of course, the patient was then able to give effect to those views when making a will. I think that the court must take the patient as he or she was before losing testamentary capacity. No doubt allowance may be made for the passage of years since the patient was last of full capacity for sometimes strong feelings mellow into indifference, and even family feuds evaporate. Furthermore, I do not think the court should give effect to antipathies or affections of the patient which are beyond reason. But subject to all due allowances, I think that the court must seek to make the will which the actual patient, acting reasonably, would have made if notionally restored to full mental capacity, memory and foresight.'

The subjective approach must be modified if the patient has been incapable from birth. In that situation, which was considered in *Re C (a patient)*[5] by Hoffman J, the patient should be assumed to be a normal decent person acting in accordance with contemporary standards of morality.

1 [1982] 2 All ER 37 at 42.
2 As to which, see above, para 5.10.
3 [1980] 3 All ER 342 at 348.
4 [1982] 2 All ER 37 at 43.
5 [1991] 3 All ER 866, where an application was made for a patient, aged 75, who had never been capable of making a will but who had inherited substantial estates from her parents. The care she had received from the community was recognised by providing that half her estate should go to mental health charities, which would receive it free of inheritance tax.

Voluntary deposit of wills

6.46 When a will is made, the testator may, if he so wishes, deposit his will at the Principal Registry[1] upon payment of a fee of £1,[2] and he will receive a certificate of deposit.[3] There is no examination of the will by the Registry when it is deposited. Indeed, it must be deposited in a sealed envelope.[4] The testator can obtain the will from the Registry only with the leave of a registrar,[5] but even although the document may remain in the Registry, the testator can still revoke it. If the will is deposited in the Registry at the date of the testator's death, the person proposing to prove the will can obtain it on production of the death certificate.[6]

1 Administration of Justice Act 1982, s 23(1)(a). If the will is lodged at a district probate registry, it will be forwarded to the Principal Registry.
2 Supreme Court (Non-Contentious Probate) Fees Order 1981, SI 1981/861.
3 The Wills (Deposit for Safe Custody) Regulations 1978 (SI 1978/1724); Administration of Justice Act 1982, s 25. A new system prescribed by ss 23–25 of the Act (not yet in force) provides not only for the deposit of wills, but also registration of wills not deposited.
4 Reg 3.
5 Reg 8.
6 Reg 9.

Wills executed in accordance with foreign formalities

6.47 Where a testator makes a will abroad, the position is governed by the Wills Act 1963, unless the will is an international will as described later.[1] The 1963 Act applies to all deaths after 1963, even if the will was made before that date. The 1963 Act seeks to save as many wills as possible. It adopts the well-established distinction of private international law between requirements of form, such as whether the will must be holograph or whether it must be witnessed, and requirements as to essential validity, such as whether the testator had full mental capacity. Where there is doubt as to the nature of the requirement, there is a tendency for it to be regarded as a requirement of form only. Thus, where a will can only be witnessed by persons holding certain qualifications, or where particular categories of testators are required to satisfy special formalities, those requirements are regarded as matters of form only.[2]

1 See below, paras 6.51–6.54.
2 Wills Act 1963, s 3.

6.48 The Act then lays down the general principle[1] that as regards formal validity, a will is to be regarded as properly executed if it was made in accordance with the *internal* law of the country or territory:
(a) where the testator was domiciled; *or*
(b) where the testator had his habitual residence; *or*
(c) of which the testator was a national, either at the time when the will was made *or* at the date of death.

1 Wills Act 1963, s 1.

6.49 In respect of immovable property, a will is also valid if it is formally valid by the law of the territory in which the property is situated, even if none of the general conditions just mentioned is satisfied.[1]

1 Wills Act 1963, s 2(1)(b).

6.50 Where a will is executed on board a ship or aircraft, it is regarded as valid if the execution conforms to the law in force in the territory 'with which, having regard to its registration (if any) and other relevant circumstances, the vessel or aircraft may be taken to have been most closely connected'.[1] This provision appears to leave ample scope for argument and dispute.

1 Wills Act 1963, s 2(1)(a).

International wills

6.51 A convention[1] was concluded in 1973 to provide a uniform law on the form of an international will, and this convention is being incorporated into the law of the United Kingdom.[2] The convention[3] lays down a number of formalities, with the intention that if they are complied with, the will will be formally valid, irrespective of the place where it is made, the location of the assets, and the nationality, domicile or residence of the testator.[4]

1 The Convention providing a Uniform Law on the Form of an International Will concluded at Washington on 26 October 1973.
2 By s 27(1) of the Administration of Justice Act 1982.
3 The essential provisions are set out in Sch 2 to the 1982 Act; see below, para 6.53.
4 Art 1.

6.52 The convention uses the concept of an 'authorised person', whose function is to be present when the will is executed, to ensure that the formalities required for making the will are complied with, and issue a certificate to that effect.[1] Where a certificate is given, it is conclusive that the will is formally valid, unless there is evidence to show that the requirements as to form were not satisfied.[2] In the United Kingdom, 'authorised persons' are solicitors and notaries public.[3]

1 The form of the certificate is given in art 10.
2 Art 12.
3 Administration of Justice Act 1982, s 28(1).

6.53 The requirements of the convention are:
(a) the will must be in writing;[1]
(b) the testator must declare in the presence of two witnesses and an authorised person that the document is his will, and that he knows the contents of it;[2]
(c) the testator must sign the will, or acknowledge his signature, in the presence of the witnesses and of the authorised person;[3]
(d) the witnesses and the authorised person shall thereupon attest the will by signing in the presence of the testator;[4]
(e) the signatures of the testator, and of the witnesses and the authorised person must be placed at the end of the will;[5] and
(f) if the will consists of several sheets, each sheet must be numbered, and signed by the testator and by the authorised person.[6]
If the formalities are not observed, the will may still be formally valid if it complies with domestic law, or is valid under the Wills Act 1963.[7]

1 Art 3.
2 Art 4.
3 Art 5(1).
4 Art 5(3).
5 Art 6(1). The original s 9 of the Wills Act 1837 required the testator's signature to be at the end. For an account of the difficulties which arose, see the 3rd edition of this book, pp 74–79.
6 Art 6(2).
7 Art 1(2).

6.54 The provisions of the Administration of Justice Act 1982 which will give effect to the convention in the United Kingdom will be brought into operation on a date to be fixed by statutory instrument.[1] When a will has been made in accordance with these provisions, it may be voluntarily deposited.[2]

1 Administration of Justice Act 1982, s 73(5), (6). No date has yet been fixed.
2 Ibid, s 28(3). See above, para 6.46.

Overcoming formal defects

6.55 Where there is no evidence as to whether or not the formalities of making a will have been complied with, effect may be given to it by the operation of the rule *omnia praesumuntur rite esse acta*. This is discussed later.[1]

1 See below, paras 18.43–18.46.

Existence without document

6.56 When a will has been validly made, both as regards the mental element and formal requirements, it will continue to exist until it is revoked. If, therefore, the document is lost or destroyed, the will, as a metaphysical concept of the testator's testamentary wishes, remains effective and the court will grant probate of the nearest reconstruction which can be made. This is described later.[1] It will also be seen later[2] that where the document cannot be found at the date of death of the testator, the court in some circumstances raises a presumption that the will has been destroyed *animo revocandi*.

1 See below, paras 18.48–18.51.
2 See below, para 18.47.

Incorporation by reference

Requirements

6.57 It is convenient to deal here with the doctrine of incorporation by reference. Under this doctrine, documents which satisfy certain conditions are regarded as forming part of the will, even though they themselves are unattested. The conditions are:
(a) the document must be in existence at the date of the will;

(b) the document must be referred to in the will as being in existence at that date; and
(c) the document must be clearly identified in the will.

The courts have, with few exceptions, demanded strict compliance with these conditions. Otherwise it would be possible for the testator to make a will in outline reserving to himself the power to alter the incorporated document at some future date. This would clearly defeat the object of the Wills Act. It is necessary to consider the conditions further.

Existence of document

6.58 A document cannot be incorporated into the will if it is not in existence at that date.[1] Where a document comes into existence after the date of the will, but before a codicil confirming it, it will be incorporated if the will in its republished form refers to it as being in existence at that time.[2] The doctrine of republication is considered in chapter 10.

1 *Singleton v Tomlinson* (1878) 3 App Cas 404.
2 *Re Lady Truro's Goods* (1866) LR 1 P & D 201; *Re Reid* (1868) 38 LJP & M 1; *Re Rendle's Goods* (1899) 68 LJP 125; *Re Phillips' Estate, Boyle v Thompson* (1918) 34 TLR 256.

Reference to existence of document

6.59 The document must not only actually be in existence when the will is made, but it must be referred to as being in existence at that time. Thus in *Re Smart's Goods*[1] the testatrix made a will in which she gave a life interest in property to a beneficiary, and subject thereto said: 'I direct my trustees to give to such of my friends as I may designate in a book or memorandum that will be found with this will.' The will was made in 1895. On the death of the testatrix a book was found written in 1898 and 1899 which was headed 'hints for executors' and which complied with the description in the will. The will was republished in 1900. The book was not incorporated, because although it was actually in existence in 1900, it was referred to in the will as being a future document. Again, in *University College of North Wales v Taylor*[2] the testator left a substantial legacy to the University College, with a direction to use the income for scholarships and prizes, the gift being conditional on compliance with 'any memorandum found with my papers'. Because this expression could refer to a document not in existence at that date, it was held to be not validly incorporated. A similar result was reached in *Re Bateman's Will Trusts, Brierley v Perry*[3] where the executors were directed to pay the income from a fund to such persons 'as shall be stated by me in a sealed letter in my own handwriting and addressed to my Trustees'.

1 [1902] P 238.
2 [1908] P 140.
3 [1970] 3 All ER 817.

6.60 A very liberal, and exceptional, decision is *Re Saxton's Estate*.[1] The testator left all his property 'to the following persons'. There was no following list of persons, but on his death lists of legacies were found, headed by the testator's note that he wished those persons to benefit. This list was held to be incorporated, but the decision is wrong in principle.

1 [1939] 2 All ER 418.

6.61 Where the document is referred to as being in existence at the time when the will is made, but cannot be found at the date of death, it is regarded as never having been incorporated, and the provision purporting to incorporate the document is without effect.[1]

1 *Re Barton, Barton v Bourne* (1932) 48 TLR 205; cf *Willoughby v Storer* (1870) 22 LT 896.

Identification of document

6.62 It was said in *Croker v Marquis of Hertford*[1] that identification is of the very essence of incorporation, but perhaps a slightly lower standard of identification is accepted than might be expected. In *Re Mardon's Estate*[2] the testatrix made a codicil in which she referred to the 'schedule hereto'. That reference was held to be sufficient. In *Re Saxton's Estate*[3] the will contained the words 'to the following persons' and the document began 'I wish to leave the following amounts'. That was held to be a sufficient cross-reference.

1 (1844) 4 Moo PCC 339 at 366.
2 [1944] P 109.
3 [1939] 2 All ER 418.

Effect of incorporation

6.63 When a document is incorporated it will normally be included in the probate. Exceptionally, however, the document will not be included in the probate if it would be unduly inconvenient to do so. Thus, in *Re Balme's Goods*,[1] where the document incorporated was a substantial library catalogue, this was omitted from probate.[2] Whether or not the incorporated document is included in the probate, it becomes testamentary, and must be construed with the will itself.[3]

1 [1897] P 261.
2 See also *Re Marquis of Lansdowne* (1863) 3 Sw & Tr 194; *Re Jones' Goods* (1920) 123 LT 202.
3 *A-G v Jones and Bartlett* (1817) 3 Price 368; *Watson v Arundel* (1877) 11 IR Eq 53.

6.64 Difficult problems arise where the document incorporated itself leaves the disposition of the property open to doubt. In *Re Jones*[1] the testator left a legacy on the terms of a deed of trust 'executed by me bearing even date with this my will and testament or any substitution therefor'. As this left room for a future document to be substituted, the whole incorporation was held by Simonds J to be ineffective. The position was more complicated in *Re Edwards' Will Trusts*.[2] The testator directed his residuary estate to be held upon the trusts declared by an identified trust instrument which was in existence at the date of the will. The trust instrument gave the testator, who was the settlor, power to direct by memorandum to whom the capital and income were to be paid, and provided that subject thereto, the fund was to be held for his wife and children. The Court of Appeal held that because the document itself satisfied the conditions it was incorporated, but excluding the offending clause enabling the settlor to appoint by memorandum.

1   [1942] Ch 328.
2   [1948] Ch 440.

Use of doctrine

6.65   Because the document will usually be admitted to probate and will always form part of the testamentary instrument, it is not an effective way of making testamentary gifts without them becoming public knowledge. The practical importance of the doctrine is in fact confined to the case where complicated questions of detail arise, and which are too bulky to be included conveniently in the will.

6.66   There is an overlap between the operation of this doctrine and revival of revoked wills.[1] In the first place a revoked will may be incorporated by reference in a later will rather than itself being revived. Thus, in *Re White, Knight v Briggs*[2] the testator by will directed his trustees to hold property on certain trusts. This will was subsequently revoked, and he made a later will leaving property on the trusts declared by the previous will. The previous will was held to be incorporated into the later. In other cases the possibility of showing that a will has not been revived or republished, but has been incorporated, must be kept in mind. This is particularly important where the previous will is in itself defective, and so has not taken effect. If it is the subject of a basic deficiency, it will not be effectively republished, but there is no reason why, as a document, it should not be incorporated if the testator's intention to that effect can be shown.

1   Considered below, para 9.11.
2   [1925] Ch 179.

Statutory will forms

6.67   Law of Property Act 1925, s 179, authorises the Lord Chancellor to publish forms to which the testator may refer in his will, and if they are incorporated in this way, they form part of the will in accordance with normal rules. The object of the rules is to enable the length of a will to be reduced by obviating the need to set out provisions at length. These are, however, inconvenient because it is preferable to have all the provisions of the will in one document, and the statutory will forms are therefore little used in practice.

CHAPTER 7

Privileged wills

The concept

The privilege

7.1 Although in most cases formalities may be thought necessary for making a will, and when the Wills Act was passed the need for those formalities was far greater than at present,[1] it is realised that in certain exceptional cases a person should be able to make a will without formality. This is where the testator is usually in grave danger, which accentuates the desire to make a will, and where he is deprived of the normal means of consultation before making his will.

1 Above, paras 6.3–6.9.

7.2 There is no general principle that a person in unusual danger or deprived of consultation may make an informal will, but s 11 of the Wills Act 1837 provides that 'any soldier being in actual military service, or any mariner or seaman being at sea, may dispose of his personal estate as he might have done before the making of this Act'. That is, he may make a will without any formal requirements whatever. A privileged will may, therefore, be nuncupative, that is, completely oral, or it may be written, and if written it need not be signed or witnessed. Although there are no formal requirements, however, it is still necessary to show an intention to make a will.[1]

1 Below, paras 7.26–7.29.

7.3 To many, the decisions on privileged wills may seem to be unduly liberal. It is then well to remember that a judge is a member of society, and must be, to a greater or lesser degree, influenced by the feelings of society. Most of the decisions on privileged wills have been made during a time of war, or shortly after the end of hostilities. At such times, if at no other, soldiers are popular and respected. In common with the society in which they lived the judges have adopted the most liberal approach to soldiers, and their wills. A second general feature of the decisions is that in this field as in others,[1] the court seeks to uphold as valid those wills where the dispositive effect accords with what the courts seek to encourage. Where an unmarried soldier wishes to benefit his parents or fiancée, or a married soldier his wife or children, the courts will be inclined even more to find for the validity of the will.

1   Eg, conditional wills: above, paras 5.30–5.33.

7.4   Whatever may have been the historical origin of the doctrine, the institution of privileged wills may be justified on pragmatic grounds. It can be a source of comfort to a soldier facing battle to know that should he not return, arrangements have been made for his affairs. Cynics have suggested that the privilege is more for the beneficiaries than the testator, for it is the persons named in the will who appear to derive all the benefit. This is to ignore the psychological benefit to the soldier in the field.

History

7.5   Immediately prior to the passing of the Statute of Frauds in 1677 there were no formal requirements for any will disposing of personalty. The Statute of Frauds altered this position by prescribing various formalities for a will disposing of personalty worth more than £30. Thereafter, the will had to be either in writing or, if nuncupative, had to be made in the presence of three witnesses and put into writing within six days of its making. The only exception to this was in respect of the wills of soldiers on actual military service and sailors at sea.

7.6   The 1837 Act preserved the position under the Statute of Frauds so far as privileged wills were concerned, so that there were no formal requirements, but these wills were only adequate to dispose of personalty.

7.7   Section 3 of the Wills (Soldiers and Sailors) Act 1918, however, extended the scope of the exception to wills of realty.[1] Accordingly, at present a privileged will may dispose of any type of property. It may also be used to appoint testamentary guardians.[2]

1   For persons dying after 5 February 1918.
2   Wills (Soldiers and Sailors) Act 1918, s 4.

Soldiers on actual military service

7.8   The first category of person who is entitled to make a privileged will is:
(a)   a soldier; who is
(b)   in actual military service.

Soldier

7.9   Although the majority of cases have concerned members of HM Forces, a person need not be in the service of the Crown to be a soldier. A soldier is any person who is doing the job of a soldier. Thus, in *Re*

Donaldson's Goods[1] a soldier in the employ of the East India Company was held entitled to the privilege, and in *Re White's Application*[2] the New South Wales Court of Appeal went further. That case concerned a British subject who was domiciled in New South Wales. During 1944 and 1945 he was employed by the United States Army in the South West Pacific as a civilian engineer. He was issued with papers which, inter alia, showed that he was given status equivalent to that of a major in the United States Army, and that in the event of capture he was entitled to be treated as an officer prisoner-of-war. The court held that a person can be treated as a soldier if he is doing the job of a soldier, and that, in this case, he was entitled to the privilege. It is, of course, by no means certain that the English courts would accept such a generous interpretation of 'soldier'. It may, however, become highly relevant in Northern Ireland[3] if a civilian involved in the conflict, such as a member of the Ulster Constabulary, endeavours to make a privileged will.

1 (1840) 2 Curt 386.
2 [1975] 2 NSWLR 125.
3 See below, para 7.18.

7.10 In principle, therefore, a member of any army is entitled to the privilege. If, however, a person is a member of an enemy army, or is engaged in military activities which are illegal according to English law, while that person might be able to make a privileged will, it is likely[1] that the court would refuse to give effect to the will on the ground of public policy.

1 There is no authority for this supposition.

'Actual military service'

7.11 Whether a person is in 'actual military service' is a question of fact, and it does not necessarily depend on the legal position of the forces concerned. Thus, almost certainly a soldier cannot make a privileged will merely because he is stationed in a country with whom we are legally at war. Continuously since the end of the 1939–45 War British soldiers have been stationed in Western Germany, mainly in conditions of effective peace, although no peace treaty was signed. It is most unlikely that a soldier serving in such circumstances now could make a privileged will.[1] Likewise, the expressions 'actual military service' and 'active service' are not coterminous, for again 'active service' is a term determining the legal status of the forces, including such matters as whether they are eligible to win certain decorations, such as the VC.

1 See, however, *Re Colman* [1958] 2 All ER 35, where such a soldier was found to be still on active service in Germany in 1954.

7.12 It was at one time thought that a soldier on actual military service was in the same position as a Roman soldier in *expeditione*.[1] A Roman soldier in *expeditione* was entitled to make a privileged will, on the basis that he was *inops consilii*, and so unable to obtain proper assistance to discuss and make a formal will. However, the respectability of the Roman analogy was discredited by Denning LJ in *Re Wingham, Andrews v Wingham*.[2] He said:

'The words of our statute are in plain English: "in actual military service". I find them easier to understand and to apply than the Latin: "in expeditione". If I were to inquire into the Roman law, I could perhaps after some research say how Roman law would have dealt with its soldiers on Hadrian's Wall or in the camp at Chester, but I cannot say how it would have dealt with an airman in Saskatchewan, who is only a day's flying from the enemy.'

1 See *Drummond v Parish* (1843) 3 Curt 522; *White v Repton* (1844) 3 Curt 818; *Re Hill's Goods* (1845) 1 Rob Eccl 276.
2 [1949] P 187.

7.13 The meaning given to the expression 'actual military service' has altered with the changing nature of warfare. Prior to 1939, a soldier had to be either serving overseas in a campaign, or to be about to serve overseas following mobilisation.[1] Thus, in *White v Repton*[2] a soldier being in barracks in peacetime was held not to be entitled to the privilege, because he might have had the same assistance as a civilian, and in *Re Stable, Dalrymple v Campbell*[3] it was said that in order to qualify, the soldier must be under orders to go to the front.

1 *Re Hiscock's Goods* [1901] P 78; *Gattward v Knee* [1902] P 99; *Re Booth, Booth v Booth* [1926] P 118; *Re Rippon's Estate* [1943] P 61.
2 (1844) 3 Curt 818.
3 [1919] P 7.

7.14 The cases arising out of the 1939–45 War extend this test markedly. Some suggest that merely by being in uniform a person is entitled to make a privileged will. Thus, in *Re Spark's Estate*[1] Hodson J decided that a soldier who was killed during an air-raid on his camp in the United Kingdom was entitled to make a privileged will. In principle, however, the circumstances in which the deceased died should be irrelevant: the relevant circumstances are those in which the will was made, but these do not appear from the report. By contrast, Henn Collins J in *Re Gibson's Estate*[2] decided that an officer of the Royal Army Dental Corps, who lived at home but attended daily at his camp, and who was killed by a bomb on his house, was not entitled to make a privileged will.[3]

1 [1941] P 115.
2 [1941] P 118n.
3 See article by R. E. Megarry (1941) 57 LQR 481.

7.15 In *Re Rowson's Estate*[1] a squadron officer, WAAF, who was in charge of a WAAF depot in England was held to be entitled to make a will. In that case, while in England, she had sent instructions to her solicitors to make for her a formal will. They had prepared a draft but it was not executed. Her instructions were treated as a valid will. Wallington J observed: 'I want to make it quite clear . . . that the few observations I wish to make are not to be understood as indicating a view, even remotely, that everybody in the WAAF is in actual military service.' He did not, however, indicate why

Squadron Officer Rowson was regarded as being in actual military service. The facts that she *had* seen active service, and *had* been mentioned in despatches were regarded as important, even though in principle they should have been just as irrelevant as the circumstances in which she died.

1 [1944] 2 All ER 36.

7.16 The most important of the cases to emerge from the 1939–45 War is *Re Wingham, Andrews v Wingham.*[1] In that case, a member of the RAF was sent to Canada for flying training and while there he made an informal will. He later died in a flying accident. At first instance it was held that because the will was made outside a theatre of war it was not privileged. This was unanimously reversed by the Court of Appeal, but on various grounds. Cohen LJ adopted as his test that 'the deceased was liable at any time to proceed to some area in order to take part in active warfare and that under these circumstances he was in actual military service'. Denning LJ went further. He said:

'The plain meaning[2] of the statutes is that any soldier, sailor or airman is entitled to the privilege, if he is actually serving with the Armed Forces in connexion with military operations which are or have been taking place or are believed to be imminent. It does not, of course, include officers on half-pay or men on the reserve, or the territorials, when not called up for service. They are not actually serving. Nor does it include members of the Forces serving in this country, or on routine garrison duty overseas, in time of peace, when military operations are not imminent. They are actually serving, but are not in actual "military" service,[3] because no military operations are afoot. It does, however, include all our men serving – or called up for service – in the wars; and women too, for that matter. It includes not only those actively engaged with the enemy but all who are training to fight him. It also includes those members of the Forces who, under stress of war, both work at their jobs and man the defences, such as the Home Guard. It includes not only the fighting men, but also those who serve in the Forces, doctors, nurses, chaplains, WRNS, ATS, and so forth. It includes them all, whether they are in the field or in barracks, in billets or sleeping at home. It includes them although they may be captured by the enemy or interned by neutrals. It includes them not only in time of war but also when war is imminent. After hostilities are ended, it may still include them, as, for instance, when they garrison the countries which we occupy, or when they are engaged in military operations overseas. In all these cases they are plainly "in actual military service". Doubtful cases may arise in peacetime when a soldier is in, or is about to be sent to, a disturbed area or an isolated post, where he may be involved in military operations. As to these cases, all I say is that, in case of doubt, the serving soldier should be given the benefit of the privilege.'

In some respects the narrower test of Cohen LJ may be preferred, as it permits a clear distinction to be drawn between cases where on the one hand the privilege should certainly be granted because fighting is in progress or imminent, and the Home Guard type of case on the other.[4] Despite some criticisms,[5] however, it seems likely that Denning LJ's test will be followed.

1 [1949] P 187.
2 When a judge refers to the 'plain meaning' of anything, it is a sure sign that it is anything but plain.
3 If the service is not military, it is difficult to know what it is.
4 *Re Anderson's Estate* [1944] P 1.
5 Eg D. C. Potter at 12 MLR 183.

7.17 It appears both from *Re Wingham* and from earlier cases that the position with regard to the privilege is the same where war is imminent though not declared as where it is in progress. Thus, in *Re Rippon's Estate*[1] a Territorial Army officer received orders in August 1939 to rejoin his battalion, whereupon he made an informal will. The Territorial Army was not embodied until 1 September, and war was not declared until 3 September, but the will was held to be privileged.

1 [1943] P 61.

Peacekeeping and similar duties

7.18 A soldier can be on actual military service even if there is no declaration of war, and even if he is only acting in support of the civil power. In *Re Anderson's Will*[1] the New South Wales court held that an Australian soldier was entitled to the privilege when under orders to proceed to Malaya following the declaration of a state of emergency, and in *Re Berry*[2] the New Zealand court held that a soldier who was sent to Korea as part of the New Zealand contingent to the United Nations force was entitled to the privilege. In *Re Jones*[3] the English courts had to determine the status of a soldier serving in Northern Ireland. In that case, a corporal of the Parachute Regiment was shot while on patrol. The court held that acting in aid of the civil power in putting down insurrection could be actual military service, and that the corporal was entitled to the privilege. If the deceased had been a member of the Ulster Constabulary, the question would have arisen as to whether he was a 'soldier'.[4]

1 (1958) 75 WN NSW 334.
2 [1955] NZLR 1003.
3 [1981] Fam 7, [1981] 1 All ER 1.
4 For the position of a 'quasi-soldier' see para 7.9.

Mariners or seamen at sea

Mariners or seamen

7.19 The second category of person entitled to make a privileged will is a mariner or seaman being at sea. The expression 'mariner or seaman' can apply to any sailor, even if he is engaged in a purely civilian capacity. Thus it has been held that in addition to members of the Royal Navy,[1] a barman on a liner[2] and a female typist on a liner[3] were both mariners or seamen.

1 Eg *Re Yates's Estate* [1919] P 93.
2 *Re Knibbs' Estate* [1962] 2 All ER 829 (although in that case there was no valid will).
3 *Re Hale's Goods* [1915] 2 IR 362.

'At sea'

7.20 The expression 'at sea' has been widely construed. It has been held that a sailor serving on board a vessel stationed permanently in harbour is 'at sea' for this purpose,[1] and in *Re Barnes' Goods*[2] it was even suggested that a pilot on duty on the Manchester Ship Canal would be regarded as being 'at sea'. However, a seaman on leave after being discharged from one ship and before joining another is not 'at sea'.[3]

1 *Re M'Murdo's Goods* (1868) LR 1 P & D 540.
2 (1926) 96 LJP 26.
3 *Re Rapley's Estate, Rapley v Rapley* [1983] 1 WLR 1069.

7.21 Members of the Royal Navy and Royal Marines when at sea are entitled to the privilege as mariners or seamen. However, s 2 of the Wills (Soldiers and Sailors) Act 1918 extended this privilege so that a member of the Royal Navy or Royal Marines can make a privileged will if he is 'so circumstanced that if he were a soldier he would be deemed to be in actual military service'.[1] On this basis, it seems that if the wider test in *Re Wingham, Andrews v Wingham* is applied, any member of the Royal Navy or Royal Marines during wartime would be entitled. In *Re Yates's Estate*[2] an officer of the Royal Navy who was ordered to join his ship told his son when bidding him goodbye at the railway station that if anything happened to him, he wanted everything to go to his wife. Something did happen to him, and this oral wish was held to be a valid will under the 1918 Act.

1 The section extends to members of the Royal Navy and Royal Marines but not to merchant seamen, who are able to rely on the 1837 Act. *Re Milligan's Goods* (1849) 2 Rob Eccl 108; *Re Parker's Goods* (1859) 2 Sw & Tr 375; *Re Hale's Goods* [1915] 2 IR 362.
2 [1919] P 93. He would also have been a seaman at sea as he had received orders to join his ship.

Airmen

7.22 Section 5(2) of the Wills (Soldiers and Sailors) Act 1918 provides that for the purpose of the privilege members of the Royal Air Force are to be treated as if they were soldiers, and *Re Wingham, Andrews v Wingham*[1] as well as other cases[2] have concerned members of the Royal Air Force. The 1918 Act does not, however, extend to other airmen.

1 [1949] P 187; see above, para 7.16.
2 Eg *Re Rowson's Estate* [1944] 2 All ER 36.

Conflict with other provisions

7.23 There are apparent inconsistencies between s 11 and several other sections of the 1837 Act. There is no general principle as to how these inconsistencies are to be resolved, it depending in each case on what the courts have thought to accord with public policy.

Infants

7.24 Section 7 of the 1837 Act declares simply: 'No will made by any person under the age of 18 years shall be valid.'[1] *Re Wernher, Wernher v Beit*[2] was concerned with an informal will made by an infant, who, had he been an adult, would clearly have been entitled to make a privileged will. It is very doubtful whether the legislature in 1837 intended s 11 to override s 7, thereby enabling a military infant to make a valid privileged will, and so thought Younger J at first instance. However, before the case reached the Court of Appeal, Parliament rushed through the 1918 Act, s 1 of which declares that the privilege has always extended to infant soldiers and infant mariners and seamen. If an infant soldier ceases to be on military service before he reaches the age of 18, he cannot make a new formal will until he reaches that age. He can, however, revoke his will before reaching that age.[3]

1 See above, para 5.1. The age of 18 was substituted for the age of 21 by the Family Law Reform Act 1969, s 3(1).
2 [1918] 1 Ch 339.
3 Family Law Reform Act 1969, s 3(3).

Revocation

7.25 One of the methods prescribed for revoking a will is by another instrument in writing 'executed in the manner in which a will is hereinbefore required to be executed'.[1] It was held in *Re Gossage's Estate, Wood v Gossage*,[2] however, that an informal privileged will can revoke an earlier formal will. Although s 11 thus overrides s 20, s 18 overrides s 11. Section 18 provides that with certain exceptions[3] a will is revoked by a subsequent marriage. In *Re Wardrop*[4] the privileged will was held to be revoked by subsequent marriage, though the reasoning seems inconsistent with *Re Gossage's Estate*.

1 Wills Act 1837, s 20.
2 [1921] P 194.
3 Below, paras 8.66–8.71.
4 [1917] P 54.

Animus testandi

7.26 Difficulty has arisen in several cases as to the mental element required for a privileged will. In principle, the deceased should intend that as a result of his words his property should devolve in the manner which he states.[1] Thus, in *Re Stable, Dalrymple v Campbell*[2] a young lieutenant was engaged during the First World War to a certain Blanche Dalrymple. To her, in a romantic moment, he said: 'If I stop a bullet everything of mine will be yours.' Another person was present,[3] and Blanche, being nicely brought up, replied: 'I wish you would not speak of such things to outside people.' Horridge J admitted the officer's words to probate, and observed in so doing that it is not necessary that a testator should think that he is making a will.

1 *Drummond v Parish* (1843) 3 Curt 522; *Re Vernon's Estate* (1916) 33 TLR 11.
2 [1919] P 7.
3 The witness was able to give evidence confirming the words spoken.

7.27 Where, however, the deceased makes an informal statement showing that he only intends at some time in the future to make a will, that statement will not amount to a will. On the other hand, such a statement will be effective if the statement shows that the deceased merely intends in the future to make a formal will repeating the terms of the present informal one.[1] Likewise, a statement that a result will occur by some other means, such as by operation of the intestacy rules, will not amount to a will, and this is so whether or not the belief or statement as to the intestacy rules is correct. In *Re Donner's Estate*[2] the deceased was discussing with a friend making a will and was told that if he died, his mother would take everything. He replied: 'That is just what I want. I want my mother to have everything', but it was held that these words did not constitute an intention to make a will, but a statement of approbation of what he understood to be the position without a will. Similarly, in *Re Knibbs' Estate, Flay v Trueman*,[3] where a sailor said 'if anything happens to me Iris will get anything I have got', Iris got nothing because this statement proceeded on the basis that Iris would take because of arrangements already made, and not as a result of these very words. By contrast, in *Re Jones*,[4] while being taken to hospital the corporal said to his officer: 'If I don't make it, make sure Anne gets all my stuff.' These words showed an adequate animus testandi, and Anne, his fiancée, was entitled.

1 *Gattward v Knee* [1902] P 99.
2 (1917) 34 TLR 138.
3 [1962] 2 All ER 829.
4 [1981] Fam 7, [1981] 1 All ER 1; see above, para 7.18.

7.28 Although the position in principle is as has just been stated, the courts are prepared in some cases to relax their requirements, and to admit to probate almost any expression of testamentary wish. It is, however, quite impossible to know in advance of the trial whether the court will relax the principle. One case where it did was *Re Spicer, Spicer v Richardson*.[1] Army pay books issued to officers and soldiers contain a page upon which a soldier may write out his will if he so wishes. In this case a soldier produced his pay book, and said that if anything happened to him, his property would go to a named person. The pay book could not be found on the soldier's death, but those present when the statement was made thought that the deceased's wishes were recorded in it. If this had been so then his oral statement could not have amounted to a will, but in the absence of production of the book, the court accepted the words spoken as a will. The decision may be contrasted with that in *Re White's Application*.[2] The document which the applicant was attempting to prove was an application form completed by the deceased for a 'Certificate of Identity of Noncombatant' issued by the United States government. Beside the word 'beneficiary' on that form, he wrote 'wife'. The court held that this probably meant the person from whom the United States government could get a good receipt in respect of items in the deceased's possession in the event of his death during service, and that the deceased did not complete the form animo testandi.

1 [1949] P 441.
2 [1975] 2 NSWLR 125; see above, para 7.9.

7.29 The facts of *Re Rowson's Estate*[1] have already been given.[2] In that case, instructions for a will were accepted as a valid will, though it is highly likely that the officer concerned intended her instructions only to amount to instructions, and not as a will itself.

1 [1944] 2 All ER 36.
2 Above, para 7.15.

The privilege reconsidered

7.30 It may be thought that the scope of privileged wills should in one respect be restricted, and in another respect extended. The restriction would involve a limitation on the period of time for which a privileged will should remain effective. There would be much to be said for an enactment that a privileged will should remain effective only for, say, twelve months after the person making it ceased to be on actual military service or at sea. He would in that time have ample opportunity to make a formal will, and so avoid the difficulties attaching to an informal one. There is, however, no such provision in English law. A privileged will remains fully effective until it is revoked or until the deceased dies.

7.31 On the other hand, it might also be thought that informal wills, similarly limited in life, could be made by any person in an emergency. A spy in an enemy prison; a round-the-world yachtsman contemplating Cape Horn; explorers in the Amazon; and spacemen cavorting around the planets should all be able to make emergency wills without any formality. Perhaps the old Roman idea could be resurrected, and anyone could make an informal will who was not able to obtain proper assistance to discuss and make a formal will.

CHAPTER 8

Revocation and alterations

8.1 An essential characteristic of a will is that the testator may revoke it at any time before his death.[1] A will can be revoked in one of three voluntary ways, or in one of two involuntary ways. To revoke a will voluntarily:

(1) the testator must have the mental capacity to revoke;

(2) he must have the intention to revoke; and

(3) he must effect the revocation:

    (a) by a document executed with the same formalities as are needed to make a will; or

    (b) by an informal declaration where the testator is entitled to make a privileged will; or

    (c) by actual destruction.

A will can be revoked by operation of law, irrespective of testamentary capacity and irrespective of intention:

(a) on marriage; and

(b) on divorce or annulment.[2]

---

1 See above, para 2.6. A will remains revocable notwithstanding that there may be an agreement not to change it, as in the case of mutual wills; see above, para 3.5.

2 Strictly this is not a revocation of the will but only of benefits to the former spouse; see below, paras 8.75–8.77.

When a will is not revoked

Change of circumstances

8.2 When considering in detail the circumstances in which a will is revoked, it is important to keep in mind that a will is not revoked in any other circumstances, even if the non-revocation will lead to a result inconsistent with that which the testator wished to achieve. This is particularly so where there has been a substantial alteration to the testator's financial position between the date when the will was made and the date of death. For example, a testator owning assets worth, say, £5,000 might leave a legacy of £4,000 to his son, and the residue to his brother. If he then wins the first prize in the Premium Savings Bond draw, and dies from the shock, his son will still receive the £4,000, but his brother will take the whole of the residue. Another example is a little less obvious. The testator might have built up a family company, and made a will when the shares were of little value, leaving them to the employees, and leaving the remainder of the estate to his wife. The company may prosper, and the shares increase in value disproportionately to the value of the remainder of the estate.

8.3 Wills should be reviewed at regular intervals, and not regarded as being made for life.

Absence of formality or intention

8.4 Assuming that a testator has the capacity to revoke his will, voluntary revocation will be effected only if there is both formality and intention. Accordingly, if the testator rips to pieces his will in a state of drunkenness, while that act will be a sufficient act of destruction to meet the formal requirements,[1] the absence of intention will prevent the will from being revoked.[2] Likewise, if there is a clear intention to revoke, but the requirements of form are not satisfied, the will remains effective. In *Re Mana Seena Veeran, Rajoo v Hussain*[3] the plaintiff and defendant were beneficiaries as well as executors and trustees of the testator's will. After his death, two letters were found written by the testator to his solicitors informing them of his intention to revoke the will. The defendant was asked to deliver the letters to the solicitors but did not do so. The solicitors therefore took no action, and the will was not revoked, although the testator considered that he had done all that was necessary. The High Court of Singapore held that the will remained valid, notwithstanding the improper act of the defendant-beneficiary.

1 See below, para 8.30.
2 *Re Brassington's Goods* [1902] P 1.
3 [1976] IJIL 1.

Capacity to revoke

8.5 In order to revoke a will, the testator must
(a) have attained the age of 18,[1] and
(b) have the mental capacity to revoke.
The same degree of mental capacity is needed to revoke a will as to make one,[2] but this probably equates the capacity to revoke a will with that to make a *simple* will. As will be seen, in the great majority of instances one will is revoked at the same time as another will is made, and questions of capacity have usually arisen in the context of the making of the new will. Nevertheless, it is clear that where a person, having made a will, subsequently ceases to have testamentary capacity, the will becomes irrevocable by him. However, the will still remains revocable by its nature because the Court of Protection can revoke a will of a person who lacks capacity as part of the process of making a new will.[3]

1   While this is strictly correct, a person could only have made a valid will under the age of 18 if he was then in a privileged position, and such a person is now given a statutory power to revoke the will even if he is under the age of 18 at the time of revocation; see below, para 8.29.
2   *Re Sabatini* (1969) 114 Sol Jo 35.
3   See above, paras 6.44–6.45.

8.6   In each of the three cases of voluntary revocation, it will be convenient to consider the requirement of intention in the context of the particular formalities.

Revocation by document

Generally

8.7   Section 20 of the Wills Act 1837 provides that no will or codicil, and no part of any will or codicil, shall be revoked otherwise than in one of two ways. The first is by actual destruction, and this is considered later. The other way is 'by another will or codicil executed in manner hereinbefore required, or by some writing declaring an intention to revoke the same, and executed in the manner in which a will is hereinbefore required to be executed'. It will be seen that s 20 contemplates the revocation either of the whole will, or of some part of it.

8.8   The declaration of intention to revoke a will may be:
(a)   express, where there is an express revocation clause; or
(b)   implied, where by making a later will containing provisions inconsistent with those in an earlier will, the testator shows an intention to revoke the earlier will to that extent.

Express revocation

Revocation clause
8.9   Almost every professionally drawn will commences with an express revocation clause.[1] Such a clause may be confined to the revocation of some part of a previous will, or to the revocation of only one of several previous testamentary instruments, so that, for example, if the testator has property in England and France, and he makes separate wills dealing with his properties in those countries, he may wish to confine his revocation clause in a subsequent will to the previous English will. However, the usual form of this clause is to revoke all previous wills.[2] Even where there has been no previous will, this clause is often included in a will for it confirms to those who are administering the estate that they need not search for an earlier will.

1   See Sherrin (1972) 122 NLJ 6. Will forms available from stationers invariably incorporate a printed revocation clause.
2   As is contained in the specimen will in Appendix C.

Nature of revoking document

8.10 The instrument in which the revocation clause is contained need not be a will, and therefore it need not be a document which is admissible to probate. The only requirement is that it should be executed in the same way as a will. Thus, in *Re Howard, Howard v Treasury Solicitor*[1] a testator had made a will in 1923 leaving his property to his son. In 1940 he executed two separate wills, both of which contained an express revocation clause. In one will he left all his property to his wife, and in the other he left all his property to his son. There was no indication which will was made first. The object of this curious procedure was so that whether his wife or son survived him, the survivor would be able to produce a will completely in his or her favour. The court held that the two wills were irreconcilable, and so neither could be admitted to probate, but they were both sufficient to revoke the 1923 will.[2]

1 [1944] P 39.
2 See also *Biddles v Biddles* (1843) 3 Curt 458; *Townsend v Moore* [1905] P 66; *Loftus v Stoney* (1867) 17 I Ch R 178.

8.11 An attested document asking for a will to be destroyed may be an effective express revocation. As will be seen,[1] where a document is to be revoked by actual destruction, the destruction must take place by the testator, or by someone in his presence. This can cause difficulties if the testator is, for example, abroad, and the will is in England. In such circumstances, the testator may execute a document revoking the will.[2] By extension it has been held that an attested letter may be construed as showing a present intention to revoke. Thus, in *Re Durance*[3] the testator was in Canada, and his will was in England. He sent a letter, attested by two witnesses, to his brother in England asking him to collect the will and to burn it. This was held to be an effective revocation.[4] It is necessary, however, to show that the testator intended the will to be revoked by the letter, and not by the following act of destruction.

1 Below, para 8.37.
2 Whether or not that document is also a will.
3 (1872) LR 2 P & D 406.
4 See also *Re Spracklan's Estate* [1938] 2 All ER 345.

Intention to revoke

8.12 Where there is an express revocation clause, this will be a very strong indication that the testator intended to revoke all previous testamentary instruments, and they will be revoked even if there is some doubt as to the testator's intentions. Thus, in *Sotheran v Dening*[1] a wife had a general power of appointment over realty. In 1877 she made a will exercising the power. In 1878 she made a new will which contained an express revocation clause, but disposed only of her personalty. It was probably her intention not to revoke the previous will in so far as it exercised the power of appointment, but this limitation of her intention could not be proved, with the result that the revocation clause was effective and the realty devolved in default of appointment.[2]

1 (1881) 20 Ch D 99.

2   See also *Cottrell v Cottrell* (1872) LR 2 P & D 397; *Re Kingdon, Wilkins v Pryer* (1886) 32 Ch D 604.

8.13   There are, however, three situations in which the previous testamentary instrument will not be revoked by the revocation clause. These are:
(a)   where a contrary intention can be proved;
(b)   in some cases where the revocation clause was inserted by mistake; and
(c)   where the doctrine of dependent relative revocation applies.

8.14   *Evidence of contrary intention*   *Re Wayland's Estate*[1] is an example of a case where the contrary intention could be proved. In that case a British subject domiciled in England made a will in Brussels in accordance with Belgian law and expressed to deal only with his Belgian property. Two years later he made a will which expressly said that it was disposing only of his property in England, but also containing a general revocation clause. It was held that the testator had no intention by this clause of revoking his previous Belgian will, so that the revocation clause was effective only to revoke the previous English will. However, had he used words which were sufficiently clear, he could have revoked even the Belgian will by a revocation clause in the English will.[2]

1   [1951] 2 All ER 1041.
2   Cf *Re Feis, Guillaume v Ritz-Remorf* [1964] Ch 106. See also *Guardian Trust and Executors Co of NZ Ltd v Darroch* [1973] 2 NLZR 143 (New Zealand Supreme Court) (testatrix, while living in New Zealand, made a will. Then moved to Australia, and there made a will containing revocation clause. Held: earlier will not revoked in so far as it related to assets in New Zealand).

8.15   The position was summarised by Langton J in *Lowthorpe-Lutwidge v Lowthorpe-Lutwidge*,[1] who said:

'It is a heavy burden upon a plaintiff who comes into court to say: "I agree that the testator was in every way fit to make a will, I agree that the will he has made is perfectly clear and unambiguous in its terms, I agree that it contains a revocatory clause in simple words: nevertheless I say that he did not really intend to revoke the earlier bequest in earlier wills." Quite obviously the burden must be heavy upon anybody who comes to assert a proposition of that kind.'

In considering the intention of the testator, it is permissible to consider declarations which he made, even although they do not form part of the will.[2]

1   [1935] P 151.
2   *Clarke v Scripps* (1852) 2 Rob Eccl 563.

8.16   *Mistake*   In determining whether the testator did intend a revocation clause to revoke a previous instrument, the court will have regard to whether the subsequent instrument is complete on its face. The distinction drawn is between a will which on its face does not appear to dispose of all the testator's property, and one which does appear to do so. Suppose that a testator owns a house in Sunderland and a house in Reading, and that he makes a will leaving the house in Sunderland to Adrian, and the house in Reading to Bernard. Suppose also that he makes a later will containing an express revocation clause, and leaving the house in Reading to Christopher. Because the later will has not purported to dispose of the house in Sunderland, the court will be more inclined to find that the express revocation clause was not intended to take effect.[1]

1 *Re Brown's Goods* [1942] 2 All ER 176; *Re Cocke's Goods* [1960] 2 All ER 289; *McKenzie v Thomas* [1968] NZLR 493; *Re Page's Wills* [1969] 1 NSWR 471; *Guardian Trust Co Ltd v Darroch* [1973] 2 NZLR 143; *Re Luck* [1977] WAR 148.

8.17 Considerable difficulty is caused where the revocation clause is included in the will by mistake. The strict rule is that if a revocation clause was included without the knowledge or approval of the testator, then it is ineffective, but that if it was included with his knowledge and approval, then it is effective, even though the testator may have misunderstood its legal effect. In *Collins v Elstone*,[1] for example, a testatrix had made a will. Later she took out a policy of assurance and wanted to make a new will leaving this policy. Although she intended to revoke her previous will only to the extent necessary to make a new will dealing with the policy, the new will contained a general revocation clause. It was held that because she intended that clause to be included in the new will, then it must take its effect notwithstanding that the testatrix thought that it only had a limited effect. This decision has been criticised in *Lowthorpe-Lutwidge v Lowthorpe-Lutwidge*[2] and while it is in accord with the general principle that mistake of legal effect is not itself a reason for failing to give effect to the terms of a will[3] it is inconsistent with the other principle that a clause should operate only so far as is necessary to effectuate the intention of the testator.[4]

1 [1893] P 1.
2 [1935] P 151.
3 See above, para 5.54.
4 *Re Lewis' Goods* (1850) 7 Notes of Cases 436; *Doe d Evers v Ward* (1852) 18 QB 197.

8.18 Where the revocation clause is included because the draftsman has misunderstood the testator's instructions, the court has power to rectify the will.[1]

1 Administration of Justice Act 1982, s 20; see above, para 5.57.

8.19 *Dependent relative revocation* The doctrine of dependent relative revocation is considered later.[1]

1 See below, paras 8.43–8.52.

Effect of absence of intention
8.20 The whole or part of a revocation clause in a will will be omitted from probate if there is no animus revocandi. A good illustration of this is *Re Morris, Lloyds Bank Ltd v Peake*[1] the facts of which are given later.[2] A further example is provided by *Re Phelan*.[3] The deceased was an Irishman. He made a will leaving all his property to the people with whom he lodged. He then appears to have been given some advice that separate holdings of

shares had to be dealt with by separate wills. So he acquired three will forms, and left each of his three blocks of shares to his landlord and landlady. The wills were all executed on the same day. However, the forms contained revocation clauses, and the deceased had not deleted them. Stirling J held that the surrounding facts showed that the deceased did not know and approve of the contents of the wills so far as they related to revocation, and he admitted the three wills to probate with the revocation clauses omitted.

1 [1971] P 62.
2 See below, paras 18.10–18.11.
3 [1972] Fam 33.

Implied revocation

The principle
8.21 There is a general rule of construction that where there are inconsistent testamentary instruments, the later instrument revokes the earlier to the extent of the inconsistency.[1] It follows that where there is no express revocation clause, but two or more testamentary instruments, there are three basic situations:
(a) the instruments are not mutually inconsistent, and all wills must be read together as the last 'will' of the deceased[2] (there is no rule that a testator revokes a previous will merely by making a later one);[3]
(b) the instruments are partly inconsistent, in which case the later instrument is completely effective, and the earlier effective only to the extent that the later is not inconsistent;[4]
(c) the two instruments are totally inconsistent, in which case the whole of the earlier will will be impliedly revoked.[5]

1 *Birks v Birks* (1865) 4 Sw & Tr 23.
2 *Simpson v Foxon* [1907] P 54; *Pepper v Pepper* (1870) IR 5 Eq 85.
3 *Simpson v Foxon*, above; *Re Wyatt* [1952] 1 All ER 1030.
4 *Lemage v Goodban* (1865) LR 1 P & D 57; *Re Petchell* (1874) LR 3 P & D 153; *Re Summers' Goods* (1901) 84 LT 271; *Re Bund* [1929] 2 Ch 455.
5 *Re Palmer's Goods, Palmer v Peat* (1889) 58 LJP 44; *Cadell v Wilcocks* [1898] P 21; *Re Bryan's Estate* [1907] P 125.

8.22 It is, in each case, a question of construction whether the previous disposition is to be revoked entirely, or whether it is to be revoked only in part. Where the later will covers practically the same ground as the earlier, the earlier will will almost always be revoked. However, there is a difference in the position of documents which are wills in the colloquial sense, that is, testamentary documents which are intended to be complete in themselves on the one hand, and of codicils on the other hand. Under the rule in *Doe d Hearle v Hicks*[1] the court will seek to construe codicils so as to interfere as little as possible with the will. In *Hearle v Hicks* itself the testator left by will his copyhold house to his wife for life. In a later codicil he left all his freehold and copyhold land to his daughter for life. It was held that as the gift in the will was clear and specific, and the terms of the codicil were general, the will would take effect to leave the house to the wife, the daughter taking the remainder of the property.[2]

1   (1832) 1 Cl & Fin 20.
2   See also *Re Stoodley, Hooson v Locock* [1916] 1 Ch 242, CA; *Re Picton, Porter v Jones*
    [1944] Ch 303 at 306; *Re Crawshay, Hore-Ruthven v Public Trustee* [1946] Ch 327 at 330,
    331; *Re Wray, Wray v Wray* [1951] Ch 425.

8.23 With this may be contrasted *Re Stoodley, Hooson v Locock.*[1] A
clergyman made numerous specific bequests and subject thereto left his
estate as to one third to the Society for the Propagation of Christian
Knowledge and as to two thirds to the vicar for church purposes. Three
years later he made a codicil leaving the residue not bequeathed by will to
Miss Mabel Locock. The words of this codicil were clear enough to revoke
the whole gift of residue in the will, for otherwise the codicil would have had
no effect.

1   [1915] 2 Ch 295.

8.24 It is common for a codicil to be worded on the basis that the will is to
be read as if a particular person's name was omitted. In general, this type of
provision will be restricted to direct beneficial interests taken under the will.
In *Re Wray, Wray v Wray*[1] the testator made a will appointing A to be his
executor, and left him a legacy. He left his residue to B, but included a
proviso that if B predeceased him, the residue should devolve as part of B's
estate. The testator subsequently made a codicil in which he directed that his
will should be read as if A's name was omitted from it and as if A were
dead. A in fact became the tenant for life under the will of B. It was held
that the codicil revoked the appointment of A as executor, and also revoked
the legacy to him, but he was not excluded from the life interest in the
residue.[2]

1   [1951] Ch 425.
2   See also *Re Spensley's Will Trusts* [1952] Ch 886.

8.25 It follows from general principles that if a gift is made by codicil, and
the gift is ineffective, the will continues to take effect, unless there is a
revocation clause.[1] The approach is illustrated by *Re Robinson, Lamb v
Robinson*[2] although that case was concerned with two wills, and not a will
and a codicil. The testatrix made a will containing certain provisions, and
subsequently made a further will leaving all her property to C. The second
will was witnessed by C's wife, and the effect was not to invalidate the
second will but to prevent C from benefiting under it.[3] Accordingly, the
provisions of the first will continued to take effect, although they would not
have done so had the second will contained a revocation clause.

1   *Ward v Van der Loeff* [1924] AC 653; *Re Ransome's Will Trusts, Moberley v Ransome*
    [1957] Ch 348 at 366, 367.
2   [1930] 2 Ch 332.
3   See above, para 6.35.

8.26 A rather different problem arises where the testator declares a
document to be 'my last will'. These words, by themselves, do not show an
intention to revoke previous wills.[1] So in *Re Hawksley's Settlement, Black v*

Tidy[2] where the testatrix made a will in 1922, a codicil to it in 1925, and a further will in 1927 described as her last will, the previous instruments remained effective. In construing the subsequent instrument, if it is not clear whether, and, if so, to what extent the testator intended by that instrument to revoke a previous instrument, the court will have regard to extrinsic evidence of the testator's intention at the time. In *Re Fairhurst*[3] the testatrix made a valid will and later made a will saying 'I wish to leave all my property and car to my nephew' X. After execution of the second will, she wrote 'emergency will: will previously made does not now stand'. The court[4] admitted that statement as evidence of the testatrix's intention to revoke the first will entirely.

1   *Kitcat v King* [1930] P 266.
2   [1934] Ch 384.
3   [1976] 1 NZLR 51.
4   The New Zealand Supreme Court.

Function of court of probate

8.27 Normally, questions of construction are dealt with in the Chancery Division after probate has been obtained.[1] It will be seen, however, that in order to decide whether a previous testamentary instrument is still effective the Family Division[2] must construe the documents before it in order to ascertain whether, and if so to what extent, an earlier instrument has been impliedly revoked by a later one.[3] There is, therefore, sometimes a double process of construction. In the first place, the Family Division makes its construction when probate is sought. Secondly, where several testamentary instruments are admitted to probate, there may still be some inconsistencies between them, and these will be dealt with by the Chancery Division. The process is cumulative, so that if a testamentary instrument has been expressly or impliedly revoked, the Chancery Division is precluded from looking at it.

1   Below, para 10.7.
2   Administration of Justice Act 1970, s 1(1).
3   *Re Murray, Murray v Murray* [1956] 2 All ER 353.

Revocation of will of privileged testator

8.28 Although there is no statutory authority equivalent to s 11 of the Wills Act 1837,[1] Warrington J held in *Re Gossage's Estate, Wood v Gossage*[2] that a person who is entitled to make a privileged will may informally revoke a will. As in the case of the making of a privileged will, it is necessary to show the requisite elements of mental capacity, and of intention, and the privilege extends only to formalities. The informal revocation can be either of an informal or of a formal will. In *Re Gossage's Estate* itself the soldier had made a formal will, and while on actual military service sent a letter to his son asking him to burn the will, the letter using words which were construed to show an intention thereby to revoke. The revocation was held to be effective.

1   See above, para 7.2.
2   [1921] P 194.

8.29 An interesting point arises with regard to the ability of a person under the age of 18 to revoke a will which was validly made while he was on actual military service. It is clear that a privileged will normally remains effective however long the testator lives after having ceased to be in a privileged position.[1] It is also clear that a privileged will of an infant is revoked on his marriage.[2] However, in general, a person under the age of 18 does not have the capacity either to make, or to revoke, a will. Accordingly, in the absence of a statutory provision, a person could make a valid privileged will while under the age of 18,[3] and, then, if he ceased to be in privileged circumstances, be unable to revoke the will voluntarily until he reached the age of 18. The point has been dealt with by s 3(3) of the Family Law Reform Act 1969, which provides that an infant may revoke a privileged will even if he could not at the time of revocation make a new privileged will. The subsection does not, however, say whether such revocation in the case of a person no longer in a privileged position must be in one of the normal ways of revocation, or whether it can be by informal declaration. Presumably informal declaration is sufficient only where the infant is still entitled to the privilege.

1 See above, para 7.25.
2 *Re Wardrop's Estate* [1917] P 54.
3 Wills (Soldiers and Sailors) Act 1918, s 1.

Revocation by actual destruction

8.30 Section 20 of the Wills Act 1837 also authorises revocation by 'burning, tearing, or otherwise destroying the same by the testator, or by some person in his presence and by his direction, with the intention of revoking the same'. It is, therefore, necessary to show:
(1) an act of physical destruction within the terms of the Act;
(2) that the act of destruction was carried out:
    (a) by the testator; or
    (b) by some other person in his presence and by his direction; and
(3) animus revocandi.

Act of destruction

Types of act
8.31 The words 'or otherwise destroying' must be read eiusdem generis with 'burning, tearing', so that it has been held that an act such as writing across the will the word 'cancelled' is not effective to revoke, even if this is done with an intention to revoke.[1] The clearest illustration of this is *Cheese v Lovejoy*.[2] In that case the testator had made his will and various codicils to it. Many years afterwards, he took them out, drew a pen through part of the will, and wrote on the back 'revoked'. In the presence of his housekeeper and maid he said that he had cancelled his will, and he then threw it into a pile of waste paper. He reckoned without the natural curiosity of most maids. After the testator left the room, the maid retrieved the will, and kept it. The testator died thinking that the will had been revoked, but the maid produced the document after his death. It was admitted to probate. The

testator had at most attempted to revoke his will by a symbolic destruction, and this was not sufficient.

1 *Stephens v Taprell* (1840) 2 Curt 458.
2 (1877) 2 PD 251.

8.32 Although the mere crossing through of a signature or other part of the will is not an effective revocation, the complete scratching out of a signature will be regarded, liberally, as a lateral cutting off, and so will be effective.[1] The word 'tearing' includes cutting.[2]

1 *Re Morton's Goods* (1887) 12 PD 141.
2 *Hobbs v Knight* (1838) 1 Curt 768; *Re Simpson's Goods* (1859) 5 Jur NS 1366; *Re Lady Slade's Goods* (1869) 20 LT 330.

Extent of act

8.33 While symbolic destruction is not sufficient, it is not necessary so to mutilate the document that it is rendered entirely illegible. There is a double test of the extent of the act of destruction: there must be *some* actual burning, tearing or other destruction; and the destruction which has actually occurred must be all that the testator intended to do by way of destruction.

8.34 Thus, it has been held that the mere tearing off of the signatures and the attestation clause may be a sufficient act.[1] If, however, some other part is torn off, that will be sufficient to revoke the will only if the part torn off is so important that the will could not fairly be allowed to stand without it. In *Re Woodward's Goods*,[2] for example, the testator made a will consisting of seven sheets of paper. He tore off eight lines of one page, and probate was granted of the remainder.[3] The decision in *Re Everest*,[4] which is discussed later,[5] is to the same effect.

1 *Re Lewis's Goods* (1858) 1 Sw & Tr 31.
2 (1871) LR 2 P & D 206.
3 Cf *Treloar v Lean* (1889) 14 PD 49; *Leonard v Leonard* [1902] P 243; *Re Green's Estate, Ward v Bond* (1962) 106 Sol Jo 1034.
4 [1975] Fam 44, [1975] 1 All ER 672.
5 Below, para 8.42.

8.35 The importance of the testator's intention as to the extent of the act of destruction is shown by *Doe d Perkes v Perkes*.[1] During a quarrel with one of the beneficiaries, the testator tore his will into four pieces. The beneficiary, choosing discretion rather than valour, apologised. The testator stopped tearing and fitted the pieces together again. It was held that when he stopped tearing the testator had not done all that he intended to do in order to revoke, and accordingly the will had never been revoked.[2]

1 (1820) 3 B & Ald 489.
2 See also *Elms v Elms* (1858) 1 Sw & Tr 155.

Partial revocation

8.36 It follows from *Re Woodward*, mentioned above, that a document may be partly revoked by actual destruction, leaving the remainder effective. In *Re Nunn's Estate*[1] a testatrix made a will, and at some time had cut a piece out of the middle of a sheet of paper, and had sewn the two remaining pieces together. She was held to have revoked the part cut out, and probate was granted of the remainder.[2]

1 [1936] 1 All ER 555.
2 The presumption that she had revoked that part animo revocandi was applied.

Presence of testator

8.37 The destruction must be by the testator, or by someone in his presence and by his direction. The concept of presence is similar to that required of witnesses to a will and construed accordingly.[1] In *Re Dadd's Goods*[2] the testatrix was on her deathbed, and said that she wished to revoke a codicil. She confirmed this to her executor and a neighbour who was called in, and they decided that the codicil should be burned. They therefore took it into the kitchen and burned it there. This was held not to be an effective revocation, as it had not been destroyed in her presence.[3]

1 See above, paras 6.25–6.26.
2 (1857) Dea & Sw 290.
3 See also *Re Bacon's Goods* (1859) 23 JP 712.

Intention to revoke

8.38 There will be no revocation where the testator had no animus revocandi at the time of destruction. In the first place, the intention and the act of destruction must be concurrent. Thus, in *Gill v Gill*[1] a husband made a will leaving everything to his wife. During an argument, the wife lost her temper and tore up the will. The husband laughed about it, and said that he would not make another one. Although he acquiesced in her act afterwards, because the will was not destroyed at his direction, and because he had no intention to revoke at the time, the will remained effective. It has been held, however, that the testator can consciously adopt his own act of destruction even if at the time of destruction he did not intend to destroy.[2]

1 [1909] P 157; see also *Re Booth, Booth v Booth* [1926] P 118.
2 *James v Shrimpton* (1876) 1 PD 431.

8.39 Mental illness or similar incapacity can be effective both to prevent revocation[1] and to provide therapy for the judges. *Re Aynsley*[2] was reported under the headline: 'Judge solves a jigsaw puzzle with torn will.' When she was suffering from such mental confusion that she did not know what she was doing, the testatrix, who was an elderly widow, tore her will into more than forty pieces. Counsel for the executors, who were propounding the will, handed the pieces to Megarry J who spent an hour putting them together again. Pleased with his success, he declared that the will was valid.

1 *Brunt v Brunt* (1873) LR 3 P & D 37; see also *Re Hine's Goods* [1893] P 282; *Re Downer's Goods* (1853) 1 Ecc & Ad 106; *Re Brassington's Goods* [1902] P 1.
2 Cited in (1973) Times, 6 February.

Mistake

8.40 It has been mentioned above that a distinction must be drawn between an act of revocation or destruction which was not intended on the one hand, and an act which was intended although there was a misunderstanding of legal effect on the other. Thus, in *Collins v Elstone*[1] where the latter applied, the revocation was held to be effective.

1 [1893] P 1; see above, para 8.17.

8.41 Where there has been destruction while the testator was under a misapprehension as to legal effect, however, the courts have shown a marked willingness to hold that such destruction was conditional on the legal result being as the testator understood it, with the result that as that was not the case, the revocation was not effective. Thus, in *Re Southerden's Estate, Adams v Southerden*[1] the testator believed, mistakenly, that on his death intestate his widow would be entitled to the whole of his property, and he therefore destroyed the will by burning.[2] As he misunderstood the effect of the intestacy rule the revocation was not effective. Again, in *Re Davies, Thomas v Thomas-Davies*[3] the testatrix thought she had made a valid second will, and in this belief she destroyed her first will. In fact the second will was not valid and the first will was held to be effective. Further cases of this nature are considered in connection with the doctrine of dependent relative revocation.

1 [1925] P 177.
2 See also *Re Carey* [1977] LS Gaz R 189.
3 [1928] Ch 24.

Revocation of part only

8.42 It is possible to intend to revoke part only of a will, without intending to revoke the remainder, and a presumption to this effect may be raised by the physical appearance of the mutilated document. In *Re Everest*[1] the testator made a will appointing executors, and after making certain bequests to his wife, left his residue to his executors upon specified trusts. While the will was in his possession, the testator cut off that part of his will which declared the trusts of residue, but he left the remainder intact. Lane J held that it was to be presumed that the testator revoked the part cut off animo revocandi, while the remainder was not revoked.[2]

1 [1975] Fam 44, [1975] 1 All ER 672.
2 See also *Re Woodward's Goods* (1871) LR 2 P & D 206; above, para 8.34.

Dependent relative revocation

8.43 Revocation of a will by destruction or by another testamentary disposition requires an intention to revoke.[1] The testator's intention may be absolute or conditional:[2] if absolute, the revocation takes effect forthwith; if conditional, it is not effective unless the condition is satisfied.

1 See above, para 8.4.
2 See generally Henderson (1969) 32 MLR 447.

8.44 Where the revocation is by an act of destruction, the testator's intention is a question of fact,[1] so that extrinsic evidence as to his declaration of intent is admissible.[2] In any other case, such as where revocation is by another will or other testamentary disposition or duly executed writing, it is a question of construction,[3] so that extrinsic evidence of the testator's intention may be admitted only to assist in the interpretation of the document.[4]

1 *Dixon v Treasury Solicitor* [1905] P 42.
2 *Powell v Powell* (1866) LR 1 P & D 209.
3 *Re Zimmer's Estate* (1924) 40 TLR 502.
4 See below, para 10.46.

8.45 There is in theory no limit to the type of condition that may be imposed, but it is customary to divide cases of conditional revocation into:
(a) cases where the revocation is conditional upon some other disposition, in which case it is known as dependent relative revocation; and
(b) other types of condition.

Where the doctrine applies

8.46 The doctrine of dependent relative revocation can perhaps be more usefully described simply as conditional revocation.[1] In practice the circumstances in which the doctrine arises can usually be summarised as where the revocation is conditional on:
(a) the execution of a new will or codicil;
(b) revival of the former will; and
(c) the intestacy rules fulfilling the testator's intention.
The doctrine is not confined to these situations and may apply in any case where the testator's intention to revoke is conditional and whether he is mistaken as to a matter of fact or law. The principle also extends to revocation of parts of a will.[2]

1 As Langton J comments in *Re Hope Brown's Goods* [1942] P 136 at 138: 'The name of this doctrine seems to me to be somewhat overloaded with unnecessary polysyllables. The resounding adjectives add very little, it seems to me, to any clear idea of what is meant. The whole matter can be quite simply expressed by the word "conditional".'
2 See below, para 8.78.

Revocation conditional on execution of new will
8.47 In a number of cases[1] a testator has revoked his will with the intention of making a new will, but he has failed to make that new will. In each case it is necessary to determine whether:
(a) the testator revoked the will, intending the revocation to be absolute, and to take effect forthwith; or
(b) the testator revoked the will, intending the revocation to be conditional, in the sense that it was only intended to take effect when the new will was made.
An illustration of the application of the doctrine in such circumstances is the decision of the Court of Appeal in *Re Jones*.[2] In 1965 the testatrix made a will leaving among the gifts substantial benefits to two nieces. In 1970 she

wished to make a new will, leaving these benefits to the children of a nephew and at the end of September 1970 she herself revoked by mutilation the 1965 will. She made arrangements to see a solicitor with a view to making a new will but she died before she was able to make it. It was held that she intended to revoke the 1965 will absolutely, and that the revocation was not, therefore, dependent on the new will being made.

1 *Thomas v Howell* (1692) 1 Salk 170; *Onions v Tyrer* (1716) 1 P Wms 343; *Re Appelbee's Goods* (1828) 1 Hag Ecc 143; *Re Mitcheson's Goods* (1863) 32 LJPM & A 202; *Powell v Powell* (1866) LR 1 P & D 209; *Re Weston's Goods* (1869) LR 1 P & D 633; *Dancer v Crabb* (1873) LR 3 P & D 98; *Dixon v Treasury Solicitor* [1905] P 42; *Re Faris, Goddard v Overend (No 2)* [1911] 1 IR 469; *Re Southerden's Estate, Adams v Southerden* [1925] P 177; *Re Botting's Estate, Botting v Botting* [1951] 2 All ER 997; *Re Bromham, Wass v Treasury Solicitor* [1952] 1 All ER 110; *Re Green's Estate, Ward v Bond* (1962) 106 Sol Jo 1034; *Re Feis, Guillaume v Ritz-Remorf* [1964] Ch 106, [1963] 3 All ER 303; *Re Addison's Estate* (1964) 108 Sol Jo 504.
2 [1976] Ch 200, [1976] 1 All ER 593.

Revocation conditional on revival of the former will
8.48 A classic illustration of these circumstances is provided by *Re Janotta's Estate*.[1] The testator made will No 1 in May, and will No 2 with practically the same persons as beneficiaries in October. The testator discussed the position with his niece, who told him that if he revoked will No 2, will No 1 would automatically be revived. Will No 2 was then revoked. The court found that the only reason for revoking will No 2 was to revive will No 1, and that will No 2 should be admitted to probate.

1 [1976] 2 WWR 312. See also *Re Bridgewater's Estate* [1965] 1 All ER 717, the facts of which and the admissibility of evidence are considered below, para 20.21.

Revocation in reliance upon the intestacy rules
8.49 Such circumstances arose in *Re Southerden's Estate, Adams v Southerden*,[1] which has already been mentioned briefly.[2] The testator made a will leaving everything to his wife. Later, he took the will and, thinking that the wife would take all his assets under the intestacy rules, burnt it. It was held that the testator revoked conditionally on the intestacy rules having the effect which he thought they had, and, as they did not, the will was not revoked.

1 [1925] P 177.
2 Above, para 8.41.

Other situations
8.50 The doctrine may apply in any other circumstances where the testator's intention to revoke is conditional. In *Re Carey*[1] the testator destroyed his will, saying that he had nothing to leave, and that it was pointless having a will. He had, however, forgotten that he might inherit under the estate of his sister. The court held that the revocation was dependent on the testator having nothing to leave, and as he had inherited from his sister, the condition was not satisfied. The court admitted a copy to probate.

1 [1977] LS Gaz R 189.

Intention

8.51 It is difficult to know exactly how far the actual intention of the testator is important. The doctrine is stated to depend entirely on the testator's intention. In many cases this is clearly true. Thus, in *Re Feis, Guillaume v Ritz-Remorf*[1] the testator had property in England and abroad, and had made a will dealing with both types of property. He then expressly revoked the will in so far as it dealt with foreign property, believing that other arrangements applied to the disposal of that property. In fact, they did not. The court refused to accept that the revocation clause was conditional upon such other arrangements applying, and therefore held the clause to be unconditionally effective.

1   [1964] Ch 106.

8.52 Nevertheless, in many cases the courts have intervened to save provisions of earlier wills where there is not the slightest evidence of the testator's actual intention. Indeed, in the typical case of a man who revokes a will because he thinks a subsequent will is valid, it never occurs to him that the subsequent will might not be valid, so that there is no actual conditional element in his intention to revoke the former will. The operation of the doctrine is, in most cases, in accordance with common sense, but it is achieved only by flagrant invention on the part of judges of an element of intention which in most cases was not present.

Presumptions where will not in existence

Will last traced in possession of testator

8.53 Where a will was last known to be in the possession of the testator, but it cannot be found when he dies, there is a presumption that the testator destroyed it animo revocandi, unless the contrary can be shown.[1] Where the will itself cannot be found but codicils to that will are found, there is no presumption that the testator intended to revoke the codicils as well as the will.[2]

1   Eg *Re Booth, Booth v Booth* [1926] P 118.
2   See the Australian decision *West Australian Trustee Executor and Agency Co Ltd v O'Connor* (1955) 57 WALR 25.

8.54 Where this presumption as to a lost will does apply, it can be rebutted by evidence to the contrary.[1] Thus, in *Re Webb, Smith v Johnston*[2] the presumption was rebutted when it was shown that the will was destroyed not by the testator, but by enemy air attack. The presumption will also be rebutted if, although there is no direct evidence that the will was destroyed by someone else, on the balance of probabilities it appears that this was so. In *Re Szylowicz's Estate*[3] the testator was a quadriplegic patient in hospital. He was unable to write, had no co-ordination, and no strength in his hands and fingers. He could hold a pen for making a mark. He executed his will, making a mark. The will could not be found among his papers and personal effects on death, but he was physically incapable of destroying the will himself. It was held that the presumption was rebutted, and probate was granted of a carbon copy.

1   *Allan v Morrison* [1900] AC 604.
2   [1964] 2 All ER 91.
3   (1978) 19 SASR 263 (South Australia).

8.55   Where the presumption of revocation applies, it is with regard to both the fact of destruction by the testator, and the intention to revoke. Thus, the presumption can also be rebutted if it can be proved that through mental incapacity or otherwise the testator did not have the animus revocandi.[1]

1   *Brunt v Brunt* (1873) LR 3 P & D 37; *Re Hine's Goods* [1893] P 282; *Re Downers' Goods* (1853) 1 Ecc & Ad 106; *Re Brassington's Goods* [1902] P 1.

8.56   There is also a rule that where an instrument revokes a will, and that later instrument is itself revoked, the earlier will is not thereby revived.[1] Difficulty can therefore arise where an instrument has been lost. If it contained a revocation clause, the previous will will be permanently revoked: if it did not, the previous will will remain effective. Extrinsic evidence may be admitted to prove the contents of the lost instrument, such as the instructions to the solicitor who drew up the document, his draft, and declarations by the testator.[2] The cases, however, are not entirely consistent.

1   *Bell v Fothergill* (1870) LR 2 P & D 148; *Barkwell v Barkwell* [1928] P 91.
2   *Barkwell v Barkwell* [1928] P 91.

8.57   In *Re Wyatt*[1] the testatrix made a will leaving everything to her husband for life, with remainder over. The will was deposited in her bank. In 1927 she gave instructions for a new will to be prepared, and, when executed, this was also deposited in the bank. Later the testatrix withdrew the will from the bank, and it was never seen again. No exact copy of the will could be produced, but the solicitor who prepared the will swore an affidavit to the effect that he usually included a revocation clause in any will which he prepared. Collingwood J held that there was not sufficient evidence to show that the 1927 will did in fact contain an express revocation clause, so that the 1925 will remained valid. On very similar facts, however, in *Re Hampshire's Estate*[2] Karminski J thought it so unlikely that a will prepared by a solicitor would not contain a revocation clause that he held that the missing will had effectively revoked the earlier one.

1   [1952] 1 All ER 1030.
2   [1951] WN 174.

8.58   The decision in *Re Ziggles*[1] is instructive. The testator made a will in 1966 leaving a substantial benefit to his wife. In 1968 he made two codicils to that will, which had the effect of reducing the amount of the wife's legacies. When the testator died in 1969, the will was found, but not the two codicils. The testator was a careful man and kept his will in a locked box, but it was not known where he kept the codicils. Goulding J started with the presumption that as the codicils were last known of as being in the hands of the testator, he had destroyed them animo revocandi. However, there were two other possible explanations for the absence of the documents. First, the testator might have lost or destroyed them accidentally. That explanation was eliminated, because it was established that the testator was a most careful man. Secondly, the testator's wife might have discovered the codicils after the testator's death, and fraudulently abstracted them. However, there was also a presumption against the fraudulent abstraction of a will, either before or after the testator's death. On the facts this latter presumption was not rebutted, so that the former presumption, that the testator himself destroyed the wills animo revocandi, operated. In the result, only the will itself was admitted to probate.

1 *Re Ziggles, Midland Bank Executors and Trustees Ltd v Ziggles* (1974) unreported.

Will found in mutilated condition

8.59 If the will is found, but in a mutilated condition, the testator is presumed to have mutilated the will with the intention of revoking it by actual destruction.[1] The presumption is rebuttable.

1 *Re Lewis's Goods* (1858) 1 Sw & Tr 31; *Magnesi v Hazelton* (1881) 44 LT 586; *North v North* (1909) 25 TLR 322.

Will last traced in possession of others

8.60 Where the will is last traced as being in the possession of others, it is rebuttably presumed not to have been revoked by the testator animo revocandi.[1] Accordingly, unless it can be shown that the will was properly revoked, probate will be admitted of a copy.[2]

1 *Finch v Finch* (1867) LR 1 P & D 371.
2 See below, paras 18.47–18.51.

Revocation by marriage

The general rule

8.61 By virtue of the substituted[1] s 18 of the Wills Act 1837, where a person marries after making a will, that will is revoked by that marriage. The revocation is automatic, and takes effect without the testator so intending, or, indeed, even contrary to his intention.[2] The rule also applies to a privileged will.[3]

1 Substituted by s 18 of the Administration of Justice Act 1982.

2   *Marston v Roe d Fox* (1838) 8 Ad & El 14; *Israell v Rodon* (1839) 2 Moo PCC 51.
3   *Re Wardrop's Estate* [1917] P 54.

8.62   For the rule to operate, the testator must have contracted a valid marriage. The rule does not apply if the marriage was void. So, in *Mette v Mette*[1] the testator made a will, and then married his deceased wife's half sister. At the time that relationship made the marriage void, and the will was not revoked.[2]

1   (1859) 1 Sw & Tr 416.
2   See also *Warter v Warter* (1890) 15 PD 152.

8.63   A will is, however, revoked by a voidable marriage, because even if the marriage is annulled, the annulment is not retrospective. In *Re Roberts*[1] the testator had made a will in favour of John, and in the following year he went through a ceremony of marriage with Eva. Eva contended that the general rule applied, and that the will in favour of John was revoked by the marriage. John contended that the marriage was void because of unsoundness of mind on the part of the testator, and that the will in his favour therefore remained effective. John would have succeeded had the marriage been void, but the Court of Appeal held that unsoundness of mind only made the marriage voidable, and that therefore the will in favour of John was revoked.

1   [1978] 3 All ER 225, CA.

8.64   Section 18 is regarded primarily as a rule of matrimonial law, and so dependent on the domicile of the testator. Accordingly, at least where the will deals with movable property, marriage will not revoke the will if the deceased was domiciled at his death outside the United Kingdom and there is no comparable provision in the law of his domicile.[1] There is some uncertainty with regard to immovable property. It has been held[2] that s 18 applies where the will deals with land in England or Wales, but this has been doubted.[3] The issues had to be decided by the High Court of New South Wales in *Re Micallef's Estate*.[4] The deceased, a man domiciled in Malta, owned land in New South Wales. After making a will dealing with that land he married, but the will remained valid according to Maltese law. The court held, under the equivalent of s 18, that the will was not revoked.

1   *Re Martin* [1900] P 211.
2   *Re Earl of Caithness* (1891) 7 TLR 354.
3   *Re Martin*, above.
4   [1977] 2 NSWLR 929.

8.65   The rule can operate to defeat the purpose of the statute. So in *Re Gray's Estate*[1] the testator was married, but went through a bigamous ceremony of marriage with a woman Edith Annie Gray in 1927. In 1958 she executed a will, being at that time unaware of the fact that her marriage was invalid. The testator's wife died in 1960, and Edith Annie then learned of the true position. She married the testator later that year, and it was held that her will was revoked, notwithstanding that when she made her will she thought that she was married.

1   (1963) 107 Sol Jo 156.

Wills in expectation of marriage

The rule
8.66 The first exception to the general rule is that a will is not revoked by marriage if it appears from the will that at the time it was made the testator:
(a)   was expected to be married to a particular person; and
(b)   intended that the will should not be revoked by that marriage.[1]

1   Wills Act 1837, s 18(3).

8.67 *Expectation of marriage*   It must be apparent from the will that the testator expected to be married to a particular person, and not merely that he expected marriage in general. In *Sallis v Jones*[1] where the last line of the will read 'this will is made in contemplation of marriage', and where the testator married a few months later, the will was revoked. Although the decision was on the forerunner of the present provisions[2] it is likely that the result would still be the same.

1   [1936] P 43.
2   The original s 18, as modified by s 177 of the Law of Property Act 1925, which continues to apply to wills made after 1925 and before 1983, provided that such 'a will expressed to be made in contemplation of a marriage . . . shall not be revoked by the solemnisation of the marriage contemplated'. Where the statutory wording was not used, a will was construed as being made in contemplation of marriage only if virtually the whole of the beneficial dispositions in it (not merely particular gifts) were given to the intended spouse. In *Re Coleman, Coleman v Coleman* [1976] Ch 1, [1975] 1 All ER 675 some beneficial dispositions to 'my fiancée' were insufficient to constitute a will made in contemplation of marriage.

8.68 The most usual way in which a testator shows that he is expecting to be married to a particular person is to refer to her as 'my fiancée'[1] or 'my future wife'.[2] However, difficulty has been caused where the testator describes a woman to whom he is not married as 'my wife'. The expression may indicate a settled state of affairs where a man lives with a woman as if they were married, and has no intention of altering the position. So, in *Re Gray's Estate*[3] the testator made a will in favour of 'my wife Edith Annie Gray' in 1935. This was revoked on the marriage in 1960, because Simon P was not satisfied that at the time when the will was made the testator had an intention to marry her. In other cases, however, the courts have accepted that to call a woman 'my wife' when she is not shows an intention to marry her. So in *Pilot v Gainfort*[4] where the testator left all his property to 'Diana Featherstone Pilot my wife', and married her three years later, the will was not revoked.[5] In *Pilot v Gainfort*, at the time when the will was made the testator was married to another woman who had disappeared, but he did not marry until she had disappeared for a total of seven years, whereafter he could have applied for a decree of presumption of death.

1   *Re Langston* [1953] P 100; *Re Coleman, Coleman v Coleman* [1976] Ch 1, [1975] 1 All ER 675; *Burton v McGregor* [1953] NZLR 487; *Public Trustee v Crawley* [1973] 1 NZLR 695; *Re Whale* [1977] 2 NZLR 1.
2   *Re Knight* (1944), not reported, but mentioned in *Re Langston*, above.
3   (1963) 107 Sol Jo 156.

4 [1931] P 103.
5 *Re Foss's Will* [1973] 1 NSWLR 180 (New South Wales Supreme Court). Gift by testator, Ian Foss, while engaged to marry Patricia Parry, 'to my wife (Mrs P Foss)'. Held: will not revoked.

8.69 *Pilot v Gainfort* should be carefully compared with *Re Gray*. In both cases at the time when the wills were made the testators were not legally in a position to marry, yet *Pilot v Gainfort* shows that a person may 'expect'[1] to marry a person when he is not at the time in a position to do so.

1 The actual decision was on the requirement in the previous provisions that the will should be in 'contemplation' of marriage. These cases were reviewed by Megarry J in *Re Coleman, Coleman v Coleman* [1976] Ch 1, [1975] 1 All ER 675. If a testator uses the s 177 wording of contemplation in a post-1982 will (he may have used a pre-1983 precedent), the question may arise as to whether this complies with the post-1982 provisions. In other words, is contemplation synonymous with expectation? It is anticipated that the courts would regard them as the same.

8.70 *Intention that will not to be revoked* If the will is to be saved from revocation, it is also necessary to show that the testator intended that it should not be revoked by the marriage. In professionally drawn wills, this is expressly stated. Where, however, there is no express statement of intention, it seems unlikely that the courts will construe an intention that a will should not be revoked from the mere fact that the will is made in expectation of marriage to a particular person.

Provisions intended not to be revoked
8.71 In some circumstances it may not be possible to discern an intention that the will in its entirety should be saved from revocation, although the testator shows that he intends a particular provision to remain operative after the marriage.[1] In order to meet this case, a further rule[2] provides that if it appears from the will that the testator:
(a) was expecting to be married to a particular person; and
(b) intended that a disposition in the will should not be revoked,
then, all the dispositions in the will take effect and are not revoked, unless the testator showed an intention that any particular provision should be revoked.

1 As in *Re Coleman, Coleman v Coleman* [1976] Ch 1, [1975] 1 All ER 675.
2 Wills Act 1837, s 18(4).

Wills conditional on marriage

8.72 A will made in expectation of marriage is not for that reason alone made conditional on marriage. In *Ormiston v Laws*[1] the testator made a will leaving a legacy to his named fiancée, but the marriage did not take place. The will was held to be unconditional, so that the woman took the legacy. Likewise, if the testator dies before there is an opportunity to marry, the will, if made only in expectation of marriage, will take effect. It is, however, open to the testator to make a will which is both conditional on and in expectation of marriage.

1 1966 SC 47.

Covenant not to revoke

8.73 A covenant not to revoke a will may be a valid covenant,[1] but an action for damages will only lie where the breach is the result of an intentional act, and not by operation of law. In *Re Marsland, Lloyds Bank Ltd v Marsland*[2] the testator made a will for the benefit of his young children, and covenanted not to revoke it. Several years later his wife died, and he remarried, making a new will partly in favour of his new wife. The children by the first marriage sued on the covenant. It was held that the covenant not to revoke did not amount to a covenant not to remarry, for that would be a covenant void for public policy, and as the revocation was by operation of law, and not by an intentional act, no action for damages would lie.

1 *Re Marsland, Lloyds Bank Ltd v Marsland* [1939] Ch 820.
2 [1939] Ch 820.

Powers of appointment

8.74 Special provisions apply where a will made before marriage exercises a power of appointment. In this case, the general rule is that the exercise of a power of appointment in a pre-nuptial will continues to be effective after the marriage, even if the remainder of the will is revoked.[1] However, as an exception to this rule, if in default of appointment the property appointed would pass to the testator's personal representatives, the exercise of the power is rendered ineffective by the marriage and will fall into his estate accordingly.[2]

1 Wills Act 1837, s 18(2), as amended by Administration of Justice Act 1982 in respect of wills made after 1982. In respect of wills made prior to 1983, the position is governed by the original s 18, where the appointment was rendered ineffective by the subsequent marriage if in default of appointment it would pass to persons who would be entitled under the pre-1926 intestacy rules.
2 Ibid.

Dissolution or annulment of marriage

8.75 By virtue of s 18A of the Wills Act 1837,[1] which applies to testators dying after 1982, where after a testator has made a will there is a decree of a recognised court[2] dissolving or annulling his marriage or declaring it void:[3]
(a) any appointment of the former spouse as executor is deemed to be omitted; and
(b) any gift to the former spouse is deemed to have lapsed.
The rule is subject to any contrary intention expressed in the will. The rule is also without prejudice to any claim the former spouse may have under the Inheritance (Provision for Family and Dependants) Act 1975.[4]

1 Inserted by the Administration of Justice Act 1982, s 18(2).

2   A decree that would be recognised in England and Wales by virtue of Part II of the Family Law Act 1986.
3   Wills Act 1837, s 18A(1)(a),(b).
4   Ibid, s 18A(2). The 1975 Act is considered in chapter 12.

8.76   If the gift to the former spouse consists of a life interest, with remainder over, the remainder is effectively accelerated to the date of death, even if it was conditional on surviving the former spouse.[1]

1   Wills Act 1837, s 18A(3).

8.77   The statement in s 18A(1)(b) that the gift to the former spouse shall be deemed to have lapsed is not to be construed as though he or she had predeceased the testator, which may have an unexpected effect on contingent gifts. In *Re Sinclair*,[1] in 1958 the testator had made a will leaving his entire estate to his wife absolutely provided she survived him for one month. If she should predecease him or fail to survive him for that period his estate was to pass to the Imperial Cancer Research Fund. The testator and his wife divorced in 1962. The testator died in 1983 without having changed his will. The question now arose whether the subsequent gift to charity should take effect. The Court of Appeal was unable to construe the word 'lapse' under s 18A(2) as synonymous with predecease. Accordingly, as the wife was still alive, the condition for the contingent gift to charity was not satisfied. The whole estate therefore devolved on intestacy.[2]

1   [1985] Ch 446, [1985] 1 All ER 1066.
2   This decision is perhaps a salutary reminder of the need for skilful will drafting. Such a clause should now provide that the contingent gift should take effect if the gift to the spouse *fails*.

Alterations and obliterations

Effect

8.78   Alterations, interlineations and obliterations are of two types: those made before the execution of the will, and those made after. Where the alteration, etc, is made before execution, the will takes effect as altered, although it is often difficult to prove that it was made before execution. Where the alteration is made after execution the position is governed by the Wills Act 1837, s 21. Effectively the section provides:
(a)   if the original words are 'apparent', they will be admitted to probate, but if they are not so apparent the obliteration will amount to a revocation by destruction of that part of the will;
(b)   the alteration will be admitted to probate if executed in compliance with the statutory formalities required for the execution of a will.

Words or effect not apparent
8.79   Words are apparent for the purposes of s 21 where they can be read from the face of the instrument, if necessary with the aid of a magnifying glass.[1] Any way of looking at the document is accepted, provided there is no physical interference with it. So, in *Ffinch v Combe*[2] the court allowed the will to be read by surrounding an obliteration with brown paper and holding

the document against a window pane. It follows that, if necessary, the will can be held up to the light, and read through the back.

1   *Re Ibbetson's Goods* (1839) 2 Curt 337; *Re Brasier's Goods* [1899] P 36.
2   [1894] P 191.

8.80   Except where the doctrine of dependent relative revocation applies, extrinsic evidence is not admissible to ascertain the state of the document before the alteration.[1] Accordingly, if the testator has pasted a strip of paper over part of the will, and written over that strip, the strip cannot be removed[2] and the effect of the instrument before alteration will not be apparent unless it is possible to read through that strip. The difference between apparent, which means 'apparent on the face of the instrument in the condition in which it was left by the testator',[3] and discoverable was illustrated by *Re Itter, Dedman v Godfrey*.[4] In that case the testatrix pasted strips of paper over parts of her will, with alterations on them. An infra-red photograph of the document was taken, and by examining this photograph it was possible to see what had been written in the first place. It was nevertheless held that the effect of the document before alteration was not 'apparent' from an examination of the will itself. The exact scope of *Re Itter* is uncertain. In that case, a new document, the photograph, had been created, and the effect of the original will was apparent not from the face of the will but from the photograph. If, however, the instrument itself is examined under ultra-violet or infra-red light, and by this process it is possible to see the state of the original will, it is difficult to see why that should not be allowed in the same way that the use of a magnifying glass.

1   *Re Ibbetson's Goods* (1839) 2 Curt 337; *Re Horsford's Goods* (1874) LR 3 P & D 211; *Re Itter, Dedman v Godfrey* [1950] P 130.
2   *Re Horsford's Goods* (1874) LR 3 P & D 211.
3   Per Sir James Hannen in *Re Horsford's Goods*, above.
4   [1950] P 130.

8.81   Where, however, the testator's intention to revoke part of the will by obliteration can be construed as conditional, if the condition is not satisfied the revocation will be ineffective under the doctrine of dependent relative revocation.[1] Where this doctrine applies the court does not regard itself as bound by s 21, and it will resort to more drastic methods of ascertaining the original state of the document. *Re Itter, Dedman v Godfrey* itself was a case of dependent relative revocation, the court accepting that the testatrix wished the provisions in the original will not take effect only if the provisions on the pasted-over strips took effect. Accordingly, the meaning of the original will was ascertained from the infra-red photograph. A further example of the application of the doctrine of dependent relative revocation is *Sturton v Whetlock*.[2] In that case the testator wished to make certain gifts to his grandchildren, to vest when they attained the age of 25. Such gifts would have contravened the perpetuity rule as it then stood[3] and accordingly the solicitor prepared the will on the basis that the gifts would vest when the grandchildren attained 21. After execution, the testator obliterated the word 'one' in 'twenty-one', and substituted the word 'five'. Probate was granted of the will as it had originally been prepared.

1 See above, para 8.43.
2 (1883) 52 LJP 29.
3 But see now Perpetuities and Accumulations Act 1964, s 4.

Execution of alteration

8.82 The second exception to the general rule laid down by s 21 that alterations after execution are ineffective is where the alterations are themselves attested. The section is rather wider than this, for it provides that an alteration is deemed to be duly executed if the signature of the testator, and of the witnesses, is made in the margin or near to the alterations, or at the foot or end of a memorandum referring to the alteration. The memorandum itself must be written on the will.

8.83 Strict observance of the formalities of execution is necessary. A hard case was *Re Shearn's Goods*.[1] In that case the testatrix properly executed her will, which was duly attested. Immediately afterwards, it was found that a small part had been omitted, and this was corrected by an interlineation. The testatrix acknowledged the document as her last will, and the two witnesses placed their initials in the margin by the interlineation. The testatrix did not herself initial the insertion, and it was held that this was not validly executed. So far as it is possible to make sense of the decision, it seems to depend on the fact that the testatrix neither signed (or initialled) the alteration herself, nor acknowledged her previous signature in respect of that alteration. While the decision does not stand alone,[2] the earlier decision of *Re Dewell's Goods*[3] seems preferable. In that case, on similar facts, the testator was held to have acknowledged his previous signature, so that it was sufficient for the witnesses alone to place their initials in the margin.[4]

1 (1880) 50 LJP 15.
2 *Re Martin* (1849) 1 Rob Eccl 712.
3 (1853) 1 Ecc & Ad 103.
4 In the light of *Wood v Smith* [1992] 3 All ER 556, the facts of which are outlined in para 6.21, it could be strongly argued that the existing signature on a will could be acknowledged after the amendments had been made and on the same occasion, so as to validate the amendments initialled by the witnesses.

Presumptions as to execution

Alterations and additions
8.84 There is a general presumption that unattested alterations, interlineations and erasures are made after execution of the will and so are ineffective.[1] This presumption may be rebutted either by evidence from the document itself or by extrinsic evidence. The following are examples of the circumstances in which the presumption has been rebutted. By internal evidence, where:
(a) without an alteration or interlineation the will does not make sense: thus, where the will was originally written out with blanks, and those blanks have been completed, they have been accepted as having been completed before execution;[2]
(b) the alteration or interlineation is proved to have been written in the same hand and with the same ink as the remainder of the document.[3] Although there is no decision, the same would be the case where a

document examiner could prove that the alteration was made either before or at the same time as the will itself.

By external evidence:

(a) in exceptional cases, such as the will of a lawyer, evidence that the testator knew the statutory requirements has been accepted as evidence that the alteration was made before execution;[4]

(b) direct proof from an attesting witness that the alterations had been made prior to execution of the will is, of course, accepted, as is the evidence of the person who prepared the will that it contained alterations when it left his hands prior to execution;[5]

(c) declarations by the testator before or at the time of execution are admissible,[6] but not subsequent declarations.

1 *Cooper v Bockett* (1846) 4 Moo PCC 419.
2 *Greville v Tylee* (1851) 7 Moo PCC 320; *Kell v Charmer* (1856) 23 Beav 195.
3 *Re Tonge's Goods* (1891) 66 LT 60.
4 *Re Jacob's Goods* (1842) 1 Notes of Cases 401; *Re Thomson* (1844) 3 Notes of Cases 441; *O'Meagher v O'Meagher* (1883) 11 LR Ir 117.
5 *Keigwin v Keigwin* (1843) 3 Curt 607.
6 *Doe d Shallcross v Palmer* (1851) 16 QB 747; *Re Foley's Goods* (1855) 2 Ecc & Ad 206; *Re Hardy's Goods* (1861) 30 LJPM & A 142; *Re Sykes' Goods* (1873) LR 3 P & D 26; *Re Jessop* [1924] P 221.

8.85 A subsequent codicil operates to republish the will[1] so that if the will was altered prior to the execution of the codicil, the codicil will republish the will as altered. It is necessary, however, to distinguish between a codicil which takes notice of the alteration, and one which does not. *Re Heath's Goods*[2] is an example of the first type of case. The testator gave a legacy of £10,000 to one of his executors. He subsequently made an unattested alteration giving him a further legacy of £1,000. Later, he made a codicil reciting the fact that he had given the executor a legacy of £11,000. On this basis it was held that probate of the will should be granted with the alteration included, for the codicil republished it in its altered form.[3] Conversely, where the codicil does not refer to the alterations, in the absence of actual evidence that the alterations were made prior to the date of the codicil, they will be presumed to have been made after the date both of the will and of the codicil.[4]

1 See below, para 9.1.
2 [1892] P 253.
3 See also *Tyler v Merchant Taylors' Co* (1890) 15 PD 216.
4 *Lushington v Onslow* (1848) 6 Notes of Cases 183; *Re Sykes' Goods* (1873) LR 3 P & D 26; *Christmas and Christmas v Whinyates* (1863) 3 Sw & Tr 81 at 89; *Rowley v Merlin* (1860) 24 JP 824.

Pencilled alterations

8.86 There is a presumption that where a will is written both in ink and in pencil, the part written in pencil is intended to be deliberative only, and not intended to have final effect. Thus, in *Re Bellamy's Goods*[1] where the will was first written out in pencil, and then parts only written over in ink, probate was only granted of the words which had been so inked over. Where, therefore, pencil alterations have been made to a will written in ink, they will be presumed to have been deliberative, and probate will not be granted of them.[2] This does not in any way modify the rule that a will can be written in whatever medium the testator wishes, so that probate will be granted of a whole will written in pencil.[3]

1 (1866) 14 WR 501.
2 *Rymes v Clarkson* (1809) 1 Phillim 22.
3 *Re Usborne's Goods* (1909) 25 TLR 519.

Alterations to privileged wills

8.87 In accordance with the general practice of stretching the rules as far as possible in favour of privileged wills, alterations in a privileged will are presumed to have been made while the testator was still in a position to make a privileged will, and so are valid without further formality.[1]

1 *Re Tweedale's Goods* (1874) LR 3 P & D 204; *Re Newland's Goods* [1952] P 71.

8.88 All the presumptions described in this section may be rebutted by contrary evidence.

Ineffectual alterations

8.89 The scope of the Act has in fact been modified slightly by the Non-Contentious Probate Rules 1987. Rule 14(2) enables the registrar to grant probate of a will with alterations which are unattested, and where there is no evidence that they were made prior to execution, where the alteration 'appears to the registrar to be of no practical importance'.

Effect of unattested alterations

8.90 Where an alteration is unattested, and it cannot be shown that it was made before the execution of the will, or later codicil, probate will be granted of the will in its original form. Where the original has been obliterated, probate will be granted with a blank space. A good illustration of this is *Re Hamer's Estate*.[1] In that case the testator made a will which contained a legacy of 'the sum of two hundred and fifty pounds'. The testator subsequently obliterated the words 'two hundred and' so that probate was granted showing a legacy of 'the sum of   fifty pounds'. Where the original words can be read, probate will be granted in the original form.

1 (1943) 113 LJP 31.

8.91 To prevent the difficulties which arise with regard to alterations, it is always prudent for the testator and witnesses to initial the alterations which are made, whether they are in fact made before the execution of the will or subsequently.

CHAPTER 9

Republication and revival

Republication

Requirements

9.1 Republication is a means of making a will take effect as if it had been written not at the date when it was written, but at the subsequent date of republication. Republication can be effected only by an act attended by the same formalities as are necessary to make a will, and, therefore, there are only two ways in which republication can take place:
(a) re-execution of the original will; or
(b) making a codicil to that will.
In both cases it must be shown that the testator intended to republish his will. The fact of re-execution of the original will leads to the presumption that the testator intended to republish although that intention may be rebutted.[1] More positive proof of intention to republish is required where a codicil is made to the will, although the standard of proof required is slight. Thus merely by referring in a codicil to the will, such as by describing it as 'the codicil to my will dated . . .' will be sufficient to republish.[2] There is no need for the codicil to contain words of express republication of the will.[3]

1 *Dunn v Dunn* (1866) LR 1 P & D 277.
2 *Re Champion, Dudley v Champion* [1893] 1 Ch 101; *Re Taylor, Whitby v Highton* (1888) 57 LJ Ch 430.
3 *Potter v Potter* (1750) 1 Ves Sen 437 at 442.

Effect

9.2 Republication was introduced into the law of wills before the 1837 Act. Under the pre-1837 law, a will was not ambulatory in respect of realty, so that it could not dispose of realty which the testator acquired between the date when the will was made, and the date of his death. It became fairly common to republish the will, so that it took effect at the date of republication, and included realty acquired in the meantime. The main reason for republication disappeared with the passing of the 1837 Act, but republication is still common.

General position
9.3 The general effect of republication was stated by the Privy Council in *Goonewardene v Goonewardene*,[1] an appeal from Ceylon on a Ceylon Ordinance which contained a similar provision to s 34 of the 1837 Act. This section provides that every will which is re-executed or republished, as well as one which is revived,[2] shall 'be deemed to have been made at the time at which the same shall be so re-executed, republished or revived'. In *Goonewardene* the Privy Council said:[3] 'the effect of confirming a will by codicil is to bring the will down to the date of the codicil, and to effect the same disposition of the testator's property as would have been effected if the testator had at the date of the codicil made a new will containing the same dispositions as in the original will but with the alterations introduced by the codicil'. With this must be contrasted the dictum of Romer J in *Re Hardyman, Teesdale v McClintock*.[4] He said:

'The authorities . . . lead . . . to the conclusion that the courts have always treated the principle that republication makes the will speak as if it had been re-executed at the date of the codicil not as a rigid formula or technical rule, but as a useful and flexible instrument for effectuating a testator's intentions . . .'

1 [1931] AC 647.
2 See below, para 9.11.
3 [1931] AC 647 at 650.
4 [1925] Ch 287.

9.4 The difficulty in understanding many of the cases is due to the fact that the courts require such a low standard of proof that the testator did intend to republish. If the codicil contains a clause formally confirming the contents of the will,[1] there is little doubt that it is republished. However, in many situations a testator makes a codicil dealing with a particular matter, and simply referring in that codicil to his will. This will usually be sufficient to republish the whole will, even though it is likely that the testator directed his attention only to the part of the will which was being altered. It would be more satisfactory to require positive proof of an intention to republish. Subject to this qualification it is possible to illustrate the operation of the rule.

1 Such a clause is often inserted as a matter of course in professional drawn codicils, although in the light of the consequences of republication the clause should be included with caution unless the contents of the whole will are reviewed by the testator.

Persons
9.5 Where the rule applies, descriptions in the will of persons will relate to those persons who fit the description at the date of republication. In *Re Hardyman, Teesdale v McClintock*[1] the testatrix made a will leaving property to the wife of her cousin. After the will was made, the cousin's wife died, and the testatrix thereafter made a codicil republishing the will in general, but without referring to this gift in particular. The cousin subsequently remarried, and it was held that his second wife could benefit.

1 [1925] Ch 287.

9.6 There is one statutory exception to the general principle. There is a presumption that in wills and other dispositions references to children and other relatives include references to illegitimate children, and to persons related through them.[1] This presumption does not apply, however, where the will was made before 1 January 1970 but republished on or after that date.[2]

1 Family Law Reform Act 1969, s 15.
2 Ibid, s 15(8). A similar provision is incorporated in the Family Law Reform Act 1987, s 19(7), in respect of wills made before 4 April 1988.

Property
9.7 The same principle applies to property. Thus, in *Re Reeves, Reeves v Pawson*[1] the testator bequeathed his interest in 'my present lease'. At the time of making the will the lease had an unexpired term of three and a half years. The testator subsequently took a new lease for twelve years and then made a codicil republishing the will. This was effective to give the beneficiary the residue of the term of the new lease. A similar result was reached in *Re Champion, Dudley v Champion*[2] where the testator devised certain freehold property 'now in my own occupation'. He later acquired some further land which he occupied with the remainder, and republished the will. The beneficiary was held to be entitled to the additional land as well as that occupied by the testator at the date of the original will.

1 [1928] Ch 351.
2 [1893] 1 Ch 101.

Exceptions to rule
9.8 *Property adeemed* The effect of gifts of property which are adeemed is considered later,[1] but, while the authorities are by no means clear, it is probably true that where the gift has been adeemed, and another asset of the same description is subsequently acquired, then republication of the will is not sufficient to save the gift. In *Re Bower, Bower v Mercer*[2] the testatrix had a power to appoint a life interest in property to her husband, and she made a will exercising the power in his favour. After she made the will she was given a further power by a new lifetime settlement made by her father, and she then republished the will. This was held to be effective to exercise both the original and the new power.[3] In *Re Viscount Galway's Will Trusts*[4] the testator made a will in 1927 leaving all his unsettled estates in certain counties to his eldest son. By virtue of the Coal Act 1938, the coal was appropriated to the State, and the owner given a right to compensation. The codicil was executed republishing the will after the date when the right to compensation arose, but it was held that the son was not entitled to this compensation. It is difficult to see the principle behind these cases.

1 Below, paras 30.36ff.
2 [1930] 2 Ch 82.
3 See also *Re Wells, Trusts, Hardisty v Wells* (1889) 42 Ch D 646; *Doyle v Coyle* [1895] 1 IR 205.
4 [1950] Ch 1.

9.9 *Contrary to testator's intention* A will is not republished where to do so would be contrary to the testator's intention. *Re Heath's Will Trusts, Hamilton v Lloyds Bank*[1] was a sympathetic decision of Harman J. In that case the testator executed a will before 1936 containing a gift to his daughter with restraint upon anticipation. By s 2, Law Reform (Married Women and Tortfeasors) Act 1935, it became impossible to create new restraints upon anticipation after 1935. After 1935 the testator executed a codicil to his will, but the judge held that if the original will was regarded as republished it would defeat the testator's intention, and accordingly he held that it had not been republished.

1 [1949] Ch 170.

Intermediate codicils

9.10 Generally a codicil republishing a will republishes it as altered by any subsequent codicils,[1] and, in some cases, as altered by even unattested alterations.[2] The decisions on unattested alterations are explicable on the basis that because the codicil refers to the will as altered the court can accept that as evidence that the alteration had been validly made before the codicil was executed. With this qualification, however, the will can only be republished in the form in which it was immediately before republication. So, in *Burton v Newbery*[3] where a gift to an attesting witness in an intermediate codicil was void, the republishing codicil did not save that irregularity.

1 *Re Fraser, Lowther v Fraser* [1904] 1 Ch 726; see also *Green v Tribe* (1878) 9 Ch D 231; *Follett v Pettman* (1883) 23 Ch D 337.
2 *Re Wollaston's Goods* (1845) 3 Notes of Cases 599; *Re Barke* (1845) 4 Notes of Cases 44; *Re Tegg* (1846) 4 Notes of Cases 531.
3 (1875) 1 Ch D 234.

Revival

Requirements

9.11 Republication is the bringing forward in time of a will which has throughout remained valid. Revival is the restoration to effect of a will or codicil which has been revoked. Section 22 of the Wills Act 1837 provides that an instrument can be revived only in the same ways as republication, namely:
(a) re-execution; or
(b) subsequent codicil.
Accordingly, to show revival, it is necessary for three elements to be shown:
(a) formal act of revival;
(b) intention that the revived instrument should have testamentary effect; and
(c) existence of document to be revived.

Intention

9.12 Stronger evidence of intention is required to revive than to republish. Accordingly, although the mere reference in a codicil to a former will is sufficient to show an intention to republish, it may not be sufficient to show an intention to revive.[1] It is necessary to show more than a mere reference, such as an express confirmation of the original will[2] or some other statement which makes this intention clear.[3] The court is very much more willing in the case of revival than in the case of republication to enquire into the actual intention of the testator.

1 *Re Smith, Bilke v Roper* (1890) 45 Ch D 632.
2 *Marsh v Marsh* (1860) 1 Sw & Tr 528; *Re Steele's Goods* (1868) LR 1 P & D 575; cf, however, *Goldie v Adam* [1938] P 85, where the word 'confirm' was described as very inappropriate to revive a will.
3 *Re Steele's Goods* (1868) LR 1 P & D 575; *Re Courtenay* (1891) 27 LR Ir 507.

9.13 It is not the case, however, that the words of the reviving instrument must contain express words of revival. Thus, in *Re Davis's Estate*[1] the testator made a will in favour of a woman to whom he was not married. He subsequently married her, and his will was revoked.[2] After his marriage he endorsed on the envelope containing the will a statement that the woman 'is now my lawful wedded wife'. This statement was signed and attested. The court accepted this as showing an intention to revive the will, Willmer J commenting not unfairly: 'I am baffled when I try to think what other intention the deceased could possibly have had except to revive the will.'

1 [1952] P 279.
2 Wills Act 1837, s 18; see above, para 8.61.

9.14 It has been held in other jurisdictions, and may be the law in England and Wales, that the testator need not have an intention to revive a will, but merely an intention that the instrument should have testamentary effect. The point arises where the testator does not know that his will has been revoked: a person cannot, strictly, intend to 'revive' a will if he thinks that it is still operative. In *Re Wan Kee Cheong*[1] the Federal Court of Malaysia held that a will revoked on marriage but confirmed by a post-nuptial codicil was revived and that it was immaterial whether the testator knew the will had been revoked by the marriage.

1 (1975) 2 MLJ 152.

Existence of document

9.15 In order to be revived, the revoked will must be physically in existence at the date of the reviving instrument.[1]

1 *Rogers and Andrews v Goodenough and Rogers* (1862) 2 Sw & Tr 342; *Re Reade* [1902] P 75.

Revocation of revoking instrument

9.16 A revoked will can be revived by re-execution, or by codicil, and in no other way.[1] Accordingly, where it was revoked by an instrument, the revocation of that revoking instrument is not sufficient to revive it.[2] For this purpose it is essential to remember that a will is revoked by a subsequent inconsistent will. In *Re Hodgkinson's Goods*,[3] by a will made in June 1881 the testator gave all his property to 'my dear friend Jane', and he appointed her to be his sole executrix. Three months later, with male fickleness, he made another will leaving, in effect, his realty to his sister, Emma, and appointed her to be his sole executrix. Will No 2 made no provision as to personalty, and it did not contain a revocation clause. The testator then revoked the second will by cutting off his signature. The effect of will No 2 was, therefore, to revoke will No 1 in so far as it related to realty. But the revocation of will No 2 did not revive will No 1. Probate was, therefore, granted of will No 1, limited to personalty.

1 Wills Act 1837, s 22.
2 *Major and Munday v Williams and Iles* (1843) 3 Curt 432; *Re Brown's Goods* (1858) 1 Sw & Tr 32; *Powell v Powell* (1866) LR 1 P & D 209.
3 [1893] P 339.

9.17 The mere fact that a codicil which revives an earlier will is stated to be a codicil to that will, does not necessarily revoke an intervening will. Whether the intervening will is revoked will depend on the terms of the first will as revived. Take a basic example:

The testator makes will No 1 in 1970; will No 2, revoking No 1, in 1980; and codicil reviving No 1 in 1990. It is clear that probate will be granted of the 1970 will and the 1990 codicil, but the fate of the 1980 will depends on the terms of the 1970 will or of the 1990 codicil. If the 1990 codicil *expressly* revokes the 1980 will, that revocation is clearly effective. If the 1970 will itself contains an express revocation clause, upon revival in 1990 it will be deemed to have been made in 1990, and so will revoke the (prior) will of 1980.[1] If neither the 1970 will nor the 1990 codicil contains an express revocation clause, the 1980 will will remain valid to the extent that it is not inconsistent with the combined 1970 will and 1990 codicil. If the court is satisfied that it is totally inconsistent, it will refuse probate of the 1980 will, but if it is not satisfied it will grant probate of all three documents, leaving the exact effect to be determined by the Chancery Division.[2]

1 *Re Pearson, Rowling v Crowther* [1963] 3 All ER 763.
2 *Re Dyke's Goods* (1881) 6 PD 205; *Re Reynold's Goods* (1873) LR 3 P & D 35; *Re Baker, Baker v Baker* [1929] 1 Ch 668.

Effect of revival

9.18 The effect of revival is the same as republication, namely the will takes effect as if it has been written at the date of revival,[1] except in those circumstances in which a republished will would not take effect as if written at the date of republication.[2] This, however, is subject to two qualifications. Revival may involve the revocation of an intermediate instrument, as has just been considered. Secondly, it is possible for only part of a document to be revived. If it is clear that the mind of the testator was directed not to the whole will but only to some part of it, then only that part will be revived.[3]

1 Above, para 9.3.
2 Above, para 9.8. The Family Law Reform Acts 1969, s 15(8), and 1987, s 19(7), provide

9.18 *Republication and revival*

that wills made before 1 January 1970 and 4 April 1988 respectively are not deemed to be made for the purpose of the respective sections by reason only of a confirming codicil executed on or after the respective dates (see para 9.6). This provision would probably apply to a pre-1970 will which was subsequently revived. It is arguable, however, that revival is not so restricted by the sections – which refer only to 'confirmation' rather than revival.

3   *Re Mardon's Estate* [1944] P 109.

The construction of wills

PART II

The construction of wills

PART II

The construction of wills

CHAPTER 10

The general principles

General considerations

The problem

10.1 The meaning of a will may not be clear. The testator may have used words which are imprecise: if there is a gift 'to John's relations', are these John's brothers and children, or are his cousins included? The testator may have used expressions which appear to be inconsistent: if there is a gift of 'my car to Albert' in one clause, and a gift of 'all my vehicles to Bernard' in another clause, does the car go to Albert or to Bernard? There may be doubt as to the person who is intended to take a benefit. If the testator leaves a legacy to 'my employees', are the people to qualify those who are employees both at the date when the will was made and at the date of death, or at either of those dates? The testator may have used a phrase that is capable of alternative interpretations: is a gift to 'the children of Henry and George' a gift to Henry's children and to George, or one to Henry's children and George's children? If there is a gift of 'my dog', and between the date of making the will and the date of death the dog dies and the testator acquires a new one, does the new one pass under that provision? Gaps may have been left in the will, which the testator intended to fill in later, but did not. Words with a precise technical meaning may have been used by a testator who was not aware of their precise meaning. As early as 1613, Coke CJ lamented: 'Wills and the construction of them do more perplex a man than any other learning, and to make a certain construction of them, this *excedit juris prudentum artem*.'[1] The law reports are full of examples of every conceivable way of making the meaning of the will uncertain and obscure.

1 *Roberts v Roberts* (1613) 2 Bulst 123 at 130.

10.2 Faced with such a situation, the obvious and natural reaction is to attempt to ascertain the testator's real meaning. But how may this be done? If one looks outside the will, the requirement that a will must be in writing is seriously threatened. It is clear, for example, that provided a word used in a will is given a clear definition in the will, then that word will be given the meaning attached to it by that definition, and not its normal meaning. Thus, if the testator gives '£1,000 to my banana', and adds a definition clause showing that wherever he uses the word 'banana' he means his son, then the son takes. If, however, there is a gift in the same terms, but no definition clause, can one admit extrinsic evidence to show that the testator always called his son 'banana'? If so, in principle it would be possible to draw a will full of such apparently meaningless phrases, leaving the meaning of all of them to be determined by extrinsic evidence. The requirement for a will to be in writing could then be made an empty formality. For this reason, the general principle is that one must deduce the testator's intention only from the will itself.

10.3   Sometimes the doubt does not appear on the face of the will itself, but only when its effect is considered in conjunction with surrounding circumstances. For example, the testator may have left '£1,000 to my nephew Arthur'. On its face, the will is clear: but when surrounding circumstances are considered there may be two nephews called Arthur. Can the surrounding circumstances of the testator's intention be adduced to show which one he intended?

Principles and rules of construction

10.4   If the court is able to deduce the testator's intention from the will, that will prevail. If the court cannot deduce his intention – and only if it cannot – it adopts the so-called 'rules of construction'. These are not in any sense rules of law which are binding on the testator: they are more rules of convenience applied by the court, more often than not in order to give some, rather than no, meaning to the will.

10.5   These rules and principles are often set forth in a neat tabulated form, and the impression is given that in any particular case a question of construction is solved by a logical application of these rules. Life is not like that. In this subject more than in any other it is important to remember how a case is tried, and in particular that all contentions are before the judge before he has to make any decision. Before he makes his decision he knows what its effect will be. The rules of construction are so numerous that he ought to be able to find some which enable him to reach the conclusion that he wishes to reach. This is not to suggest that in all such cases judges come to a decision which they wish to reach, and then construct the reasoning for it, so that when the judgment is read, it appears to be a logical sequence starting with the principles, which appear to point, inevitably, to the conclusion. While it is not suggested that all judges approach the matter in this way, and there is positive evidence that some do not, nevertheless the suspicion remains that in many cases this is what happens.

The court of construction

10.6   As will be seen, the Chancery Division of the High Court is the usual 'court of construction'. In some respects this is unfortunate. All lawyers become increasingly conscious of the exact meaning of words. It is part of the result of construing documents, distinguishing and drafting. A lawyer can see what he imagines to be a real difference between two similar words, whereas to the layman who can see no difference this is but splitting hairs. The consciousness of the meaning of words is particularly true of Chancery lawyers and Chancery judges. It is also worth recalling that the Chancery Division is used to the construction of complex trust deeds, settlements, conveyances, and commercial documents almost all of which will have been professionally prepared. Although the Chancery Division attempts, or sometimes attempts, to shake off this background when construing a 'home-made' will, it is unrealistic to expect that a lifetime's background can be put aside. This may help to explain why some decisions appear to be unduly narrow, and to lead to a result far removed from what might be thought to be the testator's intention. A judge may complain testily that 'the numerous class of persons who, in wills and otherwise, speak as if the office of language were to conceal their thoughts, have no right to complain of being taken to mean what their language expresses'.[1] Instead of indulging in such arrogance, it is better to recall that few testators set out to conceal their thoughts: lack of ability with a pen, rather than intention to obscure, is the usual cause of the difficulty, and it is lack of ability which should meet with sympathy, not irritation, on the part of the court. Fortunately, a more liberal attitude has prevailed since the often harsh and unattractive Victorian era, and effect is perhaps now more frequently given to the testator's intention. But Lord Atkin may have been a little too optimistic when, in *Perrin v Morgan*,[2] he anticipated 'with satisfaction that henceforth the group of hosts of dissatisfied testators who, according to a late Chancery judge, wait on the other bank of the Styx to receive the judicial personages who have misconstrued their wills may be considerably diminished'.

1 Knight-Bruce LJ in *Lowe v Thomas* (1854) 5 De GM & G 315 at 317.
2 [1943] AC 399 at 415, HL.

The court of construction

Division of functions

10.7 There is an apparently curious division of function between the 'court of probate', which is concerned with the validity of the will, and the 'court of construction', which is concerned with the meaning and effect of a valid will. The former function is now usually exercised by the Family Division of the High Court,[1] whereas the latter function is exercised by the Chancery Division. This division of function is the result of historical development.

1 Administration of Justice Act 1970, s 1(4)(a).

10.8 By the end of the twelfth century the ecclesiastical courts were recognised as having jurisdiction over the interpretation of a will, as well as over the validity of a will of personalty.[1] The common law courts were content not to interfere, and accepted the grant of probate by the Bishop as conclusive evidence that the will was valid. The Court of Chancery made one or two rather weak attempts to interfere with the probate jurisdiction of the ecclesiastical courts, their main interest being with regard to interpretation. In due course the Court of Chancery became the accepted court of construction of wills of personalty, while the ecclesiastical courts continued to exercise their probate function. The common law courts had never accepted the need for probate of wills of realty. Where a will disposed both of realty and personalty, and probate was granted by the church courts, this had no effect on the realty.[2] The common law courts and the Court of Chancery had concurrent jurisdiction over the interpretation of wills of realty. The Judicature Acts assigned the construction of all wills, whether of realty or personalty, to the Chancery Division and the Judicature Act 1873 assigned probate jurisdiction to the then Probate, Divorce and Admiralty Division. The Probate, Divorce and Admiralty Division was renamed the Family Division by the Administration of Justice Act 1970.

1 At that time there was no possibility of making a will of realty.
2 At common law realty devolved directly to the devisee named in the will or, if there was no will, to the heir upon intestacy, until the Land Transfer Act 1897 (now Administration of Estates Act 1925, s 1).

Effect of historical background

10.9 The ecclesiastical courts borrowed heavily from Roman law, and many of the rules of Roman law were applied in the construction of wills of personalty. When the Court of Chancery became concerned with the interpretation of wills of personalty, and the common law courts became concerned with the interpretation of wills of realty, they adopted many of the Roman-based rules of the ecclesiastical courts. Roman law has, therefore, influenced considerably the construction of wills of personalty, although it has played little part in the construction of wills of realty. The general tendency since the Judicature Acts has been for the principles of construction of realty and personalty to be equated, but some differences still remain.

Interrelation with probate court

10.10 In practice it is not always possible to separate the probate and construction functions. In the first place the Family Division has to construe a document to ensure that it is intended to operate as a will;[1] and in the second place, where two wills are inconsistent, the Family Division must construe both documents to decide the extent to which the earlier will has been impliedly revoked.[2] Further, the Family Division may have to construe the will to the extent of determining the appointment of executors.[3] Any construction of the Family Division is not binding on the Chancery Division, except to the extent that the Chancery Division is obliged to accept the will in the form in which probate has been granted. If there is any error in it, the probate can be altered only by the Family Division. In exceptional cases, such as where the estate is small, the Family Division may determine a question of construction if all parties agree.[4]

1 See above, para 5.27, and *Re Hawksley's Settlement* [1934] Ch 384.
2 See above, para 8.21, and *Re Fawcett's Estate* [1941] P 85.
3 *Re Hubbuck's Estate* [1905] P 129.
4 *Re Last's Estate* [1958] P 137.

Fundamental principles

Courts will not make wills

10.11 The function of the court is to interpret the words which the testator has used and not to make the will itself. The court can only interpret the testator's intention as expressed in the will itself,[1] and it is not the court's function 'to improve upon or perfect testamentary dispositions'.[2] There are two reasons for the courts' attitude. In the first place, it was shown earlier[3] that a testator may make a will in such terms as he wishes, even if the court does not think that he has been wise in so doing. The second reason for the attitude of the courts is that if the court departs from the words of the testator, it upsets the basic rule that the testator is himself entitled to determine the destiny of his property.

1 See *Re Rowland* [1963] Ch 1 where spouses made wills in each other's favour with contingent gifts in the event of their deaths 'coinciding'. This was construed in its strict sense of simultaneous. Consequently, the contingent gifts did not take effect when the spouses died at sea where there would have been a time-lag between their deaths.
2 Per Jenkins LJ in *Re Bailey* [1951] Ch 407 at 421.
3 Above, para 5.3.

10.12 The result of this approach is that if the words which the testator has used are clear, then subject to the limited power of the court to rectify the will,[1] effect will be given to them, even though the court might suspect that the result is not what the testator intended. Some examples of this have already been given. Thus, where the testator intended certain words to be included in his will, effect will be given to them even if he did not intend that effect.[2] In *Scalé v Rawlins*[3] the testator left three houses to his niece for life, and provided that if she should die leaving no children, the houses were then to go to his nephews. It seems clear that the testator intended that if the niece died leaving children of her own, then on her death the property should go to her children. It was held by the House of Lords, however, that because the testator had not expressly made any provision for the niece's children, they could not take. A further example is provided in *National Society for the Prevention of Cruelty to Children v Scottish National Society for the Prevention of Cruelty to Children*.[4] The testatrix, who had lived in Scotland throughout her life, gave a series of legacies to Scottish charities. In the midst of these legacies there was a legacy to 'the National Society for the Prevention of Cruelty to Children', which was the precise name of an English charity. There was no evidence that the testatrix had taken the slightest interest in the English charity. As the description fitted the English charity exactly, there was no ambiguity entitling the court to admit extrinsic evidence that the testatrix almost certainly intended the legacy to be given to the Scottish National Society for the Prevention of Cruelty to Children.

1 Under s 20 of the Administration of Justice Act 1982; see above, paras 5.56–5.59.

2 See, eg, above, para 5.54.
3 [1892] AC 342.
4 [1915] AC 207.

Will as a whole to be construed

10.13 Having established that the courts seek to interpret the intention of the testator, it is necessary to note that in general they are prepared only to interpret that intention as expressed in the will itself.[1] This means that the will as a whole must be considered, and not merely the particular part upon which doubt arises.[2] By looking at the will as a whole, other provisions in it may make it more easy to determine what the testator intended by the part in dispute. Furthermore, the testator may himself have given a definition of a word in another part of the will.[3]

1 *Lowen v Cocks* (1627) Het 63; *Bowen v Lewis* (1884) 9 App Cas 890; *Beaudry v Barbeau* [1900] AC 569.
2 *Baddeley v Leppingwell* (1764) 3 Burr 1533; *Thellusson v Woodford* (1799) 4 Ves 227 at 329; *Martin v Lee* (1861) 14 Moo PCC 142 at 153; *Crumpe v Crumpe* [1900] AC 127.
3 The so-called 'dictionary principle' discussed below, para 18.18.

Meaning of words and phrases

Usual meaning

10.14 A word or phrase is in the first place given its ordinary grammatical meaning.[1] This rule was stated by Kindersley VC in *Re Crawford's Trusts*[2] as 'a rule of universal application, which admits of no exception, and which ought never under any circumstances to be departed from'. This considerably overstates the position, which has been better described as 'the most general of rules; a rule of great utility'.[3] Consideration of the ordinary grammatical meaning is part of the enquiry to ascertain the meaning which the testator himself placed on the words,[4] but in the absence of some indication that the deceased used the words in a special sense, they are given their normal meaning.

1 *Villar v Gilbey* [1907] AC 139 at 147; *Hamilton v Ritchie* [1894] AC 310 at 313; *Higgins v Dawson* [1902] AC 1 at 12; *Gorringe v Mahlstedt* [1907] AC 225 at 227.
2 (1854) 2 Drew 230.
3 *Gether v Capper* (1855) 24 LJCP 69 at 71.
4 *Shore v Wilson* (1842) 9 Cl & Fin 355 at 563.

10.15 Although this insistence on giving effect to the strict meaning of the words used often causes a result which the testator did not intend, it seems necessary to have some such approach if the whole requirement that a will must be in writing should be preserved. Otherwise, the testator could express himself in the most vague and general terms, leaving scope for the admission of outside evidence to determine what he really intended.

10.16 The meaning which the court seeks to establish is the ordinary meaning at the time when the will was made,[1] it being remembered that with the passage of time words can alter their meaning. It follows from this that care must be exercised in the use of precedents: they can show only what meanings have in the past been given to a particular word.[2]

1   *Cave v Horsell* [1912] 3 KB 533; *Pigg v Clarke* (1876) 3 Ch D 672.
2   *Perrin v Morgan* [1943] AC 399 and the authorities referred to in that case.

Secondary meanings

10.17   The courts will adopt a secondary meaning:
(a)   where there is, in effect, a definition clause in the will itself; and
(b)   where the ordinary meaning does not make sense, but when applied to the surrounding circumstances, it appears that the testator must have used the word in some other sense.

Definition clause

10.18   The testator may, when preparing his will, as in the case of the preparation of any other document, incorporate an express definition clause attributing to certain words a specified meaning. However, even if the testator does not specifically define the meaning of the words used, the same effect may be achieved under the so-called 'dictionary principle', where it is clear to the court that the testator has attributed a specific meaning to the words he has used. An example is provided in *Re Davidson*.[1] The testator in the earlier part of his will referred to his named stepson as 'my son' and to one of his stepson's children as 'my granddaughter'. The court concluded that the testator had incorporated his own definition of children as including stepchildren. Accordingly, the residuary gift to 'my grandchildren' was held to include the children of his stepson.

1   *Re Davidson, National Provincial Bank Ltd v Davidson* [1949] Ch 670. See also *Re Helliwell, Pickles v Helliwell* [1916] 2 Ch 580; *Re Lynch* [1943] 1 All ER 168.

Where the ordinary meaning does not make sense

10.19   Where the ordinary meaning of a word does not make sense when read in the light of the surrounding circumstances, the court can attribute a meaning to the word which does make sense in those circumstances. So in *Re Smalley*[1] a testator gave his estate to 'my wife Eliza Ann Smalley'. His lawful wife's name was Mary Ann Smalley, although the testator had bigamously married and lived with Eliza Ann Mercer, who believed herself to be the testator's lawful wife. As the ordinary meaning of wife (lawful wife) did not make sense as the description and names did not match, the court attributed to the words 'my wife' the secondary meaning of 'my reputed wife'.

1   [1929] 2 Ch 112. The same result could have been reached by disregarding the words 'my wife' under the falsa demonstratio rule considered below, paras 10.38–10.43.

10.20   In *Thorn v Dickens*[1] the court was concerned with what has been described as the shortest known will, which read merely 'All for mother'. Evidence was admitted to show that the testator referred to his wife as 'mother', and the wife took.[2]

1   [1906] WN 54.

2 See also *Charter v Charter* (1874) LR 7 HL 364; *Re Bailey, Barclay's Bank Ltd v James* [1945] Ch 191.

10.21 In these cases, however, it was established that the testator habitually used these words in a particular sense. Evidence is not admitted to show that the testator used an expression in a particular sense on only an isolated occasion.[1]

1 *Re Atkinson's Will Trusts* [1978] 1 All ER 1275.

Words with more than one meaning

10.22 A word may have more than one usual or ordinary meaning. In this case the court will adopt the meaning which it regards as most probable,[1] which in effect leaves a wide discretion to the judge. An example of this is the expression 'stocks and shares'. In *Re Everett, Prince v Hunt*[2] the testatrix had made provision in her will for the disposal of her 'stocks and shares'. Her investments consisted partly of stocks and shares in limited companies, but they also included redeemable debentures[3] and government securities. Cohen J held that the gift passed only stocks and shares in the limited companies. He could have founded his decision on the basis that in that case the other investments were required for the payment of legacies, but he expressly said that he was not basing his decision on that. By contrast, in *Re Purnchard's Will Trusts, Public Trustee v Pelly*[4] Jenkins J held that the testator must be presumed to have wished to dispose of the whole of his estate, and therefore the expression 'stocks and shares' included all his investments.

1 *Perrin v Morgan* [1943] AC 399 especially the judgment of Lord Atkin at 414.
2 [1944] Ch 176.
3 Debentures are technically a loan to the company, rather than an equity participation in it.
4 [1948] Ch 312.

10.23 Further examples are provided by the use of the word 'money'. This was originally restricted to coin of the realm, but the word has now ceased to have any prima facie meaning.[1] As Goulding J has observed:[2]

'the use of a word like "money" varies between persons of different classes, possibly between different parts of the country, certainly in the mouth of one and the same individual under differing circumstances, and a judge would need to be more of a philologist than I am to feel confident in relying in all cases on his own knowledge of the contemporary use of the English language. Nonetheless, it seems to me that the House of Lords[3] has directed that a judge should apply his own knowledge of the language in the light of such context and circumstances as may assist him.'

So, where the testator made a gift of his money, but no gift of residue, the expression was held to pass all the personalty;[4] and where the testator directed his debts to be paid, and then left 'the remainder of my money', this was effective to leave also his realty.[5] In *Re Barnes' Will Trusts, Prior v Barnes*[6] there was a gift of 'my money' and a residuary gift of 'any other personal property'. The judge had no difficulty in deciding that balances with Barclays Bank, and with the Abbey National Building Society, were included. But what of premium bonds? The judge tried to put himself in the position of the testatrix, who was a 'small trader'. 'If I am . . . to apply my experience of the contemporary and vulgar use of the English language, I think on the whole that a testatrix in the position of Mrs Barnes would have included [the bonds] as part of her money. It is certainly not unfamiliar to hear persons speak of a purchase of premium savings bonds as "placing my money with Ernie".'[7]

1 *Re Trundle* [1961] 1 All ER 103, per Cross J; *Re Barnes' Will Trusts, Prior v Barnes* [1972] 2 All ER 639.
2 In *Re Barnes' Will Trusts, Prior v Barnes* [1972] 2 All ER 639 at 644.
3 The reference is to the decision of the House of Lords in *Perrin v Morgan* [1943] AC 399.
4 *Perrin v Morgan* [1943] AC 399.
5 *Re Mellor, Porter v Hindsley* [1929] 1 Ch 446; *Re Shaw, Mountain v Mountain* [1929] WN 246.
6 [1972] 2 All ER 639.
7 [1972] 2 All ER 639 at 645. The decision may be contrasted with that in *Re Plant* [1974] QD R 203 (Queensland). The testator had two accounts with the Commercial Bank of Australia and two deposit accounts with the Toowoomba Building Society. It was held that a gift of 'money in any bank account' did not include the money with the building society.

10.24 Just as a word may have more than one meaning, so may a phrase, and again the court will adopt the meaning which it regards as most probable. In *O'Connor v Perpetual Trustee Co Ltd*[1] there was a gift 'to the children of A and B'. This could have meant the children of A, and B himself, or the children of A and the children of B, but the court interpreted the expression in the latter sense.

1 (1974) 5 ALR 47 (High Court of Australia).

Technical words and symbols

10.25 Where the testator uses words which have a technical legal meaning, such as 'heir',[1] there is a strong presumption that the words will carry that technical meaning,[2] particularly if they appear in a professionally drawn will.[3] In *Re Cook*[4] the testatrix, by a home-made will, gave 'all my personal estate whatsoever' to her nephew and nieces. In fact the bulk of her estate consisted of realty.[5] Harman J nevertheless found that the realty had not been disposed of by the will and so devolved on intestacy. He commented:[6]

'It seems unlikely that she intended to dispose only of the personal estate in the lawyer's sense of that word . . . but this is a case where a layman has chosen to use a term of art. The words "all my personal estate" are words so well-known to lawyers that it must take a very strong context to make them include real estate. Testators can make black mean white if they make the dictionary sufficiently clear, but the testatrix has not done so. It may well be that she thought "personal estate" meant "all my worldly goods"; I do not know. In the absence of something to show that the phrase ought not to be so construed, I must suppose that she used the term "personal estate" in its ordinary meaning as a term of art.'

1 A gift in a will to 'my heir' would be construed in its technical sense as the person who would have inherited freehold property under a pre-1926 intestacy, unless the court can construe from the will that the testator had attributed a different meaning.
2 *Re Athill, Athill v Athill* (1880) 16 Ch D 211; *Re Fetherston-Haugh-Whitney's Estate* [1924] 1 IR 153; *Re Bourke's Will Trusts* [1980] 1 All ER 219. Although the court will sometimes first have to determine whether the word used is a technical one. For example, in *Re Drake's Will Trust* [1970] 3 All ER 32 the words 'male descendants' were not a legal term of art but a descriptive phrase, so males descended through females were included. In contrast, in *Re Du Cros' Settlement* [1961] 1 WLR 1252 'male issue' was construed as meaning male descendants in the exclusively male line.
3 *Read v Backhouse* (1831) 2 Russ & M 546; *Hall v Warren* (1861) 9 HL Cas 420. Although *Re Cook* (below) was made on a printed will form.
4 [1948] Ch 212.
5 That is, freehold property.
6 [1948] Ch 212 at 216.

10.26 The meaning of scientific technical terms is a question of fact, and they will prima facie be given the technical meaning which they bear according to the evidence of experts in that field.[1]

1 *Goblet v Beechey* (1829) 3 Sim 24; *Clayton v Gregson* (1836) 5 Ad & El 302.

10.27 Where the testator uses special words or symbols which have a recognised significance in the locality, trade or business to which the testator belonged, evidence will be given of their significance.[1] Where, however, the testator uses symbols which are known only to himself, evidence will not be admitted to prove their meaning.[2] Thus, in *Clayton v Lord Nugent*[3] the donees in the will were described by letters which referred to a card index system maintained by the testator which was not incorporated by reference. It was not possible to admit evidence of the significance of those letters.

1 *Kell v Charmer* (1856) 23 Beav 195, where the testator, a jeweller, had incorporated in his will symbols used in his trade, to represent the amounts of the intended legacies; *Shore v Wilson* (1842) 9 Cl & Fin 355 at 525; *Re Rayner, Rayner v Rayner* [1904] 1 Ch 176.
2 *Goblet v Beechey* (1829) 3 Sim 24.
3 (1844) 13 M & W 200.

Custom

10.28 Where the testator belonged to a special group of persons, and a word has a special meaning among persons of that group, the meaning of the word for that group will be taken to be the ordinary meaning of the word for the purposes of the will, and not the meaning attributed to it in common parlance. In the same way, where the testator has used the symbols of a trade to which he belonged, these symbols will be given their meaning current among persons who carry on that trade.[1] But the principle is not confined to a trade: for example, it also applies to members of a particular religious community. So in *Shore v Wilson*,[2] where the testator was a member of a dissenting sect, his expression 'godly persons' was given the meaning current among members of that sect.[3]

1 *Kell v Charmer* (1856) 23 Beav 195.
2 (1842) 9 Cl & Fin 355.
3 Cf *Re How, How v How* [1930] 1 Ch 66.

Summary

10.29   The position is, therefore:
(a)   Where the testator has expressly or impliedly defined his word, the meaning given will be in accordance with that definition. Likewise, where there is no definition, but by reference to the surrounding circumstances it can be seen that he uses the word in a special sense, the court will adopt that special sense.
Subject to that:
(b)   If the testator came from a special group, and used a word having a special significance among members of that group, the word will have that special meaning.
(c)   If the testator has used a technical word, it will be presumed to bear that technical meaning.
(d)   Subject to all the foregoing, the word will carry its ordinary general meaning, or, if it has more than one ordinary general meaning, such meaning as the court considers most appropriate in the circumstances.

Subsidiary general principles of construction

Inconsistent clauses

10.30   There is a general rule that if two parts of a will are mutually inconsistent then the later clause is to prevail.[1] The reason for this arbitrary rule is that the last clause is said to be the last expression of the testator's wish but this reasoning appears to be specious and it is perhaps better to regard the rule either as a mere rule of thumb[2] or a 'rule of despair'.[3]

1   *Paramour v Yardley* (1579) 2 Plowd 539; *Sherratt v Bentley* (1834) 2 My & K 149; *Brocklebank v Johnson* (1855) 20 Beav 205; *Re Hammond, Hammond v Treharne* [1938] 3 All ER 308.
2   Per Jessel MR in *Re Bywater, Bywater v Clarke* (1881) 18 Ch D 17.
3   Per Lord Greene MR in *Re Potter's Will Trusts* [1944] Ch 70 at 77.

10.31   Although the acceptance of the rule has been recognised for a long time,[1] because of its arbitrary nature the courts are in fact reluctant to apply it. Accordingly, the rule will not apply in any of the following circumstances:
(a)   Where upon construction of the will as a whole it appears that the testator intended the first clause to apply. This in fact gives the judge more or less complete freedom to reach whichever conclusion he wishes. If there are clauses in a will which are inconsistent, if the judge wishes to follow the former clause he has only to say that this is in accordance with the testator's intention. In many cases, however, there is no clear indication of what the testator intended. An illustration of this is *Re Bywater, Bywater v Clarke*.[2] In that case the testator bequeathed an annuity to his second wife but provided that the annuity should not be payable until the daughters of his first wife had reached the age of 21. The final clause of the will indicated that the annuity

should be paid at once and there was therefore this inconsistency. Jessel MR at first instance, basing his decision not upon the arbitrary rule but upon what he held to be the testator's intention derived from the will as a whole, held that the final clause prevailed. The Court of Appeal, however, held that the first clause prevailed, they themselves basing their decision on what they took to be the testator's intention. Where there is this type of inconsistency it is usually anyone's guess to determine from the will itself what the testator actually intended.

(b) There is Commonwealth authority that if by following the arbitrary rule an intestacy occurs then the former clause is to be preferred.[3] This is in accordance with the presumption against intestacy referred to at para 10.33.

(c) Where the inconsistency lies in a gift of the same thing to two persons both donees will take some interest in that thing. They may both take at once as joint tenants or tenants in common[4] or, if the nature of the thing so demands, they will take in succession.[5] In *Re Alexander's Will Trusts, Courtauld-Thomson v Tilney*,[6] for example, where the same bracelet was given to one person in one clause and to another person in another clause both clauses were construed together as giving both persons a half each. It seems, however, that separate considerations affect gifts of residue. In *Re Gare, Filmer v Carter*[7] where there were inconsistent gifts of residue the first of the gifts was held to prevail. There was substantial previous authority to support this decision[8] and this rule may be justified on the basis that if there are lapsed shares of the first gift of residue these would pass under the second gift. Alternatively, it may be possible to show that all lapsed legacies fall into residue.[9]

(d) If one gift is in the will and the other in a codicil the court will usually conclude that to that extent the codicil has revoked the will.[10]

1 See authorities cited in footnote 1 to para 10.30, above.
2 (1881) 18 Ch D 17.
3 *Piper v Piper* (1886) 5 NZLR 135.
4 *Ridout v Pain* (1747) 3 Atk 486; cf *Sherratt v Bentley* (1834) 2 My & K 149.
5 *Gravenor v Watkins* (1871) LR 6 CP 500; *Re Bagshaw's Trusts* (1877) 46 LJ Ch 567.
6 [1948] 2 All ER 111.
7 [1952] Ch 80.
8 *Davis v Bennett* (1861) 30 Beav 226; *Re Spencer, Hart v Manston* (1886) 54 LT 597; *Re Isaac, Harrison v Isaac* [1905] 1 Ch 427.
9 *Re Jessop* (1859) 11 I Ch R 424; *Re Gare* [1952] Ch 80.
10 *Earl Hardwicke v Douglas* (1840) 7 Cl & Fin 795; *Re Stoodley, Hooson v Locock* [1916] 1 Ch 242.

10.32 In most cases the difficulty which arises from inconsistent provisions could be resolved if the courts were prepared to admit extrinsic evidence as to the testator's intentions. It is shown later[1] that the courts will admit extrinsic evidence of a testator's intention only where there is an ambiguity. This does not apply where there is an inconsistency. It may be thought, however, that it would be far better for the courts to admit extrinsic evidence of the testator's intentions in the case of an inconsistency rather than to indulge in speculation of this unattractive kind. In *Re Bywater*,[2] for example, there was evidence that the final clause had been inserted in the will by mistake and indeed directly contrary to the testator's express instructions to his solicitor. That evidence was not admissible.

1   Below, para 10.46.
2   Above. An application could now be made to rectify the will: see above, paras 5.56–5.59.

The golden rule

10.33   The so-called golden rule is that the court will endeavour to adopt a construction which gives a sensible meaning to the provisions of the will[1] and which will not lead to an intestacy. It is, of course, accepted that a testator has a right to be capricious if he so wishes[2] and if he uses words which are clear and unambiguous then the court has no alternative but to give effect to the testator's words unless an application is made under the family provision legislation. The golden rule operates where there are at least two possible constructions. The rule was expressed by Esher MR in *Re Harrison, Turner v Hellard* in the following words:[3] 'Where a testator has executed a will in solemn form you must assume that he did not intend to make it a solemn farce – that he did not intend to die intestate when he had gone through the form of making a will. You ought, if possible, to read the will so as to lead to a testacy, not an intestacy.'

1   So, in *Re Arnould, Arnould v Lloyd* [1955] 2 All ER 316 the court could make sense of the testator's will only by construing his full stops as commas.
2   *Bird v Luckie* (1850) 8 Hare 301; *Varley v Winn* (1856) 2 K & J 700 at 707; *Jenkins v Hughes* (1860) 8 HL Cas 571 at 589; *Re Hamlet* (1888) 39 Ch D 426 at 434.
3   (1885) 30 Ch D 390 at 393.

Ejusdem generis

10.34   The so-called ejusdem generis rule provides that where a wide word is used in conjunction with and following several narrow words then the scope of the wide word will be controlled by the narrow words. In *Re Miller, Daniel v Daniel*[1] the testator made specific bequests of his books and wine, and his plate, and then made a residuary gift of 'all the rest of the furniture and effects at my residence'. By itself the word 'effects' will include all personal property but in this case the court decided that the word must be construed ejusdem generis with the preceding words books, wine, plate and furniture, so that the beneficiary did not take the share certificates and banknotes which were at the testator's residence.

1   (1889) 61 LT 365.

10.35   The ejusdem generis rule can operate only where there is no other expression of the testator's intention. If by considering the phrase or the will as a whole it appears that the general word is not to be restricted by the preceding narrow words then the ejusdem generis rule will not apply. Again it is for the courts to decide whether there is that contrary intention. Thus in *Re Fitzpatrick*[1] where there was a gift of 'my house and all my furniture and effects' the word 'effects' was not construed ejusdem generis and was held to include all the personalty of the testatrix.

1   (1934) 78 Sol Jo 735.

10.36 It has been suggested[1] that the rule is no more than an illustration of the general principle of construction that a word must be construed in a secondary sense if the will shows that this was the testator's meaning.

1 S. J. Bailey *The Law of Wills* (6th edn), p 217.

Ambiguous words do not control a clear gift

10.37 A clear gift in a will will not be reduced in scope by any subsequent words which are ambiguous or not equally clear. In *Re Freeman*[1] the testator appointed A to be one of his executors and gave him a legacy of £1,000 and a share in the residue. The appointment of A to be the executor and the specified legacy to him were revoked by a subsequent codicil. The codicil provided that B should be the executor and should have a legacy of £200 and that the will should take effect as if the name of B were inserted throughout instead of the name of A. No specific mention was made in the codicil of the share of residue given to A. There was accordingly a gift of residue to A in the will and the general statement in the codicil that the will should take effect as if the name of B were substituted for the name of A. The court held that the general statement in the codicil did not revoke the specific gift of residue in the will and accordingly A took.[2]

1 [1910] 1 Ch 681 at 691.
2 See also *Re Gouk, Allen v Allen* [1957] 1 All ER 469.

Falsa demonstratio

10.38 The full maxim is *falsa demonstratio non nocet cum de corpore constat*. The doctrine applies to all written instruments but with regard to wills there are two limbs of it. The first limb provides that where the description of a person or property is made up of more than one part, and one part is true and the other false, then if the part which is true describes the person or property with sufficient certainty the untrue part will be rejected and will not vitiate the gift.[1]

1 *Re Brocket, Dawes v Miller* [1908] 1 Ch 185.

10.39 In order to ascertain whether part of the description is true the court has regard to the will as a whole and to the surrounding circumstances. Accordingly, where there was a gift to 'my wife Caroline' and the testator had a wife Mary but lived with a woman named Caroline with whom he had gone through an invalid ceremony of marriage, the word 'wife' was held not to affect the validity of the gift and Caroline took.[1] The rule also applies to property. Thus where a gift of stock was stated to be in the joint names of a testator and/or another, and in fact the stock was standing in the name of the testator alone but all other description of it was correct, the gift was effective.[2] Further, where the testator devised all his freehold houses in a named place and it appeared that the testator had no freehold houses there but leasehold houses the gift was sufficient to pass the leaseholds.[3]

1 *Pratt v Mathew* (1856) 22 Beav 328; *Re Petts* (1859) 27 Beav 576; *Re Howe's Goods* (1884) 48 JP 743.
2 *Coltman v Gregory* (1870) 40 LJ Ch 352.
3 *Day v Trig* (1715) 1 P Wms 286.

10.40 A more extreme example is *Re Price, Trumper v Price*.[1] In that case the testatrix bequeathed 'my £400 5 per cent War Loan, 1929/1947'. She had in fact never held any War Loan but had held £400 National War Bonds which had been converted into other government securities before she made her will. It was found as a fact that she regarded as 'War Loan' any securities which represented the investments she had made to assist the country during the First World War. Accordingly, her words were sufficient to cover the proceeds of her National War Bonds, and the words 'Five per cent . . . 1929/1947' were rejected as falsa demonstratio and the word 'Loan' was read in a secondary sense to enable effect to be given to the testatrix's wishes.

1 [1932] 2 Ch 54.

10.41 The second limb of the falsa demonstratio rule is that additional words are not rejected as importing a false description if they can be read as words of restriction. So in *Wrightson v Calvert*,[1] where the testator made a gift to his grandchildren living near B, the testator had three grandchildren but only two lived near B and the third was held not to be entitled.

1 (1860) 1 John & H 250.

10.42 The usual situation in which the main part of the falsa demonstratio rule applies, that is, the first limb, is where words of the will themselves contain an accurate description as well as a further false description. The principle has, however, been extended so that if the description in the will is wholly false but the context of the will and the surrounding circumstances show unambiguously what the testator meant then the description in the will is rejected and the intention of the testator is given effect.[1] In one case there was a gift to the 'resident apothecary' but there was only a resident dispenser and he was held entitled to take.[2] In several cases a gift to the children of A has been held to take effect as a gift to the children of B provided that the context and circumstances show that that was what was intended.[3] The rule is likewise with regard to property. Thus the description 'War Loan' was held to pass holdings of Conversion Stock and Treasury Bonds[4] and a devise was held to pass the interest in the proceeds of sale of the land.[5]

1 *Morrell v Fisher* (1849) 4 Exch 591; *Cowen v Truefitt* [1899] 2 Ch 309.
2 *Ellis v Bartrum (No 2)* (1857) 25 Beav 109.
3 *Bradwin v Harpur* (1759) Amb 374; *Bristow v Bristow* (1842) 5 Beav 289; *Lord Camoys v Blundell* (1848) 1 HL Cas 778.
4 *Re Price, Trumper v Price* [1932] 2 Ch 54; *Re Gifford, Gifford v Seaman* [1944] Ch 186.
5 *Re Glassington, Glassington v Follett* [1906] 2 Ch 305.

10.43 An example of this approach is the decision in *Re Fleming's Will*

Trusts.[1] The testator held a long lease of a house, and made a will leaving 'my leasehold house 54 Narcissus Road' to named beneficiaries. Two years after making the will, the testator purchased the freehold reversion, but the leasehold interest was not merged with the freehold. The question was whether the beneficiaries were entitled to the freehold also. Templeman J held that, where the testator makes a gift of property, it is likely that he intends to give whatever estate and interest which he has in the property at the date of his death,[2] and that merely by referring to the estate or interest which he holds at the date when the will is made does not disclose a contrary intention. Accordingly, in this case the named beneficiaries took both the freehold and leasehold interests in the property.

1 *Re Fleming's Will Trusts, Ennion v Hampstead Old People's Housing Trust Ltd* [1974] 3 All ER 323.
2 See also *Struthers v Struthers* (1857) 5 WR 809; *Miles v Miles* (1866) LR 1 Eq 462; *Cox v Bennett* (1868) LR 6 Eq 422; *Saxton v Saxton* (1879) 13 Ch D 359.

10.44 *Re Price, Trumper v Price, Re Fleming's Will Trusts* and many of the other decisions show the lengths to which the court will go in order to give effect to the testator's intention. The reasoning for such decisions represents intellectual acrobatics of an unconvincing kind and while one does not quarrel with the decision itself this type of intellectual acrobatics shows the great scope which the courts in fact have if they wish to use it in order to give a decision which they consider to be fair, and in many cases it is extremely difficult for professional advisers to give firm advice as to the likely outcome of a case. Again one comes to the point[1] when in many cases the courts are able to reach their decision first and then to construct the reasoning which appears to support it.

1 Above, para 10.5.

10.45 The principles so far discussed have been evolved by the courts themselves. Two sections of the Wills Act 1837, ss 24 and 27, are very important in the construction of wills but these are considered in the next chapter, on gifts of property and gifts to persons.

Use of extrinsic evidence

General rule

10.46 The general rule is that the court is entitled to ascertain the testator's intention only from the words of the will itself, and that it may not admit extrinsic evidence of what the testator intended. There are, however, certain exceptions to this principle, when extrinsic evidence will be admitted:
(a) where the surrounding circumstances are taken into account under the armchair principle;
(b) where from the words which the testator has used the will is ambiguous on its face;
(c) where the words which the testator has used are ambiguous in the light of the surrounding circumstances;

(d)   where any part of the will is meaningless; and

(e)   to rebut certain presumptions which equity raises.

The armchair rule

10.47   In construing a will, the court has the right to ascertain all the facts which were known to the testator at the time when he made the will, and thus to place itself in the testator's position at that time. In *Boyes v Cook*[1] James LJ said: 'You may place yourself, so to speak, in [the testator's] armchair, and consider the circumstances by which he was surrounded, when he made his will to assist you in arriving at his intention.'

1   (1880) 14 Ch D 53 at 56.

10.48   The method in which the rule is applied is that the will is first construed without any reference to the surrounding circumstances. The apparent effect of the will is then applied to the surrounding circumstances so that the court can confirm to itself that the conclusion drawn from the terms of the will itself is in accordance with the circumstances existing at the date when it was made.[1] The rule is also adopted to identify more particularly the person or property named in the will. Suppose, therefore, in a will a testator makes a gift 'to the wife of my cousin John'. On its face, the effect of the will seems clear. The court is then entitled to check its conclusion by sitting in the testator's armchair. If, therefore, the testator knew that at that time John's wife had died, the will is construed as meaning any subsequent wife of John.[2]

1   *Blackwell v Pennant* (1852) 9 Hare 551.
2   See below, para 11.3.

10.49   It is by the application of this rule that it can sometimes be seen that the testator uses words in a particular way.[1] A further example is provided by *Re Fish, Ingham v Rayner*,[2] where a testator bequeathed property 'to my niece Eliza Waterhouse'. When the apparent effect of the will was checked in the light of surrounding circumstances, it appeared that he had no niece of this name, but that his wife had a grand-niece of that name. It was held that the testator used the word 'niece' in this wide sense, so that Eliza took. The armchair rule is also applied when the description of the person or property in the will is not in precise terms.[3] Thus, where the testator gives property 'to my friend Bonzo', evidence will be admitted of the testator's practice of calling a particular person by the nickname Bonzo.[4] Again, where the description of the property is vague, such as 'my estate called Ashford Hall', evidence will be admitted to show the exact extent of what the testator regarded as his Ashford Hall estate.[5]

1   Above, para 10.18.
2   [1894] 2 Ch 83.
3   *Thomson and Baxter v Hempenstall* (1849) 1 Rob Eccl 783; *Grant v Grant* (1870) LR 5 CP 727; *Kingsbury v Walter* [1901] AC 187.
4   *Mostyn v Mostyn* (1854) 5 HL Cas 155 at 168; *Re Ofner, Samuel v Ofner* [1909] 1 Ch 60.
5   *Ricketts v Turquand* (1848) 1 HL Cas 472. See also *Doe d Beach v Earl of Jersey* (1825) 3 B & C 870; *Webb v Byng* (1855) 1 K & J 580; *Re Vear, Vear v Vear* (1917) 62 Sol Jo 159.

10.50   While it is true that evidence of the surrounding circumstances in which the will was made will always be admitted[1] this evidence can be used only to confirm the apparent effect of the will, or to clarify imprecise terms in the will. It cannot be used to alter the effect of the words used in the will if they are clear and unambiguous.[2] So, in *Evans v Angell*[3] the testator devised his freehold land 'situate in the parish of C with their appurtenances'. It was found that at the date when the will was made, the testator held with that property certain pieces of land in two other parishes, all of which had been occupied as one unit. Nevertheless, because the words of the will were clear, the land in these other parishes could not pass under the devise.

1   *Re Davis' Estate* [1952] P 279.
2   *Higgins v Dawson* [1902] AC 1; *Re Rowland* [1963] Ch 1.
3   (1858) 26 Beav 202.

Ambiguity on the face of the will

10.51   Where the words used in any part of a will are ambiguous on their face, the court will admit extrinsic evidence to assist in the interpretation of the will.[1] A will is ambiguous on its face if the words used are equally applicable to two or more persons, or to two or more items of property. The rule under which extrinsic evidence may be admitted in these circumstances is new,[2] but is well illustrated by the facts of an old case. In *Doe d Gord v Needs*[3] the testator gave one of his two houses to 'George Gord the son of George Gord'; a pecuniary legacy to 'George Gord the son of John Gord'; and his other house to 'George Gord the son of Gord'. The third gift was ambiguous on its face, and in circumstances such as this, evidence would now be admissible to show which Gord was intended.[4]

1   Administration of Justice Act 1982, s 21(1)(b).
2   Ibid applies to wills of testators *dying* after 1982.
3   (1836) 2 M & W 129.
4   In *Doe d Gord v Needs* extrinsic evidence was admitted despite the general rule at that time that such evidence was generally not admissible in the case of patent ambiguities. The decision was considered to be contrary to principle.

Ambiguity in light of circumstances

10.52   A will might not be ambiguous on its face, but might be seen to be ambiguous when an attempt is made to relate it to the surrounding circumstances. For example, suppose that the testator makes a will leaving £5,000 'to my brother'. Suppose also, however, that the testator has two brothers. In this case there is said to be a latent ambiguity, and extrinsic evidence may be admitted to assist in the interpretation of the will.[1]

1   Administration of Justice Act 1982, s 21(1)(c).

10.53   A good example of the operation of the rule is *Re Jackson, Beattie v Murphy*.[1] In her will the testatrix gave property to 'my nephew Arthur Murphy'. There was no ambiguity on the face of the will, but there were two legitimate nephews Arthur Murphy, as well as one illegitimate one. There was, therefore, a latent ambiguity, and it was possible to admit extrinsic evidence of the testatrix's intention. This was that the illegitimate nephew should take, the testatrix having used the word 'nephew' in a wide sense.[2] If there had been only one legitimate nephew of this name, then at the first stage of this process, the application of the armchair principle, that nephew would have taken.[3] It was only because there were two legitimate nephews of the same name that the latent ambiguity arose. If there had been only the two legitimate nephews, and the extrinsic evidence did not indicate that either of them was entitled to take, the whole gift would have been void.

1 [1933] Ch 237.
2 The illegitimate nephew thus took, and goes down in legal history as the lucky bastard!
3 In wills made before 1970 a reference to relations was deemed to include only legitimate relations of that description. See below, para 11.12.

10.54 Evidence of the testator's intention from outside the will cannot, however, be admitted in order to *create* the ambiguity. Suppose, therefore, that a testator had one nephew, and was well disposed towards the son of a friend, whom he treated as a nephew. Suppose also that the testator, having in mind the son of the friend, left £1,000 to 'my nephew'. There would be no ambiguity, because in the circumstances surrounding the will, the language of the will would point only to the lawful nephew. Evidence could not be admitted to show that the testator intended that the gift should be to the son of the friend.[1]

1 *Re Jackson, Beattie v Murphy* [1933] Ch 237. If, however, the draftsman had incorrectly understood the testator's instructions, the will could now be rectified; see above, paras 5.56–5.58.

Meaningless provisions

10.55 Extrinsic evidence may also be admitted where any part of the will is meaningless,[1] that is, that without such evidence the court cannot give any effective meaning to it. Accordingly, if a testator uses words or symbols which have no meaning to anyone else, extrinsic evidence is admissible as to the meaning the testator attributed to those words or symbols. So, for example, if a testator gives 'o.x.x. to S', extrinsic evidence may be admitted to assist the court in interpreting what appears meaningless to anyone other than the testator.[2] It is doubtful, however, that extrinsic evidence would be admitted to fill a blank space in a will, such as 'I give my house to   '. Evidence is admissible only to assist in the interpretation of the will,[3] but if there is nothing on the will, there is nothing to interpret. It is possibly arguable that extrinsic evidence may be admitted where the testator has partly filled the space, such as a gift 'To Mr . . .'.[4]

1 Administration of Justice Act 1982, s 21(1)(a).
2 Evidence has always been admissible where such symbols are recognised in a trade (see para 10.27), as indeed these symbols were in *Kell v Charmer* (1856) 23 Beav 195. However, in respect of wills of persons dying after 1982, evidence may be admitted of symbols or signs peculiar to the testator, such as a key written on a separate card where direct evidence was not admissible before 1983: *Clayton v Lord Nugent* (1844) 13 M & W 200. However, circumstantial evidence has always been admissible, *Abbot v Massie* (1796) 3 Ves 148.
3 Administration of Justice Act 1982, s 21(2).

4 As in *Baylis v A-G* (1741) 2 Atk 239, where, under the pre-1983 rules, extrinsic evidence was not admissible in such cases.

10.56 If the will is clear, even though what is written is meaningless, in the sense of pointless, no further evidence is admissible to give purpose to it. So, for example, if the will states 'I give my wife nothing', no evidence can be admitted to show that he intended to give her, say, £10,000.

Evidence to rebut equitable presumptions

10.57 Equity raises certain presumptions against double portions,[1] the satisfaction of portion debts by legacies,[2] and legacies by portions.[3] These are, however, only presumptions of the testator's intention, and evidence may be admitted either to support or rebut the presumptions.[4]

1 See below, para 30.95.
2 See below, paras 30.96–30.102.
3 See below, paras 30.103–30.106.
4 *Hurst v Beach* (1821) 5 Madd 351; *Hall v Hill* (1841) 4 I Eq R 27; *Kirk v Eddowes* (1844) 3 Hare 509 at 51; *Re Tussaud's Estate* (1878) 9 Ch D 363.

Nature of admissible evidence

10.58 The nature of the extrinsic evidence admissible to assist the court in interpreting the will varies depending on whether the testator died before 1983 or after 1982.

In respect of persons dying before 1983
10.59 Normally only circumstantial and not direct evidence was available to assist the court in interpreting the will. The difference in the types of evidence may be illustrated by an example. If the testator gives his house to 'my angel', evidence of the fact that he habitually called his housekeeper by that endearing name would be circumstantial evidence of the testator's intention. On the other hand, the fact that when he signed his will the testator told the witnesses that he was leaving his house to his housekeeper would be direct evidence of the testator's intention.

10.60 However, direct evidence of the testator's intention was admissible where there was an equivocation, that is, a latent ambiguity which does not come to light until an attempt is made to apply a description of the beneficiary or the subject matter to the facts.[1] So if a testator gave his estate to 'my nephew Arthur Murphy', but when he died it is discovered that he has two nephews of that name, direct evidence of his intention was admissible to assist the court in determining whom he intended to benefit.[2] Similarly, if there is a gift in a will to 'my local general hospital' and on the testator's death it is discovered that there were two such hospitals, direct evidence will be available as to his intention.[3]

1 See above, para 10.52.
2 *Re Jackson, Beattie v Murphy* [1933] Ch 237.

3 *Re Nesbitt's Will Trusts* [1953] 1 All ER 936; the doctrine of falsa demonstratio was also applied.

10.61 Direct evidence was also available to rebut the equitable presumptions referred to in para 10.57, if such presumptions arose.

In respect of persons dying after 1982

10.62 Both direct and circumstantial evidence are admissible to ascertain the testator's intention.[1] The evidence may be contemporaneous with the making of the will, or prior to or subsequent to it. Accordingly, all forms of evidence are now admissible, so that it may consist, for example, of correspondence between the testator and his solicitor as to the provisions which he wished to be included in his will, or perhaps statements made in the presence of the witnesses to his will at the time he signed it.

1 Administration of Justice Act 1982, s 21(2) permits extrinsic evidence, including evidence of the testator's intention, to be admitted.

Summary

10.63 The position may be summarised as follows:

1. Is the meaning of the will apparently clear on its face? If so, in all cases reference should be made to the surrounding circumstances to see whether that description fits exactly, or subject only to insignificant misdescription,[1] one, and only one, person or item of property.
(a) If it does, that meaning will prevail, even if it is clear that this is contrary to the testator's intention.
(b) If it does not, there is either:
   (i)   a statement which is so vague that it is meaningless, in which case extrinsic evidence can be admitted;
   (ii) a patent ambiguity, in which case extrinsic evidence can be admitted; or
   (iii) a latent ambiguity when the surrounding circumstances other than the testator's intention are considered, in which case again extrinsic evidence can be admitted.
2. If extrinsic evidence is admissible and is admitted, but nevertheless no effective meaning can be given to a provision, the gift purportedly made by it fails.

1 Which can be ignored under the falsa demonstratio rule; see above, paras 10.38–10.43.

CHAPTER 11

Gifts to persons and of property

The last chapter was concerned with general principles of the construction of wills. This chapter is concerned with the application of those principles to gifts to persons, and to gifts of property, and also with the particular considerations which apply to these gifts.

I. GIFTS TO INDIVIDUAL PERSONS

Gifts to persons identified by name or description

11.1 In many cases, a gift will be to a person or persons in a defined relationship to the testator, such as 'my wife', or 'my children'; or to a person holding office by reference to that office, such as 'my housekeeper' or 'the vicar'. If nothing else is said, is the person entitled to take that person who fulfils the description at the date of the will, or at the date of death? The general rule is that where a person fulfils the description at the date of the will, that person takes. Section 24 of the Wills Act 1837 provides that with regard to the property disposed of, the will speaks from death unless there is a contrary intention,[1] but this section does not apply to the persons entitled.[2] The rules may be stated more specifically as follows.

1 Below, para 11.42.
2 *Bullock v Bennett* (1855) 7 De GM & G 283; *Gibson v Gibson* (1852) 1 Drew 42.

Person fulfilling description at date of will

11.2 Where a person fulfils the description at the date of the will, there is a presumption that that person is to take. So, in *Re Whorwood, Ogle v Lord Sherborne*[1] a testator bequeathed a cup to 'Lord Sherborne'. Lord Sherborne was alive at the time when the will was made, but predeceased the testator, leaving a son who took the title. The Court of Appeal held that the gift was to the Lord Sherborne who was alive when the will was made, and that as he himself had predeceased the testator, the gift lapsed.[2]

1 (1887) 34 Ch D 446.

2   See also *Lomax v Holmden* (1749) 1 Ves Sen 290; *Thompson v Thompson* (1844) 1 Coll
    381; *Amyot v Dwarris* [1904] AC 268. In the last of these cases, a gift to the eldest son
    lapsed, in view of the fact that the son who was the eldest at the time when the will was
    made died before the testator, even though the testator left other sons surviving him.

11.3 This principle is, however, subject to there being no contrary
intention. It may be that the court will be less willing to find a contrary
intention if the relation of the beneficiary to the testator is close.
Accordingly, there will be a strong presumption that a gift to 'my wife' or 'to
the wife of A' is a gift to the person who is the wife at the date of making
the will, and a weaker presumption if the gift is to 'the vicar'.[1]

1   But even 'wife' may be subject to a contrary intention – *Peppin v Bickford* (1797) 3 Ves 570;
    Meredith v Treffry (1879) 12 Ch D 170; *Bathurst v Errington* (1877) 2 App Cas 698.

No person fulfilling description at the date of the will

11.4 Where no person fulfils the description at the date of the will, there
are four possibilities:
(a)   the description is wrong. In this case the gift may be saved under the
      falsa demonstratio principle,[1] in which case the relevant time will be
      either the date of the will, or the date ascertained in accordance with
      (c) below;
(b)   the context indicates that the designated beneficiary could take only if
      he fulfilled the description at the date of the will. In this case, the gift
      will fail;
(c)   the context indicates that the designated beneficiary is to be
      ascertained at a specified time. This will usually be the death of the
      testator, or the death of some life tenant, but some other future date
      may be chosen.[2] In *Re Daniels, London City and Midland Executor
      and Trustee Co Ltd v Daniels*[3] there was a gift to 'the Lord Mayor of
      London for the time being', and it was held that the words 'for the time
      being' indicated the person who was Lord Mayor at the date of the
      testator's death;
(d)   the context indicates that the designated beneficiary is to be
      ascertained at some unspecified time in the future. In this case, the first
      person to fulfil the description will take.[4] So, in *Radford v Willis*,[5]
      where there was a gift 'to the husband of A', and at the date of the will
      A had no husband but later acquired one, that person took. As this
      case shows, where no person fulfils the description at the date of the
      will, and none of the preceding paragraphs applies, the courts will
      strain to save the gift by bringing it within this head.

1   Above, paras 10.38–10.43.
2   *Re Earl Cathcart* (1912) 56 Sol Jo 271.
3   (1918) 87 LJ Ch 661.
4   *Ashburner v Wilson* (1850) 17 Sim 204.
5   (1871) 7 Ch App 7.

Republication

11.5 Where a will is republished[1] and, it seems, the testator knew of the
facts, the republication can make the will speak as to persons from the date

of republication. In *Re Hardyman, Teesdale v McClintock*[2] there was a gift by will to the wife of A. The will was republished by codicil after the testator knew of the death of A's wife. A's subsequent wife was held entitled to take.

1 Above, paras 9.1–9.10.
2 [1925] Ch 287.

Description subsequently becoming inappropriate

11.6 Where a person appears to be entitled under the rules so far considered, then, unless there is a contrary intention in the will, that person continues to be entitled even if the description is no longer applicable. So in *Re Hickman, Hickman v Hickman*[1] there was a gift 'to the wife of my grandson'. At the date of the will the grandson was not married, but he subsequently married twice, the first marriage being brought to an end by divorce. The first wife became entitled under para 11.4(d) above, and in this case she continued to be entitled, although she had ceased to be the grandson's wife by the time of the testator's death.

1 [1948] Ch 624.

Gifts to persons by name

11.7 There may sometimes be a dispute between two persons of the same name. Suppose the will contains a gift to William Silver. Suppose also that there was a William Silver alive at the date of the will, but between the date of the will William Silver died, leaving a son also called William Silver. As has already been shown,[1] in the absence of a contrary intention the will would indicate William Silver the elder, and the gift would therefore lapse. Where the name of the beneficiary is accurate, the same rules apply as previously considered.

1 Above, para 11.2.

Inaccurate names or descriptions

11.8 From what was said in the previous chapter, the following procedure with regard to persons should be followed:
1. Ascertain from the face of the will the person entitled to benefit. (At this stage there has been no reference whatever to the surrounding circumstances.)
2. Attempt to identify in the surrounding circumstances which existed at the relevant date, ascertained as above, the person who fulfils the description.
   (a) if there is one such person, who was known to the testator, he will take;
   (b) if there were two or more such persons, both known to the testator,

and an equivocation arises, extrinsic evidence of the testator's intention will be admitted;[1]
(c) if there was no such person attempt to establish from the surrounding circumstances whether part, or even the whole, of the name or description was inaccurate:
  (i) if that can be done and the correct name ascertained, apply rules (a) and (b) above as if the correct name had been stated in the will;
  (ii) if that cannot be done, the gift fails.

1 Above, paras 10.52–10.53.

11.9 To illustrate the operation of these rules, we may consider the facts of *Re Halston*, *Ewen v Halston*. There was a gift to 'John William Halston the son of Isaac Halston'. When the terms of the will were applied to the surrounding circumstances at the date when the will was made it appeared that John William Halston was by then already dead, and that fact was known to the testator. It was then necessary under rule 2(c) to ascertain whether part of the description was false. Under the falsa demonstratio rule it was held that the words 'John William' could be rejected. Isaac Halston, however, had several sons, so that the expressions 'the son of Isaac Halston' gave rise to an equivocation, and by applying rule 2(b) it was possible to admit extrinsic evidence to show which son was actually intended.

1 [1912] 1 Ch 435.

Relationships

11.10 Where a person is described by a relationship to the testator, it is presumed in the absence of intention to the contrary that the testator intended:
(a) both lawful and unlawful relations;[1]
(b) blood relations; and
(c) only relations of the actual degree specified.

1 In respect of wills *made* after 1969.

Legitimate relations

Illegitimate relations
11.11 The Family Law Reform Act 1969 completely reversed the position with regard to illegitimate relations. In respect of wills made before 1970, there is a presumption that illegitimate relations do not take. In respect of wills made after 1969, there is a presumption that they do take. The Family Law Reform Act 1987 effectively[1] re-enacted the provisions of the 1969 Act and abolished most of the exceptions to it in respect of wills made after 3 April 1988.[2] It is therefore necessary to consider dispositions[3] by a will or codicil *made*:[4]
(a) before 1970;

(b) after 1970 but before 4 April 1988;
(c) after 3 April 1988.

1 The 1987 Act nowhere refers to 'illegitimate' or 'illegitimacy' but, rather, to disregarding the fact that persons were or were not married to each other (see below, para 11.16).
2 The Act was brought into force by Family Law Reform Act 1987 (Commencement No 1) Order 1988 (SI 1988 No 425).
3 The two Acts apply to *dispositions* in a will or codicil made after the relevant date. A will made before the relevant date which is merely republished by a confirming codicil (in contrast to actual dispositions in the codicil) made on or after the relevant date is not treated as made at the later date for the purposes of the Acts: 1969 Act, s 15(8) and 1987 Act, s 19(7).
4 It is the date the will or codicil was made, not the date of death, that counts. Hence the pre-1987 Act provisions will be relevant for many years.

11.12 *Pre-1970 dispositions* It was laid down in *Hill v Crook*[1] that if illegitimate relations are to be treated as legitimate, and so to take, there must be either:
(a) no legitimate relatives to satisfy the description; or
(b) intention appearing from the will itself to include illegitimates.
If there are no legitimate relations at the relevant date[2] illegitimate ones can take unless the testator contemplated future legitimate relations.[3] Any knowledge of the testator that a woman was past childbearing or a man was incapable of procreating children will be taken into account.[4]

1 (1873) LR 6 HL 265.
2 Ie usually at the date of the will; see above, para 11.2.
3 *Dorin v Dorin* (1875) LR 7 HL 568; *Re Brown, Penrose v Manning* (1890) 63 LT 159; *Re Dieppe, Millard v Dieppe* (1915) 138 LT Jo 564.
4 *Paul v Children* (1871) LR 12 Eq 16; *Re Eve, Edwards v Burns* [1909] 1 Ch 796; *Re Brown, Penrose v Manning* (1890) 63 LT 159; *Re Wohlgemuth, Public Trustee v Wohlgemuth* [1949] Ch 12.

11.13 In order to take, however, an illegitimate person must show that no legitimate person could take, and it is not sufficient to establish in the mind of the court the probability that the illegitimate person was intended. So, in *Re Fish, Ingham v Rayner*,[1] which was mentioned earlier,[2] the testator left property 'to my niece Eliza Waterhouse'. He had no nieces, but two grandnieces, both called Eliza Waterhouse. As one was legitimate and the other illegitimate, the legitimate one took, even though the Court of Appeal appeared to think that the illegitimate one was intended.

1 [1894] 2 Ch 83.
2 Above, para 10.49.

11.14 An intention on the part of the testator to include illegitimate relations may appear on the face of the will. So, in *O v D*[1] an illegitimate girl was described in one clause as 'my daughter'. In another clause there was a gift to 'my children', and she was entitled to join with legitimate children in taking.[2] It must, however, be shown that the testator treated the claimant himself as legitimate, not that he treated other illegitimate relations as legitimate.[3]

1 [1916] 1 IR 364.
2 See, however, *Re Jodrell, Jodrell v Seale* (1890) 44 Ch D 590.
3 *Mortimer v West* (1827) 3 Russ 370; *Re Wells' Estate* (1868) LR 6 Eq 599. See also *Re Jackson, Beattie v Murphy*, above, para 10.53.

11.15 *Dispositions after 1969 but before 4 April 1988* Section 15(1) of the Family Law Reform Act 1969 provides that, in a will made on or after 1 January 1969, a reference to a child or relative includes an illegitimate child or relative. For the purposes of the legislation a will is made at the time it is signed, not when the testator dies. A will executed before 1970 is treated as having been made before then even if confirmed by a post-1969 codicil.[1] The section applies only where the illegitimate person is the beneficiary or where the beneficiary claims through an illegitimate person.[2] Accordingly, if the testator provides for a gift 'to my son but if he dies without children to the RSPCA', the contingent gift to the charity will take effect if the son dies leaving only illegitimate children. It is further provided that where the word 'heir' is used or an entail is created, there is still a presumption against illegitimate persons taking.[3]

1 Family Law Reform Act 1969, s 15(8).
2 Ibid, s 15(2).
3 Ibid.

11.16 *Post-3 April 1988 dispositions* Section 19 of the Family Law Reform Act 1987 made further changes to these rules of construction and abolished most of the exceptions.[1] A will or codicil executed on or before, but confirmed by codicil executed after, 3 April 1988 is not treated for these purposes as made after that date.[2] Section 19 provides that references (whether express or implied) to any relationship between two persons shall, unless a contrary intention appears, be construed without regard to whether or not the father and mother of either of them, or the father or mother of any person through whom the relationship is deduced, have or had been married to each other at any time. Under the new rule of construction there is no longer any restriction that the reference should be to a person who is to benefit or be capable of benefiting under the dispositions. The new provisions apply also to the construction of 'heir' or 'heirs' and to any expression which is used to create an entailed interest,[3] but it does not extend to the devolution of any property which would otherwise devolve along with a dignity or title of honour.[4]

1 In accordance with the Law Commission Second Report on Illegitimacy, Law Com No 157.
2 See above, para 11.11 and footnotes.
3 Family Law Reform Act 1987, s 19(2).
4 Ibid, s 19(4).

Legitimated children
11.17 Under the Legitimacy Act 1976, in the case of the will of a testator who dies after 1975,[1] the general principle is that a legitimated person takes the same benefit that he would have had he been born legitimate, subject to a contrary intention.[2] The rule applies regardless of whether legitimation occurs before or after the testator's death.[3]

1 Legitimacy Act 1926, ss 3 and 5 continue to apply to testators dying before 1 January 1976: 1976 Act, Sch 1, para 2. For the previous law see the 4th edition of this book.
2 1976 Act, s 5(4), (5). This extends to property limited to devolve along with any dignity or title of honour in respect of children born after 28 October 1959: ibid, Sch 1, para 5.
3 For deaths before 1 January 1976 legitimation must have occurred before the death: 1926 Act, s 3(1).

11.18   Section 5 of the Act sets out (with examples) two rules of construction which, subject to a contrary intention, apply to wills of testators *dying* after 1975. The rules relate to a disposition by will where entitlement depends on the date of birth of a child or children. Such a disposition is to be construed as though:

(a)   the legitimated child had been born on the date of the legitimation; and

(b)   two or more children legitimated on the same date had been born on that date, in the order of their actual births,

but these rules do not affect any reference to the actual age of a child.[1]

1   1976 Act, s 5(4).

11.19   Section 5(5) sets out some examples of the application of these rules. The first is a gift to the children of A 'living at my death or born afterwards'. If the testator dies after 1975 and after his death A legitimates a child born prior to 1976, that child is entitled to take as a child born after the testator's death, even though he does not fall within the description of a child of A living at the testator's death. A further example is of a gift to the children of A 'living at my death or born afterwards before any one of such children for the time being in existence attains a vested interest, and who attain the age of 21 years'. A's legitimated child is entitled to take under the gift if he is legitimated before any other child attains a vested interest and himself provided he actually attains the age of 21, which is calculated from the date of his birth, not of his legitimation. The same examples would apply if the reference were to grandchildren instead of children.[1]

1   Ibid, s 5(5) Example 3. A further example is given in s 5(5) Example 4, of a gift to A for life 'until he has a child' and then to his child or children.

Adopted children

11.20   Under the Adoption Act 1976 the general principles are that a child adopted by a married couple is treated as a child of that marriage and that a child adopted in other circumstances is treated as though he had been born to the adopter in wedlock.[1] The adopted child is thus treated as the child of his adopter or adopters and of no other person, and is effectively transplanted into his new family for all purposes.[2] Accordingly, references to children in wills of testators *dying* after 1976 will, subject to any contrary intention, be construed so as to include adopted children, regardless of whether the adoption order is made before or after the testator's death.[3]

1   1976 Act, s 39(1), (2) and (4), which applies to an adoption order made by a court in any part of the UK, the Isle of Man or the Channel Islands and to certain foreign adoptions: s 38.

2   This includes an application under the Inheritance (Provision for Family and Dependants) Act 1975, where a child ceases to qualify as an applicant if he is adopted before the application is made: *Re Collins* [1990] 2 All ER 47.

3   1976 Act, ss 42(1), 46(3) and 72(1). The Adoption Act 1958, ss 16 and 17 apply to testators dying before 1 January 1976, and provisions containing a reference to those sections continue to apply: 1976 Act, s 73(1) and Sch 2, para 6.

11.21   Section 42 of the Act sets out (with examples) two rules of construction similar to those for legitimated children. The rules apply to

wills of testators *dying* after 1975, subject to a contrary intention, and relate to a disposition by will where entitlement depends on the date of birth of a child or children. Such a disposition is to be construed as though:
(a) the adopted child had been born on the date of adoption;[1] and
(b) two or more children adopted on the same date had been born on that date, in the order of their actual births,
but the rules do not affect any reference to the actual age of a child.[2] The examples are similar to those for legitimated children.[3]

1 For adoptions by one of the child's natural parents see example in s 43 of the 1976 Act.
2 Ibid, s 42(2).
3 See above, para 11.19.

11.22 Subject to any contrary provision in the will, an adoption does not affect the descent of or devolution of any property limited to devolve along with any peerage or dignity or title of honour.[1]

1 Adoption Act 1976, s 44.

Relationship by blood and affinity

11.23 Relationship arising by marriage is known as relationship by affinity. The presumption is that where a relationship is specified in a will, the only persons to take are the relations by blood, and not by affinity.[1] This is subject to the same exceptions as in the case of legitimate relations, namely relations by affinity may be included if there are no relations by blood,[2] or if there is an intention that they should. There may be a considerable difficulty in knowing whether a contrary intention is shown. In several cases a niece by affinity has been called for the purposes of a specific bequest or legacy 'my niece A', but such person has been held not entitled to share in a subsequent gift to 'my nephews and nieces'.[3] These decisions have not been followed in others,[4] so that little may be said by way of general rule, each decision depending on its context.

1 *Hibbert v Hibbert* (1873) LR 15 Eq 372; *Hussey v Berkeley* (1763) 2 Eden 194; *Smith v Lidiard* (1857) 3 K & J 252; *Merrill v Morton* (1881) 17 Ch D 382.
2 *Frogley v Phillips* (1861) 3 De GF & J 466; *Hogg v Cook* (1863) 32 Beav 641; *Adney v Greatrex* (1869) 38 LJ Ch 414; *Sherratt v Mountford* (1873) 8 Ch App 928; *Re Gue, Smith v Gue* (1892) 61 LJ Ch 510.
3 *Smith v Lidiard* (1857) 3 K & J 252; *Wells v Wells* (1874) LR 18 Eq 504.
4 *Re Gue, Smith v Gue* (1892) 61 LJ Ch 510; *Re Cozens* 1928 SC 371. It will often depend on whether the court will adopt the 'dictionary principle': see above, para 10.18.

11.24 It is also difficult to state the position affecting relations of the half-blood. In *Re Reed*[1] it was said that there is a presumption that relations of the half-blood are included and that 'the context must be overriding to exclude the half-blood'. On the other hand, in some cases the context has very easily displaced the presumption. So where the testator said 'my own brothers and sisters' this was held sufficient to exclude stepbrothers and stepsisters.

1 (1888) 57 LJ Ch 790.

11.25 The emphasis placed on blood relationships is illustrated by *Re Barlow's Will Trusts*.[1] In that case the testatrix conferred a benefit on her 'family'. She had no issue and it was held that the expression meant those related to her by blood.

1 [1979] 1 All ER 296.

Degree of relationship

11.26 There is a presumption that the testator only intended relations of the exact degree to benefit. Thus, if he refers to nieces, it is presumed he meant nieces and not, for example, greatnieces.[1] Again the presumption may be displaced by the context or contrary intention.

1 *Seale-Hayne v Jodrell* [1891] AC 304; *Re Cozens* 1928 SC 371.

Incorrect statement of relationship

11.27 The falsa demonstratio rule applies, whereby it may be possible to ignore incorrect descriptions.[1]

1 See above, paras 10.38–10.45.

Particular words

11.28 There has been a considerable amount of litigation as to the meaning of particular words used to designate beneficiaries. It is not intended even to begin to give an exhaustive statement of the position, but as illustrations five examples may be taken.

'Children'

11.29 The word 'children' prima facie means immediate descendants, and not grandchildren or remoter issue.[1] If, however, it can be shown that the testator has confused the strict meaning of the word children with remoter issue, grandchildren will be entitled to take.[2] A child en ventre sa mère is included in the description of children born or living at a particular date if it is to the child's own benefit that he should be included.[3] The position of legitimated and adopted children has already been considered.

1 *Loring v Thomas* (1861) 1 Drew & Sm 497.
2 *Wyth v Blackman* (1749) 1 Ves Sen 196; *Re Marshall* [1957] Ch 507.
3 *Villar v Gilbey* [1907] AC 139; *Elliot v Joicey* [1935] AC 209; *Re Stern's Will Trusts* [1962] Ch 732.

'Descendants'

11.30 The expression 'descendants' is not a term of art, so that it will in general be construed as meaning anyone who is descended from a particular individual, however that descent is traced. Accordingly, if there is a gift to 'the male descendant of Rupert', all such descendants will take even if they have their descent through a female.[1] The word will not include collateral relations unless there is a clear definition clause in the will to that effect.[2]

1 *Re Drake, Drake v Drake* [1971] Ch 179, [1970] 3 All ER 32. Cf *Oddie v Woodford* (1821) as reported in 3 My & Cr 584; *Bernal v Bernal* (1838) as reported in 3 My & Cr 559n; *Re Du Cros' Settlement, Du Cros Family Trustee Co Ltd v Du Cros* [1961] 3 All ER 193; *Allen v Crane* (1953) 89 CLR 152 (Australia).
2 *Re Thurlow, Riddick v Kennard* [1972] Ch 379, [1972] 1 All ER 10.

'Survivors'

11.31 Where property is to be divided among the survivors of a particular group, the prima facie meaning of that expression is that they should be living at and after[1] the moment of distribution.[2] In the case of an immediate gift, the moment of distribution is, for this purpose, the death of the testator, but in other circumstances it may be the death of a life tenant. Thus, a gift to 'the surviving children of Winnie' means a gift to such of her children as are living at the date of death of the testator, but a gift to 'Winnie for life, with remainder to her surviving children' enables the children living at the death of Winnie to take. Until that time, their interest does not vest, so that if they predecease Winnie they will take no benefit, even if they survive the testator.[3] The context of the will may, of course, show that the word is used in a special or secondary sense.

1 *Elliot v Joicey* [1935] AC 209 at 218; see also *Re Castle, Public Trustee v Floud* [1949] Ch 46.
2 *Cripps v Wolcott* (1819) 4 Madd 11.
3 *Re McKee, Public Trustee v McKee* [1931] 2 Ch 145.

'Issue'

11.32 The technical meaning of the word 'issue' is descendants in every degree.[1] In one case[2] the testator left a legacy to his daughter for life and thereafter to her children, but there was a gift over if the daughter should die without leaving 'issue her surviving'. The daughter had a son, and that son had two children. The son predeceased the daughter, but the gift over did not take effect because the son's children were 'issue' of the daughter. However, the meaning of the word 'issue' may be restricted to 'children', where the context so indicates. Thus, a gift to 'the issue of our marriage' has been confined to the children of the marriage[3] and wherever the testator uses an expression which shows that he used the word other than in its technical meaning, the word will bear that meaning. An example of this occurred where the testator used the expression 'issue of such issue'.[4]

1 *Westwood v Southey* (1852) 2 Sim NS 192; *Edyvean v Archer* [1903] AC 379; *Re Burnham, Carrick v Carrick* [1918] 2 Ch 196; *Re Swain, Brett v Ward* [1918] 1 Ch 399; *Re Hipwell, Hipwell v Hewitt* [1945] 2 All ER 476; *Re Chilver Estate, Selkirk v White* [1974] 6 WWR 198 (British Columbia).
2 *Perpetual Trustee Co Ltd v McKendrick* [1973] 2 NSWLR 784 (New South Wales). See also *Westwood v Southey*, above.

3 *Re Noad, Noad v Noad* [1951] Ch 553.
4 *Pope v Pope* (1851) 14 Beav 591; *Fairfield v Bushell* (1863) 32 Beav 158.

'Next of kin'

11.33 The expression 'next of kin' simpliciter does not have a technical meaning, but merely denotes the most nearly related relative or kin. On the other hand, the expression 'statutory next of kin' indicates the persons who would be entitled to succeed to the property on intestacy, and in the proportions and subject to the same conditions as they would have taken under the intestacy rules.[1] Although the expression has this meaning by statute,[2] the statutory definition is nevertheless subject to a contrary intention being shown. If there is more than one person in the same degree of kinship, all those persons will in general take, but this also is subject to no contrary intention being shown. So, where the testator left land to 'the nearest female in the direct line of kinship', and the nearest female kin were three great-granddaughters, it was held that the eldest great-granddaughter took to the exclusion of the others.[3]

1 *Re Hart's Will Trusts, Public Trustee v Barclays Bank Ltd* [1950] Ch 84; *Re Kilvert, Midland Bank Executor and Trustee Co Ltd v Kilvert* [1957] Ch 388; and see *Re Krawitz's Will Trusts, Krawitz v Crawford* [1959] 3 All ER 793.
2 Administration of Estates Act 1925, s 50.
3 *Re Rogers' Will, Mitchell v Thomas* [1973] 2 NSWLR 312 (New South Wales).

II. GIFTS TO GROUPS OF PERSONS

Gifts by number

11.34 A testator may attempt to identify the beneficiaries by describing them as members of a class or group, and adding their number, such as a gift to 'the four children of A'. Clearly in this case no problem arises if A in fact has four children, but what is the position if he has three or five? The position is as follows:
(a) The relevant date is the same as for individuals, so that usually regard is paid to the position when the will is made.
(b) The court considers the surrounding circumstances to see with which of the members of the class the testator was acquainted. If that number corresponds to the number specified in the will, those persons will take.[1] This is part of a more general rule that where persons are misdescribed in number, an attempt should be made from the surrounding circumstances to see whether it is possible to say which of the class were meant. In *Re Mayo, Chester v Keirl*,[2] for example, there was a bequest to the three children of A. A had four children, but the testator had admitted paternity only of the younger three. The eldest child did not take.
(c) Where it is not possible to say which of the class is meant, all persons who answer the description take. Thus, in *Sleech v Thorington*[3] the testatrix left a gift to 'the two servants living with me at my death'. She in fact had three servants, all of whom took.

1   *Newman v Piercey* (1876) 4 Ch D 41.
2   [1901] 1 Ch 404.
3   (1754) 2 Ves Sen 560.

Class gifts

Nature of rule

11.35   Special rules apply to gifts which are, strictly so-called, 'class gifts'. The general object of these rules is to facilitate the distribution of the estate or fund at the earliest opportunity. The general situation may be described by an example. Suppose a testator leaves a fund to 'my sisters'. Suppose also that he has three sisters alive at the date of his death, and two born afterwards. There are two possibilities: the gift may be divided between the three who are alive at the date of his death; or the fund may be retained until it is impossible for any more sisters to be born, and then distributed. It is a fundamental principle of English property law that property and assets of every description should circulate as much as possible, and not be tied up. In accordance with this thinking, the class is deemed to close at the earliest opportunity, that is, at the date of death of the testator. On the example given, the two sisters born afterwards take nothing.

11.36   Although the purpose behind the class-closing rules can be clearly understood, they are nevertheless curious. They may be excluded by an expression of contrary intention[1] but apart from that they do not even purport to be an interpretation of the testator's intention. They are, frankly, and blatantly, rules of convenience.[2]

1   *Scott v Earl of Scarborough* (1838) 1 Beav 154; *Hodson v Micklethwaite* (1854) 2 Drew 294; *Re Kebty-Fletcher's Will Trusts* [1969] 1 Ch 339, [1967] 3 All ER 1076.
2   *Re Emmet's Estate, Emmet v Emmet* (1880) 13 Ch D 484 at 490. See also Bailey (1958) Camb LJ 39 at 42. Although sometimes the rule was effective in preventing gifts from failing for breach of the perpetuity rule at a time when it was not permissible to 'wait and see', ie prior to the Perpetuities and Accumulations Act 1964.

Statement of the rule

11.37   The classic statement of the nature of a class is that of Lord Davey in *Kingsbury v Walter*,[1] where he said 'prima facie a class gift is a gift to a class, consisting of persons, who are included and comprehended under some general description and . . . it may be none the less a class because some of the individuals of the class are named'. Examples of 'classes' are gifts 'to all my sisters';[2] 'to the grandchildren of A',[3] 'to the children of A including his son B';[4] and 'to my late husband's nephews and nieces other than A and B'.[5]

1   [1901] AC 187.
2   *Weld v Bradbury* (1715) 2 Vern 705.
3   *Re Knapp's Settlement, Knapp v Vassall* [1895] 1 Ch 91.
4   *Re Jackson, Shiers v Ashworth* (1883) 25 Ch D 162.
5   *Dimond v Bostock* (1875) 10 Ch App 358.

The rule may be stated as follows:
11.38   1(a) Where the shares of members of the class are to vest at birth, the class will remain open indefinitely, unless:
(b)(i)   a member of the class was born before the testator's death; *or*
(b)(ii) a member of the class was born before the end of some intermediate period of limitation.
2. Where the shares of members of the class are to vest upon the happening of any event other than birth and where the exceptions within rule 1(b) apply, the class closes when the first member becomes entitled to an interest in possession.
3. No person may take a benefit after the class has closed.[1]

---

1   The rule governing the position where the gift to the class is postponed or is subject to the members of the class attaining a qualifying age, is known as the rule in *Andrews v Partington* (1791) 3 Bro CC 401.

The particular situations likely to arise
11.39   These are as follows:
(a)   Immediate gift to a class without qualification – eg 'to all my grandchildren'. If the testator has a grandchild alive at his death, the class closes at his death (rule 1(b)(i)) but if he has no grandchildren alive then, all grandchildren whenever born will take (rule 1(a)).
(b)   Immediate gift to class with qualification – eg 'to all my grandchildren who attain the age of 21'. The class will close at the date of death of the testator if any grandchild attained the age of 21 during the testator's lifetime (rule 1(b)(i)). If grandchildren are alive during the testator's lifetime, but have not reached the age of 21 by his death, the class closes when the first one reaches that age (rule 2). It will be seen that rule 1 can apply only where vesting is to be at birth, and not at some other time. This is quite illogical.
(c)   Mediate gift without qualification – eg 'to A for life, with remainder to all my grandchildren'. The class will close on the death of A (the time when a child may acquire an interest in possession) if there is any grandchild then alive (rule 1(b)(ii)), but if there is no grandchild upon the death of A, the class will remain open indefinitely (rule 1(a)).
(d)   Mediate gift with qualification – eg 'to A for life, with remainder to all my grandchildren who attain 21'. The class will close on the death of A if there is any grandchild aged 21 (rule 2). The class cannot close earlier than the death of A, because until then no member of the class can obtain an interest in possession. If there is no grandchild who has attained 21 at the death of A the class will close when the first grandchild does so (rule 2).

Effect of closing rule

11.40   Where there is a gift, whether immediate or mediate, with qualification, all persons who may attain that qualification at the date when the class closes are prima facie included. Thus if there is a gift 'to all my grandchildren who attain the age of 21' and at the testator's death there are four grandchildren aged 23, 19, 10 and 2, the class then closes because one has fulfilled the qualifying conditions. Each of the others *then alive* will participate if they in due course attain the qualifying age. Thus, when the class closes, the minimum amount payable to each member of the class is ascertained and one quarter of the fund can be paid to the eldest forthwith. If one of the others dies before attaining the age of 21, his share lapses, and is divided among the others. Thus the eldest, who would already have received one quarter, will receive a further third of the lapsed quarter.

Contrary intention

11.41 It has been mentioned[1] that the rules can be excluded by a contrary intention: the result is often an inelegant game of coin tossing to see whether the testator in fact had a contrary intention.[2] A good example is *Re Edmondson's Will Trusts, Baron Sandford v Edmondson*.[3] There was, in effect, a gift to 'such of my grandchildren, whenever born, as should attain the age of 21'. At the time of the gift there were two children, and one grandchild, a few months old. By the time of the application to the court, there were eight grandchildren, with the possibility of more to follow. Was the class to close, the eldest grandchild having reached the age of 21? Or was it to remain open, and so admit any grandchild who might be born in the future? At first instance[4] Goulding J held that the class closed: the Court of Appeal held that it did not.[5] The decision of the Court of Appeal centred on the proposition that an expression such as 'born or hereafter to be born' was merely a general reference to the future, not sufficient to exclude the rule, whereas the expression 'whenever born' was sufficiently specific and emphatic to exclude the rule. This type of dispute shows a detachment from reality meriting approval from the medieval Schoolmen, but from no one else. It is possible to formulate the principle that *Andrews v Partington*[6] should be excluded only if it can be shown that the testator appreciated the nature of the problem that would arise by its exclusion, that is, that the shares of persons with vested interests might have to be retained in case further members of the class come to reduce the size of each share. But in this sphere no rule is likely to be satisfactory, for the mind of the testator is rarely directed to the problem – and the mind of the draftsman not much more frequently.

1   Above, para 11.3.
2   Sherrin (1972) 122 NLJ 144.
3   [1972] 1 All ER 444, CA.
4   [1971] 3 All ER 1121.
5   The court was concerned with two documents, but there was no dispute that for the purposes of one of them the class did close.
6   (1791) 3 Bro CC 401.

III. GIFTS OF PROPERTY

The relevant date

The general rule

11.42 The general rule is that a reference to a person in a gift by will is to the person who fulfils that description at the date of the will.[1] So far as references to property are concerned, the rule is the reverse. By virtue of the Wills Act 1837, s 24, unless there is a contrary intention, a will must be construed with reference to the property comprised in it, to speak and take effect as if it had been executed immediately before the death of the testator. Accordingly, a gift of 'all my stocks and shares' will include all stocks and shares owned by the testator at the date of his death, even if he acquired some of them after the date of the will. The reason for s 24 was probably the rule relating to leaseholds. Before 1837, a gift of a leasehold interest would pass only that interest in existence at the date of the will. If, therefore, after the date of the will the lease expired and the testator was granted a new lease before his death, the new lease would not pass, because it was a different, new interest. By virtue of s 24, therefore, a new lease will pass provided the words of the will are appropriate to describe it.[2]

1 Above, para 11.2.
2 If, for example, the testator refers not merely to his leasehold property, but to the property demised by a lease dated 1960, the property will not pass if between the date of making the will and the date of death the term expires, and a new lease is granted.

Contrary intention

11.43 Section 24 reads: 'Every will shall be construed with reference to the [property] comprised in it, to speak and take effect as if it had been executed immediately before the death of the testator, unless a contrary intention shall appear by will'. In the light of this, suppose a testator makes a gift of 'my present car'. Does one apply the section narrowly, and read this clause as if the will had been executed just prior to death, or does one interpret the words 'my present' as imparting a contrary intention, and to indicate the car owned at the date of the will? Although s 24 does not distinguish between general and specific gifts, the courts will be far more ready to find a contrary intention in specific gifts than in general gifts. A gift of 'my house and land at A', where the word 'my' forms an essential part of the description, will be regarded as a specific gift, whereas a gift of 'all my houses and lands at A' will be regarded as general. This distinction is important. If the testator uses the word 'my' or some other possessive adjective, that may convert an otherwise general gift into a specific one.

11.44 The confusion which abounds in this field is illustrated by some of the many cases which have been concerned with the use of the word 'now'. There have been three approaches.

To ignore it
11.45 In *Wagstaff v Wagstaff*,[1] where there was gift of an article 'which I now possess', the expression 'which I now possess' was treated as meaning 'which I possess'. An alternative route to reach the same result is to construe such words not as an essential part of the description, but as mere additional description, which may be rejected. So, in *Re Willis, Spencer v Willis*[2] there was a devise to the testator's wife of 'all that my freehold house and premises situate at Oakleigh Park, Whetstone, in the County of Middlesex, and known as "Ankerwyke", and in which I now reside'. Between the date of the will and the date of death the testator acquired two other plots which

he enjoyed with the house. Eve J asked whether the expression 'in which I now reside' was 'an essential part of the gift, or [was] simply added as an additional description, inaccurate at the date when the will came into operation'. Deciding on the facts that the latter was the case, he held that the two additional plots passed with the house to the wife.

1 (1869) LR 8 Eq 229.
2 [1911] 2 Ch 563.

To interpret 'now' expressly as referring to the deemed time of execution, that is, immediately before death

11.46 In *Hepburn v Skirving*,[1] for example, a gift of 'all the shares which I now possess in the Union Bank of Calcutta' was read as referring to assets held immediately before death.

1 (1858) 32 LTOS 26.

To interpret 'now' as imputing a contrary intention

11.47 So, in *Re Fowler, Fowler v Wittingham*[1] there was a gift of 'my house and land wherein I now reside'. Between the date of the will and the date of death further fields were acquired, and added to the grounds, but they did not pass under the gift. Similarly, in *Re Edwards, Rowland v Edwards*[2] there was a gift of 'my house and premises where I now reside'. After the date of the will, part of the property was let, but the beneficiary was entitled to the whole premises occupied as at the date of the will.

1 (1915) 139 LT Jo 183.
2 (1890) 63 LT 481.

11.48 A good explanation of the contrary intention rule was given by Stuart VC in *Lady Langdale v Briggs*.[1] He said:

'Where . . . a testator by a will . . . devises lands by the description of "all the lands now vested in me" and in the same will speaks of other lands which shall be vested in him at the time of his death, the language affords sufficient evidence of an intention to distinguish after acquired lands from lands vested at the time of the date and making of his will . . .'

1 (1855) 3 Sm & G 246 at 254.

11.49 Although there are the three approaches, it will be appreciated that the result of following either of the first two will be the same. It is in cases such as this where the great freedom of action given to the judge is seen. Again, take the example of a gift of 'the house in which I now reside'. The judge may follow the first or second course and take the house as it stands at the date of the will,[1] or he may take the words as relating to the date of the will.[2] The construction of the will as a whole may control the judge's discretion, but if it is unfettered, one may speculate on the reasons which may lead a judge to one decision or to the other. This is of course speculation, but it may be expected that the court will be influenced by any material alteration in the value of the asset, and by the destruction of the property. Suppose the testator makes a gift of 'my car'. Suppose also that at the date of the will the car was an old model worth £500, but that this was subsequently sold and a Rolls-Royce worth £50,000 purchased by the testator shortly before his death. It may well be that if the beneficiary was a casual friend, the gift would be construed as one relating to the date of the will, whereas if it is to the testator's son it may speak from death. If this contention is correct, it shows how considerations which are technically irrelevant may affect the result, but nevertheless enable a just result to be reached.

1 Eg *Hutchinson v Barrow* (1861) 6 H & N 583; *Noone v Lyons* (1862) 1 W & W (Eq) 235.
2 *Re Midland Rly Co* (1865) 34 Beav 525; *Re Champion, Dudley v Champion* [1893] 1 Ch 101.

Scope of a general gift

Nature of a general gift

11.50 A general gift may be a gift of all the testator's assets, such as 'all my property';[1] or a gift of all the testator's assets of a particular nature, such as 'all my realty'; or a gift of the testator's residuary estate, or of his residue of a particular nature, such as 'all my property remaining after the payment of my legacies' or 'all my personal property remaining after the payment of my legacies'. The characteristic of all general gifts is that no particular item of the specified property is identified.

1 *Re Bridgen, Chaytor v Edwin* [1938] Ch 205.

Interests included

11.51 In the absence of a contrary intention, a general gift will include all interests of the testator in the property comprised in the gift, whether legal or equitable.[1] It will also include all interests, whether vested or contingent, and whether in possession, in remainder or in expectancy. So in *Re Egan, Mills v Penton*[2] where the word 'money' was given a very wide meaning[3] a gift of 'money in my possession at my death' passed a reversionary interest held at the date of death.

1 *Atcherley v Vernon* (1723) 10 Mod Rep 518; *Potter v Potter* (1750) 1 Ves Sen 437; *Capel v Girdler* (1804) 9 Ves 509.
2 [1899] 1 Ch 688.
3 See above, para 10.23.

11.52 In some cases technical words are used which, strictly, are applicable only to realty alone or to personalty alone, but which appear to apply to both realty and personalty. For example, the word 'devise' is strictly applicable only to realty, and 'bequest' to personalty. What, then, is the effect if the testator says: 'I bequeath all my property to X', and dies leaving both realty and personalty. Such technical words, or technical words of limitation, will be a factor in showing whether a gift is of all property, or is to be restricted,[1] but usually more force is given to the general nature of the gift than to the technical words used.[2] In the example given, it could be expected that the words would be sufficient to pass both realty and personalty.[3]

1 *Fullerton v Martin* (1853) 1 Eq Rep 224; *Prescott v Barker* (1874) 9 Ch App 174; *Kirby-Smith v Parnell* [1903] 1 Ch 483.
2 *Ackers v Phipps* (1835) 3 Cl & Fin 665.
3 *Barclay v Collett* (1838) 4 Bing NC 658; *Hamilton v Buckmaster* (1866) LR 3 Eq 323; *Stein v Ritherdon* (1868) 37 LJ Ch 369; *Lloyd v Lloyd* (1869) LR 7 Eq 458; *Longley v Longley* (1871) LR 13 Eq 133.

Property given to a spouse and then to issue

11.53 A testator who makes his own will sometimes attempts to give successive absolute interests in property. This most frequently arises when a testator makes an absolute gift to his wife with a provision that on her death the property is to pass to their children.[1] The problem of construction is then whether the wife receives the property absolutely, so that the children receive nothing (as successive absolute interests are not possible), or whether she receives a life interest with remainder to the children. Section 22 of the Administration of Justice Act 1982 addresses the problem. It provides that, for deaths after 1982, except where a contrary intention is shown, a gift by a testator to his spouse is presumed to be absolute provided two requirements are satisfied:

(a) The gift to the spouse is made 'in terms which in themselves would give an absolute interest to the spouse'. A gift of 'my estate to my wife', for example, would meet this requirement. On the other hand, a gift of 'my estate to my wife for life' is clearly not in absolute terms and is therefore outside the section.

(b) The testator by the same instrument purports to give his *issue* an interest in the same property. A gift of 'my house, Homeacre, to my wife absolutely and after her death to my children equally' satisfies the section. If, however, the gift over is to someone other than the testator's issue, the second requirement is not met.

If the successive gifts do not satisfy these requirements, the testator's intention will have to be determined under the pre-1983 law.

1 See Law Reform Committee, 19th Report, Interpretation of Wills, Cmnd 5301 (1973), paras 60–62 and 65.

Property subject to a power of appointment

Powers subject to Wills Act, section 27

11.54 It is not intended to discuss here the law relating to powers of appointment, but it may be useful to summarise the classification of powers. Powers may be classified according to:

(1) *the width of class of possible appointees*:
   (a) general – eg 'to such persons as X shall select';
   (b) special – eg 'to such of my children as X shall select';

    (c) hybrid – eg 'to such persons, other than Y, as X shall select'.
(2) *the method of exercise*:
    (a) by deed only;
    (b) by will only;
    (c) by deed or will.
(3) *the number of persons who must join in or concur*:
    (a) exercisable by the donee of the power alone;
    (b) exercisable by the donee of the power jointly with another, that is, where there are two donees; and
    (c) exercisable by the donee of the power, either with the consent of, or subject to veto by, another.

In principle, there may be any combination of these possibilities. Section 27 of the Wills Act 1837, which deals with the exercise of powers of appointment, governs property 'which he [the testator] may have power to appoint in any manner he may think proper'. It is necessary to consider to which powers the section applies.

Width of class of possible appointees: general power only

11.55 The general meaning of 'in any manner he may think proper' refers to the class of possible objects. Accordingly it is established that a special power is not within the scope of the section.[1] It also seems that a hybrid power is excluded.[2] It would seem, however, that in certain circumstances a hybrid power can become a general power. Thus, if only one person (not being the donee of the power) is excepted, and that person dies[3] or if the excepted person does not exist,[4] then the power will be, or will become, general. Presumably, by applying s 24, the relevant date is the date of death of the testator, so that if a power is hybrid when the will is made, but has become general by the date of death, that power will fall within s 27.

1 *Cloves v Awdry* (1850) 12 Beav 604; *Re Penrose, Penrose v Penrose* [1933] Ch 793.
2 *Re Byron's Settlement, Williams v Mitchell* [1891] 3 Ch 474; *Re Harvey, Banister v Thirtle* [1950] 1 All ER 491; *Re Jones, Public Trustee v Jones* [1945] Ch 105.
3 *Re Byron's Settlement, Williams v Mitchell* [1891] 3 Ch 474.
4 *Re Harvey, Banister v Thirtle* [1950] 1 All ER 491.

Method of execution: by will

11.56 Section 10 of the Wills Act 1837 provides that the formalities required for making a will are sufficient formalities to exercise a power of appointment by will, even if the instrument creating the power requires additional formalities. Subject to that, any requirement as to execution contained in the instrument creating the power takes precedence over the Wills Act provisions. Accordingly, if a power is exercisable by deed only, it cannot be exercised at all by will. A power exercisable by will only, or by deed or will, can fall within s 27.[1] Also, in accordance with the general principle that the requirements contained in the instrument creating the power take priority, if the instrument of creation requires express reference to the power, that power does not come within s 27, for if the testator must refer to the power, he does not, within the terms of s 27, have a power to appoint 'in any manner he may think proper'.[2]

1 *Re Powell's Trusts* (1869) 39 LJ Ch 188.
2 *Phillips v Cayley* (1889) 43 Ch D 222; *Re Davies, Davies v Davies* [1892] 3 Ch 63; *Re Lane, Belli v Lane* [1908] 2 Ch 581.

More than one person to join in

11.57 Where the power of appointment is to be exercised by two persons, it can be validly exercised by the joint will of those persons. In *Re Duddell, Roundway v Roundway*[1] a power was executed by two persons. They made a joint will which was admitted to probate on the death of the first to die. It was held that provided the survivor did not revoke the will, and it was also admitted to probate on his death, that would be a good exercise of the joint power. Whether the power has to be exercised by a joint will, or whether it can be exercised by two separate wills, depends on the requirements of the instrument creating the power.

1 [1932] 1 Ch 585.

11.58 As the words 'in any manner' in s 27 refer to the objects of the power, it is thought that if the exercise of a power is subject to consent, then, provided that consent is given, there may be a valid exercise under s 27.

Operation of section 27

11.59 Section 27 provides that in respect of those powers which are subject to it, a general devise or a general bequest shall, in the absence of a contrary intention, operate as an exercise of the power without any express reference to the power being made.

11.60 To exercise a power of appointment under s 27, a general gift need not be of the whole of the testator's estate, or, indeed, of the whole of his realty or personalty. So far as realty is concerned, the section applies to a general devise of the whole of the testator's real estate; to his real estate in any particular place or in the occupation of any particular person; and to the real estate of the testator 'otherwise described in any general manner'. In the case of personalty, it applies to a general bequest of the personal estate of the testator, or to any bequest of personal property described in any general manner.

11.61 In order for a power to be exercised by a general gift, the property subject to the power must come within the description of the gift. So, where the testator has a general power of appointment over shares, this power would be exercised by a gift of all his property; or of all his personalty; or of all his investments; but it would not be exercised by a gift of all his furniture. The principle has been developed that the power will be exercised by the narrowest gift in the will sufficient to cover the property subject to the power. So, in *Re Doherty-Waterhouse*[1] the testator had a power of appointment over stock, and by his will made a gift of 'all my stock to X' and 'all the residue of my property to Y'. Both gifts, by themselves, would have been sufficient to exercise the power, but the stock passed under the former.

1 [1918] 2 Ch 269.

11.62 Section 27 applies only in the absence of a contrary intention, but the courts will be slow to find such a contrary intention. This is shown by numerous cases concerned with wills which appear to refer only to property which belongs to the testator. Thus a gift of property 'which I possess or to which I am entitled' will be sufficient to include property over which the testator has a power of appointment.[1] Likewise, a gift of 'all my stock' will exercise a general power of appointment over stock.[2]

1 *Re Jacob, Mortimer v Mortimer* [1907] 1 Ch 445.
2 *Re Doherty-Waterhouse, Musgrave v De Chair* [1918] 2 Ch 269.

Powers outside section 27

11.63 In the case of a power within s 27, there is a presumption that the power is intended to be exercised. In the case of a power outside the section, the burden of proof is reversed: it is upon the person claiming that the power has been exercised to prove that it has been.

11.64 In the case of a non-s 27 power, there must always be an expression of intention to exercise the power. But it was stated in *Re Weston's Settlement, Neeves v Weston,*[1] and the same applies to any non-s 27 power, that a special power may be exercised in any one of four ways, that is, by express exercise; by reference to the power itself even if there is no express exercise of it; by reference to the property subject to the power; or by showing an intention to exercise the power in any other way.

1 [1906] 2 Ch 620.

11.65 It seems that the testator need not intend actually to exercise the power: his intention must be to transfer the property to the beneficiary. Thus, if a person has a special power over property, and specifically disposes of that property, he is deemed to have intended to exercise the power.[1] If, however, the property is mentioned only generally, that will not be sufficient to exercise the power.[2] In this case it is necessary to show that the testator had no property of his own which could pass under the general words.[3]

1 *Forbes v Ball* (1817) 3 Mer 437; *Davies v Davies* (1858) 28 LJ Ch 102; *Elliott v Elliott* (1846) 15 Sim 321; *Re David's Trusts* (1859) John 495; *Re Mackenzie, Thornton v Huddleston* [1917] 2 Ch 58.
2 *Re Huddleston, Bruno v Eyston* [1894] 3 Ch 595.
3 *Bennett v Aburrow* (1803) 8 Ves 609; *Re Mattingley's Trusts* (1862) 2 John & H 426.

Scope of gift of residue

11.66 A residuary gift is a gift of such of the testator's property that he has not purported to dispose of by specific gifts. If the will itself does not dispose of the whole of the testator's property, that part which is not disposed of devolves in accordance with the intestacy rules.

11.67 Provided that the words of the gift are sufficient, and no contrary intention is shown, a residuary gift will include all property and all interests in property which are not effectively otherwise disposed of. If, therefore, a person is given a life interest, and there is no gift in remainder, upon the death of the life tenant, the property will fall into residue. Likewise, if there is a gift to a person upon attaining the age of, say, 21, and no prior gift of that property, the income until the beneficiary attains the age of 21 will form part of residue.[1]

1 Subject to the rules with regard to intermediate income.

11.68 Where a specific gift fails for any reason, such as lapse, then in the absence of a contrary intention the property subject to that gift will fall into residue. The result is the same whatever the reason for the failure of the specific gift. The testator may, of course, expressly provide for certain eventualities. Thus, '£1,000 to A but if he predeceases me, then to B'. Alternatively, the testator may show a contrary intention to prevent it falling into residue, in which case it would devolve as on intestacy, but such a contrary intention is often hard to establish. It is clear that the mere attempt to leave the property elsewhere is not a sufficient contrary intention.[1] Furthermore, where the testator uses conventional expressions such as, 'I give all my property not otherwise disposed of' the words 'otherwise disposed of' are treated in the absence of a contrary intention as meaning 'otherwise effectively disposed of', and previous specific gifts which have lapsed will therefore come within the residuary gift.

1 *Re Spooner's Trust* (1851) 2 Sim NS 129.

11.69 Where the whole residuary gift fails, then the residuary property passes as on intestacy. Where, however, part of the residuary gift fails, the effect of the gift depends on the testator's intention. If there is no expression of his intention, then the undisposed of part devolves as on intestacy.[1] So if a testator makes a gift of the residue 'to my three nephews equally' and one of them predeceases him, that third share will lapse and devolve as on intestacy. Alternatively, the testator may show an intention for that part to fall back into residue, and so, in effect, be added to the other parts. Accordingly, if the residue is to be divided among four people, and one predeceases the testator, the share of that person will, if there is a sufficient expression of intention, be added to the shares of the other three.[2] So, for example, if the testator had given his residue 'equally to such of my three nephews as shall survive me' and one of them predeceased him, the residue would be divided equally between the two survivors.

1 *Sykes v Sykes* (1868) 3 Ch App 301; *Re Bentley, Podmore v Smith* (1914) 110 LT 623; *Re Forrest, Carr v Forrest* [1931] 1 Ch 162.
2 *Re Woods* [1931] 2 Ch 138.

PART III

Intestacy

CHAPTER 12

Total intestacy

12.1 The rules relating to beneficial entitlement on intestacy are designed to reflect the wishes of the average testator, and are in fact based on an analysis of a large number of wills. Thus, the three most common situations are where the deceased left a spouse, but no children and no near relatives, in which case the spouse takes all; where the deceased left a spouse and children, in which case, provided the total estate exceeds £75,000, the property is divided between the spouse and children; and where the deceased left neither spouse nor children, in which case near relatives benefit.

12.2 The intestacy rules are changed from time to time, but in the case of deaths after 31 May 1987 they are governed by the Administration of Estates Act 1925[1] and the Family Provision (Intestate Succession) Order 1987.[2] The account of the intestacy rules in this chapter is confined to the case where the deceased died after 31 May 1987. The provisions of the 1925 Act, as amended, are reproduced in Appendix A. Although it has been modified by subsequent Acts, the Administration of Estates Act 1925 remains the basis of the law.[3] In addition to making provision for a total intestacy, the rules also deal with the case of a partial intestacy, that is, where the testator makes a will which for one reason or another fails effectively to dispose of the whole of his assets.

1 As amended by the Intestates' Estates Act 1952 and the Inheritance (Provision for Family and Dependants) Act 1975.
2 SI 1987/799, made under s 1 of the Family Provision Act 1966.
3 The Law Commission has recommended that the present law should be changed, particularly the provisions relating to the surviving spouse and the rules relating to hotchpot considered later (Law Commission No 187, *Distribution on Intestacy* (1989)). Referring to the report, the Lord Chancellor, Lord Mackay of Clashfern, announced on 1 July 1993 that The Government has not accepted the first recommendation, namely that a surviving spouse should in all circumstances receive the whole of the intestate's estate. The Government has, however, decided to accept the Commission's other recommendations, which concern the hotchpot rule, survivorship clauses and provision for cohabitants, and will introduce legislation to implement them when a suitable legislative opportunity occurs.' Lord Mackay continued 'The Government is concerned to provide additional protection for a surviving spouse in order to enable him or her in the great majority of cases, where the size of the intestate's estate permits it, to remain in the former matrimonial home and to have a sufficient surplus on which to live. To this end I will make an order as soon as practicable to increase the statutory legacy payable to a surviving spouse on intestacy from £75,000 to

£125,000 in the case of the lower legacy, and from £125,000 to £200,000 in the case of the higher legacy' (Press Release No 149.93).

Statutory trust for sale

12.3 Section 33(1) of the Administration of Estates Act 1925 provides that the personal representatives hold all the deceased's property upon trust for sale. The personal representatives have a power to postpone sale for as long as they think proper. There are three qualifications to the general requirement to sell:

(a) Any reversionary interest is not to be sold until it falls into possession, unless the personal representatives 'see special reason' for sale. A reversionary interest is one from which the intestate is not receiving the income or enjoying possession.[1] So if property is settled on A for life with remainder to B, and B dies intestate during A's lifetime, his interest in remainder is not to be sold until A's death.

(b) 'Personal chattels' are not to be sold unless the proceeds are required for administration purposes because there are insufficient other assets, or because the personal representatives again 'see special reason' for the sale.[2] The expression 'personal chattels' is considered later.[3]

(c) Where the intestate's assets include an interest in a dwellinghouse in which the intestate's surviving spouse was resident at the time of the intestate's death, that interest is not to be sold within twelve months of the first grant of representation to the intestate's estate, without the consent of the surviving spouse, unless sold in the course of administration owing to lack of other assets.[4] This is considered below.[5]

1   Administration of Estates Act 1925, s 33(1).
2   Ibid.
3   Below, para 12.11(a).
4   Intestates' Estates Act 1952, Sch 2, para 4(1).
5   Below, para 12.16.

12.4 From the fund produced by the sale, the personal representatives pay the funeral, testamentary and administration expenses, debts and other liabilities of the deceased and, in the case of a partial intestacy, they also pay the legacies bequeathed by the will.[1] The residue of the trust money and property is referred to as 'the residuary estate of the intestate'.[2] This is held for distribution among the persons entitled to it, except that it will remain invested where a minority or life interest arises.

1   Administration of Estates Act 1925, s 33(2).
2   Ibid, s 33(4).

Rights of the surviving spouse

Ascertainment

12.5 To qualify as a surviving spouse on an intestacy, that person must have:

(a)   survived the intestate, even by a very short period;[1] and
(b)   been married to the intestate at the time of death.

1   The Law Commission has recommended that the spouse should inherit under the intestacy rules only if he or she survives the intestate by fourteen days (Law Commission No 187, *Distribution on Intestacy* (1989)). The Government proposes to implement this recommendation 'when a suitable legislative opportunity occurs': see para 12.2, footnote 3.

The spouse must have survived the intestate

12.6   This is a question of fact. However, where both spouses have died in circumstances rendering it uncertain which survived the other, neither is deemed to have survived the other.[1] This is in contrast to the normal commorientes rule, whereby persons who die in such circumstances are deemed to die in order of seniority.[2]

1   Administration of Estates Act 1925, s 46(3) inserted by Intestates' Estates Act 1952. See below, para 30.33.
2   Under Law of Property Act 1925, s 184. See below, para 30.28.

The surviving spouse must have been married to the intestate at the time of his or her death

12.7   The status of a spouse under a polygamous marriage is not entirely clear,[1] but such a spouse may qualify following the analogy that a party to a polygamous marriage is treated as a spouse for the purposes of s 1(1)(a) of the Inheritance (Provision for Family and Dependants) Act 1975.[2]

1   See Hartley (1969) 32 MLR 135.
2   *Re Sehota, Surjit Kaur v Gian Kaur* [1978] 3 All ER 385, [1978] 1 WLR 1506.

12.8   A person will not qualify as a surviving spouse if his or her marriage to the intestate was void or has been dissolved by a decree absolute of divorce or annulled by a decree of nullity declared absolute before the death of the intestate. A decree of judicial separation does not dissolve the marriage, but it is provided[1] that if, while a decree of judicial separation is in force and the separation is continuing, either of the parties to the marriage dies intestate, any property as to which he or she dies intestate shall devolve as if the other party to the marriage had predeceased the intestate.

1   Matrimonial Causes Act 1973, s 18(2), re-enacting Matrimonial Proceedings and Property Act 1970, s 40(3), if either party to the marriage dies intestate after 13 August 1970. Before that date this provision applied only where a judicially separated wife had died intestate.

Entitlement

12.9   The entitlement of the surviving spouse depends on which of three situations applies:
(a)   if the intestate leaves neither issue, nor parent, nor brother or sister of the whole blood or their issue;[1]
(b)   if the intestate does leave issue (whether or not there are also relatives);
(c)   if the intestate does not leave issue, but does leave a parent, or brother or sister of the whole blood or their issue.

1 A relation of the 'whole' blood is distinguished from a step-relation, who is of the 'half blood'.

Intestate leaving neither issue, nor near relative
12.10 If the intestate leaves neither issue, nor a relative of the class specified above, the residuary estate is held upon trust for the surviving spouse absolutely.

Intestate leaving issue
12.11 Where the intestate leaves issue as well as a spouse, the spouse is entitled to:
(a) the 'personal chattels' absolutely. The expression 'personal chattels' is defined by s 55(1)(x) of the Administration of Estates Act 1925 and means, broadly, articles of household or personal use or ornament, such as clothes, furniture, jewellery, motor cars and domestic animals. The expression does not include any article used by the intestate at the date of his or her death for business purposes, nor does it include money or securities. It is, therefore, necessary to have regard both to the nature of the asset itself, and also to the purpose for which it was used at the date of death. If an antique dealer keeps part of his stock at home, that stock will not fall within the expression, but if he retires, and continues to keep at home those items which were formerly part of his stock, those items will be treated as personal chattels.

The expression 'personal chattels' is also commonly found in wills, and most of the decisions have been on the meaning of this expression in wills. While all expressions in wills are construed in the context of the will itself, these decisions serve to illustrate the meaning of the expression for the purposes of the intestacy rules.

Personal chattels can sometimes represent a disproportionate part of the value of an estate. For example, in *Re Crispin's Will Trusts*[1] the testator had, in his youth, assisted one Todhunter in building up and maintaining a collection of clocks. When Todhunter died, he left the collection of clocks to the testator, who for the remainder of his life maintained the collection, and carried out necessary works of repair, but did not materially add to it. He died testate, leaving to his sister his personal chattels as defined in the 1925 Act. The probate value of the clocks was £51,000 out of a gross estate of £83,000. The Court of Appeal held that a clock was, in the ordinary sense of the word, an article of furniture and it was immaterial where it was kept, what use, if any, it was put to, or whether it formed part of a collection. Accordingly, the collection passed under the specific bequest of personal chattels.[2]

If the article is used partly for personal purposes and partly for business purposes, it seems that it is to be classified according to the main purpose to which it was put when the deceased died. In *Re MacCulloch's Estate*[3] the testator owned a yacht named *Patricia of Camelot*,[4] which he moored at a country waterside property. The testator and his wife used the property, and the yacht, for their own purposes for part of the time, and he let out the property with the yacht for the remainder of the time. As the court said, it was 'one of those happy arrangements for the combination of business and pleasure which are dear to the hearts of successful businessmen'. The testator left to his wife, inter alia, all 'articles of personal, domestic or household use or ornament'. The court held that the predominant use of the yacht was commercial, so that it did not pass to the wife under this provision.

(b) a 'statutory legacy of £75,000[4a] absolutely, this sum to be paid free of deduction for inheritance tax[5] or costs.

(c) interest on the statutory legacy at 6% pa from the date of death to the date of payment.[6] This interest is payable primarily out of the income of the estate[7] but if there is insufficient income, the balance is payable out of capital. (This is in contrast to a legacy under a will which, in the absence of contrary provision and subject to certain exceptions, is payable one year from the date of death.[8]) Where the interest has to be made good out of capital, this will lead to disadvantageous taxation results, with the result that the spouse might well wish to disclaim her right to interest.[9]

(d) a life interest in one half of the residue. Thus, after setting aside from the residuary estate the personal chattels, the statutory legacy, and interest on it, the residuary estate is divided into two halves. One is held upon trust for the issue absolutely, and the other upon trust for the spouse for life, with remainder to the issue.

1 *Re Crispin's Will Trusts, Arkwright v Thurley* [1975] Ch 245, [1974] 3 All ER 772.
2 See also *Re Chaplin* [1950] Ch 507, [1950] 2 All ER 155, where a 60-foot motor yacht was held to be a personal chattel, and *Re Reynolds' Will Trusts, Dove v Reynolds* [1965] 3 All ER 686 and *Re Collins's Settlement Trusts, Donne v Hewetson* [1971] 1 All ER 283, where stamp collections were held to be included in the expression. In the latter case, the collection was worth about £15,000 out of a total estate of about £25,000.
3 (1981) 44 NSR (2d) 666, Nova Scotia.
4 The wife, Patricia, had played Queen Guinevere in the Broadway production of *Camelot*.
4a This statutory legacy is to be increased to £125,000, probably from the end of 1993: see para 12.2, footnote 3.
5 In any event a legacy to a surviving spouse is now exempt from inheritance tax: IHTA 1984, s 18. See below, para 35.21.
6 Administration of Justice Act, 1977, s 28; Intestate Succession (Interest and Capitalisation) Order 1977.
7 Intestates' Estates Act 1952, s 1(4).
8 See below, para 31.32.
9 See below, para 31.59 and see paras 30.10, 31.7, 36.19.

Intestate leaving no issue, but near relative

12.12 Where the intestate leaves, in addition to the spouse, a parent, or brother or sister of the whole blood, or their issue, the spouse is entitled to:
(a) the personal chattels, as defined above;
(b) a statutory legacy, in this case of £125,000[1];
(c) interest on the statutory legacy, as above; and
(d) one half of the residue. This right is to one half of the capital, and not merely, as in the case where there are issue, to a life interest in one half. The other half of the residue is divided between the parents, or if there are none, the brothers and sisters of the whole blood.

1 This statutory legacy is to be increased to £200,000, probably from the end of 1993: see para 12.2, footnote 3.

The spouse's own property

12.13 Where property is vested in the names of the deceased and the surviving spouse as beneficial joint tenants, the surviving spouse automatically becomes entitled to the deceased's share by survivorship. Accordingly the deceased's share does not form part of the estate and reduce the surviving spouse's entitlement. However, even where the matrimonial home or other asset was vested solely in the name of the deceased, it may still be shown that by virtue of contributions made by the spouse, the deceased came to hold the property upon trust for himself or herself and the spouse.[1] This may reduce the amount for which the surviving spouse needs to give credit on taking a transfer of the property,[2] as it is only the deceased's equitable interest in the property which will form part of the estate.[3]

1 See *Gissing v Gissing* [1971] AC 886, [1970] 2 All ER 780; *Re Densham* [1975] 3 All ER 726; *Eves v Eves* [1975] 3 All ER 768.
2 See below, para 12.17.
3 See further, (1981) LS Gaz, 1 July, p 752, and (1981) LS Gaz, 26 August, p 890.

Right to require capital payment in lieu of life interest

12.14 A surviving spouse who becomes entitled to life interest under the intestacy has a right to require the personal representatives to pay a capital sum in lieu of the life interest.[1] This right must be exercised within twelve months from the date on which a grant of representation is obtained, unless the court extends the period for special reasons.[2] The notice exercising the right must be in writing, and is revocable only with the consent of the personal representatives.[3] To safeguard the situation where the surviving spouse is also the sole personal representative, the spouse must in that case give notice of election to the Principal Registrar of the Family Division, and this notice is entered in a public register.[4] The surviving spouse may make this election even if he or she is a minor, and although the election is valid, the capital can be paid only when the spouse reaches the age of 18.[5] The capitalised value is ascertained by an actuarial valuation based on the age of the surviving spouse and interest rates prevailing at the date of election. The precise method of calculation is prescribed by statutory instrument.[6]

1 Administration of Estates Act 1925, s 47A, added by the Intestates' Estates Act 1952.
2 Ibid, s 47A(5).
3 Ibid, s 47A(6).
4 Ibid, s 47A(7).
5 Ibid, s 47A(8).
6 Intestate Succession (Interest and Capitalisation) Order 1977.

12.15 Where the surviving spouse and the issue are all of full age and capacity, they can capitalise the spouse's life interest for whatever sum they agree among themselves, thereby removing the necessity for using the statutory provisions.[1] Whether the statutory procedure is followed, or the life interest redeemed by agreement, there will often be practical and tax advantages in redeeming it. The practical advantage is that the whole estate may be distributed forthwith; the tax advantage is that the surviving spouse does not have a life interest in a trust fund which would be aggregated with the surviving spouse's estate for inheritance tax purposes on his or her death.[2] If the spouse's interest is capitalised by agreement, it will normally be achieved by a deed of variation effected within two years of the date of death of the intestate so that it is deemed to have been effected by the deceased for inheritance tax and capital gains tax purposes.[3]

1 Under the rule in *Saunders v Vautier* (1841) Cr & Ph 240.
2 See below, paras 35.41–35.42.
3 Under IHTA 1984, s 142 for inheritance tax purposes and TCGA 1992, s 62(6)(b) for capital gains tax purposes. See below, paras 37.9ff.

Right to matrimonial home

12.16 The surviving spouse is given special rights where part of the residuary estate includes an interest in a dwellinghouse in which the surviving spouse was resident at the time of the intestate's death. The spouse has a right by notice in writing to require the personal representatives to appropriate to him or her that dwellinghouse in or towards satisfaction of any absolute interest which he or she has in the intestate's estate,[1] or in or towards the capital value of a life interest which the spouse has elected to have redeemed.[2] The spouse may, therefore, make an election on the basis just discussed, and then require that capital entitlement to be satisfied by a transfer of the house. This right may be exercised only within twelve months from the grant of representation being issued,[3] unless this period is extended by the court.[4] It is for this reason the personal representatives may not sell the property within the twelve months without the written consent of the surviving spouse, unless, through lack of other assets, it is needed for the purposes of administration.[5]

1 Intestates' Estates Act 1952, Sch 2, para 1(1), but the right cannot be exercised after the death of the surviving spouse: ibid, Sch 2, para (3)(1)(b).
2 Ibid, para 1(4).
3 Ibid, para 3(1)(a).
4 Ibid, para 3(3).
5 Ibid, para 4(1).

12.17 Where the property is to be transferred, it is transferred at its open market value.[1] Before committing himself or herself, the spouse may require the deceased's interest in the property to be valued, and to be notified of that value, before deciding whether to exercise the right.[2] The open market value is determined at the date of appropriation, and not at the date of the deceased's death, and at times of rapid changes in property values this can make a substantial difference.[3] If the value of the house at the date of appropriation would exceed the amount of the surviving spouse's entitlement under the intestacy rules, he or she is still entitled to take the house on paying the difference.[4]

1 Administration of Estates Act 1925, s 41.
2 Intestates' Estates Act 1952, Sch 2, para 3(2).
3 In *Robinson v Collins* [1975] 1 All ER 321 the former matrimonial home was appropriated to the spouse at £8,000 – its value at the date of appropriation – and not at £4,200, the value at the date of death.
4 *Re Phelps* [1980] Ch 275, [1979] 3 All ER 373, CA.

12.18   It is not necessary for the deceased to have owned the property outright. It is sufficient if he had only an equitable interest in it, for example as a beneficial tenant in common. The right is not generally exercisable where the interest of the deceased was leasehold with less than two years to run from the date of death, or where the lease contains a provision enabling the landlord to determine it within that period.[1] The surviving spouse does, however, have the right to take a short lease where an application can be made for a long lease or the freehold under the Leasehold Reform Act 1967.[2] Even where the surviving spouse has no right to take over a short lease, it may be advantageous to do so in the hope, for example, of obtaining a new or protected tenancy. In such cases the personal representatives may wish to exercise their general power of appropriation in favour of the spouse under s 41 of the Administration of Estates Act 1925.[3] In practice the surviving spouse will frequently be given statutory protection to possession of the matrimonial home held on a short tenancy. This may arise in the case of a protected or statutory tenant under the Rent Act 1977,[4] an assured periodic tenancy under the Housing Act 1988[5] or secure periodic tenancy under the Housing Act 1985.[6]

1   Intestates' Estates Act 1952, Sch 2, para 1(2).
2   Leasehold Reform Act 1967, s 7(8).
3   See below, Chapter 10.
4   Rent Act 1977, s 2(1)(b) and Sch 1, Part I, as amended by the Housing Act 1980, ss 76, 152, Sch 26 and the Housing Act 1988, s 39 and Sch 4.
5   Housing Act 1988, s 17.
6   Housing Act 1985, ss 79, 80, 87–91.

12.19   In some cases the right of the surviving spouse is exercisable only if the court is satisfied that the exercise of the right will not diminish the value of the remainder of the assets in the residuary estate, or make them more difficult to dispose of.[1] The application to the court may be made either by the personal representatives or by the spouse.[2] The consent of the court is necessary in the following circumstances:
(a)   where the dwellinghouse forms part only of a building, and an interest in the whole of the building is comprised in the residuary estate;
(b)   where the dwellinghouse is held with agricultural land and an interest in the agricultural land is comprised in the residuary estate;
(c)   where the whole or a part of the dwellinghouse was at the time of the intestate's death used as a hotel or lodging house; and
(d)   where part of the dwellinghouse was at the time of the intestate's death used for non-domestic purposes.[3]

1   Intestates' Estates Act 1952, Sch 2, para 2.
2   Ibid, para 4(2).
3   Ibid, para 2.

12.20   The right itself is not expressly to require a transfer of the matrimonial home, but the 'dwellinghouse in which the surviving husband or wife was resident at the time of the intestate's death'. This will usually be the matrimonial home, but need not be.[1] It seems, however, that 'resident' is not equivalent to merely 'living'. 'Residence' normally implies some degree of permanence or regularity[2] and this will probably be the case here.

1   In this respect the reference in the Intestates' Estates Act 1952, Sch 2, s 5 to the 'matrimonial home' is misleading.
2   For cases by analogy, see *Re Young* (1875) 1 TC 57; *Rogers v Inland Revenue* (1879) 1 TC 225; *Lloyd v Sulley* (1884) 2 TC 37; *Levene v IRC* [1928] AC 217.

12.21   Where the spouse is also a personal representative the right to take the home would appear at first sight to conflict with the rule that a trustee may not purchase trust property. It is specifically provided that this rule does not prevent the exercise of the right where the spouse is one of two or more personal representatives.[1] Where, however, the spouse is the sole personal representative it would be necessary to apply to the court for consent, or obtain the consent of all other persons entitled, provided that they were all sui juris.

1   Intestates' Estates Act 1952, Sch 2, para 5(1).

12.22   As in the case of election to redeem a life interest, a spouse who is a minor has the same right as an adult spouse to insist that the matrimonial home is transferred to him or her, and also, where the personal representatives wish to sell within twelve months from the grant of representation, a spouse who is a minor may give a valid consent.[1]

1   Intestates' Estates Act 1952, Sch 2, para 6(2).

Rights of issue

12.23   Where the intestate leaves issue, the issue will take:
(a)   if there is also a surviving spouse, the balance of the residuary estate after the spouse's interest (that is, after payment of the statutory legacy, half the capital balance of the residuary estate and the interest in remainder in the other half, in which the surviving spouse has a life interest);
(b)   in any other case, the whole of the residuary estate.
In either case, the whole or part of the residuary estate to which the issue are entitled is held upon 'the statutory trusts'. These are prescribed by the Administration of Estates Act 1925, s 47.

The statutory trusts

12.24   Property held upon the statutory trusts for issue[1] is to be divided in equal shares among such of the children of the intestate who are alive at the date of the death of the intestate, and who either attain the age of 18 or marry under that age. Where a child predeceases the intestate, but leaves issue living at the date of death of the intestate, then those issue, if they attain the age of 18 or marry under that age, will take the share in the residuary estate which their parent would have taken had he attained a vested interest. The issue therefore take 'per stirpes'.[2]

1   This includes issue in gestation. Administration of Estates Act 1925, s 55(2).
2   Which means through each stock of descent, but so that no issue take whose parent is living at the intestate's death and so capable of taking: Administration of Estates Act 1925, s 47(1)(i).

12.25 It will be seen that in order to benefit under the statutory trusts, the beneficiary must:
(a) be alive at the date of death of the intestate; and
(b) either attain the age of 18, or marry under that age.
Consider the following example where Arthur has died intestate, a widower, leaving a net residuary estate of £120,000. Arthur is survived by his sons Barry and Charles. His daughter Diana has predeceased him leaving a surviving daughter Fiona and two grandchildren, George and Harry, who are the children of Diana's son Eric, who also predeceased Arthur. The residuary estate will be divided as follows:

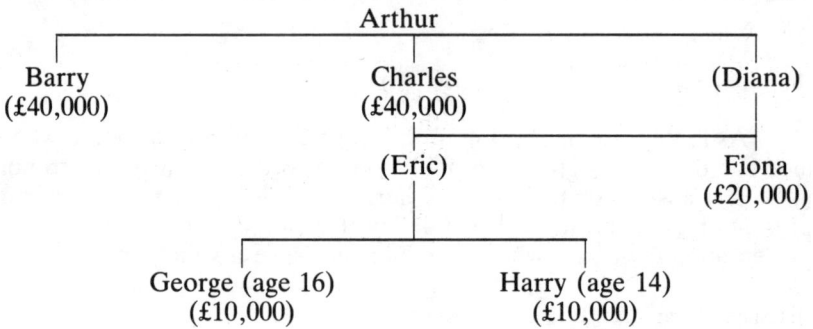

This example assumes that George and Harry both attain the age of 18 or marry under that age. If, however, Harry, although alive at the death of Arthur, dies before attaining the age of 18 or marrying (and without himself leaving issue to take), his contingent entitlement to £10,000 would accrue on his death to George, assuming that he in turn attains the age of 18 or marries under that age; if he does not, Fiona will take the whole of Diana's one-third share.

12.26 A minor who marries thereby attains a vested interest, but although he can give a valid receipt for income, he cannot give an effective receipt for capital. Accordingly, the personal representatives will wish for their own protection to retain the capital as bare trustees for the minor until he attains his majority.

12.27 The effect of requiring that a beneficiary shall be alive at the date of death of the intestate is the same as the operation of the class closing rules[1] in that the minimum amount which may accrue to each beneficiary is ascertained at the date of death of the intestate. If a beneficiary who is alive at that date nevertheless fails to attain a vested interest by attaining the age of 18, or marrying under that age, as from the date when the contingent beneficiary dies, the estate is distributed as if that beneficiary had never been alive. Suppose, then, that Edward left a wife Deirdre and an infant son, so that Deirdre takes a life interest in the residue. If before attaining a vested interest the son dies, from that date Deirdre will become entitled to the whole estate.

1 Above, para 11.38.

Hotchpot

Requirement to bring into hotchpot

12.28 In an attempt to satisfy the presumed intention of the deceased to achieve equality among his children, certain statutory rules of hotchpot are applied where a person has died intestate.[1]

1 Under Administration of Estates Act 1925, s 47(1)(iii). The Law Commission does not consider that these rules serve any useful purpose and recommends that they should be abolished (Law Commission No 187, *Distribution on Intestacy* (1989), para 47). The Government proposes to implement this recommendation 'when a suitable legislative opportunity occurs': see para 12.2, footnote 3.

12.29 Where money or property has been paid or transferred to a child by way of advancement, or on the occasion of the marriage of that child, that money or property is to be treated as having been paid on account of the share of that child on intestacy, with the result that it is to be brought into hotchpot.[1] The provision also applies where the money or property was settled for the benefit of the child, even if the child received only a life or lesser interest. However, the section does not apply where there is a contrary intention which is either expressed or appears from the circumstances of the case.

1 Administration of Estates Act 1925, s 47(1)(iii). The separate rule that issue must bring into hotchpot benefits received under a will on a partial intestacy is considered below, at para 13.7.

Advancements

12.30 Accordingly, whenever a child of the intestate has received at any time during his lifetime any money or property from the intestate, it is necessary to see whether it was paid or transferred by way of advancement. The expression 'advancement' implies that the payment has been made to establish the child in life, or to provide permanent provision for him.[1] There is a presumption that a large sum paid at one time is an advancement, whereas a small sum is not.[2] A mere casual payment is excluded.[3] Whether a payment was large will be considered both in the abstract, and also by reference to the size of the estate of the intestate.[4] A payment made on the occasion of the marriage of the child will, in the absence of contrary intention, automatically be treated as an advancement, irrespective of the purpose for which it was paid, or its size.[5] Where an advancement has to be brought into hotchpot, the gift is valued as at the date of death of the intestate, and not at the date of the gift.[6]

1 *Boyd v Boyd* (1867) LR 4 Eq 305; *Taylor v Taylor* (1875) LR 20 Eq 155; *Re Hayward, Kerrod v Hayward* [1957] Ch 528, [1957] 2 All ER 474; *Hardy v Shaw* [1975] 2 All ER 1052.
2 Per Jessel MR, *Taylor v Taylor* (1875) LR 20 Eq 155 at 158.
3 Ibid, at 157.
4 Per Goff J, *Hardy v Shaw* [1975] 2 All ER at 1056.
5 Administration of Estates Act 1925, s 47(1)(iii).
6 So in *Hardy v Shaw*, below, para 12.32, Harold and Vera had to bring into account the value of the shares at Margaret's death.

Contrary intention

12.31 Whether there has been an actual advancement or a payment on the marriage of the child, the child will not be required to bring the amount into hotchpot if the intestate indicated a contrary intention. The onus of proving this contrary intention lies with the child. The test is positive rather than negative. It is whether the intestate intended to prefer the child to whom the payment was made over the other child or children both at the point of time at which the recipient child took the benefit, and as regards the amount and nature of that benefit.

1   *Re Lacon, Lacon v Lacon* [1891] 2 Ch 482.

12.32   The matter was considered in *Hardy v Shaw*.[1] In 1952 the whole of the share capital in a family company was owned by Arthur Shaw, who held 1,000 shares, his son Harold, who held 600 shares, and his two daughters Vera and Mary, who each held 600 shares. Late in 1952 Mary married a man of whom Arthur disapproved, and she ceased to work in the company. Arthur stated that she should have no further shares in the company. Under his will, Arthur left all his shares in the company to his widow Margaret. In her lifetime Margaret gave Harold and Vera 499 shares each, keeping 2 for herself. She subsequently died intestate and the question was whether the two blocks of 499 shares which had been transferred to Harold and Vera should be brought into hotchpot. Goff J held first that the transfers were made by way of advancement. Although at the time Harold and Vera were middle-aged, and had no particular need, the transfers could be regarded as making permanent provision for them. Secondly, Goff J held that there was no contrary intention. It was clear that Margaret intended that, so far as the business itself was concerned, Harold and Vera were to be preferred to Mary, but there was no indication that Margaret intended Harold and Vera to be preferred so far as the whole of the expected inheritance was concerned. Indeed, there was no evidence that Margaret had ever considered what should happen on her death. Accordingly, Harold and Vera were required to bring into account the value of the two blocks of shares.

1   [1975] 2 All ER 1052.

Grandchildren

12.33   Because of the terms of the Act, it is necessary for an advancement to be brought into hotchpot only if it was to the child of the deceased. If a substantial gift was made to remoter issue, such as a grandchild, then even if that grandchild claims because his father predeceases the intestate, he will not have to bring into account that gift. On the other hand, if his father received an advancement, that must be brought into account against the father's share.

12.34   The operation of these rules may be illustrated by an example. Andrew has died intestate, a widower, leaving a net residuary estate of £120,000. He is survived by his two adult sons, Barry and Charles, and two minor grandchildren, Eric and Freda, the children of his deceased daughter, Diana. During his lifetime, Arthur made advancements of £20,000 to Barry and £10,000 to Diana, and a gift of £5,000 to Freda. The estate will be distributed as follows:

	£
Net residuary estate available for distribution:	120,000

Add advances to children to be brought into account:

		£	
	Barry	20,000	
	Diana	10,000	30,000

Hotchpot pool to be divided . . .				150,000

Entitlement	Barry	Charles	Diana's estate	£
	£	£	£	
⅓ of £150,000	50,000	50,000	50,000	
Less advances	20,000	—	10,000	
Payable out of the net residuary estate	30,000	50,000	40,000 =	120,000

Eric and Freda will then receive £20,000 each, on the statutory trusts; Freda, being a grandchild, does not have to bring into account the gift made to her.

Administrative provisions

12.35 Where the statutory trusts operate, the trustees are given the usual powers of maintenance and advancement, and the duty to accumulate surplus income.[1] When an infant marries, and so acquires a vested interest, he can then give a receipt for income, but not for capital.[2] The personal representatives are given an express power to permit any infant contingent beneficiary to use any personal chattels subject to the trusts[3] but there is no power enabling them to allow beneficiaries to reside in any house forming part of the estate.[4]

1 Administration of Estates Act 1925, s 47(1)(ii).
2 Ibid.
3 That is, if they are not taken by the surviving spouse.
4 Administration of Estates Act 1925, s 47(1)(iv).

Rights of other relatives

Parents

12.36 If the intestate leaves a spouse but no issue, then the parents take equally, or the survivor of them outright, the half share of the residue not taken by the surviving spouse.[1] If the intestate leaves neither spouse nor issue, the parents take the entire estate equally, or the survivor of them outright.[2]

1 Above, para 12.12.
2 Administration of Estates Act 1925, s 46(1)(iii), (iv).

Brothers and sisters of the whole blood

12.37 If the intestate leaves a spouse, but not issue or parents, then the brothers and sisters of the whole blood, or their issue, will take the half share of the residue not taken by the surviving spouse,[1] on the statutory trusts. If the intestate leaves neither spouse nor issue nor parents, then the brothers and sisters of the whole blood, or their issue, will take the entire estate on the statutory trusts.[2]

1 Above, para 12.12.
2 Administration of Estates Act 1925, s 46(1)(v).

Remoter relatives

12.38 Where there is no spouse, issue, parent, or brother or sister of the whole blood, the following are entitled. If there is only one person in a category, he takes all, and no person in a lower class can take if there is any person in the previous class:
(a)   brothers and sisters of the half blood on the statutory trusts;
(b)   grandparents in equal shares;
(c)   uncles and aunts of the whole blood upon the statutory trusts;
(d)   uncles and aunts of the half blood on the statutory trusts.
All relationships here described are blood relationships. Thus the wife of an uncle, bearing the courtesy title 'aunt', cannot take.

12.39 The statutory trusts for brothers and sisters, and uncles and aunts, are the same as the trusts for issue. Thus deceased members of the class may be represented by their issue, and entitlement is dependent upon attaining the age of 18 or marrying under that age,[1] but the hotchpot rule is inapplicable.

1 Administration of Estates Act 1925, s 47(3).

12.40 In certain family circumstances it is possible for a person to trace his or her entitlement on intestacy by more than one route to the intestate. There is no English authority on the situation, but there are Commonwealth authorities to the effect that a double share cannot be claimed.[1]

1 *Re Adams* (1903) 6 OLR 697; *Troop v Robinson* (1911) 45 NSR 145 (Nova Scotia); *Re Cullen's Estate* [1976] 14 SASR 456 (South Australia).

The Crown

12.41 Where there is no one in the foregoing categories entitled to take, the estate goes to the Crown, or Duchy of Lancaster or Duchy of Cornwall as bona vacantia. The Crown may at its discretion provide for persons who were actually dependent on the intestate whether related or not, and for such other persons for whom the intestate may have been expected to provide.[1]

1 Administration of Estates Act 1925, s 46(1)(iv).

Special provisions as to children

Adopted children

12.42 Where a child is adopted under an adoption order made in England and Wales, or where a child is adopted elsewhere and the adoption is recognised by the law of England and Wales, and the death occurs after 1975,[1] the adopted child is regarded as the lawful child of the adopter, and not of any other person (including its natural parents).[2] As a result, an adopted child has the same entitlement under the intestacy of its adoptive parents as a child born in lawful wedlock. Likewise, if the adopted child dies intestate, his adoptive parents will have the same entitlement as if the child were their own legitimate child. Further, where a child is adopted by a married couple, it becomes a brother or sister of the whole blood of any other child, including an adopted child, of the couple. In any case of adoption other than by a married couple, the adopted child will become the brother or sister of the half blood of any other children of the adopter.

1 Where the death occurred between 1949 and 1975, see the first edition of this book.
2 Except when adopted by one of its natural parents.

Legitimated children

12.43 A legitimated child[1] is entitled to take any interest on intestacy as if he had been born legitimate.[2] Further, where the entitlement of any other person depends on the status of a legitimated child, that other person takes in exactly the same way as if the legitimated child had been born legitimate.[3] Legitimation is no longer of significance for the purpose of intestate succession in respect of an intestate dying on or after 4 April 1988 as, from that date, illegitimacy is no longer a bar to taking on intestacy.

1 A legitimated child is one whose parents married each other after the child's birth.
2 Legitimacy Act 1976, s 5(1)–(3), applying to deaths of persons intestate on or after 1 January 1976. The previous law was governed by the Legitimacy Act 1926, ss 3–5 (now repealed), applying to deaths of persons intestate on or after 1 January 1926.
3 Ibid.

Illegitimate children

12.44 At common law, illegitimate persons were not recognised for the purpose of intestate succession. Apart from the provisions relating to adoption and legitimation outlined above, this position continued until the Family Law Reform Act 1969.

The Family Law Reform Act 1969
12.45 The 1969 Act provides that in respect of persons dying on or after 1 January 1970, a child had the same rights under his parents' intestacy as if he had been born legitimate.[1] Similarly, where an illegitimate child died after 1969, each of the parents were to have the same rights as if the child had been born legitimate.[2] These provisions were limited in that they did not extend beyond the parent and child relationship. Accordingly, an illegitimate

child could not take on the intestacy of any other children of his parents or grandparents or his parents' brothers and sisters. Conversely, neither could any of those persons take on the intestacy of an illegitimate child. These limitations sometimes resulted in an intestate's estate passing as bona vacantia to the Crown, even where he or she had been living together with such persons as one family.

1   Family Law Reform Act 1969, s 14(1).
2   Ibid, s 14(2). A father of an illegitimate child was presumed to have predeceased his child, thus requiring the father to establish paternity before he could take on his child's intestacy (s 14(4)).

The Family Law Reform Act 1987

12.46   The common law rule has now been completely reversed by the Family Law Reform Act 1987, which applies where the intestate dies after 3 April 1988. The 1987 Act provides that references to any relationship between two persons are to be construed without regard to whether or not the father and mother of either of them or the father and mother of any persons through whom the relationship is deduced, have or had been married to each other at any time.[1] Accordingly, on the death of a person intestate after 3 April 1988, an illegitimate child can succeed in exactly the same way as a legitimate child. The purpose of the Act is to provide that for nearly all purposes the legal status of a child will be the same whether or not his parents are married to each other.[2] Therefore, on the death of a person intestate after 3 April 1988, an illegitimate child is entitled to take on the intestacy as if he were legitimate. Conversely, on the death of an illegitimate child, his relatives will be entitled as if he were born legitimate.

1   Family Law Reform Act 1987, ss 1 and 18.
2   These provisions do not apply to devolution of a dignity or title of honour: ibid, s 19(1), (4).

12.47   There may still be practical difficulties in identifying a child's father: he may have been a stranger in the night. It is therefore provided that for the purpose of these provisions a child is presumed not to have been survived by his father or by any person related to him only through his father, unless the contrary is shown.[1] Accordingly, on the death of the child intestate, the onus which was already placed on the person claiming to be the father of such a child to establish his paternity under the 1969 Act,[2] is extended to all relatives of the child on the father's side who seek to establish a claim on the child's intestacy.

1   Family Law Reform Act 1987, s 18(2).
2   See above, para 12.45, n 2.

Children born as a result of artificial insemination by donor

12.48   Where a child is born following artificial insemination by a donor other than the mother's husband, at common law the child was of necessity illegitimate. Following the Family Law Reform Act 1969, if the identity of the father was known, a claim on the intestacy of the father or child could be made by the survivor of them.

12.49 However, following the Family Law Reform Act 1987, a child born to a married woman after 3 April 1988 as a result of artificial insemination by donor is presumed to be the child of that woman and her husband.[1] This presumption is rebuttable only by establishing that the husband did not consent to the artificial insemination.[2] The presumption is limited to the case of a married couple so that a child born by this method to an unmarried woman remains in law the child of the donor.

1 Family Law Reform Act 1987, s 27(1), an exception being succession to any dignity or title of honour, (s 27(3)).
2 Ibid, s 27(1).

Other problems of parentage

12.49A The advances of reproductive medicine posed further legal problems, to be resolved by the Human Fertilisation and Embryology Act 1990.[1] For example, it is possible for a fertile female donor to provide an infertile woman with an ovum which is fertilised in the laboratory with sperm of the donee's husband. The fertilised embryo is then implanted in the donee's womb and she can give birth to the child in the normal way. Alternatively, sperm and eggs may be placed in the donee's womb to enable fertilisation and pregnancy to continue otherwise as normal. In these circumstances, who is the child's mother? The donor or the woman who gave birth to the child? Section 27 of the 1990 Act provides that the mother who gives birth to the child should in law be the child's mother.

1 Implemented in pursuance of the Report of the Committee of Inquiry into Human Fertilisation and Embryology (The Warnock Committee) (1984) Cmnd 9314.

12.50 It is further provided that where a child is being or has been carried by a woman as a result of the placing in her (on or after 1 August 1991) of an embryo or of sperm and eggs, if, at the time of the relevant procedure, she was married and her husband was not the donor, then he shall be treated as the child's father unless he did not consent to that procedure.[1] If the woman's husband did not consent, the donor of the sperm is not to be treated as the father of the child[2] or of any other person.[3] If this provision does not apply (for example, because the woman is not married) but the procedure took place in the course of licensed treatment provided for her and a man together, and that man was not the donor, he is to be treated as the father of the child.[4]

1 Human Fertilisation and Embryology Act 1990, s 28(2).
2 Ibid, s 28(6)(a).
3 Ibid, s 28(4).
4 Ibid, s 28(3), (4).

12.51 The 1990 Act further provides that where the sperm of a man, or any embryo the creation of which was brought about by his sperm, was used after his death he is not to be treated as the father of the child. This would apply whether or not the man was the woman's husband (who had given his express consent) or some other person.[1]

1   Human Fertilisation and Embryology Act 1990, s 28(6)(b). Implemented in pursuance of para 10.9 of the Warnock Report. This therefore confirms that the child will not be able to make a claim against the father's estate under the intestacy rules as he is not deemed to be living or in gestation at the intestate's death.

Variation of intestacy rules

12.52   The intestacy rules are statutory, and cannot be varied directly. In *Re Snider*,[1] which was a case of partial intestacy, the testator made a will in 1967, containing a recital that he had been living apart from his wife and children since 1933 and a statement that he did not wish them to benefit from his estate. This statement did not, however, prevent them from taking under the intestacy rules. The testator should, of course, have made a valid will leaving his property directly to those whom he wished to benefit.

1   (1974) 46 DLR (3d) 161 (Ontario).

Disclaimer

12.53   It will be seen[1] that it is clearly established that a person may disclaim a benefit under a will. In *Re Scott*[2] the deceased, who died partially intestate, was survived by her brother and sister, who were next of kin. The brother and sister both executed instruments disclaiming their benefit under the intestacy rules, and the court had to decide whether the interest which they had disclaimed passed to the Crown as bona vacantia, or passed to the persons who would have been the deceased's next of kin had the brother and sister both predeceased her. Walton J held that the next relatives were entitled. In *Re Scott* it was assumed that the interest could be disclaimed, but it has been suggested[3] that just as the intestacy rules cannot be directly altered by a provision in the will[4] they cannot be altered by an instrument of disclaimer. This suggestion is based on the fact that the intestacy rules are statutory, but it seems almost certain that *Re Scott* will be followed, and that the right to make an effective disclaimer of an interest on intestacy will be upheld.

1   Below, para 30.1.
2   *Re Scott, Widdows v Friends of the Clergy Corpn* [1975] 2 All ER 1033.
3   Goodhart 'Disclaimer of Interests on Intestacy' [1976] 40 Conv (NS) 292. See also Oughton 'Disclaimer of Interests on Intestacy – An American Viewpoint' [1977] Conv 260; Pinkerton 'Disclaimer of Interests on Intestacy – Some Thoughts from Northern Ireland' [1978] Conv 213.
4   See *Re Snider*, above, para 12.52.

CHAPTER 13

Partial intestacy

Meaning

13.1 A partial intestacy occurs when a person dies leaving a will which effectively disposes of some, but not all, of his property. The test is not whether there is a will, but whether there is a will effectively disposing of property.[1] Thus, if a person makes a will appointing executors, but not effectively disposing of any part of his property, the executors hold the property upon the trusts declared by the total intestacy rules.[2]

1 Property is defined to include any interest in real or personal property: Administration of Estates Act 1925, s 55(1)(xvii).
2 *Re Ford, Ford v Ford* [1902] 2 Ch 605; *Re Cuffe, Fooks v Cuffe* [1908] 2 Ch 500; *Re Skeats, Thain v Gibbs* [1936] Ch 683.

Operation of will

13.2 In general, in the first instance full effect is given to the will, and the intestacy rules are then applied as a second stage to the extent that the will has not disposed of the property.[1] The operation of the intestacy rules does, however, cause difficulty. Partial intestacy is governed by s 49 of the Administration of Estates Act 1925, which Danckwerts J has described[2] as being 'as bad a piece of draftsmanship as one could conceive'. Some of the difficulties which arise from that draftsmanship are now considered.

1 Administration of Estates Act 1925, ss 33(7), 49(1).
2 In *Re Morton, Morton v Warham* [1956] Ch 644 at 647.

Will dealing with undisposed of property

13.3 This heading might be considered curious: how can a will deal with property which is undisposed of? The legislation envisages that sometimes this can happen, for the opening part of s 49(1) provides that the rules as to intestacy shall have effect as respects property undisposed of 'subject to the provisions contained in the will'. The expression was considered by the Court of Appeal in *Re Thornber*,[1] where it was shown that the expression 'subject to the provisions contained in the will' means provisions which remain operative and effective. In this case the testator directed his trustees to pay his wife an annuity out of the residue of his estate and to accumulate the surplus income for the period of 21 years, or until the earlier death of his wife, for the benefit of his children. He died without issue, and the question arose whether the surplus income should be treated as undisposed of, and not subject to the terms of the will, or whether it should be accumulated in accordance with the testator's direction. The Court of Appeal held that the trustees should not accumulate. Romer LJ said:

> 'when you have ascertained what interest has been undisposed of by the testator you then look at the will to see whether as regards that interest he has given any directions, and, if he has, those directions must be attended to. For instance, it is conceivable that a testator bearing in mind the provisions of the Administration of Estates Act 1925 might insert a direction something to this effect in his will: "In the event of any of my property being undisposed of by this my will and the provisions of s 49 taking effect I direct that any such property shall be dealt with" in a particular way; but the provisions in this testator's will relating to accumulation are not provisions relating to any interest of which the testator had failed to dispose.'

It is, therefore, necessary to draw a distinction between an interest which has not been disposed of effectively, and other directions in the will providing for the possibility of a partial intestacy. The line is often a fine one.

1 [1937] Ch 29.

13.4 As has been seen,[1] it is also necessary to distinguish the position where in his will the testator gives directions as to property undisposed of, and where he seeks to alter the intestacy rules as such.

1 Above, para 12.52, and *Re Snider*, discussed there.

Trust for sale

Does a statutory trust for sale arise?

13.5 The provisions as to total intestacy in the Administration of Estates Act 1925 are dealt with in two parts. Part III of the Act[1] deals with the *administration* of the intestate's estate, while Part IV[2] deals with the *distribution* of the estate. Although the general intention seems to have been to apply so far as appropriate all the rules as to intestacy to partially intestate estates, s 49 only applies 'this Part', that is, Part IV, to such estates and there is no corresponding provision applying Part III. There is, then, no statutory provision for the whole of the deceased's property to be held upon a trust for sale. While, however, there is no provision applying all the administrative provisions to a partial intestacy, s 33 on its terms does apply to the extent that any property is undisposed of, subject to the provisions of the will.[3] There will, then, usually be a trust for sale of that part of the property which is undisposed of, although it seems that the will could validly direct that no trust for sale should arise.

1 Administration of Estates Act 1925, ss 32 to 44.
2 Ibid, ss 45 to 52.
3 Ibid, s 33(7). Cf Williams and Mortimer *Executors Administrators and Probate* p 875.

Which trust for sale?

13.6 It may be necessary to decide which of an express trust for sale and a statutory trust for sale shall apply, for there will not be more than one effective trust for sale in respect of the same property.[1] It is important to know which applies, for the terms of the trust may differ. The position seems to be that if the will contains an express trust for sale of the whole of the property, but a partial intestacy arises because a share in the proceeds of sale is undisposed of, the express trust for sale in the will operates. If, however, the property undisposed of in the will is not subject to a trust for sale, the statutory trust for sale applies to that property, subject to a contrary direction in the will. It is possible, then, for the will to create an express trust for sale in respect of part of the property, and for there to be a statutory trust for sale in respect of another part.

1 *Re Plowman, Westminster Bank Ltd v Plowman* [1943] Ch 269; *Re Taylor's Estate and Will Trusts, Taylor v Taylor* [1969] 2 Ch 245.

Hotchpot

Benefits to be brought into hotchpot

13.7 In three situations, benefits have to be brought into hotchpot in applying the rules as to partial intestacy.[1]
(a) The surviving spouse must bring into account the beneficial interests received under the operative provisions of the will, except that personal chattels specifically bequeathed are left out of account.[2]
(b) Children must bring into account substantial benefits which they received from the deceased during his lifetime. This is the general rule which applies in the same way as on total intestacy.[3] This rule does *not* require account to be taken of substantial benefits given by the deceased in his lifetime to remoter issue.
(c) Children *and* remoter issue must bring into account beneficial interests acquired under the operative provisions of the will.[4]
The issues which arise must now be considered in greater detail.

1 The Law Commission does not consider that these rules serve any useful purpose and recommends that they should be abolished (Law Commission No 187, *Distribution on Intestacy* 1989, para 55). The Government proposes to implement this recommendation 'when a suitable legislative opportunity occurs': see para 12.2, footnote 3.

2 Administration of Estates Act 1925, s 49(1)(aa), which applies only to post-1951 deaths.
3 See above, para 12.29.
4 Administration of Estates Act 1925, s 49(1)(a).

Benefits of spouse

13.8 It will be recalled that in the case of total intestacy, a spouse may become entitled to benefit from the estate in four respects:[1] the statutory legacy; interest on the statutory legacy; personal chattels; and an absolute or a life interest in half the remainder. In the case of a partial intestacy, it is necessary to value the total beneficial interests received under the will, with the exception of personal chattels which are specifically bequeathed. That aggregate is then used to reduce the statutory legacy, of £75,000, or £125,000, so that if the benefit under the will exceeds the limit of the statutory legacy, none is payable. Where the statutory legacy is reduced, but not eliminated, the interest to which the spouse is entitled is calculated on the reduced amount of the legacy. Accordingly, the rule does not reduce the spouse's entitlement other than to the statutory legacy with interest. It does not therefore reduce the entitlement to undisposed of personal chattels or the interest in the residue.

1 See above, paras 12.9–12.12.

13.9 In so far as they relate to life interests, the rules are curious.
(a) Where the spouse takes a life interest under the will, that interest is actuarially valued, and is added to the other benefits, if any, which the spouse received under the will. The actuarial value of the life interest will, therefore, totally or partly eliminate the entitlement to the statutory legacy.
(b) If the benefits under the will exceed the amount of the statutory legacy, the remaining benefits are ignored and do *not* reduce the absolute or life interest in the remainder.

Successive interests to children and remoter issue

13.10 Suppose that the will creates a life interest for the son of the testator, with remainder to the issue of that son. What is to be brought into account? Section 49(1)(a) requires that there shall be brought into account 'any beneficial interests acquired by any issue of the deceased'. This does not necessarily mean that the interests of the issue are to be separately valued, and brought into account at that valuation. In *Re Young, Young v Young*,[1] where there was, in effect, a gift to the testator's son for his life, and thereafter for his issue, Harman J made a surprising decision. He held that it was necessary to treat the whole fund which was given by the deceased to the son and the descendants of the son as one gift, and that it was the capital value of that fund that was to be brought into account. In effect, then, the son had to bring into account the capital value of the fund, even though he enjoyed only a life interest in it. A different approach was adopted by Danckwerts J in *Re Morton, Morton v Warham*.[2] In this case the fund was limited not merely to the son, and his issue, but other persons were also entitled to take a benefit. There was no question, then, on any view, of including the whole value of the fund. However, Danckwerts J approached the problem of valuation in more general terms. He said:[3]

> 'the life interests or less interests which are brought in at a valuation, must be brought in at a valuation appropriate to the nature of the interest . . . and they cannot be brought in as if they were equivalent to an absolute interest in the capital. To value the interest as being equivalent to a gift of capital in a case where a person takes no more than a life interest seems to be contrary to fairness, common sense and everything else.'

1 [1951] Ch 185.
2 [1956] Ch 644.
3 Ibid, at 648, 649.

13.11 In a later decision[1] Danckwerts J is stated to have taken it for granted that the interests of the remoter issue should be brought into account as well as that of the child. If this is so the difference between his approach and that of Harman J is as to valuation, and not as to the nature of the interest to be brought into account. At the heart of the dispute is the fact that when separate interests exist in the same property, the aggregate value of those interests will only rarely be equivalent to the value of the property itself. The present position of the authorities appears to be that:

(a) a child must give credit for benefits received both by himself and by his children or remoter issue under the will;

(b) if the child and his issue are the only persons who could benefit, the child must give credit for the whole capital value of the fund; but

(c) if persons other than the child and his issue can benefit, then, subject to what is said below, each interest is to be valued, and the child must give credit for the aggregate of the values of his interest and that of his issue.

While this approach produces a fair stirpital distribution, it seems to stretch the legislation well beyond its apparent meaning.

1 *Re Grover's Will Trust, National Provincial Bank Ltd v Clarke* [1971] Ch 168 per Pennycuick J at 178.

Interest liable to divesting

13.12 The problem has been considered so far on the basis that the first interest is an absolute life interest. Suppose, however, that the interest is less than an absolute life interest, and that some person other than the child and his issue may become entitled? In general, it is suggested that the interest must be valued having full regard to its terms, and not as a life interest. In two cases, however, the life interest was not absolute, but was held on protective trusts, with the result that the spouse of the child could have benefited. Both in the first case, *Re Young*,[1] and in the later decision, *Re Grover's Will Trusts, National Provincial Bank Ltd v Clarke*,[2] Harman and Pennycuick JJ, respectively, blithely disregarded the fact that the interests were held on protective trusts, and treated them for this purpose as absolute life interests.

1 [1951] Ch 185; above, para 13.10.
2 [1971] Ch 168.

Example

13.13 The application of the rules may be illustrated by an example. Andrew died in 1993 leaving a net estate of £150,000. By his will he left his wife his car, worth £5,000, and an annuity of £1,000 pa. He also left legacies to his two sons, Bernard and Cedric, of £9,000 and £11,000 respectively. In his lifetime, he had made an advancement of £2,000 to Bernard. The actuarial value of the widow's annuity is £14,000.

	£	£
Net estate		150,000
Legacies and bequests		
Specific bequest to wife	5,000	
Bernard	9,000	
Cedric	11,000	25,000
		125,000
Set aside fund to provide annuity		16,000
		109,000
Widow's statutory legacy	75,000	
Less value of annuity under will (NB car is *not* brought into account)	14,000	61,000
		48,000
Half residue to provide for wife's life interest		24,000
Balance available for children		24,000
Entitlement of children is:		
Half share of residue		24,000
Add		
Advance to Bernard	2,000	
Legacies to children	20,000	22,000
Hotchpot pool available for distribution		46,000

	Bernard £	Cedric £	
$\frac{1}{2} \times$ £46,000	23,000	23,000	
Less advancement	2,000	—	
	21,000	23,000	
Less legacies	9,000	11,000	
Payable	12,000	12,000 =	24,000

On the death of the wife, there will be available for the children the fund set aside to provide for the annuity, and the capital of the life interest fund.

Foreign situated property

13.14 Where a person dies domiciled abroad leaving property situated in England or Wales as well as property situated abroad, in applying the partial intestacy rules to the property situated abroad, the value of the property situated abroad must be brought into account.[1]

1 *Re Osoba, Osoba v Osoba* [1979] 2 All ER 393, CA, per Goff LJ at 400.

Disclaimer and intestacy

13.15 A disclaimer of an interest under a will does not prevent the person disclaiming taking a benefit under the intestacy rules. In many cases it will make no difference to his position. If a wife is entitled to a statutory legacy of £75,000, and is given a legacy of £5,000, in principle her position is the same whether she receives £5,000 under the will and £70,000 on intestacy, or disclaims her legacy under the will and receives £75,000 on intestacy. In some cases, however, it can be in her interest to disclaim and take on intestacy. These situations are discussed later.[1] It is appropriate to note here, however, *Re Sullivan, Dunkley v Sullivan*.[2] In that case the widow was entitled to receive under the will certain royalties, but the effect of the will was to treat these as capital. She disclaimed the legacy under the will and became entitled on intestacy. However, the provision in the will affecting the royalties no longer took effect, so that the widow received them as income, as part of her life interest.

1 Below, para 30.11.
2 [1930] 1 Ch 84.

Property undisposed of after direction for excessive accumulation

13.16 Where a will directs the payment of an annuity from a specified fund, and the income from the fund exceeds that which is required for the annuity, there is a presumption that the excess income is to be accumulated. However, this implied direction can be effective only for 21 years.[1] Thereafter, the surplus income will devolve as on intestacy, unless there is a contrary intention in the will, in which case it will pass to the residuary beneficiaries.[2]

1 *Cooper v Cooper* (1874) LR 7 HL 53; *Re Hammond's Estate* [1953] SCR 550; *Berry v Geen* [1938] AC 575; *Re Bennett, Franks v Bennett* [1975] Tas SR 1 (Tasmania); *Re Martin* (1979) 98 DLR (3d) 570 (Ontario).
2 For an example, see *Cathcart's Trustees v Foresterhill Hospital* 1977 SLT 114.

Intestacy after life interest

Application of partial intestacy rules

13.17 In some cases, a partial intestacy arises after the death of a life tenant. Suppose a testator dies leaving the whole of his estate to his wife for life, but makes no provision as to the distribution of the fund after her death. There is no property undisposed of on the death of the deceased, but there is on the death of the wife. There are two possibilities. If effect is given to the will, the personal representatives are obliged to apply the intestacy rules at that time. On this basis, the wife's estate will be entitled to the statutory legacy, less the value of the life interest, together with interest at 6% pa from the date of death. In *Re McKee, Public Trustee v McKee*[1] the testator gave the residue of his estate to his wife for life, with remainder to such of his brothers and sisters as should be living at her death. All his brothers and sisters had died before the death of his wife, so that an intestacy arose at that time. The Court of Appeal held that the intestacy rules should be applied on her death, and that her estate should receive the statutory legacy and interest. (The intestacy rules in force at the time did not require the spouse to bring into account benefits received under the will, although she would have to bring them into account were the case to be decided on the same facts now.)

1 [1931] 2 Ch 145.

13.18 The other possibility is to give the wife her statutory legacy at once. On this basis her life interest under the will is actuarially valued, and is brought into hotchpot at that figure. This result was reached by Goff J in *Re Bowen-Buscarlet's Will Trusts, Nathan v Bowen-Buscarlet*,[1] where the wife was left a life interest in the whole residuary estate, but there was no provision as to what should happen after her death. The decision in *Re Bowen-Buscarlet* is to be preferred to that in *Re McKee*, and will probably now be followed.

1 [1972] Ch 463, [1971] 3 All ER 636.

13.19 The effect of following *Re Bowen-Buscarlet* is in practice to require different methods of calculation according to whether the life interest is in a fund greater or less than the amount of the statutory legacy. If the fund is less than the amount of the statutory legacy the widow can claim immediate payment of the whole fund. Suppose, for example, that Bernard dies leaving a net estate of £120,000, which he directs to be held on trust for his wife Celia, for life, but that he makes no gift over on her death. There are no children. Celia is entitled to say that she has a charge on the fund for a statutory legacy of the full amount of the estate. The charge is postponed to her life interest, but she can merge the two, and claim immediate payment.[1] Suppose, however, that the facts are the same, but that Bernard left two children, so that the wife's statutory legacy is £75,000. In this case, an actuarial valuation is made of the wife's life interest under the will, and the normal intestacy rules applied. Suppose that the life interest is worth £20,000. The wife cannot be compelled to disclaim her life interest under the will, and it seems that she is entitled to insist on the income from £120,000 being paid to her for life, but also to an immediate capital payment of £55,000. The only way in which this could be produced would be for the personal representatives to sell the reversionary interest. But as the aggregate of the value of the life interest and the value of the reversion will not be equal to the value of the fund, the reversionary interest may not produce enough to pay the £55,000 in full. There is no problem if the widow disclaims her life interest under the will, and takes the capital sum of £75,000.

1 [1971] 3 All ER 636 at 640.

13.20 *Re Bowen-Buscarlet* has been followed, and extended, by the Queensland Supreme Court in *Re Wade*.[1] In that case, in the events which happened, the testator left his residuary estate upon trust for his wife for life, but with no effective remainder over. The court held that the partial intestacy rules had the effect of creating a charge over the property for the benefit of the spouse, and that she was entitled to merge that interest with her life interest under the will. The court also held, however, that as the distribution on intestacy notionally occurred on the termination of the life interest, it was not necessary for the spouse to bring the value of her life interest into account.

1 [1980] Qd R 70.

Valuation of life interest

13.21 Whenever it is necessary to bring into account the value of a life interest, it is appropriate to take the actuarial value of the life interest at the date of the deceased's death. If the interest is not taken in possession at the date of death of the deceased, the value of the life interest is ascertained at the date when it does fall into possession.[1] An actuarial valuation is made, even though on the facts which happen it would be possible to calculate the exact amount received.[2]

1 *Re Morton, Morton v Warham* [1956] Ch 644.
2 *Re Thomson Settlement Trusts, Robertson v Makepeace* [1953] Ch 414 and (1956) 72 LQR 483. This will, of course, be the situation where the actuarial valuation is not actually made until after the death of the life tenant.

The extent of testamentary freedom

Part IV

The extent of testamentary
freedom

CHAPTER 14

Restrictions on testamentary freedom

The fundamental problem

14.1 In much the same spirit as people refer, quite inaccurately, to an Englishman's home being his castle, people also seem convinced that a person has an inalienable right to leave his property to whomsoever he wishes. Both notions were derived from the nineteenth century, but are commonly thought to represent immutable principles of English law. In neither case is this so.[1] So far as testamentary freedom is concerned, long before the nineteenth century there was a period at which severe restrictions were imposed. And the provisions of other legal systems, by which a fixed proportion is given to a surviving wife and children, show that complete testamentary freedom is by no means the only principle, and perhaps by no means the norm, even among Western legal systems.[2]

1 See Mellows (1963) 2 Solr Qtrly 109.
2 A principle of *legitio portio*, whereby close relatives are entitled to a fixed proportion of the family assets, applies to most EC countries. This automatic right often means that assets become fragmented between the family, and is one of the principal reasons the EC common agricultural policy is distorted by the needs of the small farmer, in particular by the limits on quotas. Such a policy is often inappropriate in the UK where testamentary freedom permits the retention of larger, more economical farm units.

14.2 There are two broad issues. First, legal systems which provide for the transmission of property on death may either allow complete testamentary freedom or make some overriding provision for the nearest relatives, such as wives and children. Secondly, if a legal system is to make some overriding provision for relatives, this may be either on the basis of a fixed entitlement, such as giving the wife a right to one third of the estate, or it may be in the discretion of the court.

14.3 If a legal system resolves to restrict a person's freedom to dispose of his estate on his death as he wishes, it must then determine whether, say, a wife or child should have a fixed right to part of the estate or only a right in the discretion of the court. If a fixed right is conferred, the rules must be blunt: they perhaps cannot cater adequately for each situation. A slightly absurd result ensues if a wife, although rich, is nevertheless entitled to receive in addition a percentage of her late husband's estate, even if he would have preferred his limited resources to be applied for his destitute niece. But there are disadvantages also in the discretionary system.

14.4 It is of the essence of the discretionary system that the applicant must persuade the court that the deceased failed to make reasonable provision for him. This frequently involves consideration of the conduct of the deceased, and of the principal contestants, often to the great distress of all. Take a typical situation. The husband marries, and after some years separates from his wife and thereafter lives with a mistress. He makes substantial provision by will for his mistress, and the wife seeks to interfere with the will. A slanging match between wife and mistress can easily follow. The wife may allege that the mistress is a wanton who lured the husband away, and that she ought to receive nothing: in her turn the mistress may allege that the wife was a complete shrew who positively drove the husband away.

14.5 Despite this, and the other disadvantages of the often substantial costs of the application – substantial because full enquiry must be made – and of the time involved in dealing with an application, the advantages still probably lie with the discretionary system. Only the discretionary system can deal adequately with the particular conditions of each individual case. Nevertheless, the question remains open.

Historical background

14.6 The history of the English law of wills since the Norman Conquest falls into three phases: fixed rights of the family; complete testamentary freedom; discretionary rights of the family. So far as personalty is concerned, in the thirteenth century the general rule was that a man could leave by will only one third of his property if his wife and children survived him; one half if either his wife or children but not both survived him; and the whole of his estate if he was survived by neither. These restrictions ceased to apply over much of the country in the fourteenth century, but the position was governed by local custom. The restrictions were not abolished in the ecclesiastical province of York until 1704, and in the City of London until 1724. Complete testamentary freedom as to personalty existed throughout the country from that date until the passing of the Inheritance (Family Provision) Act 1938.

14.7 Wills of personalty had been under the control of the church courts, but a similar trend appears with regard to wills of realty. At first, it was thought essential that freehold land should remain in the family. In feudal times land represented both power and wealth, and in most places a freehold estate devolved automatically upon the heir. Again, exceptions existed in particular localities, such as the City of London, usually as the result of a royal charter. In 1540, however, the Statute of Wills allowed all freehold land to be devised, subject to restrictions in the case of land held by military tenures, and these restrictions themselves disappeared with the passing of the Act for the Abolition of Military Tenures 1660. Thereafter, there was complete testamentary freedom as to realty, again until the Inheritance (Family Provision) Act 1938.

The family provision legislation

Basis of legislation

14.8 The Inheritance (Family Provision) Act 1938 followed earlier legislation in New Zealand and Australia[1] and it applied to persons dying between 13 July 1939 and 31 December 1952. The Act was superseded by the Intestates' Estates Act 1952, which applied to persons dying between 1 January 1953 and 31 December 1966. This, in turn, was superseded by the Family Provision Act 1966, in respect of persons dying between 1 January 1967 and 31 March 1976. The present legislation is the Inheritance (Provision for Family and Dependants) Act 1975,[2] which applies where the death occurs on or after 1 April 1976.

1 The earliest legislation was the New Zealand Family Protection Act 1908.
2 The Act enacts, with minor amendments, the draft bill appended to the Law Commission's Report entitled Family Provision on Death (Law Com No 61).

14.9 The 1938, 1952 and 1966 Acts had certain constant features. These were that they gave to the courts a discretion, to award *maintenance* for certain *dependants* out of income, but each Act extended the scope of the previous one. Thus, the 1952 Act extended the legislation to cover total intestacies, and the 1966 Act extended the power to award lump sum payments. The 1975 Act keeps the fundamental notion of the court having a discretion, but in the important case of husband and wife it has moved away from the idea of providing maintenance for a dependant, to one of giving to the surviving spouse financial provision, either from income or from capital, of an amount which is fair, whether or not that amount is required for the surviving spouse's maintenance. In other cases, however, it will be seen that the concept of providing for the maintenance of a dependant has been preserved. In the remainder of this chapter it is proposed to deal only with the provisions of the 1975 Act, and not the earlier Acts.

Applications under the 1975 Act

14.10 In order to succeed in an application under the 1975 Act the applicant must:
(a) prove that the deceased died domiciled in England and Wales;[1]
(b) prove that he has a locus standi, that is, that he is a member of one of the specified classes of applicants which are set out in s 1(1) of the Act; and
(c) convince the court that the will of the deceased, or the intestacy rules, or a combination of both, do not make reasonable financial provision for the particular applicant.

1 The legislation does not extend to Scotland or Northern Ireland: s 27(2).

Domicile of deceased

14.11 The Act applies only where the deceased died domiciled in England and Wales. Curiously, there is no power for the court to interfere if the deceased was not domiciled in England and Wales, even if he had been resident here for many years. This approach distinguishes the legislation from recent Acts in other fields, where the basic concept of domicile is often extended to include one of deemed domicile, based on residence for a number of years.[1]

1 Eg Inheritance Tax Act 1984, s 267, by virtue of which a person is treated as being domiciled in the United Kingdom for the purposes of inheritance tax if he was resident here for 17 out of the previous 20 years.

14.12 The burden of proof is upon the applicant to prove the domicile of the deceased, with the result that the application will not succeed where substantial doubt exists as to the deceased's domicile. Thus, in *Mastaka v Midland Bank Executor and Trustee Co Ltd*[1] a daughter made an application in respect of the estate of her late mother. The mother had married a Russian, from whom she had been separated for a considerable period, and of whom she had heard nothing. There was no evidence before the court to show that the Russian was either alive or dead. At that time, a married woman automatically took the domicile of her husband, so that if the man had been alive at the date of her death she would have died domiciled in the USSR. The court held that the daughter had not proved that the deceased's domicile was English, and accordingly she failed in her application.

1 [1941] Ch 192, [1941] 1 All ER 236.

14.13 The domicile of the applicant is irrelevant.

Jurisdiction

14.14 Proceedings under the Act may be commenced in the Family Division or the Chancery Division of the High Court[1] or in the county court. The latter's jurisdiction is no longer limited,[2] but appropriate cases will be transferred to the High Court.[3]

1 The Law Commission had recommended that all applications to the High Court should be made only in the Family Division.
2 Under the County Courts Act 1984, s 25, county court jurisdiction was limited to estates not exceeding £30,000. The limit was removed from 1 July 1991 by the Courts and Legal Services Act 1990, ss 1 and 120, and the High Court and County Courts Jurisdiction Order 1991 (SI No 724).
3 The criteria for the transfer of proceedings are governed by the 1991 Order, ibid, and include the financial substance of the action, its importance and whether any questions of general public interest are raised, the complexity and the likelihood of a more speedy trial (although there will be no transfer on that ground alone).

Class of persons who may apply

14.15 An application can be made by:[1]
(a) a wife or husband[2] of the deceased;
(b) a former wife or former husband of the deceased who has not remarried;
(c) a child of the deceased;

(d) a person, other than a child of the deceased, who was at some time treated by the deceased as a child of the family[3] in relation to a marriage to which the deceased had at some time been a party;

(e) a person who was being maintained by the deceased immediately before the death of the deceased, and who does not fall within any of the previous categories.

1 Inheritance (Provision for Family and Dependants) Act 1975, s 1(1).
2 These words necessarily mean the widow or widower of the deceased.
3 The expression 'child of the family' is found also in s 52(1) of the Matrimonial Causes Act 1973.

Wife or husband

Generally

14.16 An applicant in this category must prove that he or she was validly married to the deceased, and that the marriage was subsisting at the date of death of the deceased. A marriage certificate is accepted as prima facie evidence of a valid marriage unless this is challenged, when further evidence is required. In *Re Watkins, Watkins v Watkins*[1] a husband deserted his wife in 1922 and was never heard of again. The wife remarried in 1948. In view of the length of time which had elapsed, and of the fact that the first husband's family, with whom the wife kept in touch during that period, had heard nothing of him, the court presumed that the first husband was dead, so that her second marriage in 1948 was valid. She therefore had a locus standi to make an application in respect of the estate of her second husband.[2] In *Re Sehota, Surjit Kaur v Gian Kaur*,[3] where the deceased had contracted polygamous marriages with two wives, the court held that the first wife could make an application against the estate of the deceased, who by his will had left his entire estate to his second wife.

1 [1953] 2 All ER 1113.
2 Cf *Re Peete, Peete v Crompton* [1952] 2 All ER 599. Where a marriage was voidable or void, the other party to it may nevertheless be able to make an application under the provisions noted below.
3 [1978] 3 All ER 385.

Voidable marriage

14.17 A party to a voidable marriage with the deceased will be treated as a husband or wife provided that the marriage was not annulled during the lifetime of the deceased.[1]

1 Although this is not specifically stated in the legislation it would seem to follow from s 25(4).

Void marriage

14.18 A party to a void marriage with the deceased will be treated as a husband or wife if he or she can prove that:
(a) the applicant entered into the marriage in good faith;
(b) the marriage of the applicant and the deceased was not dissolved or annulled during the lifetime of the deceased; and

(c)   the applicant has not entered into a later marriage during the lifetime of the deceased.[1]

1   1975 Act, s 25(4).

Judicially separated spouses

14.19   Where a decree of judicial separation is made, the parties to that marriage remain spouses, and in principle, upon the death of one of them, the other can make an application. However, a judicially separated spouse may be barred from applying for provision by an order of the court made on the application of the other spouse on or after the date of judicial separation.[1]

1   1975 Act, s 15(1), (4), as amended by the Matrimonial and Family Proceedings Act 1984.

'Spouses' in other circumstances

14.20   A purported spouse may not come within any of these categories. For example a party to a bigamous marriage may not be able to show that he entered into it in good faith. In this case, the purported spouse will nevertheless usually be able to make an application, but under the heading of 'Other persons maintained by the deceased' noted below.[1] The distinction is, however, important, because the provision for an applicant spouse is more liberal than that for an applicant in the residuary category.[2]

1   See below, para 14.25.
2   Because of the higher standard of reasonable financial provision required for a spouse than for other categories of applicant.

Former husband or former wife

Generally

14.21   A former spouse of the deceased can apply under this heading if he or she can show:

(a)   that the applicant had been validly married to the deceased;[1]
(b)   that during the lifetime of the deceased, the marriage was dissolved or annulled by a decree of divorce or nullity; and
(c)   that the applicant has not remarried, whether before or after the death of the deceased.[2]

While, therefore, remarriage bars the right of a former spouse, it will have been noted that there is no similar bar under the preceding category to spouses who remarry.

1   1975 Act, s 25(1).
2   For the purposes of this condition, the applicant is treated as having remarried even if that remarriage is void or voidable: s 25(5).

Exclusion order

14.22   As in the case of an order made following a decree of judicial separation,[1] the court can make an order at the time of granting a decree of divorce or nullity, or at any time thereafter, excluding the right of either spouse to make an application in respect of the estate of the other.[2]

1   See above, para 14.19.

2 1975 Act, s 15(1). If the order is made before the decree nisi is made absolute, it only takes effect when the decree is made absolute: s 15(2).

Child of the deceased

14.23 A child of the deceased, of any age, can make an application.[1] In addition to a lawful child of the whole blood, an application can be made under this heading by a legitimated child, an adopted child, an illegitimate child and a child en ventre sa mère at the date of the deceased's death, whether the deceased is the father or mother of that child.[2] A stepchild of the deceased cannot apply under this category, but in appropriate circumstances can apply in the following category.

1 1975 Act, s 1(1)(c).
2 Ibid, s 25(1).

Children in other circumstances

14.24 Any person who has at any time been treated by the deceased as a child of the family in relation to any marriage to which the deceased was a party[1] can make an application.[2] The applicant can be of any age.

1 It is not necessary for the treatment to have occurred during the marriage provided it was in relation to the marriage: *Re Debenham* [1986] 1 FLR 404.
2 1975 Act, s 1(1)(d).

Other persons maintained by the deceased

14.25 In order to have a locus standi under this heading, the applicant must show:
(a) that he does not come within any other category;
(b) that the deceased was wholly maintaining him, or was making a substantial contribution towards his reasonable needs;[1]
(c) that he was being maintained by the deceased immediately before the death of the deceased;[2] and
(d) that the deceased was not receiving full valuable consideration for maintaining him;[3] and perhaps
(e) that the deceased had assumed responsibility for the maintenance of the applicant.
It is necessary to consider each of these requirements.

1 1975 Act, s 1(3).
2 Ibid, s 1(1)(e).
3 Ibid, s 1(3).

Not within other categories
14.26 In order to come within the preceding four categories, the applicant must have had a legally recognised relationship to the deceased, but in order to come within this final category, it is not necessary for the applicant to have any relationship to the deceased. Where the deceased maintained his

mistress, the mistress can make an application. Where the test of maintaining is satisfied, a mere friend can also make an application. It is not necessary for the applicant and the deceased ever to have lived under the same roof.[1]

1 The Law Commission has recommended that this category of applicant should be living with the deceased in the same household immediately before the date of death: *Family Law: Distribution on Intestacy*, Law Comm No 187 (1989) Part IV. It also recommended that the protection for cohabitees should be improved by removing the necessity for them to prove dependence on the deceased. The Government proposes to implement these recommendations 'when a suitable legislative opportunity occurs': see para 12.2, footnote 3.

Maintenance of the applicant
14.27 Immediately before his death, the deceased must have been wholly maintaining the applicant, or have been making a substantial contribution towards his needs. The requirement will be satisfied if the deceased provided accommodation for the applicant, even if that accommodation was shared with the deceased.[1]

1 *Re Wilkinson* [1978] 1 All ER 221; *Jelley v Iliffe* [1981] Fam 128, [1981] 2 All ER 29, CA; *Bishop v Plumley* [1991] 1 All ER 236, CA.

Maintenance immediately before death
14.28 The deceased must have been maintaining the applicant 'immediately' before his death. Although no minimum period is specified, the concept of maintaining denotes an element of recurrence or continuance. In *Re Beaumont, Martin v Midland Bank Trust Co Ltd*[1] Megarry V-C said that this is concerned not with the facts at the moment before death, but with the normal and habitual state. This approach was followed in *Jelley v Iliffe*,[2] where the Court of Appeal held that the test is satisfied if the deceased was making a substantial contribution in money or money's worth towards the reasonable needs of the applicant on a settled basis or arrangement, which either was still in force immediately before the deceased's death, or would have lasted until the death but for the approach of death and the consequent inability of either party to continue to carry out the arrangement.

1 [1980] Ch 444, [1980] 1 All ER 266.
2 [1981] Fam 128, [1981] 2 All ER 29, CA.

14.29 It follows that if what had been a settled state of affairs had come to an end for other reasons before the deceased died, the deceased would not have been maintaining the applicant immediately before the death. In *Kourkgy v Lusher*[1] the applicant had begun to work for the deceased as his secretary in 1951. She became his mistress in 1969, and, apart from one short interval, she continued to be so until 1979. The deceased generally lived with the applicant, but went on holiday with his wife in 1977 and again in 1979. He appears to have decided that he liked his wife after all, because after the holiday in June 1979 he went back to live with his wife, rather than returning to his mistress. He died a month later. Wood J held that the deceased was not maintaining the applicant 'immediately' before his death, so that she did not have a locus standi.

1 (1981) 4 FLR 65. In *Layton v Martin* [1986] 2 FLR 227 the claim was refused where the

relationship had ended two years before the death. See also *Sen v Headley* [1991] Ch 425, [1991] 2 All ER 638, CA, where the issue before the court was whether the doctrine of donatio mortis causa applied to land (see below, para 34.39), the plaintiff having to rely on the doctrine as she was unable to pursue a claim under s 1(1)(e) as she was not being maintained by the deceased *immediately* before his death.

Maintenance not for full valuable consideration

14.30 If the applicant can show that the deceased was wholly or substantially contributing to his maintenance immediately before his death, it is also necessary for the applicant to show that he did not give to the deceased full valuable consideration for the maintenance. A person might provide full valuable consideration where he and the deceased shared resources which they provided equally.[1] If, however, the value of the deceased's contribution was greater than that of the applicant, the consideration provided by the applicant, although valuable, would not be 'full'. In *Re Wilkinson*[2] the deceased persuaded the applicant, her sister, to live with her. The deceased paid all the household expenses, and the deceased and the applicant shared the cooking and household tasks. The court held that the services provided by the applicant, when measured in financial terms, were less than the value of the maintenance provided by the deceased, so that the applicant had a locus standi.[3]

1 See eg *Re Beaumont, Martin v Midland Bank Trust Co Ltd* [1980] Ch 444, [1980] 1 All ER 266.
2 [1978] 1 All ER 221.
3 In *Bishop v Plumley* [1991] 1 All ER 236, CA, the deceased and the applicant lived together as man and wife for ten years before the deceased's premature death. The Court of Appeal considered that the applicant's exceptional devotion to and care of the deceased during his illness during the last three years of his life did not disqualify the applicant: it did not amount to full valuable consideration for the maintenance she had received in the form of being provided with secure accommodation.

Assumption for responsibility for maintenance

14.31 It will be seen[1] that in considering an application by a person in this category, the court is directed to have regard to various factors, including 'the extent to which and the basis upon which the deceased assumed responsibility for the maintenance of the applicant'. In *Re Beaumont*[2] Megarry V-C held that, in the light of this provision, s 1(1)(e) must be construed as if there were implied into it the condition that the deceased had assumed responsibility for the maintenance of the applicant. He said that this involves an act demonstrating an assumption of responsibility, and not the mere act of maintaining. The court held, on the particular facts, that the deceased and the applicant were two people who had chosen to pool their individual resources without either undertaking any responsibility for maintaining the other.

1 See below, para 14.71.
2 *Re Beaumont, Martin v Midland Bank Trust Co Ltd* [1980] Ch 444, [1980] 1 All ER 266.

14.32 However, in *Jelley v Iliffe*[1] the Court of Appeal refused to follow the approach in *Re Beaumont*, holding that the bare fact of maintenance generally raised a presumption that the deceased had assumed the responsibility for maintaining the applicant. Where the deceased did assume the responsibility for maintaining the applicant, the applicant will have no locus standi if the deceased abandoned that responsibility in his lifetime. Abandonment of responsibility was one of the grounds for the decision in *Kourkgy v Lusher*.[2]

1 [1981] Fam 128, [1981] 2 All ER 29, CA.
2 (1981) 4 FLR 65; above, para 14.28.

Reasonable financial provision

14.33 When the applicant has shown that the deceased died domiciled in England and Wales, and that he, the applicant, falls within one of the five special specified categories, he must then show that the disposition of the deceased's estate effected by his will, or by the law relating to intestacy, or, in the case of partial intestacy, the combination of the two, was not such as to make 'reasonable financial provision' for the applicant.[1] It will be noted in particular that the court is not bound to assume that the intestacy rules make reasonable provision for the deceased's dependants. In effect, therefore, the court is given power to prescribe special intestacy rules for each particular estate.

1 1975 Act, s 1(1).

14.34 The 1975 Act makes a distinction between the meaning of 'reasonable financial provision' for a spouse and for one of the other categories of applicant.

Provision where application by spouse

14.35 Where the application is by the husband or wife of the deceased, the expression 'reasonable financial provision' means such financial provision as it would be reasonable in all the circumstances of the case for the applicant to receive, whether or not that provision is required for the maintenance of the applicant.[1] Although, as will be seen,[2] the court will have to have regard, inter alia, to the financial position of the applicant, the legislation does not require the provision to be limited in any way to the needs of the applicant. Indeed the starting point is the amount which the applicant could have expected to have received on a divorce.[3]

1 1975 Act, s 1(2)(a).
2 Below, para 14.51.
3 1975 Act, s 3(2). The 'imaginary divorce' guideline is considered below, paras 14.36–14.37.

The imaginary divorce guideline
14.36 One of the particular guidelines to be taken into account in respect of applications by spouses is the amount which the applicant could have expected to have received if the marriage had ended by divorce on the date of death of the deceased.[1] The guideline does not, however, set out in detail how the court should approach the imaginary divorce. The guideline cannot be taken literally as it fails to take into consideration the vital distinction that where a marriage ends on death the deceased has no future needs and,

conversely, no future earnings. In *Re Bunning*[2] Vinelott J assessed the provision for the applicant wife on the basis of what she would have received in an imaginary divorce on the day of her husband's death, by taking into account his future needs without 'foreknowledge of [his] imminent death'.

1 1975 Act, s 3(2), introduced following a recommendation of the Law Commission, Law Com No 61, paras 33–34, to enable the court 'to adopt an approach similar to that adopted in divorce proceedings'.
2 [1984] Ch 480 at 496.

14.37 However, this imaginary divorce guideline is only one of a number of particular guidelines which are to be taken into account when endeavouring to ascertain what constitutes reasonable provision for the applicant. As Oliver LJ commented in *Re Besterman*:[1]

'However, the figure resulting from the section 25 [ie of the Matrimonial Causes Act 1973] exercise is merely *one* of the factors to which the court is to "have regard" and the overriding consideration is what is "reasonable" in all the circumstances. Where the estate is very substantial, it is suggested that it would "be a curious result that a party to a happy and contented marriage who has behaved impeccably should be thought to be entitled to a lesser provision from a husband than one who has, perhaps, behaved quite improperly and whose marriage has, in consequence, ended in divorce and dissension".'

Oliver LJ further remarked that this may be an 'inevitable consequence of the two different exercises which the Court is directed to carry out' in respect of applications under s 25 of the Matrimonial Causes Act 1973 and under the 1975 Act. In *Re Besterman* the husband had left a net estate in excess of £1.4 million. Apart from his personal chattels, the only provision in the will for the wife, to whom he had been happily married for eighteen years, was a yearly income of £3,500 to supplement her widow's pension of £400 pa. The balance of the estate was left to Oxford University. The trial judge awarded the widow a lump sum of £238,000, which the Court of Appeal increased to £378,000.

1 [1984] Ch 458 at 469.

14.38 It seems that the law is moving towards a position in which, in due course, a surviving spouse will be entitled in the ordinary case to a part of the deceased's estate in any event, as a form of matrimonial property.

14.39 Where a decree of judicial separation had been made and it was continuing in force at the date of the deceased's death, the application is not treated as being made by a surviving spouse, but as coming within the class now to be considered.

Provision where application by former spouse

14.40 The Court of Appeal has said[1] that where an application is made by a former spouse, and on the dissolution of the marriage financial arrangements between the parties had been settled by the court or by agreement, the application should not succeed if there has been no change of circumstances. If, however, there has been a material change of circumstances, as where an order was made for the deceased to make periodical payments to the applicant and the payments have come to an end on his death, the court will entertain an application.[2] It may also do so if there has been a substantial change in the financial circumstances, as in the case of a policy of insurance on the life of the deceased maturing on his death.

1 In *Re Fullard* [1982] Fam 42, [1981] 2 All ER 796, CA.
2 *Whiting v Whiting* [1988] 2 All ER 275: an application to vary a periodical payments order does not impose a 'clean break' unless there are compelling reasons for doing so.

14.41 Where financial arrangements were not settled on the divorce, an application by a former spouse comes within the category now to be considered. With one exception,[1] the test of reasonable financial provision for a former spouse is not that applicable to a spouse, but is the lower standard applicable to the other categories of applicant.

1 Under s 14(1) of the 1975 Act it is provided that where within twelve months of the date on which a decree of divorce or nullity has been made absolute or a decree of judicial separation has been granted a party to the marriage dies and either: (a) an application for a financial provision order under ss 23 and 24 of the Matrimonial Causes Act 1973 has not been made by the other party to that marriage; or (b) such an application is pending at the death of the deceased, then, if an application for an order under s 2 of the Act is made by the other party the court has power if it thinks just to do so to treat that party for the purposes of that application as if the decree of divorce or nullity of marriage had not been made absolute or the decree of judicial separation had not been granted as the case may be. In the case of a decree of judicial separation, the provision is applicable only if the separation has continued: s 14(2).

Provision in other cases – maintenance

14.42 In the case of applications by every applicant other than the spouse of the deceased, the expression 'reasonable financial provision' means such financial provision as it would be reasonable in all the circumstances of the case for the applicant to receive *for his maintenance*.[1] There is no statutory definition[2] of maintenance, but the courts have evolved the following principles.

(a) Maintenance does not mean mere subsistence.[3]
(b) The concept denotes payments which directly or indirectly enable the applicant to discharge the recurrent cost of daily living. It does not generally include substantial capital benefit.[4] In *Re Dennis, Dennis v Lloyds Bank*[5] the testator gave to his son, the applicant, £90,000 with which to purchase a farm. The deceased died within seven years of making the gift, and capital transfer tax[6] became payable in respect of the £90,000. The son made an application for a lump sum with which to discharge the capital transfer tax liability. Browne-Wilkinson J held that in these circumstances the lump sum which the applicant sought did not come within the description of maintenance.
(c) The appropriate level of support is not to be determined solely by reference to the financial position of the applicant, but regard must

also be paid to his social position and station in life.[7] 'What would be a reasonable provision for the widow of, for instance, a farm labourer would, in ordinary circumstances, be unreasonable provision for the widow of a wealthy man.'[8]

(d) The appropriate level of support is also to be determined in the light of the standard of living which the deceased encouraged the applicant to adopt. In *Malone v Harrison*[9] the applicant was a mistress, but not the sole mistress, of the deceased. For twelve years, from the age of 23, 'it was the deceased's pleasure to visit and relax with her and to take her abroad frequently and regularly, where she was treated as his wife'. The deceased objected to her working to support herself, and bought her a car as well as flats in England and Malta. The court took fully into account the generosity which the deceased had shown the applicant.[10]

(e) Maintenance may denote the well-being, health and financial security of the applicant and his immediate family, even if the only way in which this can be ensured is by the provision of capital. In *Re Christie*[11] the deceased had a son and a daughter. She made a will leaving her London house to her daughter and her Essex house to her son, with the residue to be divided between them. After making the will she sold the Essex house, and bought another, but the new house did not pass under the specific devise.[12] The court held that the deceased always intended that the son should have one house, and that, in the circumstances, the will did not make reasonable provision for him.

1 1975 Act, s 1(2)(b).
2 As the 1975 Act makes no other reference to maintenance, recourse may be had to cases which have previously considered its meaning, as did Goff LJ in *Re Coventry, Coventry v Coventry* [1980] Ch 461 at 484, 485. Maintenance is rather more than keeping a person above the breadline, which would be equating the meaning to mere subsistence level: Stamp J in *Re E, E v E* [1966] 2 All ER 44, quoted by Goff LJ in *Re Coventry*.
3 *Re C* [1978] LS Gaz R 1233; *Re Christie, Christie v Keeble* [1979] Ch 168, [1979] 1 All ER 546; *Re Wood, Wood v Wood* [1982] LS Gaz R 774.
4 Although the award of a lump sum may be the most effective way of enabling the applicant to meet recurrent costs.
5 [1981] 2 All ER 140.
6 The forerunner of inheritance tax.
7 *Re Chatterton* [1980] Conv 150; *Re Inns, Inns v Wallace* [1947] Ch 576, [1947] 2 All ER 308.
8 *Re Inns, Inns v Wallace* [1947] Ch 576 at 581 per Wynn Parry J.
9 [1979] 1 WLR 1353.
10 See also *Bosch v Perpetual Trustee Co Ltd* [1938] AC 463.
11 [1979] Ch 168, [1979] 1 All ER 546.
12 Under the doctrine of ademption; see paras 30.36ff.

14.43 However, the decision in *Re Christie* was not followed in *Re Coventry, Coventry v Coventry*[1] where the Court of Appeal said that the approach adopted in *Re Christie* 'came dangerously near to equating [maintenance] with well-being or benefit'.[2] *Re Coventry* shows that there are limits on the power of the court to widen artificially the meaning of 'maintenance' in an attempt to achieve what might more generally be thought to be a fair result.[3]

1 [1980] Ch 461, [1979] 3 All ER 815, CA.
2 Per Oliver J in *Re Coventry* at first instance: [1979] 2 All ER 408 at 415.

3 See also *Allcorn v Harvey and Woodcock* [1980] CA Transcript 289, noted at 131 NLJ 242 where the court refused to follow *Re Christie*.

Objective test

14.44 In all cases, the question whether reasonable financial provision was made for the applicant is to be determined objectively, that is, according to the actual facts as known to the court.[1] The test is not whether the deceased thought that he was acting reasonably; nor whether he did in fact behave reasonably according to the circumstances known to him. Under the previous legislation there was doubt whether the test was objective or subjective, but following the decision in *Re Goodwin, Goodwin v Goodwin*[2] it was generally thought that the test was objective.[3] That case is still good law. The testator made a will leaving various legacies, and then leaving his residuary estate to his wife. He anticipated that this would amount to between £8,000 and £9,000, but after the payment of estate duty[4] it in fact amounted only to £1,500. Although the testator might be said to have acted reasonably, the court made an order in favour of the widow. Megarry J said:[5]

'The question is simply whether the will or the disposition has made reasonable provision, and not whether it was unreasonable on the part of the deceased to have made no provision or no larger provision for the dependant. A testator may have acted entirely reasonably; he may have taken skilled advice on the drafting of his will, intending to make a fully reasonable provision; and yet through some blunder of the draftsman (perhaps as to the incidence of estate duty) or by some change of circumstance unknown to the testator in his lifetime, the provision in fact made may have been wholly unreasonable. Conversely, the testator may have acted wholly unreasonably in deciding what provision to insert in the will, but by some happy accident, such as the lapse of a share of residue which then passed to the widow on intestacy, the provision in fact made may be entirely reasonable. In my judgment, the question is not subjective but objective. It is not whether the testator stands convicted of unreasonableness, but whether the provision in fact made is reasonable.'

1 1975 Act, s 3(5).
2 [1969] 1 Ch 283, [1968] 3 All ER 12.
3 See also *Millward v Shenton* [1972] 2 All ER 1025; *Re Parkinson* (1975) Times, 4 October, CA.
4 A forerunner of inheritance tax.
5 [1969] 1 Ch 283 at 287, [1968] 3 All ER 12 at 15.

The relevant date

14.45 It is not clear whether the test of reasonableness is to be determined as at the date of death of the deceased or as at the date of hearing of the application. One would expect that the relevant date would be the date of death, and that if the provision was reasonable at that date the court could not interfere. However, s 3(5) of the 1975 Act requires the court to 'take into account the facts as known to the court at the date of hearing'. It is suggested that these words mean that the court must take into account all the facts which it knows as to the circumstances prevailing at the date of death. Two situations may be contrasted. Suppose that the deceased was survived by his wife and daughter; that the daughter was in well-paid and secure employment; and that the wife was of modest means. In general it might be thought that the daughter would not succeed in an application. If, however, she could show that at the date of death of the deceased she was suffering from a terminal illness, as a result of which she would have to give up work, she might well succeed even if neither she nor the deceased knew of that illness at the date of his death. The fact of the illness is a fact known to the court at the date of hearing. If, however, the daughter was in good health when the deceased died, but subsequently contracted the illness, then it seems that, strictly, the court cannot make an order in her favour.

14.46 In practice this distinction may well be unreal. It is necessary only to show that any provision was slightly unreasonable to give the court jurisdiction to make an order. When it has jurisdiction the court can take full account of events which have occurred up to the date of the hearing. To revert to the example, if the daughter could show that the deceased ought to have made some provision, if only 50p a week, and she then contracted the illness, the court would have jurisdiction and could award her a much larger sum.

14.47 Although the relevant date is generally the date of death, a change in the circumstances of the applicant or the estate between the date of death and the date of hearing is to be taken into account by the court. The fact that, say, the applicant wins the first prize on a premium bond between the date of death and the date of the hearing is a relevant factor; conversely, the fact that the estate had received a similar prize after the date of death[1] would be taken into consideration. Likewise, the court must take into account circumstances at the date of death which are likely to affect the applicant in the future.[2] A claim under the 1975 Act is personal to the applicant,[3] so that if the applicant dies during the course of the proceedings the action comes to an end and is not enforceable by the applicant's personal representatives for the benefit of the estate.[4] Such a claim neither gives rise to nor becomes a cause of action unless an order has been made in respect of it before the death of the applicant. Until then it remains no more than a hope or contingency – of no surviving value to the applicant's estate.[5]

1 Premium bonds continue to qualify for prizes for one year from the date of the holder's death if not cashed by the personal representatives before then.
2 *Re Schroeder* [1972] QWN 10 (Queensland). The applicant was the husband of the deceased. Held that the deceased should have anticipated that the business would probably decline to the point at which the applicant could barely support himself.
3 The principle is the same as that applied to a claim for financial provision under the Matrimonial Causes Act 1973.
4 *Whytte v Ticehurst* [1986] Fam 64, [1986] 2 All ER 158.
5 *Re Bramwell, Campbell v Tobin* [1988] 2 FLR 263.

Deceased's inability to make provision

14.48 Because an objective test is adopted, a provision may be unreasonable even if the deceased could not have altered it. In *Re Franks, Franks v*

Franks[1] a woman who had been previously married left a small part of her estate to her second husband, and the substantial balance to her son by her first marriage. She then had a child by her second husband, and died two days later. Even though it was not practicable for her to alter her will to make provision for her new baby, it was held that the child could successfully make an application.

1 [1948] Ch 62, [1947] 2 All ER 638.

Matters to be taken into account

The court's discretion

14.49 The court is directed[1] to have regard to certain factors:
(a) in deciding whether financial provision has in fact been made; and
(b) if it has not, whether to exercise its powers under the Act; and
(c) if reasonable financial provision has not been made, and the court considers that it should exercise its powers, in deciding in what manner it should exercise its powers.

It by no means follows that merely because reasonable financial provision has not been made for the applicant that an order will be made in his favour. Thus, suppose that the deceased made provision for his son, and that the court finds that that was unreasonable. If after the deceased's death the son's financial position greatly improves, the court might well not make an order in his favour. The court, thus, has a dual discretion. Even when it is satisfied that reasonable financial provision was not made, it has to decide whether to exercise its powers; and, if so, how to do so. The factors to which the court must have regard are divided into general guidelines, which have to be taken into account with all applications, and particular guidelines which apply to particular applicants.

1 By s 3 of the 1975 Act.

The general guidelines

14.50 The matters which are taken into account for all applicants are as follows.[1]

1 Set out in s 3(1) of the 1975 Act.

Financial position of applicant
14.51 The court considers the financial resources and the financial needs which the applicant has or is likely to have in the foreseeable future.[1] If the applicant is capable of working, his earning capacity is taken into account whether or not he is in fact working.[2]

1 1975 Act, s 3(1)(a).
2 Ibid, s 3(6).

Financial position of other applicants
14.52 If any other person is making an application, the financial resources, including earning capacity, and financial needs of the other applicants are also taken into account.[1]

1 1975 Act, s 3(1)(b).

Financial position of beneficiaries
14.53 The court also takes into account the financial position of the persons who would be beneficially entitled to the deceased's estate if no order is made.[1]

1 1975 Act, s 3(1)(c).

14.54 By taking into account these three sets of facts, therefore, the court has before it a picture of the financial resources and needs of everyone who is likely to be affected by an order.

The deceased's obligations and responsibilities
14.55 The court then takes into account the obligations and responsibilities which the deceased had towards the applicant, any other applicant, and those entitled under his will or under the intestacy provisions.[1] These obligations and responsibilities are moral as well as financial and legal.[2] In a number of decisions on the earlier legislation, the court had to consider whether the deceased owed a moral obligation, and those cases are equally relevant under the present Act.

1 1975 Act, ss 3(1)(c), 25(1).
2 In *Re Haig, Powers v Haig* [1979] LS Gaz R 476 the decision was based on what was 'the morally reasonable thing to have done'. The Act does not expressly refer to moral obligation although the legislation in some other jurisdictions does. Thus, s 117 of the Eire Succession Act 1965 gives the court power to make an order in favour of a child of the testator if the court 'is of the opinion that the testator has failed in his moral duty to make proper provision for the child in accordance with his means, whether by will or otherwise'.

14.56 In the first place, it is clear that a moral obligation may be recognised to a person regardless of the nature of the relationship with the deceased. So, where a testator made provision for a mistress of 20 years' standing his moral obligation was recognised.[1] The moral obligation to a person named in the will may be recognised even if that person would not himself be able to make an application.[2]

1 *Re Joslin, Joslin v Murch* [1941] Ch 200.
2 *Re Joslin, Joslin v Murch*, above; *Re E, E v E* [1966] 2 All ER 44.

14.57 Secondly, the moral obligation of a parent to his child will often be treated as coming to an end when the applicant becomes the moral responsibility of another. So, in *Re Andrews, Andrews v Smorfitt*[1] a daughter of the deceased lived with a married man for 40 years, and had six children by him. She never married. At the age of 69 she made an application in respect of her late father's estate, but the court held that by establishing a permanent relationship with the man, the daughter ceased to have any moral claim on the deceased. A parent may be under a special moral obligation where through penury or other disadvantage he was not able to give the child a good start in life.[2]

1 [1955] 3 All ER 248.
2 *Re Stubbe Estate* [1973] 1 WWR 354 (Canada).

14.58 Generally, a moral obligation will be owed by one spouse to the other, but, exceptionally, this will not be so. In *Re Gregory, Gregory v Goodenough*[1] the husband and wife married in 1926. In 1927 they had a daughter, and the husband left the wife. He did not pay any maintenance to his wife or daughter, and cohabited with another woman. The other woman died in 1950 and the husband then asked his wife to come back. She refused because she was at the time looking after her mother. Shortly thereafter, the daughter went to live in South America and in 1955 the wife joined her there. From 1958 the husband wrote letters to his wife asking her to return. She did not do so and rarely answered his letters. He died in 1968, worth about £2,500, having left his wife nothing. The wife applied unsuccessfully to the county court, and her appeal to the Court of Appeal was unanimously dismissed. Although it was accepted that the husband was solely responsible for the breakdown of the marriage in 1927, he was held to have owed no moral obligation in respect of services or assistance in his later years. The other reasons for the decision were the length of the separation itself, and the fact that the wife had not relied in any way on the deceased for maintenance or support.

1 [1971] 1 All ER 497.

14.59 This decision is to be contrasted with that in *Re W*.[1] The deceased and the applicant married in 1934. In 1939 they both joined HM Forces and spent their leaves together. In 1942 the wife was discharged from military service and from that date the marriage began to break down. In 1946 the wife obtained a divorce from the deceased, but she was not maintained by him. When he died in 1972 the wife made an application. The court held that the deceased should have maintained his wife, and that it was only because of her gentle and compliant nature that she had not obtained the maintenance to which she was entitled. As a result of not maintaining his former wife the deceased had been able to accumulate capital. The deceased's estate amounted to £28,000, and the registrar had recommended that she should be given £14,000. However, Rees J considered that this was too much as the applicant was now aged 75, and he awarded her £11,000 from the estate. This was sufficient to enable her to buy an annuity of £1,750 a year, and leave some capital over.

1 (1975) 119 Sol Jo 439; Law Soc Gaz 14 May 1975.

14.60 The moral obligation owed by a testator may depend partly on relationship, and partly on the need of the applicant. Thus, while the conduct of an applicant may disentitle him, this depends not only on the conduct itself, but on the degree of need. The stronger the need, the more reprehensible must have been the applicant's conduct if he is to be disentitled.[1]

1 *Hughes v National Trustees Executors and Agency Co of Australasia Ltd* (1979) 23 ALR 321 (High Court of Australia).

The size and nature of the deceased's net estate

14.61 The meaning of the expression 'net estate' is considered in detail later,[1] but generally it means the deceased's assets as at the date of his death, after the deduction of his debts and liabilities. The concept is important, because the court can alter the destination of the net estate only. If the bulk of the deceased's estate is in unrealisable form, that will be taken into account. Further, the court appears to be reluctant to interfere with small estates. In *Re Howell, Howell v Lloyds Bank Ltd*[2] and *Re Gregory, Gregory v Goodenough*,[3] where the estates were both less than £3,000, the Court of Appeal stated that they would be very slow to interfere with the testator's disposition of his estate, but in principle there is no reason for the size of the estate to affect the court's approach.

1 Below, paras 14.76–14.77.
2 [1953] 2 All ER 604.
3 [1971] 1 All ER 497.

14.62 Where the value of the estate has increased between the date of death and the date of hearing, it seems that the assets of which the deceased was competent to dispose at his death will be valued at the date of the hearing.[1] In respect of other items which comprise the net estate, the value is generally taken at the date of death.[2]

1 See 1975 Act, s 3(5). On the previous legislation, see *Lusternik v Lusternik* [1972] Fam 125, [1972] 1 All ER 592.
2 Ibid, ss 2(1), (2), 9(1), 10(3). See however s 11(3).

Any physical or mental disability of any applicant, or of any beneficiary

14.63 Although specified separately in the legislation,[1] physical or mental disability will also affect the degree of moral obligation owed by the deceased where the disability existed during the lifetime of the deceased, and also it will usually be relevant to the financial needs of the person under disability.

1 1975 Act, s 3(1)(f).

14.64 It used to be thought that a testator was entitled to make no or little provision for dependants who were being cared for under the National Health Service.[1] However, in *Re Pringle, Baker v Matheson*[2] it was held that even though the testator's mentally defective son was being cared for in a National Health Service home, it was nevertheless reasonable for the testator to make some provision for him, and in *Millward v Shenton*[3] it was held that a testatrix should have made provision for a son aged 52 who was totally incapacitated, and who was entirely dependent on social security payments.[4]

1 *Re Watkins, Watkins v Watkins* [1953] 2 All ER 1113.
2 [1946] Ch 124.
3 [1972] 2 All ER 1025, CA.
4 See also *Sivyer v Sivyer* [1967] 3 All ER 429, where half the deceased's estate was awarded

to a girl who was in the care of the local authority; *Re Wood, Wood v Wood* [1982] LS Gaz R 774, where the court awarded a lump sum to a mentally subnormal applicant living permanently in hospital; and *Re Collins* [1990] Fam 56, [1990] 2 All ER 47.

14.65 On the other hand, it has been held that where the applicant is in receipt of a social security pension or allowance and the only result of provision from the estate would be to reduce that allowance, then it is not unreasonable for the deceased to make no provision for the applicant.[1] The courts are alive to the problem, and in *Re Canderton, Canderton v Barclays Bank Ltd*[2] the court divided the benefit between income and capital so that social security payments were affected to the least extent.

1 *Re E, E v E* [1966] 2 All ER 44.
2 (1970) 114 Sol Jo 208.

14.66 Conversely, where there is no physical or mental disability, that may lessen the deceased's moral obligation to the applicant. So, in *Re Coventry*[1] the Court of Appeal said that applications by able-bodied and comparatively young men needed to be approached with caution.

1 [1980] Ch 461, [1979] 3 All ER 815, CA.

Any other relevant matter
14.67 The court is also directed to have regard to 'any other matter, including the conduct of the applicant or any other person, which in the circumstances of the case, the court may consider relevant'.[1] The conduct of the applicant, or of a beneficiary, is relevant as going to the strength or otherwise of the moral obligation owed by the deceased. Clearly, a person who consistently behaves badly towards the deceased can expect to get less than he otherwise might.

1 1975 Act, s 3(1)(g).

14.68 One matter which the court is likely to consider relevant is the source of the deceased's funds. So, in *Sivyer v Sivyer*[1] the deceased owed moral obligations to his widow, who was his third wife, and to his daughter by his second wife. The deceased had a net estate of about £4,000, and died intestate. The widow would, under the intestacy rules, have taken the total estate, and an application was made on behalf of the daughter. Pennycuick J was at first minded to award the daughter £2,000, but increased this to £2,500 solely because most of the deceased's wealth was derived from his second wife, the girl's mother.[2]

1 [1967] 3 All ER 429.
2 See also *Re Pointer, Pointer and Shonfield v Edwards* [1941] Ch 60, [1940] 4 All ER 372; *Re Clayton, Clayton v Howell* [1966] 2 All ER 370.

14.69 Under the legislation previously in force the court was directed to have regard to any statement which the deceased left giving reasons for making, or not making, any specific disposition.[1] Under the 1975 Act an oral or written statement made by the deceased is admissible in evidence.[2]

1 Inheritance (Family Provision) Act 1938, s 1(7).

2 It is admissible under the Civil Evidence Act 1968, s 2. See s 21 of the 1975 Act, although the court is not specifically required to have regard to the deceased's reasons under s 3.

14.70 The court will consider any statement which the deceased leaves. All that this statement can do, however, is to bring to the notice of the court facts which might not otherwise have come to light. A statement can be a dangerous instrument because if the deceased leaves a statement containing facts which are inaccurate, that in itself may indicate that the deceased is not making reasonable financial provision for the applicant.[1] An example of this occurred in *Re Clarke, Clarke v Roberts*.[2] The testator married at the age of 49, when he was still a bachelor living with his mother. His wife was a schoolteacher aged 36. After the marriage, the parties lived with the testator's mother for seven months, but she made his wife feel unwanted. In his will the testator left his wife £1,000, and said: 'I hereby declare that the reason why I have not made further provision in this my will for [my wife] is that having before our marriage after due consideration agreed that the matrimonial home should be in the home of my mother who is a partial invalid she has seen fit to leave me and set up a home by herself.' However, Plowman J found that the true position was that the wife went to live in the mother's house as a temporary measure, intended to last only long enough to get the mother used to the idea that her 49-year-old bachelor son had got married, and that it was not intended to be a permanent arrangement. Indeed, the judge said that had the case been a matrimonial dispute, he would have found the husband to have been in constructive desertion of the wife. He therefore rejected the reason given in the will, and awarded one half of the income of the estate to the wife for the rest of her life, or until remarriage.

1 *Re Borthwick, Borthwick v Beauvais* [1949] Ch 395, [1949] 1 All ER 472.
2 [1968] 1 All ER 451.

Particular guidelines

14.71 In addition to the general guidelines just considered, the court is also directed to have regard to specific factors, depending on who makes the application. These other considerations are as follows:

Application by	*Additional matters to be considered*
1. Husband or wife (where no decree of judicial separation in force at date of death)[1]	(1) Age of applicant[2] (2) Duration of marriage (3) Contribution made by applicant to the welfare of the family of the deceased, including any contribution made by looking after the home or caring for the family (4) The amount which the applicant could have expected to have received if the marriage had been determined by a decree of divorce on the date of death of the deceased (the 'imaginary divorce' guideline)

Application by	*Additional matters to be considered*
2. (1) Husband or wife where decree of judicial separation in force at the date of death (2) Former husband or wife[3]	(1), (2) and (3) above
✓ 3. Child of the deceased[4]	The manner in which the applicant was being educated or trained; or the manner in which the applicant might expect to be educated or trained

4. Person accepted by deceased as a child of the family[5]	(1) The manner in which the applicant was being educated or trained; or the manner in which the applicant might be expected to be educated or trained
	(2) Whether the deceased had assumed any responsibility for the applicant's maintenance, and, if so:
	  (a) the extent to which the deceased had assumed that responsibility
	  (b) the basis upon which he had assumed that responsibility
	  (c) the length of time for which he had discharged that responsibility
	  (d) whether in assuming and discharging that responsibility the deceased did so knowing that the applicant was not his own child
	(3) The liability of any other person to maintain the applicant

5. Other person maintained by the deceased[6]	(1) The extent to which the deceased assumed responsibility for the maintenance of the applicant (2) The basis upon which he assumed that responsibility (3) The length of time for which he had discharged that responsibility.

1 1975 Act, s 3(2).
2 For the relevance of age, see *Re W* (1975) 119 Sol Jo 439, above, para 14.59.
3 1975 Act, s 3(2).
4 Ibid, s 3(3).
5 Ibid.
6 Ibid, s 3(4).

Applications by spouses

While each case is considered on its own facts, it may be helpful here to summarise certain general trends which emerge from the cases with regard to applications by spouses.

14.72 In general, the deceased will have owed a moral obligation to the applicant, and the applicant will therefore be entitled to some provision from the deceased's estate. The decision in *Re W*[1] has been noted.[2] Perhaps more striking is *Re Bonassera*.[3] At the age of 50, the deceased, who had been married before, married the applicant, a young woman half his age who was 'a vivacious young girl who wanted dining and dancing'. In due course the applicant left the deceased because he was not giving her the good times she desired. The deceased made a will leaving his estate of £22,000 to be divided equally between his children by his first marriage, and his mistress, whom Walton J described as 'a Junoesque brunette'. The court held that although the deceased did not morally owe the applicant much, he did owe her something, and the applicant was therefore awarded £2,000 from the estate.[4] It is only in very rare circumstances that it will be found that the deceased did not owe his spouse a moral obligation, but the decision in *Re Gregory, Gregory v Goodenough*[5] has been noted.[6]

1 (1975) 119 Sol Jo 439; Law Soc Gaz 14 May 1975.
2 Above, para 14.59.
3 (1974) Times, 11 May. The case is reported in the Home News section of the newspaper, not the Law Report.
4 The costs of the case were estimated at £3,000.
5 [1971] 1 All ER 497.
6 Above, para 14.58.

14.73 Where a moral obligation does exist, and the estate is small, the courts have a tendency to award the total estate to the spouse, particularly where there is no other applicant or beneficiary with a moral claim. *Re Goodwin, Goodwin v Goodwin*,[1] which has been noted in another context,[2] is an example of this. Another example is *Re Parkinson*.[3] In that case the testator married the applicant in 1961, and he died in 1973. His estate consisted of his house, valued at £3,500, its contents, valued at £100, and cash of about £300. He made a will leaving the applicant a life interest in the house and contents, with a provision that on her death or remarriage the house was to go to the Royal Society for the Prevention of Cruelty to Animals. The wife made an application for provision from the estate, asking that she should have the whole interest in the house. She said that she wished to live in it. The county court judge held that the widow would be no better off[4] by having the whole interest in the house, and he refused to interfere with the will. The widow appealed, but by the time the case came to the Court of Appeal two facts had changed. First, by appealing, the widow had ensured that the costs could not be met out of the deceased's personalty, so that the house would have to be sold in any event. Secondly, she said that she no longer wished to continue living in the house. Lord Denning MR thought that the testator's provision in his will was not reasonable and he thought that she should receive the whole of the residuary estate. James LJ concurred, with some reluctance. He said that the courts should be careful not to vary the wishes of the testator save within the strict limits provided by the legislature[5] and that the courts had a duty not to encroach on the freedom of the individual to dispose of his property by will further than the legislature required in the Acts. Bridge LJ also concurred, but said that he would not have concurred if the competing claim to the residuary estate had been advanced by a party who could be regarded as having a moral claim on the bounty of the deceased.

1 [1969] 1 Ch 283, [1968] 3 All ER 12.

2   Above, para 14.43.
3   (1975) Times, 4 October, CA.
4   The judge must have been thinking only in income terms.
5   The case was decided under the 1966 Act.

14.74   Where the estate is not small, the tendency is to award the spouse one half of the estate, or one half of the income from the estate. In *Re Clarke, Clarke v Roberts*,[1] which was noted above,[2] the spouse was awarded one half of the income of the estate. In that case the spouse was still young, and was working. Where the spouse is of more advanced years there is a great tendency to award half of the capital. It has been seen that in *Re W*[3] the starting point in the court's calculations was one half of the estate. However, the court also takes into account the income which can be purchased with that capital. Another example of the approach of equal division is *Re Shanahan, De Winter v Shanahan's Legal Personal Representatives*.[4] The applicant was the first wife of the deceased whom he married in 1927 and by whom he had four children. She obtained a divorce from him in 1956, with an order for maintenance. In 1965 the deceased married his second wife, and later made a will leaving her all his property. The first wife made an application and was granted half the estate. Both first and second wives were at the end of their working lives. Wife No 1 had no capital; wife No 2 had £6,000. Wife No 1 had a national insurance retirement pension of £250 pa; wife No 2 had a pension from her job as a teacher and a national insurance pension of £1,100 pa. Both as regards capital and income, wife No 2 was better off, but the court divided the estate between them.

1   [1968] 1 All ER 451.
2   Above, para 14.70.
3   (1975) Times, 22 April, [1975] LS Gaz R 70.
4   [1973] Fam 1.

14.75   Finally, where the spouse is old, the court may reduce the amount which that spouse might otherwise receive, because a larger amount of income can be purchased in the form of an annuity. This was the approach under the previous legislation,[1] under which the spouse could only be awarded maintenance. However, as payment of capital may be awarded under the 1975 Act, this may not be such an important factor and the question of age simply considered as a particular guideline.[2]

1   As in *Re W* -- above, para 14.58.
2   Under the 1975 Act, s 3(2)(a).

The net estate

Meaning

14.76   As will be seen, the court has power to order reasonable financial provision to be made from the 'net estate' of the deceased. Basically, this means all the property which the deceased owned at the date of his death and which he could have disposed[1] of by his will, less:
(a)   his funeral, testamentary and administration expenses;

(b) his debts and liabilities; and
(c) any inheritance tax payable out of his estate on his death.[2]
The value of the net estate is to be taken as at the date of the proceedings, not at the date of death.[3]

1 He is treated as being able to dispose of property even if he does not in fact have the mental capacity to do so: 1975 Act, s 25(2).
2 Ibid, s 25(1). Definition of 'net estate': (a).
3 *Re Kozdrach* [1981] Conv 224.

14.77 The amount of inheritance tax which is to be deducted is that which is payable after the court has made its order. In particular, this is important because although generally inheritance tax is payable on all the deceased's net assets, it is not payable on property which devolves upon his spouse.[1] Accordingly, the inheritance tax liability is calculated as if the will of the testator itself gave effect to the provisions of the court's order.[2]

1 Inheritance Tax Act 1984, s 18.
2 Ibid, s 146.

Powers of appointment

14.78 In the case of property which the deceased did not own outright, but over which he had a power of appointment the position is as follows:

Type of power	Whether property included in net estate	Authority
(a) General power, exercisable by deed or will, whether or not power exercised	yes	s 25(1), Definition of 'net estate': (a), being property of which deceased had power to dispose by his will
(b) General power, exercisable by deed but not by will. Power not exercised	yes	s 25(1), Definition of 'net estate': (b), to include such a power not exercised
(c) General power, exercisable by deed, but not by will. Power exercised	no	
(d) Special power, whether exercisable by deed, or will or either	no	s 25(1), Definition of 'net estate': (a) which specifically excludes a special power
(e) Hybrid power	no	

Property subject to nomination

14.79 Where a nomination[1] is in force at the date of the deceased's death, and it relates to money, that money forms part of the net estate.[2] If there is a nomination in force at the date of death affecting property other than money, that property, to the extent of its value at the date of death of the deceased, also forms part of the net estate.[3] In either case the amount of inheritance tax payable in respect of it is deducted.[4]

1 See above, para 2.14.
2 1975 Act, s 8(1).
3 Ibid.
4 Ibid, s 8(1), (3).

Donatio mortis causa

14.80 It will be seen that a donatio mortis causa is a gift made in the donor's lifetime in contemplation of death and conditional upon the death occurring.[1] Where the deceased made a donatio mortis causa the amount of money concerned, or the value of the property concerned, as at the date of death of the deceased, forms part of the net estate.[2] Inheritance tax payable in respect of it is deducted.[3]

1 See chapter 34, below.
2 1975 Act, s 8(2).
3 Ibid, s 8(2), (3).

Property held on joint tenancy

14.81 Where any property[1] was held by the deceased and one or more other persons on a beneficial joint tenancy, the court may order that the deceased's severable share shall 'to such extent as appears to the court to be just in the circumstances of the case' be treated as part of the net estate.[2] The value which may be taken into the net estate is the value of the share immediately before the death of the deceased. This will usually be less than the value of a proportionate part of the whole. For inheritance tax purposes,[3] the value of a share in a jointly owned asset is generally discounted by between 10 and 15 per cent.[4] It remains to be determined whether the same approach will be adopted for the purposes of the family provision legislation.[5]

1 The provision is not restricted to land: 1975 Act, s 9(4).
2 Ibid, s 9(1).
3 Subject to certain anti-avoidance rules concerning 'related property': Inheritance Tax Act 1984, s 161.
4 This is to reflect the fact that the owner of a share in an asset does not have complete control over the asset, and may be involved in delay, difficulty and expense in realising it.
5 It is arguable that the value of a share should not be reduced where it passes to a sole surviving beneficial joint tenant as, based on the facts considered at the date of the hearing rather than at the date of death (see above, para 14.45), the survivor has become the absolute owner.

14.82 Where the joint owners do not have an equal likelihood of survival, this will not make any difference to the value of the share where a beneficial joint tenancy can be severed. If, however, there is a contractual obligation not to sever, the fact that the deceased had a reduced chance of surviving can be taken into account. There is no restriction on the circumstances which the court can consider in deciding to what extent the deceased's share is to be taken into account.

14.83 The amount of inheritance tax payable in respect of the deceased's share is to be deducted.[1]

1 1975 Act, s 9(2).

Anti-avoidance legislation

14.84 It will be seen that, in certain circumstances, the court can upset dispositions or contracts made by the deceased with a view to avoiding the effect of the legislation.[1] Where the court takes action under those provisions, the amount added back is treated as part of the net estate.[2]

1 See below, chapter 15.
2 1975 Act, s 25(1), definition of 'net estate': (e).

The court's order

The effect of the order

14.85 Once an order is made it is deemed to have had effect from the deceased's death for all purposes.[1] A memorandum of the order is endorsed on the grant of representation under which the estate is being administered.[2] When an order is made, the successful applicant is placed in the position of a beneficiary.[3] Accordingly, the successful applicant will not receive the full benefit awarded if a direct beneficiary under the will who took a comparable benefit would not have done. Accordingly, if the value of the estate falls, the successful applicant's benefit may abate.[4]

1 1975 Act, s 19(1).
2 Ibid, s 19(3).
3 Ibid, s 19(1).
4 *Re Pointer, Shonfield v Edwards* [1946] Ch 324, [1946] 2 All ER 409; *Re Jennery, Jennery v Jennery* [1967] Ch 280, [1967] 1 All ER 691; *Royal Trust Co v Downton* (1977) 19 Nfld & PEIR 455. Cf *Union-Fidelity Trustee Co of Australia Ltd v Montgomery* [1976] 1 NSWLR 134 where it was held on the comparable legislation that when the value of the estate fell, an annuity awarded to a widow did not abate with other legacies, but took priority. As to abatement, see below, paras 30.53ff.

The powers of the court

14.86 The court may make any one or more of the following orders where it is satisfied that the deceased did not make reasonable financial provision for the applicant.
(a) An order for periodical payments.[1] This is the traditional way of providing maintenance for a dependant out of the estate. The order may relate to the whole income of the net estate, or any smaller amount.[2] If less than the whole of the income is to be paid to the

applicant, the applicant's entitlement may be expressed in terms of a fixed sum; or of a proportion of the income of the whole net estate; or of the income to be produced from a sum of capital to be appropriate for this purpose.[3]

An order for periodical payments is not bound to cease on remarriage where it is made in favour of a spouse,[4] but it will cease on remarriage where it is made in favour of a former spouse.[5]

(b) An order for the payment of a lump sum to the applicant out of the estate.[6] In the case of an application by a husband or wife of the deceased, the court will often order a lump sum payment to be made. In the case of other applications, where the object is to provide for the maintenance of the applicant, the power to award a lump sum is particularly important where the estate is small, and the income produced is negligible.

(c) An order for the transfer to the applicant of property.[7] This power can be used in respect of both property which the deceased owned, and, in the case of action taken under the anti-avoidance provisions,[8] property which is owned by others.

(d) An order for the settlement of property for the benefit of the applicant.[9] Again, this can be property which the deceased owned, or, exceptionally, property owned by others.

(e) An order for the acquisition out of property comprised in the estate of other property, and for the transfer of that other property to the applicant, or for the settlement of that other property.[10] Under this provision the court might order the personal representatives to purchase a house, or an annuity for the applicant, and to transfer that asset to the applicant.

(f) An order for the variation of a settlement[11] made on the parties to a marriage to which the deceased was one of the parties.[12] The variation must be for the benefit of the surviving party to that marriage, or any child of that marriage, or any person who was treated by the deceased as a child of the family in relation to that marriage.

These powers correspond to the powers which the court has in making financial provision in matrimonial proceedings.

1 1975 Act, s 2(1)(a).
2 Ibid, s 2(2).
3 Ibid, s 2(2), (3).
4 Ibid, s 2(1)(a).
5 Ibid, s 19(2).
6 Ibid, s 2(1)(b).
7 Ibid, s 2(1)(c).
8 Ibid, ss 10, 11: see below, para 15.33.
9 Ibid, s 2(1)(d).
10 Ibid, s 2(1)(e).
11 Whether ante-nuptial or post-nuptial, and whether or not made by will.
12 1975 Act, s 2(1)(f).

14.87 The court also has power to order an applicant to make an adjusting payment into the estate. Thus, in *Re Kozdrach*[1] the court made an order for the transfer to the applicant of a house in which she had lived with the deceased on condition that she paid £9,000 into the estate.

1 [1981] Conv 224.

Supplementary orders

14.88 In addition to these specific powers, the court has a very wide power to include in any order such supplemental provisions as it thinks fit.[1] An example under the previous legislation of how this power might be exercised is *Re Lidington, Lidington v Thomas*,[2] where the court made an order in favour of the deceased's widow on condition that she continued to maintain the deceased's infant children.[3] A further example could be that if the court gave a house to the applicant, it might give the devisee some compensating benefit.

1 1975 Act, s 6.
2 [1940] Ch 927.
3 See also *Re Pointer, Pointer and Shonfield v Edwards* [1941] Ch 60, [1940] 4 All ER 372.

Index-linked orders

14.89 The power of the court to award periodical payments is probably wide enough to enable the court to make an order for the payment of an annual amount which automatically increases with changes in the Index of Retail Prices. Such orders are being made in some Commonwealth jurisdictions,[1] but there is no reported case in which the English court has done so.

1 *Re Z* [1979] 2 NZLR 495 (New Zealand Court of Appeal); *White v Barron* (1980) 30 ALR 51 (High Court of Australia); *Goodman v Windeyer* (1980) 31 ALR 23 (High Court of Australia).

Interim orders

14.90 Where an applicant is in immediate need of financial assistance, he can apply for an interim order, and the court has power to make provision for him even though the merits of the substantive application have not been determined.[1] Before making such an order, the court must be satisfied that there is property forming part of the net estate of the deceased which can be made available to meet the needs of the applicant.[2]

1 1975 Act, s 5.
2 Ibid, s 5(1)(b).

14.91 Upon making an interim order, the court is entitled to impose such conditions as it thinks fit, for example by requiring the repayment to the estate of the amount provided if the substantive application is subsequently rejected.

14.92 As the making of an application has the practical effect of freezing the estate until it is dealt with, it is unsatisfactory that beneficiaries under the will who are in immediate financial need do not themselves have the power to apply for an order for an interim distribution of payments.[1]

1 See the remarks of Cross J in *Re Ralphs* [1968] 3 All ER 285.

Variation of orders

14.93 Where the court has made an order for periodical payments to be made to an applicant, the court has a wide power to vary that order.[1] However, the variation can affect only property from which the income is being used to make periodical payments[2] and on an application to vary an order, no new property can be brought into the net estate.[3]

1 1975 Act, s 6.
2 Ibid, s 6(2), (6).
3 Ibid, s 6(9).

14.94 An application for the variation of an order can be made by the applicant; by any person who would be entitled to make an application even if he did not do so originally; the personal representatives; any persons affected as trustees; and any beneficiary under the will as drawn by the testator, or any person who would be entitled under the intestacy rules.[1]

1 1975 Act, ss 6(5), 25(1).

Time limit

The general rule

14.95 As a general rule, an application must be made to the court within six months from the date when probate or letters of administration to the deceased's estate are first taken out.[1] For this purpose, a grant limited to settled land[2] is left out of account.[3] If there are separate grants to real estate and to personal estate, the first grant is also left out of account.[4] Accordingly, the time limit runs from the date when there is for the first time a grant to the whole of the deceased's general estate.

1 1975 Act, s 4.
2 As to grants limited to settled land, see below, para 24.11.
3 1975 Act, s 23.
4 Ibid.

14.96 It was held under the previous legislation that where a grant of administration is made because no will is found, but that grant is subsequently revoked because a will comes to light, the six-month period runs from the date of the grant of probate.[1] It remains to be seen whether this decision would be followed under the present legislation. It is, however, clear that where a will is proved in common form, and is subsequently proved in solemn form[2] the six-month period runs from the date of the original grant in common form.[3] The reason for the time limit is to enable the personal representatives to distribute the estate with reasonable expedition.

1 *Re Bidie, Bidie v General Accident Fire and Life Assurance Corpn Ltd* [1949] Ch 121, [1948] 2 All ER 995, CA.
2 As to grants in solemn form, see below, paras 24.4–24.10.
3 *Re Miller, Miller v de Courcey* [1968] 3 All ER 844.

Late applications

14.97 An application can be made after the expiration of the six-month period only with the permission of the court.[1] The 1975 Act does not specify the grounds on which the court may grant permission, but the following principles emerge from the cases.
(a) The discretion is unfettered, and is to be exercised judicially in accordance with what is just and proper.[2]
(b) The time limit is a substantive requirement, and not one of procedure only. The time limit will not, therefore, be extended lightly.[3]
(c) The onus is on the potential applicant to show that there are sufficient grounds for the case to be taken outside the general rule, and so deprive the beneficiaries who are protected by it.
(d) It is material to consider how promptly the application is made, and how promptly the potential applicant warns the personal representatives, perhaps by letter, that an application will be made. Thus, if the warning is given within the six-month time limit, but for some good reason the proceedings are not commenced until a short while after time runs out, the court is likely to extend the time.
(e) It is also material to consider whether negotiations had been entered into with a view to settling the potential applicant's claim. If negotiations had been commenced within the time limit, and time had run out while they were proceeding, the court is likely to extend the time. Further, if negotiations were commenced after the expiry of the time limit without any of the parties affected taking the point that time had expired, that might also encourage the court to extend the time.
(f) It is material to consider whether or not the estate had been distributed before a claim under the Act is made or notified. The end of the six months marks a change from a period where any distribution by the personal representatives is made at their own risk[4] to a period when there is statutory protection for the distribution.[5]
(g) If, in the event of the court refusing to extend the time, the potential applicant would have a remedy against someone else, that may encourage the court to refuse to extend the time. This usually arises where the potential applicant consulted a solicitor in good time, but the solicitor failed to commence the application within the six-month period.[6]
(h) It is also material to consider whether, in the event of the court extending the time, the substantive application is likely to succeed.[7]
These principles are not exhaustive.[8]

1 1975 Act, s 4.
2 *Re Ruttie, Ruttie v Saul* [1969] 3 All ER 1633, [1970] 1 WLR 89. Principles (a) to (g) were all

enunciated in *Re Salmon, Coard v National Westminster Bank Ltd* [1981] Ch 167, [1980] 3 All ER 532 by Megarry V-C.
3 See also *Re Gonin, Gonin v Garmeson* [1979] Ch 16, [1977] 2 All ER 720.
4 *Re Simson, Simson v National Provincial Bank Ltd* [1950] Ch 38, [1949] 2 All ER 826.
5 1975 Act, s 20(2).
6 *Re Greaves, Greaves v Greaves* [1954] 2 All ER 109; *Re Bone, Bone v Midland Bank Ltd* [1955] 2 All ER 555; *Re Trott, Trott v Miles* [1958] 2 All ER 296; *Re McNare, McNare v McNare* [1964] 3 All ER 373; *Re Kay, Kay v West* [1965] 3 All ER 724.
7 *Re Dennis, Dennis v Lloyds Bank* [1981] 2 All ER 140.
8 *Re Dennis*, above.

14.98 Although there is no reported decision, it is likely that the principles will be followed where a person wishes to apply to the court to rectify a will[1] and the six-month period has expired.

1 Under s 20 of the Administration of Justice Act 1982; see above, para 5.59.

Protection for personal representatives

14.99 Where the court makes an order varying the provisions of the will, or of the intestacy rules as applicable to the deceased's estate, the personal representatives will be protected for distributing the deceased's estate in accordance with the order; and, indeed, they will be liable if they do not do so.[1]

1 This follows from the general principle that a person is absolutely protected if he acts in accordance with an order under the seal of the court.

14.100 In the case of a substantive order, the court will have investigated the size of the net estate, and its order will be made accordingly, but in the case of an interim application, the court will not necessarily know the extent of the net estate. However, personal representatives will not generally be liable to any creditors or other persons if they make payment in accordance with the court's order, even if the estate subsequently proves to be insufficient to meet all the liabilities.[1] As an exception to this general rule, however, the personal representatives will be liable if at the time of making payment they have reasonable cause to believe that the estate is not sufficient.[2] In this case they should refer the matter back to the court.

1 1975 Act, s 20(2).
2 Ibid.

14.101 Further, personal representatives are not liable for distributing the estate after the six-month period on the ground that they should have taken into account the possibility that an application would be made to the court out of time.[1] Of course, they ought not to make a distribution if proceedings are known to be imminent. The Act does not specifically provide that personal representatives should not distribute within the six-month period, but where there is a person who could make an application they will probably be liable for distributing within that period.[2]

1 1975 Act, s 20(1).
2 See *Re Simson, Simson v National Provincial Bank Ltd* [1950] Ch 38 at 43.

14.102 Under separate provisions, protection is also conferred on persons who are affected by orders made by the court under the anti-avoidance provisions considered in the next chapter. That protection is considered in the context of those provisions.

Nature of applicant's interest

14.103 It seems that a person who is entitled to make an application has no rights in the estate itself until an order is made, when he has the same rights as a beneficiary.[1] The question came before the court in South Australia in *Re Gough's Estate, Gough v Fletcher*.[2] The testator had made provision for his widow, but she made an application seeking further provision. The executor proposed to realise part of the testator's real estate to pay estate duty and other charges, and the applicant sought an injunction to restrain the sale pending the hearing of her application. The court held that the executor 'owes the legal duty to exercise his discretion properly and according to law to the beneficiaries rather than to applicants for testator's family maintenance'. Although laying down this principle, the court granted the injunction because there were other assets available to meet the estate duty and charges, and it appears that the court considered that it was in the interest of the beneficiaries as a whole for the realty not to be sold.[3]

1 As to the nature of the beneficiary's interest generally, see below, paras 29.1ff.
2 (1973) 5 SASR 559.
3 Zelling J managed the sweeping, and untenable, observation that: 'it is obvious that unless compelled to do so, no-one would convert land into money with inflation running at its present rate'.

CHAPTER 15

Safeguarding and defeating the dependants

Introduction

15.1 The family provision legislation is surprisingly unsophisticated. Until the Inheritance (Provision for Family and Dependants) Act 1975 came into force, there was no anti-avoidance legislation, and the testator was left with considerable scope to defeat any likely application by his dependants. The 1975 Act contains certain anti-avoidance provisions, which will be considered in this chapter, but even they leave a determined testator in a position in which he can take a number of steps to defeat the claims of his dependants.[1] First, however, it is proposed to consider one course open to the testator which does not depend on the anti-avoidance provisions at all.

1 See Sherrin 'Defeating the Dependants' [1978] Conv 13; and articles at (1977) 121 Sol Jo 551, and (1979) 123 Sol Jo 661.

Acquisition of foreign domicile

15.2 It has been seen[1] that the court does not have power to intervene if the deceased died domiciled outside England and Wales even if he left property here.[2] He may in any event wish to acquire a foreign domicile for tax or other reasons, but a distant journey is not necessary. Acquisition of a domicile in Jersey, the Isle of Man or even Scotland[3] will be sufficient to oust the jurisdiction of the court.[4] If the deceased takes the simple expedient of acquiring a foreign domicile, it will not be relevant to consider any of the anti-avoidance provisions now to be described.[5]

1 Above, para 14.11.
2 Inheritance (Provision for Family and Dependants) Act 1975, s 1(1).
3 Ibid, s 27(2).
4 It has been shown earlier, at para 14.11, ante, that in other branches of the law anti-avoidance provisions have the effect of deeming a person to be domiciled in England and Wales, even if he is in fact domiciled elsewhere.
5 Although the testator may find that he has jumped out of the frying pan into the fire, as he may be obliged under the relevant foreign law to leave a proportion of his estate to his close family.

Lifetime dispositions

The rule

15.3   Where an application is made to the court under the family provision legislation, the court can make provision only out of the deceased's 'net estate', which is, subject to the qualifications noted earlier,[1] the assets which the deceased owned at the date of his death, after deducting his debts and liabilities. If there was no further provision in the legislation, an obvious way in which the deceased could defeat his dependants would be for him to dispose of all his assets in his lifetime. This situation is dealt with by s 10 of the 1975 Act. It provides that in certain circumstances, where the deceased transferred property in his lifetime, the transferee, as well as the deceased's estate, can be ordered to make financial provision for the applicant. The Act refers to the transferee as the 'donee', and the term is used in this chapter, but it is misleading, because the transferee is still referred to as the donee even if he provided some, but not full, valuable consideration for the disposition.

1   Above, paras 14.76–14.84.

15.4   By virtue of s 10, the court can order the donee to make financial provision for the applicant if it is satisfied that:
(a)   the deceased made a disposition; and
(b)   the deceased made that disposition not less than six years before the date of his death; and
(c)   the deceased made the disposition with the intention of defeating an application for financial provision under the 1975 Act; and
(d)   the deceased was not given full valuable consideration for the disposition; and
(e)   by exercising its powers, the court would facilitate the making of financial provision for the applicant.

Disposition
15.5   On general principles, 'disposition' means the parting with any type of proprietary right. It includes the payment of money, and is widely defined to include also 'any conveyance, assurance, appointment or gift of property of any description, whether made by an instrument or otherwise'.[1] The definitions expressly exclude:
(a)   a provision in a will, because this is subject to the general provisions of legislation;
(b)   a nomination, because this is subject to the special provision of sub-s 8(1);[2]
(c)   a donatio mortis causa, because this is the subject of the special provision of sub-s 8(2);[3]
(d)   an appointment made in the deceased's lifetime in exercise of a special power of appointment. The lifetime exercise of a special power of appointment is excluded even if it arose under a settlement created by the deceased himself.[4]

1   Inheritance (Provision for Family and Dependants) Act 1975, s 10(7).
2   Above, para 14.79.

237

3 Above, para 14.80.
4 See definition of 'net estate': s 25(1): (a), which specifically excludes a special power of appointment. See above, para 14.78.

15.6 In addition to the matters which are expressly excluded from the definition of 'disposition', two other exceptions may be noted:
(a) the creation of liabilities is not itself a disposition;[1] and
(b) if the deceased gave to the person whom he wished to benefit the opportunity to exploit a situation, that would not be a disposition. Suppose that the deceased was in a position to obtain for himself a profitable trading contract with a third party, but arranged for his friend, whom he wished to benefit, to have that contract, he would not be making a disposition in favour of his friend.

1 A separate provision has the effect that the creation of some, but not all, liabilities can be avoided: below, paras 15.24ff.

Date of disposition
15.7 The disposition comes within s 10 only if it was made within six years before the date of the death of the deceased. No rules are prescribed to determine when a disposition is made, but it may well be that where an assurance of a legal estate is preceded by an enforceable and unconditional contract, the disposition will be treated as being made at the time of the contract. Where there is no prior contract, the date of the disposition will be the time it is perfected under the general law. It remains to be decided whether, in the case of a disposition requiring registration, the disposition will be treated as being made when the deceased has done everything which is due for him to do, or only when the registration is completed.[1]

1 *Re Rose, Midland Bank Executor and Trustee Co Ltd v Rose* [1949] Ch 78, [1948] 2 All ER 971; *Re Rose, Rose v IRC* [1952] Ch 499, [1952] 1 All ER 1217, CA; cf *Re Fry, Chase National Executors and Trustee Corpn Ltd v Fry* [1946] Ch 312, [1946] 2 All ER 106.

15.8 The enjoyment of property after a disposition does not affect the disposition.[1] Accordingly if the deceased conveyed his house to his friend more than six years before his death, but continued to live in it until his death, the disposition would be outside the section. Or suppose that more than six years before his death the deceased created a settlement under which he took an interest for life. Even though he enjoyed the settled property until his death, he would be treated as having made the disposition more than six years before his death, so that the disposition into settlement could not be upset. If, when creating the settlement, he conferred on himself a special power of appointment he could direct the destination of the settled property shortly before his death by exercising that power, without the exercise of the power being a disposition.

1 Although it would then be a 'gift with reservation' for inheritance tax purposes, under FA 1986, s 102.
2 See above, para 15.5(d).

15.9 The Act does not apply to dispositions made before 1 April 1976.[1]

1 Inheritance (Provision for Family and Dependants) Act 1975, ss 10(8), 27(3).

Intention
15.10 Section 10 applies only where the disposition was made with the intention of defeating an application for financial provision under the 1975 Act. This condition is satisfied if on the balance of probabilities the court is of the opinion that the deceased intended to defeat an application, or to reduce the amount of the provision which might otherwise be made.[1] It is expressly provided[2] that this need not have been the deceased's only intention in making the disposition.

1 Inheritance (Provision for Family and Dependants) Act 1975, s 12(1).
2 Ibid.

Full valuable consideration
15.11 A disposition, even if made within six years from the date of death of the deceased, and even if made with the intention of defeating an application, will not be within the section if the deceased received full valuable consideration for it. The consideration can have been provided by the donee, or by any other person.[1]

1 Inheritance (Provision for Family and Dependants) Act 1975, s 10(2)(b).

15.12 It seems that if the deceased received consideration, it is to be valued at the time when it was furnished. This is important where benefit is to be enjoyed at some time in the future. Suppose that the deceased has an expectation of life of five years. The present value of a right to receive future property will depend on various factors, including interest rates and investment yields at the time, but the present right to receive £100,000 in five years' time might be worth only £50,000. If, therefore, the deceased sold to his friend for £50,000 the right to receive his house, worth £100,000 on his death, that disposition would be for full valuable consideration and could not be challenged under s 10.

15.13 The expression 'full valuable consideration' is also used in the context of determining whether the deceased was maintaining an applicant[1] and it was shown[2] that an agreement to provide services can be a valuable consideration. Whether that consideration is 'full' depends on the circumstances of the case.

1 Inheritance (Provision for Family and Dependants) Act 1975, s 1(3).
2 Above, para 3.2.

15.14 Marriage is not treated as valuable consideration for this purpose.[1]

1 Inheritance (Provision for Family and Dependants) Act 1975, s 25(1).

Facilitating provision
15.15 The final condition is that the exercise of the powers would facilitate the making of financial provision. All that this appears to mean is that if the donee is worthless, there is no point in the court making an order.

Factors to be considered

15.16 If the conditions just discussed are satisfied, the court is entitled to make an order if it thinks fit. In considering whether and in what manner to exercise its powers, the court is directed to have regard to:[1]
(a) the circumstances in which the disposition was made;
(b) any valuable consideration which was given for it;
(c) the relationship, if any, of the donee to the deceased;
(d) the conduct of the donee;
(e) the financial resources of the donee; and
(f) all the other circumstances of the case.

1 Inheritance (Provision for Family and Dependants) Act 1975, s 10(6).

The order

15.17 Where the court is entitled to exercise its powers, and decides to exercise them, it can order the donee to make financial provision for the applicant, but there are limits on the amount of the provision which the donee can be ordered to make.

Disposition of money

15.18 If the disposition by the deceased was of a sum of money, the donee cannot be required to make greater provision than that sum of money, less any inheritance tax which the donee paid in respect of it.[1] If the donee spent the money, by acquiring an asset which has appreciated, the limit is still the original sum of money. Thus, if the deceased gave to the donee £10,000, and the donee bought a picture which is worth £50,000 by the date of death of the deceased, the donee can be required to provide only £10,000. Likewise, if the donee invested the money, and accumulated the interest, he cannot be required to make provision out of the interest.

1 Inheritance (Provision for Family and Dependants) Act 1975, s 10(3).

Disposition of other property

15.19 If the disposition was of property other than money, the donee can be required to make provision up to the value of the property at the date of death of the deceased, after deducting any inheritance tax which the donee paid in respect of it.[1] The form which the transaction takes can, therefore, be of great importance. Suppose that the deceased wanted to benefit the donee by enabling the donee to travel round the world. If the deceased gave the donee money, the donee can be required to make provision up to the amount of that money under the rule just considered. If, however, the deceased bought the tickets, and gave the tickets to the donee, then provided that the deceased died after the donee had used the tickets, the donee could not be called upon to make any provision. This is because the property which was given, namely the tickets, are worthless at the date of the deceased's death. Similarly, if the deceased gave to the donee a short leasehold property, and that lease runs out before the date of death of the deceased, then even if the donee renews the lease he will not be required to make provision. In this case, the property which was given, namely the original lease, has ceased to exist at the date of death of the deceased, and so it cannot have any value.

1 Inheritance (Provision for Family and Dependants) Act 1975, s 10(4).

15.20 If the deceased wishes to dispose of an appreciating asset, he would usually do better to give the donee money, and allow the donee to purchase the asset from him with that money. This might be achieved simply by a cross-cheque transaction.

Related transactions

15.21 There is no provision under which the court can look at a series of transactions, and base its order on their overall effect.[1] Suppose the deceased has a pair of Ming vases valued individually at £50,000, but as a pair at £250,000. If the deceased gives the donee £100,000 and allows the donee to purchase from him each vase in a separate transaction for £50,000, the donee will have furnished full valuable consideration for each disposition, and the court will have no jurisdiction, even though the effect of the two sales, taken together, is to give the donee a benefit of £150,000.[2]

1 Cf the 'associated operations' provisions in the tax legislation. See, for example, Inheritance Tax Act 1984, s 268.
2 Under ibid, for inheritance tax purposes the deceased would be deemed to have made a transfer of value equivalent to the loss to his estate, ie the full value of £250,000.

Donee parting with property

15.22 The court can make an order where the donee received a sum of money, even if the donee no longer has that money. Likewise, where the donee received property, but has himself disposed of the property, the court can make its order. In this case, the amount of the order is limited to the value of the property at the time the donee disposed of it.[1] If, however, the donee has himself died, and his personal representatives have disposed of the property, they are not liable.[2]

1 Inheritance (Provision for Family and Dependants) Act 1975, s 10(4).
2 Ibid, s 12(4).

Ancillary provisions

15.23 Where the court is asked to order the donee to make provision for the applicant, it may come to light that the deceased made other dispositions which are also capable of being the subject of an order. In this case, either the donee, or any other applicant, can ask the court to make a similar order in respect of those other dispositions.[1] The donee is given this right so that the burden of making financial provision for applicants can be spread fairly among all donees who have had such benefits. The court also has a wide power to make supplemental orders for securing a fair adjustment of the rights of all persons affected.[2]

1 Inheritance (Provision for Family and Dependants) Act 1975, s 10(5).
2 Ibid, s 12(3).

Contracts to leave property by will

Introduction

15.24 It will be appreciated that there are two main elements in the concept of the net estate: first, the deceased's gross assets, and secondly his liabilities. The provision just discussed is related to attempts by the deceased to reduce the net estate by removing some of the gross assets. The provision now to be considered is related to attempts to reduce the net estate by increasing liabilities. It has been seen[1] that, in general, a contract to leave property by will is interpreted as an obligation to procure that the property will pass to the promisee in any event. The obligation is a liability of the estate, and must be discharged before the net estate is ascertained.[2] Accordingly, a person might seek to avoid the claims of his dependants by entering into lifetime obligations that property will be transferred on death to those whom he wishes to benefit. Section 11 of the 1975 Act is designed to nullify such attempts.

1 Above, paras 3.1ff.
2 *Schaefer v Schuhmann* [1972] AC 572, [1972] 1 All ER 621, PC.

The rule

15.25 Section 11 provides that if certain conditions are satisfied, the court can modify the effect of a contract entered into by the deceased to leave his property by will. These conditions are that:[1]
(a) the deceased made a contract by which he agreed either to leave a sum of money, or property, to a person by his will, *or* that a sum of money or property would be paid or transferred to a person out of his estate; and
(b) the contract was made with the intention of defeating an application for financial provision under the 1975 Act; and
(c) at the time when the contract was made, full valuable consideration was not given or promised by the donee; and
(d) by exercising its powers the court would facilitate the making of financial provision for the applicant.

1 Inheritance (Provision for Family and Dependants) Act 1975, s 11(2).

The contract
15.26 It will be appreciated that, curiously, the Act does not extend to all contracts, but only those which relate to the passing of property on death. It seems that for the purposes of this legislation, a person can have an 'estate' only on death.[1] Accordingly, a contract to transfer property in one's lifetime is not within the provision. More surprisingly, the creation of any other type of liability is not within the provision, even if it was for the purpose of defeating the dependants.

1 See Inheritance (Provision for Family and Dependants) Act 1975, ss 2(1); 25(1); 25(2);

25(3). Cf the definition of 'estate' for inheritance tax purposes: Inheritance Tax Act 1984, s 5.

15.27 Accordingly, as the net estate of a person is ascertained by deducting all liabilities,[1] whether or not they were created for full consideration, and the creation of an obligation or liability to be given effect to in a person's lifetime is not within the anti-avoidance provisions relating to dispositions[2] or to contracts to leave property by will,[3] a person can, for example, enter into a deed of covenant to pay to the donee in his lifetime a sum of money which exceeds his total net asset value. As payment will not be made, on death it seems that the covenantee will have the benefit of a liability which must be satisfied before the 'net estate' is ascertained. To this statement, however, there is one caveat. In reading the majority opinion in *Schaefer v Schuhmann* Lord Cross observed[4] that: 'Whether contracts made by a testator not with a view to excluding the jurisdiction of the court under the Act[5] but in the normal course of arranging his affairs in his lifetime should be liable to be wholly or partially set aside by the court under legislation of this character is a question of social policy on which different people may reasonably take different views.' The purport of this dictum may be incontrovertible, but Lord Cross slips in the distinction between contracts made with a view to excluding the jurisdiction of the court, and contracts made in the normal course of arranging one's affairs. But he gave no indication of how the distinction should be drawn, or operated. A person who wishes to create a genuine liability, but solely for the purpose of defeating the dependants, is now on notice that the courts will seek to find a loophole in favour of the dependants. Whether they will be able to do so remains to be seen.

1 Inheritance (Provision for Family and Dependants) Act 1975, s 25(1).
2 Above, para 15.4.
3 Above, para 15.25.
4 [1972] AC 572 at 600.
5 The Act was the Testator's Family Maintenance and Guardianship of Infants Act 1916–1954, of New South Wales.

Time limit
15.28 By contrast to s 10, which applies only where the disposition was made within six years from the date of death, s 11 applies irrespective of the period of time which elapsed between when the contract was made and the date of death. It does not, however, apply where the contract was made before 1 April 1976.[1]

1 Inheritance (Provision for Family and Dependants) Act 1975, ss 11(6); 27(3).

Intention
15.29 As in the case of a disposition of property, it is only necessary for the court to be satisfied that on the balance of probabilities the deceased intended to defeat an application under the Act, or to reduce the amount which would otherwise be available; and the contract is caught by the section even if the deceased had other intentions as well.[1] Where no consideration was given or promised when the contract was made, the court is required to presume that the contract was made with the intention of

defeating an application, although this presumption is capable of being rebutted.[2]

1 Inheritance (Provision for Family and Dependants) Act 1975, s 12(1).
2 Ibid, s 12(2).

Full valuable consideration

15.30 Section 11 does not apply where the contract was for full valuable consideration, given or promised. It seems that if the donee promised consideration, but did not fulfil that promise, the section will still not operate.[1] Apart from this, the position is the same as that in respect of dispositions of property.[2]

1 Inheritance (Provision for Family and Dependants) Act 1975, s 11(2)(c).
2 Above, paras 15.11–15.14.

Facilitating provision

15.31 This condition is the same as in the case of dispositions of property.[1]

1 Above, para 15.15.

Factors to be considered

15.32 In determining whether and in what manner to exercise its powers, the court is to have regard to the circumstances in which the contract was made, the relationship, if any, of the donee to the deceased, the conduct and financial resources of the donee and all the other circumstances of the case.[1] Although not specifically mentioned, one of the most relevant circumstances will be the value of any consideration furnished, even if it was not full consideration.

1 Inheritance (Provision for Family and Dependants) Act 1975, s 11(4).

The order

Payment made or property transferred

15.33 Personal representatives are not required to delay the administration of an estate in case an application is made, and they are expressly exonerated from liability if they distribute property before they have notice of the making of an application.[1] It may well be, therefore, that payment will have been made, or property transferred, in pursuance of the contract before the court makes its order. In this case the court can order the donee to make financial provision for the applicant.[2] If a sum of money was paid, the donee cannot be ordered to provide more than that sum.[3] If property has been transferred, the provision cannot exceed the value of the property but in this case, the property is valued at the date of the hearing.[4] If the donee furnished consideration, the amount or value of that consideration must be deducted from the sum of money or value of the property.

1 Inheritance (Provision for Family and Dependants) Act 1975, s 12(4).
2 Ibid, s 11(2). If the personal representatives have distributed, assets can be traced into the hands of the beneficiaries.
3 Ibid, s 11(3).
4 Ibid.

Payment not made, or property not transferred

15.34 Where the money has not been paid, or the property has not been transferred, the order consists of a direction to the personal representatives either not to pay or transfer, or to pay or transfer only a specified amount.[1] The personal representatives are fully protected by complying with such a direction.[2] Where an order is made, the court can make supplemental provisions for securing a fair adjustment of the rights of the persons affected.[3]

1 Inheritance (Provision for Family and Dependants) Act 1975, s 11(2).
2 Ibid, s 11(5).
3 Ibid, s 12(3).

Third party asset holding

15.35 An effective way for a person to defeat applications under the Act is to ensure that he never owns certain assets, even if arrangements are made for him to benefit from them, and even if he has control over them. Suppose, for example, that a person sets up a trust with a nominal sum of £5, and under the terms of the trust (a) the income is payable to him for life, (b) the trustees have power to release capital to him and (c) he has a restricted power of appointment.[1] Suppose also that that person is one of the trustees or, even,[2] the sole trustee. Suppose then that that person arranges that money-making possibilities which become available are exploited not by him personally but by the trustees of the trust. Even if he is not the sole trustee, he is in practice likely to be able to influence the manner in which the trust property is applied, and to retain a substantial measure of control over it. However, the assets subject to the trust will never have formed part of his estate, so that the court will be powerless to make an order in respect of it.

1 The power must not be a general testamentary power: see s 25 of the 1975 Act, and above, para 14.78.
2 Although this might be too provocative to the court.

15.36 A significant proportion of the population is already, unwittingly, in a somewhat comparable position. Most private sector pension schemes are based on discretionary trusts, but the provisions of the pension scheme may well confer upon the member of the scheme benefits of a value greater than the whole of his own personal capital. However, in the case of the usual scheme the court will not be able to interfere with the discretion of the trustees of the pension fund.[1]

1 Most such schemes provide an automatic pension for the surviving spouse and payment for children of the deceased who are minors. If the deceased dies before drawing his pension, however, a capital payment is made by the trustees to such person as the deceased may have nominated in his lifetime. See further, and for a statement of the position with regard to

public sector schemes, Rosettenstein 'Occupational Pensions and the 1975 Inheritance Act' (1979) 123 Sol Jo 661.

Abnegation of moral responsibility

15.37 It has been seen[1] that in *Re Beaumont, Martin v Midland Bank Trust Co Ltd*[2] Megarry V-C said that for a person in the fifth category to succeed, he must show not only that the deceased maintained him, but also that the deceased assumed a responsibility to maintain him. The Court of Appeal in *Jelley v Iliffe*[3] said that the bare fact of maintenance usually raises a presumption that the deceased assumed a responsibility for maintaining the applicant, but there was no suggestion that this presumption could not be rebutted. Accordingly, it seems that a person who is proposing to maintain another can defeat a possible application by that other by making it clear at the outset that he does not undertake any responsibility for maintaining him.[4]

1 Above, paras 14.31–14.32.
2 [1980] Ch 444, [1980] 1 All ER 266; above, para 14.31.
3 [1981] Fam 128, [1981] 2 All ER 29, CA.
4 See Cadwallader 'Inheritance Act Applications by Financial Dependants: a Loophole?' (1981) 125 Sol Jo 175.

15.38 A similar result is likely to be achieved where the deceased and the applicant agree that they shall be free to deal with their own property on death as they wish. This will not exclude the court's jurisdiction, but the court is unlikely to make an order in favour of the applicant.[1]

1 See eg *Re Beaumont* [1980] Ch 444, [1980] 1 All ER 266; above, para 14.31. See also *Re Marquis' Estate* [1980] 30 NBR (2d) 93 (New Brunswick), where a man and woman married late in life, and expressly agreed that on death their estates would pass to their children, and not to each other. The man died leaving only his personal effects to the wife. The court refused to make an order in favour of the wife.

15.39 For the person who forgot to establish either of these bases at the commencement of a relationship, the moral is to follow *Kourgy v Lusher*[1] and to abandon the responsibility for maintaining the applicant shortly before death.

1 (1981) 4 FLR 65; above, para 14.29.

PART V

Probate

CHAPTER 16

Grants of representation

Introduction

16.1 A grant of representation is an order of the court which confirms or confers the authority of the personal representatives to administer the estate of the deceased, and which indicates the terms on which the estate is to be administered. In every case the grant issues under the court seal and so takes effect as a court order, even though in most cases grants are obtainable by a quasi-administrative process of lodging certain documents, described later, at the offices of the Principal Registry of the Family Division of the High Court at Somerset House, or at the offices of the district registries of the High Court, or at probate sub-registries.

16.2 There are several types of grant, all of which are described in detail later, but they fall into three broad categories:
(a) probate, which can be issued only where there is a will, and only to one or more of the executors named in the will;
(b) administration with will annexed (usually known as administration cum testamento annexo), which is issued where there is a will, but no proving executors;
(c) administration, which is issued where there is an intestacy.

16.3 Where an executor is appointed by the will, and subsequently takes out probate, his authority dates from the death of the testator, so that in his case the grant of probate confirms his authority. In the other cases, the personal representative has no authority prior to the grant, and derives his authority from the grant itself.[1] But in either case, the personal representative can prove his authority only by production of his grant.

1 The date on which a personal representative acquires his authority may be critical. For example, an administrator is unable to commence an action on behalf of the estate until the grant of administration has been issued: *Ingall v Moran* [1944] KB 160, [1944] 1 All ER 97. See below, paras 25.16–25.19.

16.4 As well as establishing the personal representative's authority, the grant of representation also indicates the terms on which the estate is to be administered. In the case of probate or letters of administration with the will annexed, the court must be satisfied that the last effective will or wills of the deceased have been deposited with it, and when these types of grants are issued, a copy of the will is attached to the grant. In the case of a total intestacy, the court must be satisfied that the person applying for the grant is the person entitled to it under the Probate Rules.[1]

1 Non-contentious Probate Rules 1987, rr 20 and 22.

16.5 Where a copy of the will is attached to a grant, that copy is the only document on which the personal representatives and all others interested can rely. If, therefore, part of the will of the deceased was invalid because, for example, it did not comply with the formal requirements of the Wills Act 1837, or because it was the product of an insane delusion, that part will be omitted from the probate copy. Likewise, where a question of construction arises, the Chancery Division has regard not to the will as actually written by the deceased, but to the probate copy of the will.

16.6 Because any grant is an order of the court, both the personal representative named in it, and any purchaser from him, are fully protected, even if it should not have been issued. If, therefore, a later will is found, a grant of probate of the earlier will remains fully effective until it is revoked by a further order of the court.

16.7 A person to whom probate has been granted is known as the executor. A person acting under a grant of letters of administration with will annexed, or of letters of administration simpliciter, is known as an administrator. Both executors and administrators are known as personal representatives.

16.8 To conclude this general introduction, it may assist to give an illustration of a grant of probate and of a grant of letters of administration simpliciter (see Appendix C). A copy of the will as proved is attached to the probate, for that is the executor's authority as to the manner in which the estate is to be distributed, but the copy is not shown in the illustration. Examples of the oaths leading to these grants are shown in Appendix C.

Historical background

16.9 It was a natural extension of the jurisdiction of the church courts over the administration of wills of personal property that they should also deal with disputes as to the validity of wills. The origin of this jurisdiction cannot be traced with certainty, but by the late twelfth or early thirteenth century, the church courts are found pronouncing as to the validity of wills.[1] At the beginning of the fifteenth century, the jurisdiction of the church courts was accepted to the extent that the common law courts treated as conclusive a grant of probate, that is, the declaration that the will had been proved to the satisfaction of the bishop as being the last effective will of the deceased.[2] The Court of Chancery made an undetermined attempt to encroach upon the jurisdiction of the church courts, but fairly quickly concentrated on questions of interpretation, leaving the jurisdiction to grant probate firmly in the hands of the church courts. The only rivals to the church courts were certain local courts, such as the London Court of the Hustings, which had customary testamentary jurisdiction. A will was normally proved in the Court of the Ordinary, that is, the bishop, of the place where the testator resided, but in certain circumstances grants were issued by the court of the archbishop of the province.

1 Holdsworth, HEL, Vol I, 625–626, 640; Pollock & Maitland, HEL, Vol II, 339, 340; Plucknett *Concise History of the Common Law* (8th edn) 740.
2 Holdsworth, HEL, Vol III, 539, 540.

16.10 It first became possible to make a will of realty in 1540,[1] but the common law courts recognised only the will itself as evidence of the devise.[2] There was no common law equivalent of probate for wills of realty. Where the same will governed both realty and personalty, the church courts granted probate, but the common law courts continued to pay regard, in respect of the realty, only to the will itself.

1 Above, para 14.7.
2 Accordingly freehold property passed direct to the devisee from the date of death – until the Land Transfer Act 1897, see para 23.1.

16.11 By the Court of Probate Act 1857, the jurisdiction of the church courts and of such local courts as exercised testamentary jurisdiction was transferred to the newly-created Court of Probate, which was thenceforth the only court in which the validity of wills of personalty could be challenged, or in which grants of probate could be obtained. The Court of Probate was not given jurisdiction to grant probate of wills of realty only, though where probate of a will of realty and personalty was granted in solemn form[1] this was accepted as evidence of a devise of realty. The jurisdiction of the Court of Probate was transferred by the Judicature Act 1873 to the Probate, Divorce and Admiralty Division of the High Court. The position with regard to wills of realty was made the same as that with regard to personalty by the Land Transfer Act 1897, which required a grant of probate for wills of realty, and provided that such grant should be conclusive. The relevant provisions of the Judicature Act 1873 and the Land Transfer Act 1897 were subsequently repealed and re-enacted, and now appear as s 25 of the Supreme Court Act 1981.

1 Ie proved as a result of proceedings. See below, para 20.4, for the distinction between proof in common form and proof in solemn form.

16.12 The last change was effected by the Administration of Justice Act 1970, which renamed the Probate, Divorce and Admiralty Division the Family Division. Logically, all probate business should be assigned to the Chancery Division, but this, apparently, would have caused too much administrative inconvenience. Thus, all non-contentious probate business continues to be dealt with in the Family Division and contentious business in the Chancery Division.

CHAPTER 17

The appointment of executors and administrators

17.1 This chapter is concerned with the persons who are entitled to one of the three basic types of grant of representation, namely, probate, letters of administration, or letters of administration with will annexed. The persons who are entitled to special types of grant are described in chapter 19.

Executors

17.2 An executor is a person appointed by will to administer the property of the testator and to carry into effect the provisions of the will.[1] In the same way as a trustee, an executor should be appointed for his personal qualities, such as his knowledge of the deceased's family and affairs, his trustworthiness and business acumen, and his general common sense. As a result of the personal nature of the appointment, two rules emerge:

(a) in principle, an executor can be appointed only by the testator, in his will; and

(b) the office is personal, and so can be exercised only by the person appointed by the will.

There are, however, exceptions to both principles.

1 This is the definition of *Williams on Wills* (6th edn) p 172.

Appointment of executors otherwise than by the testator

The exceptional circumstances in which an executor can be appointed otherwise than by the testator himself are now considered.

By nominated person

17.3 A testator may, instead of appointing an executor himself, nominate some other person to make the appointment.[1] This power to nominate must be given in an instrument executed as a will. The power may indicate the persons who may or may not be nominated, but in the absence of any provision to the contrary in the power, the person who is given the power may nominate himself.[2] Although the power to appoint an executor can be delegated, the power to make a will cannot.

1   *Re Cringan's Goods* (1828) 1 Hag Ecc 548; *Jackson and Gill v Paulet* (1851) 2 Rob Eccl 344.
2   *Re Ryder's Goods* (1861) 2 Sw & Tr 127.

During minority or life interest

17.4   Although, as will be shown, where a minority or life interest arises a grant of letters of administration can be granted only to two or more administrators,[1] there is no such rule affecting executors. Accordingly, a grant of probate can be made to a sole executor even if a minority or life interest arises under the will. However, in the case of a grant of probate in such circumstances, the person entitled to a life interest, or the guardian of a minor who is interested, may apply to the court for the appointment of a co-executor, and the court has a discretion to make such an appointment.[2]

1   Supreme Court Act 1981, s 114(2).
2   Ibid, s 114(4).

In respect of settled land

17.5   The curious provisions as to special personal representatives in respect of settled land are considered later.[1] In general terms, the testator may appoint as special personal representatives the persons who are the trustees for the purposes of the Settled Land Act 1925, and if he does not do so, he is deemed to have appointed them.[2] This is the only statutory provision under which a person is ever 'deemed' to be appointed as executor. Special personal representatives, or any person entitled to a beneficial interest under the settlement, may apply to the court for the appointment of a special personal representative if there is none, or an additional personal representative if there is only one, and the court has a discretion to make such appointment.[3]

1   Below, paras 24.11–24.14.
2   Administration of Estates Act 1925, s 22.
3   Ibid, s 23(2).

Chain of representation

17.6   Section 7 of the Administration of Estates Act 1925 provides[1] that an executor of a sole or last surviving executor of a testator is also the executor of that testator. Suppose that A and B take out a grant of probate of the will of X. On the death of A, B carries on as sole executor. If on B's death C takes out a grant of probate of B's will, C will be B's executor by virtue of the grant, and also A's executor by virtue of s 7, where he is described as being an executor by representation to A's estate. The result would be the same if B was from the outset X's sole executor. The reasoning – which is specious – for this rule is that just as X had full confidence in his own choice of executors, so he ought to have like confidence in their choice of successor.

1   In sub-s (1).

17.7   There are two aspects of this principle:
(a)   so long as the chain of representation is unbroken, the last executor in the chain is the executor of every preceding testator;[1] and
(b)   a proving executor automatically becomes executor by representation of every preceding testator, and he cannot accept one executorship and refuse any preceding executorship.[2] In the example just postulated, C must either renounce completely, or accept the executorship of both X and B.

1   Administration of Estates Act 1925, s 7(2).
2   *Re Perry's Goods* (1840) 2 Curt 655; *Brooke v Haymes* (1868) LR 6 Eq 25.

17.8   An executor by representation is in the same position as the original executor. He thus has the same rights in respect of the estate of the original testator as the original executor would have had were he still living, and he is accountable to the same extent.[1]

1   Administration of Estates Act 1925, s 7(4). See further (1980) 77 Law Soc Gaz 265.

17.9   The chain of representation applies only to a succession of proving executors. The chain is therefore broken:
(a)   by an intestacy; or
(b)   in the event of a testator making a will, by his failure to appoint an executor under that will; or
(c)   by the failure of a person appointed executor to prove the will,[1] unless there is another executor of that will who does prove; or
(d)   where there is *any* difference in the number of executors.
This last point may be illustrated by a further example. Suppose that Edward dies, appointing Fred and George to be his executors. Suppose also that only George proves the will, and that he dies leaving Henry his proving executor. Henry becomes the executor by representation of Edward. If Fred dies, or renounces probate, Henry's position is secure. If, however, Fred subsequently proves the will with George[2] the identity of representatives is broken at that time, and Henry will then cease to be executor by representation of Edward's estate.

1   Administration of Estates Act 1925, s 7(3). The practice of the church courts in such cases was to grant letters of administration cum testamento annexo (see *Thomas v Baker* (1753) 1 Lee 341). However, this practice will probably not now be followed. In the Canadian case *Re Sharon* [1979] 5 WWR 547, a testator died having made a will appointing two executors, but neither proved the will. One of the persons appointed as executor himself died, and his executor sought probate of the testator's will. The court refused to make a grant.

2   The original grant would have reserved him the power to prove at some subsequent time: see below, para 17.20.

17.10   Where a person obtains a limited grant of probate[1] and he dies, appointing a full executor who proves, that executor is the executor by representation of the original testator.[2] On the other hand, if a person takes a limited grant to the estate of a full executor, he does not become the executor by representation of the original testator.[3]

1   Below, para 19.7.
2   *Re Beer's Goods* (1851) 2 Rob Eccl 349.
3   *Re Bayne's Goods* (1858) 1 Sw & Tr 132; *Re Bridger's Goods* (1878) 4 PD 77.

17.11   If, during the minority of a beneficiary, or the subsistence of a life interest, the court appoints[1] an additional personal representative to act with him, that additional personal representative is not included in the chain of representation.[2]

1   Under Supreme Court Act 1981, s 114(4).
2   Ibid, s 114(5).

17.12   Where a Scottish confirmation is obtained,[1] that does not operate as a grant of probate for the purposes of this rule so that a Scottish grant will not cause the chain of representation to pass through it.[2] It appears, however, that a Northern Ireland grant of probate is treated as a grant of probate.[3]

1   See below, para 18.61.
2   Administration of Estates Act 1971, s 1(3).
3   Ibid, s 1(4).

17.13   The rule is of considerable practical importance. If a person becomes executor by representation, he becomes so automatically, and no further formality is required. If a deceased's estate is not fully administered, and there is no executor by representation, the whole procedure of a new grant – in this case letters of administration de bonis non[1] – must be followed.

1   See below, paras 19.12–19.18.

The office of executor

Personal nature

17.14   The general principle mentioned at the beginning of this chapter, that the office of executor is personal, is shown by the fact that it is non-assignable.[1] Even if the executor employs agents to carry out part of the work[2] he must always make the executive decisions.[3] The general rule is broken by the operation of the chain of representation, which in effect causes a devolution of the office.

1 *Re Galbraith's Goods* [1951] P 422; *Re Skinner* [1958] 3 All ER 273.
2 Under Trustee Act 1925, s 23.
3 Parker and Mellows *The Modern Law of Trusts* (3rd edn) p 239.

Persons who may be appointed

17.15 A testator may appoint whoever he likes to be his executor. Thus, he can appoint a minor, a person of unsound mind, a bankrupt[1] or a foreigner.[2] If the person under this incapacity is one of two or more executors, probate is granted to the others, with power reserved[3] to the one under disability to prove when the disability ceases. If he is the sole executor, a grant of administration is made to his guardian or other person on his behalf. He may still apply for probate when the disability ceases.[4]

1 *R v Raines* (1698) Carth 457; *Hill v Mills* (1691) 1 Show 293. This is subject to the Wills Act 1968, s 1(1).
2 Status of Aliens Act 1914, s 17, as amended.
3 See below, para 19.38.
4 See below, paras 19.29 and 19.36.

17.16 Special rules apply where the person appointed is an infant or person of unsound mind. So far as an infant is concerned, probate cannot be issued until he reaches the age of 18[1] and his appointment as executor by the will does not give him any interest in the deceased's property until probate is granted subsequent to his attaining 18.[2] Accordingly, he cannot even dispose of such items as personal chattels for which a grant is not normally required.[3] Similarly, probate will not issue to a person of unsound mind or to a person suffering from some physical disability if the court is satisfied that he is incapable of managing his affairs.[4]

1 Supreme Court Act 1981, s 118.
2 Ibid.
3 See below, ch 25.
4 Non-contentious Probate Rules 1987, r 35.

17.17 A corporation sole[1] may be an executor.[2] Where a corporation aggregate which is a trust corporation is appointed, the grant of probate may be to that corporation in its own name and it may act as a sole executor, or jointly with an individual executor.[3] In the case of a corporation aggregate which is not a trust corporation, it cannot take a grant in its own name, but probate will be granted to its nominee.[4] However, before such grant is issued, it must be shown that the corporation has power under its constitution to act as personal representative[5] and it is necessary to lodge with the court a copy of the resolution appointing the nominee.[6]

1 For example, the bishop for the time being of a diocese.
2 *Re Haynes' Goods* (1842) 3 Curt 75.
3 Supreme Court Act 1981, s 115(1). The rule also applies to bodies incorporated in other EC states if they comply with certain conditions: Public Trustee (Custodian Trustee) Rules 1975; *Re Bigger* [1977] Fam 203, [1977] 2 All ER 644.
4 *Re Hunt's Goods* [1896] P 288; Non-contentious Probate Rules 1987, r 36(1),(2).
5 *Practice Direction* [1956] 1 All ER 305, [1956] 1 WLR 127 and Non-Contentious Probate Rules 1987, r 36(1).

6 Non-contentious Probate Rules 1987, r 36(2)(b), unless the nominee holds an official
position and his name is included in a list filed with the senior district judge: ibid, r 36(2)(a).

17.18 Where an unincorporated body is appointed, such as a firm of
solicitors, in the absence of a contrary intention shown on the face of the
will, the grant is made to partners of the firm at the date of death.[1]

1 *Re Horgan* [1971] P 50, [1969] 3 All ER 1570; cf *Re Fernie's Goods* (1849) 6 Notes of Cases
657. Care should be taken, however, not to appoint 'one of the partners' of the firm as this
would fail for uncertainty.

Numbers of executors

17.19 A testator may appoint only one executor, and in that case that
executor will have full power to deal with the estate. He may appoint any
number of executors, but probate can only be granted to four executors in
respect of the same property.[1] Subject to this principle, there is no
restriction on numbers. So, four persons can be appointed executors in
respect of personal property and four persons to deal with realty, or the
assets can be split between them in any other way the testator wishes. In *Re
Holland's Estate*[2] a testator appointed four persons to be his general
executors, and a fifth to be his literary executor. Bucknill J, on appeal from
the registrar, refused to grant probate save and except the literary works to
the four, and to grant probate limited to literary works to the fifth, on the
ground that under the will the general executors were appointed executors
of the whole estate, so that in respect of the literary works there were in fact
five executors.

1 Supreme Court Act 1981, s 114(1).
2 [1936] 3 All ER 13.

17.20 Where more than one person is appointed executor, there need be
no collaboration between them in obtaining a grant. Anyone can apply for
probate without consulting the others.[1] Probate will be granted to that one
alone, with power reserved to the others to prove subsequently. Until such
time as the others prove, the one who has probate has full authority.

1 However, the proving executor or executors must formally give notice to the other
executors of the application for the grant: Non-contentious Probate Rules 1987, r 27(1), (2).

Modes of appointment of executors

Express appointments

17.21 In general, no problem arises with an express appointment. If,
however, the appointment is not clear, the rules which apply to uncertainty
of executor are:
(a) where there is a person who fits exactly the name and description given

in the will, the court will not admit extrinsic evidence to show that some other person was intended;[1]
(b)   the court will always have regard to the surrounding circumstances existing at the time when the will was made; in other words, it will apply the armchair rule;[2]
(c)   extrinsic evidence of the testator's intention will be admitted to identify the executor where there is an ambiguity either on the face of the will, or when the will is considered in the context of the surrounding circumstances.[3]

If the executor is appointed by reference to his office, then in the absence of evidence to the contrary, probate will be granted to the holder of that office at the date of death, and not at the date of the will.[4]

1   *Re Peel's Goods* (1870) LR 2 P & D 46.
2   *Grant v Grant* (1869) LR 2 P & D 8; *Re De Rosaz's Goods* (1877) 2 PD 66; *Re Twohill's Goods* (1879) 3 LR Ir 21; *Re Brake's Goods* (1881) 6 PD 217. See paras 10.47ff.
3   Administration of Justice Act 1982, s 21. See paras 10.51ff.
4   *Re Jones' Estate* (1927) 43 TLR 324.

Implied appointments

17.22   An executor may be appointed by implication, in which case he is known as the 'executor according to the tenor of the will'. For a person to be appointed as executor according to the tenor, it must be shown that the testator intended him to discharge the major functions of an executor. In *Re Adamson*[1] the principal duties of an executor were stated to be:
(a)   getting in the assets of the deceased;
(b)   payment of funeral expenses and debts (including payment of inheritance tax[2]);
(c)   payment of legacies; and
(d)   accounting for the residuary estate.

1   (1875) LR 3 P & D 253.
2   In this case estate duty (a precursor to inheritance tax) was not specifically mentioned. Estate duty was not substantially introduced until the Customs and Inland Revenue Act 1889.

17.23   What the testator envisaged that a person would do is a question of construction, but the following are examples of cases where a person has been held to be so appointed:
(a)   *Re Russell's Goods*,[1] where the testator appointed trustees 'to carry out my will';
(b)   *Re Baylis's Goods*,[2] where a person was given all the testator's personalty, upon trust for sale and conversion, coupled with a direction to pay debts and funeral and testamentary expenses;
(c)   *Re Fawcett's Estate*,[3] where the will contained the words 'all else to be sold and proceeds after death . . . B will do this';
(d)   *Re Cook's Goods*,[4] where a person was appointed 'to pay all my just debts'. This must be carefully distinguished from the situation where a legatee is directed to pay debts, in which case the effect of the will may be only to make the legacies subject to the payment of debts.[5]

A person is not appointed an executor according to the tenor merely because he is the universal or residuary beneficiary.[6]

1   [1892] P 380.
2   (1865) LR 1 P & D 21.
3   [1941] P 85.
4   [1902] P 114. The decision has been followed in *Bradbury v Sparkes* (1979) 22 Nfld & PEIR 163.
5   *Re Murphy's Goods* (1868) 18 LT 63.
6   *Re Jones's Goods* (1861) 2 Sw & Tr 155; *Re Pryse's Goods* [1904] P 301.

17.24   Once it is clear that a person is appointed an executor according to the tenor, hs is in exactly the same position as any other executor. Thus, where a person is expressly appointed executor, and another is appointed executor according to the tenor, probate will be granted to them both.[1]

1   *Re Brown's Goods* (1877) 2 PD 110; *Re Lush's Goods* (1887) 13 PD 20; *Re Wright's Goods* (1908) 25 TLR 15.

Conditional appointments

17.25   An appointment may be made subject to a condition precedent or a condition subsequent. Thus, the appointment may be conditional upon a child attaining a specified age;[1] or upon another named person refusing to act as executor.[2] *Re Lane's Goods*[3] is an example of appointment subject to a condition subsequent. The will provided that if the executor should go abroad, his appointment should lapse, and another should take his place. The court gave effect to this provision.[4]

1   *Re Langford's Goods* (1867) LR 1 P & D 458.
2   *Re Betts's Goods* (1861) 30 LJPM & A 167.
3   (1864) 33 LJPM & A 185; see also *Re Freeman's Estate* (1931) 146 LT 143.
4   See also *Re Kavanagh's Estate* (1977) 16 SASR 342 (South Australia).

Limited appointments

17.26   A testator may appoint executors to deal with property only of a special designation. There may be geographical limitation, such as an appointment to deal with 'all my land in London', or 'all my property in Wales'. The appointment may be limited to 'all my personalty'.[1] An appointment may also be for a limited time. The usual examples are during the absence abroad of another person; during the minority of a child; or during the widowhood of the spouse. The appointment may, however, be limited as regards time in any way, so that it can commence in the future. Thus, an appointment of Simon if and when he shall qualify as a solicitor would be valid.

1   *Re Wallich's Goods* (1864) 3 Sw & Tr 423.

17.27   Special rules apply to settled land.[1]

1   See below, chap 24.

Executor de son tort

17.28 An 'executor de son tort' is a person who acts as if he had been appointed an executor although in fact he is not appointed as such, either expressly or by implication. He cannot obtain a grant of probate. The position of an executor de son tort is considered later.[1]

1 See below, chap 27.

Ineffective appointments

17.29 The court has a discretionary power to refuse to allow a properly appointed executor to take a grant of probate, and to grant to some other person letters of administration cum testamento annexo.[1] This power has been exercised where the person appointed to be the executor is of bad character;[2] where he is imprisoned;[3] and where he is of ill health or unsound mind.[4] The power may also be exercised where there is such hostility between the named executor and the sole or principal beneficiary that the administration of the estate or the interests of that beneficiary are likely to suffer.[5]

1 Supreme Court Act 1981, s 116(1).
2 *Re Wright's Goods* (1898) 79 LT 473.
3 *Re S's Estate* [1968] P 302, [1967] 2 All ER 150.
4 *Re Atherton's Goods* [1892] P 104; *Re Galbraith's Goods* [1951] P 422, [1951] 2 All ER 470n.
5 In *Re Bowerman* (1978) 87 DLR (3d) 597, the testator named his sister as executrix and left his entire estate to his common law wife. As the sister was hostile to the common law wife, the Ontario court granted letters of administration to the common law wife.

Acceptance and renunciation

Acceptance

17.30 The normal way of accepting office is by applying for probate, but just as slight acts will be sufficient to make a person liable as an executor de son tort,[1] so slight acts will be sufficient to enable the court to find that an executor has accepted office. Examples of such acts are taking possession of some of the deceased's goods; collecting or releasing debts;[2] and advertising for claims against the estate under Trustee Act 1925, s 27.[3] On the other hand, acts of mere humanity, such as arranging for the burial of the corpse[4] or feeding the deceased's children or cattle[5] will not be sufficient to show that a person has accepted office.

1 Below, para 27.2.
2 *Stokes v Porter* (1558) 2 Dyer 166b; *Pytt v Fendall* (1754) 1 Lee 553.
3 *Long and Feaver v Symes and Hannan* (1832) 3 Hag Ecc 771.
4 *Harrison v Rowley* (1798) 4 Ves 212.
5 *Long and Feaver v Symes and Hannan* (1832) 3 Hag Ecc 771.

17.31 Apart from the case where he has actually accepted office, a person appointed in the will to be an executor cannot be compelled to take out a grant of probate. This is so even if during the lifetime of the testator he agreed to act as executor.[1]

1 *Doyle v Blake* (1804) 2 Sch & Lef 231; see Lord Redesdale at 239.

17.32 Where the person appointed as executor takes no action, and another person wishes to apply for a grant, a citation may issue against the executor to compel him to decide whether to accept or refuse. Where he has intermeddled a citation may be issued against him to compel him to take a grant,[1] failure to comply with which can lead to contempt of court.[2]

1 See eg *Re Biggs's Estate* [1966] P 118.
2 Contempt lies in failure to comply with an order to take a grant issued as a result of the citation.

Renunciation

17.33 Section 5 of the Administration of Estates Act 1925 provides, in effect, that a person who is appointed to be an executor may renounce probate, and that if he does so, he loses all his rights as executor and that as regards representation, the will is read as if he had never been appointed executor. A renunciation of the office of executor does not affect any other appointment which he is given in the will, so that where a person who is appointed executor and trustee renounces probate he is still entitled to act as trustee.[1]

1 *Re Gordon, Roberts v Gordon* (1877) 6 Ch D 531; *Re Clout and Frewer's Contract* [1924] 2 Ch 230.

17.34 With one exception the renunciation must be of the whole office. He cannot, therefore, renounce office as respects certain property only and, as has been shown, he cannot accept one executorship, and renounce other executorships which devolve with it under the chain of representation. In this case the executor may consider renouncing probate and applying for a grant of letters of administration. The position with regards to this is as follows. If an administrator renounces his rights, he cannot without the leave of the court obtain a grant of administration in a lower capacity.[1] By contrast, where an executor renounces probate he does not thereby renounce any right to apply for letters of administration in some other capacity[2] unless he expressly renounces such right.[3]

1 Non-contentious Probate Rules 1987, r 37(2).
2 For example, as a statutory beneficiary an intestacy or as a creditor: *Re Toscani's Estate* [1912] P1 (creditor).
3 Non-contentious Probate Rules 1987, r 37(1).

17.35 The exception to the principle that a person must renounce entirely or not at all applies to settled land. Under the Administration of Estates Act 1925, s 23(1), a person who is appointed general executor may renounce his office in respect of settled land without renouncing it in respect of other property.

17.36 For the purposes of the Administration of Estates Act 1925, s 5, and the Non-contentious Probate Rules 1987, the term 'renunciation' means a formal renunciation in writing, signed by the person who renounces, and lodged at the probate registry. Until that time the renunciation is ineffective and may be retracted at will.[1] Once a formal renunciation has been made, it may be retracted only with the consent of the court.[2] The court has adopted the principle of allowing the retraction of a renunciation only if it can be shown to be for the benefit of the estate or of those interested under the will. In *Re Gill's Goods*[3] an executor who renounced received incorrect legal advice as to the effect of renunciation. He applied to retract, but was not allowed to do so, because it could not be shown that this would be for the benefit of the estate.[4] Where the court grants leave to retract, the retraction is made without prejudice to the previous acts and dealings of any other personal representatives who had taken out a grant of representation.

1 *Re Morant's Goods* (1874) LR 3 P & D 151.
2 *Melville v Ancketill* (1909) 25 TLR 655.
3 (1873) LR 3 P & D 113.
4 See also *Re Stiles's Goods* [1898] P 12; *Re Heathcote's Estate* [1913] P 42.

Administration with will

17.37 Where the deceased left a will, but there is no proving executor, a grant of administration cum testamento annexo is made. The long-established principle is that the right to a grant of administration should follow the right of property.[1] In accordance with this principle, the order of priority of grants of administration with will annexed is:[2]
1 Trustees of the residuary estate (because their function is most nearly equated with that of the executor. They take no benefit as such, and occupy a fiduciary position.)
2 Persons having a life interest in the whole of the residue; or in the residuary realty or residuary personalty.
3 (a) ultimate residuary beneficiaries, whether entitled absolutely, or only on the happening of a contingency. Beneficiaries with a vested interest are preferred to those with only a contingent interest;[3] or
 (b) where the residue is not wholly disposed of by will, the persons who take substantially the whole of the residue or who are entitled on intestacy, including the Treasury Solicitor acting on behalf of the Crown as the person entitled to the assets as bona vacantia or, in either case, the personal representative of any such person.[4] Thus, where the deceased leaves his estate to be divided into two equal shares, and one share lapses, the persons entitled to a grant will be equally the person entitled to the other share, and the person entitled on intestacy.
4 (a) specific legatees;
 (b) specific devisees;
 (c) creditors; or

(d)   the personal representative of any such person.
5   (a)   contingent beneficiaries;
(b)   persons who have no interest under the will, but who would be
entitled on intestacy.

1   *Re Gill's Goods* (1828) 1 Hag Ecc 341; see also Non-contentious Probate Rules 1987, r 20.
2   Non-contentious Probate Rules 1987, r 20.
3   Ibid, r 20(e).
4   Subject to preference being given to living persons. See ibid, r 27(5) and below, para 17.53.

Right to grant where total intestacy

17.38   Where there is no will, the following persons and in the following
order are entitled to a grant of administration:[1]
(a)   The surviving spouse, or if he or she has not taken out a grant before
death, his or her personal representative. Exceptionally, if the
surviving spouse has died without taking a beneficial interest in the
whole estate of the deceased, his or her personal representative has no
prior right to apply for a grant.
(b)   The children of the deceased, or the issue of any child who died during
the lifetime of the deceased.[2]
(c)   The father and mother of the deceased.
(d)   The brothers and sisters of the whole blood, or the issue of any brother
or sister.
If there is no person within these categories then any of the following may
apply if they have a beneficial interest in the estate. This can be the case
only where the deceased did not leave a surviving spouse:[3]
(e)   The brothers and sisters of the half blood, or the issue of any of them.
(f)   Grandparents.
(g)   Uncles and aunts of the whole blood, or the issue of any of them.
(h)   Uncles and aunts of the half blood, or the issue of any of them.
If there is no person in any of the above categories, or if they have all been
cleared off, then a grant may issue to:[4]
(i)   the Treasury Solicitor, claiming bona vacantia on behalf of the Crown;
or
(j)   a creditor; or
(k)   any person who has no immediate beneficial interest in the estate, but
who may have such an interest in the event of an accretion to the
estate. This will apply where the estate is so small that it is taken
wholly by the spouse, but where, in the event of an increase in the size
of the estate, others would then acquire a beneficial interest.

1   Non-contentious Probate Rules 1987, r 22.
2   Children includes illegitimate as well as legitimated and adopted children by virtue of the
Family Law Reform Act 1987, ss 1, 18.
3   Non-contentious Probate Rules 1987, r 22(1).
4   Ibid, r 22(2)–(4).

17.39   In each case it is for the applicant for the grant to prove his
entitlement. A neat illustration of this arose in *Re Seaford, Seaford v
Seifert*.[1] In that case a wife obtained a decree nisi of divorce in March 1965,

and in July 1965 her solicitors applied for the decree to be made absolute. It was found as a fact that the respondent husband took an overdose of sodium amytal tablets at some time between 9 pm, 5 July and 4 am, 6 July. The decree was in fact made absolute at 10 am on 6 July, but there is an old rule[2] that a judgment or order takes effect from the first moment of the day on which it was made. As the wife could not prove that the husband died before 00.01 am, Cairns J held that she had not discharged the burden of proof upon her, and refused to make a grant in her favour. However, the decision was reversed by the Court of Appeal[3] on the ground that as the deceased had undoubtedly died by 4 am, no effective application for a decree to be made absolute could be made, so that the doctrine of relation back did not apply.

1 [1967] 2 All ER 458 (first instance).
2 Ibid, at 461.
3 [1968] 1 All ER 482.

Grants in special circumstances

Power to depart from order

17.40 The rules just considered, as to the persons entitled to grants of administration either with or without the will annexed, are subject to the overriding discretion of the court to make a grant of administration to such persons as it thinks fit. This power is conferred by s 116 of the Supreme Court Act 1981, which gives the court a discretion to depart from the normal order, and to make a grant of administration to such person as it considers expedient, in cases where it appears to be necessary or expedient by reason of the insolvency of the estate 'or of any other special circumstance'.[1]

1 In *Re Jones* [1973] 2 NZLR 402, the intestate, a Maori rejoicing under the name of Juicy David Jones, was survived by two sons, neither of whom wanted to apply for a grant. The New Zealand Administration Act 1969 did not provide for this situation, and the court granted letters of administration to the intestate's brother under its inherent jurisdiction.

17.41 Section 116 of the 1981 Act replaced earlier provisions,[1] and the scope of the section can be illustrated by cases under those Acts. The cases may be grouped into the following categories.

1 Court of Probate Act 1857, s 73; Judicature Act 1925, s 162.

Person entitled incapable of acting
17.42 Where the person entitled to a grant is incapable of acting, he will often be prepared to renounce, leaving the person next entitled in a position to obtain the grant. The person with the prior right may not be prepared to renounce, however, if he has no confidence in the person with the inferior right. In this case, he may appoint nominees to apply for a grant. In *Re Davis' Estate*[1] the person with the prior right was the sole executrix, and person entitled to the whole of the estate. Ill health prevented her from acting, and her nominees were successful in obtaining a grant. The court

will, however, probably be reluctant to exercise its discretion in such circumstances unless the unsuitability of the person next entitled can be proved, or unless, as in *Re Davis's Estate*, the person next entitled has no beneficial interest.

1   [1906] P 330.

Considerations of public policy

17.43   Just as public policy demands that a person who has caused the death of a person by certain acts, such as murder and manslaughter, cannot take a benefit,[1] so by committing such an act the wrongdoer also may lose the right to a grant of representation. In *Re Crippen's Estate*[2] Crippen was convicted of murdering his wife, and was subsequently executed. His wife died intestate, and in normal circumstances her husband would have been entitled to a grant, and, as he was dead, that right would have devolved on his personal representatives. In this case, however, a grant was made to the next of kin of the wife, and not to the personal representatives of the husband.

1   See below, paras 30.63ff.
2   [1911] P 108.

17.44   *Re Crippen's Estate* was followed in *Re S*,[1] where a husband made a will appointing his wife to be his sole executrix and beneficiary. The wife was convicted of the manslaughter of her husband and a grant was made to the deceased's daughters. Baker J appeared to place equal weight on the fact of the wife's conviction and the fact that because she was serving a term of life imprisonment it was 'quite impossible'[2] for her to act as executrix.

1   [1967] 2 All ER 150.
2   Ibid, at 152. However, the judge appears to have overstated the position: the wife could have appointed agents, herself taking the basic decisions in prison.

Person entitled refusing to act

17.45   Where a person having a right to apply for a grant refuses to do so, but also refuses to renounce, the person next entitled may cite him to accept or refuse a grant,[1] or, where he has already intermeddled, he may be cited to accept a grant.[2] However, a citation to accept or refuse a grant may be issued only at the instance of a person having an inferior right to a grant.[3] A citation to an executor who has intermeddled to take a grant may also be issued at the instance of anyone interested in the estate.[4] Where it is not possible to use this procedure, or in other cases where it is expedient to do so, an application may be made under s 116. Thus, in *Re Knight's Goods*[5] where a person had a claim for damages for personal injuries, and was unable to proceed because the next of kin failed to apply for a grant, he successfully applied for the appointment of the Official Solicitor as administrator. The Official Solicitor, however, can be appointed only with his consent. Where he refuses consent, a grant may be made to the claimant's nominee.[6]

1   See below, para 18.60.
2   Ibid.

3 Non-contentious Probate Rules 1987, r 47(1).
4 Ibid, r 47(3).
5 [1939] 3 All ER 928.
6 *Re Simpson's Estate* [1936] P 40.

17.46 Special problems have arisen where a solicitor who is a sole practitioner dies, and no grant is taken out to his estate. In these circumstances, the court will entertain applications from a nominee of The Law Society for a grant.[1] Similar considerations would presumably apply in the case of the death of sole practitioners in other professions.

1 *Practice Direction* [1965] 1 All ER 923; *Re Morgans* (1931) 145 LT 392, [1931] All ER Rep 440.

Person entitled unsuitable

17.47 The most frequent example of unsuitability to take a grant is mental or physical illness, but any other factor, such as a completely irrational approach to the estate, will make the applicant unsuitable. A case which contained both aspects is *Re Biggs' Estate*.[1] The testator appointed by his will a husband and wife as joint executors. The estate was small, and the husband gave effect to the terms of the will, but without obtaining probate. Subsequently, it became necessary to obtain a grant, and the executor refused. As he had, by administering the estate, intermeddled, a citation was issued to him to take a grant. He failed to appear to the citation, and an order was made that he should apply for and obtain a grant of probate. The executor ignored that order, and an application was made for his committal for contempt. When the hearing of the summons for committal was heard, it appeared that the executor was over 70 and seriously ill, but furthermore, that he had developed an overbearing sense of hostility to the estate, so that, according to Rees J. he had 'allowed his sense of grievance to overcome his judgment'. This sense of hostility is illustrated by the executor's attitude towards the articled clerk who served the court order on him. In his affidavit, the articled clerk said:

> 'I had made several visits to the citee's house without being able to meet him, and on June 14 I could get no reply except that a man whom I assumed was Mr Glew [the citee] was standing behind the front door shouting abusive language and threats which were directed to me and a colleague who was with me, and I could not persuade him to open the door. Finally, I propelled the copy order . . . through the letter box, and I could see as I did so that it came into contact with Mr Glew who was immediately behind the door. Mr Glew at once opened the door, picked up the copy order at the same time and he then proceeded to kick the copy order into the gutter of the road outside his house. I and my colleague retreated quickly down the road but Mr Glew and his wife pursued us and it was only due to the intervention of a police constable that we were able to escape them.'

The court was therefore faced in this case with the situation where an executor had intermeddled, but it discharged its previous order and exercised its power under the forerunner of s 116 to pass over the executor, and to make a grant to the applicant.

1 [1966] P 118.

Other cases
17.48 It is not possible to give an exhaustive categorisation of the 'special circumstances' for the purposes of s 116. Other examples in which the power has been used are where, during wartime, the person entitled was an enemy alien,[1] and where, following a dispute between the next of kin as to who should take a grant, a grant was made to their nominee.[2]

1 *Re Schiff's Estate* [1915] P 86; *Re Grundt's Estate* [1915] P 126; *Re Sanpietro's Estate* [1941] P 16.
2 *Re Morgans* (1931) 47 TLR 452.

Restrictions on section 116

17.49 It seems that s 116 governs only situations which are not otherwise specifically provided for, and that it cannot be used to override other statutory provisions. This was established in *Re Hall*.[1] Section 114 of the Supreme Court Act 1981 requires that where a minority or life interest will arise, a grant of administration (but not of probate) must be made to two persons or to a trust corporation.[2] In *Re Hall* the deceased had died intestate at the age of 79, survived by several brothers and sisters. One of the brothers applied for a grant, and the other brothers and sisters all renounced. Over 40 years before his death he had entered into a deed of separation and his wife then went to Canada with their child. Nothing had been heard of either of them since. Willmer J held that as there was a possibility of the wife still being alive, and being entitled to a life interest, two administrators should be appointed. Accordingly, both the applicant and his wife were appointed.

1 [1950] P 156.
2 See below, para 17.54.

17.50 Further, according to Willmer J in *Re Edwards-Taylor's Goods*,[1] the expression 'special circumstance' relates only to circumstances affecting the estate or its administration, not to circumstances affecting the beneficiary. While this dictum may go too far, it is clear that the court will not use s 116 to interfere even indirectly with beneficial ownership. In *Re Edwards-Taylor's Goods* the beneficiary who was entitled to a considerable fortune under the will was said to be immature and unfitted to look after the money. An attempt was made to obtain a limited grant in favour of a trust corporation, but that was unsuccessful.

1 [1951] P 24 at 27.

General discretion of the court

17.51 In addition to the power under s 116, the court has an inherent discretion to make a grant to whomsoever it wishes[1] but almost certainly it will now rely entirely upon s 116.

1 *Re Schwerdtfeger's Goods* (1876) 1 PD 424.

More than one person entitled

17.52 It is common for more than one person of the same degree to be entitled to a grant. For example, if the deceased has died intestate without leaving a surviving spouse but leaving several children surviving, each child has an equal right to apply for a grant of letters of administration. Any person so entitled may make an application without notice to the others of the same degree and may obtain a grant in his own name alone.[1] Where another person of the same degree wishes to prevent this happening, he may enter a caveat.[2]

1 Non-contentious Probate Rules 1987, r 27(4).
2 See below, paras 18.55–18.59.

Disagreement as to person to take

17.53 Where there is a dispute between those entitled, the court adopts the following principles:
(a) The primary rule is that the grant is to be made to the person who is likely to deal with it best from the point of view of the creditors and beneficiaries.[1] Although usually expressed in this way, however, the result is that in effect all appointments will be regarded as likely to do equally as well for the beneficiaries and creditors unless there is a reason for *not* appointing a particular person. Examples of such reasons are the bankruptcy or insolvency of the applicant,[2] his general badness of character,[3] and, during wartime, his status as an enemy alien.[4]
(b) Subject to that, the court will issue the grant to the person who has the largest beneficial interest; or the person whom the majority of members of the same degree favour.[5]
(c) It used to be said that the eldest child would be preferred to the younger ones, unless the majority of them favoured another child,[6] and that subject to the same exception, sons would be preferred to daughters.[7] It is doubtful whether these considerations still operate.
(d) 'Live interests are preferred to dead.' Rule 27(5), Non-contentious Probate Rules 1987, provides that as a general principle administration shall be granted to a living person rather than to the personal representative of a dead person entitled in the same degree. Thus, if a widower has two sons, one of whom predeceases him, administration will be granted to the son who survives in preference to the personal representative of the one who predeceases.
(e) If one applicant is of full capacity, and another is not, then the one of full age will be preferred to those representing the one who is not.[8]

1 *Warwick v Greville* (1809) 1 Phillim 123 at 125.
2 *Hill v Mills* (1691) 1 Show 293; *Bell v Timiswood* (1812) 2 Phillim 22; *Re Bowron's Goods* (1914) 84 LJP 92.
3 *Re Frost's Estate* [1905] P 140.
4 *Re Sanpietro's Estate* [1941] P 16.
5 *Budd v Silver* (1813) 2 Phillim 115.
6 *Warwick v Greville* (1809) 1 Phillim 123.

7 *Iredale v Ford and Bramworth* (1859) 1 Sw & Tr 305.
8 Non-contentious Probate Rules 1987, r 27(5).

Number of administrators

17.54 When an application is made for a grant of administration, the applicant in his oath must swear whether, to the best of his knowledge and belief, a life interest or minority arises under the will or intestacy. The court acts on this oath, and where there is a minority or life interest, s 114 of the Supreme Court Act 1981 requires the grant to be made to two persons or to a trust corporation. This rule does not apply to probate. It seems that in such a case it is necessary to have two administrators, even if the estate is insolvent.[1] Where there is only one administrator, either because the existence of a life interest or minority has subsequently become known, or because another administrator has died, then the court may appoint an additional administrator upon the application of any person interested.[2]

1 *Re White* [1928] P 75; cf *Re Herbert* [1926] P 109 to the contrary.
2 Supreme Court Act 1981, s 114(4).

17.55 Section 114(1) of the Supreme Court Act 1981 also provides that neither administration nor probate shall be granted to more than four persons in respect of the same property.[1]

1 See above, para 17.19, for position as to probate.

Grants to special persons

The Crown

17.56 Section 46 of the Administration of Estates Act 1925 limits the class of persons who can succeed to the property of an intestate to those who are descended from one of his grandparents.[1] In the absence of any relations within that class, more distant relations cannot take, and the Crown is entitled. In such circumstances the grant is made to the Treasury Solicitor. Where the deceased was resident in the Duchy of Lancaster or the Duchy of Cornwall, the grant is made to the solicitor to the appropriate Duchy.

1 See above, para 12.41.

Creditors

17.57 If no other person makes an application for a grant, a creditor may do so. The creditor's right is the lowest in priority, and he must therefore first cite everyone having a prior right (excluding the Crown where it has no beneficial interest) before he can take a grant himself. Where the creditor believes that the deceased left no relatives entitled to take, he is required to cite, in general terms, all persons claiming a right to share in the estate, and to serve that citation by means of advertisement. A copy of the advertisement must be delivered to the Treasury Solicitor.

17.58 Any creditor is entitled to apply, even if his debt is unenforceable as being barred by the Limitation Acts.[1] Creditors whose debts accrued after death or who took an assignment of the debt after death[2] are entitled to apply. A liquidator is entitled to apply for a grant to the estate of a contributory[3] on the winding up[4] and a trustee in bankruptcy of a creditor may obtain a grant.[5] If there is a dispute between creditors, preference will generally be given to the one:
(a) who has the greatest debts;[6]
(b) who is favoured by the majority of creditors.

1 *Coombs v Coombs* (1866) LR 1 P & D 288.
2 *Newcombe v Beloe* (1867) LR 1 P & D 314.
3 A contributory is a member of the company liable to contribute towards its deficiency on winding up.
4 Companies Act.
5 *Downward v Dickinson* (1864) 3 Sw & Tr 564.
6 *Re Smith's Goods* (1892) 67 LT 503.

Assignee

17.59 Where the only person who is entitled to the beneficial interest in the estate assigns that interest, the assignee stands in the position of the assignor for the purposes of applying for a grant.[1] The same rule applies where there is more than one person entitled to the estate, and they all assign to the same assignee. Where there is more than one assignor, the assignee stands in the position of the assignor with the highest priority. An assignee is only entitled to a grant where he is entitled to the whole beneficial interest. Where a person is entitled only to part of the beneficial interest, the assignee does not thereby become entitled to take a grant.

1 Non-contentious Probate Rules 1987, r 24.

Attesting witness

17.60 Where a beneficiary named in a will, or his spouse, attests the will, he is generally not entitled to take his beneficial interest.[1] By attesting the will, he also loses his right to a grant in his capacity as a beneficiary, although this does not invalidate his appointment as an executor or disentitle him to apply for a grant in some other capacity.[2]

1 See above, paras 6.35ff.
2 Non-contentious Probate Rules 1987, r 21.

Where deceased domiciled abroad

17.61 Where the deceased did not die domiciled in England, the court will grant administration either to the person who is actually entrusted with the administration of the estate by the law of the deceased's domicile, or to the person entitled to administer in accordance with that law.[1] The court will require an affidavit of law showing the entitlement of the applicant. In special cases, an application may be made under s 116 to enable a grant to be made to the person who would have been entitled had the deceased died domiciled in England.

1 Non-contentious Probate Rules 1987, r 30; *Re Kaufman's Goods* [1952] P 325.

Why the rush?

17.62 In some cases difficulty is caused because the person entitled to a grant refuses to apply for it.[1] However, far more difficulties are caused because there is a struggle between two or more persons to obtain a grant. There are, in appropriate cases, sound practical reasons for this. Thus:

(a) Where the estate is large enough to pay all debts and legacies, the personal representative may pay himself his legacy forthwith, even if he is not in a position to pay the other legacies until some time later.

(b) He may by becoming a personal representative perfect a previously imperfect gift. The rule known as the rule in *Strong v Bird*[2] is to the effect that a previously incomplete gift will be completed when the donee becomes personal representative.[3] The rule applies both where the personal representative becomes executor[4] and where he becomes administrator.

(c) He may have little confidence in the qualities of the other persons who may be entitled to a grant, and prefer to attend to the administration himself.

But the major reason is usually non-legal – it is the power lust which leads to the desire to gain control; or the opportunity which this gives to enable the personal representative to poke into other people's affairs; or the desire to be seen as the distributor of largesse – other people's. There need be little surprise, therefore, that there are a large number of reported decisions arising from contests to become personal representative.

1 Eg *Re Biggs's Estate*, above, para 17.47.
2 (1874) LR 18 Eq 315.
3 *Strong v Bird* (1874) LR 18 Eq 315; *Re Stewart, Stewart v McLaughlin* [1908] 2 Ch 251.
4 *Re James, James v James* [1935] Ch 449.

CHAPTER 18

Non-contentious probate

Definition

18.1 The practice of probate, which for this purpose includes obtaining grants of administration, is divided into two categories: contentious and non-contentious. Contentious business involves a contested action, such as to prove the validity of an alleged will,[1] while in non-contentious business a grant is made upon the affidavit of the applicant, but without a formal hearing. The great majority of business is non-contentious.

1 See below, para 20.1, for a full statement of the matters which are described as contentious business.

Documents admissible to probate

18.2 Every document which is executed in accordance with the formal requirements of the Wills Act 1837, as amended, is entitled to be admitted to probate if it has a testamentary character. A document has a testamentary character if:
(a)   it disposes of property; or
(b)   if it appoints an executor;
and perhaps:
(c)   it revokes a will; or
(d)   it appoints a guardian.[1]
In every case, however, it is necessary to show that there was adequate mental capacity on the part of the testator, and that he intended that the document should operate on death.

1 In *Re Blow* (1978) 82 DLR (3d) 721 (Ontario) the court refused to grant probate of a memorandum which complied with the formal requirements for a will, but which was intended only as a guide to the executors in the exercise of their discretion. It was not intended itself to have any dispositive effect.

Disposal of property

18.3   In general, a document may be admitted to probate only if it disposes of property in England or Wales. If the document does not dispose of such property, but disposes of property exclusively elsewhere, the general rule is that that document will not be admitted to probate. The rule is because probate or letters of administration operate as orders of the court, and in principle the court has no jurisdiction over property outside England and Wales. There are, however, two exceptions to this rule:

(a)   Where there is a special reason for obtaining a grant. The court may issue a grant where no English property is involved. This will be done only where it is needed for a particular purpose, and that purpose must be recited in the affidavit leading to the grant. In *Re Wayland's Estate*,[1] the facts of which were given at para 8.14, the court admitted to probate the will disposing only of Belgian property, because the effect of this had been called into question by the revocation clause in the subsequent English will.

(b)   Where the will disposing of foreign property is referred to in another will dealing with English property, and it is necessary for both to be admitted to probate so that they can be read together.[2] Where the wills can be read separately, the foreign will is not admitted to probate.[3]

1   [1951] 2 All ER 1041.
2   *Re Lord Howden's Goods* (1874) 43 LJP 26; *Re Astor's Goods* (1876) 1 PD 150; *Re Bolton's Goods* (1887) 12 PD 202; *Re Callaway's Goods* (1890) 15 PD 147; *Re Seaman's Goods* [1891] P 253; *Re Fraser's Goods* [1891] P 285.
3   *Re Murray's Goods* [1896] P 65; *Re Todd's Estate* [1926] P 173.

18.4   Examples of cases where probate is granted of wills dealing only with foreign property are where the grant is required for production to a foreign court, or where the personal representative wishes to commence proceedings in England. In *Carter and Crost's Case*[1] an executor who had obtained probate in Ireland was compelled to take out an English grant before he could sue in the English courts even to recover Irish assets.[2]

1   (1600) Godb 33.
2   See also *Whyte v Rose* (1842) 3 QB 493.

Appointment of executors

18.5   A document which merely appoints executors is admissible to probate. This frequently happens in the case of codicils which have no other function.

Revocation of will

18.6   In *Re Durance's Goods*,[1] considered above,[2] the testator in Canada sent an attested letter to his brother in England asking him to collect the will and destroy it. This was effective to revoke the will, and Lord Penzance made a grant of administration with the letter of revocation annexed. In *Toomer v Sobinska*,[3] however, the court made a grant of letters of administration, without the revoking instrument annexed, but incorporating in the grant a note that it was made as a result of the revocation of the earlier will. The latter approach is better, and was followed in *Re Howard, Howard v Treasury Solicitor*.[4] Even if the document is not admissible to probate, it is an effective revocation.

1 (1872) LR 2 P & D 406.
2 Above, para 8.11.
3 [1907] P 106.
4 [1944] P 39.

Appointment of guardian

18.7 The power to appoint a testamentary guardian is conferred by the Guardianship of Minors Act 1971. There is no decision whether a document which only appoints a guardian is admissible to probate, although, for evidential reasons, it would be most desirable to do so. Under the pre-1926 law, it is clear that a document only appointing a guardian was not admissible.[1]

1 *Re Morton's Goods* (1864) 3 Sw & Tr 422; *Re Tollemache's Estate* [1917] P 246.

Need to prove all testamentary instruments

18.8 The executor is under a duty to propound all testamentary instruments unless there is any serious reason to doubt their validity. The problem often arises where there is a dispute over the will, and agreement is reached between the parties concerned that one document should be left out. In *Re Watts's Goods*[1] a testator made a will after he had been found lunatic by inquisition. Almost all the persons interested in the estate agreed that the will should be ignored, and an application was made for letters of administration. Sir Herbert Jenner refused the application on the basis[2] that: 'The consent of parties interested proves nothing; no person's consent can make a will no will.'

1 (1837) 1 Curt 594.
2 Ibid at 595.

18.9 The rule has been followed. So, in *Re Muirhead's Estate*[1] the testator made a will appointing his wife to be the sole executrix, and giving her all his property. He then made what appeared to be a valid codicil giving his secretary half his estate. There were certain negotiations between widow and secretary, which are only hinted at in the report, but the widow tried to avoid proving the codicil by citing the secretary to prove it. The secretary did not appear to the citation, and the widow sought probate of the will alone. This was refused. Cairns J decided that the will and codicil should both have been brought before the court in an application for probate in solemn form.

1 [1971] P 263, [1971] 1 All ER 609.

Probate of part of a will

No animus testandi

18.10 If a document or part of a document was not executed animo testandi it will not be admitted to probate. This has been held to apply where a clause has been inserted by fraud[1] or by forgery.[2]

1 *Barton v Robins* (1769) 3 Phillim 455n; *Allen v M'Pherson* (1847) 1 HLC 191.
2 *Plume v Beale* (1717) 1 P Wms 388; *Re Raphael, Raphael v D'Antin* [1973] 3 All ER 19 (order pronounced against a purported will where one of the executors named in it had been convicted of forging it).

18.11 Where a mistake has been made, it is necessary to draw a clear distinction between two situations. If the testator knew and approved of a particular word or phrase, then that cannot be omitted from probate, even though it produces a result contrary to the testator's intention. If, on the other hand, part of the will is included without the knowledge or instructions of the testator, that part will be omitted. An illustration of the former principle is *Collins v Elstone*.[1] The testatrix was misinformed as to the effect of a revocation clause. It was held, however, that as she knew that that clause was in the will, it must stand.[2] The second principle is illustrated by *Re Boehm's Goods*,[3] where the name of a legatee was wrongly inserted in a will, and the will was not read over to the testator before execution. The name was omitted from probate.[4]

1 [1893] P 1.
2 This was criticised in *Lowthorpe-Lutwidge v Lowthorpe-Lutwidge* [1935] P 151. See above, para 8.17.
3 [1891] P 247.
4 *Re Oswald's Goods* (1874) LR 3 P & D 162; *Morrell v Morrell* (1882) 7 PD 68; *Re Moore's Goods* [1892] P 378; *Re Reade's Goods* [1902] P 75.

18.12 A good illustration of the rule is *Re Morris*.[1] By clause 3 of her will the testatrix made provision for her housekeeper, and by clause 7 gave a total of 20 pecuniary legacies. Sub-clause 7(iv) was a pecuniary legacy to the housekeeper. The testatrix wrote to her solicitor saying that she wished to revoke the provisions in favour of her housekeeper, and to make new provisions for her. The codicil should have read: 'I revoke clauses 3 and 7(iv)' but owing to an error in the solicitor's office it in fact read 'I revoke clauses 3 and 7'. Latey J admitted the codicil to probate, but omitting the '7' in the revocation clause, basing his decision on two grounds. First, the testatrix did not know and approve the contents of the codicil and, secondly, the testatrix was not to be bound by a mistake which the draftsman had made where the mind of the draftsman had never really been applied to the words introduced, and never adverted to their significance and effect.[2] The judge admitted that attempts to reconcile all the earlier cases had, in the past, 'produced intellectual gymnastics, if not acrobatics'. He followed the dictum of Sachs J in *Crerar v Crerar*[3] that the court must 'consider all the relevant evidence available and then, drawing such inferences as it can from the totality of that material, it has to come to a conclusion whether or not those propounding the will have discharged the burden of establishing that the testatrix knew and approved the contents of the document which is put forward as a valid testamentary disposition'.

1   *Re Morris, Lloyds Bank Ltd v Peake* [1971] P 62.
2   Such a clerical error could now be rectified under s 20, Administration of Justice Act 1982, but this remedy was not available in respect of testators dying before 1983; see above, para 5.56.
3   (1956) unreported, but see (1956) 106 LJ 674.

18.13   The general rule remains that 'there is no difference between the words which a testator himself uses in drawing up his will, and the words which are bona fide used by one whom he trusts to draw it up for him'.[1] If, therefore, a word is used intentionally, even though its significance is not appreciated, the testator will be bound by it. But it seems that the courts will now be reluctant to hold a testator bound by words which the draftsman clearly inserted contrary to the intention of the testator.

1   Per Lord Blackburn in *Rhodes v Rhodes* (1882) 7 App Cas 192 at 199, 200.

18.14   There is one qualification to the rule that a word or phrase may be omitted if inserted without the testator's knowledge or intention. The court will not make the omission if to do so would alter the meaning of what remains.[1]

1   *Re Horrocks, Taylor v Kershaw* [1939] P 198, CA; *Rhodes v Rhodes* (1882) 7 App Cas 192.

18.15   In general, the court can omit, but it cannot insert. Accordingly, even in the most obvious case, the court cannot go further than to grant probate with a blank, leaving the court of construction to give meaning to the document in that form if it is able to do so.[1] However, in some cases the court has power to rectify the will in order to give effect to the testator's intentions,[2] and where this power is exercised, probate will be granted of the will as rectified.

1   *Re Schott's Goods* [1901] P 190; cf *Re Bushell's Goods* (1877) 13 PD 7. For a good example of this at a time when the court had no power to rectify the will, see *Re Reynette-James, Wightman v Reynette-James* [1975] 3 All ER 1037.
2   Administration of Justice Act 1982, s 20; above, paras 5.56ff.

18.16   If a clause is invalid because of an insane delusion, that clause will be omitted, even though probate may be granted of the remainder of the document. So in *Re Bohrmann's Estate*,[1] the facts of which were stated earlier,[2] probate was granted of the will and all codicils, except the part of the last codicil affected by the insane delusion.

1   [1938] 1 All ER 271.
2   Above, para 5.15.

Offensive material

18.17   In certain circumstances, the court will omit from probate words which are of no testamentary effect, whose omission will not alter the meaning of the remainder of the will, and which are offensive. Thus, words have been omitted because they are libellous or scandalous.[1] In *Re Bowker's Goods*[2] Lord Merrivale P omitted words relating to the mode of disposal of the bodily remains of the deceased on the ground that they were 'offensive and objectionable, and repugnant to the members of the deceased's family, and unless omitted would be broadcast in the press and particularly in the locality where the deceased was well known and where the dependent and other members of the family lived'. The court will, however, be reluctant to exercise its power even where the words cause offence,[3] particularly where there is any suggestion that the excision of the offending words might affect the construction of what remains. In *Re Rawlings' Estate*[4] there was a gift on certain trusts with the direction: 'do not in any way give, lend or have anything to do with that rascal her husband, or any of her family, except Cyril her son', and on an application to omit the words 'that rascal', Sir Boyd Merriman P took the view that those words might be relevant to the construction of what remained, and refused to omit them.

1   *Re White's Estate* [1914] P 153; *Re Maxwell* (1929) 140 LT 471; *Re Hall's Estate* [1943] 2 All ER 159.
2   [1932] P 93.
3   *Re Honywood's Goods* (1871) LR 2 P & D 251; *Re Caie's Estate* (1927) 43 TLR 697.
4   (1934) 78 Sol Jo 338.

18.18   Words will also be omitted from the probate copy where it is in the interest of national security.[1] This may be expected to happen in particular where a soldier manages to make and send an uncensored formal or privileged will from a theatre of war.

1   *Re Heywood's Estate* [1916] P 47.

Importance of probate copy

18.18A   Once probate has been granted, questions of construction will, in principle, depend on the probate copy. In general, reference cannot be made to the original will[1] except to see whether the probate copy is correct.[2] Exceptionally, however, the court will look at the original will in order to determine questions of construction. So, in *Re Battie-Wrightson, Cecil v Battie-Wrightson*[3] a clause which contained reference to a bank was omitted from probate. A later clause, which was included, referred to 'the said bank'. The court referred to the original will to determine the identity of the bank. In any case where the Chancery Division goes behind the probate copy, it is to some extent usurping the jurisdiction of the probate court, but that may be expected in view of Chancery's history of taking jurisdiction where it can.

1   *Havergal v Harrison* (1843) 7 Beav 49; cf *Oppenheim v Henry* (1853) 9 Hare 802n; *Gann v Gregory* (1854) 3 De GM & G 777.
2   *Compton v Bloxham* (1845) 2 Coll 201; *Shea v Boschetti* (1854) 18 Beav 321.
3   [1920] 2 Ch 330.

Time for obtaining a grant

18.19 A grant of probate or letters of administration with will annexed may be obtained at any time after seven days from the date of death, and a grant of letters of administration may be obtained at any time after fourteen days from death.[1] These time limits are intended to ensure that adequate time is given to look for any will, or any further will. The time limits may be waived if two registrars agree.[2] The papers to lead to a grant may be lodged before these periods have expired, but the grant itself must not pass the court seal within the prescribed periods.

1 Non-contentious Probate Rules 1987, r 6(2).
2 Ibid.

18.20 There is generally no limit on the time after death in which a grant may be obtained, and, indeed, in the case of certain types of grant, such as administration de bonis non,[1] the application is often made several years after death. The one exception to this principle is that where a person who has intermeddled has, after citation, been ordered to take a grant within a certain period,[2] if he fails to do so he is guilty of contempt.[3]

1 See below, paras 19.12ff. A grant de bonis non is made where an executor acting under a probate dies before the administration of the estate is complete, and a further grant is necessary so that another person can complete the administration. This commonly arises where it is necessary to complete title to a property where all the original personal representatives have died before the sale.
2 See below, para 18.60(a).
3 *Re Biggs' Estate* [1966] P 118.

18.21 The penalties for acting without a grant are mentioned later.[1]

1 Below, chap 25.

Obtaining a grant in common form

18.22 It has already been explained that a grant of probate or letters of administration is an order of the court, and the decision whether to make a grant is accordingly a judicial act. But in most cases of the routine common form grants, the procedure, although theoretically a judicial act, is in fact far more administrative than judicial. The applicant for the grant, either personally[1] or through his solicitor,[2] lodges with the appropriate probate registry or probate sub-registry certain papers. These are considered by the registrar and his staff, and if they are in order, the applicant receives the grant through the post about ten days or a fortnight after the papers were lodged.

1 Non-contentious Probate Rules 1987, r 5.
2 Ibid, r 4.

The documents required are described in the following paragraphs.

In all cases

Executor's or administrator's oath
18.23 This is the document on which the grant is based. In it, the executor or administrator swears as to the date and place of death of the deceased; the age of the deceased; the domicile of the deceased; whether the deceased held settled land under a settlement arising before his death and not terminating on death, so that any necessary reference to settled land may be made in the grant; and his own entitlement to take a grant. In common form business, the facts deposed to in the oath are taken as sufficient proof, so that no corroboration is required. It is not even necessary to support the fact of death by production of the death certificate (though as it is not necessary to produce a corpse in order to get a death certificate, this is perhaps not as surprising as it may seem). The oath also states the amount of the estate, but where the estate does not exceed £125,000 it can be sworn as not exceeding that figure.[1]

1 Inheritance Tax (Delivery of Accounts) Regulations 1981, SI 1981/880 as finally amended by SI 1991/1248: see below para 18.27.

18.24 For readers of this book unfamiliar with such oaths, two illustrations are included in the Appendix at paras 00 and 00.[1]

1 Examples of the grants issued following these oaths are given in Appendix C.

Inland Revenue account
18.25 *Generally* This document is prepared solely to determine whether and, if so, how much inheritance tax is payable. It specifies each asset owned by the deceased, and shows its gross value, and any debts which are charged on it. It also gives details of general debts and liabilities, and funeral expenses. In the case of assets where the exact value is open to some doubt, such as the deceased's house, the personal representatives give their estimate of the value, usually on the low side, leaving adjustments to be made later. Where inheritance tax is payable it must, in general, be paid before the papers are lodged for the grant except on land and business assets.[1]

1 Payment of tax on land and business assets can be paid by instalments, the first commencing 6 months from the date of death: Inheritance Tax Act 1984, s 227. Any instalments that have fallen due must be paid before probate will issue.

18.26 In most cases some adjustment is necessary to the Inland Revenue account, either because further assets or liabilities come to light in the course of the administration, or because the value of an asset has to be altered. This is done by means of a corrective account, which can be submitted to the Capital Taxes Office at any time after grant.

18.27 *Small estates* Where the gross value of the estate does not exceed £125,000, no Inland Revenue account is required if:[1]
(a) the estate comprises only property which has passed under the deceased's will or intestacy, or by nomination, or beneficially by survivorship;

(b) not more than £15,000 of the estate consists of property situated outside the United Kingdom;[2]
(c) the deceased died domiciled in the United Kingdom; and
(d) the deceased had not made in his lifetime any chargeable transfers for the purpose of inheritance tax.

If these conditions are satisfied, and a grant is obtained without an Inland Revenue account having been delivered, the Inland Revenue have the right to serve notice on the personal representatives within 35 days from the issue of the grant calling for an account. The Revenue issue some notices as part of their procedure for monitoring the working of the arrangements, and not because of suspicions.[3]

1 Inheritance Tax (Delivery of Accounts) Regulations 1981, SI 1981/880, as ultimately amended by SI 1991/1248. These Regulations apply only if the deceased died after 1 April 1981. The amount has increased from time to time to the current level to allow a margin below the inheritance tax threshold, currently £150,000.
2 The amount has increased from time to time to the current level.
3 Inland Revenue Press Release of 22 June 1981.

In cases of probate, or administration with will

The will

18.28 The original will must be referred to in the oath, and must be lodged when the application for the grant is made. Once lodged, the will is retained by the registry. A photocopy is available for public inspection at the Principal Registry, but not the original will.

18.29 There is some doubt whether the will, once lodged, can ever be released from the registry. In *Re Todd's Estate*[1] the applicant sought to prove the will abroad after it had been proved in England, and the court directed that the original could be released for this purpose provided a sealed copy was retained in the registry. In *Re Greer*,[2] however, it was held that the court had no power to allow the will to be sent out of the jurisdiction for the purpose of proceedings abroad. Probably the court will allow a will to be sent abroad only if it is required to prove it abroad, and the English court is satisfied that the foreign court will not accept a sealed copy.

1 [1926] P 173.
2 (1929) 45 TLR 362.

18.30 Where the will is held abroad, and cannot be brought here, as where it has been proved in a foreign court and that court will not release it, probate here can be granted of an authenticated copy of the foreign will.[1]

1 Non-contentious Probate Rules 1987, r 54(2).

18.31 Sometimes the will, although not validly revoked, will not be in existence. It may, for example, have been destroyed without compliance with the provisions of the Wills Act as to revocation, or it may have been lost.[1] In this case, provided its contents can be reconstructed, probate will be granted of the best document available. So probate may be granted of a copy, or of a draft, or of a document which is a reconstruction from oral evidence.[2]

1 There is, however, a presumption that in certain circumstances a will which has been lost has been destroyed animo revocandi; see above, para 8.53.
2 See below, paras 18.48 and 18.49.

18.32 Where the original will is in existence, it must be lodged at the registry, even if it is not in the custody of the applicant. Where the applicant cannot obtain the will he may obtain an order requiring it to be lodged. It has been held that a solicitor cannot exercise a lien over a client's will to the extent of refusing to produce it until his costs are paid.[1]

1 *Ex p Law* (1834) 2 Ad & El 45.

Probate and letters of administration – special cases

The following documents are not generally required but will be required in the circumstances mentioned.

Copy will
18.33 When probate is granted, a photocopy of the will is attached to the probate or letters of administration, and a further photocopy is made available for public inspection. If the will is not suitable for photographic reproduction, an engrossment of the will suitable for photographing must be lodged. If a will has been rectified[1] or if parts of the document are not admissible to probate, as in the case of inadmissible alterations or insertions, a copy of the will in the form in which it is to be proved must be lodged.[2]

1 Under Administration of Justice Act 1982, s 20: see above, chapter 5.
2 Non-contentious Probate Rules 1987, r 11.

Translation of the will
18.34 A will is valid even if written in a foreign language. Where the will is written in a language other than English, a translation must be lodged, together with an affidavit by the translator verifying the translation. The executor is sworn to the foreign will, but the photocopy of the will attached to the probate is of the translation and not the original.

Affidavit as to due execution
18.35 Where the will contains an attestation clause purporting to show that the formal requirements of the Wills Act have been complied with, then, in the absence of any other circumstances giving rise to doubt, that will be accepted as sufficient evidence that the will is formally valid.

18.36 Where, however, there is no, or a defective, attestation clause, or there are some circumstances leading to doubt, an affidavit of due execution is necessary.[1] This is an affidavit from one of the attesting witnesses, or from someone else who was present at the time, to the effect that the formal requirements were observed. If it is not possible to trace anyone to make an affidavit, it may still be possible to satisfy the court under the rule omnia praesumuntur rite esse acta.[2]

1   Non-contentious Probate Rules 1987, r 12.
2   See below, para 18.43.

Affidavit of plight and condition

18.37   In some circumstances an affidavit is required as to the condition of the will at the time when it was executed. In the first place this will be required where there is an alteration, obliteration or interlineation which is not authenticated by the signature or initials of the testator and witnesses in the margin.[1] The affidavit is required so that the registrar can decide whether to allow the will in that form to be admitted to probate. The usual evidence is an affidavit from someone who saw the will before or at the time of execution with those alterations.

1   Non-contentious Probate Rules 1987, r 14.

18.38   An affidavit is also required where from the face of the will it appears that some other document may have been pinned to it. Pin marks, or the indentation made by a paperclip, are sufficient to require an affidavit of condition, because if the documents were attached at the time of execution, that might be sufficient to make both of them testamentary documents.[1] The registrar will usually require to see the documents which were attached. Thus solicitors should be careful to tell clients not to punch the will or to attach any covering letter to it by means of a pin or paperclip.

1   See above, para 6.11.

18.39   If there is evidence of some attempt to tear or destroy the will, an affidavit of condition may also be required.[1]

1   Non-contentious Probate Rules 1987, r 15.

Administration, or administration with will

Guarantee

18.40   Section 120 of the Supreme Court Act 1981 provides that before granting letters of administration, the court may require one or more persons to act as sureties.[1] The sureties guarantee that they will make good any loss which any person interested in the administration of the estate may suffer in consequence of a breach by the administrator of his duties. At the time of requiring the guarantee to be given, the court fixes the limit of liability. Once a guarantee is given, it automatically applies for the benefit of every person interested in the administration of the estate.[2] However, before any such person takes action against the sureties, he must obtain the leave of the court. The section does not apply where the administration is granted to the Treasury Solicitor, and to certain other public or diplomatic officers.[3]

1   See further (1980) Law Soc Gaz 1275.
2   Supreme Court Act 1981, s 120(2).
3   Ie the Public Trustee, the Solicitor of the Duchy of Lancaster or of the Duchy of Cornwall; the Chief Crown Solicitor for Northern Ireland; and to certain consular officers where the Consular Conventions Act 1949, s 1, applies.

Special cases

Privileged wills

18.41   Where an informal will is to be proved, it must be accompanied by an affidavit showing the circumstances in which it is alleged that the deceased was entitled to make an informal will. This may arise where it is alleged the will complies with formalities of a foreign law under the Wills Act 1963[1] or is made by a privileged testator who is a soldier or seaman.[2]

1   Non-contentious Probate Rules 1987, r 17(b); see above, paras 6.47–6.50.
2   Ibid, r 17(a); see chap 7, above.

Affidavit of law

18.42   An affidavit is sometimes required as to the law of a foreign country. Thus, where a person applies for the grant of administration to the estate of a person who died domiciled abroad on the ground that he is the person entitled by the law of domicile to administer, an affidavit of law is required to show that he is in fact so domiciled. Such an affidavit must be by a barrister or advocate who practises or has practised in that country, or by some other person who is able to satisfy the court that he has knowledge of the law of the country in question.[1]

1   Non-contentious Probate Rules 1987, r 19.

Presumption of due execution

18.43   The court will in some circumstances apply the maxim omnia praesumuntur rite esse acta and admit a document to probate accordingly.[1] The classic statement of the doctrine is that of Lindley LJ in *Harris v Knight*, where he said:[2] 'The maxim expresses an inference which may reasonably be drawn when an intention to do some formal act is established; when the evidence is consistent with that intention having been carried into effect in a proper way; but when the actual observance of all due formalities can only be inferred as a matter of probability.'

1   *Re Sims, Sims v Faulkner* (1972) 116 Sol Jo 356.
2   (1890) 15 PD 170 at 179.

18.44   When this dictum is analysed it may not be of very great assistance. The first part requires the establishment of an intention to do a formal act, that is, to make a will. This intention will be presumed in the absence of evidence to the contrary if the document appears on its face to be a will.

The second element in the dictum is that the evidence must be consistent with the intention having been carried into effect. The making of any will is consistent with an intention to make it. The final element is that the actual observance of all due formalities can only be inferred. One can therefore state rather more simply that the maxim will apply whenever there is a document which on its face appears to be a will and where its appearance is consistent with the formal requirements of the Act having been observed. The maxim is particularly useful where the only witnesses and other persons present at the time of execution are dead, or cannot be traced, or where their evidence is unreliable. Indeed, in *Rolleston v Sinclair*,[1] an Irish case, it was said that the maxim can be adopted only in these circumstances.

1 [1924] 2 IR 157.

18.45 Another example of the operation of the rule is *Re Denning, Harnett v Elliott*.[1] That case was concerned with an application for probate of a single sheet of paper, on one side of which was a dispositive part signed by the deceased, and on the reverse were the signatures of two unidentified persons without any attestation clause. In admitting the document to probate, Sachs J said that there was 'no other practical reason why those names should be on the back of the document unless it was for the purpose of attesting the will'.

1 [1958] 2 All ER 1.

18.46 The presumption can be used only where there is no evidence pointing to wrongful execution. So in *Re Bercovitz*[1] there was a signature of the testator and of two witnesses at the top of the document, and the signature of the testator alone at the bottom. This pointed to non-compliance with the provisions of the Wills Act,[2] and the maxim did not apply to save the will. In this case Philimore J said[3] that the strength of the presumption varies with all the circumstances, it being strong where the document is in regular form, and weaker where it is unusual. *Re Denning, Harnett v Elliott*,[4] however, shows the lengths to which the court will sometimes go in admitting a document to probate.

1 [1961] 2 All ER 481, [1961] 1 WLR 892.
2 The operative signature on wills of testators dying before 1983 had to be at the 'foot or end' of the will. Under the Administration of Justice Act 1982, however, the signature needs simply to be such that it appears to be intended to give effect to the will. See above, paras 6.18ff.
3 [1961] 2 All ER 481 at 485, [1961] 1 WLR 892 at 894.
4 [1958] 2 All ER 1; above, para 18.45.

Lost wills

18.47 It has been seen[1] that a will, once validly made, will remain in effect in law even if the document itself has ceased to exist. It has also been seen[2] that where a will was last known to be in the possession of the testator, the testator is presumed to have destroyed it animo revocandi although this presumption is capable of being rebutted. Accordingly, where an attempt is made to prove a reconstruction of a lost will, it is necessary to show:

(a)   that the deceased had executed a will;
(b)   that the will was executed in accordance with legal requirements;
(c)   that the reconstruction corresponds to the original will; and
(d)   that if the loss of the will raises a presumption of revocation animo revocandi, then that presumption is rebutted.[3]

1   Above, para 6.56.
2   Above, paras 8.53–8.58.
3   *Palmer v Smedley* [1974] 1 NZLR 751 (New Zealand Supreme Court).

The reconstruction

18.48   Where an attempt is made to prove a lost will, its contents must be reconstructed in the most accurate manner possible. If it was professionally prepared, the solicitor may have retained a draft of the will, or a copy. If there is no document in existence, an epitome is prepared from the recollection of persons who had read the will. In *Sugden v Lord St Leonards*[1] the court was concerned with the estate of Lord St Leonards, a former Lord Chancellor. Towards the end of his life he made numerous wills, the last being made in 1870, with eight codicils to it. On his death in 1875, the codicils were found, but not the will, and an attempt was made to reconstruct the will. His daughter had acted as his secretary for a number of years, and she gave evidence that Lord St Leonards had asked her to read the will over to him so many times that she was able to write out from memory its main provisions. The Court of Appeal admitted to probate the daughter's reconstruction.

1   (1876) 1 PD 154.

18.49   In *Re Yelland*[1] the testatrix had made a will in 1951, leaving her husband a life interest, with remainder to her daughter Florence and the children of Florence. The testatrix died in 1952, and shortly after her death her husband threw the will on the fire, and obtained a grant of letters of administration on the wholly false basis that the testatrix had died intestate without issue. The husband died in 1972, and after his death a dispute arose between the executrix of the will of the husband and Florence, and Florence attempted to prove the will which had been destroyed. Florence had read the will only once, for about five minutes, and this was over 20 years before the case, yet she claimed to be able to remember the exact terms of the will. Oliver J thought it most unlikely that Florence could have remembered the exact and literal terms, but nevertheless he admitted her reconstruction to probate as representing the substance of the testamentary dispositions contained in the will.

1   (1975) 119 Sol Jo 562.

Evidence of the reconstruction

18.50   It was at one time thought that the burden of proof required to obtain probate of a lost will was equivalent to that in criminal proceedings,[1] but this view was rejected in *Re Yelland*[1a], where the court adopted the ordinary test in civil cases of considering the balance of probabilities. The task of the person seeking to prove the lost will is aided where the result is one which the testator is likely to have intended. In both *Sugden v Lord St Leonards*[2] and *Re Yelland*[3] the result was one which the court considered likely to have commended itself to the testator. Where the evidence of the contents of the will is that of the beneficiary, the court will need to be satisfied that there were no suspicious circumstances,[4] but in both *Sugden v Lord St Leonards* and *Re Yelland* the only evidence was that of the beneficiary.[5]

1 *Woodward v Goulstone* (1886) 11 App Cas 469. See also *Harris v Knight* (1890) 15 PD 170; *Re Wipperman, Wissler v Wipperman* [1955] P 59, [1953] 1 All ER 764.
1a See above, para 18.49.
2 Above, para 18.48.
3 Above, para 18.49.
4 See above, Chapter 5.
5 See also *Re Phibbs' Estate* [1917] P 93; below, para 20.15.

18.51 It will be seen[1] that declarations made by the testator himself as to the contents of his will are admissible in evidence.

1 Below, paras 20.16–20.24.

Formalities of execution

18.52 It is not only necessary to prove the contents of the lost will, but also that it was duly executed, although the maxim omnia praesumuntur rite esse acta will often assist. In *Re Yelland*[1] the two witnesses to the will had both died, but one of the witnesses had told a neighbour that she had witnessed the testatrix's will, and that statement was admitted under the Civil Evidence Act 1968.

1 (1975) 119 Sol Jo 562.

18.53 A more striking illustration of the operation of the presumption is *Re Webb, Smith v Johnston*.[1] In that case Faulks J said: 'The court will not allow defective memory alone to overturn a will which is upon the face of it duly executed; if the witnesses are utterly forgetful of the facts, the presumption omnia praesumuntur rite esse acta will prevail.' In *Re Webb, Smith v Johnston* an application was made to obtain probate of the draft of a will when the original had been lost. The original had probably been destroyed when the testatrix's solicitor's office was destroyed by a bomb in 1940. The draft showed that the will had been attested by a Mrs Mackins, and by a solicitor, since deceased. No other person was found who was present when the will was made. Mrs Mackins said in evidence that she did not remember the document at all, and that she remembered only having been called to the deceased's shop on one occasion and 'that a little man in a Homburg hat was there'. The judge accepted that this little man was the other solicitor, and admitted the will to probate.

1 [1964] 2 All ER 91.

Rebuttal of presumption of revocation

18.54 The rebuttal of the presumption that the testator destroyed the will animo revocandi, where it was last in his possession, has been considered previously.[1]

1 See above, para 8.54.

Caveats

18.55 A caveat is a notice to the registrar not to seal a grant without first giving notice to the person who lodged the caveat. A caveat may be lodged by any person. Once entered, it remains effective for six months, though it can then be renewed.[1]

1 Non-contentious Probate Rules 1987, r 44.

18.56 If a caveat has been entered, the applicant for the grant will be notified of the caveat, and if he wishes to proceed he must seek to have the caveat removed by, in the curious expression, 'warning' it. A warning to a caveat is issued by the registrar at the instigation of the applicant for the grant, and requires the caveator to enter an appearance to the warning within eight days of service. If the caveator does not enter an appearance, the caveat is removed and the grant will issue. If the caveator wishes to persist, the procedure depends on whether the caveator merely wishes to stop the applicant obtaining a grant, or whether he has some contrary interest. In the former case, he issues a summons for directions, which is heard by a registrar. In the latter case, he enters an appearance which gives details of his interest. In either case, at that stage, contentious business begins.

18.57 A caveat may be withdrawn by the caveator.

18.58 The rules[1] provide that a caveat may be entered by any person. It is usually used:
(a) where the caveator disputes the validity of a will which is about to be proved by another; *or*
(b) where the caveator wishes to prevent one person entitled in the same degree as himself from obtaining a grant alone, as, for example, where there are two brothers both equally entitled to a grant; *or*
(c) where the caveator wishes to show that the applicant is unfit to take a grant, or for some other reason a grant ought to be issued under s 116; *or*
(d) where the caveator just wishes to be notified of the grant, for such purposes as commencing proceedings against the estate, or for making an application under the family provision legislation.[2]

1 Non-contentious Probate Rules 1987, r 44.
2 So that the caveator will be warned, but he will not be justified in entering an appearance on these grounds. A better procedure is to make a standing search under ibid, r 43; see below, para 18.63.

18.59 A caveat is only a warning put upon the file of the Probate Registry which prevents proceedings to obtain probate or administration without notice to the caveator.[1] Although it may lead to proceedings, it does not constitute a step in proceedings. Accordingly, the caveator cannot be ordered to provide security for costs.[2]

1 *Re Emery, Emery v Emery* [1923] P 184.
2 *Rose v Epstein* [1974] 2 All ER 1065; affd [1974] 3 All ER 745, CA.

Citations

18.60 Citations are used both in contentious and non-contentious business, but for the sake of convenience, both are dealt with here. A citation is issued by the court at the instigation of a person interested for a variety of purposes.
(a) In the case of a person who has intermeddled, but, although entitled, has not applied for a grant: this is known as a citation to take a grant. Failure to take a grant once an order has been made following a citation is contempt, though the court may pass over the citee if it thinks fit.[1]
(b) In the case of a person who has a prior right to a grant of administration, to compel him to accept or refuse a grant. If he fails to do so, he loses his right to a grant, and the person next entitled can apply.
(c) To set aside a will of which probate in common form has been granted: in this case, the executors and all persons interested are cited to propound the will. This merely requires the executors to prove the will in solemn form. It is not applicable where it is sought to have the grant revoked.[2]
(d) To compel an executor or administrator to bring in a grant of representation so that it can be revoked, as, for example, where a will, or a later will, is discovered.
(e) To persons 'to see proceedings': this type of citation requires persons who are not made parties to a probate action to take notice of the proceedings so that they may be bound by the result as res judicata.

1 *Re Biggs' Estate* [1966] P 118.
2 *Re Jolley, Jolley v Jarvis* [1964] P 262.

Re-sealing

18.61 Where a person dies domiciled in Scotland, a confirmation (the Scottish equivalent of probate) is treated in England and Wales as a grant of representation without further formality.[1] If the Scottish grant is made to persons who were not nominated by the deceased, it is treated as a grant of letters of administration.[2] Likewise a grant of probate or letters of administration made in Northern Ireland in respect of a person dying domiciled there is treated as valid in England and Wales without the need for re-sealing.[3]

1   Administration of Estates Act 1971, s 1(1), which came into force on 1 January 1972; Non-contentious Probate (Amendment) Rules 1971.
2   Administration of Estates Act 1971, s 1(2).
3   Ibid, s 1(5). The converse is also true; ibid, s 2.

18.62   Grants of representation issued in certain Colonial or former Colonial territories may be re-sealed in England.[1] Once the seal of the English court is impressed on the grant, it takes effect as if it were a grant of the English court, and has operation accordingly.

1   Colonial Probates Act Application Order 1965. Documents which are not grants of representation but which, in their own country, have equivalent effect may also be re-sealed: see Registrar's Direction (1982) Law Soc Gaz Vol 79 17 March, p 337. For procedure, see Non-contentious Probate Rules 1987, r 39.

Standing search

18.63   A person who does not wish to delay the issue of a grant of representation to an estate, but who needs to know if a grant has been issued, can make a standing search. This may be useful, for example, in order to commence proceedings against the estate or to make a claim under the family provision legislation. A notice in a prescribed form can be lodged at or posted to any registry or sub-registry.[1] The applicant will then be sent an office copy of any grant issued within twelve months before and six months after the date of the search.[2]

1   Non-contentious Probate Rules 1987, r 43. The prescribed fee, currently £2, must accompany the notice.
2   The period may be extended for successive periods of six months by repeated applications for extension: ibid, r 43(3).

CHAPTER 19

Special grants

19.1 In the usual case, a grant of representation, whether of probate, letters of administration simpliciter, or letters of administration with will annexed, is unlimited as to both property and time. It therefore enables the personal representative to deal with the whole of the deceased's assets, and to complete fully the administration of his estate. In some cases, however, more restricted grants are issued. These may be divided into the following categories:
(a)   grants with a special purpose;
(b)   grants limited as to property;
(c)   grants limited as to time;
(d)   other special types of grant; and
(e)   grants relating to settled land.

Grants with a special purpose

Grants ad colligenda bona

19.2   Where the assets of the estate consist of perishables, or other assets which need quick attention, but no person applies for probate or administration, a grant ad colligenda bona may be obtained. This grant is intended to give the administrator power only to get in the estate of the deceased, and to do such acts as are necessary in order to preserve it, and it is usually limited in this way. A grant in these terms does not give a power to invest money collected in, or to sell the assets, even where a sale is necessary because the asset is wasting. If it is anticipated that powers of this nature will be required, they may be expressly included in the grant upon application being made to the court.[1]

1   For illustrations of the circumstances where such extended grants were made, see *Re Wyckoff's Goods* (1862) 32 LJPM & A 214; *Re Schwerdtfeger's Goods* (1876) 1 PD 424; *Re Stewart's Goods* (1869) LR 1 P & D 727; *Re Bolton's Goods* [1899] P 186.

19.3   A grant of administration ad colligenda bona will be made only where it is necessary in order to protect the estate. A graphic illustration of the power is provided by *IRC v Stype Investments (Jersey) Ltd*.[1] In May 1979 Sir

Charles Clore conveyed his Hereford estate, which was worth £21 million, to Stype Investments (Jersey) Ltd, a company incorporated in Jersey, to hold as bare trustees for Sir Charles. Two days later the Jersey company contracted to sell the property to the Prudential Assurance Co Ltd, and ultimately completed that sale. In the meantime, in July 1979 Sir Charles died. There was no doubt that, at his death, the equitable interest in the property, subject to the contract for sale, was an asset of Sir Charles's estate, but the executors named in his will, who were foreign residents, delayed for a considerable time in applying for a grant, and no capital transfer tax[2] was paid. Accordingly, on the application of the Inland Revenue, the court granted letters of administration ad colligenda bona to the Official Solicitor.[3]

1 [1982] 3 All ER 419, CA.
2 The forerunner of inheritance tax.
3 For a further example, see *Re Cohen* [1975] VR 187.

Grants ad litem

19.4 Two special types of grant may be issued in connection with legal proceedings. The most usual is a grant of administration pendente lite, which gives the administrator full powers of administration, other than to distribute residue, except that his powers cease on the termination of the action. This type of grant is discussed at para 19.22. The other type of grant in connection with legal proceedings is a grant ad litem. An administrator ad litem has power merely to represent the estate in proceedings. He has no power over the assets of the estate. This type of grant is usually made only where it is necessary to make the estate a defendant to an action, but the persons, if any, entitled to a grant will not take one out. Thus, in *Re Knight's Goods*[1] where a person wished to bring a claim against the estate for personal injuries under the Law Reform (Miscellaneous Provisions) Act 1934, but was unable to do so because the next of kin refused to apply for a grant, a grant ad litem was made to the Official Solicitor.[2]

1 [1939] 3 All ER 928.
2 The Official Solicitor can be appointed only with his consent, which was given in this case.

19.5 Where proceedings are in progress, and it is necessary to make the estate a party to the action, every Division of the High Court has power to appoint a person to represent the estate, and the acts of such a person bind the estate in the same way as if he had been a personal representative.[1] This procedure is, however, applicable only where the action is in progress, and the former procedure must be adopted where the estate is to be the defendant.

1 RSC Ord 15, r 5.

19.6 A simpler alternative procedure to enable proceedings to be commenced against an estate where no grant of representation has been obtained is provided for in s 2 of the Proceedings Against Estates Act 1970, considered below.[1]

1 At para 26.59. This alternative, however, is not available for an action to be brought *by* (as opposed to against) the estate or to an action which would not have lain against the deceased himself, such as a claim for family provision.

Grants limited as to property

Limited probate

19.7 Although there may not be more than four executors or administrators in respect of the same item of property, a testator may appoint executors of only certain assets, or assets in a specified area.[1] Where this is done, the executors so appointed obtain probate limited to that property. This type of grant is made usually in respect of literary works, where a special literary executor is appointed, and where the deceased left property both in England and elsewhere, and appoints separate executors of the English estate. Thus, in *Re Von Brentano's Estate*[2] the deceased, who was domiciled in Germany, made two wills, one dealing with English realty and appointing English executors, and the other dealing with the remaining assets in England and abroad. Limited probate was granted in respect of the English realty. In the case of settled property, if the settlement continues following the death, a special grant will be taken out limited to the settled property.[3]

1 *Re Falkner's Estate* (1915) 113 LT 927.
2 [1911] P 172.
3 See below, paras 24.11–24.16.

Section 113 grants

19.8 Section 113 of the Supreme Court Act 1981 gives the court power to grant probate or letters of administration of realty and personalty separately, and to limit in any way which it thinks fit a grant of realty. The section also gives a special power to make a grant in respect of a trust estate only. With the exception of the power in respect of trust estates, grants may not be issued separately under this section if the estate is insolvent.

19.9 Although the power to make separate grants exists, it will be exercised only where there is very good reason.[1] An example of the type of circumstance in which this power will be exercised is where a grant is needed only to complete title. Thus, in *Re Butler's Goods*[2] the testator died holding leasehold property, and title could be made only with the aid of a grant. A grant was made limited to that specified property.[3] The power may be, but is not necessarily, used where a will is made exercising a power of appointment. Limited grants have been issued restricted to the property devolving under general powers of appointment.[4] Alternatively, a general grant may be issued but with probate of only so much of the will as relates to the power of appointment.[5] The result is the same in either case.

1 *Re Lady Somerset's Goods* (1867) LR 1 P & D 350.
2 [1898] P 9.

3 See also *Re Baldwin's Goods* [1903] P 61; *Re Ratcliffe's Goods* [1899] P 110; *Re Agnese's Goods* [1900] P 60.
4 *Re Russell's Goods* (1890) 15 PD 111.
5 *Re Poole's Estate, Poole v Poole* [1919] P 10.

19.10 The power to make a separate grant in respect of trust estates is useful. Where the deceased was the last surviving trustee of a trust fund the whole of the legal title to that fund would have been vested in him, and would normally pass to his general personal representatives, who would be bound to give effect to the terms of the trust. If a separate grant, limited to the trust fund, is taken out, the representative under that grant would be entitled to appoint a new trustee or new trustees of the trust under the Trustee Act 1925, s 36(1). Representation limited to a trust fund may be granted to a beneficiary if the deceased sole trustee has no personal representatives, or if he has representatives and they agree.[1]

1 *Re Ratcliffe's Goods* [1899] P 110; *Pegg v Chamberlain* (1860) 1 Sw & Tr 527.

Grants 'save and except' and caeterorum

19.11 Both of these grants are made where a limited grant either has been or will be made. If under the terms of a will an executor is appointed of a specified item of property, such as the testator's literary works, as we have seen the executor is entitled to a grant limited to that property. Where the general executors wish to take out a grant before the limited grant is issued, they will take a grant save and except the literary works. If, however, the grant in respect of the literary works has already issued, they will take a grant caeterorum. The effect of these grants is exactly the same, and they differ only according to whether they precede or succeed the limited grant.

Grants de bonis non

19.12 A grant de bonis non administratis may be applied for where, following a grant of probate or letters of administration, the representative has not completed the administration of the estate, and there is no representative by the chain of representation. Under this type of grant, the administrator has full power to complete the administration of the estate.

19.13 Before a grant de bonis non can be issued it must be shown:
(a) that a previous grant has been made to the deceased's estate. If part of the estate has been administered, but without a grant having been taken out, an original grant must be obtained, and not a grant de bonis non;
(b) that there is no remaining personal representative;
(c) that part of the estate is left unadministered.
The second requirement, that there must be no remaining personal representative, means that a grant de bonis non must not be issued where there is a surviving personal representative, or where there is an executor by representation.[1] If, therefore, there are two personal representatives, and one dies, the whole power will pass to the survivor, and there will be no case

for a de bonis non grant. Again, if the sole or last surviving executor dies, and the executor appointed by his will proves, so that the chain of representation operates, there will be no case for a grant de bonis non.

1   Above, para 17.6.

19.14   Although de bonis non grants are usually issued following the death of the personal representative, they may also be issued where a previous grant is revoked. This has happened where the court revoked a grant of letters of administration because the administrator disappeared[1] and where the administrator permanently left the jurisdiction.[2]

1   *Re Loveday's Goods* [1900] P 154.
2   *Re Sakers's Estate* [1909] P 233; *Re French's Estate* [1910] P 169; *Re Thomas's Estate* [1912] P 177.

19.15   If the last surviving personal representative holds assets in the capacity of trustee only, such as where the administration of the estate had come to an end,[1] a grant de bonis non will not be necessary. If a sole surviving trustee dies, his personal representatives will have power to appoint a new trustee under Trustee Act 1925, s 36(1). In respect of realty and leaseholds, however, a personal representative will continue to hold in that capacity until he makes a formal assent to himself, to vest the property in himself in the capacity of trustee.[2]

1   See below, paras 22.5ff, for a more detailed statement of the position.
2   *Re King's Will Trusts, Assheton v Boyne* [1964] Ch 542.

19.16   A grant de bonis non involves the same full procedure as for obtaining any grant of administration, so that an Inland Revenue account of the whole of the estate (and not merely of the unadministered part) must be sworn, and a guarantee obtained.

19.17   Where the deceased personal representative was an executor, or administrator with will the grant will be of administration cum testamento annexo et de bonis non administratis, and if he was an administrator simpliciter he will be an administrator de bonis non administratis.

19.18   A grant de bonis non can be made only to the persons who would have been entitled to the original grant, either of administration or administration with will.[1]

1   Ie, the persons who would have been entitled to apply had no previous grant been made. See above, paras 17.37 and 17.38.

Grants limited as to time

Limited probate or administration with will

19.19   Just as a will may limit the property to which it is subject, so it may limit the time for which a person is to act as executor. Limited probate would be granted accordingly. The only situation where this is at all usual is where a person is appointed to act as executor during the minority of the principal beneficiary.

Where will not available

19.20 Where the original will is in existence but it cannot be produced, as where it is held by a foreign court, and there is an urgent need to obtain a grant of representation, a grant of administration with will annexed may be issued, limited until the original or a more authentic copy of the will is brought into the registry.[1] Similarly, where a will is known to have been in existence after the date of the testator's death, but cannot subsequently be found, administration will be granted 'till the will be found'.[2] This situation must be carefully distinguished from that where the testator is known to have made a will, but it was not known to be in existence after his death. In this case, there is a presumption that it was revoked.[3]

1 *Re Lemme's Goods* [1892] P 89; *Re von Linden's Goods* [1896] P 148.
2 *Re Wright's Goods* [1893] P 21.
3 See above, para 8.53.

Administration durante absentia

19.21 Where the personal representative remains out of England and Wales[1] the court may grant administration durante absentia to a creditor or any person interested in the estate. There are two types of grant durante absentia. The earlier type, as the name shows, determines automatically upon the return to the jurisdiction of the original representative,[2] but for it to have this effect, an appropriate limitation must be included in the grant. The more common type of grant does not determine on the return of the original representative, or on his death.[3] Where, however, a grant durante absentia has been made, and the representative under that grant is a party to proceedings, then in the event of the original representative returning to the jurisdiction he is also made a party to the proceedings.[4]

1 Even if the personal representative is in Scotland: *Taynton v Hannay* (1802) 3 Bos & P 26.
2 *Slaughter v May* (1704) 1 Salk 42.
3 *Taynton v Hannay* (1802) 3 Bos & P 26.
4 Judicature Act 1925, s 164(3).

Administration pendente lite

19.22 The circumstances in which a grant ad litem will be made were explained at para 19.4. Section 117 of the Supreme Court Act 1981 gives power to appoint an administrator pendente lite where there is any dispute as to the validity of a will[1] or as to the right to administer.[2] Section 117 enables the court in these circumstances to appoint 'an administrator'. It has been held[3] that this overrides the provisions of s 114, which requires two administrators to be appointed in the case of a minority or life interest, so that in *Re Haslip*[4] appointment was made to only one administrator, even though there was a life interest.[5] Two administrators pendente lite may, of course, be appointed if it is so desired.

1   See *Hewson v Shelley* [1914] 2 Ch 13.
2   *Frederick v Hook* (1690) Carth 153.
3   On the corresponding provision in the Judicature Act 1925.
4   [1958] 2 All ER 275n; following *Re Lindley's Goods* [1953] P 203. However, in *Re Hall* [1950] P 156, a grant to a single administrator was refused (see above, para 17.49), so that the power to grant administration to only one person exists only under s 117.
5   See above, para 17.54.

19.23   Administration pendente lite will be granted only where it can be shown that the appointment is necessary.[1] Thus, if there is an executor whose appointment is not in dispute, even if there is a dispute as to the remainder of the will, probate will be granted to that executor and a grant pendente lite will not issue. Likewise, where only a codicil is in dispute, probate will issue to the executor named in the will. Thus, in *Re Day's Estate*[2] there was no dispute as to the validity of a will, but proceedings were brought as to the validity of a codicil. The codicil affected only a comparatively small part of the estate. The court refused to appoint an administrator pendente lite, but found in favour of the will, and granted probate to the executors upon their giving an undertaking not to administer the property the subject of the codicil, except in order to safeguard it. This left the validity of the codicil to be determined at a later date. A grant pendente lite can issue only where proceedings have actually been commenced, and the entry of a caveat, warning of a caveat, or entry of appearance to a warning[3] is not sufficient for this purpose.[4]

1   *Horrell v Witts and Plumley* (1866) LR 1 P & D 103.
2   [1940] 2 All ER 544.
3   See above, para 18.56.
4   *Salter v Salter* [1896] P 291.

19.24   Although there is no theoretical restriction on appointing as administrator pendente lite a person who is a party to the action,[1] administration is in practice granted only to an independent person. This is usually a professional person with no interest in the outcome of the proceedings, or alternatively the joint nominee of the parties.[2]

1   *Re Griffin, Griffin v Ackroyd* [1925] P 38.
2   *Stratton v Ford* (1754) 2 Lee 49; *Re Shorter's Goods* [1911] P 184.

19.25   Where an administrator pendente lite is appointed, the Chancery Division may still appoint a receiver, though it will seldom do so.[1] The probate court, however, will, when deciding upon the appointment of an administrator pendente lite, take into account the same considerations as the Chancery Division does when asked to appoint a receiver. These are the size and nature of the estate, and the fitness of the proposed administrator.[2]

1   *Re Oakes, Oakes v Porcheron* [1917] 1 Ch 230.
2   *Re Bevan, Bevan v Houldsworth* [1948] 1 All ER 271.

19.26   Once an administrator pendente lite is appointed, he has all the powers of a general administrator, except that of distributing the residue. Although s 117(2) provides that the only restriction on the administrator's power is on the distribution of residue, some of the older cases indicate that the administrator should not pay disputed debts or legacies.[1] It is not clear how far an administrator pendente lite is subject to these limitations after 1925. He may be sued by a creditor in the same way as an ordinary representative.[2]

1 *Charlton v Hindmarsh* (1860) 1 Sw & Tr 519; *Whittle v Keats* (1866) 35 LJP & M 54.
2 *Re Toleman, Westwood v Booker* [1897] 1 Ch 866.

19.27 The grant is limited to the duration of the proceedings, and the administrator's powers therefore come to an end on the termination of those proceedings. The person primarily entitled to the grant at that time then applies.

19.28 As an exception to the general position affecting personal representatives, an administrator pendente lite is entitled to remuneration, which is fixed by the court, and the account for his administration must be passed by the court.[1]

1 Supreme Court Act 1981, s 117(3).

Administration durante minore aetate

19.29 By virtue of s 118 of the Supreme Court Act 1981 a minor cannot take a grant, either of probate or of administration. Accordingly, where a minor is the sole executor of a will, administration with will annexed is granted to his guardian or such other person as the court thinks fit for his 'use and benefit'. Where the minor has no beneficial interest in the estate, administration will be granted to one administrator, but where he also has a beneficial interest, administration must be granted to two administrators, or a trust corporation.[1] Likewise, where a minor would be entitled to administration, administration durante minore aetate is made for the minor's use and benefit. As a minor can only be entitled to a grant of administration because he has a beneficial interest, the grant must be made to two individuals, or to a trust corporation.

1 Supreme Court Act 1981, s 114(2).

Persons entitled to the grant
19.30 Where the minor is appointed sole executor, and has no interest in the residuary estate, the person entitled to the residue is entitled to the grant.[1]

1 Non-contentious Probate Rules 1987, r 32(1).

19.31 Where the minor has a beneficial interest in the residue under the will, or is entitled on intestacy, the parent of the minor who has parental responsibility for him will be entitled to the grant.[1] Such parent will be:

(a)   if the minor's parents were married when the minor was born, both of them have parental responsibility[2] and either or both of them are entitled to take out the grant;

(b)   if the parents were not married when the minor was born, the mother has parental responsibility[3] but the father can obtain parental responsibility by court order or by a parental responsibility agreement with the mother.[4]

Alternatively, the grant may be issued to the guardian of the minor appointed by the court or to his testamentary guardian.[5] Further, the district judge or registrar has an overriding discretion to make an order appointing any person to obtain the grant, who may be appointed jointly with or to the exclusion of any of the persons mentioned above.[6]

1   Non-contentious Probate Rules 1987, r 32(1).
2   Children Act 1989, s 2(1).
3   Ibid, s 2(2).
4   Ibid, s 4.
5   Ibid, s 5.
6   Non-contentious Probate Rules 1987, r 32(2).

19.32   Where only one person is competent and willing to take out the grant, that person may nominate another person to act with him, subject to the right of the court to reject the person nominated.[1]

1   Non-contentious Probate Rules 1987, r 32(3).

Effect of the grant

19.33   A grant durante minore aetate is usually limited expressly until the minor attains the age of 18. On his attaining that age, the grant automatically ceases, and the minor may then apply for probate. Where the minor does prove the will, the intervention of the durante minore aetate grant does not break the chain of representation.[1]

1   Administration of Estates Act 1925, s 7(3).

19.34   An administrator durante minore aetate has all the powers of an ordinary administrator, and he can therefore sell the estate in the course of administration, and complete the administration.[1] However, he exercises all his powers on behalf of the minor, and is accountable to the minor. The minor may, therefore, require the administrator to give him a full account of his administration, even if the minor has no beneficial interest in the estate.[2]

1   *Re Cope, Cope v Cope* (1880) 16 Ch D 49.
2   *Fotherby v Pate* (1747) 3 Atk 603; *Taylor v Newton* (1752) 1 Lee 15; *Harvell v Foster* [1954] 2 QB 367.

19.35   It is, of course, only appropriate to apply for a grant of this nature where the minor is the sole executor. Where he is the joint executor, the other executors are entitled to prove the will, with power to the minor to join in when he attains the age of 18. Provided he does prove at that time, again the chain of representation is not broken.[1]

1   See *Re Reid's Goods* [1896] P 129.

Administration during mental incapacity

19.36 The position where the person entitled to a grant is suffering from mental incapacity is similar to that where the person entitled is a minor. Administration, either simple or with will, as appropriate, will be granted for the use and benefit of the person under the incapacity. An application for a grant for the use and benefit of a person who is incapable of managing his affairs but is not resident in an institution must be accompanied by a certificate from his doctor showing, inter alia, that the patient is unlikely to become capable of managing his own affairs within three months.[1]

1 *Practice Direction* [1969] 1 All ER 494.

Persons entitled to the grant
19.37 Entitlement is in the following order of priority:[1]
(a) the person authorised by the Court of Protection to apply;
(b) the lawful attorney of the incapacitated person, acting under a registered power of attorney;
(c) the person entitled to the residuary estate of the deceased.
Further, the district judge or registrar has overriding discretion to make an order appointing any two or more persons to obtain the grant.[2] Where a grant is required to be made to not less than two administrators and there is only one person competent and willing to take out a grant, that person may nominate another person to act with him, subject to the right of the court to reject the person nominated.[3]

1 Non-contentious Probate Rules 1987, r 35(2).
2 Ibid, r 35(4).
3 Ibid, r 35(3).

19.38 If more than one person is entitled to a grant, and only one is suffering from incapacity, the grant is made to the others, with power reserved to the one under incapacity to join in when the disability ceases.

Incapacity arising after grant
19.39 Where the incapacity occurs after a grant has been made to a sole representative, the court will impound the grant, and make a grant to another limited to the period of the incapacity, and to the unadministered property.[1] Where the incapacity is of one of two or more representatives, the court will usually revoke the grant, making a new grant to the executor not under incapacity, with power to the other to join in when the disability ceases.[2]

1 See Registrar's Direction dated 16 July 1956.
2 *Re Shaw's Estate* [1905] P 92.

19.40 In *Re Galbraith's Goods*[1] there were two executors, and both became incapable by reason of old age. On the application of a relative, the probate was revoked, and a new grant de bonis non was issued to another. A grant de bonis non will be issued only where the representatives will not recover from the incapacity.

1 [1951] P 422.

Miscellaneous grants

Double probate

19.41 It has been shown[1] that where in his will the testator appoints more than one executor, any of the executors may obtain a grant without consulting the others, provided the first gives notice to the others, and in this event power will be reserved to the others to apply for a grant later. Where that person subsequently does apply for a grant, it will be called 'double probate'. The earlier grant is not called in.

1 Above, para 17.20.

Cessate grant

19.42 Where a grant limited as to time has been made, and has ceased to have effect because that period has expired, the subsequent grant is known as a cessate grant. Thus, if a testator appoints one person to be his executor for, say, five years, and then appoints another, that other will, after the five-year period has expired, obtain a cessate grant. Theoretically, the cessate grant is a renewal of the whole original grant, whereas a grant de bonis non is a grant of only so much of the estate as is unadministered, but in practice cessate grants and grants de bonis non have the same effect.

Grants to attorneys

19.43 A person entitled to a grant of probate or administration may appoint an attorney to take out the grant on his behalf.[1] The grant is usually limited for the use and benefit of the principal, and until such time as he himself shall apply for a grant. While his grant is in force, the attorney has full power to administer the estate.[2] When he comes to distribute the residue, he may himself either distribute to the beneficiaries entitled, or pay it over to the principal if, by the law of domicile of the principal, the principal is obliged to perform the functions of executor or administrator.[3]

1 Non-contentious Probate Rules 1987, r 31. If the person entitled to the grant is an executor, notice of the application must be given to any other executor (r 31(2)) and where the person entitled is mentally incapable, r 35 is to apply (r 31(2)). A general power of attorney given in accordance with the Powers of Attorney Act 1971 is sufficient, as is an enduring power of attorney; alternatively, a power limited to taking out the grant may be given.
2 *Re Rendell, Wood v Rendell* [1901] 1 Ch 230.
3 Ibid; *Re Achillopoulos, Johnson v Mavromichali* [1928] Ch 433.

19.44 The grant will be revoked if and when the principal applies for a grant, or the principal dies.[1] However, where there are two principals, and they jointly appoint one attorney, the death of one only of the principals will not in itself revoke the grant, though it will be revoked if the survivor appoints a different attorney.[2]

1 *Pipon v Wallis* (1753) 1 Lee 402; *Re Cassidy's Goods* (1832) 4 Hag Ecc 360; *Suwerkrop v Day* (1838) 8 Ad & El 624; and see *Re Dinshaw's Goods* [1930] P 180.
2 *Re Dinshaw's Goods*, above.

19.45 The usual provisions of the Powers of Attorney Act 1971 governing attorneys will apply to attorney administrators, and protection will be conferred thereby.

19.46 Where the principal was appointed executor, the attorney takes a grant of administration with will annexed, but nevertheless, for the purposes of the chain of representation, he is regarded as standing in the stead of the executor himself, so that the chain of representation is not broken by a grant of administration with will to an attorney administrator, even if his principal never himself proves the will.[1]

1 *Re Murguia's Goods* (1884) 9 PD 236.

Settled land

19.47 Special rules apply to the persons entitled to a grant in respect of settled land, known as special personal representatives, and grants in respect of settled land are the most frequent types of grant which are made where there is a limitation to a particular type of property. It will, however, be more convenient to defer consideration of them until the devolution of settled land itself is discussed.[1]

1 Below, chap 24.

CHAPTER 20

Contentious business

Definition

20.1 There is no statutory definition of contentious business, although the expression is used in the same sense as the definition of a probate action in the Rules of the Supreme Court. This is:[1] 'an action for the grant of probate of the will, or letters of administration of the estate, of a deceased person or for the revocation of such a grant, or for a decree pronouncing for or against the validity of an alleged will, not being an action which is non-contentious or common form probate business'. It will be seen that care needs to be exercised in the use of the expression contentious business, because some aspects of the non-contentious procedure, particularly with regard to caveats and citations, may have an element of contention in them, although they are excluded from this definition. Contentious business is usually commenced by writ of summons, which is discretionary and is not issuable as of right. Contentious business is dealt with in the Chancery Division.[2]

1 RSC Ord 76, r 1(2).
2 Supreme Court Act 1981, Sch 1, para 1(h).

20.2 Contentious business falls into three categories:
(a) actions as to the validity of a will, which are actions to prove the will in solemn form;
(b) actions between two or more applicants for the right to take a grant of representation; and
(c) actions to revoke a grant, previously made in common form.
The same action may consist of any combination of these elements.

20.3 It is not proposed to consider here the procedure followed in a probate action, but to deal only with the entitlement to require a will to be proved in solemn form; evidence in contentious cases; and costs. Much of what is said with regard to the types of evidence which are admissible applies also to non-contentious business. The use of citations in contentious business was referred to at para 18.60.

Proof of will in solemn form

At instance of executor

20.4 Probate in common form is an order of the court and therefore everyone acting under it is protected as long as those acts were done while it was in force. As will be seen, however, the executor can be required to prove the will in solemn form, and where this is anticipated it will be more convenient for the executor himself to apply for probate in solemn form at the outset. It is, therefore, advisable for the executor to seek probate in solemn form if there are doubts as to its validity, or as to the validity of a codicil, or if it is anticipated that there will be opposition to the will. As a general principle, the longer the time which elapses from the death, the more difficult will be the proof.

20.5 Apart from the more obvious case where the executor may apply for probate in solemn form, it may be noted that this procedure is often adopted where it is sought to obtain probate of a lost will, and the consent of persons having a contrary interest cannot be obtained. In these circumstances, it is open to the court to grant probate on motion, and it will do so where the issue is clear,[1] but if an attempt is made to obtain a grant on motion, the judge may well refuse to deal with the question on motion, and to require an action to be brought.[2]

1 See eg *Re Penson's Estate* [1960] CLY 1232.
2 *Re Apted's Goods* [1899] P 272; *Re Pearson's Goods* [1896] P 289.

At instance of other persons interested

20.6 Anyone who has a contrary beneficial interest to the will being propounded, that is, as being entitled on intestacy, or under an earlier will, or a person named as executor in another will may require the executor to prove the will in solemn form. Thus, the following classes of persons may require probate in solemn form:
(a) persons entitled to any share of the estate on intestacy. They are entitled to insist on this right even if they have stood by while probate in common form was granted,[1] or even if they have received a legacy under the will;[2]
(b) a beneficiary under the will. This is so that he can be sure of his own position, but as a condition of allowing him to take action to require probate in solemn form, he will be obliged to pay his legacy into court until the result of the action is known;[3]
(c) a beneficiary under a previous will; and
(d) an executor under a previous will.
A creditor is not allowed to insist on solemn form probate, as he is concerned only to be paid his debt, which will be paid out of the estate irrespective of whether any will is valid.[4]

1 *Re Jolley, Jolley v Jarvis* [1964] P 262.
2 *Bell v Armstrong* (1822) 1 Add 365 at 374.

3 *Braham v Burchell* (1826) 3 Add 243.
4 *Burroughs v Griffiths* (1754) 1 Lee 544; *Menzies v Pulbrook and Ker* (1841) 2 Curt 845.

20.7 A person so interested may take action either before the will has been proved at all, or after it has been proved in common form.[1] The action is commenced by the person opposing the will, but the person propounding the will can insist that the opposer shows that he has some interest in the estate. This interest, however, may be very slight,[2] and the mere possibility of an estate is sufficient.[3]

1 *Re Jolley, Jolley v Jarvis* [1964] P 262.
2 *Hingeston v Tucker* (1862) 2 Sw & Tr 596.
3 *Kipping and Barlow v Ash* (1845) 1 Rob Eccl 270.

20.8 An assignee of an interest under a will is in the same position as the assignor so far as being able to take action for probate in solemn form. So, in *Wintle v Nye*,[1] Colonel Wintle was only able to take action against Mr Nye by taking an assignment of a beneficial interest in a small part of the estate.

1 [1959] 1 All ER 552; see above, para 5.38.

Effect of probate in solemn form

20.9 When proved in solemn form, the will becomes res judicata and will bind all those who had notice of it. In *Re Barraclough, Barraclough v Young*[1] Payne J expressly approved the earlier dictum of Sir Cresswell Cresswell in *Young v Holloway*[2] in the following terms: 'The general principle, as I collect it, is this, that where a party has had full notice, and has had the opportunity of availing himself of the contest, he will be bound by the decision.' The principle applies if the party concerned has the opportunity to oppose the proceedings, whether or not he actually did so. *Re Barraclough, Barraclough v Young* was concerned with a will made in favour of a second wife, under which no reference was made to the child of the first marriage. The executrix under the will commenced proceedings to prove the will in solemn form, the daughter of the first marriage being a defendant to the action. The defendant claimed that the deceased was not of sound mind, memory and understanding in that he was suffering from the insane delusion that she was not his lawful child. The defendant was of virtually no means, and obtained a legal aid certificate to enable her to be represented in the proceedings. In the usual way, the legal aid certificate was subject to a condition that at the close of pleadings the papers would be considered by counsel, who would advise as to merits. Counsel advised adversely to the defendant, and her legal aid certificate was discharged. Having been abandoned by the legal aid authority, a compromise was reached whereby she withdrew her opposition on the basis that the plaintiff executrix would not seek an order for costs against her. The action was dealt with on that basis, and probate in solemn form was granted. However, some people never give up. The daughter subsequently obtained another opinion of counsel which was favourable to her, and sought to reopen the question. Payne J held that although he had jurisdiction[3] to set aside the proof in solemn form, as in the present case the action had been compromised, he would not do so. The daughter had had the opportunity of persisting in her opposition.[4]

1 [1965] 2 All ER 311 at 316.
2 [1895] P 87.
3 Under Ord 36, r 33.
4 See also *Young v Holloway* [1895] P 87; and *Re West, Tiger v Handley* [1948] WN 432.

20.10 Accordingly, probate in solemn form will be set aside only where it was obtained by fraud,[1] or a later will is discovered, or the party opposing has been prevented by some unavoidable accident from taking part in the proceedings.[2]

1 *Priestman v Thomas* (1884) 9 PD 70; *Birch v Birch* [1902] P 62.
2 Per Payne J in *Re Barraclough, Barraclough v Young* [1965] 2 All ER 311 at 316. See also *Re Langton's Estate* [1964] P 163.

Evidence in probate actions

Attesting witnesses

20.11 The best evidence which the court will accept of the due execution of a will is that of an attesting witness, so that a person propounding a will must call one of the attesting witnesses, unless they cannot be traced or are dead. This applies even if there is other evidence of due execution.

20.12 An attesting witness is regarded as a witness on behalf of the court, and not of either party.[1] Accordingly, if the executor calls one of the attesting witnesses, who gives evidence against proper execution, he may cross-examine that witness.[2] If at the same time as giving evidence as to due execution of the will the witness can also testify as to collateral matters, such as the capacity of the testator, and whether he knew and approved the contents of the will, the witness is treated as a witness of the court in respect of these matters also.[3] Probate may be granted in solemn form if one attesting witness speaks in favour of the will,[4] but if one speaks against the will, both must be called, if available.

1 *Jones v Jones* (1908) 24 TLR 839; *Oakes v Uzzell* [1932] P 19.
2 *Coles v Coles and Brown* (1866) LR 1 P & D 70; *Re Fuld (No 2)* [1965] P 405.
3 *Re Webster, Webster v Webster* [1974] 3 All ER 822n.
4 *Bowman v Hodgson* (1867) LR 1 P & D 362; *Owen v Williams* (1863) 32 LJP M & A 159.

20.13 Where neither of the attesting witnesses is available, the evidence of some other person who was also present at the time of execution may be admitted. The evidence of such a person is admissible, even if he takes a benefit under the will, and had for that reason refrained from attesting the will himself.[1]

1 *Mackay v Rawlinson* (1919) 35 TLR 223.

20.14 Even if the action is contested, the witnesses are allowed to remain in court until the judge directs to the contrary.[1]

1 *Re Nightingale, Green v Nightingale* [1975] 1 WLR 80.

Other evidence

20.15 If no attesting witness can be traced, and no other person can be found who was present at the time of execution, the court will admit the next best evidence that is available. Of this it is possible to give only examples. In *Re Phibbs' Estate*[1] the testator sent his will by registered post to his solicitor at Dublin, at the time of the civil disorder in Ireland. The letter never arrived and it was presumed to have been destroyed in a post office fire in Ireland. There was no record of who had witnessed the will. The testator's nephew, and the principal beneficiary who was a clerk to a solicitor, had both read through the will after execution and were able to remember the contents. Probate was granted. In *Palin v Ponting*[2] the will had first been proved in common form, and as part of that process, one of the attesting witnesses had sworn an affidavit of due execution. The witness was not available at the time of the application for probate in solemn form, and that previous affidavit of due execution was admitted in evidence. And in *Re Powe's Estate*[3] a solicitor who prepared the will was allowed to produce as a witness a note prepared by him at the same time.

1 [1917] P 93.
2 [1930] P 185.
3 [1956] P 110.

Declarations by the testator

Generally
20.16 The general rule with regard to the construction of wills is that the intention of the testator must be deduced from the will itself, and extrinsic evidence is admitted only in certain circumstances.[1] In addition to the circumstances in which extrinsic evidence is admissible to assist in the construction of the will, in the following three sets of circumstances declarations made by the testator are admissible.

1 See above, paras 10.46ff.

20.17 *Where the declaration is made by the testator in writing, and signed by him* In this case the declaration is within the terms of the Civil Evidence Act 1968, and is evidence of the statements contained in it.[1]

1 *Re Bridgewater's Estate* [1965] 1 All ER 717, a decision on the Evidence Act 1938.

20.18 *To show the state of mind of the testator* The types of situations in which this arises are:
(a) Where there is doubt whether a testamentary act has been done with the necessary animus testandi or animus revocandi. Thus evidence has

been admitted to show whether the testator signed a will animo testandi;[1] whether he destroyed a will animo revocandi;[2] and whether the presumption that a will known to have existed cannot be found at death has been revoked animo revocandi could be rebutted.[3]

(b)   Whether a particular document is in fact intended to be a will, or some other type of instrument. Thus in *Re Slinn's Goods*[4] where an elderly widow executed a deed in which she granted her savings to her niece, and it was not apparent from the face of the document whether it was intended to operate as a deed inter vivos or a will, the court admitted evidence that the woman had said that she wanted to settle her affairs, to show that it was intended as a will.

(c)   Whether, in the case of an allegation of unsoundness of mind, the testator had mental capacity.

(d)   Whether, in the case of an allegation of fraud, the will was consistent with the testator's desires.[5]

1   *Re Slinn's Goods* (1890) 15 PD 156.
2   *Giles v Warren* (1872) LR 2 P & D 401.
3   *Keen v Keen* (1873) LR 3 P & D 105.
4   (1890) 15 PD 156; and see above, para 2.10.
5   *Doe d Ellis v Hardy* (1836) 1 Mood & R 525; *Doe d Shallcross v Palmer* (1851) 16 QB 747.

20.19   *Exceptionally, to show that a will or codicil has been made or revoked in accordance with the formal requirements of the Wills Act* This last category causes difficulty. In general, declarations by the testator are not admissible to prove compliance with formal requirements. They are, however, admissible:

(a)   where the declaration comes within the Civil Evidence Act 1968;

(b)   to support (and presumably, therefore, to rebut) a presumption of due execution. Thus, in *Clarke v Clarke*[1] the testator made a holograph will which contained an attestation clause. He asked two illiterate farmhands to act as witnesses, and they signed the will with crosses. They died before the testator, and the court admitted in evidence a statement made by the testator to his wife at the time showing that he knew of the requirements for attestation.

1   (1880) 5 LR Ir 47.

20.20   An example of the application of two of these rules is *Re Bridgewater's Estate*.[1] The testator made two wills, one on 27 March 1960 and the other on 29 March 1960, to which he referred as his 'old will' and his 'new will' respectively. In August 1960 his solicitor sent the new will to him, together with an accompanying letter, and the testator replied: 'Thank you for your note with enclosure; you will find the old will has been deposited at the Municipal Bank, the new one having been destroyed.' On his death in 1962 neither will was found. The applicant, who was named as executor in both wills, claimed that notwithstanding the presumption that the new will was revoked because it could not be found, the testator had destroyed the new will only because he thought that the old will would thereby be revived, and that therefore the doctrine of dependent relative revocation would operate to save the new will.[2] Scarman J held that the letter from the testator was evidence of the testator's intention to destroy the new will with a view to setting up the old one. He held that the letter was also admissible under the Evidence Act 1938 as evidence of actual destruction. On this basis, the applicant was successful, and probate was granted of the new will.[3]

1 [1965] 1 All ER 717.
2 For consideration of this doctrine see paras 8.43ff.
3 It had been held in *Powell v Powell* (1866) LR 1 P & D 209 that the doctrine of dependent relative revocation could apply in circumstances such as this.

Where will lost or destroyed

20.21 There is no doubt that where a will has been lost, or is destroyed without animus revocandi, and an attempt is being made to reconstruct it for probate purposes, declarations made by the testator before or at the time of making the will are admissible as evidence of its contents. As Sir J P Wilde said in *Johnson v Lyford*:[1] 'It would often be impracticable to judge of the quality and nature of acts done if the statements of the person doing them immediately preceding or accompanying those acts were excluded from view.' There is, however, some doubt as to the admissibility of declarations made after the will was made.

1 (1868) LR 1 P & D 546.

20.22 The classic authority is *Sugden v Lord St Leonards*,[1] to which reference has already been made.[2] It will be recalled that the daughter gave evidence that she could recall the contents of the will from having repeatedly read it over to the deceased. In addition, she gave evidence of conversations with Lord St Leonards after the making of the will, which indicated the contents. The court thought it inconceivable that he would have died intestate, and it accepted the daughter's evidence. In the Court of Appeal the decision was upheld, but Mellish LJ dissented from the majority, and said that while he agreed with the result, the evidence of the conversations after the making of the will should not have been admitted.

1 (1876) 1 PD 154.
2 See above, para 18.48.

20.23 The decision was doubted by the House of Lords in *Woodward v Goulstone*[1] and it has been subsequently doubted by the Court of Appeal.[2] In the most recent decisions, *Sugden v Lord St Leonards* has been followed by the Court of Appeal,[3] and at first instance,[4] as well as being supported, obiter, by the Lord Chief Justice of Northern Ireland.[5] Although the position cannot be regarded as settled, it seems that *Sugden v Lord St Leonards* remains binding, though it will not be extended.

1 (1886) 11 App Cas 469.
2 *Atkinson v Morris* [1897] P 40 at 50; *Barkwell v Barkwell* [1928] P 91 at 97.
3 *Re MacGillivray's Estate* [1946] 2 All ER 301.
4 *Re Wipperman, Wissler v Wipperman* [1955] P 59.
5 *Re Gilliland's Goods* [1940] NI 125.

20.24 Although declarations by the testator as to the contents of a lost will may be admissible, the testator's declarations as to the execution of that will are generally not admissible.[1] In *Palmer v Smedley*[2] the testator had said on several occasions that prior to going overseas he had made a will leaving everything to his wife, but there was no trace of the will on his death. The court refused to admit the epitome to probate because there was no evidence that the will had been executed, although it did admit the testator's declarations as to the contents of the will.

1 See above, para 20.19, and the exceptions to this general principle noted there.
2 [1974] 1 NZLR 751 (New Zealand Supreme Court).

Costs

20.25 It is an implied term of the relationship between the executor and the estate that he is entitled to be paid out of the estate such costs as are incurred by him in establishing or maintaining his position. The position was summarised by Jessel MR in *Turner v Hancock*,[1] who said that the right of an executor to his costs rests 'substantially upon contract and [will] only be lost or curtailed by such inequitable conduct on the part of [the executor] as may amount to a violation or culpable neglect of his duty under the contract'.[2]

1 (1882) 20 Ch D 303 at 305.
2 See also *Re Plant's Estate* [1926] P 139, especially at 146.

20.26 Accordingly, as long as an executor acts reasonably, his position with regard to costs is protected. *Re Speke's Estate, Speke v Deakin*[1] is an example of a case where an order for costs was made against the executors. They had proved a will and two codicils in common form, and after the grant a third codicil was also found. The principal beneficiary under the third codicil asked the executors to prove that codicil, but they refused, saying that it had been made without the knowledge and approval of the testator. In some circumstances, where the evidence was abundantly clear, this attitude might have been proper, but in this case the judge described their attitude as 'perfect folly'. He condemned them to pay the costs personally.[2]

1 (1913) 109 LT 719.
2 For another example, see *Thomas v Jones* [1928] P 162.

20.27 From one point of view the general rule is unsatisfactory. Although, in the absence of culpable behaviour, an established executor is entitled to his costs, where a will is being proved for the first time, the person propounding the will cannot know until the outcome of the case whether in fact he is the executor. A person who is nominated in the will is not automatically entitled to his costs if he fails to establish the validity of the will,[1] and in this case the costs are in the discretion of the court.[2]

1 *Re Barlow's Estate* [1919] P 131.
2 See RSC Ord 65, r 1. See also *Davies v Jones* [1899] P 161.

20.28 So far as the costs of other parties are concerned, the position is:

(a) in all cases, costs are in the discretion of the court;[1] subject to this:
(b) where the costs have been incurred through the fault of the testator, or of the persons interested in residue, the court will order the costs to be paid out of the estate;[2]
(c) where a party is unsuccessful, but brought the proceedings reasonably, he may not have an order for costs made against him;[3]
(d) in all other cases the court will usually award costs to the successful party.

An example of a case where the costs are incurred through the fault of the testator would be where the will on its face is not clear, and judicial action is necessary to resolve the doubt. It does not include 'fault' in a more general sense, such as failing to make provision for certain classes of beneficiary who may have a moral claim on the estate,[4] or by telling persons in his lifetime that he had made provision for them, whereas he had in fact not done so.[5]

1 *Mitchell and Mitchell v Gard and Kingwell* (1863) 3 Sw & Tr 275 at 278; *Twist v Tye* [1902] P 92 at 93; *Re Cutliffe's Estate, Le Duc v Veness* [1959] P 6.
2 *Spiers v English* [1907] P 122.
3 *Spiers v English* [1907] P 122 at 123.
4 Subject to the right of an applicant to apply under the family provision legislation.
5 *Re Cutliffe's Estate, Le Duc v Veness* [1959] P 6 at 19.

CHAPTER 21

Revocation of grants

Power to revoke

21.1 Section 121 of the Supreme Court Act 1981 confers upon the High Court power to revoke grants, as well as to make them. Section 121 is in general terms, and does not specify the circumstances in which a grant will be revoked, but a body of law has developed so that there is now little doubt as to when a grant will be revoked. The court also has power to amend a grant.[1]

1 Non-contentious Probate Rules 1987, r 41.

When grants will be revoked

21.2 There are two principles which the court applies in deciding whether to revoke a grant:
(a) the person truly entitled to a grant shall prevail; and
(b) the court has regard to the interests of the beneficiaries under the will or on intestacy.[1]
By applying these principles, it appears that a grant will be revoked in the following circumstances.
(a) Where the 'deceased' is in fact alive.[2]
(b) Where the grant has been made to the wrong person. Thus in *Re Bergman's Goods*[3] a grant was made to a person who claimed to be a relative, and who, had he in fact been a relative, would have been entitled to the grant. It was revoked when it was found that he was illegitimate. Again, in *Re Moore's Goods*,[4] where a man and a woman had lived together as man and wife, and, upon the man's death, the woman obtained a grant of administration as his 'widow', that grant was revoked upon it being shown that she had not been legally married.[5]
(c) Where on the facts as known at the time of the grant it was properly made, but facts subsequently coming to light show it to have been improper. This will apply if, after a will is proved, a codicil is discovered appointing a different executor, or if a completely new will is discovered. It will also apply if it subsequently appears that the deceased married after making the will.[6]

311

(d) If the grant was obtained in contravention of the appropriate procedural requirements. This includes cases where a grant has been inadvertently issued after the entry of a caveat, but without notice to the caveator;[7] where a person in a lower order of entitlement has obtained a grant of administration without citing all those with a higher right;[8] and where a grant was mistakenly issued less than the prescribed time from the date of death.[9]

(e) Where the grant was obtained through fraud on the court.[10]

(f) Where, in the case of a grant in solemn form, a person having an opposing interest was, through unavoidable accident, precluded from taking part in the proceedings.[11]

(g) Where, after a will has been proved in common form, the executors attempt to prove it in solemn form, but are unable to do so.

(h) Where one of two representatives becomes incapable of acting, so that a new grant may be made to the other.[12] Where, however, a sole representative becomes incapable, the grant will usually be impounded during the period of incapacity, and not revoked.[13]

(i) Where the representative has permanently left the jurisdiction, or otherwise cannot be found.[14]

The first seven of these grounds are within the first principle, namely proper entitlement, and the last two are within the second principle, of the court acting to safeguard the interests of the beneficiaries.

1 See *Re Galbraith's Goods* [1951] P 422.
2 *Re Napier's Goods* (1809) 1 Phillim 83; *Re Bloch's Estate* (1959) Times, 2 July.
3 (1842) 2 Notes of Cases 22.
4 (1845) 3 Notes of Cases 601.
5 See also *Re Langley's Goods* (1851) 2 Rob Eccl 407.
6 *Priestman v Thomas* (1884) 9 PD 210.
7 *Trimlestown v Trimlestown* (1830) 3 Hagg Ecc 243.
8 *Ravenscroft v Ravenscroft* (1671) 1 Lev 305.
9 *Trimlestown v Trimlestown*, above; *Blackborough v Davis* (1700) 1 Salk 38.
10 *Priestman v Thomas* (1884) 9 PD 70; *Birch v Birch* [1902] P 62; *Re Barraclough, Barraclough v Young* [1967] P 1, [1965] 2 All ER 311.
11 See *Re Barraclough, Barraclough v Young* [1965] 2 All ER 311 at 316.
12 *Re Phillips' Goods* (1824) 2 Add 335; *Re Shaw's Estate* [1905] P 92; see above, Chapter 19.
13 *Re Cooke's Goods* [1895] P 68.
14 *Re Bradshaw's Goods* (1887) 13 PD 18; *Re French's Estate* [1910] P 169; *Re Thomas's Estate* [1912] P 177.

21.3 Where a grant of letters of administration is made, it will state who is entitled to administer the deceased's estate.[1] If it subsequently transpires that that statement is wrong, the grant should be revoked if the statement is inconsistent with the true entitlement.[2] For example, if the grant stated that the testator died a bachelor, and that those entitled to his estate were his brothers, the grant would be revoked if it came to light that he was in fact married and was survived by his spouse. If, however, the statement in the grant is not inconsistent with beneficial entitlement, then it need not be revoked. Thus, where the grant stated that the deceased died a spinster leaving seven nephews and nieces, and it subsequently transpired that the children of a predeceased nephew were also entitled to share, it was not necessary for the grant to be revoked.[3]

1 See illustration below, Appendix C.

2 *Re Ivory, Hankin v Turner* (1878) 10 Ch D 372.
3 *Re Ward, National Westminster Bank Ltd v Ward* [1971] 2 All ER 1249.

Procedure on revocation

21.4 The Non-contentious Probate Rules[1] envisage that in most cases an application for revocation will be made by the party to whom the grant was made, and they provide that a grant is to be revoked on the application of some other party only in exceptional circumstances. This, however, applies only to non-contentious business. Where an application is made to compel revocation, and the person to whom the grant was made actively resists, the matter will be contested, and will come within the definition of contentious business.[2]

1 Non-contentious Probate Rules 1987, r 41.
2 See above, paras 20.1–20.2.

21.5 In general, the court will not make a new grant until the old grant has been revoked.[1] Where the application for revocation is made by some person other than the person to whom the grant was issued, he may issue a citation to the grantee requiring him to bring in his grant to the registry.[2] However, s 121 of the Supreme Court Act 1981 enables the court to call in a grant on its own initiative, and to revoke a grant without it being called in, if it cannot be obtained.[3] Further, a personal representative is always under an obligation to deliver up his grant when called upon to do so by the court.[4] A theoretical distinction is drawn between the situation where a grant is called in and cancelled, and one where, because it cannot be produced, it is revoked but not cancelled.[5] No practical difference results from this distinction.

1 *Re Hornbuckle's Goods* (1890) 15 PD 149.
2 See above, para 18.60.
3 Eg if it has been lost, or cannot be traced.
4 Administration of Estates Act 1925, s 25(c), substituted by Administration of Estates Act 1971, s 9.
5 *Re Thomas's Estate* [1912] P 177.

Amendment

21.6 The court has power to amend a grant,[1] but this power will be exercised only where a non-substantial error has been made on the grant, such as a mistake in the date or place of death of the deceased, or in the name or address of the grantee. All questions of substance must be dealt with by revocation, and the issue of a new grant. It should be noted, however, that the court will not revoke a grant if there is any other way of achieving a proper result. If, therefore, after a grant has been made of a will, a codicil is discovered, a separate grant will be made of that codicil, without disturbing the existing grant in respect of the will, unless the codicil appoints different executors.[2]

1 Non-contentious Probate Rules 1987, r 41.
2 In which case the grant will be revoked.

Misconduct on part of grantee

21.7 It will be noted that in the list of circumstances given above in which the court will revoke a grant, no reference was made to revocation on the ground of the representative's misconduct. This is because the beneficiaries will usually be protected by some other means. In particular, the representatives can be compelled to make on oath an inventory and account under Administration of Estates Act 1925, s 25, and an action will lie against them at the instance of the beneficiaries in the case of default.[1]

1 *Hill v Bird* (1648) Sty 102; *Re Cope's Estate* [1954] 1 All ER 698.

Effect of revocation

21.8 A grant of probate or administration, being an order of the court, confers full protection on those acting under it while it remains in force, and it is specifically provided that even if it was improperly issued, a purchaser acting under it will be protected, even if he had knowledge of the impropriety.[1] This is particularly important with regard to settled land. Where it appears on the face of the will that a grant of special representation should have been made to the trustees for the purposes of the Settled Land Act,[2] but in fact a general grant is issued, the purchaser from the general personal representatives is protected, and obtains a good title.[3]

1 Law of Property Act 1925, s 204.
2 See below, paras 24.22–24.25.
3 *Re Bridgett and Hayes' Contract* [1928] Ch 163; *Re Taylor's Estate* [1929] P 260 at 263.

21.9 There is no single provision which protects persons who have relied upon a grant which is subsequently revoked, but a series of separate provisions which go a long way towards having the same effect. These are described in the next five paragraphs.

Administration of Estates Act 1925, section 27
21.10 Sub-section (2) provides that if a payment has been made to a personal representative, and his grant is subsequently revoked, the receipt of the personal representative at that time is a good discharge. This sub-section also enables a representative, upon revocation of his grant, and upon his accounting to the new personal representative, to reimburse himself for those payments which he made while the grant was in force, and which were proper to be made in the administration of the estate.

Administration of Estates Act 1925, section 37
21.11 Under this section, a 'conveyance' of either realty or personalty to a 'purchaser' is declared to be valid, notwithstanding the subsequent revocation of the grant. The word 'conveyance' is used in a very wide sense,

and is defined[1] to 'include' a mortgage, lease, vesting instrument and every other assurance 'by any instrument'. It is not clear whether the handing over of chattels, where no instrument is involved, would be within the section. The section clearly contemplates a written means of transferring title, but as the definition is stated to 'include' such instruments, it may well be that the definition is wide enough to embrace the physical handing over.

1 Administration of Estates Act 1925, s 55(1).

Law of Property Act 1925, section 204
21.12 The protection conferred upon a purchaser, even where he knows of the irregularity, has already been mentioned.

Administration of Estates Act 1925, section 39(1)(iii)
21.13 This sub-section confers upon personal representatives the statutory powers given to trustees for sale. It provides that all contracts entered into by personal representatives within these powers as trustees for sale are enforceable by and against the personal representatives for the time being, so that a contract entered into by a personal representative whose grant is revoked will be binding upon the new representative.

Administration of Estates Act 1925, section 17
21.14 This section applies only to the revocation of temporary grants, and not to the revocation of permanent ones. Under it, the court may direct that proceedings pending by or against a temporary representative whose grant is revoked may be continued by or against the new representative. This power is, however, within the discretion of the court.

21.15 The effect of the provisions described above is to confer adequate protection upon purchasers, which means any person who acquires an interest in property for valuable consideration.[1] Unfortunately, the provisions do not deal expressly with the position of a person who receives property without consideration, as, for example, the person entitled under a will. What is the position of a person to whom an assent is made in accordance with the terms of the will, and upon a new will being discovered the grant is revoked? The principle in *Hewson v Shelley*[2] assists. In that case letters of administration had been granted to the widow of a man who was thought to have died intestate. The administratrix in the course of administration sold part of the estate. Subsequently, a will was discovered, the grant of administration revoked, and probate of the will granted to the executors named in it. They instituted an action against the purchaser to recover the land on the ground that the original grant was void ab initio, and they were successful at first instance. The decision was reversed by the Court of Appeal, who held that the grant was not void ab initio but that the revocation took effect only from the date of revocation. Although the case is concerned with the position of a purchaser, and its result has now been given statutory authority, the principle would appear to apply to any disposal. The transferee would obtain a good title, but it seems that upon the grant being revoked, an action would lie at the instance of the new representatives for the recovery of that asset.[3]

21.15 Revocation of grants

1 Administration of Estates Act 1925, s 55(1).
2 [1914] 2 Ch 13, CA.
3 *Re Diplock's Estate, Diplock v Wintle* [1948] Ch 465, [1948] 2 All ER 318.

PART VI

The position of the personal representatives

CHAPTER 22

The personal representative's office

Functions of personal representatives

22.1 At the outset of this section of the book, on the administration of estates, it may be useful to outline the functions of a personal representative. Broadly following the usual chronological order, a personal representative must:

(a) ascertain the assets and liabilities of the deceased;

(b) pay the inheritance tax, if any, on the net value of the assets, as so ascertained;

(c) obtain a grant of probate or letters of administration, where it is proposed to take out a grant;[1]

(d) collect in the assets, including (where appropriate) first registering the grant of representation with the appropriate authorities, such as banks, building societies, registrars of companies in which the deceased held stocks and shares, etc;

(e) realise at least sufficient of the assets to pay all debts and liabilities of the estate, and, where assets are not to be transferred in specie, to pay pecuniary legacies;

(f) examine each of the debts and liabilities, and to pay such of them as are properly payable. This will include agreement of the deceased's liability for income tax, capital gains tax and inheritance tax up to the date of death;

(g) pay the pecuniary and specific legacies;

(h) make any adjustment necessary to the Inland Revenue account of the deceased's estate which may become necessary in view of further assets or liabilities coming to light, and pay any additional inheritance tax which is exigible. Upon payment of all tax on the estate as finally agreed, the personal representative will apply for and obtain a clearance certificate to the effect that all tax properly payable in respect of the assets declared has been paid;[2]

(i) agree and discharge all liabilities of the administration itself (as distinct from the liabilities of the deceased which were dealt with under (f)). These will include payment of the funeral account; reimbursement of any expenses incurred by the personal representative; payment of his remuneration, if by virtue of a charging clause he is entitled to make a charge for his services; payment of legal and any other professional

fees incurred during the course of the administration; and the payment
of any income tax and capital gains tax which is payable in respect of
events occurring since the death of the deceased;

(j)   prepare the estate accounts, giving details of all assets received,
      payments made, and the balance due to the residuary beneficiaries;

(k)   transfer the residue to the residuary beneficiaries, or, if the personal
      representative is to hold that residue on trust, assent to the vesting of
      that property in himself as trustee.

There are many possible variations in this order, but this list will serve as a
sufficient outline. Other chapters of this book deal with obtaining the grant
of probate or letters of administration,[3] and the management of assets prior
to the grant.[4] It is not proposed to discuss here the incidence of inheritance
tax, or the personal representative's liability therefor, but the remainder of
the items mentioned above are considered in the following chapters.

1   See below, paras 25.1–25.9, for a discussion of the circumstances in which a personal
    representative need not apply for a grant.
2   Unless no inheritance tax account was required (see above, para 18.27), in which case the
    personal representatives will in the ordinary case be automatically discharged: Inheritance
    Tax (Delivery of Accounts) Regulations 1981, SI 1981/880, as finally amended by SI 1991/1248.
3   See above, paras 18.1 et seq.
4   See below, paras 25.10ff.

The administration period

22.2   Generally speaking, a personal representative holds office during the
administration period. There is, however, no statutory definition of the
administration period for general purposes. Some assistance may be derived
from the Income and Corporation Taxes Act 1988, s 695, which is considered later. It will be seen that the definition in this section stops at item
(j) in the list given above, and would not include (k). The Privy Council has
adopted this interpretation[1] in the context of New Zealand legislation.[2]

1   *Lilley v Public Trustee of the Dominion of New Zealand* [1981] AC 839.
2   The Law Reform (Testamentary Promises) Act 1949, under which a family provision
    application must be made before the 'final distribution' of the estate.

22.3   The general statement that a personal representative holds office
during the administration period is subject to these qualifications:

(a)   a personal representative may be sued after he has ceased to function
      as such for acts committed during the period of administration;[1]

(b)   in special cases grants may be obtained many years after the
      completion of the administration period; and

(c)   in many cases it is more appropriate to ask whether a person is a
      personal representative in respect of a particular asset or in respect of a
      particular liability than to ask the question in a more general sense.

The last two points need elaboration.

1   See below, para 28.56.

22.4   We have seen that in some cases a further grant of representation can be obtained after the completion of the administration period in the sense given above. Thus, if a minor is entitled to a grant, administration may be entrusted to a person for his use and benefit, leaving the minor to obtain a grant upon attaining the age of 18.[1] If the administration is complete by that time, this will involve the administrator in the liability only to give to the former infant an account of his administration. Likewise, where, for example, an asset falls into the estate, and the original representatives are no longer alive, a grant de bonis non may be necessary. Suppose, therefore, that Albert makes a will leaving his house to his nephew Basil for life, with remainder to Clarence. Suppose also that Albert dies in 1940, Clarence in 1950 and Basil in 1960. The administration of Clarence's estate may have been completed within a year or so after his death, without his personal representatives necessarily having any knowledge of the reversionary interest to which his estate would be entitled. If one or more of his personal representatives was alive at the date of death of Basil, then he could deal with the house at that time in accordance with Clarence's will, but if no personal representative was then alive a grant de bonis non to the estate of Clarence would be necessary, unless there was an executor acting under the chain of representation. On these considerations alone, therefore, it indicates that it is often better to consider in respect of a particular asset whether a person is acting as personal representative.

1 See above, para 19.29.

Personal representative or trustee?

22.5 The function of a personal representative is essentially to wind up an estate and distribute assets, whereas the function of a trustee is essentially to hold assets until a specified event happens. In many cases the same persons are appointed by will to be executors and trustees, either because a trust is expressly created by will, or because a trust will arise by operation of law in that one or more of the beneficiaries may be under 18, and so unable to give a good discharge. In this type of case there will be a normal progression from acting as personal representative to acting as a trustee. There is, however, considerable doubt as to the point of time at which the transition takes place, and whether formalities are necessary to mark the transfer in status.

Importance of distinction
22.6 It is important to know whether a person is acting as personal representative or as trustee for the following reasons.
(a) In respect of personal property, personal representatives have several authority, while trustees have only joint authority.[1] Thus *George Attenborough & Son v Solomon*[2] was concerned with the dealing by one of two persons with silver plate. One executor alone would have had power to sell the plate in the course of the administration of the estate, but it was held that as the dealing occurred over ten years after the administration had ceased, the personal representative had by then become a trustee, so that he alone could give no title to it.[3] This distinction applies only to pure personalty: in respect of realty, and leaseholds,[4] the authority of both personal representatives and trustees is joint.

(b)   A sale by a sole, or sole surviving, personal representative will be sufficient to overreach equitable interests, whereas a sale by a sole trustee will not be sufficient for this purpose.[5] Where, therefore, title is proposed to be made by a sole trustee, the purchaser must insist on the appointment of a co-trustee, to enable him to obtain a title free of overreachable equities.[6]

(c)   A new trustee can be appointed of an existing trust by the existing trustees, or, if there are none, by the personal representatives of the last surviving trustee.[7] There is no similar provision in respect of executors and administrators, so that if the only or last surviving personal representative dies, and there is no executor by representation, then if the estate is not fully administered a new grant de bonis non must be obtained.

(d)   Certain rights and liabilities may be exercised only in respect of the deceased's estate, and not in respect of trust property. For example, where a guarantee is given by a surety, it makes him liable only in respect of acts done during the administration of the estate.[8]

(e)   Actions against personal representatives in respect of personal estate may be brought within twelve years from the cause of action arising,[9] whereas actions by beneficiaries to recover trust property or in respect of breach of trust cannot be brought later than six years from the accruer of the right of action.[10] These limitations apply in neither case where there is fraud, or retention by the trustee or personal representative of the property.[11]

1   *Jacomb v Harwood* (1751) 2 Ves Sen 265.
2   [1913] AC 76.
3   This case is discussed further, below, para 22.11.
4   Administration of Estates Act 1925, ss 23(1), 54.
5   Unless the sole trustee is a trust corporation. See Law of Property Act 1925, s 27(2) and Settled Land Act 1925, s 18(1).
6   Subject to the provisions of the Law of Property (Joint Tenants) Act 1964.
7   Trustee Act 1925, s 36.
8   See on the position of an administration bond, which was replaced by the guarantee, *Harvell v Foster*, below, paras 22.13–22.16.
9   Limitation Act 1980, s 22; except in respect of actions to recover arrears of interest on legacies, when the period is six years.
10   Limitation Act 1980, s 21(3).
11   Ibid, s 21(1), (2).

Principles

Before examining the cases, it may assist to formulate the conclusions which it is suggested can be drawn from them. These are described in the four paragraphs that follow.

22.7   It is necessary to draw a distinction between the office of a personal representative and the functions which attach to that office.

(a)   Where the grant is limited as to time, the office of personal representative will terminate at the expiration of that period. It will also terminate if the grant is revoked by the court, unless, presumably, it is replaced by another grant to the same person but in a different capacity. In all other cases the office of personal representative will last for the duration of the life of the executor or administrator, although, as it terminates on his death, it will not devolve to his estate. There is,

therefore, a distinction between the time during which the personal representative holds his office, and the administration period.
(b)   The functions which attach to that office are those comprised in the list with which this chapter began.

22.8   A person may be both personal representative and trustee at the same time, although he cannot hold the same item of property in both capacities simultaneously. Accordingly, after the administration of the estate has been completed the person holds property as trustee, but he nevertheless retains his office of personal representative, and so he can act if, for example, further property falls into the estate.

22.9   In respect of any item of property, a personal representative will cease to hold as such and will thereafter hold as trustee:
(a)   in the case of land, if, and only if, he executes an assent in his favour in the capacity of trustee;
(b)   in the case of pure personalty:
   (i)   if he executes an assent in his favour as trustee; or
   (ii)   upon the completion of the administration, whichever occurs first.

22.10   For the purposes of the last rule, it is a question of fact in all cases whether the administration has been completed, although there will probably be a presumption that when all the items listed at the beginning of this chapter have been dealt with, the administration is complete.

22.11   We can now turn to the cases which either support these principles or are at least consistent with them. *George Attenborough & Son v Solomon*[1] is clear authority that provided a person does hold as trustee, then he has authority over assets jointly with trustees, and not individually. In that case the testator appointed his two sons to be his executors and trustees. He left to them part of the estate beneficially, in respect of which no question arose, and part to be held upon trust for his daughter. The testator died in March 1878, and the residuary account was prepared in March 1879, all debts and legacies having been paid before that time. One of the assets forming part of the residue which was to be held upon trust for the daughter consisted of silver plate, which had always been in the sole custody of one of the sons.[2] In March 1892 he pledged the plate to secure a loan, the lender having no notice that it consisted of trust property. The son who pledged the plate subsequently died, and the other son brought an action against the lender to recover the plate, on the basis that he had no title to it. If the sons had had several authority, the action could not have succeeded, because each could have made title, and the lender took without notice of the rights of the beneficiaries. The plaintiff did, however, succeed, both in the Court of Appeal and in the House of Lords. Viscount Haldane LC found as a fact that:

'the executors considered that they had done all that was due from them as executors by 1879, and were content when the residuary account was passed that the dispositions of the will should take effect. That is the inference I draw from the form of the residuary account; and the inference is strengthened when I consider the lapse of time since then, and that in the interval nothing was done by them purporting to be an exercise of power as executors . . . It follows that under these dispositions the residuary estate, including the chattels in question, became vested in the trustees as trustees.'

It will be noted that Lord Haldane took into account, when making his decisions on the facts, that a residuary account had been prepared; the interval of time since then; and the attitude of the personal representatives themselves.

1   [1913] AC 76.
2   It was the duty of the other son to see that the asset was brought under joint control, and an action would have been brought against him for failing to do so.

22.12   The next case is *Re Ponder, Ponder v Ponder*.[1] In that case, a widow was granted letters of administration to her late husband's estate. She had discharged the debts and had ascertained the residue, and had divided it into the separate funds which were required under the pre-1926 Statutes of Distribution. Sargant J held that she had assumed the character of trustee in respect of that property, and so advantage could be taken of the statutory powers[2] for appointing new trustees.[3]

1   [1921] 2 Ch 59.
2   At that time, under the Trustee Act 1893.
3   The appointment then had to be made with the assistance of the court. It can now be made without the intervention of the court under the Trustee Act 1925, s 36.

22.13   *Re Ponder, Ponder v Ponder*[1] was called into question in *Harvell v Foster*.[2] In that case the testator's daughter was appointed the sole executrix of his will. She was married but under 21, and so could not take probate.[3] Accordingly, a grant of letters of administration with will annexed was granted to her husband for her use and benefit during her minority.[4] An administration bond was given. The husband received the net residue of almost £1,000, which under the terms of the will belonged to the daughter, his wife. He gave her £300, turned her out of the matrimonial home, and disappeared. When she attained the age of 21, the daughter had the bond assigned to her, and, her husband not being traceable, she brought action on the bond against the sureties. The terms of the bond required the husband 'well and truly to administer the estate according to law' and 'to make or cause to be made a just and true account of the administration of the estate'. At first instance Lord Goddard CJ[5] dismissed the action. Relying upon *Re Ponder, Ponder v Ponder* he held that once the net residue was in the husband's hands, he became a trustee of it, and as the sureties to the bond were liable only in respect of acts done by the husband qua administrator, they were not liable.

1   [1921] 2 Ch 59.
2   [1954] 2 QB 367.
3   Under the rules then in force.
4   As to this type of grant, see above, para 19.29.
5   [1954] 1 QB 591.

22.14   The decision was reversed on appeal. The exact ground of the decision is uncertain. In the first place considerable importance was attached

to the wording of the bond itself. Lord Evershed MR said, 'upon the failure
. . . of her husband to account for the proceeds of the realisation of the
testator's estate, having in fact misappropriated it to his own use, the latter
was shown not to have "well and truly administered" the estate "according
to law" *within the true meaning and interest of the bond*'.[1] It may be that the
court regarded the expression 'well and truly administer' for the purposes of
the bond as being rather different from administration for more general
purposes. Secondly, the court was clearly influenced by the fact that the
grant was for a limited time only. In this connection, Lord Evershed
observed that 'the present is not an "ordinary" case, for the husband, by the
terms of his appointment as administrator, ceased altogether to have that
character' when the daughter attained 21. It is difficult to see the theoretical
justification for any reliance being placed on this point. Thirdly, Lord
Evershed drew a distinction between the office as such, which, where the
grant is not limited as to time, 'the personal representative, once appointed,
retains for all time', and the duties or functions of office, which will be
exhausted.

1 Emphasis supplied.

22.15 Lord Evershed then said that a personal representative may retain
that office and nevertheless hold assets qua trustee. Indeed, accepting that
the widow in *Re Ponder, Ponder v Ponder*[1] had become a trustee, Lord
Evershed said that 'it does not necessarily follow that she had therefore
altogether cast off her duties and capacity as administratrix'. But difficulty is
caused by the application of this distinction to the facts in question. There
would have been no difficulty in saying that after the residue had been
ascertained, the husband held as trustee, although he could still be sued as
personal representative for acts done during the period leading up to the
ascertainment of the residue. But Lord Evershed went much further. He
said, in an important passage:

> 'we are unable to accept the view . . . that because a personal
> representative who has cleared the estate becomes a trustee of the net
> residue for the persons beneficially interested, the clearing of the
> estate necessarily and automatically discharges him from his obliga-
> tions as personal representative and, in particular, from the obligation
> of any bond he may have entered into for the due administration of the
> estate. We would add that, in our view, the duty of an administrator as
> such must at least extend to paying the funeral and testamentary
> expenses and debts and legacies (if any) and where, as here,
> immediate distribution is impossible owing to the infancy of the person
> beneficially entitled, retaining the net residue in trust for the infant.'

Lord Evershed recognised the possibility that an express appointment of
trustees of the fund *could* be made under the Administration of Estates Act
1925, s 42, but subject to this the personal representative would hold as such
until the minor reached majority.

1 [1921] 2 Ch 59.

22.16 For present purposes, the most important aspect of *Harvell v Foster*[1]
is the remarks made upon the decision in *Re Ponder, Ponder v Ponder*:[2]

'If Sargant J in *Re Ponder, Ponder v Ponder* is to be taken to have decided that once a personal representative, by clearing the estate, has discharged all his functions other than those of a trustee for the persons beneficially interested in the net residue, and has thus become a trustee for those persons, he must be regarded, merely by virtue of such clearance, to have discharged himself from all his obligations as personal representative, because the capacities of personal representative and trustee are mutually exclusive, then we think the proposition too widely stated.'

The Court of Appeal refused to say whether they thought *Re Ponder, Ponder v Ponder* was correctly decided on its own facts, and also refused to define exactly the moment at which the personal representative would become trustee. If *Harvell v Foster* is to be regarded as authority that a personal representative can be sued as such while holding property as trustee, then it may be unobjectionable, for this merely recognises the distinction made above. But the clear doubt which it casts on *Re Ponder* is objectionable, not so much in itself, but more because the court refused to substitute what the proper test was.

1 [1954] 2 QB 367.
2 [1921] 2 Ch 59.

22.17 In *Re Cockburn's Will Trusts*[1] Danckwerts J was asked to decide whether an administrator, who had cleared the estate and a period of about ten years had elapsed therefrom, could exercise the statutory power of appointing new trustees. He was firm. 'I feel no doubt about the matter at all. Whether persons are executors or administrators, once they have completed the administration in due course, they become trustees holding for the beneficiaries either on an intestacy or under the terms of the will, and are bound to carry out the duties of trustees.' He then dealt with *Harvell v Foster*. 'My attention has been called to the observations made in *Harvell v Foster* which are obiter so far as they cast any doubt on the decision of Sargant J and which, with all respect, I should have thought were not justified.' But were they obiter? Perhaps one cannot be quite so certain.

1 [1957] Ch 438, [1957] 2 All ER 522.

22.18 The most important case relating to land is *Re King's Will Trusts*,[1] where, ironically, the plaintiff and the defendant were both partners in the same firm of solicitors. The testatrix died in 1939, and her will was proved by Henry and Cecil, two of the executors named in it. The administration account was finalised in 1951, but Henry and Cecil did not execute an assent of land in their favour as trustees. Cecil died in 1953, leaving Henry as the sole surviving executor and trustee and in the same year Henry appointed Basil to be a co-trustee. Henry died in 1958, and his will was proved by the defendant, who thereby also became the executor by representation[2] of the will of the testatrix. In 1959 Basil appointed the plaintiff to be a trustee of the will, and Basil thereafter died. The question was whether the legal estate was held by the plaintiff or the defendant. Previously, the practice of many conveyancers had been to follow *Re Ponder*,[3] and to accept a personal representative as having power to appoint trustees if he was in fact acting in the capacity of a trustee. In *Re King's Will Trusts*, however, Pennycuick J regarded himself as bound by s 36(4) of the Administration of Estates Act 1925. This provides that 'An assent to the vesting of a legal estate shall be in writing, signed by the personal representative, and shall name the person in whose favour it is given, and shall operate to vest in that person the legal estate to which it relates; and *an assent not in writing* or not in favour of a named person *shall not be effectual* to pass a legal estate . . .'[4] It was argued that because the appointments of trustees had been by deed, there would be an implied vesting of the legal estate in the new trustees under Trustee Act 1925, s 40. Pennycuick J said, however, that s 40 operated only where the person making the appointment held the property in his capacity as a trustee. In this case, at the time of the 1953 deed of appointment, the legal estate was held by Henry as personal representative, although he held as trustee, and could confer upon himself and the new trustee the right to insist on a transfer of the legal estate.[5] Thus, it was held that the legal estate remained with the defendant.

1 [1964] Ch 542.
2 See above, para 17.6.
3 [1921] 2 Ch 59.
4 Emphasis supplied.
5 [1964] Ch 542 at 545.

22.19 The decision in *Re King's Will Trusts* has been criticised,[1] particularly because it has rendered defective many titles which were previously thought to be good. The decision has, however, more recently been followed.[2] It will be appreciated that *Harvell v Foster* is the decision which makes it difficult to give a coherent statement of the law. Subject to this, and with the other cases in mind, it is thought that the cases are at least consistent with the principles suggested in paragraphs 22.7 to 22.10, above.

1 See eg Walker (1964) 80 LQR 328; Garner (1964) 28 Conv (NS) 298.
2 In *Re Edwards' Will Trusts* [1982] Ch 30, [1981] 2 All ER 941, CA.

Nature of the personal representative's estate

Distinct from personal estate

22.20 For most purposes the position of a person as personal representative is kept quite distinct from his position in his personal capacity, and it is almost as if the 'personal representative' is constituted by law as a separate legal entity. For example, if the personal representative becomes bankrupt, the property which he holds as personal representative cannot be touched by the trustee in bankruptcy.[1] If the personal representative is sued in his personal capacity, the judgment creditor generally has no right against the assets of the estate. The only major circumstance in which this distinction is broken is where the personal representative has been guilty of some improper act or inaction, and he is sued on that ground, when his personal effects can be taken in execution.

1 Insolvency Act 1986, s 283(3)(a).

22.21 It would perhaps be more accurate to speak of the personal representatives for most purposes constituting a separate legal entity, with the entity unchanged despite alterations in the persons comprising them. Thus, where two executors are appointed, and one dies, the survivor is bound by the acts of both of them. One aspect of this is dealt with in the Administration of Estates Act 1925, s 39(1)(iii), which provides that when a contract is entered into by personal representatives, then their successors as personal representatives are fully bound by that contract.[1]

1 See above, paras 21.9–21.15, for further circumstances where changes in personal representatives do not affect obligations.

22.22 The most general statement of the rule is contained in s 62(3) of the Taxation of Chargeable Gains Act 1992, which deals with the liability of the estate to capital gains tax. It provides that 'in relation to property forming part of the estate of a deceased person the personal representatives shall for the purposes of this Act be treated as being a single and continuing body of persons (distinct from the persons who may from time to time be the personal representatives)'.

22.23 These twin principles, that:
(a) capacity as personal representative is generally kept entirely distinct from personal capacity; and
(b) generally, account is not taken of changes in the persons who are from time to time personal representatives,
lead to several other more detailed rules.

No merger of estates

22.24 The Law of Property Act 1925 has an infuriating habit of frequently saying what it means only indirectly, when direct expression would be quite easy. Section 185 of the Act, re-enacting a provision of the Judicature Act 1873, provides that 'there is no merger by operation of law only of an estate the beneficial interest in which would not be deemed to be merged or extinguished in equity'. The situation here contemplated is where the personal representative owns an interest in land in his personal capacity and then acquires a further interest in the same land in his representative capacity. The common law rule was that where a freeholder subsequently acquired a lease, that lease became automatically merged in the freehold. The section considered here modifies that rule.

22.25 The approach of equity was that merger was not presumed where it was not in the interest of the party that it should take place, or even where it was only consistent with the duty of the party that it should not take place.[1] Accordingly, merger does not take place where there are the different capacities of personal and representative entitlement.[2] Although merger does not take place at first, if the personal representative is also beneficially entitled, and he acquires beneficially the estate's interest in the property, merger may then take place.

1 *Chambers v Kingham* (1878) 10 Ch D 743; *Capital and Counties Bank Ltd v Rhodes* [1903] 1 Ch 631 at 653; cf *Manks v Whiteley* [1912] 1 Ch 735 (overruled sub nom *Whiteley v Delaney* [1914] AC 132); *Re Radcliffe, Radcliffe v Bewes* [1892] 1 Ch 227 at 231.
2 *Re French-Brewster's Settlement* [1904] 1 Ch 713; *Re Hodge, Hodge v Griffiths* [1940] Ch 260 at 265.

Bankruptcy of personal representative

22.26 Where a personal representative becomes bankrupt, his estate vests automatically in the trustee in bankruptcy on appointment.[1] However, the bankrupt's estate expressly excludes any property held by him on trust for any other person.[2] Consequently, the trustee in bankruptcy does not have recourse to any assets held by the bankrupt personal representative in that capacity.

1 Insolvency Act 1986, s 306.
2 Ibid, s 283(3)(a).

Personal debts of personal representative

22.27 Generally, the assets of the estate cannot be taken in satisfaction of a debt due from the personal representative personally.[1] In one case, where an administrator took possession of the deceased's chattels, and used them for three months, it was held that they could not be taken in execution for the administrator's own debt.[2] However, it seems that where a substantial period has elapsed in which the assets have been in the hands of the personal representative, equity will not intervene to prevent those goods being taken in satisfaction of the representative's personal debts.[3]

1 *Farr v Newman* (1792) 4 Term Rep 621 at 645.
2 *Gaskell v Marshall* (1831) 1 Mood & R 132.
3 *Ray v Ray* (1815) Coop G 264; though this case may be explicable on the basis that the facts raised an inference of a gift by the testator's creditor to the executor – see Fry J in *Re Morgan, Pillgrem v Pillgrem* (1881) 18 Ch D 93 at 101.

22.28 The general rule applies even where the debt is incurred by the personal representative in his personal capacity while acting on behalf of the estate. In *Re Morgan, Pillgrem v Pillgrem*[1] an executor carried on a business previously carried on by the testator, the will giving a power for this to be done.[2] The executor carried on the business in his own name, and the assets used in it appeared to be those of the executor personally, but even so the judgment creditor was held not entitled to take the assets on a warrant of execution.

1 (1881) 18 Ch D 93.
2 As to the general position where the personal representative carries on the deceased's business, see below, paras 28.10ff.

22.29 There is no exception to the converse rule, that a personal representative is not ipso facto liable to have his own goods taken in satisfaction of the debts of the estate.

No disposition by will

22.30 On the death of a personal representative, others may remain, and whether or not they do, the personal representative cannot leave the deceased's assets by will, even if they are left upon the same trusts as are declared by the deceased's will.[1] Powers of disposition will therefore pass to the next person to be appointed personal representative either by a further grant, or by an executor being entitled by virtue of the chain of representation.

1 *Bransby v Grantham* (1557) 2 Plowd 525.

Dispositions inter vivos

22.31 The personal representative has full power of disposition inter vivos, save that in the case of freehold and leasehold land, this power must be exercised jointly.[1] It is, however, established that where the personal representative acting in his personal capacity makes a disposition of property, and the extent of the property passed is not clear, there will be a presumption against it including property of which he is personal representative. Thus, in *Knight v Cole*[2] Holt CJ held that where an executor who executed a deed of release by which he released all actions and rights of action 'which he had for any cause whatever', he had in fact released only actions which were personal to him, and not actions which he had on behalf of the estate.

1 See above, para 22.6(a).
2 (1690) 1 Show 150.

Taxation

22.32 The provision of s 62(3) of the Taxation of Chargeable Gains Act 1992, in respect of capital gains tax, has already been mentioned, and the effect is that the personal representative's liability for capital gains tax is kept quite distinct from his personal liability, so that his personal liability cannot be affected in any way by the fact that he also becomes liable qua personal representative. Likewise for the purposes of income tax and inheritance tax, the estate is taxed quite separately from the representative, whose personal liability is unaffected by his representative capacity.

CHAPTER 23

Realising assets

Devolution of assets

23.1 As their name suggests, personal representatives originally held only personal estate, and, indeed, since the time when the office of executor became recognised, only the personal estate automatically devolved upon him. At common law realty devolved directly to the devisee named in the will or, if there was no will, to the heir upon intestacy. The position was altered by the Land Transfer Act 1897, but this has been repealed and the position is now governed by s 1 of the Administration of Estates Act 1925.

23.2 Sub-section 1(3) lays down the general principle that 'the personal representatives shall be the representative of the deceased in regard to his real estate to which he was entitled for an interest not ceasing on his death as well as in regard to his personal estate'. Logically, therefore, executors and administrators should be, but are not, called real and personal representatives.

23.3 The devolution of realty is governed by sub-s 1(1) of the Administration of Estates Act 1925, by which real estate devolves on the personal representative 'in like manner as before the commencement of this Act chattels real devolved on the personal representative from time to time of a deceased person'. This is another piece of legislative obscurity. Its general meaning is clear enough, but there is no definition of chattels real. They clearly include leaseholds[1] but otherwise one is thrown back on the somewhat loose definition of Coke, who described them as such chattels as concern or savour of the realty.[2] Fortunately, the point is not important. All assets to which the deceased was entitled at his death, other than for an interest ceasing on his death[3], now devolve on the personal representative, either by virtue of the common law or by virtue of the statute.

---

1 See Administration of Estates Act 1925, s 55(1)(xxiv), and Law of Property Act 1925, s 205(1)(xxvii).
2 Co Litt 118 b.
3 Where the deceased was tenant for life under a Settled Land Act settlement, the legal title vests in his ordinary personal representative, notwithstanding that the deceased's beneficial interest ceased on his death: see below, para 24.17.

23.4 There are two riders to this general statement. First, the extract from sub-s 1(1) given above contains the phrase 'personal representative from time to time', which indicates that where there is a change in personal representatives, such as upon the revocation of a grant and the issue of a new one, then the assets held by the old personal representative automatically vest in the new one. Secondly, the provisions of s 1 and the general rule as to the devolution of personal estate must be read subject to s 9. Under this section, where the deceased dies intestate, all his property, both real and personal, vests in the President of the Family Division until a grant of administration is made, whereupon it automatically vests in the administrator. This section is considered later.[1]

1 Below, paras 25.16–25.19.

Special types of property and person

Trust property

23.5 Where the deceased was one of two or more trustees the trust property will be held by the trustees as joint tenants, so that on the death of the deceased the ius accrescendi will apply to vest the whole title in the surviving trustees. If, however, the deceased was the sole, or sole surviving trustee, the property will devolve upon his personal representatives. This has always been the case so far as personalty is concerned, and is declared to be so as far as realty is concerned by the Administration of Estates Act 1925, s 3.[1] The ius accrescendi will also apply where the deceased was himself one of two or more personal representatives. However, where he was the sole or sole surviving personal representative, the property of the estate will not devolve upon his personal representatives, so that a new grant will be required.[2]

1 Sub-s 3(1)(ii).
2 Above, para 19.12.

Joint property

Joint tenancy
23.6 The ius accrescendi was recognised as an incident of a joint tenancy of the goods in the same way as a joint tenancy of the legal estate,[1] and in this case the whole title passes upon the death of one to the survivor.

1 See Co Litt 182a; Swinb Pt 3, s 6, pl 1; *Harris v Fergusson* (1848) 16 Sim 308; *Crossfield v Such* (1853) 8 Exch 825.

23.7 Where the asset owned jointly is land, it must be held upon a legal joint tenancy, whether or not the equitable interests are also joint, so that the legal title will automatically accrue to the survivor.[1] For this reason, the Administration of Estates Act 1925, s 3(4), provides that 'the interest of a deceased person under a joint tenancy where another tenant survives the deceased is an interest ceasing on his death and shall devolve to his successor'. There is no similar requirement, however, that chattels must be held upon a joint tenancy. Where the joint owners are tenants in common, either because that was their express intention, or because in the circumstances equity presumes[2] a tenancy in common, the personal representatives of the deceased tenant in common will themselves stand in the same position as the deceased.

1 Litt 280; Co Litt 181a.
2 For the circumstances in which equity presumes a tenancy in common, reference must be made to the standard textbooks on equity.

23.8 In this connection the decision in *Young v Sealey*[1] should be noted. This illustrates that even where equity raises a presumption of a tenancy in common, that presumption may be rebutted by contrary evidence. In that case a woman held a joint account with her nephew. During her lifetime, she alone made payments into the account, and withdrawals from it. Evidence was admitted to rebut the presumption which equity would raise that the woman and her nephew held upon trust for the woman alone, and it was shown that the woman intended the whole beneficial interest to pass to her nephew on her death. Evidence will always be admitted to show that an apparent beneficial joint tenancy was intended to be a beneficial tenancy in common.

1 [1949] Ch 278.

Joint mortgages
23.9 Where two or more persons lend money on mortgage, there is an equitable presumption that they are to hold as tenants in common.[1] Accordingly, when one of the lenders dies, it is prima facie necessary for his personal representatives to join with the other lenders in giving a discharge when the load is repaid.[2] To overcome this difficulty, it became the practice in mortgage deeds to include a 'joint account clause', which was a clause declaring that the money being lent belonged to the lenders as joint tenants beneficially. So far as the mortgagor was concerned, he could rely on this clause, and in the event of the death of one of the lenders, he could presume that the ius accrescendi applied, and so take a good discharge from the survivor alone. Such a clause is now unnecessary in a mortgage of land, for it is deemed to be included by statute.[3] The joint account clause, either express or deemed to be incorporated by statute, operates only as between mortgagor and mortgagees, and does not affect the rights of mortgagees inter se. As a result, although the survivor can give the mortgagor a good discharge, the survivor is then bound to account to the estate of the deceased lender for his share.[4]

1 *Petty v Styward* (1631) 1 Rep Ch 57; *Rigden v Vallier* (1751) 2 Ves Sen 252 at 258; *Morley v Bird* (1798) 3 Ves 628 at 631; *Vickers v Cowell* (1839) 1 Beav 529.
2 *Petty v Styward*, above; *Vickers v Cowell*, above.
3 Law of Property Act 1925, s 111.
4 *Re Jackson, Smith v Sibthorpe* (1887) 34 Ch D 732.

Husband and wife
23.10 Where property was jointly used or occupied by husband and wife, then even if the title to that property is vested in only one of them, it is necessary to consider whether the other had acquired an equitable interest

in it[1] before determining what interest devolves on the personal representatives of the first spouse to die.

1   *Gissing v Gissing* [1971] AC 886, [1970] 2 All ER 780, HL; *Re Densham* [1975] 3 All ER 726; *Eves v Eves* [1975] 3 All ER 768; *Bristol and West Building Society v Henning* [1985] 2 All ER 606, CA.

Partnership property

23.11   Where land is held by partners, they must hold as joint tenants at law, and the ius accrescendi will apply to vest the legal estate in the survivors upon the death of one of the partners.[1] The survivors will therefore hold the legal estate upon trust to give effect to the beneficial interests of the partners, including the estate of the deceased.[2] Partnership chattels are regarded both at common law and in equity as being held by the partners in common, so that the jus accrescendi does not apply. However, the surviving partner or partners have the right to realise the assets of the partnership for the purpose of paying the partnership debts. Once the debts of the partnership have been ascertained, the executors of the deceased partner have a lien over the surplus assets for the proportion due to the estate.[3]

1   Law of Property Act 1925, s 34.
2   Ibid, ss 34 to 36; Partnership Act 1890, s 22.
3   *Re Bourne, Bourne v Bourne* [1906] 2 Ch 427, CA.

23.12   Where the deceased was one of only two partners, his death will ipso facto bring the partnership to an end. Even where there were more than two partners, prima facie the death of one will bring the partnership to an end. This, however, leads to complications, and partnership agreements often provide that where there are more than two partners, the partnership will continue notwithstanding the death of one of them, and such agreements are binding on the personal representatives. The partnership agreement may specify the rights and liabilities of the deceased's estate. In the absence of such provision, if the other partners continue to trade, the surviving partners may each deduct a 'salary'[1] but subject thereto the personal representatives of the deceased partner have the option either to take the deceased's share of profits as if he were still alive, or to charge the surviving partners interest on the capital belonging to the deceased and used by them for partnership purposes.

1   Partnership Act 1890, s 42(1).

23.13   If the partnership continues, for income tax purposes the trade is regarded as having ceased on the death of the deceased partner, and a new trade as having been commenced the day after.[1] This effect can be avoided if the surviving partners, and the personal representatives of the deceased partner, give notice to the Inspector of Taxes within two years from the date of death that they require the trade to be regarded as having continued throughout.[2] The personal representatives of the deceased partner must, however, be satisfied that in giving such a notice, the estate will be benefited or at least that it does not suffer. Failure to do this will render them personally liable in an action for breach of trust.

1   Income and Corporation Taxes Act 1988, s 113.
2   Ibid, s 113(6).

Property subject to power of appointment

23.14   Section 3(2) of the Administration of Estates Act 1925 provides that where the deceased exercised by will a general power of appointment over realty, then for the purposes of devolution that property shall pass on his death to his personal representatives, who take it to give effect to the terms of the appointment. A similar provision makes property which was entailed, and is disposed of in accordance with the Law of Property Act 1925, s 176,[1] devolve upon the deceased's personal representatives. Section 3(2) applies only to realty. At common law personal property over which the deceased had a power of appointment did not devolve upon the personal representatives of the appointor, and there is no statutory provision to alter this position.[2]

1   This is the section by which a person of full age may bar an entail by will, and so dispose of it.
2   *O'Grady v Wilmot* [1916] 2 AC 231.

Corporator sole

23.15   On the death of a corporator sole, such as a bishop, his interest in the corporation's property, both real and personal, is regarded as an interest ceasing on death. Accordingly, it does not pass to his personal representatives, but devolves to his successor.[1]

1   Administration of Estates Act 1925, s 3(5).

Options and powers of selection

23.16   Where the deceased held an option, this may, according to its true construction, be either personal to the deceased or transmissible to his personal representatives.[1] In many instances the option is regarded as being transmissible. So, in *Re Adams and Kensington Vestry*[2] the deceased's executor was held entitled to exercise an option to purchase the freehold land of which the deceased held the lease.[3]

1   *Skelton v Younghouse* [1942] AC 571; *Re Avard, Hook v Parker* [1948] Ch 43; cf *Belshaw v Rollins* [1904] 1 IR 284.
2   (1883) 24 Ch D 199; on appeal (1884) 27 Ch D 394.
3   The executor has also been held entitled to exercise an option in respect of stocks and shares: *James v Buena Ventura Nitrate Grounds Syndicate Ltd* [1896] 1 Ch 456.

23.17   The rules governing the exercise of a power of selection given to the deceased are more stringent. The basic situation is that the deceased is given, usually under the will of another, a power to select articles and dies before exercising the power of selection. The rules are as follows.

(a) Where the power of selection was as to the articles themselves, and no selection was made in the deceased's lifetime, then there is no property to pass to his personal representatives, who accordingly cannot exercise the power.[1] So in *Re Madge, Pridie v Bellamy*[2] a testator left to his widow such articles of a specified character as she should select within two months of his death. She died within two months of his death, and her personal representatives were held not entitled to exercise the power, even within the two-month period.

(b) (i) Where the power is not as to the article itself, but is only as to the degree of the gift, this can usually be exercised by the personal representatives. So in *Jones v Cherney*[3] a person was granted by will a lease of either 40 or 60 years as he should elect. Upon his death before election, his personal representatives were held entitled to choose.

   (ii) This is subject to the general rule that where selection must be made within a specified time, or on a specified occasion, it must then be made, and personal representatives cannot make the selection later.[4]

1 *Morris v Levesay* (1594) 1 Roll Abr 725.
2 (1928) 44 TLR 372.
3 (1680) Freem KB 530.
4 Co Litt 145a.

Leaseholds

23.18 Leaseholds will devolve upon the personal representatives in the usual way.[1] Likewise, weekly, monthly or yearly tenancies will also devolve on the personal representatives.[2] Accordingly, before possession can be recovered by the landlord, a notice to quit must be served either on the personal representatives or, in the case of an intestate prior to the issue of letters of administration, upon the President of the Family Division.[3]

1 See above, paras 23.1–23.4; Administration of Estates Act 1925, s 1(1).
2 *Doe d Shore v Porter* (1789) 3 Term Rep 13; *Rees d Mears v Perrot* (1830) 4 C & P 230; *Abbey v Barnstyn* [1930] 1 KB 660.
3 Under Administration of Estates Act 1925, s 9; see below, para 25.16.

Devolution of tenancies protected by statute

Residential premises

Categories of tenancy

23.19 The legislation which confers security of tenure on the tenants of residential accommodation divides the tenancies into the following categories:

(a) protected, where the tenant occupies by virtue of a contract[1] with the landlord, and the full protection of the Rent Act applies;[2]

(b) statutory, where the tenant occupies after the protected, contractual, tenancy expires;[3]

(c) assured, where the tenancy is of a property constructed after 8 August 1980, by a landlord specially approved for this purpose;[4]
(d) secure, where the tenancy is granted by a housing association or certain public bodies;[5]
(e) long, where the tenancy is granted for a term of more than 21 years.[6]

1 Including a lease or tenancy.
2 Rent Act 1977, s 1.
3 Ibid, s 2.
4 Housing Act 1980, s 56.
5 Ibid, s 28(1).
6 Rent Act 1977, s 152(1).

Transmission
23.20 The general principle is that statutory rights of occupation pass on the death of the tenant to his spouse if she was residing with him at the date of his death or, if there is no spouse, to other members of his family who were residing with him. The transmission of the right occurs directly on death, and does not pass through the deceased's estate. The position with regard to each type of tenancy is as follows.

23.21 *Statutory* A statutory tenancy cannot be transmitted by will,[1] but there may be a statutory right of transmission for the surviving spouse or member of the family living with the deceased. The policy of the Housing Act 1988 is to phase out protected and statutory tenancies under the Rent Act 1977. However, as existing tenancies are preserved, this will take a long time to achieve and the old rules will therefore be relevant for some time. The right to succession varies depending on whether the tenant dies before or after the commencement date of the Housing Act 1988.[2]

(a) *The first successor, the original tenant dying before 15 January 1989.* In respect of deaths before this date,[3] the first successor is the surviving spouse (if any) of the original tenant if residing in the dwellinghouse immediately before the death of the original tenant. If there is no such surviving spouse, the first successor is a person who was 'a member of the original tenant's family' residing with him for six months immediately before his death.
(b) *The first successor, the original tenant dying after 14 January 1989.* The spouse of the deceased tenant is entitled to be the first successor, but the right is extended to a person living with the original tenant as his or her wife or husband.[4] The test is therefore now one of cohabitation only. If there is no person treated as a spouse, the first successor will be a member of the original tenant's family residing with him in the dwellinghouse for two years immediately before his death. A successor in this category acquires not a statutory tenancy but an assured tenancy from which no further succession may be claimed.
(c) *The second successor, the first successor dying before 15 January 1989.* On the death of the first successor any surviving spouse takes priority if residing in the dwellinghouse at the date of death of the first successor. In the absence of such a spouse, the successor is a member of the first successor's family who resided with him for six months immediately prior to his death. There is no further transmission after the second successor.[5]

(d) *The second successor, the first successor dying after 14 January 1989.*
    Where the first successor (not being the spouse or a person treated as
    the spouse of the original successor) took an assured tenancy by way of
    succession, no second succession is possible.[6] Where the first successor
    (being a member of the family of the original tenant) succeeded before
    15 January 1989, but died on or after that date, or where the first
    successor (being the spouse or a person treated as a spouse of the
    original tenant) succeeded on or after that date, one more succession is
    possible. This succession is only available to a person who is a member
    of the original tenant's family and a member of the first successor's
    family and residing in the dwellinghouse with the first successor for two
    years immediately before the death.[7] If the second successor takes, it
    constitutes an assured periodic tenancy,[8] from which no further
    succession may be claimed.

1 *John Lovibond & Sons Ltd v Vincent* [1929] 1 KB 687.
2 For an excellent exposition of the Housing Act 1988, see Jill Martin *Residential Security* (1989).
3 But after 28 November 1980, when the amendments containing in Housing Act 1980, s 76,
   came into effect.
4 Rent Act 1977, Sch 1, para 2(2) (inserted by Housing Act 1988, Sch 4, para 2).
5 Ibid, Sch 1, para 10.
6 Housing Act 1988, s 17(2)(c).
7 Rent Act 1977, Sch 1, para 6, as substituted by Housing Act 1988, Sch 4, para 6.
8 Housing Act 1988, s 39(5).

23.22 *Protected* On the death of a protected tenant, that is, where the
contractual tenancy is still subsisting, the contractual tenancy will devolve on
the personal representatives, but the right to a statutory tenancy is
transmitted to the same persons as would be entitled if the original tenant
had a statutory tenancy.[1]

1 *Moodie v Hosegood* [1952] AC 61, [1951] 2 All ER 582.

23.23 *Assured* There is no provision for the statutory transmission of an
assured tenancy. Accordingly, on the death of the original tenant, the
tenancy will devolve on his personal representatives.

23.24 *Secure* A secure tenancy can be transmitted in the same way as a
statutory tenancy, but it can only be transmitted once.[1]

1 Housing Act 1980, s 30.

23.25 *Long* A long tenancy will devolve on the personal representatives
for the residue of the term for which it was granted.

Agricultural cottages

23.26 An agricultural worker who occupies a farm cottage or other tied
residential accommodation will usually have the protection conferred by the
Rent (Agriculture) Act 1976[1] in respect of licences and tenancies granted
before 16 January 1989, when one transmission only is allowed under the
Act. Licences and tenancies granted after that date are 'assured' agricultural

tenancies under the Housing Act 1988,[2] when a statutory periodic tenancy arises on the death of the agricultural worker.[3]

1 Rent (Agriculture) Act 1976, s 4(2).
2 Housing Act 1988, s 34.
3 Ibid, s 5(3). See further Rodgers *Agricultural Law* (Butterworths 1991), pp 234–56.

Agricultural holdings

23.27 Where the deceased had a lease of agricultural land, that lease will devolve on his personal representatives in the usual way. If, however, the deceased was in occupation of the land by virtue of a tenancy which was protected by the Agricultural Holdings Act 1948, the tenancy will devolve on the personal representatives, but the landlord can serve a notice to quit within three months from the death of the tenant.[1] Notwithstanding this, if the tenancy was granted before 12 July 1984, a close member of the family has the right to apply to the agricultural lands tribunal for an order directing the landlord to grant a new tenancy to that person, and if that application is successful, the landlord's notice to quit is of no effect.[2]

1 Agricultural Holdings Act 1948, s 24(2)(g), substituted by the Agriculture (Miscellaneous Provisions) Act 1976, s 16. Agricultural Holdings Act 1984, s 2, abolished succession rights for all new tenancies granted on or after 12 July 1984; this provision is now incorporated in Agricultural Holdings Act 1986, s 34(1).
2 See further Rodgers *Agricultural Law* (Butterworths, 1991) pp 151–69.

23.28 A person who wishes to claim a new tenancy must show that:
(a) the tenancy of which he is claiming transmission was granted before 12 July 1984;[1]
(b) he is a close relative of the deceased tenant;[2]
(c) in general, he derives his principal livelihood from agriculture;[3]
(d) he does not occupy any other farm;[4] and
(e) he is suitable to take a grant of a new tenancy, having regard to his training and practical experience in agriculture, and his age, health and financial standing.[5]

1 Agricultural Holdings Act 1986, s 34(1).
2 Ibid, ss 35(2), 36(3).
3 Ibid, s 36(3). A widow is deemed to have so derived her livelihood: ibid, s 36(4).
4 Ibid, s 36(3): he must not himself be the occupier of a commercial unit of agricultural land.
5 Ibid, s 39(2).

Registration and notice

Registered land

23.29 Section 41 of the Land Registration Act 1925 provides that registered land is within the expression 'real estate' for the purposes of s 1 of the Administration of Estates Act 1925, so that although the legal estate devolves upon the personal representative, he cannot deal with it until he becomes the registered proprietor. One of two courses is open to a personal representative in respect of registered land.

(a) He may lodge with the Land Registry the land certificate together with the probate or letters of administration, whereupon the land certificate and register will be altered to show the personal representative as registered proprietor.[1] As that transaction will not be for value, the registrar will also note on the title that until the property is sold, it remains liable for the payment of any inheritance tax outstanding, although this note will not be made if a clearance certificate relating to that land is also lodged.[2]

(b) He may wait until the property is sold, or until it is to be transferred to the person entitled either in accordance with the terms of the will or on intestacy.[3] In the case of sale, the purchaser will be registered as proprietor upon lodging with the registry the land certificate (still showing the deceased as registered proprietor), the grant of representation, and the transfer executed by the personal representative. In the case of a transfer to the beneficiary an assent will be used instead of a transfer, but otherwise the procedure is the same. In the latter case the same note that the land is subject to the payment of any inheritance tax will be made on the register unless a clearance certificate is lodged.

Where the deceased was a joint registered proprietor,[4] the registrar will delete his name from the register upon proof of death being given, by production of either a death certificate or the grant of representation.[5]

1 Land Registration Act 1925, s 41(1).
2 Inheritance Tax Act 1984, s 237.
3 Land Registration Act 1925, s 37(1), (2).
4 That is, a beneficial joint tenancy where the survivor can give a valid receipt.
5 Land Registration Rules 1925, r 172.

Stocks and shares

23.30 The position is similar where the deceased held stocks and shares. These will devolve on death upon the personal representatives who may deal with them in one of three ways:

(a) register themselves as owners, by production of the grant of representation, together with the share certificate. Where the company has notice of the death, it will usually not make any further payment of dividends until the personal representatives are registered, although dividends held back pending registration will be paid to the personal representatives upon registration; or

(b) execute forms of transfer in favour of a purchaser or beneficiary, which will be registered upon the share certificate being lodged with the company and production of the grant. Unless the articles of association otherwise provide, the personal representatives may transfer the stocks or shares without first being registered as owners;[1] or

(c) where the personal representative is beneficially entitled, instead of executing a transfer in favour of himself, he may procure his beneficial registration by completing a document known as a letter of request and lodging this with the certificate and grant.[2]

There is no provision for notice of any outstanding liability for capital transfer tax to be endorsed on a share certificate or upon the register of members of the company.

1   Article 31 of Table A, set out in the Companies (Alteration of Table A, etc) Regulations 1984, SI 1984/1717, prescribed pursuant to Companies Act 1985, s 8. *Re Greene, Greene v Greene* [1949] Ch 333.
2   As stock transfers executed after April 1987 vesting shares in the beneficiaries entitled are exempt from stamp duty, it makes little difference whether a transfer or letter of request is used: Stamp Duty (Exempt Instruments) Regulations 1987, SI 1987/516.

Leasehold property

23.31   If there is no provision to the contrary in the lease, the personal representatives are not required to notify the landlord of the devolution of the title to them, nor are they required to obtain the landlord's consent for the transfer of the lease to the person entitled under the will or on intestacy, or upon sale.[1] Nevertheless, the landlord will usually wish to know where the legal estate in the lease lies, so that he can take any action for arrears of rent and serve any notices[2] required to be served in accordance with the terms of the lease. Furthermore, in most cases, the landlord will wish to control the person who will be occupying the property. Two clauses will therefore frequently be found among the lessee's covenants in the lease, namely:

(a)   that the tenant shall not assign, underlet or part with the possession of the premises; or that he shall not do so without the consent of the lessor; and

(b)   that following any permitted assignment, or other devolution, notice must be given of that assignment or devolution within a prescribed time.

The first type of covenant applies only to voluntary dispositions, so that it does not prevent the lease vesting in the personal representatives on death.[3] However, the landlord's consent is probably required before the personal representatives can give effect to the terms of the will.[4] The second type of clause does require notice of devolution of death to be given to the landlord, provided that the clause in the lease requiring notice to be given is not confined on its terms to dispositions inter vivos.

1   *Doe d Mitchinson v Carter* (1798) 8 Term Rep 57 at 60.
2   The lease may contain provision for the landlord to determine the term upon giving notice; or he may wish to serve notice for repairs to be carried out.
3   *Fox v Swann* (1655) Sty 482; *Doe d Goodbehere v Bevan* (1815) 3 M & S 353.
4   *Re Wright, ex p Landau v Trustee* [1949] Ch 729.

Choses in action

23.32   Where the deceased was owed a debt, or had the benefit of some other chose in action, the personal representatives must protect their position by giving notice of the devolution to the debtor or other person under obligation.[1]

1   *Dearle v Hall* (1823) 3 Russ 1; *Loveridge v Cooper* (1823) 3 Russ 1.

Devolution on separate representatives

23.33   Where the testator appointed different personal representatives in respect of different types of property, the relevant property will devolve automatically on the appropriate representative. This is most likely to arise where there are different representatives of settled land, and this is considered in the next chapter. The other situations in which this may be met are where the testator appoints a separate literary executor, and where he appoints separate representatives in respect of realty and personalty.

23.34 In the latter case, care needs to be taken where one of the assets was a mortgage. Section 3(1)(ii) of the Administration of Estates Act 1925 provides that for the purposes of that part of the Act the expression 'real estate' includes land held by way of mortgage, so that it devolves to the personal representatives under s 1(1). The provision is unnecessary, because a mortgage can take effect only as a mortgage by demise, subject to provision for cesser on redemption,[1] or as a charge by deed by way of legal mortgage,[2] in both of which cases the mortgage would devolve as a chattel real upon the personal representatives under the general law. However, s 3 applies only to devolution, and not to the nature of the property devolved. The mortgage will devolve upon the personal representative entitled to personalty[3] unless the mortgagor's right of redemption was barred at the date of death of the deceased, when it will devolve as realty.[4]

1 Law of Property Act 1925, s 85(1).
2 Ibid.
3 See *Coote on Mortgages* (9th edn) pp 870ff.
4 Law of Property Act 1925, ss 88, 153(3).

Contractual rights

Personal and non-personal contracts

23.35 We are concerned here with rights of action which had accrued to the deceased prior to his death. It is necessary first to draw a distinction between personal contracts, which terminated on the death of the deceased, and non-personal contracts which accrue for the benefit of the estate. The more common examples of personal contracts are contracts between employer and employee,[1] principal and agent,[2] and artist and the person commissioning him.[3] Where the contract is personal, it will be discharged by death unless there is an express provision to the contrary.[4] It may be necessary for adjustments to be made under the Law Reform (Frustrated Contracts) Act 1943.

1 *Farrow v Wilson* (1869) LR 4 CP 744, esp at 746.
2 Ibid; and *Graves v Cohen* (1929) 46 TLR 121.
3 *Robinson v Davison* (1871) LR 6 Exch 269.
4 *Farrow v Wilson*, above.

23.36 A contract which is not of its nature personal may be brought to an end by the death of one of the parties, if there is an express or implied agreement to that effect. So in *Neal v Hanbury*[1] Thomas Neal had the right to receive an annuity of £5. He was described as being 'a very lewd, dissolute man', and the annuity was made conditional upon him behaving civilly to the payer's wife. It was held that this annuity was personal to him, and therefore died with him. Where a contract which is not of a personal nature is not discharged by death, the position depends on whether it was broken in the deceased's lifetime.

1   (1701) Prec Ch 173.

Contract broken in deceased's lifetime

23.37   At common law the rule was actio personalis moritur cum persona[1] so that, where a personal contract had been broken in the lifetime of the deceased, although the deceased himself could have sued, his personal representatives could not. This rule was altered by Law Reform (Miscellaneous Provisions) Act 1934, s 1(1). The essential words of this section are that 'on the death of any person after [25 July 1934] all causes of action[2] . . . vested in him shall survive . . . for the benefit of his estate'. The terms of this section are wide enough to include actions for breach of personal contracts. There are two qualifications to this principle:
(a)   exemplary damages may not be awarded;[3] and
(b)   the general rule of public policy that personal representatives cannot sue where money arises from the felonious act of the deceased. So in *Beresford v Royal Insurance Co Ltd*[4] the personal representatives of an assured were held not entitled to sue for moneys under a life policy on his life because his death was caused by his own suicide.

1   *Raymond v Fitch* (1835) 2 CrM & R 588.
2   See *Sugden v Sugden* [1957] P 120, CA.
3   Law Reform (Miscellaneous Provisions) Act 1934, s 1(2).
4   [1938] AC 586.

Representative's position

23.38   Where the contract was broken before the death of the deceased, or where it was not personal and remained in force at his death, personal representatives stand in the position of the deceased, even though they are not mentioned in the contract. There are numerous examples of this. To give but one, in *Beswick v Beswick*[1] the widow was entitled to enforce the contract even though on its face it referred just to the parties themselves, no mention being made of their personal representatives.

1   [1966] Ch 538.

Rights of action in tort

Generally

Survival of actions
23.39   Section 1(1) of the Law Reform (Miscellaneous Provisions) Act 1934 also saves rights of action in tort, and declares that all causes of action[1] subsisting in the deceased at the time of his death – except actions for

defamation – survive for the benefit of his estate.[2] This applies whether or not action was commenced by the deceased himself.

1   See *Kelly v Kelly and Brown* [1961] P 94.
2   This includes a right to a contribution: *Ronex Properties Ltd v John Laing Construction Ltd* [1983] QB 398, [1982] 3 All ER 961, CA.

23.40   Where proceedings were not commenced by the deceased, they may be commenced by the personal representatives. The normal rules apply, but where the action is for negligence, nuisance or breach of duty, and the claim is for damages for personal injury, whether or not any other relief is sought, proceedings must be commenced within three years from the date when the cause of action arose or from the date on which the deceased knew of the cause of action.[1] If the deceased did not himself commence proceedings, the personal representatives can bring an action within three years from when they acquired knowledge.[2] An action for damages under the Fatal Accidents Act 1976 can be brought within three years from when the persons for whose benefit the action is brought first acquired knowledge.[3]

1   Limitation Act 1980, s 11.
2   Ibid, ss 11(5), 14.
3   Ibid, ss 12, 14.

Damages

23.41   The normal rules as to remoteness and quantum of damages apply, with few exceptions. Damages are recoverable for the pain and suffering of the deceased between the wrong and the date of death,[1] and damages are also recoverable for loss of expectation of life.[2] There are two qualifications to the normal rules. First, exemplary damages cannot be awarded.[3] Secondly, apart from funeral expenses, which can be awarded,[4] damages are to be calculated without reference to any loss or gain to the estate as a result of the death. On this basis, payments received under insurance policies do not reduce the amount of damages awarded, but on the other hand, where the deceased had an interest ceasing on his death, such as a life interest in a trust fund, no damages are awarded for the reduction in the period for which he had enjoyed that interest.

1   *Rose v Ford* [1937] AC 826.
2   Ibid; see also *Wise v Kaye* [1962] 1 QB 638, CA; *Andrews v Freeborough* [1967] 1 QB 1, [1966] 2 All ER 721.
3   Law Reform (Miscellaneous Provisions) Act 1934, s 1.
4   Ibid, s 2(3).

Fatal accidents

Right of action

23.42   The Fatal Accidents Act 1976 provides that where the death of a person is caused by the wrongful act of another, an action will lie against the person causing the death if the deceased could himself have brought an action against him had he survived.[1] The action must normally be brought by the personal representatives,[2] who must have a grant before proceedings are instituted,[3] but this is only a device of convenience. Whereas other tortious (and contractual) actions are brought or continued for the benefit of the estate, actions brought by the personal representatives under the Fatal Accidents Act are brought for the benefit of the deceased's close relatives, or those living with him.[4]

1 Fatal Accidents Act 1976, s 1A, substituted by Administration of Justice Act 1982, s 3.
2 Substituted s 2.
3 See below, para 25.00.
4 Fatal Accidents Act 1976, s 1(2), (3), substituted by Administration of Justice Act 1982, s 3.

Damages

23.43 The fundamental principle of the Acts is '*to compensate the recipient on a balance of gains and losses for the injury sustained by the death*'.[1] For this purpose 'injury' means pecuniary loss only[2] and, in order to succeed, it is necessary for the plaintiffs to show actual pecuniary loss, or the loss of a reasonable possibility of pecuniary advantage.[3] Payments under private and various state insurance schemes are ignored[4] but otherwise pecuniary advantages or disadvantages to the dependants as a result of the death are taken into account. In particular, where action is brought both under the Law Reform Act and under the Fatal Accidents Act, then if the persons entitled to the estate are the same persons as those entitled as dependants, the amount of an award under the Fatal Accidents Act will be reduced by the award under the Law Reform Act.[5] However, any benefits which accrue to the estate by virtue of the death are ignored.[6]

1 Per Lord Wright, *Davies v Powell Duffryn Associated Collieries Ltd* [1942] AC 601 at 617.
2 *Blake v Midland Rly Co* (1852) 18 QB 93.
3 *Duckworth v Johnson* (1859) 4 H & N 653; *Barnett v Cohen* [1921] 2 KB 461.
4 Fatal Accidents (Damages) Act 1908; Fatal Accidents Act 1959, s 2.
5 *Davies v Powell Duffryn Associated Collieries Ltd*, above.
6 Fatal Accidents Act 1976, s 4, substituted by Administration of Justice Act 1982, s 3.

Bereavement

23.44 Where a claim is brought under the Fatal Accidents Act 1976, the wife or husband of the deceased, or the parents of the deceased if he was an unmarried minor, may claim damages for bereavement in an amount which is fixed from time to time by statutory instrument but which is at present £7,500.[1]

1 In respect of causes of action arising on or after 1 April 1991 (£3,500 prior to that date): Fatal Accidents Act 1976, s 1A, substituted by Administration of Justice Act 1982, s 3 and increased by the Damages for Bereavement (Variation of Sum) (England and Wales) Order 1990, SI 1990/2575.

General powers of personal representatives

23.45 Personal representatives have very wide powers to get in the assets of the deceased; preserve and maintain them pending distribution or disposal; and to dispose of them. In most cases it will be found that the personal representatives have the power to take the action which they wish to take in connection with the administration of the estate, but where the power does not exist, the court nevertheless has jurisdiction to confer the power in a special case.[1]

1 Trustee Act 1925, s 57.

Powers to get in assets

To take proceedings

23.46 Where the assets of the deceased are not in the possession of the personal representatives, the person having custody of them will usually be prepared to hand them to the personal representative upon production of evidence of his authority, namely the grant of representation, or, in some cases, of the will itself. Where the personal representatives cannot obtain the assets upon request, they have the right to take proceedings.

23.47 There are two types of proceedings which the personal representatives may wish to take:
(a) where rights of action have devolved upon them, but in respect of which the deceased himself did not commence proceedings. Subject to the exceptions noted above,[1] all rights of action of the deceased devolve to his representatives; and
(b) where it is necessary for them to take proceedings to recover assets. They have a general power to sue to recover assets.[2]
Before proceedings of either type are commenced, personal representatives, to safeguard their own position, will usually be advised to apply to the court at the outset for directions.[3] It will be remembered that an asset of the estate is the right to recover void or voidable dispositions made by the deceased, such as lifetime gifts made by the deceased while under undue influence.[4] The power to take proceedings extends to taking such proceedings as the deceased could have taken in order to maximise the value of the estate.[5]

1 Above, paras 23.35–23.40.
2 *Cobbett v Clutton* (1826) 2 C & P 471.
3 If they do not do so they may not be able to obtain their costs from the estate.
4 See above, paras 5.46–5.47. It may be presumed from the fiduciary relationship of the parties; it may also be proved as a matter of fact, as in *Re Craig, Meneces v Middleton* [1971] Ch 95, [1970] 2 All ER 390.
5 *Heslop v Burns* [1974] 3 All ER 406. (Dwellinghouse devolving upon executors, but occupied for 20 years by a family for whom the deceased intended to provide a home. Held: house occupied by family as licensees, and executors were entitled to possession.)

To levy distress

23.48 Ordinary actions in respect of arrears of rent expressly come within the general power to sue just considered. There is a special statutory power to levy distress. Section 26(4) of the Administration of Estates Act 1925 confers upon personal representatives the right to distrain for arrears of rent due to the deceased in the same way as he might have done had he been living. This sub-section confers a special right to distrain, for it is not necessary for the personal representatives themselves to be the reversioners. Thus, it appears that a deceased's general personal representatives may levy distress even if the reversion devolves upon his special representatives. Provided that the tenant is still in possession, the personal representatives can exercise this power even within six months after the determination of the term.

To give receipts

23.49 In general, personal representatives each have entire authority over the whole of the estate,[1] and a receipt or release given by one personal representative will be good.[2] In respect of land, if there is only one personal representative he can give a valid receipt for capital money, although if there are two or more proving executors, they will all have to join in.[3]

1 *Ex p Rigby* (1815) 19 Ves 463; *Owen v Owen* (1738) 1 Atk 494.
2 *Jacomb v Harwood* (1751) 2 Ves Sen 265.
3 Law of Property Act 1925, s 27(2).

Powers of management

23.50 The principal powers of management are:
(a)   to invest in authorised securities[1] or in accordance with the terms of the will, whichever is wider;
(b)   to operate a bank account;[2]
(c)   to deposit money in a deposit account[3] and to deposit documents with a banker or depositary.[4] There is no express power to enable a personal representative to deposit articles of value, but it is doubtful whether, if he exercised reasonable care, he would be liable for any loss which resulted;
(d)   to insure any building or other property to three-quarters of its full value against damage by fire.[5] The statutory power is unsatisfactory. In the first place it is often desirable to insure to the full reinstatement value. Secondly, it is often desirable to insure against other risks as well. Thirdly, the statutory power does not extend to any property which the personal representative is bound to transfer forthwith to a beneficiary.[6] Accordingly, it is better practice to include wider powers of insurance in the will;
(e)   to pay calls on shares;[7] to take up rights issues of shares, or to renounce the rights;[8] and to concur in schemes for the amalgamation or reconstruction of a company, or for the modification of the rights attaching to shares;[9]
(f)   in respect of land, all the powers of trustees for sale of land;[10]
(g)   in respect of debts and disputes very wide powers to compromise or abandon, provided such action is taken in good faith.[11]
Personal representatives also have the general power of trustees to appoint agents.[12]

1 Under the Trustee Investments Act 1961.
2 Trustee Act 1925, s 11(1).
3 Ibid.
4 Ibid, s 21.
5 Ibid, s 19.
6 Ibid, s 19(1).
7 Ibid, s 11(2).

8   Ibid, s 10(4).
9   Ibid, s 10(3); *Re Walker's Settlement* [1935] Ch 567; Trustee Investments Act 1961, s 9(1).
10   Administration of Estates Act 1925, s 39(1)(ii).
11   Trustee Act 1925, s 15.
12   Ibid, s 23.

Powers in connection with disposal

23.51   The main powers are, first, to raise money on mortgage, for the payment of the debts and liabilities of the deceased, and the administration expenses.[1] Where this is done, the appropriate adjustment has to be made between the various beneficiaries so that there is no alteration in the incidence of liabilities. Secondly, there is a power to sell.

(a)   Personal representatives have a wide power to sell assets if the proceeds are required for the purpose of administration, even if the assets are specifically bequeathed.[2]

(b)   They have a power to sell assets in order to raise capital for the payment of legacies.[3]

(c)   Where there is a total or partial intestacy, the undisposed-of property is held upon a trust for sale[4] with full power to postpone. However, personal representatives are directed not to sell reversionary interests or personal chattels unless there is some special reason for doing so.

(d)   In respect of land, personal representatives have all the powers of trustees for sale.[5]

(e)   Personal representatives have a wide discretion as to the method of sale. They can sell assets separately or together; subject to or free from charges and incumbrances; and by private contract or by auction.[6]

The protection conferred upon purchasers from personal representatives is considered later.[7]

1   Administration of Estates Act 1925, s 40.
2   *Re Cohen* [1960] Ch 179 at 188.
3   Trustee Act 1925, s 16(1).
4   Administration of Estates Act 1925, s 33.
5   Ibid, s 39(1)(ii).
6   Trustee Act 1925, s 12.
7   Below, para 33.16.

23.52   Personal representatives are under the same restrictions as trustees with regard to purchasing the property of the estate.

Individual powers of personal representatives

23.53   The powers just discussed are those exercisable by all personal representatives acting together or, where there is only one personal representative, by that person acting alone. Difficulty can arise where there is more than one personal representative and one only of those personal representatives purports to act by himself. The position is as follows.

(a)   In the case of pure personal property, executors generally have several authority. Accordingly, one executor can sell pure personal property without the consent or concurrence of the others.[1] This principle has been extended, so that if a debt is owed to the estate, one executor can settle an account with the debtor, and that settlement will be binding on the other executors, even if they disagree.[2] Further, where the estate is sued, if one executor submits to judgment, that submission is binding on the co-executors.[3]

(b) Where one personal representative has done an effective act, no subsequent act will be effective if it is inconsistent with it. If, therefore, one personal representative claims on behalf of the estate that a debt is statute barred, an acknowledgment of the debt by another personal representative is ineffective.[4]

(c) The act of all personal representatives together is sometimes required by statute,[5] and where stocks and shares in a private company are held, the articles of association of the company will usually require all personal representatives to act together.[6]

(d) One of two or more executors can enter into a contract binding the estate for the sale of freehold or leasehold land, although he can complete the contract only with the concurrence of the co-executors or an order of the court.[7]

(e) It is uncertain whether one administrator acting without his co-administrators is in the same position as one executor acting without his co-executors,[8] but in the most recent decision, in *Fountain Forestry Ltd v Edwards*,[9] the court assumed, without deciding, that one administrator could enter into a contract binding on his co-administrator.

(f) A person can enter into a contract on a specific basis, that basis being made fundamental to the existence of the contract. If he does so, and that purported fundamental basis does not exist, there is no contract, although other rights may arise. The point was neatly illustrated in *Fountain Forestry Ltd v Edwards*. Letters of administration to the deceased's estate were granted to his widow and to his son. The son entered into a contract for the sale of real property, signing the contract, and adding beneath his signature the words 'for self and Mary Jones Edwards'. Subsequently, the widow, who had not been consulted about the sale, refused to join in the conveyance, and the contracting purchasers sought a decree of specific performance. Brightman J held[10] that the son had purported to bind the estate only on the assumption, which he warranted to be correct, that he had authority to sign for the widow. As he had no authority, there was no contract to be enforced. The contracting purchasers did, however, have a right to sue the son for breach of warranty of authority. It seems that if the son had merely signed in his own name, without warranting that he had authority from his co-administrator, then a decree of specific performance would have been granted.

1 *Anon* (1536) 1 Dyer 23*b*, in *margin*; *Kelsack v Nicholson* (1596) Cro Eliz 478, 496; *Jacomb v Harwood* (1751) 2 Ves Sen 265; *Cole v Miles* (1852) 10 Hare 179.
2 *Smith v Everett* (1859) 27 Beav 446, 29 LJCh 236.
3 *Lepard v Vernon* (1813) 2 Ves & B 51; *Simpson v Gutteridge* (1816) 1 Madd 609; *Warner v Simpson* [1958] 1 QB 404, [1958] 1 All ER 44. There is an exception to the rule if the executors file separate defences: *Baldwin v Church* (1716) 10 Mod Rep 323; *Elwell v Quash* (1730) 1 Stra 20; *Re Midgley, Midgley v Midgley* [1893] 3 Ch 282.
4 *Re Chamandy* (1975) 58 DLR (3d) 332.
5 *Barton v North Staffordshire Rly Co* (1888) 38 Ch D 458; *Barton v London and North Western Rly Co* (1889) 24 QBD 77.
6 See eg Table A, art 29 prescribed under SI 1985/805 pursuant to Companies Act 1985, s 8.
7 This is not expressly stated in the legislation. Prior to 1898, leaseholds as well as pure

personalty vested in the executors, and could be sold by one of two executors under the general principle noted above. Between 1898 and 1926 the position was governed by the Land Transfer Act 1897, under which, in general, the powers of personal representatives as to personalty were extended to realty, but all representatives were required to join in the transfer of realty. In this period, therefore, one of two or more representatives could contract to sell, and could convey, leaseholds but not freeholds. Section 2 of the Administration of Estates Act 1925 provides that the personal representatives' powers to sell apply to realty, but under sub-s 2(2) all representatives have to join in the conveyance.

8 *Hudson v Hudson* (1735) Cas temp Talb 127; *Jacomb v Harwood* (1751) 2 Ves Sen 265; *Warwick v Greville* (1809) 1 Phillim 123; *Stanley v Bernes* (1828) 1 Hag Ecc 221; *Smith v Everett* (1859) 27 Beav 446, 29 LJ Ch 236.

9 [1975] Ch 1, [1974] 2 All ER 280.

10 Following *Sneesby v Thorne* (1855) 7 De GM & G 399.

Power to contract with oneself personally

23.54 A personal representative, in that capacity, can contract with himself in his personal capacity. This is illustrated by *Rowley Holmes & Co v Barber*.[1] In that case, in 1954 the testator, a solicitor, had taken into employment a legal executive. By his will the testator left the practice to the legal executive and appointed him to be his executor. When the testator died the legal executive could not carry on the practice himself, and he sold it to another solicitor. The legal executive continued in employment with the purchaser until he was made redundant. The question was whether, for the purpose of claiming a redundancy payment, the legal executive had been in continuous employment only since the sale of the practice to the purchaser, or since 1954 when he first entered employment with the testator. The court held that a personal representative had power to contract with himself in his personal capacity; that on the death of the testator he had as executor continued to employ himself personally in the practice, and that his employment had therefore been continuous since 1954.

1 [1977] 1 All ER 801.

Other powers of trustees

23.55 Section 69 of the Trustee Act 1925 provides that, except where there is an express statement to the contrary, the provisions of the Act apply to executors and administrators, and accordingly the other powers conferred by the Act will apply to personal representatives. These will include the statutory powers of maintenance and advancement.[1]

1 Trustee Act 1925, ss 31, 32.

23.56 Under this principle, personal representatives may find s 57 of the Trustee Act 1925 particularly helpful. This section confers on the court power to authorise trustees, and so personal representatives, to enter into a wide range of transactions in respect of any property held by them.[1] In *Perpetual Trustee Co Ltd v Godsall*[2] the court of New South Wales used the local equivalent of s 57 to assist personal representatives. The testator left his house and contents to his wife for life, on the condition that she should pay all the costs of maintaining it. The widow was financially unable to do so. The court made an order enabling the personal representatives to sell the house, purchase a smaller house, allow the widow to reside in it, and invest the income surplus to that required to maintain the smaller house in an accumulating fund for the benefit of the remainderman.[3]

1 See, generally, *Re Downshire Settled Estates* [1953] Ch 218 at 248, CA.
2 [1979] 2 NSWLR 785.
3 The last point arose as recompense for delapidations which had arisen, and which had resulted in the testator's house being worth less.

CHAPTER 24

Devolution of settled land

The problem

24.1 It is not difficult to mount a convincing argument in support of the proposition that the concept of the strict settlement of land should have been abandoned long ago and replaced with a new type of settlement based largely, but not entirely, on the trust for sale.[1] Only a lawyer could appreciate the fine, but sometimes vital, distinction[2] between a strict settlement and a trust for sale. A testator who makes his own will leaving his house to his wife for life and then to his children equally would hardly have conceived that he was invoking the elaborate machinery of the Settled Land Act 1925 – followed on his wife's death by a trust for sale governed by the rather different provisions of the Law of Property Act 1925.

1 The concept of settled land is based on a wish that the land should not be sold – although paradoxically that objective may be effectively achieved only by means of a trust for sale. Section 106 of the Settled Land Act 1925 renders void any provision that attempts or tends to prevent a tenant for life from exercising his power of sale. A sale may, however, be effectively prevented by means of a trust for sale by requiring the consent of not more than two persons to any sale (under the Law of Property Act 1925, s 28(1)) and ensuring that those persons will not give their consent as it would be detrimental to their interests to do so: *Re Inns* [1947] Ch 576. See also *Re Herklot's Will Trusts* [1964] 1 WLR 583.
2 The distinction is simply a matter of wording. If a testator gives his house to his trustees 'upon trust to my son for his life and then to his children' a strict settlement arises on the testator's death. On the other hand, if he leaves his house to his trustees 'upon trust to sell or retain the same for my son for life and then to his children', the testator has created an immediate trust for sale.

24.2 Where land is settled within the meaning of the Settled Land Act 1925, the scheme of the Act is to distinguish between land which ceased to be settled on the death of a life tenant, and land which will remain settled after his death. In respect of land which ceases to be settled on the death, the Act:
(a) provides that the land vests in the deceased's *general* personal representatives; who
(b) vest it in the person absolutely entitled under the settlement.
In respect of land which remains settled after the death of the life tenant, it
(a) provides that the land vests in the *special* personal representatives; who
(b) vest it in the person next entitled under the settlement.
These principles now require elaboration.

Land ceasing to be settled land

Following the death of life tenant

24.3 It is essential to distinguish between land which ceases to be settled on the death of a tenant for life, and land which remains settled. To decide this, it is necessary to look at the position not at the time when the tenant for life was alive, but at the moment immediately after his death. If immediately after the death the land is not settled land, within the terms of the Settled Land Act 1925, s 1,[1] of which the most common example is land limited for persons in succession,[2] then it will cease to be settled. This is so even though the person ultimately entitled is entitled because of the terms of the settlement. Suppose land is settled upon trust for Victoria for life, with remainder to Edward for life, with remainder to George absolutely. Upon the death of Victoria the land remains settled. If the position is considered immediately after Victoria's death, the land is still limited for persons in succession, namely Edward for life, with remainder to George. However, on the death of Edward, the land ceases to be settled. Considered immediately after his death, the land is no longer limited in succession, but is held for George absolutely.

1 In general terms, Settled Land Act 1925, s 1, defines 'settled land' as land limited in trust for any persons by way of succession; or limited in trust for any person in possession for an entailed or similar interest; or limited in trust for any person contingently on the happening of any event; or land charged by way of family arrangement. The Schedule to the Law of Property (Amendment) Act 1926 excludes land held upon trust for sale.
2 Settled Land Act 1925, s 1(1)(i).

24.4 This principle was established by the important decision in *Re Bridgett and Hayes' Contract*.[1] In that case land was held, in essence, upon trust for A for life, with a direction for it to be sold on the death of A and the proceeds of sale held for specified beneficiaries. It was held that the land ceased to be settled land on the death of A, so that the legal estate vested in his general personal representatives.[2] Land which was settled will cease to be settled following the death of a tenant for life if the remainderman then becomes fully entitled. This is subject to two exceptions and where these apply the land will remain settled. They are:
(a) if any charge exists under the settlement, or any power of charging is still capable of being exercised;[3]
(b) if the person who is absolutely and beneficially entitled is a minor,[4] in which case the land will continue to be settled until the minor attains the age of 18.[5]

1 [1928] Ch 163.
2 See also *Re Bordass' Estate* [1929] P 107; *Re Birch's Estate* [1929] P 164.
3 Settled Land Act 1925, s 3(a).
4 Ibid, s 3(b).
5 Ibid, s 1(1)(ii)(d) and s 2.

24.5 If the remainderman, during the lifetime of the tenant for life, himself created a settlement of his remainder, that will cause the land to remain settled, even though the original settlement would then come to an end.[1]

1 *Re Taylor's Estate* [1929] P 260.

Where trust for sale arises

24.6   If following the death of a tenant for life the land becomes subject to an express trust for sale, the land ceases to be settled land and should be conveyed to the trustees of the settlement as trustees for sale. This is the result of the unhappy Settled Land Act 1925, s 36(1), which provides that

> 'if and when . . . settled land is held in trust for persons entitled in possession under a trust instrument in undivided shares, the trustees of the settlement (if the settled land is not already vested in them) may require the estate owner in whom the settled land is vested . . . to convey the land to them . . . as joint tenants.'

The use of the expression 'settled land' in the opening part of the section is unfortunate, for the definition of settled land is restricted to 'land not held upon trust for sale'.[1] However, it has been held that the effect of the trust for sale in putting an end to the settlement is ignored for the purposes of s 36,[2] so that the section can be interpreted as if it read 'land which was previously settled land'.

1   Schedule, Law of Property (Amendment) Act 1926.
2   *Re Cugny's Will Trusts, Smith v Freeman* [1931] 1 Ch 305 at 309.

24.7   Suppose, therefore, that land is limited upon trust for Peter for life, and thereafter for Queenie and Quince in undivided shares, for general purposes the land will cease to be settled on the death of Peter, although it will remain settled for the purposes only of s 36. In such circumstances, the land will cease to be settled for the purposes of the Administration of Estates Act only if there is no outstanding charge taking priority over the trust for sale. So, in *Re Norton, Pinney v Beauchamp*,[1] land was held upon trust for A for life and then, subject to certain rent charges and portions charged on the land, upon trust for sale. Romer J held that upon the death of A, the land remained settled land.

1   [1929] 1 Ch 84.

24.8   A further difficulty arises under the Settled Land Act 1925, s 36. Section 36(2) provides that when land is vested in the trustees of the settlement, they hold upon a statutory trust for sale.[1] This sub-section refers to 'settled land', but, as in the case of sub-s 36(1), it seems that this means 'land which was previously settled'. In *Re Cugny's Will Trusts*,[2] in essence, land was settled upon trust for A for life, with remainder to B and C in undivided shares. It was held that following the death of A, s 36(2) applied, and the trustees of the settlement were entitled to have the legal estate vested in them as trustees for sale. However, it was also held that in accordance with the principle in *Re Bridgett and Hayes' Contract*[3] the land had ceased to be settled on the death of A, for the purposes of the Administration of Estates Act, with the result that it devolved first on the general personal representatives of A. To put it at its lowest, there is the highly inelegant result that at the same time the land was not settled land, so that it devolved on the general personal representatives, but that it was settled land, so that s 36(2) applied. It is possible to reconcile this only by saying that the expression 'settled land' means 'settled land' for the

Administration of Estates Act, but that it means 'land which was previously settled land' for the purposes of the Settled Land Act, s 36. In any event, in *Re Cugny's Will Trusts* the land was regarded as settled land only for the purposes of s 36, and for no other.

1 Settled Land Act 1925, s 36(6).
2 [1931] 1 Ch 305.
3 [1928] Ch 163; see above, para 24.4.

24.9 It should be noted that whereas generally land remains settled land if there are any charges outstanding, s 36(2) operates even if there are any such charges, and that the trustees for sale take subject to them.

Summary

24.10 The position may therefore be summarised as follows. For the purposes of the Administration of Estates Act, land will cease to be settled if:
(a) the person entitled following the death of the tenant for life is entitled absolutely and beneficially;
(b) he is of full age;
(c) there are no outstanding charges, or powers of creating charges; and
(d) there are no derivative interests.
Even where land ceases to be settled for the purposes of the Administration of Estates Act, it may remain settled for the purposes, and only for the purposes, of the Settled Land Act, s 36.

Special personal representatives

Special probate

24.11 The Administration of Estates Act 1925, s 22(1) provides that a testator may appoint as his special executors the persons who are the trustees of the settlement at the date of his death. If he does not make that appointment, they are nevertheless deemed to be his special executors. Accordingly, where the deceased left a will, and there are trustees of the settlement in existence at the date of his death, they will be his special executors, either by virtue of the express, or alternatively because of the deemed, appointment.

24.12 Section 30(3) is another section in the Settled Land Act which causes difficulty. It applies to settlements made by will, and provides that where there are no trustees of the settlement, the personal representatives of the deceased settlor shall be deemed to be the trustees of the settlement until others are appointed. From this section, it would be expected that where the settlement arose by will, and there are no express trustees of the settlement at the date of death of the tenant for life, then the personal representatives of the deceased settlor would be the special executors of the deceased tenant for life. This, indeed, was the decision in *Re Gibbings's Estates*.[1] In that case a settlor died in 1890, appointing his wife and son to be his executors, and devising land upon trust for his wife for life and, in the events which happened, thereafter for his children equally. On the death of the wife, after 1925, it was held that the deceased's son, as surviving executor of his will, was the special executor of the wife.

1   [1928] P 28.

24.13   Notwithstanding the decision in *Re Gibbings's Estates*,[1] the Probate Registry draws a distinction between cases where the personal representatives of the deceased settlor have expressly appointed themselves as trustees of the settlement, and where they have not. It is only in the former case that special probate will be granted: in the latter case it is only possible to obtain a grant of special administration with will annexed. The only possible justification for this silly distinction is the argument that s 30 applies for the purposes of the Settled Land Act only, so that it cannot also apply for the purposes of s 22 of the Administration of Estates Act. There would seem to be no merit in this argument at all.

1   [1928] P 28.

24.14   The Administration of Estates Act 1925, s 22, refers to 'the persons, if any, who are at his death the trustees of the settlement'. Accordingly, if there are no trustees of the settlement at that time, but some are appointed after the death but before the application for the grant, they will not be special executors, though they can apply for special administration with will annexed.

Special administration

24.15   Where a deceased life tenant dies wholly intestate so that he has neither appointed nor is deemed to have appointed[1] special executors, the order of priority for a grant of special administration is as follows:[2]
(a)   the trustees of the settlement at the time of application for the grant;
(b)   if there are no such trustees, and the settlement arises under a will or intestacy, the personal representatives of the settlor; and
(c)   the general personal representative of the deceased.
Although special probate can be granted only where the trustees are in existence at the date of the death of the life tenant, special administrators can be appointed where they are appointed trustees after the death but before the application for the grant.

1   Under Administration of Estates Act 1925, s 22; see above, para 24.11.
2   Non-contentious Probate Rules 1987, r 29.

Type of grant

24.16   It will have been seen that there may be a grant of special probate, special administration with will annexed, or special administration simpliciter, but, although there are these different types of grant, the position of the special personal representative under them is exactly the same. Whatever the basic type of grant, it will usually be the normal type of grant limited to particular property, namely, settled land.[1] Accordingly, the general personal representatives will obtain a grant 'save and except settled land', or a grant 'caeterorum', depending on whether the general grant precedes or succeeds the limited grant.[2]

1 See above, para 19.7.
2 See above, para 19.11.

Devolution of settled land

Land ceasing to be settled

24.17 Where land ceases to be settled land, for the purposes of s 22 of the Administration of Estates Act, it will vest in the general personal representatives of the deceased. This is the principle of *Re Bridgett and Hayes' Contract*.[1] There will be no need for a special grant, but although it is rarely used in these circumstances, the court nevertheless has a power to grant representation limited to settled land, under s 113 of the Supreme Court Act 1981. Thus, in *Re Mortifee's Estate*[2] the tenant for life died intestate, and upon his death the remainderman became absolutely entitled. The tenant for life had no known kin. A grant of letters of administration save and except settled land was made to the Treasury Solicitor, and a grant limited to the settled land was made to the remainderman.

1 [1928] Ch 163.
2 [1948] P 274.

24.18 Where the land for most purposes ceases to be settled, but remains settled for the purposes of s 36 of the Settled Land Act, the land will vest in the general personal representatives, but they will be required to transfer it to the trustees of the settlement as trustees for sale, if they do not require it for the purposes of administration.[1]

1 Settled Land Act 1925, s 36(1), (2).

Land remaining settled

24.19 If the land was settled previous to the death of the deceased, and remains settled thereafter, the legal estate will vest automatically on his death in his special executors, if he had any. If he has none, the legal estate will vest in the usual way in the President of the Family Division[1] until a grant of representation with or without will is made, when it will vest in the special administrators. If the land is not required for the purposes of administration by the special administrators, they will execute a vesting assent in favour of the next person entitled under the settlement.

1 See below, para 25.16.

Powers of special personal representatives

24.20 The provisions of Part III of the Administration of Estates Act 1925, which apply generally to the administration of assets, apply to special personal representatives. They may, therefore, sell the settled land, or mortgage it for the purposes of raising money for the payment of inheritance tax in respect of the settled land itself, or for the costs of the administration of that land.[1] Special personal representatives have an express power to dispose of the settled land without the concurrence of the general representatives, and likewise the general representatives may dispose without the concurrence of the special representatives.[2]

1 Administration of Estates Act 1925, s 36.
2 Ibid, s 24(1).

24.21 Where a person is entitled to a grant of administration, and he is not a trustee of the settlement, he may renounce his right to special administration, without renouncing his right to general administration.[1] This is contrary to the normal rule that where there is a renunciation, it must be renunciation of the whole entitlement to a grant. Likewise, where a grant has been made including settled land, the administrator may apply for the revocation of the grant in respect of settled land without revoking it in respect of other property.[2] These provisions are designed to encourage the trustees of the settlement to take special administration. Further to this end, it is also provided that the trustees of the settlement or any person beneficially interested under the settlement may apply to the court for the appointment of a special or additional personal representative in respect of the settled land. In the absence of special circumstances, the court must appoint such persons as will secure that the representatives after the appointment are the same as the trustees of the settlement.[3] This provision is also contrary to another general rule, namely that additional personal representatives cannot usually be appointed.[4]

1 Administration of Estates Act 1925, s 23(1)(a).
2 Ibid, s 23(1)(b).
3 Ibid, s 23(2).
4 Above, para 17.2.

The position of purchasers

24.22 As the provisions affecting special personal representatives are somewhat complicated, purchasers may in some circumstances encounter difficulty. This difficulty is usually connected with the fact that a grant of representation does not specify the land in respect of which it is made.

24.23 In the first place, suppose that a grant of special representation ought to have been made, but was not made. For example, if land was limited to A for life, with remainder to B for life, and with remainder to C absolutely, and on the death of A a general grant was obtained to A's estate. There should, of course, have been either a general grant save and except settled land, together with a special grant limited to settled land, or alternatively a general grant expressly including settled land. But if neither of these courses was followed, perhaps because at the time of application for the grant the general personal representatives did not know of the existence of the settled land, and a general grant was issued without reference to settled land, would the purchaser be safe in accepting title from them?[1] On these facts it is clear that a special grant should have been obtained; on the other hand, any grant is an order of the court, and a person is entitled to rely upon it. The latter is generally assumed to be correct, and the purchaser is thought to be protected. This was said in *Re Bridgett and Hayes*,[2] although because in that case the land had ceased to be settled land the statement was obiter.[3]

1 Although the fact that the land had been settled would be evident to a purchaser from the vesting deed which would form part of the title, he would assume that the settlement had come to an end so that the grant had properly been taken out by the general personal representatives. See above, paras 24.3–24.10.
2 [1928] Ch 163.
3 See also *Re Taylor's Estate* [1929] P 260 at 263.

24.24 The second difficulty is more substantial. Suppose that a person is the life tenant under two settlements, one of which comes to an end on his death, and the other of which continues. A special grant should be taken out in respect of the land comprised in the settlement which continues, and a general grant to the remainder. Suppose on these facts that a general grant save and except settled land is granted to A and B, and a grant limited to settled land is made to C and D. Then suppose that through some confusion the immediate title to the land which remains settled is:

vesting deed in favour of deceased;
general grant in favour of A and B,

what is the position of a purchaser from A and B? Conversely, suppose that title to the land which ceased to be settled is deduced as:

vesting deed in favour of deceased;
special grant in favour of C and D,

what is the position of a purchaser from C and D?

24.25 In these two cases A and B on the one hand, and C and D on the other, are purporting to sell land which is not vested in them. Can the purchaser be protected? It seems that he can properly protect himself only by examining the equitable interests, to confirm that the correct grant has been made, but this would breach the principle of separation of legal estate and equitable interests. On the other hand, it is just possible that the situation is saved by the Administration of Estates Act, s 36. This provides that 'a personal representative may assent to the vesting in any person who . . . may be entitled thereto',[1] and that an assent by the personal representatives 'shall operate to vest in that person the estate or interest to which the assent relates'.[2] One might suppose that these sections can apply only if the property is vested in the personal representatives in the first place, but if in fact they enable personal representatives to transfer a title which they do not have, the difficulty just postulated would be resolved (although greater difficulties would arise in its place). There is no satisfactory answer to this problem, and if and until it is resolved, the purchaser is at risk.

1 Sub-s (1).
2 Sub-s (2).

CHAPTER 25

Position of personal representatives without a grant

Where no grant is required

25.1   In general a grant of probate or letters of administration is necessary to enable the personal representatives to administer the estate. In particular cases, however, assets can be dealt with without the need for a grant. The assets about to be discussed can be, and usually are, dealt with under the terms of a grant, so that advantage is taken of the special provisions only where it is not proposed to take out a grant. The special provisions are described in this first section.

Administration of Estates (Small Payments) Act 1965

25.2   In order to enable small estates to be administered with little expense and formality, numerous statutes have enabled nearly fifty statutory and similar authorities to pay over to persons beneficially entitled assets in their hands without the necessity of producing a grant of probate or letters of administration. These statutes have been amended by the Administration of Estates (Small Payments) Act 1965, to impose a uniform limit on the amount which may be so paid. The limit is currently £5,000.[1]

---

1   Section 7(2). Under the Act the limit was £500, but the Treasury had power to fix a higher limit. The limit was increased in 1975 to £1,500 and increased again to the current limit in 1984 by the Administration of Estates (Small Payments) (Increase of Limit) Order 1984, SI 1984/539.

Assets falling within these provisions
25.3   The list is set out in the First Schedule of the Act, which includes:
(a)   National Savings products, such as National Savings Bank accounts, Savings Certificates, premium bonds and certain holdings of government stocks;
(b)   Trustee Savings Bank deposits;
(c)   building society accounts and deposits with friendly societies;
(d)   arrears of salary or superannuation benefits due to employees of government departments and local government. This will therefore include such sums due to deceased members or former members of

HM forces and includes their personal effects. It also extends to such amounts held on behalf of deceased public servants, such as policemen.

Payment is discretionary
25.4 While the authority concerned may make payment without production of a grant, it is not obliged to do so, and different authorities have different regulations as to the circumstances in which they will pay.

Protection of payer
25.5 As will be seen,[1] if payment is made of the assets of an estate without production of a grant, the payer may render himself an executor de son tort and liable to pay the sum again to the appointed personal representative. However, many of these provisions expressly protect the payer against this danger.[2]

1 See below, paras 27.1ff.
2 As an example, s 27 of the Industrial and Provident Societies Act 1965 exonerates the society committee from paying to the true personal representative provided payment is made to any person appearing to the committee at the time of payment to be entitled to the payment.

Nominations

25.6 A nomination is a direction by a person who holds certain types of investment to the authority in which that investment is made requiring payment to be made on the death of the investor to the person nominated. Payment is made to the nominee on proof of death only. A nomination may be made by a minor once he has attained the age of 16, and by any adult. It may be revoked or varied by a subsequent nomination, and is revoked on marriage. A nomination is not, however, revoked by will. In every case a nomination must be in writing, and in most cases an attesting witness is required. The form of nomination is usually held by the authority in which the investment is made, and so its existence will come to light when an application is made by the personal representative to deal with the asset after grant, even if he previously did not know of its existence.

25.7 Nominations are the only method of testamentary disposition available to minors who are not entitled to make a privileged will. There is often a danger, however, that the existence of the nomination is forgotten by the investor, and this disadvantage is particularly serious because a nomination is not revoked by a subsequent will.

25.8 There are two broad types of nomination, the distinction depending on the financial limits:
(a) nominations made prior to May 1981 in respect of various National Savings products, such as National Savings Certificates, National Savings Bank accounts and government stocks held on the National Savings Bank Register, where there is no financial limit;[1] nominations in respect of these assets cannot be made after April 1981; and
(b) nominations in respect of Trustee Savings Banks,[2] friendly societies,[3] and industrial and provident societies,[4] where the limit is £5,000.[5] A

nomination for an amount above the prescribed limit is valid to the extent of the limit.

If a nomination complies with the requirements of the Wills Act 1837, it may be proved as a will.[6]

1 Post Office Savings Bank Act 1954, s 7.
2 Trustee Savings Bank Act 1954, s 21(3).
3 Friendly Societies Act 1896, ss 56, 57; Friendly Societies Act 1955, s 5.
4 Industrial and Provident Societies Act 1965, ss 23, 24.
5 The Administration of Estates (Small Payments) (Increase of Limit) Order 1984, SI 1984/539.
6 *Re Baxter's Goods* [1903] P 12.

Persons domiciled abroad – insurance policies

25.9 The general requirement as to a grant of representation applies to any assets situate in England and Wales, even if the deceased died domiciled abroad. As an exception to this principle[1] a grant is not required for the payment of the proceeds of a policy of assurance on the life of a person domiciled abroad.[2] This does not, however, exempt the policy moneys from inheritance tax, which may still be payable.[3]

1 Under Revenue Act 1884, s 11.
2 Revenue Act 1889, s 19.
3 *Haas v Atlas Assurance Co Ltd* [1913] 2 KB 209.

Executor's authority prior to grant

25.10 The executor derives his authority from the will, and the probate merely confirms his rights. Generally, however, the executor can prove his right only by taking a grant of probate. The result is that he can do any act without a grant except:

(a) sue to judgment where it is necessary to show his title as executor; and
(b) in practice, make title.

Thus, it has been held that an executor without a grant may levy distress for unpaid rent,[1] pay and release debts, receive payments, sell chattels, and pay legacies.[2] On the other hand, before he has taken out a grant he may be sued by a creditor of the testator.[3]

1 *Whitehead v Taylor* (1839) 10 Ad & El 210.
2 *Wankford v Wankford* (1699) 1 Salk 299; *Woolley v Clark* (1822) 5 B & Ald 744.
3 *Mohamidu Mohideen Hadjiar v Pitchey* [1894] AC 437.

25.11 Although the probate is only evidence of the executor's authority an unproved will can be admitted in evidence to prove that the testator had made a will. In *Whitmore v Lambert*[1] a contractual tenant of a dwellinghouse died leaving a will naming his widow as sole beneficiary and executrix. She did not prove the will and the question arose whether she could put the unproved will in evidence to show her entitlement to remain in possession of the premises.[2] In holding that she could do, Evershed MR said:[3]

'a person appointed executor or executrix by will can do a number of things, and justify doing them, in relation to the property which was in the possession of the deceased, by virtue of the will before that will is proved: even though, because the executor or executrix dies, it never is proved, or capable of being proved by virtue of s 5 of the Administration of Estates Act. One such thing which the executor may do or justify doing is entering upon property which was in the ownership and occupation, or in the occupation only, of the deceased.'

Unfortunately, the Master of the Rolls did not classify further the other things which could and could not be done.

1 [1955] 2 All ER 147, [1955] 1 WLR 495.
2 The question was relevant for the purposes of a provision of the Rent Acts then in force.
3 [1955] 2 All ER 147 at 151, [1955] 1 WLR 495 at 501.

25.12 The first of the two situations in which the executor needs a grant is to sue to judgment. Any executor before grant can begin any action, and he can continue any action commenced by the deceased, provided it does not lapse on death.[1] He must obtain probate before judgment, if the action depends on his title as executor, but probate is not needed in any other case. If, therefore, it is necessary only to show possession and not title, as in the case of an action for trespass, the action can be completed without a grant.[2]

1 *Meyappa Chetty v Supramanian Chetty* [1916] 1 AC 603, PC; *Biles v Caesar* [1957] 1 All ER 151.
2 *Oughton v Seppings* (1830) 1 B & Ad 241.

25.13 The second situation where the grant is needed is to make title. So far as land is concerned, on the death of the testator the legal estate vests in the executor, and if he executes a conveyance of it, that will vest the legal estate in the purchaser. But, the purchaser will, as a matter of practice, insist on proof of title, which can be provided only by the probate. Accordingly, in *Re Stevens, Cooke v Stevens*[1] a purchaser was held entitled to refuse to complete until probate was obtained. Further, s 36(5) of the Administration of Estates Act 1925 provides that where a personal representative makes an assent or conveyance of a legal estate, the person in whose favour it is made is entitled to demand that a notice of that assent or conveyance is endorsed on the grant. A purchaser may well not complete before he is able to secure the endorsement of that notice, and to examine the probate to see that no endorsement has been made on it in favour of any other person.[2]

1 [1897] 1 Ch 422.
2 *Re Miller and Pickersgill's Contract* [1931] 1 Ch 511.

25.14 The absence of a grant can have other unexpected disadvantages. Where a tenancy of business premises comes to an end, the tenant is usually entitled to a new tenancy under the provisions of the Landlord and Tenant Act 1954. In exceptional circumstances, the court must refuse to grant a new tenancy, but, in that event it must issue to the tenant a certificate of refusal,[1] and the tenant is then entitled to compensation from the landlord. In *Sims-Hilditch v Simmons*[2] the tenant died, and his widow obtained a grant of probate of his will in Jersey. The landlord served notices determining the tenancy and the widow sought a declaration that the notices were invalid. The court refused the application and Goulding J held that in ordinary circumstances the tenant would have been entitled to a certificate for compensation. However, in this case, the widow had not obtained a grant in England and Wales, and the court could not recognise her as 'the tenant'. She was accordingly not able to obtain the certificate until a United Kingdom grant had been extracted. This was so even though the landlords did not object to the issue of the certificate: Goulding J held that the parties could not, as it were, contract out of the provisions of the law.

1 Landlord and Tenant Act 1954, s 37.
2 In *Re Crowhurst Park, Sims-Hilditch v Simmons* [1974] 1 All ER 991.

25.15 Even where he does not need to sue, or to make title, a personal representative will usually wish to take out a grant. This is because although he may think that he has the last will, and that he is appointed executor under it, he cannot know that this is so until probate has been granted. In most cases, therefore, the executor will wish to obtain protection for distributing the estate in the manner provided for by the will which a grant gives.

Administrator's authority prior to grant

25.16 Although the executor's authority stems from the will, in general an administrator, whether an administrator simpliciter or an administrator with will annexed, has no authority before the grant is issued. Between the date of death and the date of grant, the legal title to all the assets of the deceased vests in the President of the Family Division[1] – for want of a better repository of the legal estate.

1 Administration of Estates Act 1925, s 9, there called the Probate Judge.

25.17 Perhaps the most striking illustration of the position prior to grant is provided by *Ingall v Moran*.[1] The deceased was killed during the war by the negligence of an army lorry driver. The limitation legislation then in force required any action to be commenced within one year of death.[2] The deceased was killed on 19 September 1941, and the action was commenced by the deceased's father, claiming as administrator, on 17 September 1942. He did not in fact take out a grant until November 1942. The action was dismissed, because the father had no authority to bring the action prior to the grant, and this defect was not cured by the subsequent grant. Further, it was then too late for him to start another action. In *Finnegan v Cementation Co Ltd*[3] a widow brought an action under the Fatal Accidents Act arising out of the death of her husband. The death occurred in Eire and the widow took out a grant in Eire. It appeared, however, that the head office of the defendants was in England and that the action should be here. No grant of administration had been taken out in England and the writ was set aside. Again, in *Burns v Campbell*[4] where an administrator who had obtained a Northern Ireland grant issued a writ in England before the Northern Ireland grant had been resealed here,[5] it was held that the subsequent resealing did not have any retroactive validity, so that the writ was defective. A final example is provided by *Fred Long & Sons Ltd v Burgess*[6] where a widow, who was a contractual tenant, died. The landlord served notice to quit on the President of the Probate, Divorce and Admiralty Division[7] and immediately that expired, he commenced proceedings for possession against the widow's two sons who were in occupation. When the case was heard, the sons had no grant of administration, and the case was adjourned to enable them to apply for it. The Court of Appeal, however, held that even by obtaining the grant the sons were not helped because the notice to quit had expired before the grant was issued.

1   [1944] KB 160.
2   Public Authorities Protection Act 1893, as amended by Limitation Act 1939, s 21, subsequently repealed by Law Reform (Limitation of Actions, &c) Act 1954, ss 1, 8(3), Sch.
3   [1953] 1 QB 688.
4   [1952] 1 KB 15.
5   Resealing is not now necessary; see above, para 18.61.
6   [1950] 1 KB 115.
7   The predecessor in this respect of the Family Division.

25.18   *Long v Burgess*[1] shows that where an interest has been lawfully determined prior to the grant, no action can be taken when the grant has been obtained. There is, however, a limited doctrine of relation back, to enable the administrator to take action on behalf of the estate in respect of wrongful acts done before the grant. So, after he has obtained the grant, the administrator can sue a person who wrongfully appropriates the assets of the estate between the date of death and the date of grant.[2]

1   [1950] 1 KB 115.
2   *Foster v Bates* (1843) 12 M & W 226; *Tharpe v Stallwood* (1843) 5 Man & G 760; *Re Pryse's Goods* [1904] P 301, CA.

25.19   It follows from what has been said that an administrator has no power whatever to execute an assent or conveyance before obtaining his grant,[1] although where a recital of entitlement was contained in the assent or conveyance, the purchaser would presumably in due course obtain the legal estate under the doctrine of 'feeding the estoppel'.[2]

1   *Morgan v Thomas* (1853) 8 Exch 302.
2   See eg *Rawlyns' Case* (1587) Jenk 254; *Mackley v Nutting* [1949] 2 KB 55; *Universal Permanent Building Society v Cooke* [1952] Ch 95.

CHAPTER 26

Discharge of debts and liabilities

Assets

26.1 As well as bearing its colloquial meaning of any item of property, the word 'assets' is used in the technical sense of the property which is liable for the payment of the deceased's debts and liabilities.

What property is assets?

26.2 The Administration of Estates Act 1925, s 32(1), provides that the following items of real and personal estate are available as assets:
(a) property of the deceased, to the extent of his beneficial interest in it;
(b) property which is subject to a general power which the deceased exercised by will; and
(c) entailed property held by the deceased and which he disposed of under the power contained in the Law of Property Act 1925, s 176.

The section provides that these items are assets for the payment of debts and liabilities, but it appears that the liabilities must arise out of obligations entered into by the deceased during his lifetime, and not obligations incurred by the personal representatives.[1] Section 32 is not, however, comprehensive, and the following other items of property are available.

1 *Re St George's Steam Packet Co, Hamer's Devisees' Case* (1852) 2 De GM & G 366.

Property acquired after death
26.3 Assets falling into the estate after death are included, such as a premium bond prize won after the date of death, or income arising after death.[1] This would therefore include entitlement under the estate of another person who survived the deceased.[2]

1 *Re Tong, Hilton v Bradbury* [1931] 1 Ch 202. See also *Bromfield v Chichester* (1773) 2 Dick 480; *James v Dean* (1805) 11 Ves 383; *Randall v Russell* (1817) 3 Mer 190; *Fitzroy v Howard* (1828) 3 Russ 225; *Giddings v Giddings* (1827) 3 Russ 241; *Fosbrooke v Balguy* (1833) 1 My & K 226; *Bevan v Webb* [1905] 1 Ch 620; *Re Thomson, Thomson v Allen* [1930] 1 Ch 203.
2 Normally such a gift would lapse in the absence of contrary intention, see para 30.15, but

the will may have provided otherwise. If the gift is to a child or other issue of the testator and saved from lapse by virtue of the Wills Act 1837, s 33, in respect of deaths after 1982, it will not fall into the estate but pass direct to the beneficiaries so saving the gift from lapse. Prior to 1983, it would have fallen into the estate of the deceased and would therefore have been available for creditors: *Re Pearson* [1920] 1 Ch 247.

Property appointed

26.4   Although s 32 refers to property subject to a general power being disposed of by will, it is necessary to consider this further. There are in each case two questions to be asked: does the property devolve upon the personal representative; and is it available for the payment of debts? The possible permutations are as follows.

26.5   *Real property appointed by will*   A testator is deemed to have been entitled at his death to an interest in any realty which is subject to a power of appointment where his will operates as an appointment of that property.[1] Accordingly, it is within the terms of the Administration of Estates Act 1925, s 1(1), and devolves upon the personal representatives. It is available for the payment of debts under s 32.

1   Administration of Estates Act 1925, s 3(2).

26.6   *Personalty appointed by will*   At common law personalty appointed by will did not devolve upon the personal representatives of the appointor, but upon the appointee.[1] There is no provision of the Administration of Estates Act which alters this position. However, it has been held that the personal representatives can give a valid receipt for it[2] and can use it for the payment of debts under s 32.[3] If the personal representatives do not take it, the creditors, as they could before 1926, can still take action to satisfy their claims out of the appointed property.[4] This rule is based on the notion that as it was a general power, the testator could have exercised it in favour of the creditors, and it would be inequitable for the testator to give a benefit to volunteers while his creditors remained unsatisfied.[5] This reasoning is taken to its logical conclusion in *Beyfus v Lawley*,[6] where it was held that the testator cannot prefer creditors by appointing in favour of one of them. The appointment under the will operates as a legacy, even though made in favour of a person who is a creditor, and the other creditors may intervene.

1   *O'Grady v Wilmot* [1916] 2 AC 231, HL.
2   *Re Hoskin's Trusts* (1877) 5 Ch D 229; on appeal 6 Ch D 281, CA; *Re Peacock's Settlement, Kelcey v Harrison* [1902] 1 Ch 552; *O'Grady v Wilmot*, above.
3   See also *Canada Life Assurance Co v Couture Estate and Holy Redeemer Catholic Church* [1975] 1 WWR 191 (Manitoba). In that case an insurance policy was issued on terms that the proceeds on maturity were to be payable to a person designated by the grantee of the policy. The grantee made a will leaving all his residue, and the policy, to charity. It was held that the will was a valid designation of the policy proceeds, but that they fell into the estate rather than going to the charity direct. The proceeds were, therefore, available for the payment of debts, and also legacies.
4   *Thompson v Towne* (1694) 2 Vern 319; *Hinton v Toye* (1739) 1 Atk 465; *Bainton v Ward* (1741) 2 Atk 172; *Townshend v Windham* (1750) 2 Ves Sen 1 at 9; *Jenney v Andrews* (1822) 6 Madd 264; *Williams v Lomas* (1852) 16 Beav 1; *Platt v Routh* (1840) 6 M & W 756; *Fleming v Buchanan* (1853) 3 De GM & G 976 at 979; *Re Hadley, Johnson v Hadley* [1909] 1 Ch 20; *Re Pryce, Lawford v Pryce* [1911] 2 Ch 286.
5   *Townshend v Windham*, above; *Re Phillips, Lawrence v Huxtable* [1931] 1 Ch 347.
6   [1903] AC 411.

26.7 *Property appointed by deed* The scope of the rule allowing creditors to intervene was extended under the pre-1926 rules to allow them to claim property which was appointed by deed.[1] In *Townshend v Windham*[2] Lord Hardwicke said that the rules had to be the same for appointment by will and by deed. If not 'the justice intended by the court in these cases would be avoided in every instance; as then it would be putting it barely on the form of the conveyance'. It is uncertain, however, how far this rule applies, but the general view is that it applies only to an appointment by deed which operates on death and not during the testator's lifetime. This is because the creditor's action is to 'intercept' the fund in transitu[3] and in the case of an appointment which is operative inter vivos the transfer is complete. The 1925 legislation has not altered this position.[4]

1   *Townshend v Windham* (1750) 2 Ves Sen 1; *George v Milbanke* (1803) 9 Ves 190; *Pack v Bathurst* (1745) 3 Atk 269; *Troughton v Troughton* (1748) 3 Atk 656.
2   (1706) 2 Ves Sen 1.
3   *O'Grady v Wilmot* [1916] 2 AC 231 at 248, 273 and 279.
4   *Re Phillips, Lawrence v Huxtable* [1931] 1 Ch 347.

26.8 *Property not appointed* Property which is subject to a general power of appointment is available for the payment of creditors if the testator did not exercise the power and if he is entitled in default of appointment. The property is not available if he is not entitled in default.[1]

1   *Holmes v Coghill* (1802) 7 Ves 499; on appeal (1806) 12 Ves 206.

26.9 *Property subject to a special power* This is not available for creditors[1] unless, presumably, the deceased was entitled in default of appointment and no appointment was made.

1   Per Lord Hardwicke in *Townshend v Windham* (1750) 2 Ves Sen 1 at 9.

Donationes mortis causa
26.10 Property which is the subject of a donatio mortis causa has been held to be liable for the payment of debts if all other property has been exhausted.[1]

1   *Smith v Casen* (1718) 1 P Wms App 406; *Ward v Turner* (1752) 2 Ves Sen 431; *Re Korvine's Trust* [1921] 1 Ch 343.

Debts due from personal representative
26.11 If the deceased was owed a sum of money from a person whom he appoints to be his executor, and releases that debt in the will, the cause of action on the debt is extinguished when the testator dies, because at common law the executor cannot sue himself. However, the executor is under an equitable obligation to those interested in the estate to account for the amount of the debt and it is therefore available for the payment of creditors.[1]

1   *Izon v Butler* (1815) 2 Price 34; *A-G v Holbrook* (1823) 12 Price 407; *A-G v Hollingworth* (1857) 2 H & N 416; *Sidney v Sidney* (1873) LR 17 Eq 65; *Re Wedmore, Wedmore v Wedmore* [1907] 2 Ch 277; *Stamp Duties Comr v Bone* [1977] AC 511, [1976] 2 All ER 354, PC.

Property not available

Property not in hands of executor

26.12 There is a theoretical distinction between property which is available for the payment of debts, and property for which the personal representative is liable. All property within s 32 is available for the payment of debts, but a personal representative is responsible only to take reasonable care to safeguard the assets.[1] Accordingly, if the assets are stolen through no fault of his, or if, being perishable, they cease to exist through no fault of his, the personal representative is not liable.[2] In practice this has the result of making the assets unavailable.

1 Below, para 28.32.
2 *Jenkins v Plombe* (1705) 6 Mod Rep 181.

Trust property

26.13 Section 32 makes property liable for the payment of debts to the extent of the deceased's beneficial interest. Trust property, therefore, is not available. In *Re Webb, Barclays Bank Ltd v Webb*,[1] for example, the deceased effected a policy of assurance on his own life. The beneficiary of the policy, according to its terms, was his infant son. The deceased paid the premiums, but it was held that as he held the policy on trust for his son, the proceeds did not form part of his estate.[2]

1 [1941] Ch 225.
2 See also *Re Gordon* [1940] Ch 851, which turned on the rules of a friendly society; *Re Sinclair's Life Policy* [1938] Ch 799.

Foreign property

26.14 The general rule is that 'assets in any part of the world shall be assets in every part of the world'.[1] All assets, wherever situated, are therefore liable for the payment of debts. But a similar distinction must be drawn to that with regard to assets not in the hands of the executor: a personal representative is liable only to the extent of assets which he has or ought to have under his control as the English personal representative. The ability of the personal representative to use foreign assets for the payment of English debts will depend on whether, by the law of the country in which the assets are situated, they can be used for the discharge of English liabilities.

1 Per Lord Lyndhurst in *A-G v Dimond* (1831) 1 Cr & J 356.

Debts and liabilities

Power to settle and compromise

26.15 The Trustee Act 1925, s 15, confers upon personal representatives wide powers in respect of debts. These are:
(a) to allow any debt or claim on any evidence which they think sufficient;
(b) to allow time for payment of any debt;

(c) to agree to the settlement of any debt by compromise, compounding or in any other way; and

(d) to abandon any debt or claim.

So long as the personal representative exercises these powers in good faith, he is not responsible for any loss which arises as a result.

Admissible debts

26.16 Subject to the general provisions of the Trustee Act 1925, s 15, the personal representative is responsible for paying funeral expenses; expenses incurred in the administration of the estate; debts which were outstanding at the date of death; and liabilities which arose as a result of actions of the deceased in his lifetime.

Funeral expenses

26.17 Funeral expenses are payable out of the estate before any other debt.[1] Even in the case of an insolvent estate, the necessary funeral expenses take first priority.[2] Where the estate is insolvent, the personal representative is allowed to incur only those expenses which are absolutely necessary.[3] In *Shelly's Case*[4] these were said by Lord Holt to be the cost of the coffin, ringing the church bell, and the fees of the parson clerk and undertaker, but they also include the cost of digging the grave. Where the estate is solvent, the personal representative will be allowed all expenses which are reasonable having regard to the circumstances and quality of the deceased. In one case[5] £600 was allowed in 1691 on the funeral of a wealthy local celebrity.

1 *R v Wade* (1818) 5 Price 621 at 627.
2 *Re Walter, Slocock v Official Receiver* [1929] 1 Ch 647.
3 *Re Wester Wemyss, Tilley v Wester Wemyss* [1940] Ch 1, CA.
4 (1693) 1 Salk 296.
5 *Offley v Offley* (1691) Prec Ch 26, Case 28.

26.18 In all cases the extent of the allowable expenses depends on the facts, and it is difficult to extract a clear principle. The cost of a tombstone has been disallowed.[1] In *Paice v Archbishop of Canterbury*[2] Lord Eldon allowed the cost of mourning rings distributed among the deceased's relations and friends, and in *Pitt v Pitt*[3] a widow was allowed her mourning expenses, although a contrary result was reached in *Johnson v Baker*.[4]

1 *Bridge v Brown* (1843) 2 Y & C Ch Cas 181.
2 (1807) 14 Ves 364.
3 (1758) 2 Lee 508.
4 (1825) 2 C & P 207.

Debts

26.19 In general all debts due from the deceased are payable by his personal representatives. If the personal representatives pay a debt which they are not obliged to pay, they will be in breach of their duty, so if a debt has been held in an action to be statute barred, it may not be paid.[1] As an exception to this rule, personal representatives are not obliged to plead the Limitation Act as a defence, so therefore have a discretion to pay a statute-barred debt.[2] They are not entitled, however, to pay a debt which is unenforceable due to non-compliance with the requirements of the Statute of Frauds, where they still exist, or the Law of Property Act 1925, s 40.[3]

1 *Re Midgley, Midgley v Midgley* [1893] 3 Ch 282, CA.
2 *Norton v Frecker* (1737) 1 Atk 524 at 526; *Stahlschmidt v Lett* (1853) 1 Sm & G 415.
3 *Re Rownson, Field v White* (1885) 29 Ch D 358, CA. The Law of Property Act 1925, s 40, has now been replaced by the Law of Property (Miscellaneous Provisions) Act 1989, s 2, in respect of contracts made on and after 28 September 1989.

Contractual obligations

26.20 Personal contracts are frustrated by death and accordingly do not bind the personal representatives.[1] If, however, the deceased had broken a personal contract during his lifetime, and judgment had been given against him, that judgment is binding on the estate.[2] Other contracts are binding upon the personal representatives. If, for example, the deceased had contracted to redecorate a house, the personal representatives must arrange for this to be done at the expense of the estate, or for the contract to be terminated by consent.[3] The obligations under a lease[4] and in respect of a business carried on by the deceased[5] are considered later.

1 *Farrow v Wilson* (1869) LR 4 CP 744 at 746; *Robinson v Davison* (1871) LR 6 Exch 269; *Graves v Cohen* (1929) 46 TLR 121.
2 *Phillips v Homfray* (1883) 24 Ch D 439.
3 *Quick and Harris v Ludborrow* (1615) 3 Bulst 29; *Re Rushbrook's Will Trusts* [1948] Ch 421.
4 Below, paras 28.22–28.23.
5 Below, paras 28.10–28.11.

Liability in tort

26.21 In general all causes of action subsisting against the deceased survive his death. However, actions for defamation[1] do not survive. Previously, if proceedings had not been commenced before the death of the deceased, they had to be commenced within six months of a grant of representation being made.[2] This rule was, however, abolished by the Proceedings Against Estates Act 1970.[3]

1 Law Reform (Miscellaneous Provisions) Act 1934, s 1.
2 The proceedings could have been commenced within this six-month period even if they had become statute barred in the deceased's lifetime: *Airey v Airey* [1958] 2 All ER 571.
3 See Ogus (1969) 32 MLR 551.

Liabilities for tax due to date of death

26.22 Many obligations of the deceased can be ascertained within a short time of death,[1] but this does not apply to liabilities for income tax and capital gains tax. The amount of the liability for income tax depends on the total income of the deceased for the period from the preceding 6 April to the date of death. This has to be agreed with the Inspector of Taxes, as well as any liability outstanding in respect of previous fiscal years.

1 A notable exception is a Lloyd's 'name', whose underwriting liability is ascertained on a three-yearly account.

Social security benefits

26.23 In many instances a person obtains in his lifetime social security benefits to which he is not entitled. Where this comes to light after his death, the amount of the overpayment is recoverable from the personal representatives to the extent of the assets in their hands.[1] The overpayment usually comes to light when it appears from a grant of representation that the deceased had capital assets, although he had informed the social security authorities that he did not do so.[2]

1 Social Security Act 1986, s 53(2); *Secretary of State for Social Services v Solly* [1974] 3 All ER 922, CA.
2 Lord Denning MR in ibid, at 925, commented that at that time about £1 million was recovered annually from personal representatives.

Inheritance tax

26.24 For inheritance tax purposes, a person is deemed to dispose of all his property immediately before death, and tax becomes payable as a result of that disposition.[1] The tax is paid from the estate as a first charge, after only the funeral and testamentary expenses.

1 Inheritance Tax Act 1984, s 4(1).

Time for payment

26.25 The rule governing the time for payment of debts was stated by Uthwatt J in *Re Tankard, Tankard v Midland Bank Executor and Trustee Co Ltd*[1] in the following terms: 'it is the duty of executors, as a matter of the due administration of the estate, to pay the debts of their testator with due diligence having regard to the assets in their hands which are properly applicable for that purpose, and in determining whether due diligence has been shown regard must be had to all the circumstances of the case'. Personal representatives should, when acting with due diligence, give special attention to debts which carry interest, and threats by creditors to sue for payment. If the cost to the estate is increased without cause, for example by interest accruing when there were ample funds from which the debt could be discharged, or by an order for costs being made against the estate unnecessarily, the personal representative will be liable to make good that loss out of his own pocket.[2] It does not follow, of course, merely because interest accrues or costs are incurred that the personal representative has not acted with due diligence. He may have had insufficient assets to make earlier payment, or he may have been waiting until all liabilities were known so that he could see whether the estate was solvent.

1 [1942] Ch 69.
2 Below, paras 28.26ff.

26.26 Subject to this 'due diligence' rule, it appears that the normal rule applies that the personal representatives cannot be called upon to make payment within one year from death. This rule is discussed below[1] in connection with legacies.

1 See paras 31.24–31.25.

Solvent estates

26.27 An estate is solvent if there are sufficient assets for the payment of the funeral, testamentary and administration expenses, and for the payment of the creditors in full.[1] Where the estate is subject to the payment of an annuity[2] the annuitant may insist that the annuity is valued, and the capital value treated as a debt due from the estate.[3]

1 *Re Leng, Tarn v Emmerson* [1895] 1 Ch 652 at 658.
2 That is, where the annuity was given in the deceased's lifetime, and does not arise under the will.
3 *Re Pink, Elvin v Nightingale* [1927] 1 Ch 237 at 241.

26.28 If the estate is solvent, the creditors are not concerned with the source of the funds from which they are paid, as they will all be paid in full. The beneficiaries may well be affected, however, particularly where debts are charged on assets, and this topic is accordingly dealt with in connection with the distribution of the estate to the beneficiaries.[1]

1 Below, paras 32.19 et seq.

26.29 It is prudent to distribute the assets among creditors on the basis that the estate is insolvent – that is, to follow the statutory order for payment – until it becomes quite clear that the assets are more than sufficient to discharge all liabilities.[1]

1 *Re Milan Tramways Co, ex p Theys* (1884) 25 Ch D 587; *Re Pink, Elvin v Nightingale* [1927] 1 Ch 237; *Re McMurdo, Penfield v McMurdo* [1902] 2 Ch 684.

Insolvent estates

Methods of administration

26.30 An insolvent estate may be administered in any one of three ways:
(a) by the personal representatives in the usual way, without the intervention of the court;
(b) under an administration order, which can be obtained from the court either by personal representatives or creditors, or other persons interested;[1] or
(c) following an order for the administration of the estate in bankruptcy.[2] The petition may be either by the personal representatives, or by any creditor whose debt would have been sufficient to support a bankruptcy petition against the deceased if he had remained alive.[3] The effect of an administration order in bankruptcy is that the deceased's estate vests in the Official Receiver until a trustee in bankruptcy is appointed.[4]

1 In accordance with RSC Ord 85.
2 Under the Administration of Insolvent Estates of Deceased Persons Order 1986, SI 1986/
   1999, made under Insolvency Act 1986, s 421.
3 The conditions to be satisfied are contained in Insolvency Act 1986, s 265.
4 Ibid, ss 292–297, as amended.

Priority of debts

26.31 The priority of debts is governed by the Administration of Estates
Act 1925, s 34(1), which provides that where the estate is insolvent, it shall
be administered in accordance with Part I of the First Schedule. This
Schedule has the following effect:
(a) funeral, testamentary and administration expenses have priority;
(b) subject to this, the same rules apply as they do to the administration of
     the assets of persons who have been adjudicated bankrupt.
There is no statutory definition of testamentary and administration
expenses. They include the expense of obtaining a grant of representation;
costs incurred in the collection, maintenance or disposal of the deceased's
assets; costs of obtaining legal advice as to the construction of any will and
the administration of the estate; payments of other liabilities arising since
the date of death, such as rent; and other expenses to which the personal
representatives are put in carrying out their functions as such.[1]

1 *Sharp v Lush* (1879) 10 Ch D 468 at 470; cf *Re Rooke, Jeans v Gatehouse* [1933] Ch 970.

26.32 If the personal representatives are involved in litigation and an order
is made for their costs to be paid out of the estate, these costs will be an
administration expense. If the costs of other parties are also directed to be
paid out of the estate, the personal representatives have priority unless, in
exceptional circumstances, a contrary order is made by the court.[1]

1 *Re Griffith* [1904] 1 Ch 807; *Re Burden* (1974) 46 DLR (3d) 342 (Ontario).

The statutory order

26.33 Where an estate is insolvent, the order of priority of debts is
determined by the bankruptcy rules in accordance with the priority set out
below. The personal representatives must pay the debts in each class pari
passu so that any shortfall is borne rateably among the members of the class.
Further, the order for the payment of debts is statutory and applies before
any effect is given to the terms of the will. Accordingly, the testator cannot
alter the priorities by directions contained in his will. The statutory order of
priority is as follows.

26.34 *Specially preferred debts*
(a) Money or property belonging to any friendly society which came into
     the possession of the deceased in his capacity as an officer of the
     society,[1] even if he had ceased to be an officer of the society by the
     time of his death.[2]

(b)   Money or property belonging to any Trustee Savings Bank which at the date of death of the deceased was held by him in his capacity as an officer or employee of the bank.[3]

(c)   Where the deceased was at the date of his death subject to military law, and he had in his possession money or property subject to s 2 of the Regimental Debts Act 1893.

1   Friendly Societies Act 1974, s 59.
2   *Re Eilbeck* [1910] 1 KB 136.
3   Trustee Savings Bank Act 1954, s 61.

26.35   Preferred debts

(a)   *Inland Revenue.* In respect of income tax deducted by the deceased under PAYE from his employees' remuneration paid during the twelve months before his death.[1]

(b)   *Customs and Excise.* In respect of VAT for the period of six months to the date of death;[2] car tax due from deceased falling due within twelve months of the death; any amount due at his death and which became due within twelve months of his death in respect of general betting duty or bingo duty, general betting duty and pool betting duty recoverable from an agent collecting stakes, or gaming licence duty.[3]

(c)   *National insurance contributions.* Arrears of Class 1 and Class 2 contributions due within twelve months before his death;[4] arrears of Class 4 contributions as assessed on the deceased up to 5 April before his death,[5] but not exceeding in the whole one year's assessment.[6]

(d)   *Pension scheme contributions.* Arrears of state and occupational pension scheme contributions.

(e)   *Remuneration of employees.* Arrears of wages of employees for the period of four months before the date of death of the deceased subject to a limit of £800 per employee.[7] Any amount owed by way of accrued holiday pay in respect of any period of employment, to an employee whose employment by the deceased had been terminated before the deceased's death.

1   Insolvency Act 1986, s 387(b), as amended.
2   Ibid, Sch 6, para 3.
3   Under Betting and Gaming Duties Act 1981, ss 12(1), 14, Sch 2.
4   Under Social Security Act 1975.
5   Ibid.
6   Although the preferential claim does not have to be made in respect of the last fiscal year before death.
7   Insolvency Proceedings (Monetary Limits) Order 1986, SI 1986/1996.

26.36   Ordinary debts
These are all debts which do not fall into any other class.

26.37   Interest on preferential and ordinary debts arising since death
If there is any balance remaining after clearing the preferential and ordinary debts, it is next applied to pay the interest on those debts from the date of death until the date of payment. The ordinary debts rank equally with preferential debts for this purpose.[1] The rate will be that specified in the Judgments Act 1838, s 17 (currently 15 per cent[2]) or the rate otherwise applicable to that debt, whichever is the greater.

1 Insolvency Act 1986, s 328(4), as modified by SI 1986/1999.
2 Judgment Debts (Rates of Interest) Order 1985, SI 1985/437.

26.38 *Deferred debts*

(a) Loans made to a person who is either engaged in or is about to be engaged in a business if the lender is to receive interest varying with the profits of a business.[1]

(b) Payment due for the price of the goodwill of a business, where the price is payable in the form of a share of the profits.[2]

(c) Money or other property lent by a husband to his wife for the purposes of her trade or business; and money or property lent by a wife to her husband for any purpose.[3] Where the relationship of husband and wife does not exist, the loan may still be deferred within category (a). Thus, in *Re Meade, ex p Humber v Palmer*[4] a woman lent the deceased £7,000 which he used in his riding academy. This sum was intended to provide benefit for both of them, and the Court of Appeal held that the debt came within the first category, and was therefore deferred.

1 Partnership Act 1890, s 2.
2 Ibid, s 3.
3 Insolvency Act 1986, s 329.
4 [1951] Ch 774.

Failure to observe priority order

Superior class

26.39 A personal representative will be personally liable if he fails to observe the order of priority and pays an inferior debt, such as an ordinary debt, before any superior debts of which he has had notice have been paid in full. If he had no notice of the superior debt at the time, however, he will escape liability.[1]

1 *Harman v Harman* (1686) 3 Mod Rep 115, 2 Show 492.

Same class

26.40 If the personal representative pays a debt in full when there is insufficient to pay all the debts in that class in full, he will be personally liable to the other creditors in that class; in such a situation all debts in the same class must be paid proportionately. The personal representative's right of preference and retainer, of a debt in the same class, which included a debt owed to himself, was abolished after 1971.[1] However, he may be protected under para 26.41, below.

1 By Administration of Estates Act 1971, s 10(1).

A personal representative who has no reason to believe the estate to be insolvent

26.41 A personal representative who pays a debt in full in good faith at a time when he had no reason to believe the estate to be insolvent, will not be liable to creditors of the same class (including himself) who lose out in consequence.[1] This provision, for example, enables a personal representative to pay tradesmen's bills at an early stage in the administration.[2]

1   Administration of Estates Act 1971, s 10(2).
2   Law Commission No 31, para 8.

Position of secured creditors

26.42   A creditor who has security for his debt in the form of a mortgage, charge or lien over property of the deceased is in an advantageous position. The fact that he is secured in this way gives him certain rights over the property charged. Depending on the nature of the charge, he may have a power of sale,[1] or the power to appoint a receiver and to apply to the court for an order for sale.[2] These powers may be exercised notwithstanding the death of the deceased, and they apply irrespective of the provisions of the will.

1   See eg Law of Property Act 1925, s 101.
2   Ibid, s 91.

26.43   Where the value of the security is more than adequate to cover the amount of the debt, the creditor is adequately protected, whether or not the estate is insolvent. If, for example, a lender has a mortgage over the deceased's property, he may exercise his power of sale, assuming it has arisen, and thus repay himself in full. He is therefore unaffected by the statutory order for the payment of debts. To give an extreme case, if the lender took a legal mortgage to secure a debt which would rank as a deferred debt, then subject to the security being of sufficient value to satisfy the debt, the creditor will be paid in full, even if there are no assets for the preferred creditors.

26.44   If the estate is insolvent, and the value of the security is not sufficient to cover the whole of the debt the creditor has the choice of:
(a)   realising his security, and proving for the balance of his claim;[1]
(b)   valuing his security and proving for the balance;[2] or
(c)   surrendering his security and proving for the whole debt.[3]
In most cases only the first course will be desirable. If the second is adopted, the personal representative or trustee in bankruptcy, depending on the type of administration, has the right to have the security redeemed at the value placed on it by the creditor, or sold, but this right can only be exercised for six months from being required by the creditor to make his election.[4] The creditor will thus be restricted in the action which he can take and will usually wish to sell outright, where he has the power to do so.

1   Insolvency Act 1986, s 322(1); Insolvency Rules 1986, SI 1986/1925, rr 6.109 and 6.119.
2   Insolvency Rules 1986, rr 6.96 and 6.98.
3   Ibid, r 6.109(2).
4   Ibid, r 6.117(4).

26.45 The existence of security in the case of a solvent estate will affect the rights of beneficiaries, and this aspect is considered later.[1]

1 See below, paras 32.1ff.

Contingent liabilities

Generally

26.46 Contingent liabilities may present considerable difficulties to the personal representative. There is no general rule of law that a personal representative is liable only for those debts of which he knows, or for those liabilities which have crystallised.[1] In principle, whenever a liability becomes apparent, then, provided it is still not statute barred, the personal representative is liable to satisfy the claim to the extent of the assets which have passed through his hands.

1 Although certain protection is conferred by Trustee Act 1925, ss 26, 27; below, paras 26.50–26.53, 26.56–26.57.

26.47 The deceased may have given a guarantee in respect of the payment of a debt by another, or a bond for the performance by another of some obligation, and at the date of death there may be no indication at all that the principal debtor may default. The deceased may have been the holder of shares in a company which were not paid up in full. In this case, if the company goes into liquidation the shareholders will be called upon to pay the difference between the amount actually paid up on the shares and the full amount due. At the date of death the company may be flourishing and show no signs of going into liquidation.[1] Again, the deceased may have taken a lease of certain property, and as such remain liable throughout the length of term for the lessee's covenants, notwithstanding that the lease has been assigned.[2] These are just some of the many circumstances in which at the time of death and during the administration period there may be contingent liabilities which have not actually become debts.

1 See eg *Taylor v Taylor* (1870) LR 10 Eq 477; *Knatchbull v Fearnhead* (1837) 3 My & Cr 122; *Newcastle Banking Co v Hymers* (1856) 22 Beav 367; *Re Bewley's Estates, Jefferys v Jefferys* (1871) 24 LT 177.
2 As to leases, see below, paras 26.49–26.54, 28.22–28.23.

26.48 The general rule is that the personal representative is liable for the satisfaction of all such liabilities as and when, if at all, they crystallise into debts.[1] He may have rights to recover assets from legatees, but if the legatees have parted with the assets, or disappeared, this right may be worthless. Is, then, the cautious personal representative bound to retain a large part of the estate, almost indefinitely, to satisfy any claims if and when they are made? Special provisions apply to leases, which will be examined first, and then the general position considered further.

1 *Nector and Sharp v Gennet* (1590) Cro Eliz 466; *Eeles v Lambert* (1648) Sty 38; *Hawkins v Day* (1753) Amb 160; *Pearson v Archdeaken* (1831) Alc & N 23.

Leases

26.49 It is necessary to consider separately the position of the personal representative who is liable as such because he is an assignee by operation of law of the lease; and his position where he enters into possession of the demised property and so also becomes liable by virtue of the doctrine of privity of estate.

Liability as assignee

26.50 The Trustee Act 1925, s 26, deals with the position where a personal representative, or trustee, is liable in his capacity as such for any rent or other covenant in a lease; for any rent or other covenant arising out of a rentcharge; or any covenant for indemnity given in respect of rent or other obligation under a lease or rentcharge. The section provides that where the personal representative discharges all liability which has accrued and been claimed to the date of distribution, and sets aside any fixed sum which the deceased agreed to lay out, even if it is to be paid at some time in the future, then he may pass on the property to the beneficiary entitled, or sell it, without making any further provision for liabilities to arise. Where the property is passed on in this way, the personal representative is not personally liable under any subsequent claim, although the lessor or grantor has the right to follow assets into the hands of the beneficiaries where any further liability does arise.[1]

1   Trustee Act 1925, s 26(2).

26.51 Section 26 only protects personal representatives who discharge all liabilities which accrue due, and make provision for any further fixed sum to be paid while the lease is still vested in them.[1]

1   *Re Bennett, Midland Bank Executor and Trustee Co Ltd v Fletcher* [1943] 1 All ER 467; *Re Owers, Public Trustee v Death* [1941] Ch 389.

26.52 It will be seen that s 26 provides adequate protection for personal representatives as assignees by operation of law.

Liability after entry into possession

26.53 By entering into possession of the property the personal representatives become liable under the terms of the lease in their personal capacity by virtue of the doctrine of privity of estate, and the protection of the Trustee Act, s 26, does not assist them.[1] Where they incur liability in this way, they should set aside a fund to meet any further liability.[2] This fund belongs to the residuary beneficiaries (assuming it was taken from residue), subject to such claims, and the residuary beneficiaries are entitled to have it transferred to them when any claims are statute barred.[3] This can work harshly, however, on the residuary beneficiaries where the lease is the subject of a specific gift, or is sold. While another person enjoys the benefit of the lease, they suffer the retention out of the funds due to them of the contingency fund.

1   *Re Owers, Public Trustee v Death* [1941] Ch 389.
2   *Re Lewis, Jennings v Hemsley* [1939] Ch 232.
3   *Re Lewis*, above.

Other liabilities

26.54 In the case of liabilities under leases or rentcharges outside the Trustee Act, s 26, and in the case of other contingent liabilities, the personal representative can adopt one of several possible courses:

(a) Obtain indemnity and distribute. The Administration of Estates Act, s 26(10), expressly empowers a personal representative as a condition of making any assent in favour of a beneficiary to require security for the discharge of outstanding debts and liabilities. Unless an indemnity is secured in some way, such as by a mortgage or bond, the personal representative always runs some risk in proceeding in this way, as the beneficiary himself may be lost to trace or become bankrupt. The personal representative would still be liable, and the indemnity worthless. The personal representative must clearly be guided by the character of the indemnifier and the nature of the liability. If an unconditional assent has been made, the right to demand an indemnity is then lost.[1]

(b) Distribute under order of court. Where the estate is administered under an order of the court, then, provided the court has been given full knowledge of all relevant facts known to the personal representative, he will be fully protected.[2] Such an order can be made only in the course of an administration action, but this can be commenced at any time, even when most of the estate is distributed.

(c) Retain fund. Where the fund is retained to meet possible liabilities, it can work hardship on the residuary beneficiaries, as mentioned above.[3]

1 *Re Bennett, Midland Bank Executor and Trustee Co Ltd v Fletcher* [1943] 1 All ER 467.
2 *Dean v Allen* (1855) 20 Beav 1; *Smith v Smith* (1861) 1 Drew & Sm 384; *Dodson v Sammell* (1861) 1 Drew & Sm 575; *Waller v Barrett* (1857) 24 Beav 413; *Re Sanford's Trust, Bennett v Lytton* (1860) 2 John & H 155; *Addams v Ferick* (1859) 26 Beav 384; *Williams v Headland* (1864) 4 Giff 505; *England v Lord Tredegar* (1866) LR 1 Eq 344; *Re King, Mellor v South Australian Land Mortgage and Agency Co* [1907] 1 Ch 72; *Re Johnson, Johnson v King Edward Hospital Fund for London* [1940] WN 195.
3 Above, para 26.53.

Unknown debts and liabilities

26.55 The general principle is that a personal representative is liable to pay any debts to the extent of the assets which have passed through his hands, even if, acting in good faith and without notice of the debts, he has distributed the whole of the assets to the beneficiaries.[1] This remains the position where the personal representative does not advertise for liabilities, but he can obtain statutory protection against claims by advertising.

1 *Chelsea Waterworks (Governor and Co) v Cowper* (1795) 1 Esp 275; *Norman v Baldry* (1834) 6 Sim 621; *Smith v Day* (1837) 2 M & W 684; *Knatchbull v Fearnhead* (1837) 3 My & Cr 122; *Hill v Gomme* (1839) 1 Beav 540.

26.56 Section 27 of the Trustee Act 1925[1] applies both to personal representatives and trustees. It provides that they may obtain protection by:

(a)   in the case of land giving notice of the intended distribution in the London Gazette[2] and in a newspaper circulating in the district in which the land is situate; and

(b)   in the case of personalty, by giving notice only in the Gazette;[3] and

(c)   in either case by giving in special cases such further notices as the court would have directed in an administration action.

The notices must require any person interested to send to the personal representatives particulars of their claim within the time specified in the notice, which must not be less than two months from its publication. Where a special case does arise, the personal representative will only be safe in applying to the court for directions as to the notices which it requires.[4]

1   As amended by the Law of Property (Amendment) Act 1926.
2   Trustee Act 1925, s 68(4).
3   The section does not expressly say that this single notice is sufficient, but this seems to follow from the wording of the section.
4   *Re Bracken, Doughty v Townson* (1889) 43 Ch D 1; *Re Letherbrow, Hopp v Dean* [1935] WN 34; *Re Holden, Isaacson v Holden* [1935] WN 52.

26.57   A personal representative may then distribute the estate taking into account:

(a)   claims of which he has, apart from the advertisement, actual or constructive notice,[1] irrespective of whether the claimant replies to the advertisement; and

(b)   claims which appear as a result of the advertisement.

The personal representative is not liable for any other claim, although the section does not prevent any other claimant from following the assets into the hands of the beneficiaries. By following the statutory procedure, the personal representative is given the same protection as if he had administered the estate under an order of the court.[2]

1   *Re Land Credit Co of Ireland, Markwell's Case* (1872) 21 WR 135; Law of Property Act 1925, s 199.
2   *Clegg v Rowland* (1866) LR 3 Eq 368; *Hunter v Young* (1879) 4 Ex D 256.

26.58   There is a curious proviso to the section, which provides that the section does not free the personal representative 'from any obligation to make searches . . . which an intending purchaser would be advised to make'. This will involve the personal representative in making all the searches which would normally be made at any stage of a routine purchase. These will be:

(a)   *in the case of unregistered land*:
   (i)   in the land charges register against the names of all estate owners since 1 January 1926, including the deceased and himself, for land charges which have been registered;
   (ii)   in the land charges register against the beneficiary to whom it is to be assented, to ensure that he is not bankrupt; and
   (iii)   in the local land charges register, for local land charges.

(b)   *in the case of registered land*:
   (i)   in the Land Registry;
   (ii)   in the land charges register against the beneficiary, and in the local land charges registers, as above.

(c)   *in the case of an equitable interest in registered land*:

(i)   in the land charges register against the beneficiary.
(d)   *in the case of personalty*:
(i)   in the land charges register against the beneficiary.
It will be seen that in each case it is probably wise to make a search in the land charges register, because this will show whether the beneficiary is bankrupt.

Need for personal representative in office

26.59   Section 2 of the Proceedings Against Estates Act 1970[1] makes provision for proceedings to be commenced against the estate of a person where no grant of probate or letters of administration has been obtained. A writ or originating summons can be issued against the estate of the deceased and having then commenced the proceedings, the plaintiff must apply to the court for an order appointing the Official Solicitor, or some other person, to represent the estate in the proceedings. The court may limit the authority of the person appointed to accepting service of the proceedings and entering an appearance.[2] In that case, when that has been done, the person appointed becomes functus officio, and the proceedings cannot be continued or enforced until some other person is appointed to represent the estate, or until a personal representative is appointed.[3] This is a simpler alternative procedure to obtaining a grant ad litem, considered above.[4]

1   As extended by RSC Ord 15, r 6A.
2   Rule 5A.
3   *Re Amirteymour* [1978] 3 All ER 637, CA.
4   At paras 19.4–19.6. The simpler alternative, however, is not available where an action is to be brought by (cf against) the estate or where no action would have lain against the deceased himself, such as an application for family provision.

CHAPTER 27

Executor de son tort

Definition

27.1 The expression 'executor de son tort' is occasionally used in the sense of a personal representative who improperly administers the assets of the estate,[1] but the usual meaning is that of a person who is not the personal representative of the deceased but who acts in one or more respects as if he were.[2] This is frequently described as intermeddling with the property of the deceased, and, indeed, this definition has been adopted by the Administration of Estates Act 1925,[3] where it provides that, in respect to liability for the payment of inheritance tax,[4] the term personal representative 'includes any person who takes possession of or intermeddles with the property of a deceased person without the authority of the personal representatives or of the court'.

1 See eg Lord Dyer in *Stokes v Porter* (1558) 2 Dyer 166b.
2 *Peters v Leeder* (1878) 47 LJQB 573.
3 Section 55(1)(ix).
4 Section 55(1)(ix) refers to liability to estate duty. By virtue of Inheritance Tax Act 1984, s 275, this includes inheritance tax.

27.2 It is not, however, every act with regard to the deceased's property which will make a person an executor de son tort, for a distinction is drawn between, on the one hand, intermeddling and, on the other, acts of necessity or humanity. The acts of humanity are generally confined to feeding the deceased's cattle or wife,[1] and arranging for his funeral in a manner suitable to the estate.[2] The acts of necessity are likely to be acts of preservation, such as locking up the deceased's valuables, and maintaining his property.[3] Other acts will constitute a person executor de son tort, even if they are very slight. The mere act of taking a Bible or bedstead,[4] or of taking only sufficient of the deceased's goods to satisfy a debt[5] have been held to be sufficient.[6]

1 *Long v Symes* (1832) 3 Hag Ecc 771 – but not necessarily in that order.
2 *Harrison v Rowley* (1798) 4 Ves 212.
3 *Laury v Aldred and Edmonds* (1612) 2 Brownl 182.
4 *Robbins's Case* (1601) Noy 69.
5 *Read's Case* (1604) 5 Co Rep 33b; *Serle v Waterworth* (1838) 4 M & W 9.

6   See also *Stokes v Porter* (1558) 2 Dyer 166b; *Stamford's Case* (1574) 2 Leon 223.

27.3   It seems that the mental state of the executor de son tort is irrelevant, provided he has full mental capacity. Accordingly, he may still be liable however innocently he may have acted.[1] However, if a person has an honest belief that he is beneficially entitled to the deceased's property, and takes possession of it in that belief, he is not an executor de son tort.[2]

1   Per Lord Halsbury in *New York Breweries Co Ltd v A-G* [1899] AC 62, HL.
2   *Femings v Jarrat* (1795) 1 Esp 335; *Re O'Reilly (No 2)* (1981) 123 DLR (3d) 767n (Ontario).

27.4   A person who is entitled to a grant of probate or letters of administration and who does act prior to the grant can be cited to take a grant,[1] but once there is a properly constituted personal representative, in most circumstances there cannot also be an executor de son tort. As an exception to this, however, if a person is in possession of assets which he received from the deceased in his lifetime as a result of a fraudulent disposition, and he disposes of those assets, he thereby makes himself liable as executor de son tort.[2]

1   Above, para 18.60; see also below, para 27.11.
2   *Stamford's Case* (1574) 2 Leon 223; *Hawes v Leader* (1610) Cro Jac 270; *Edwards v Harben* (1788) 2 Term Rep 587.

27.5   Although liability as an executor de son tort usually arises as a result of physical interference with chattels, it need not do so. Thus, in *New York Breweries Co Ltd v A-G*[1] the deceased, who died domiciled in America, owned shares in an English company. The American executors did not obtain a grant of probate in England, as they could have done, and the English company knew that they had not obtained a grant, and had no intention of doing so. Nevertheless the company, at their request, registered the deceased's shares in the American executors' names, and paid dividends to them. In so doing the English company was held to have acted as executors de son tort. At first instance Wills J, having regard to the nature of the property, had said that the company had not intermeddled. Commenting on this in the House of Lords, Lord Halsbury said: 'In what way could a person, dealing with this particular class of property, otherwise intermeddle with the estate? The appellants have done that which, as I say, has created a new title in somebody else . . . they have done a legal act, and by virtue of that legal act they have enabled it to be dealt with by somebody else, and made available by him for any purpose he desires.' In consequence, the company rendered itself liable to pay the estate duty[2] on the English estate, for which the personal representatives were responsible. Although the result of the case avoids an unduly fine distinction between choses in action and other property, the act of the company has to be regarded as the equivalent of physically taking possession.[3]

1   [1899] AC 62.
2   A forerunner of inheritance tax.
3   As was recognised by Lord Halsbury in this case.

27.6   Where a person takes part in arrangements which transfer assets from the jurisdiction of the English court to that of another court, it seems that that act in itself will constitute that person as an executor de son tort. The facts of *IRC v Stype Investments (Jersey) Ltd*[1] have already been given.[2] In that case, Stype, a Jersey company, held land which had belonged to Sir Charles Clore, as nominee for him, subject to a binding contract for sale. Sir Charles died prior to completion of the sale. The property, subject to, and with the benefit of, the contract for sale, was an asset situated in England, and had no further events occurred, the property would have devolved on the English personal representatives when they were constituted. However, after the death of Sir Charles, the Jersey company completed the sale and received, in Jersey, the proceeds of sale. The proceeds of sale therefore became an asset situated in Jersey, and came under the control of the Jersey personal representatives when constituted. In effect, the Jersey company had transferred control from the English personal representatives, when constituted, to the Jersey personal representatives, when constituted, and, following the *New York Breweries*[3] case, the Court of Appeal held that it had become an executor de son tort. Consequently, Stype rendered itself liable to pay the substantial capital transfer tax[4] on the English estate.

1   [1982] 3 All ER 419, CA.
2   Above, para 19.3.
3   [1899] AC 62.
4   The immediate forerunner of inheritance tax.

Effect of acts

Creditors

27.7   Section 28 of the Administration of Estates Act 1925 governs the position of anyone who, in defraud of creditors, or without valuable consideration, obtains any assets of the deceased. It provides that he is liable to account for those assets, after deducting any debt properly due to him from the deceased at the time of his death, and any payment made by him which might properly be made by a personal representative. Accordingly, where the executor de son tort uses the assets of the deceased's estate to pay debts and liabilities, the creditors will be properly paid, and will not be liable to refund the sums received. Likewise, the executor de son tort receives credit for those payments. It follows that where the executor de son tort applies all the deceased's assets in the discharge, in proper order, of the debts, he will not be liable beyond the scope of those assets.[1]

1   *Hooper v Summersett* (1810) Wight 16; *Yardley v Arnold* (1842) Car & M 434.

Rightful representatives

27.8   Where a person has intermeddled, and has therefore made himself liable as executor de son tort, and subsequently a grant of probate or letters of administration is made to another person, some of his acts will bind the true representatives. It seems that in order to bind the true representatives, the acts done must either:

(a) involve making payments or disposing of assets to a third party who reasonably believes that the executor de son tort has lawful authority to act as executor;[1] or

(b) be acts which the rightful representative was bound to do, and not merely acts which he was entitled to do.[2]

1 *Mountford v Gibson* (1804) 4 East 441; *Thomson v Harding* (1853) 2 E & B 630.
2 *Buckley v Barber* (1851) 6 Exch 164.

27.9 An illustration of the first situation is given in *Mountford v Gibson*.[1] In that case the deceased had purchased, but not paid for, goods which had been delivered to him. The vendor asked the deceased's widow, shortly following his death, for the return of the goods, and she returned them accordingly. In so doing, the widow made herself liable as executrix de son tort. Letters of administration were subsequently granted to another person, who sued the vendor. The vendor claimed that the goods had been handed over by the widow, whom he was entitled to regard as executrix de son tort. It was held that because the return of the goods by the widow was an isolated act, and that she had done no other act which would make her liable, the vendor had no sufficient cause for believing that she had authority to act, and the administrator succeeded.

1 (1804) 4 East 441.

27.10 With regard to the second category of acts mentioned above, it is necessary to draw a distinction between payments and other acts. Under the Administration of Estates Act 1925, s 28, the executor de son tort is entitled to credit for all payments which the personal representatives might properly have made, even if they were not obliged to do so. So far as other acts are concerned, it seems that only those which the personal representatives were bound to do will bind them.[1]

1 *Buckley v Barber* (1851) 6 Exch 164.

Liability

To take grant

27.11 Where the executor de son tort is entitled to a grant of probate or letters of administration, the acts which he has done will probably amount to an acceptance of office by conduct, so that he cannot thereafter renounce his right. Accordingly, if he is an executor he may be cited to take a grant, or if he is entitled to letters of administration he may be cited to accept or refuse a grant.[1] Where, however, he is not entitled to a grant, he cannot be compelled to apply for one.[2]

1 Above, para 18.60.
2 *Re Davis's Goods* (1860) 4 Sw & Tr 213.

To account

27.12 His primary liability is to render an account for assets which he has received. His liability here is less than in the case of a properly constituted representative. The properly constituted representative is liable to account both for assets which he has received, and for those he ought to have received,[1] whereas the liability of an executor de son tort is restricted by s 28 'to the extent of the real and personal estate received or coming to his hands, or the debt or liability released'.[2] It is, in fact, only by accounting to the rightful executor, and handing the balance of the assets to him, that the executor de son tort can obtain his discharge.[3] The liability to account is to both the rightful representatives and the creditors of the estate.[4] *New York Breweries Co Ltd v A-G*[5] is an example of an action by a creditor, in that case the Crown.

1 Below, paras 28.26ff.
2 This was the position even before the Administration of Estates Act 1925: *Coote v Whittington* (1873) LR 16 Eq 534.
3 *Curtis v Vernon* (1790) 3 Term Rep 587.
4 *Fyson v Chambers* (1842) 9 M & W 460.
5 [1899] AC 62.

To pay inheritance tax

27.13 An executor de son tort is liable to pay inheritance tax in respect of the property with which he intermeddles.[1] Accordingly, the Jersey company in *IRC v Stype Investments (Jersey) Ltd*[2] was liable for the tax in respect of the proceeds of sale of the land, even though those proceeds of sale had come under the control of the Jersey personal representatives.

1 Inheritance Tax Act 1984, ss 199(4) and 200(1), (4).
2 [1982] 3 All ER 419, CA; above, paras 19.3 and 27.6.

CHAPTER 28

The liability of personal representatives

28.1 The chest may puff out with pride when the executor learns with gratification of his appointment. In other situations, his appointment may have come only after a long struggle.[1] Yet caution, not enthusiasm, is to be counselled. In general, unless there is some contrary provision in the will, the personal representative may be liable to make good out of his own pocket any loss which arises as a result of his unauthorised acts, even if they were done honestly. Further, again unless there is some contrary provision in the will, the personal representative may not derive any benefit[2] from acting as such. Gratification of his power lust may be his only reward.

1 See above, para 17.62.
2 Although the office of personal representative can confer certain advantages: see above, para 17.62.

28.2 This chapter indicates the extent of the personal representative's personal liability. He may become liable:
(a) in contract, for contracts made by him during the administration of the estate;
(b) under the doctrine of privity of estate for lessee's covenants under a lease;
(c) in devastavit, if he misappropriates assets of the estate; maladministers the estate; or fails to safeguard the assets;
(d) in breach of trust.

Liability in contract

Contract carrying personal liability

28.3 A personal representative may in the course of the administration of the estate enter into two types of contract, namely contracts made on the basis that his liability is to be limited to the net assets of the estate, and contracts made without any such limitation. In order to limit the liability to the assets of the estate, two conditions must be satisfied:
(a) the fact that the liability is to be limited must be established; and

(b)   the contract must be an authorised contract.

Limitation of liability

28.4   The liability of the personal representative may be limited by an express limitation, in which case no problem arises, by contracting 'as executor' of the deceased, or 'as personal representative' of the deceased, or by expressly contracting in pursuance of the statutory power conferred by the Administration of Estates Act 1925, s 39.

28.5   Most of the reported decisions relate to contracts which the personal representative entered into as a result of some transaction of the deceased. Indeed, Mellish LJ in *Farhall v Farhall*[1] referred to them as all having in common that 'the consideration for the promise of the executor was a contract or transaction with the testator'. In *Powell v Graham*,[2] for example, the testator had contracted with a woman that if she entered his employment as his nurse, and was still serving in that capacity at the date of his death, he would pay her £20. The woman became his nurse, and was still so acting when he died. The payment was not made on death, but the deceased's executor promised that whenever he, in his capacity as executor, was asked for the £20, he would pay it to her. The executor was held to be not personally liable on the contract, but only to the extent of the assets of the deceased.[3] Although most of the reported decisions relate to contracts following transactions with the deceased, there is no reason in principle that the rule should be so restricted.

1   (1871) 7 Ch App 123 at 127.
2   (1817) 7 Taunt 580.
3   See also *Dowse v Coxe* (1825) 3 Bing 20.

Authorised contracts

28.6   The liability of the personal representative is limited only where the contract which he makes is authorised. It is, therefore, important to know what contracts are authorised, but it is impossible to give a comprehensive list. The position is stated in the Administration of Estates Act 1925, s 39, which provides that personal representatives have:
(a)   all the powers which personal representatives had before the Act came into force;[1] and
(b)   all the powers conferred upon trustees for sale.[2]
To these must be added:
(c)   powers conferred by the Trustee Act 1925;[3] and
(d)   powers conferred by the will itself.

1   Section 39(1)(i).
2   Section 39(1)(ii).
3   Trustee Act 1925, s 69(1), provides that except where otherwise expressly provided, the provisions of the Act applicable to trusts apply also to executorships and administratorships.

28.7   The effect of making these contracts a charge upon the estate – which is the result of making an authorised contract – is that they are considered to be either necessary for the purposes of administration, or otherwise for the general benefit of the estate. It follows that where an executor effectively limits his liability in this way, and the estate has no assets, there is no asset or fund to which the party contracting with the executor can have recourse.

28.8 A personal representative cannot restrict his liability by contracting as executor if the contract is unauthorised. This is because he must not involve the estate in unauthorised contracts,[1] which will often be burdensome, or to its disadvantage. A strict view is taken so far as contracts by a personal representative to borrow money are involved. In some cases, for example, to raise money to pay inheritance tax prior to grant, and so before realisation of assets, contracts to borrow money are authorised, but in most cases they are not. Thus, in *Farhall v Farhall*[2] where the personal representative borrowed money 'as executrix', James LJ held that this was not a charge on the estate, but only on the representative. He maintained that to hold otherwise would be to give executors the power to charge debts on the estate to an unlimited extent. This decision must, however, be treated with caution: whether or not a contract to borrow is authorised will depend on the circumstances of each case.

1 *Farhall v Farhall* (1871) 7 Ch App 123; *Owen v Delamere* (1872) LR 15 Eq 134.
2 (1871) 7 Ch App 123.

Funeral expenses

28.9 It is necessary to mention separately funeral expenses. There is a rule that if no other person is liable, an executor is liable for funeral expenses to the extent of the assets in his hands by virtue of an implied contract with the undertaker for the provision of a funeral in accordance with the circumstances and station in life of the deceased.[1] Where the order for the funeral is given by someone other than the personal representative, the person giving the order to the undertaker will generally become liable, but he will have a right of indemnity against the estate. Taking these principles together, the position is as follows.
(a) If the personal representative gives the order for the funeral, in his capacity as such, he will be liable only to the extent of the assets.
(b) If the personal representative gives the order without restricting his liability, he will be personally liable to the undertaker for the whole funeral account[2] but will have a right of recourse against the estate to the extent of the assets.[3]
(c) If someone else gives the order, he is liable to the undertaker. Unless he paid the account gratuitously, he can recover against the executor to the extent of the assets of the estate.
(d) If someone else arranges the funeral, but upon the basis that he accepts no liability for it, the executor will be liable on the implied contract to the extent of a funeral appropriate to the circumstances of the deceased, and to the extent of the assets of the deceased.

1 *Tugwell v Heyman* (1812) 3 Camp 298; *Rogers v Price* (1829) 3 Y & J 28; *Corner v Shew* (1838) 3 M & W 350; *Rees v Hughes* [1946] KB 517 at 524.
2 *Brice v Wilson* (1834) 8 Ad & El 349n; *Walker v Taylor* (1834) 6 C & P 752; *Corner v Shew* (1838) 3 M & W 350.
3 See below, para 28.18 as to this right of recourse.

Trading contracts

Generally
28.10 Where the deceased carried on a business in his personal capacity –
and the rules now to be discussed have no application if he carried on
business by means of an incorporated company – then if it was carried on at
a profit, or is capable of being carried on at a profit, the business may well
have some goodwill. For this purpose, goodwill may be regarded as little
more than the likelihood that customers will continue to resort to the
business, and will depend on such matters as the location of the business,
the personality of the deceased, and the length of time for which the
business had been established. It is by no means unusual for the value of the
goodwill to be the only asset of any size of a business. In most cases the
goodwill will be lost completely if the business is closed down for more than
a few days. It is, therefore, usually important for the business to be
continued after the testator's death. On the other hand, the function of
personal representatives is to distribute assets, and not primarily to carry on
a trade.

28.11 The general rule of law, which applies both to testate and intestate
estates, is that personal representatives are entitled to carry on the
deceased's business:
(a) if the business, which here means the goodwill, is of value; and
(b) to such extent only as will enable the business to be sold to the best
     advantage of the estate.
Where these business conditions are satisfied, and the personal representative carries on the business, the expenses of so doing are an administration
expense, and along with, for example, funeral expenses[1] rank in priority to
other liabilities. The personal representative is liable to trade creditors, but
may, therefore, obtain a full indemnity from the assets of the estate. If the
business is carried on for longer than the time needed to dispose of the
business, it is necessary to consider the position of the creditors and of the
personal representative.

1 Although funeral expenses are payable in priority to other administration expenses.

Position of creditors – pre-death debts
28.12 Where the debts arose before the death of the deceased, they
become liabilities of the estate in the normal way. The executor will be
entitled to recover the administration expenses from the estate as a first
charge, and these will include expenses of carrying on the business with a
view to its disposal as a going concern, but the trade creditors will rank with
other creditors in taking priority next.

28.13 In general, and subject to one exception, if the personal representative prolongs the trading, and is entitled to an indemnity from the estate, his
right of indemnity is postponed to rights of the trade creditors existing at the
date of death. The one exception to this principle is where the creditors at
the date of death expressly sanction the continuance of the business at their
risk. This exception was established in *Dowse v Gorton*[1] and was
summarised by Buckley LJ in *Re Oxley*,[2] where he said:

'In order to introduce the principle of *Dowse v Gorton* it must I think be established that the old creditor has so acted, either by claiming (as he did in that case) the assets of the continued business or by affirmative acts by which he so adopts the action of the executors in carrying on the business, as to shew that he has abandoned that which is prima facie his right . . . and that he has assented to another course, namely, that the fund to which he is entitled to look shall be risked in trade with the result that there may be loss or there may be further additions made for his benefit. It is necessary I think to shew an active affirmative assent. Mere standing by with knowledge and doing nothing is not sufficient.'

1 [1891] AC 190.
2 [1914] 1 Ch 604.

Creditors' post-death debts

28.14 A personal representative who carries on the deceased's trade, whether for the purpose of speedy realisation, or upon a longer term, and whether or not he is authorised by the will, makes himself personally liable to the creditors, who may sue him. There are several reported cases in which the personal representative has been made bankrupt as a result.[1] It seems that this is so even if the personal representative holds himself out as carrying on the business qua personal representative.[2] The primary right of the creditor in respect of post-death contracts is, therefore, to sue the personal representative personally and not as personal representative. In some circumstances, however, he will also have a right against the estate under the principle of subrogation. This is considered below.[3]

1 *Ex p Garland* (1804) 10 Ves 110; *Owen v Delamere* (1872) LR 15 Eq 134; *Re Percy's Goods, Fairland v Percy* (1875) LR 3 P & D 217.
2 *Labouchere v Tupper* (1857) 11 Moo PCC 198.
3 See para 28.19.

Position of beneficiaries

28.15 The pre-death debts will always be liabilities of the estate, and the beneficiaries will always take subject thereto.[1] The same rule applies in respect of post-death debts incurred for the purpose of realisation. In respect of other post-death debts, the position varies according to the terms of the will.

1 Provisions of the will can alter the incidence of liability.

28.16 *Authority in will* Where the will authorises the personal representative to carry on the business longer than for mere realisation, or without restriction as to length of time, the personal representative will have a right of indemnity against the assets of the estate which must be satisfied before the beneficiaries can take. It is necessary to deduce from the will clear authority in that respect[1] and a restrictive interpretation is usually made. Thus, in *McNeillie v Acton*,[2] where there was a simple direction to the personal representative to carry on the testator's business, it was held that that provision authorised the employment only of the capital which was in the business at the date of death, and that the personal representative had no right of recourse to other assets.[3] As well as by explicit authority, a power to continue the business may be given where there is a trust for sale and conversion of the deceased's assets, coupled with a power to postpone sale. This is sufficient to enable the personal representative to continue the business indefinitely[4] unless there is a provision requiring sale within a specified time.[5]

1 *Kirkman v Booth* (1848) 11 Beav 273 at 280.
2 (1853) 4 De GM & G 744.
3 See also *Cutbush v Cutbush* (1839) 1 Beav 184; *Thompson v Andrews* (1832) 1 My & K 116.
4 *Re Crowther* [1895] 2 Ch 56; *Re Ball* [1930] WN 111.
5 *Re Smith* [1896] 1 Ch 171.

28.17 *Intestacy* It will be recalled that the Administration of Estates Act 1925, s 33(1), provides that where any property devolves as on intestacy, the personal representatives hold that property upon trust for sale and conversion 'with power to postpone such sale and conversion for such a period as the personal representatives, without being liable to account, may think proper'. The effect of this provision is to give personal representatives power to carry on a business longer than for mere realisation,[1] but probably only until the estate is distributable. In the case of an express trust for sale under a will, where there was a power to postpone, it was held that that power ceased to operate when the estate was divisible,[2] and there seems to be no reason why the same rule should not apply on intestacy.[3] It has been suggested[4] that the power to postpone in the case of intestacy only authorises the personal representatives to use assets employed by the deceased in carrying on his business at the date of death, but there is no authority as to this.

1 *Re Crowther* [1895] 2 Ch 56.
2 *Re Crowther*, above; *Re Ball* [1930] WN 111.
3 *Re Ball*, above.
4 *Re Crowther*, above.

Indemnity and subrogation

28.18 If the personal representative carries on the business longer than is necessary for realisation, and if he does so with the authority either of the will or of the Administration of Estates Act, s 33(1), he has a right of indemnity from the estate which ranks after the liabilities as at the date of death but before the beneficiaries have been paid. If the assets are insufficient, the personal representative bears the difference from his own pocket. Where the testator authorised the personal representative to carry on the business, but the authority is limited to assets employed by the deceased in the business at the date of death, the personal representative's right of indemnity is likewise confined.

28.19 In those cases where the personal representative has a right of indemnity, creditors in respect of post-death debts have a claim against the estate by subrogation. This right, however, extends only to the assets in respect of which the personal representative could exercise his right[1] and with the same degree of priority.[2] It follows that the only circumstance in which the post-death creditors can proceed against the estate and take priority over the pre-death creditors is where the latter expressly authorised the personal representatives to continue to trade.

1 *Ex p Garland* (1803) 10 Ves 110; *Re Beater, ex p Edmonds* (1862) 4 De G F & J 488.
2 *Cutbush v Cutbush* (1839) 1 Beav 184; *Thompson v Andrews* (1832) 1 My & K 116; *Strickland v Symons* (1884) 22 Ch D 666; *Moore v M'Glynn* [1904] 1 IR R 334.

Trading profit

28.20 It will be shown later in this chapter that a personal representative is for most purposes in the same position as a trustee. As a result, the personal representative cannot make any profit from his office unless, generally, he is authorised to do so in the will itself. The general rule is that a trustee could spend the whole of his waking hours in carrying on the business, without being entitled to be paid a penny.[1] A personal representative is, therefore, often faced with the choice either of carrying on the business – for the profit of the beneficiaries if he is successful, or at his personal expense if he is not – or of abandoning the business. He can, however, be protected, or be entitled to remuneration for his services, if all the beneficiaries are sui juris and he is able to make an agreement with them to this effect.

1 *Robinson v Pett* (1734) 3 P Wms 249; *Williams v Barton* [1927] 2 Ch 9; *Dale v IRC* [1954] AC 11.

Summary of order for payment of debts

28.21 The order in which assets of the estate will be applied in the discharge of trading debts is:
(1) Debts incurred by the personal representatives in carrying on the business only until such time as it can be realised. This ranks first, as it is an administration expense.
(2) Pre-death debts, unless the personal representatives have been given an express authority from the creditors to continue to use the assets for trading.
(3) The amount required to indemnify the personal representatives for the business carried on for longer than is necessary for realisation, where this has been done with authority. The amount will be paid either to the personal representatives, or to creditors who exercise a right of subrogation.
(4) Pre-death debts where the pre-death creditors expressly authorised the personal representatives to carry on the business at their risk.
It will be seen that personal representatives will suffer:
(a) under (1) above, to the extent that the assets of the estate are insufficient to meet the debts;
(b) under (3) above, to the extent that the assets of the estate are insufficient to meet the debts; and
(c) to the total extent of unauthorised trading, unless they have an effective right of recourse against the beneficiaries under an indemnity agreement.

Liability under a lease

28.22 A personal representative can only limit his liability, by express agreement, if that liability is purely contractual. Special considerations arise in the case of a lease, where the relationship will be by virtue of contract and of estate. The lease vests in the executor upon the death of the deceased, and in an administrator upon the making of a grant.[1] If the personal representative does nothing more, he is liable as an assignee but only to the extent of the assets of the estate.[2] So, in *Youngmin v Heath*[3] a woman who was the tenant of two furnished rooms died intestate. Her administrator did not enter into possession of the rooms, and did not take any benefit from them. Her tenancy continued after her death, until it was determined by the administrator giving notice, and the Court of Appeal held that the administrator was liable for the rent from the date of death until the termination of the tenancy, but only to the extent of the deceased's assets in his hands.

1 See above, para 23.18.
2 *Rendall v Andreae* (1892) 61 LJQB 630; *Whitehead v Palmer* [1908] 1 KB 151.
3 [1974] 1 All ER 461.

28.23 In addition to any contractual liability, the personal representative becomes liable by virtue of the doctrine of privity of estate if he enters upon the demised premises. In this case his liability is not limited, and he may be sued in his personal capacity both in respect of rent for the period from which he entered[1] and for breach of covenant.[2] It follows that where the personal representative has entered into possession, the lessor may sue him:

(a) *as personal representative*, in which case the claim is limited to the assets of the estate; and

(b) *personally*, in which case, generally, there is no limit to the liability.

There is a curious upper limit on the personal representative's personal liability for rent: he is entitled to limit his liability to the value of the premises if that is less than the rent.[3] If the personal representative seeks to limit his liability in this way, he is accountable not only for the amount actually received, but also for the amount which he might have received by the exercise of reasonable diligence.[4] Therefore, if the letting value of the premises is decreased because the personal representative fails to comply with the repairing covenants in the lease, his liability will be for the letting value which would have been produced if the premises had been kept in a good state of repair.[5]

1 *Re Owers, Public Trustee v Death* [1941] Ch 17 and [1941] Ch 389.
2 *Buckley v Pirk* (1695) 1 Salk 316; *Tilny v Norris* (1700) 1 Ld Raym 553.
3 *Helier v Casebert* (1665) 1 Lev 127; *Rendall v Andreae* (1892) 61 LJQB 630.
4 *Re Bowes, Earl of Strathmore v Vane* (1887) 37 Ch D 128; *Whitehead v Palmer* [1908] 1 KB 151.
5 *Hornidge v Wilson* (1840) 11 Ad & El 645.

Plene administravit

28.24 The basic rule is that a personal representative is liable to creditors who had claims outstanding at the date of death to the extent of assets in his hands, or assets which ought to be in his hands. If a creditor institutes proceedings against the estate, and the personal representative does not have assets to meet the claim, he can protect himself from personal liability only by entering one of two pleas, namely:

(a) plene administravit, ie that the estate has been fully administered; or

(b) plene administravit praeter, ie that the estate has been fully administered with the exception of certain assets.[1]

If the personal representative fails to enter this plea, he is conclusively presumed to have assets sufficient to satisfy any judgment which the creditor obtains.[2] Where the personal representative enters this plea, the burden of proof lies upon the creditor to show that the personal representative had, or ought to have had, sufficient assets at the time of the commencement of proceedings to meet the judgment in full.[3]

1 *Thompson & Sons v Clarke* (1901) 17 TLR 455; *Re Marvin* [1905] 2 Ch 490; *Lacons v Warmoll* [1907] 2 KB 350 at 360.
2 *Wheatley v Lane* (1669) 1 Sid 397; *Cousins v Paddon* (1835) 2 Cr M & R 547; *Re Higgins's Trusts* (1861) 2 Giff 562.
3 *Mara v Quin* (1794) 6 Term Rep 1; *Britton v Jones* (1837) 3 Bing NC 676; *Stroud v Dandridge* (1844) 1 Car & Kir 445; *Webster v Blackman* (1861) 2 F & F 490.

28.25 The point arose in *Midland Bank Trust Co Ltd v Green (No 2)*.[1] A father granted an option to his son and then transferred the property to his wife, thereby frustrating the option agreement. The son commenced proceedings against the father for damages for breach of contract, and after the death of his father, the proceedings were continued against the defendant, his personal representative. The son obtained a judgment against the defendant for damages. The father's estate was in the region of £9,000, and the son's claim for damages was in the region of £100,000. The personal representative had not raised the plea after judgment and the defendant was therefore liable in the full amount of the judgment. While the rule is one of pleading, it has the effect of altering the substantive law.

1 [1979] 1 All ER 726.

Devastavit

28.26 A personal representative must preserve, protect, and properly administer the assets of the estate with due diligence.[1] Further, he is under a general statutory obligation to administer the estate of the deceased in accordance with law.[2] Any failure to do so amounts to devastavit, or a wasting of the assets,[3] and an action will lie against the personal representative personally. There are three types of devastavit:
(a) misappropriation of assets by the personal representative;
(b) maladministration; and
(c) failure to safeguard assets.

1 *Re Tankard* [1942] Ch 69.
2 Administration of Estates Act 1925, s 25(a), substituted by Administration of Estates Act 1971, s 9.
3 Bac Abr Exors I 1.

Misappropriation

28.27 Little explanation of this is necessary. The most obvious example is where the personal representative uses the assets of the estate in the payment of his personal liabilities.[1] Other examples are the fraudulent disposal of the assets, such as the collusive sale of part of the estate at an undervalue,[2] or putting part of the assets into his own pocket.

1   *Re Morgan* (1881) 18 Ch D 93; *Ricketts v Lewis* (1882) 20 Ch D 745.
2   *Rice v Gordon* (1848) 11 Beav 265.

Maladministration

Misapplication
28.28   Maladministration for this purpose means applying the assets, albeit in good faith, otherwise than in the order provided by statute and any will. Accordingly, if the personal representative uses all the assets of the estate in the payment of ordinary creditors, and fails to discharge a preferential debt, that creditor has an action against him.[1] The same principle applies if the personal representative pays legacies, leaving insufficient for creditors or paying residuary beneficiaries leaving insufficient for specific legatees.

1   *Wheatley v Lane* (1669) 1 Saund 216a.

Unjustified expenses
28.29   Expenses incurred in the course of the administration must in all the circumstances be reasonable. If legal advice is required, it may be reasonable to consult a solicitor, but not to take the opinion of silk.[1] The personal representatives should, for example, incur funeral expenses only to a standard suitable to the estate and quality of the deceased, and greater expense will constitute devastavit.[2] In each case it is for the personal representative to be able to show that the expenses which he incurred were reasonably necessary.

1   Queen's Counsel.
2   *Shelly's Case* (1693) 1 Salk 296; *Stag v Punter* (1744) 3 Atk 119.

Wasting the assets
28.30   It is also devastavit for a personal representative to give away an asset of value, or, within certain limits, to pay debts which he is not bound to pay. *Thompson v Thompson*[1] is an example of the former situation. In that case the deceased held leasehold property which had a greater value than the rent payable under it. In those circumstances the lease could have been sold at a premium, but the personal representative surrendered the lease without consideration. He was held liable. Where the converse applies, that is, where the rent exceeds the realisable value, the personal representative will also be liable in devastavit if he fails to take steps so far and as quickly as possible, to surrender or assign the lease.[2]

1   (1821) 9 Price 464.
2   *Rowley v Adams* (1839) 4 My & Cr 534.

28.31   As has been shown[1] the position with regard to the payment of debts is governed by the Trustee Act 1925, s 15. That gives power to a trustee or personal representative[2] to pay or allow any debt or claim on such evidence as he thinks fit, and this will be a good defence provided the power is exercised in good faith. He is entitled to pay statute-barred debts[3] and he is not obliged to plead the Limitation Act in the case of actions brought by creditors against the estate.[4] However, a debt must not be paid where a court has declared it to be barred.[5]

1 Above, para 26.15.
2 Trustee Act 1925, s 69.
3 *Re Midgley, Midgley v Midgley* [1893] 3 Ch 282, CA.
4 *Williamson v Naylor* (1838) 3 Y & C Ex 208; *Lowis v Rumney* (1867) LR 4 Eq 451.
5 *Midgley v Midgley* [1893] 3 Ch 282; *Re Rownson* (1885) 29 Ch D 358.

Failure to safeguard assets

28.32 The personal representative must take reasonable steps to maintain the value of the estate, and of its assets. At one time a personal representative was liable for the loss of assets once they had come into his hands, even if they were lost without fault.[1] The modern rule, however, was stated by Jessel MR in *Job v Job*[2] as follows: 'An executor or administrator is in the position of a gratuitous bailee who cannot be charged with the loss of his testator's assets without wilful default.'[3] In *Job v Job* the testator was a watchmaker, as was the executor's son. The executor had to dispose of the testator's stock in trade, and handed it to his son for disposal in the ordinary course of trade. The executor was held not to be guilty of wilful default, so that he was not liable when the son became bankrupt.

1 *Crosse v Smith* (1806) 7 East 246.
2 (1877) 6 Ch D 562.
3 As to the meaning of 'wilful default', see *Re Leeds City Brewery* [1925] Ch 532; *Re City Equitable Fire Insurance Co* [1925] Ch 407; *Re Vickery* [1931] 1 Ch 572.

28.33 Further examples of this type of devastavit are failure to pay debts when the personal representative is able to do so, with the result that the creditor involves the estate in expense when he sues;[1] failure to get in assets until they are irrecoverable, as where the personal representative fails to sue until the debt becomes statute barred[2] – unless he had reasonable grounds for thinking that the debt would not be recovered even if he did sue;[3] and loss caused by failure to sell an asset at the proper time.[4]

1 *Seaman v Dee* (1672) 2 Lev 40; *Hancocke v Prowd* (1670) 1 Wms Saund 328.
2 *Hayward v Kinsey* (1701) 12 Mod Rep 568.
3 *Clack v Holland* (1854) 19 Beav 262; *Re Brogden* (1888) 38 Ch D 546.
4 *Phillips v Phillips* (1676) Freem Ch 11; *Fry v Fry* (1859) 27 Beav 144.

Liability for breach of trust

Liability

28.34 The object of the rules relating to devastavit is to keep the value of the estate, after payment of proper debts and administration expenses, as high as possible, for the benefit of both creditors and beneficiaries. But by accepting office as personal representative, a person also becomes liable as a trustee. There is an overlap between liability for devastavit and liability for breach of trust. For example, paying the wrong beneficiaries, and failing to take reasonable care of assets, would be both devastavit and breach of trust. Liability for breach of trust is, however, wider than for devastavit, so that an executor will be liable for breach of trust if, for example, he makes a profit from his office which is not authorised by the will, even if the estate itself does not lose,[1] or if he makes an unauthorised investment of the assets of the estate.[2]

1 *Williams v Barton* [1927] 2 Ch 9.
2 *Re Salmon* (1889) 42 Ch D 351; *Re Emmet's Estate* (1881) 17 Ch D 142.

28.35 Again the executor will be liable for breach of trust if he fails to observe the terms of the will. Thus, if he is directed by the will to sell and convert the assets into authorised investments, he will be liable for any loss which results from failure to do so, unless he had a power to postpone, and genuinely exercised his discretion to postpone.[1] It is not possible to give an exhaustive statement of the circumstances in which a breach of trust will be committed, and for a more comprehensive statement reference should be made to standard books on trusts.

1 *Marsden v Kent* (1877) 5 Ch D 598.

28.36 Where the personal representative in default is ordered to make a payment into the estate in respect of damages for breach of trust, he will usually also be liable to pay interest. Unless the personal representative has derived personal benefit from the breach, the interest will generally be at the rate paid on funds in court on short-term investment account.[1]

1 *Bartlett v Barclays Bank Trust Co Ltd* [1980] Ch 515, [1980] 1 All ER 139.

28.37 In one respect there is an important difference between the liability of executors and the liability of other trustees. A trustee of a trust created inter vivos is under an obligation to inform the beneficiary of his interest under the trust,[1] but where the trusts arise under a will or on intestacy there is no similar duty.[2] This is because a will, together with the probate, and a grant of administration are public documents open to public inspection.

1 *Hawkesley v May* [1956] 1 QB 304.
2 *Re Lewis, Lewis v Lewis* [1904] 2 Ch 656.

Benefit from office

28.38 As in the case of other trusts, the general rule is that a personal representative is entitled to be refunded from the estate the expenses to which he has been put, but that he is entitled to no remuneration. To be allowable the expenses must in the circumstances be reasonable[1] and must not arise from his own default.[2] Where the personal representative is involved in court proceedings he has a choice. He may participate in the proceedings, when, upon the conclusion of the matter, the court may make such order as to costs as it thinks fit. Alternatively, and preferably, he can at the outset apply to the court for directions. If he does so, then whatever the outcome, he will be allowed an indemnity from the estate.[3]

1 *Potts v Leighton* (1808) 15 Ves 273; *Hide v Haywood* (1741) 2 Atk 126.
2 *Field v Peckett (No 3)* (1861) 29 Beav 576.
3 See Lord Radcliffe, *Chettiar v Chettiar (No 2)* [1962] 2 All ER 238 at 245.

28.39 The most usual way in which a personal representative is entitled to remuneration is by virtue of a charging clause included in the will. The normal form of charging clause enables a professional person acting as a trustee to make a charge for the time and services incurred and rendered by him in connection with the administration, whether or not it was necessary for a professional person to attend to those matters. However, a charging clause ranks as a legacy, and it will be ineffective if the executor witnessed the will,[1] or if there are insufficient assets in the estate to enable any legacies to be paid.[2]

1 See above, para 6.41.
2 If there are sufficient funds to meet the general legacies in part only, the charges will abate with them in the absence of any contrary intention; see para 30.58.

28.40 The court has a general power to authorise remuneration, but it will only exercise this power where the personal representative is able to render exceptional services in the discharge of his duties,[1] or otherwise it is for the benefit of the estate.

1 *Boardman v Phipps* [1967] 2 AC 46, HL.

28.41 If the will contains no charging clause, and no order is obtained from the court authorising payment, the personal representative may reach agreement with the beneficiaries with regard to his remuneration. If all the beneficiaries are ascertained, and are sui juris, and they all agree, they can together authorise the personal representative to be paid out of the estate.

Liability for acts of agents and co-representatives

Agents
28.42 Personal representatives are given an express power to appoint agents by the Trustee Act 1925, s 23, which provides:

'Trustees or personal representatives may, instead of acting personally, employ and pay an agent, whether a solicitor, banker, stockbroker, or other person, to transact any business or do any act required to be transacted or done in the execution of the trust, or the administration of the testator's or intestate's estate, including the receipt and payment of money, and shall be entitled to be allowed and paid all charges and expenses so incurred, and shall not be responsible for the default of any such agent if employed in good faith.'

This power is wide enough to allow personal representatives to appoint agents to do acts which they themselves could have done, and the section represents a marked change from the pre-1926 position, when an agent could be appointed only if it was reasonably necessary to do so, or a man of ordinary prudence would have appointed an agent had he been dealing with his own affairs.[1]

1 *Re Weall* (1889) 42 Ch D 674; *Re Parsons, ex p Belchier* (1754) Amb 218; *Re Speight, Speight v Gaunt* (1883) 22 Ch D 727.

28.43 Although s 23 is clear in allowing the appointment of agents, the extent of the personal representative's liability for the acts of the agent is less clear. It will be recalled that s 23(1) concludes with the words that the person employing the agent 'shall not be responsible for the default of any such agent if employed in good faith'. On the other hand, s 30 of the same Act provides that a trustee – and this includes a personal representative – shall be chargeable only for money and securities actually received by him, and shall not be responsible for any other loss 'unless the same happens through his wilful default'.[2] On the one hand it would appear that the person appointing the agent is absolved from liability if the appointment is made in good faith, while on the other hand it might appear that failure to exercise firm control over the agent may in itself amount to 'wilful default', such as to make the personal representative liable. The inconsistency may be reconciled on the basis that a personal representative will be responsible for any loss arising through the fault of an agent who is not appointed in good faith, but that if he is appointed in good faith, the personal representative will remain liable if he is guilty of wilful default in failing to exercise reasonable supervision over the agent.[3]

1 Trustee Act 1925, s 69.
2 As to the meaning of 'wilful default', see cases cited above, para 28.32n.
3 See further the discussion in Parker and Mellows *The Modern Law of Trusts* (3rd edn) p 239.

Co-representatives

28.44 Rather different considerations apply where loss arises through the default not of an agent but of a co-representative. Where the loss arises through the act of a co-representative alone, the position appears to be governed by s 30, which will usually absolve the others. The others may themselves be liable, however, if they have been guilty of wilful default in failing to procure that assets were brought under their joint control, or in failing to take account of the acts of their co-executor. In this case they will be jointly liable.

Right to sue all the personal representatives

28.45 The beneficiary or creditor who loses as a result may sue all the personal representatives jointly, or any of them individually. In the latter case there will be rights of contribution so that the ultimate position of the personal representatives inter se is that they each contribute to the liability. There is, however, no right of contribution where the fault occurs solely through the act of the one who is sued, and the others have not been guilty of wilful default, or where there has been fraud;[1] where one of the personal representatives was a solicitor and the wrongful act was done on his advice and under his influence;[2] where one personal representative alone benefits from the breach;[3] and to a limited extent where one personal representative is also a beneficiary.[4] Again reference should be made to the books on trusts for a detailed statement of the position in these cases.

1   *Bahin v Hughes* (1886) 31 Ch D 390.
2   *Lockhart v Reilly* (1856) 25 LJ Ch 697; *Head v Gould* [1898] 2 Ch 250; *Re Partington* (1887) 57 LT 654.
3   *Bahin v Hughes*, above.
4   *Chillingworth v Chambers* [1896] 1 Ch 685, CA.

Accounts

28.46   Where mismanagement or misappropriation is alleged, a person who is interested in the estate may seek an order for an account. The order may provide for the account to be in common form, under which the personal representatives must account for the money which they themselves have received.[1] Alternatively, the order may provide for the account to be taken on the footing of wilful default, in which case the personal representatives must account both for the money which they have received and also for the money which they would have received but for their own default. It is necessary to prove an act of wilful default before an order will be made on the latter basis,[2] and even where such an act is proved the court will order the account to be taken on the footing of wilful default only if it is reasonable to infer that breaches of trust unknown to the plaintiff or to the court have occurred. So, in *Re Tebbs, Redfern v Tebbs*[3] personal representatives admittedly sold land forming part of the estate for less than its full market value. However, the honesty of the personal representatives was not in question, and there was no indication of any other improper transactions having been made. Accordingly, Slade J ordered an account to be taken on the footing of wilful default so far as the land was concerned, and an account to be taken in common form of the remainder of the estate.

1   *Pybus v Smith* (1790) 1 Ves 189, 193; *Shepherd v Towgood* (1823) Turn & R 379, 388; *Barber v Mackrell* (1879) 12 Ch D 534; *Re Stevens, Cooke v Stevens* [1898] 1 Ch 162.
2   *Sleight v Lawson* (1857) 3 K & J 292; *Re Youngs, Doggett v Revett* (1885) 30 Ch D 421; *Re Stevens* [1897] 1 Ch 422, 432.
3   [1976] 2 All ER 858.

Relief from liability

28.47   Where a personal representative would otherwise be liable to beneficiaries or creditors, he may in certain circumstances be relieved from liability. These circumstances are:
(a)   where there is a relieving clause in the will;
(b)   where the court makes a relieving order;
(c)   where there is agreement with the beneficiaries.

Clause in will

28.48   The testator can restrict the liability of his personal representatives by including in the will a provision to this effect. The usual form of clause used to this effect restricts liability to wilful and individual fraud or wrongdoing on the part of the person to be made liable, and relieves him from liability for mistakes made in good faith or for the acts or defaults of co-representatives or agents. The effect of such a clause is to restrict liability so far as beneficiaries are concerned, but it cannot affect the position of creditors of the estate at the date of death. They have a right to be paid irrespective of any provisions of the will.

Order of court

28.49   The Trustee Act 1925, s 61, enables the court to grant relief to a trustee or personal representative,[1] either wholly or in part, where he has acted:
(a)   honestly, that is, in good faith;
(b)   reasonably; and
(c)   ought fairly to be excused.
When these conditions are satisfied the court has a power, but not a duty, to relieve from liability, and in this case the relief may be against both beneficiaries and creditors. Each case depends on its own circumstances, and the courts refuse to lay down any rules to govern the situations in which the power will be exercised.[2] A good example, however, is *Re Kay*,[3] where the personal representative of the will of the testator who died leaving an estate of over £22,000, and had apparent claims of only about £100, paid a legacy of £300, and only thereafter learned of liabilities which exceeded the value of the estate. In the circumstances of the case it was held reasonable for him to assume that with an estate of this size liabilities would not approach the value of the estate, so that he could safely pay the legacy. The court therefore granted him relief.

1   The protection afforded to trustees by s 61 is extended to personal representatives by Trustee Act 1925, s 69(1).
2   See Byrne J in *Re Turner* [1897] 1 Ch 536; and Romer J in *Re Kay* [1897] 2 Ch 518 at 524.
3   [1897] 2 Ch 518.

28.50   In general it is more difficult for a personal representative who is entitled to take the benefit of a charging clause, or who is a professional trustee, to obtain relief than one who is unpaid. So, in *Re Rosenthal, Schwarz v Bernstein*[1] the executors paid from residue part of the estate duty in respect of realty. Estate duty on realty was, in principle, payable by the donee,[2] but in this case the property had been transferred to the donee without provision being made for the duty. The residuary beneficiary objected to the payment being made from residue and one of the executors, who was a solicitor, sought relief under s 61. Plowman J held that although he had acted honestly, he had not shown that he had acted reasonably, or that he ought fairly to be excused. Had relief been granted, the residuary beneficiary, who was the deceased's widow, would have suffered. It does not, however, follow that the court will refuse to grant relief under s 61 to a professional trustee. In *Re Cooper (No 2)*[3] the two executors were the senior partner in a Toronto law firm, and one of his partners. The whole of the conduct of the administration of the estate was left in the hands of the senior partner, who stole $C180,000 and was sentenced to seven and a half years' imprisonment. The court held that the junior partner acted honestly and reasonably, and had no reason to suspect the fraud of his senior partner, and therefore granted the relief under the local equivalent of s 61.

1 [1972] 3 All ER 552.
2 Finance Act 1894, s 9(1), although now, in the absence of contrary provision, inheritance tax is borne out of the residue of the estate: Inheritance Tax Act 1984, s 211.
3 (1978) 21 OR (2d) 579 (Ontario).

Agreement of beneficiaries

28.51 Where a beneficiary has agreed to or concurred in a breach of trust, he cannot afterwards bring an action in respect of it.[1] The agreement or concurrence must be at a time when the beneficiary was sui juris, and had full knowledge of the relevant facts, and was not acting under any undue influence.[2] Likewise the beneficiaries will not be able to take action if, after having learned of a wrongful act on the part of the personal representative, they acquiesce in it, or give the personal representative a release.[3]

1 *Nail v Punter* (1832) 5 Sim 555.
2 *Thomson v Eastwood* (1877) 2 App Cas 215.
3 *Ghost v Waller* (1846) 9 Beav 497.

28.52 Similarly, where the beneficiary instigated[1] or requested the personal representative to do a wrongful act with the intention of obtaining a personal benefit from it, or if he concurred in a breach of trust and actually derived a personal benefit from it, not only is that beneficiary estopped from suing the personal representative, but the personal representative may be able to claim an indemnity from the beneficiary.[2] Further, the court has power under the Trustee Act 1925, s 62, to impound a beneficiary's interest if he instigates or concurs in a wrongful act, whether or not with a view to obtaining personal benefit.

1 *Trafford v Boehm* (1746) 3 Atk 440.
2 *Montford v Cadogan* (1816) 19 Ves 635; *Fuller v Knight* (1843) 6 Beav 205.

Limitation of actions

Claims by creditors

28.53 The limitation rules so far as creditors are concerned are entirely statutory. In respect of causes of action outstanding at the death of the deceased, proceedings in simple contract or tort must be commenced, in the usual way, within six years from the date when the cause of action arose,[1] and proceedings on a covenant within twelve years.[2]

1 Limitation Act 1980, ss 2, 5.
2 Ibid, s 8.

28.54 The usual rule as to acknowledgment of debts applies, so that a creditor may rely upon an acknowledgment of the debt made by the deceased or his personal representatives within the period of six or twelve years, as the case may be.[1] To be effective the acknowledgment must be in writing, and signed by the person making it, and it must be made to the person who is making the claim. Accordingly, the inclusion of the debts in the Inland Revenue account, or in an affidavit of assets and liabilities made for probate purposes, does not amount to an acknowledgment;[2] nor does a simple direction in the will to pay the debt.[3] An acknowledgment by one only of several personal representatives is sufficient.[4]

1   Limitation Act 1980, ss 29 to 31.
2   *Bowring-Hanbury's Trustee v Bowring-Hanbury* [1943] Ch 104; *Howard v Hennessey* [1947] IR 336.
3   *Rose v Rose* (1979) 28 Nfld & PEIR 181.
4   *Re Macdonald* [1897] 2 Ch 181; see, however, *Astbury v Astbury* [1898] 2 Ch 111; and, above, para 23.53.

28.55   Creditors are able to commence proceedings against the estate even if no personal representatives are constituted at the time,[1] and this can be particularly important where the limitation period is about to expire. If, however, the limitation period expires shortly after the death of the deceased, a creditor may be able to take advantage of the Canadian decision in *Carpenter v Rose*.[2] In that case the testator had given in his will a general direction for the payment of debts. The court held that that direction constituted the executors as express trustees of a part of the estate sufficient to pay the debts, and that, as that property was in their possession, no limitation period ran.[3]

1   RSC Ord 15, r 15.
2   (1979) 28 Nfld & PEIR 184.
3   For the corresponding English provision, see s 21(1)(b) of the Limitation Act 1980.

Claims by beneficiaries

28.56   A beneficiary who wishes to claim either personalty or realty of which the deceased was possessed when he died must bring his action within twelve years from the date on which he became entitled,[1] and to recover arrears of interest the action must be brought within six years.[2] Where the existence of the right of action is concealed by fraud the period is extended until the beneficiary has discovered it, or could with reasonable diligence have discovered it.[3] The period is also extended where the beneficiary is under a disability.[4] These statutory periods do not apply, however, if the action is based on the fraud of the personal representative,[5] or if the action is for the recovery of property or the proceeds of property which the personal representative still has in his possession or has converted to his own use. In these cases there is no statutory period, though, no doubt, the equitable doctrine of laches would prevent action by a beneficiary if he delayed unreasonably in bringing proceedings once he learned of the facts.[6]

1   Limitation Act 1980, s 22(a).
2   Ibid, s 22(b).
3   Ibid, s 32. See also *G L Baker Ltd v Medway Building and Supplies Ltd* [1958] 2 All ER 532.
4   Ibid, s 28.

5 Ibid, s 29.
6 An attempt was made to raise this defence in *Re Howlett* [1949] Ch 767.

28.57 One of the differences between the position of a personal representative and the position of a trustee is that in the latter case the normal period of limitation is six years and not twelve from when the right of action arose.[1] It can, therefore, be important to know whether the proposed defendant was acting as a personal representative or as a trustee at the relevant time. Accordingly, it is beneficial for the personal representative to assent to the vesting of assets in himself as trustee at as early a stage as possible if there is any possibility of proceedings subsequently being taken against him.

1 Limitation Act 1980, s 21.

PART VII

The position of the beneficiaries

PART III

The position of the beneficiaries

CHAPTER 29

Rights of beneficiary during administration

A beneficial interest?

29.1   In general terms it is customary to regard the legal title and equitable interest in the deceased's property as devolving separately on his death. According to this view, the legal title passes to the personal representatives, and the beneficial interest to the beneficiaries, subject to the right of the personal representatives to sell the assets for the purposes of the administration of the estate. While it is permissible to think in these terms so far as concerns the deceased's property considered as a whole, it is not accurate to regard each asset in a similar way. So far as each asset is concerned it is necessary to distinguish between the period before the residue is ascertained, and the period thereafter.

Before residue ascertained

29.2   For many purposes a personal representative is regarded as a trustee, in that he is made liable in the same way as a trustee. Thus, in *Re Marsden, Bowden v Layland*[1] Kay J said: 'An executor is personally liable in equity for all breaches of the ordinary trusts which in Courts of Equity are considered to arise from his office.' The position of a trustee need not be the exact corollary of that of the beneficiary[2] but there is this sense in which a personal representative may be regarded as a trustee. However, to call a person a trustee can lead to confusion, for in any particular case it is necessary to know the duties which arise from the alleged trusteeship. Thus, although a personal representative is subject to the trusts of the office, those trusts 'might just as well have been termed "duties in respect of the assets" as trust'.[3]

1   (1884) 26 Ch D 783 at 789.
2   As in the case of calling a vendor a trustee of the property for a purchaser, following exchange of contracts. The vendor does indeed owe the purchaser fiduciary duties, but the normal trustee–beneficiary relationship certainly does not exist.
3   Per Lord Radcliffe, *Stamp Duties Comr (Queensland) v Livingston* [1965] AC 694, PC.

29.3   If the phrase 'duties in respect of the assets' is substituted for trusts, it becomes easier to understand the attitude of equity. It was that equity did not recognise the residuary beneficiary as having any beneficial interest in the assets during the administration of the estate, although the personal representatives could be compelled to discharge their duties in respect of those assets. In the eyes of equity the whole property devolved upon the personal representatives without distinction between legal and equitable interests. In this way, it was possible for equity to impose duties on the personal representative without creating or recognising a separate equitable interest.

29.4 The position was reviewed by the Privy Council in *Stamp Duties Comr (Queensland) v Livingston*,[1] which was heard on appeal from the High Court of Australia. A testator had died domiciled in the State of New South Wales, leaving property in Queensland. Under the terms of his will, the testator's widow was entitled to a share of the residue which included the Queensland property. The widow herself died before the estate was administered. If the widow held a beneficial interest in the Queensland property at the date of her death, duties would have been payable on her death, but not otherwise.[2] The Privy Council held that because the estate was not administered by the time of her death, and the residue not ascertained, she did not have a beneficial interest in that property. All she had was the right to secure the proper administration of the estate. Accordingly no duty was payable.[3]

1 [1965] AC 694.
2 The provisions of Australian law differ substantially from those applying in the UK. Inheritance tax would be payable by a UK domiciliary in such circumstances. See below, para 29.13.
3 See also *Lord Sudeley v A-G* [1897] AC 11, HL; and article by S. J. Bailey (1965) CLJ 44; cf *R v Myre* (1974) 46 DLR (3d) 298, below, para 29.10.

29.5 Equity could have treated the assets of the estate as a present, though fluctuating, trust fund held for the benefit of those interested in the estate. It did not do so, although this would, perhaps, have been logical. Part of the difficulty with the *Livingston*[1] decision is to know where the beneficial interest in the property lies during the administration period. The decision shows that it is not with the beneficiaries: and presumably, because they can derive no benefit from it, it is not with the personal representatives. The difficulty was recognised. In *Livingston* Lord Radcliffe said:

'Where, it is asked, is the beneficial interest in those assets during the period of administration? It is not, ex hypothesi, in the executor: where else can it be but in the residuary legatee? This dilemma is founded on a fallacy, for it assumes mistakenly that for all purposes and at every moment of time the law requires the separate existence of two different kinds of estate or interest in property, the legal and the equitable. There is no need to make this assumption. When the whole right of property is in a person, as it is in an executor, there is no need to distinguish between the legal and equitable interest in that property, any more than there is for the property of a full beneficial owner.'

Lord Radcliffe's argument does not convince. Although there is no *need* to distinguish between the legal estate and equitable interest in the case of a full beneficial owner, it is possible to regard such a person as having both the legal estate and equitable interest. So long as the personal representatives can obtain no benefit from their office, the same reasoning does not apply to them. The question remains: where can the beneficial interest be regarded as being during the administration period?

1 *Stamp Duties Comr (Queensland) v Livingston* [1965] AC 694.

29.6 The failure to regard the beneficiary as having any proprietary interest in the residuary estate was to the advantage of the beneficiary in *Livingston*,[1] but it is more likely to work to disadvantage. *Eastbourne Mutual Building Society v Hastings Corpn*[2] was concerned with the position of a person entitled under the intestacy rules before completion of the administration. Under the relevant compulsory purchase legislation then in force,[3] when a local authority declared an area to be a clearance area, it was entitled to purchase the land in that clearance area at site value compensation only, that is, making no payment for the house or other building erected on the land. Where, however, the house was occupied by a person who acquired it between certain specified dates 'or by a member of his family [who] was entitled to an interest in the house',[4] full market value compensation was payable. In this case a woman acquired the property during the specified dates and died intestate. The value of the estate was small, and her husband became entitled to the whole of it, but no grant of representation was ever made. However, the husband continued to occupy the house. Relying on *Livingston*, and without further explanation, Plowman J held that the husband did not have an 'interest' in the house, with the result that only site value compensation was payable, and not full compensation. The decision is particularly hard because had the husband applied for a grant, and assented to the property in his favour, full compensation would have been payable.

1 *Stamp Duties Comr (Queensland) v Livingston* [1965] AC 694.
2 [1965] 1 All ER 779.
3 Housing Act 1957, s 61.
4 See ibid, Sch 2 Part II, para 4(2).

29.7 Related considerations arose in *Lall v Lall*.[1] A son was the registered owner of a house. He claimed that he was the beneficial owner, whereas his mother claimed that he held the house as trustee for his late father. If the mother's contention was correct, the beneficial interest in the house would form part of the husband's estate, and she would be entitled to have the house appropriated to her as part of her statutory share.[2] No grant of representation had been made. The mother was in occupation of the house and the son commenced proceedings for possession. Buckley J held that although the mother had the right to claim the house as part of her statutory share if it formed part of her husband's estate, nevertheless she had no locus standi to defend the son's action for possession. She had no interest in the property recognisable by law.

1 [1965] 3 All ER 330.
2 See above, paras 12.16–12.22.

29.8 A somewhat similar situation to *Lall v Lall*, although raising different issues, arose in *Barclay v Barclay*.[1] The testator gave express directions for the sale of his bungalow, and for the division of the proceeds in five equal shares between his sons and daughters-in-law. One of the sons lived in the bungalow, and refused to move out. The plaintiff, who was a daughter-in-law, took out letters of administration, and wished to sell with vacant possession. The Court of Appeal held that none of the beneficiaries had any right in the bungalow itself, but only in the proceeds of sale. Accordingly, the plaintiff was entitled to an order for possession. However, in the course of his judgment, Lord Denning MR said:[2] 'An equitable tenancy in common arises wherever two or more persons become entitled to the possession of property (or the rents and profits thereof) in undivided shares. They may become so entitled by grant, or under a will.' Lord Denning suggests, therefore, that an equitable interest in the property itself could arise under the will if it is appropriately worded. Much will depend on the object of the provision in the will.

1 [1970] 2 QB 677, [1970] 2 All ER 676, CA.
2 [1970] 2 All ER 676 at 678, CA.

29.9 These cases, and the present position, cannot be regarded as satisfactory. It would be far better if the beneficiary was regarded as having a defeasible equitable interest in the assets of the estate. Although this would cause, perhaps, some difficulty, it would avoid the hardship in the *Eastbourne Mutual Building Society* case and *Lall v Lall*, and it would also accord more with the other rights of the beneficiary to be considered later.

After residue ascertained

29.10 It seems that once the residue has been ascertained, the personal representatives will hold the property on trust for the beneficiary, even if there has been no formal assent to either themselves or others qua trustees. This is the converse of *Livingston*. In *Livingston* Lord Radcliffe quoted two extracts from the House of Lords decision in *Barnardo's Homes v Special Income Tax Comrs*.[1] In that case,[2] Viscount Finlay said: 'the legatee of a share in the residue has no interest in any of the property of the testator *until the residue has been ascertained.*[3] His right is to have the estate properly administered and applied for his benefit when the administration is complete.' In the same case, Viscount Cave said:

'When the personal estate of a testator has been fully administered by his executors, and the net residue ascertained, the residuary legatee is entitled to have the residue, as so ascertained, with any accrued income, transferred and paid to him; but until that time he has no property in any specific investment forming part of the estate or in the income from any such investment, and both corpus and income are the property of the executors and are applicable by them as a mixed fund for the purposes of administration.'

So in *R v Myre*[4] the beneficiary who was entitled to the testator's net residuary estate died after the residue had been ascertained but before it was distributed. It was held that the Canadian equivalent of inheritance tax was payable in respect of that residuary estate on the death of the beneficiary, whereas on the authority of *Stamp Duties Comr (Queensland) v Livingston*[5] no tax would have been payable under Canadian law if the residuary estate had not been ascertained.

1 [1921] 2 AC 1.
2 The particular income tax issue in that case is no longer good law; see below, para 29.23.
3 Author's italics.
4 (1974) 46 DLR (3d) 298 (Canadian Federal Court).
5 [1965] AC 694; see above para 29.4.

29.11 There is no rule of law to determine when the residue is ascertained: this is a question of fact.[1] It is not necessary for all liabilities of the estate to have been discharged, provided funds have been set aside to meet those liabilities.[2] The essential point is whether the exact amount due to the residuary beneficiaries is known.[3]

1 *IRC v Smith* [1930] 1 KB 713; *Corbett v IRC* [1938] 1 KB 567.
2 *IRC v Smith*, above.
3 Other than, perhaps, the precise amount of interest to be earned on moneys held pending distribution.

An inchoate right

29.12 Although during the administration period the beneficiary does not have, until the residue is ascertained, an interest in the assets, he has more than a mere right to compel proper administration. He has an inchoate right. The results from this are as follows.

Inheritance tax on gift

29.13 For inheritance tax purposes, the general rule is that tax is payable on the property which is transferred on the death on each occasion on which it is transferred. If, therefore, John dies leaving all his property to his son Samuel, and then Samuel dies leaving all his property to his daughter, Lucy, tax is payable both on the death of John and on the death of Samuel. Because the provisions of United Kingdom inheritance tax differ substantially from the position in Australia, the actual decision in the *Livingston* case would not apply for inheritance tax purposes. If, therefore, Samuel died before the administration of John's estate had been completed, inheritance tax would be payable on the value of Samuel's rights under John's will.[1]

1 If inheritance tax had been paid on John's estate and Samuel had died within five years of John's death, quick succession relief would be available under Inheritance Tax Act 1984, s 141. If, however, the deaths occur within two years of each other, by means of a variation under Inheritance Tax Act 1984, s 142, a double charge to tax may be avoided altogether: see below, para 37.15.

Transmissible interest

29.14 As long as the beneficiary survives the deceased, he will acquire a transmissible interest, and the doctrine of lapse will not apply.[1] Accordingly, if George dies on 1 January, leaving a legacy of £1,000 to Harry; if Harry dies on 2 January the £1,000 given to Harry will devolve to his estate. Accordingly, the benefit under the will of George can be left by will, or disposed of inter vivos.

1 See below, para 30.15.

29.15 An example of the transmission of the right is *Re Leigh's Will Trusts, Handyside v Durbridge*.[1] The testatrix made a will leaving 'all shares which I hold and any other interest or assets which I may have in Sheet Metal Prefabricators (Battersea) Limited'. She had never owned any shares or interest in that company, but her husband had owned 51 per cent of the shares in that company, and he also had the benefit of a loan account with it. The husband died intestate, and at the date of her death the testatrix was the sole administratrix and beneficiary under the unadministered estate. Buckley J held that the words used were sufficient to pass to the legatee under the will of the testatrix the chose in action in respect of the husband's estate.[2] There is, therefore, the rather absurd result that although during the period of administration the beneficiary has no 'interest' in the assets, he nevertheless has rights in them which he can dispose of inter vivos or by will.

1 [1970] Ch 277, [1969] 3 All ER 432.
2 The decision has its difficulties: see (1970) 86 LQR 20 (Baker).

Possession with consent

29.16 The provisions of the Administration of Estates Act 1925, s 43, are noted later.[1] Section 36(10) of the Act requires a personal representative to give an assent in favour of a beneficiary, in effect as soon as is convenient, and without necessarily waiting for the discharge of liabilities if other provision has been made for them. Section 43 provides that before giving an assent in favour of any person 'entitled', the personal representative may permit that person to take possession without prejudice to the right of the personal representative to retake possession if he needs to do so for the purpose of the administration of the estate. On a broad view, the beneficiary is therefore entitled to take possession of the land with the consent of the personal representative. On the narrow view, what does 'entitled' mean in this section? This may come near to going beyond the recognition of a mere inchoate right.

1 Below, para 33.15. The assets can be bequeathed separately: *Re Leigh's Will Trusts* [1970] Ch 277, [1969] 3 All ER 432.

Effect of assent

29.17 It is also significant that the Administration of Estates Act 1925, s 36(2), provides that an 'assent shall relate back to the death of the deceased' unless a contrary intention appears. It seems, however, that this section, applying the common law rule to the same effect,[1] does not apply to an assent of the residuary estate.[2]

1   *IRC v Hawley* [1928] 1 KB 578.
2   *Barnardo's Homes v Special Income Tax Comrs* [1921] 2 AC 1; *Corbett v IRC* [1938] 1 KB 567.

Other rights

To compel due administration

29.18   The beneficiary has the right to compel due administration of the estate. This in effect gives him three possible courses of action. First, he may apply by originating summons for the determination of certain questions which the court will deal with without ordering full administration. These include:

(a)   the ascertainment of any class of creditors or beneficiaries;
(b)   the ascertainment of the rights or interests of creditors or beneficiaries;
(c)   the furnishing by the personal representatives of accounts, and the vouching of those accounts;
(d)   directing the personal representatives to do or abstain from doing any particular act;
(e)   the determination of any question arising in the administration of the estate.[1]

This power is also available to the personal representatives themselves. Alternatively, he may apply for the administration of the estate. Again this application may be made by either beneficiary or personal representative. In fact, an administration order is often made at the request of the personal representative, as a means of securing his own protection, but the court will also act at the request of a beneficiary if it considers it necessary in order to protect the interests of the beneficiaries generally or of creditors. The personal representatives act under responsibility to and supervision of the court. Finally, a beneficiary may sue the personal representatives for devastavit. This was considered at paras 28.26 to 28.33.

1   RSC Ord 85, rr 1, 2.

Information and accounts

29.19   It is considered that a beneficiary under a will or upon intestacy has the same rights to information and accounts as does the beneficiary under a trust, except that a personal representative is under no obligation to inform the beneficiary of his entitlement.[1]

1   *Re Lewis, Lewis v Lewis* [1904] 2 Ch 656.

29.20   In general, all knowledge or information coming to personal representatives is held by them in their fiduciary capacity. They can use it only for the benefit of the estate and the beneficiaries are entitled to it.[1] In *O'Rourke v Darbishire*,[2] a case on trusts, Lord Wrenbury said: 'a beneficiary has a right of access to the documents which he desires to inspect upon what has been called in the judgments in this case a proprietary right. The beneficiary is entitled to see all trust documents, because they are trust

417

documents and because he is a beneficiary.' The same would seem to apply to a beneficiary under a will. As an exception to the general principle, the beneficiary is not entitled to inspect those parts of trust documents which give reasons for the exercise of a discretion,[3] nor may they in general question the exercise of a discretion where it has been exercised in good faith.[4] In the same way, the beneficiaries are entitled to production of accounts.[5] Strictly, their right is to be able to inspect accounts, and they are entitled only to have copies prepared for them at their own expense.[6] Nevertheless the better and more satisfactory practice is for copies of accounts to be prepared by the personal representatives, and supplied to the residuary beneficiaries.

1 *Phipps v Boardman* [1965] Ch 992, CA.
2 [1920] AC 581.
3 *Re Londonderry's Settlement, Peat v Walsh* [1965] Ch 918.
4 *Re Beloved Wilkes' Charity* (1851) 3 Mac & G 440; *R v Archbishop of Canterbury and Bishop of London* (1812) 15 East 117.
5 *Kemp v Burn* (1863) 4 Giff 348; *Re Cowin, Cowin v Gravett* (1886) 33 Ch D 179; *Re Tillott, Lee v Wilson* [1892] 1 Ch 86; *Re Page, Jones v Morgan* [1893] 1 Ch 304 at 309.
6 *Ottley v Gilby* (1845) 8 Beav 602.

Income interests

29.21 Where a beneficiary is entitled to an income interest only, then subject to any provisions in the will to the contrary he can insist that a balance is held by the personal representatives between his interests and the interests of those who will be entitled in remainder.[1] This can be particularly important where the deceased owned a controlling shareholding in a private company. The personal representatives, by exercising the rights attaching to the shares, might be able to procure the company to maintain high dividends, or to retain the income and so increase the capital value of the shares.[2]

1 This is the general rule where property is held in trust for persons in succession. See Parker and Mellows *The Modern Law of Trusts* (4th edn) p 289.
2 See *Re Campbell, Rowe v McMaster* [1973] 2 NSWLR 146 (New South Wales).

29.22 If the deceased carried on a business on his own account, and authorised the personal representatives to carry on the business, they will impliedly have a discretion to improve and build up the business. In doing so, they may retain income and use it for the purposes of the business, but if they do so, that retained income must be kept separately in the accounts of the business, so that when it is in due course paid out, the life tenant will be entitled to it. This is an aspect of a wider rule that whenever the personal representatives properly carry on any business, the life tenant is entitled immediately only to such amount as the personal representatives in the prudent management of the business decide to distribute. In *Re Richards*[1] the testator, who was a farmer, left his residuary estate, which included his farming business, to be held on trust for his widow for life, with remainders over. The executors were authorised by the will to carry on the business, which they did, and they improved it by adding substantially to the quantity and quality of the livestock. It was held that the widow could not compel the sale of the additional stock, but that when it was sold the proceeds were to be payable to her and not to the remaindermen.

1 [1974] 2 NZLR 60 (New Zealand).

Tax treatment

29.23 The particular income tax issue in the *Dr Barnardo's* case[1] is no longer good law. It will be seen[2] that, under current law,[3] a residuary beneficiary is regarded as being entitled to the income of the residue of the estate from the date of death, although the rules for calculating it vary depending on whether the residuary beneficiary is entitled to the residue absolutely or for life only.

1 *Barnardo's Homes v Special Income Tax Comrs* [1921] 2 AC 1.
2 Paras 36.12ff.
3 Income and Corporation Taxes Act 1988, ss 695–702.

29.24 The current income tax position is, in effect, to strengthen the notion that the beneficiary has almost an interest in the property. This is also the position with regard to capital gains tax. Where an asset is transferred to a beneficiary in accordance with the terms of the will, or in accordance with the intestacy rules, the beneficiary is treated, retrospectively, as having acquired the asset at the date of death of the deceased, and the personal representatives are then not regarded as having had any chargeable interest in the asset.[1]

1 Taxation of Chargeable Gains Act 1992, s 62(1)(a).

29.25 The result of all these provisions is that a beneficiary has most of the rights of the owner of an equitable interest in property, although *Livingston*[1] constitutes a formidable barrier to the final logical step being taken.

1 *Stamp Duties Comr (Queensland) v Livingston* [1965] AC 694, above, para 29.4.

CHAPTER 30

Failure of benefit

In this chapter it is proposed to consider the various circumstances in which a beneficiary will not receive the benefit to which at first sight he appears to be entitled under the will or under the intestacy rules.

Disclaimer

Right to disclaim

30.1 A beneficiary cannot be forced to accept a gift under a will. If authority for this obvious proposition is needed, it is provided by Abbot CJ in *Townson v Tickell*,[1] where he said: 'The law is not so absurd as to force a man to take an estate against his will.' Disclaimer may be made by deed, writing under hand only,[2] conduct, or even as a result of contract,[3] though any document is admissible so that evidence of the disclaimer is available. Where the gift is to a body corporate, or to an unincorporated association, the gift can be effectively disclaimed by a resolution of that body or association.[4] The position of disclaimer of entitlement on intestacy has already been considered.[5]

1 (1819) 3 B & Ald 31.
2 *Re Jung* (1979) 99 DLR (3d) 65 (British Columbia).
3 *Begbie v Crook* (1835) 2 Bing NC 70; *Re Birchall, Birchall v Ashton* (1889) 40 Ch D 436; *Re Clout and Frewer's Contract* [1924] 2 Ch 230.
4 *Townson v Tickell* (1819) 3 B & Ald 31; *Re Moss* (1977) 77 DLR (3d) 314 (British Columbia).
5 Above, para 12.53.

30.2 A disclaimer once made is usually retroactive to the date of death of the deceased.[1] Until the disclaimer has been made, however, the beneficiary has a right to have the asset transferred to him.[2] The general rule is that a disclaimer can be made at any time before the beneficiary has derived any benefit from the asset, but not afterwards. By accepting a benefit, the beneficiary affirms the gift. However, if the gift is of a life interest, it may be that the beneficiary can disclaim the income of some years after having accepted the income for previous years.[3]

1 *Re Parsons, Parsons v A-G* [1943] Ch 12, CA.
2 Unless it is required in the course of the administration of the estate.
3 *Re Coulson* (1977) 16 OR (2d) 497 (Ontario); below, para 30.9.

Retraction of disclaimer

30.3 A disclaimer made without consideration may be retracted where it has not been acted upon by the personal representatives, or the other parties have not altered their position in reliance upon it.[1] In *Re Young*,[2] for example, a tenant for life had refused to accept the income from the property for some time, but then changed his mind. He was held entitled to receive the income from the time when he changed his mind, but not before. In all other circumstances, a disclaimer once given is final and cannot be retracted.

1 *Re Young, Fraser v Young* [1913] 1 Ch 272; *Re Cranstoun's Will Trusts* [1949] Ch 523.
2 [1913] 1 Ch 272.

Reasons for disclaiming

30.4 A beneficiary who does not want an asset to which he is entitled will usually accept it, and then give it away or sell it. A gift is rarely disclaimed, therefore, merely because the beneficiary does not like it. There are better reasons for disclaiming.

Unacceptable conditions
30.5 A gift by will may be subject to conditions. In general, a person may not accept a conditional gift without becoming subject to the condition, and this may make the gift in that form unacceptable. As will be seen, in some circumstances, where the beneficiary disclaims the gift, he might be entitled to the property on intestacy, in which case he may take free from any conditions. It is, however, necessary to distinguish the case where a gift is made subject to a condition, and a gift where the testator by his will charges the subject matter with the payment of a legacy. In the latter case, the person who ultimately receives the property, under whatever title, will take it subject to that charge. Suppose, for example, that a testator leaves his house to his son subject to the payment of a legacy of £5,000 to his sister, and, after other specific gifts, leaves his residue to his son. If the son disclaims the house, hoping to take it free from the legacy as part of the residue, he will be disappointed, for the legatee will be entitled to be paid. If the facts are the same, but the gift of residue is to the testator's daughter, if the son disclaims the daughter will take the house, subject to the legacy charged on it.[1]

1 *Wilson v Wilson* (1847) 1 De G & Sm 152.

Onerous property and disclaimer of part
30.6 Another reason for disclaiming a gift is because it is onerous, that is, subject to liabilities which more than outweigh the value of the property. An example is property held on a lease which will expire shortly, and under which the tenant is responsible for substantial delapidations.

30.7 Sometimes it is difficult to know whether a beneficiary can disclaim one of two gifts. The principle is easy to state. If upon a true construction of the will two assets are intended to be taken together or not at all, then one of them alone cannot be disclaimed, and where several assets are given under one heading, then some of those assets alone cannot be disclaimed. Thus, where there is a gift of residue, the whole of the assets comprising the residue must be taken or none at all.[1] In other cases, the beneficiary may disclaim one asset and accept another. In *Guthrie v Walrond* Fry LJ said:[2] 'It appears to me plain that when two distinct legacies or gifts are made by will to one person, he is, as a general rule, entitled to take one and disclaim the other, but that his right to do so may be rebutted if there is anything in the will to show that it was the testator's intention that that option should not exist.'

1 *A-G v Brackenbury* (1863) 1 H & C 782 at 791; *Hawkins v Hawkins* (1880) 13 Ch D 470; *Parnell v Boyd* [1896] 2 IR 571.
2 (1883) 22 Ch D 573 at 577.

30.8 Although these principles are clearly established, difficulty may be experienced in applying them. In *Re Lysons, Beck v Lysons*,[1] for example, a gift of a leasehold house and its furniture was held to constitute two independent gifts, so that the beneficiary could accept the furniture and disclaim the lease, but in *Re Joel, Rogerson v Joel*[2] there was a contrary result on similar facts. It is a question of construction in each case.

1 (1912) 107 LT 146.
2 [1943] Ch 311.

30.9 The reason for the general rule that a beneficiary must either disclaim the whole of a gift, or accept it in its entirety, is so that he cannot select the advantageous parts of the gift, and cast the burden of the disadvantageous parts on others. It seems, however, that there can be partial disclaimer where it does not have the effect of placing any other person at a disadvantage. If, therefore, a beneficiary is left a life interest in property, he can disclaim the income for some years, but not for others.[1] Where there are two or more joint beneficiaries, a disclaimer may be made only by all of them.[2]

1 See *Re Young, Fraser v Young* [1913] 1 Ch 272, above, para 30.3; *Re Coulson* (1977) 16 OR (2d) 497 (Ontario).
2 *Re Schär* [1951] Ch 280. If all joint beneficiaries do not wish to disclaim, the one who does can release his interest to the others.

Income tax saving
30.10 Interest on legacies is regarded as separate from the legacies themselves, so that the interest may be waived without affecting the right to the legacy itself. In *Dewar v IRC*[1] a beneficiary was entitled to a legacy of £1 million. This was not paid by the end of the executor's year, and he therefore became entitled to interest from that time. He refused to accept the interest, and was held not to be assessable on it. The principle applies, however, only while no identifiable income for the legatee has come into existence.[2]

1 [1935] 2 KB 351, CA.
2 See *Spens v IRC* [1970] 3 All ER 295, discussed above, para 36.19.

To take on intestacy

30.11 If the beneficiary is entitled both to a specific legacy, and also to the residue, or on intestacy, it is sometimes in his interest to disclaim the specific legacy and to take under the residuary gift or the intestacy rules. This can be a particularly useful way of obtaining free of conditions property which is left in the will subject to conditions. It is clear that the beneficiary may disclaim where he intends to take in this way. However, this will not free assets from legacies which the deceased charged on them.[1]

1 *Wilson v Wilson* (1847) 1 De G & Sm 152; above, para 30.5.

Inheritance and capital gains tax saving

30.12 One of the most common reasons for disclaiming is to mitigate inheritance tax and capital gains tax. As will be seen,[1] entitlement to an estate under a will or on intestacy can be disclaimed within two years of the date of death whereupon it is treated for the purpose of these taxes as though the benefit had never been received.[2] In practice, a deed of variation is more likely to be used, but there are circumstances where a disclaimer is more advantageous and may be the only option available.[3]

1 Below, paras 37.9ff.
2 Inheritance Tax Act 1984, s 142, and Taxation of Chargeable Gains Act 1992, s 62(6), respectively.
3 See below, para 37.11.

Because it is the decent thing to do

30.13 A beneficiary may have moral inhibitions about accepting the gift. In *Re Moss*[1] the testator, who had been a lifelong member of the Jehovah's Witnesses, left all his property to the local congregation of that body. About five months before his death, the testator, then aged 76, was chewing tobacco on the lawn of 'Kingdom Hall', the local congregation's premises, for which distasteful act he was excommunicated. He did not revoke his will, but after his death the congregation considered that as they had excommunicated the testator, it would be wrong to accept his estate of $C21,000, and they resolved to renounce it.

1 (1977) 77 DLR (3d) 314 (British Columbia).

Deeds of variation

30.14 By means of a deed of variation made by the beneficiaries entitled to an estate under a will or on intestacy, it is possible to redirect the estate for inheritance and capital gains tax purposes. Deeds of variation are considered later,[1] and provided they are effected within two years of the date of death and notice given to the Revenue within six months of the deed, the variation is deemed to have been effected by the deceased so that it is written back into the estate. These provisions therefore provide substantial scope for post-death tax planning.

1   Below, paras 37.9ff.

Lapse

The general principle

30.15   Until the testator dies, his will has no effect.[1] If the beneficiary is no longer alive at the date of the testator's death, the beneficiary's estate will not in general take any benefit under the will, and the gift in the will is of no effect. Although the will may contain alternative provisions providing what is to happen on the predecease of a beneficiary[2] a mere declaration against lapse will be of no effect.[3] Where a legacy other than a gift of residue lapses, the property which is the subject of that gift falls into residue, and where a gift of residue lapses, the property devolves as on intestacy.[4] To the general rule as to lapse there are the following exceptions:
(a)   in respect of gifts of entails;
(b)   in respect of gifts to the children or other issue of the testator;
(c)   in respect of gifts in satisfaction of a moral obligation;
(d)   in respect of certain gifts to charity;
(e)   where there are substitutory provisions in the will.

1   Except for mutual wills, considered above, paras 4.6 et seq.
2   See below, para 30.26.
3   *Re Ladd, Henderson v Porter* [1932] 2 Ch 219; see also article at 78 LQR 90. A provision in the will that 'if any beneficiary dies before me the gift shall not lapse' does not itself save the gift from lapse unless a substitutionary gift can be construed from the will as a whole, for example that the gift should fall into the estate of the predeceasing beneficiary.
4   *Re Pugh's Will Trusts, Marten v Pugh* [1967] 3 All ER 337.

Gift of entails

30.16   Section 32 of the Wills Act 1837[1] provides that if an entail of realty is devised to a person who predeceases the testator but who leaves issue who would take under the entail, then the gift does not fail. In this case the devise takes effect as if the death of the devisee occurred immediately after the death of the testator.[2] The general provision of the Law of Property Act 1925, s 130(1),[3] applies statutory provisions relating to entails of realty to entailed interests in personalty, with the result that s 32 now applies to all entailed gifts whether of realty or personalty. The provisions of s 32 are clearly sensible. If a testator leaves an entailed interest he clearly intends to benefit not only the immediate beneficiary but his heirs. Section 32 may be displaced by a contrary direction on the part of the testator.

1   As substituted by Administration of Justice Act 1982 in respect of deaths after 1982.
2   So that it effectively passes to the beneficiary, thus saving the gift from lapse. In respect of persons dying before 1983, under the original s 32 the entailed interest would pass into the estate of the predeceasing devisee.
3   By which personal property was made entailable for the first time.

Gifts to children and issue

Scope of section 33

30.17 Section 33, as substituted by the Administration of Justice Act 1982, provides that where a testator makes a gift in favour of his child or remoter issue, and that child or issue predeceases him, the gift will be saved from lapse if the beneficiary named in the will himself left issue living at the date of death of the testator. The section does not apply if it appears from the will that the deceased had a contrary intention. It seems that such a contrary intention will be presumed from the fact that a gift to the beneficiary named in the will was only of an interest, such as a life interest, determinable on the death of the beneficiary. A child who had been conceived prior to the testator's death, but who is born living thereafter is treated for this purpose as if he had been living at the date of death of the testator.[1] An illegitimate child or issue is treated for all purposes of s 33 as a legitimate child or issue.[2]

1 Wills Act 1837, s 33(4)(b), as substituted by Administration of Justice Act 1982 in respect of deaths after 1982.
2 Ibid, s 33(4)(a), as substituted ibid.

Application of class-closing rules

30.18 Suppose that a testator leaves his property to 'my children'. He has three children, one of whom predeceases him leaving issue who survive him. If the gift is a class gift, then under the ordinary rules relating to class gifts[1] the property would be divided between the two children who survive the testator.[2] However, the substituted s 33 provides[3] that, unless a contrary intention is apparent from the will, in such circumstances the issue of the predeceased child who are living at the date of death of the testator take in his place.

1 See above, paras 11.35ff.
2 *Viner v Francis* (1789) 2 Cox Eq Cas 190.
3 Wills Act 1837, s 33(2).

Effect of the section

30.19 Where the section applies to a gift, that gift takes effect as if it were directly to the issue of the predeceased beneficiary who are living or are en ventre sa mère at the date of death of the testator. The entitlement is stirpital, so that the issue take the share which their parent would have taken had the parent survived the testator.[1]

1 Wills Act 1837, s 33(3).

Contrary intention

30.20 Section 33 applies 'unless a contrary intention appears by the will'. It seems that the testator need not intend to exclude s 33, because he may not know of its existence, but merely intend that the gift to the issue shall not take effect.[1] In *Re Meredith, Davies v Davies*,[2] a decision on the original s 33,[3] the testator bequeathed £100 to his son, and the residue to his five children, including his son. The son predeceased the testator, leaving issue, so that the gift was saved from lapse, but the testator thought that the gift had lapsed. He therefore made a codicil which recited the death of the son, and, as he thought, the lapse of the gift to the son, and gave £100 to each of his children. Taking the will and the codicil together as comprising the testator's 'will', it was held that the testator had expressed a contrary intention.[4]

1 Per Romer J in *Re Meredith* [1924] 2 Ch 552 at 556.
2 [1924] 2 Ch 552.
3 Which, in this respect, was to the same effect as the substituted s 33.
4 See also *Re Mores' Trust* (1851) 10 Hare 171.

30.21 Where the testator shows that only his *surviving* children are to benefit, that will also constitute a contrary intention. For example, in *Re Horton*[1] the testatrix directed her executors to 'divide the residue of my estate in three equal shares among my *surviving* children'. One child predeceased her leaving issue, but the gift was not saved from lapse.

1 (1979) 88 DLR (3d) 264 (British Columbia).

30.22 Section 33 will not operate if a contrary intention is apparent from the will, however that intention appears, but it is unlikely that the court will deduce a contrary intention from an omission rather than a positive statement. In *Re McNeill*,[1] a Newfoundland decision, the testatrix left her property to her brothers and sisters. Under the Newfoundland (but not the English) legislation a gift to a brother or sister will be saved from lapse if the brother or sister dies leaving issue. One brother and one sister died. The testatrix then made a codicil leaving the share of the deceased brother to his son, but made no mention of the share of the deceased sister. It was held that the failure to mention the share of the deceased sister did not constitute an expression of contrary intention, with the result that, by the Newfoundland equivalent of s 33, the gift to the deceased sister was saved from lapse.

1 (1980) 109 DLR (3d) 109, 25 Nfld & PEIR 297.

Gifts in satisfaction of moral obligation

30.23 The principle was laid down in some early cases that where the gift was made with the intention of discharging a moral obligation, it would not lapse. As long as there is a moral obligation existing at the testator's death, the rule applies even though there is no legally enforceable obligation. The rule has been held to apply to statute barred debts[1] and debts barred by a discharge in bankruptcy.[2] There is no statutory authority for the principle, and its extent is uncertain.[3]

1 *Williamson v Naylor* (1838) 3 Y & C Ex 208; *Philips v Philips* (1844) 3 Hare 281; *Re Leach's Will Trusts* [1948] Ch 232.
2 *Re Sowerby's Trusts* (1856) 2 K & J 630; *Turner v Martin* (1857) 7 De GM & G 429.
3 *Stevens v King* [1904] 2 Ch 30; see also article at 78 LQR 88/89. Many of these cases can possibly be explained on the basis that the court has construed an intention from the will that the gift should not lapse.

General charitable gifts

30.24 Where a gift is made to a charitable institution which ceases to exist in the testator's lifetime, that gift may take effect as a gift of general charitable intent, and be applicable cy-pres.[1]

1 This doctrine is not explained in this book, and readers are referred to the textbooks on trusts.

Gifts to corporations

30.25 If the testator leaves a gift to a corporate body, and that body ceases to exist before the death of the testator, the gift will lapse. However, the court has power, within certain time limits, to declare the dissolution of a company to be void, or to restore a defunct company to the register.[1] Where such action is taken after the death of the testator, the effect is as if the company had remained in being and the gift will be saved from lapse. So, in *Re Servers of the Blind League*[2] an order for the dissolution of a body corporate was set aside, and so defeated a claim by the Crown.[3]

1 Under Companies Act 1985, ss 651, 653.
2 [1960] 2 All ER 298, [1960] 1 WLR 564.
3 See also *Re Montreal Trust Co and Boy Scouts of Canada (Edmonton Region) Foundation* (1979) 88 DLR (3d) 99 (British Columbia).

Substitutory provisions

30.26 Gifts are most frequently prevented from lapsing not by the application of any of the foregoing rules, but because the testator has expressly provided what is to happen in the event of predecease of the beneficiary. To obviate the difficulties which may arise, it is always advisable for the testator to say expressly what he wishes to happen. thus, in many cases he will wish to provide '£1,000 to my daughter Wendy, but if she shall predecease me, to her son Winkle'. By making this type of substitutory provision the testator has confirmed his intention to override the operation of ss 32 and 33, and he will prevent the unexpected results which sometimes flow from the application of these sections. However, the substitutory provision may not be expressed in a manner which gives it the desired effect. So, in one case[1] there was a gift of residue in shares with a provision that if a beneficiary should die 'before receiving the benefits given him or her by this my will', that share should be divided among the survivors. One beneficiary died two days after the grant of probate. It was held that a person 'received' the benefit at the end of the executor's year[2] or on completion of the administration of the estate, whichever first occurred, so that in this case lapse was not prevented.

1 *Re Ramsden, Borrie v Beck* [1974] 5 WWR 554 (British Columbia).
2 It is arguable whether this is correct.

Commorientes

The rule

30.27 It is for every person who claims to be entitled to a part or the whole of the testator's estate to prove that entitlement, and as part of that burden he must, as a general principle, prove that he survived the testator. As has been shown, if the beneficiary did not survive the testator, in general[1] the gift will lapse. This caused difficulty where the deaths of testator and beneficiary were virtually simultaneous. In some pre-1926 cases, the personal representatives of a deceased beneficiary were held to be unable to succeed if they could not prove that the beneficiary outlived the testator.[2] At common law there was no presumption as to who died first. The court firmly declared in *Wright v Netherwood*[3] that it was more reasonable to consider the parties as all dying at the same time rather than 'to resort to some fanciful supposition of survivorship on account of degrees of robustness'. Accordingly, none of the parties could prove he had survived the others and so none could take under the wills of any of the others.

1 Above, para 30.15.
2 *Underwood v Wing* (1855) 24 LJ Ch 293; on appeal sub nom *Wing v Angrave* (1860) 8 HL Cas 183; *Re Nightingale, Hargreaves v Shuttleworth* (1927) 71 Sol Jo 542.
3 (1793) 2 Salk 593n.

30.28 This position was altered by the Law of Property Act 1925, s 184, which provides that where after 1925 'two or more persons have died in circumstances rendering it uncertain which of them survived the other or others, such deaths shall for all purposes affecting the title to property, be presumed to have occurred in order of seniority, and accordingly the younger shall be deemed to have survived the elder'. The scope of this section was clarified in *Hickman v Peacey*.[1] In this case two brothers were killed while in a house which was destroyed by a high-explosive bomb during an enemy air attack. They had each made a will leaving a legacy to the other. It was argued that the evidence indicated that both brothers died simultaneously, so that the circumstances did not render it 'uncertain' which of them died first. If this had been accepted, s 184 would have had no application. The House of Lords, by a majority, and reversing the Court of Appeal, held that s 184 did apply. Lord Macmillan said:[2] 'All that is necessary in order to invoke the statutory presumption is the presence in the circumstances of an element of uncertainty as to which of the deceased survived.' The House of Lords held that although the evidence suggested that the deaths were simultaneous, there was still an element of uncertainty as to the exact moment when each brother died, and this was sufficient to operate the section.

1 [1945] AC 304.
2 Ibid, at 325.

30.29 The Scottish decision in *Lamb v Lord Advocate*[1] has made a welcome contribution to the topic. In that case, on the Scottish equivalent of s 184,[2] the Court of Session held that the provision applied only where the order of deaths is uncertain, and that the court must first be satisfied that, on the evidence before it, the order of deaths is in fact uncertain. Accordingly, if on the balance of probabilities the actual order of deaths emerges, the court will give effect to that without resorting to s 184. In *Lamb v Lord Advocate* a husband and wife were both killed when the house in which they were staying caught fire. The husband, who was the elder, had been gassed in the First World War, and was in poorer health than the wife. The circumstances in which they died could not be established with certainty, but the court found that the most likely explanation of the circumstances was that the wife, who was the more active of the two, managed to get out of the house to summon assistance, and having done so went back into the house to help her husband. By that time the husband was asphyxiated, and the wife then died herself. Although it could not be said for certain that the wife survived the husband, it was established on the balance of probabilities that she did so. There was, therefore, no scope to invoke the statutory presumption. This approach is preferable to that which had been stated in *Hickman v Peacey*,[3] namely that s 184 should be applied whenever there is *any* element of uncertainty, but the decision is not binding in the English courts.[4]

1   1976 SLT 151.
2   Succession (Scotland) Act 1964, s 31(1).
3   [1945] AC 304, HL.
4   See also *Re Harlow* (1977) 72 DLR (3d) 323. The deceased had had a brother and a sister. The brother was last heard of in 1941; the deceased died in 1966; and the sister died in 1968. The Ontario Court of Appeal held that the brother should be presumed dead, and that, by applying the presumption, the brother was to be regarded as having predeceased both the deceased and the sister. There was, therefore, no element of uncertainty, and no scope for the local equivalent of s 184 to apply.

30.30   *Hickman v Peacey*[1] does not expressly say that s 184 applies where death is simultaneous. It seems that if it could be proved conclusively that both deaths were simultaneous, to the very moment, then the section would not apply, but the effect of *Hickman v Peacey* is that for all practical purposes it may never be possible to prove simultaneity of death to the very moment.[2]

1   [1945] AC 304.
2   *Re Bate, Chillingworth v Bate* [1947] 2 All ER 418.

Exceptions to the rule

Order of the court
30.31   Section 184 itself incorporates the words 'subject to any order of the Court'. It is doubtful, however, whether those words have any meaning. In *Re Lindop, Lee-Barber v Reynolds*[1] Bennett J said that they did not give the court a discretion not to operate the section because it might be unfair. Subsequently it has been said that the words are obscure, if not meaningless.[2]

1   [1942] Ch 377.
2   See *Hickman v Peacey* [1945] AC 304 at 314; *Re Bate, Chillingworth v Bate* [1947] 2 All ER 418.

Inheritance tax

30.32 The effect of s 184 is to cause the property to pass from elder to younger, and then from younger to the person entitled under his will or upon intestacy. The property therefore is transferred twice, and inheritance tax would normally be payable on each transfer. However, for inheritance tax purposes only, where it cannot be known which of two or more persons survived the others or other, they are assumed to have died at the same instant.[1]

1 Inheritance Tax Act 1984, s 4(2), so that neither is deemed to survive the other, so preventing a double charge to tax. However, because of the interaction between s 4(2) and s 18 (spouse exemption), if spouses die in commorientes circumstances the estate of the elder effectively arrives with the ultimate beneficiaries free of tax!

Intestate spouses

30.33 Where an intestate has died with his or her younger spouse in circumstances rendering the order of their deaths uncertain, the presumption that they have died in order of seniority does not apply. The intestate is presumed to have died without leaving a surviving spouse.[1] Accordingly, in the absence of issue, the intestate's estate passes to his or her side of the family rather than passing through the surviving spouse's estate to his or her side of the family.[2] This exception to the general rule only applies where the elder spouse has died intestate. Where a spouse has died *testate* in commorientes circumstances leaving his or her estate to the survivor, s 184 does operate to attribute their deaths in order of seniority. Consequently the whole of the elder spouse's estate will pass to the younger spouse and in turn devolves in accordance with the terms of the surviving spouse's will or intestacy.[3]

1 In respect of deaths after 1952: Administration of Estates Act 1925, s 46(3), incorporated by Intestates Estates Act 1952, s 1(4) and Sch 1. Also see above, para 12.6.
2 Prior to 1953, in the absence of issue, the elder spouse's estate not infrequently ended up with his or her mother-in-law.
3 This danger, like most others, can be easily avoided by the appropriate drafting of the will, such as by incorporating a 30-day survival clause. Survival clauses must themselves be carefully drafted to avoid their own pitfalls: see paras 8.77, 37.88.

Presumption of death

30.34 The doctrines of lapse[1] and commorientes[2] apply where it is known that one or more persons have died. In other circumstances it may not be known whether a person is alive or dead. In these circumstances, where it is proved both that for a period of seven years no news of a person has been received by those who would naturally hear of him if alive and that all appropriate inquiries and searches have been made, then:
(a) there is a presumption of law that that person is dead; and
(b) the court will grant leave to presume death.[3]
There is *no* presumption that:
(a) the person died at any particular time; or
(b) that he continued alive to the end of the seven-year period.

1 See above, para 30.15.
2 See above, para 30.27.
3 *Re Callicott's Goods* [1899] P 189; *Re Bowden's Goods* (1904) 21 TLR 13.

30.35 The presumption can be invoked to show either that a beneficiary is dead, or that the testator or intestate is dead. A graphic illustration is provided by *Kamouh v British Aircraft Corpn.*[1] Antoine Kamouh was a dealer in munitions of war and operated from Paris and London. He negotiated large contracts with countries of the Middle East, received big commissions, and became a multimillionaire. In 1968 Antoine negotiated a deal between the government of Libya and the British Aircraft Corporation for the supply of an air defence system for Libya at a cost of £120 million. Antoine negotiated for himself a commission of £11.5 million if the deal went through, but the revolution in Libya stopped it. However, this activity had its disadvantages. Antoine was repeatedly threatened, and was generally accompanied by a bodyguard. He was last seen in Paris in 1973. After receiving a telephone call, he went out alone, saying he had an appointment and would be back in two hours. He was not seen again. His family heard nothing of him, and his bank accounts were not touched. His brother, however, sought to make a claim for the commission; obtained in the Lebanon a grant of administration to his estate; and commenced proceedings. The High Court gave leave to presume death, and the brother obtained an English grant of administration.[2] Other circumstances in which the presumption is invoked are generally less dramatic.

1 (1982) Times, 17 July.
2 The court had previously held that the Lebanon grant did not entitle the brother to sue in the English court as administrator: *Kamouh v Associated Electrical Industries International Ltd* [1980] QB 199.

Ademption

30.36 The expression ademption is used in several situations. Its common use, and that with which this chapter is concerned, is where an asset bequeathed or devised by will ceases to be subject to the testator's power of disposition, or ceases to conform to the description given in the will. In the simplest case, if the testator makes a bequest to David of 'my white Rolls-Royce', and between making the will and dying the testator sells that car, then David receives nothing. Alternatively, if the testator is killed in an accident with the car, which is then totally written off, David will not be entitled to any insurance proceeds paid for the loss of the car. Where the doctrine applies, the gift will be adeemed even if the ademption is caused by an act of the testator, and the testator does not know that his act will have that effect.[1]

1 *Re Freer, Freer v Freer* (1882) 22 Ch D 622; *Jones v Green* (1868) LR 5 Eq 555. See also *Re Dupont* (1978) 79 DLR (3d) 754 (Manitoba). The testator made a specific bequest of money on deposit. Subsequently, the testator ceased to be capable of managing his own affairs, and his estate was placed in the hands of the Manitoba Public Trustee. The Public Trustee did not know of the terms of the will, withdrew the money, and invested it elsewhere. It was held that the gift had been adeemed, notwithstanding that the Public Trustee, as the alter ego of the testator, did not know that his action would have that effect.

Doctrine applies to specific gifts

30.37 Ademption operates on specific legacies only, and not on general legacies. It will be shown[1] that generally a gift of money is not specific, though it may be if a particular sum – eg 'the £50 note which I keep under my mattress' – is indicated. If there is no estate, or the estate is insolvent, then even in the case of general legacies the beneficiary will receive nothing – but that is termed abatement and not ademption.

1 Below, para 31.5.
2 See below paras 30.53 et seq.

30.38 Because of this distinction between general and specific legacies the courts have often shown a reluctance to find that a gift is specific. Where there is room for any doubt, if the asset can be replaced, and there is no inevitable description pointing to the testator, the gift will usually be regarded as general. This is illustrated by *Re Gage, Crozier v Gutheridge*.[1] In that case the testator bequeathed to his niece 'the sum of £1,150 Five per Cent War Loan 1929/47 stock and to M.G. the sum of £500 New South Wales Five per Cent stock now standing in my name'. At the time of making the will the testator held £1,150 of this War Loan Stock, but had disposed of it before his death. Clauson J held that the two parts of the clause were disjunctive, so that the words 'now standing in my name' applied only to the New South Wales stock. Accordingly, while the gift of New South Wales stock was specific, the gift of War Loan was held to be general, so that the executors were directed to purchase £1,150 of this stock for the beneficiary.

1 [1934] Ch 536.

30.39 A warning has, however, been given in *Re Rose, Midland Bank Executor and Trustee Co Ltd v Rose*[1] that in each case the will as a whole must be construed, so that where there is evidence of an intention to make a specific gift, that will of course prevail.

1 [1949] Ch 78.

Changes in nature of asset

Generally

30.40 Once it is established that a gift is specific, there is usually no doubt whether it has been adeemed or not: either the asset exists and forms part of the estate, or it does not. Difficulty does, however, arise where the asset changes its nature. The test was stated by Cozens-Hardy MR in *Re Slater, Slater v Slater*[1] in these words: 'You have to ask yourself, where is the thing which is given? If you cannot find it at the testator's death, it is no use trying to trace it unless you can trace it in this sense, that you find something which has been changed in name or form only, but which is substantially the same thing.' Whether the change is of form only is in all cases a question of fact.[2]

1 [1907] 1 Ch 665, CA.
2 *Re Bridle* (1879) 4 CPD 336 at 341.

30.41 The application of the doctrine may be illustrated by reference to stocks and shares. Where after a reorganisation of the capital structure of a company the testator continues to hold stocks and shares in that company, even if the new securities carry different rights and are of different quantity, the gift will not be adeemed. Thus, it has been held that there is no ademption if bonds are converted into shares[1] or if shares are subdivided, as, for example, where four 25p shares are issued to shareholders in place of each £1 share,[2] or if shares in a reconstituted company are issued to replace the holding in the previous company.[3] In these cases there has been:

(a) a unity of the company issuing the security, in the sense that it has been either the same company or a new company formed just to take over the old;

(b) a similarity in the nature of the security itself;[4] and

(c) a similarity in the quantity of the holding before and after the change.

It seems that if any of these three unities is missing, the gift will be adeemed. Thus, where the company is not merely reconstructed but is amalgamated with a larger organisation, whether or not as a result of a take-over bid, ademption will take place. In *Re Slater, Slater v Slater*[5] a gift of shares in a private water company was adeemed when the company was taken over by the Metropolitan Water Board. A gift of stock is also adeemed when it is converted into cash. So, in *Harrison v Jackson*[6] a gift of stock was adeemed, when the holding was redeemed by the company by repayment in cash to the stockholders. Where there is some element of increment, such as the issue of additional shares as part of the reorganisation, the additional shares will not pass under the gift, though the gift of the other shares will not be adeemed.[7]

1 *Re Pilkington's Trusts* (1865) 6 New Rep 246.
2 *Re Greenberry, Hops v Daniell* (1911) 55 Sol Jo 633; *Re Clifford, Mallam v McFie* [1912] 1 Ch 29.
3 *Re Leeming* [1912] 1 Ch 828.
4 Although admittedly this to some extent begs the question.
5 [1907] 1 Ch 665, CA.
6 (1877) 7 Ch D 339.
7 *Re Kuypers, Kuypers v Kuypers* [1925] Ch 244. See also *Re Cudeck* (1977) 78 DLR (3d) 250. In that case the testator bequeathed the proceeds of a specific deposit made on a specified date or at any time thereafter. He (a) cashed it (b) redeposited part (c) cashed that and (d) put the money in his safe deposit box. It was held that the gift had not been adeemed. The money could still be identified, and the testator had kept it apart from his general funds.

Changes by Act of Parliament

30.42 The principle of ademption applies even to changes which are forced upon the testator. Some, but not all, of the company changes just described may in effect be forced upon the testator, but compulsory changes are more usually effected by Act of Parliament. These changes are of two broad types: changes of substance, and changes in the legal nature of the asset without effecting any physical change.

30.43 An example of the first type of case is provided by *Re Anderson, Public Trustee v Bielby*.[1] The testator owned shares in one of the local railway companies, and by the Railways Act 1921, the undertaking of this company was transferred to one of the national railway companies. A specific gift of the shares in the local company was adeemed. However, the legislation may, and it might be thought, always should, include a provision to prevent ademption. *Re Jenkins, Jenkins v Davies*,[2] for example, was concerned with the gift of a holding in the Swansea Harbour Trust. This holding was converted by the Great Western Railway Act 1923 into GWR stock, which would normally have adeemed the gift. There was, however, a general section in the 1923 Act by which references to the Swansea Harbour Trust in, inter alia, wills and codicils were to be construed as references to the GWR stock substituted for it.

1 (1928) 44 TLR 295.
2 [1931] 2 Ch 218.

30.44 The operation of the doctrine of ademption is important having regard to the various nationalisation measures. An early example is provided by an Act in 1833 for the abolition of slavery in Jamaica. Upon abolition, the owners of the slaves were entitled to payment from a compensation fund. In *Richards v A-G of Jamaica*[1] a former owner made a specific gift of his share in the compensation fund. By the law of Jamaica, slaves had been regarded as realty, and could only be devised as such, and at the time there were different formalities for wills of realty and wills of personalty. In this case, if the share in the compensation fund was regarded as representing the slaves, and so as realty, then the will would not be effective, but if as a gift of personalty it would be effective. It was treated as personalty.[2] A more recent example arises under the Coal Act 1938. By virtue of this Act, coal and coal mines vested in the Coal Commission, and the owner received compensation money. In *Re Viscount Galway's Wills Trusts*[3] Harman J held that a gift of property, which would have included the coal, did not pass the compensation money, which accordingly went to the residuary legatee. In general, therefore, nationalisation will involve either the issue of new stock or monetary compensation. In the former case, unless there is some excepting provision, or in any case in the latter, the gift will be adeemed, subject to what is said below[4] about contrary intention.

1 (1848) 6 Moo PCC 381.
2 See also *Frewen v Frewen* (1875) 10 Ch App 610.
3 [1950] Ch 1.
4 Below, para 30.50.

Ademption following conversion

30.45 Considerable difficulty has arisen from s 35 of the Law of Property Act 1925. Before 1 January 1926 it was possible for two or more persons to own land concurrently. A share in land was realty. By s 35, whenever more than one person holds land concurrently, there is a statutory trust for sale, under which the interest of the owner is in the proceeds of sale. The owner's interest is therefore converted into personalty. If, then, there was a pre-1926 will leaving in terms applicable to realty a share in land, and the testator dies after 1925, what is the effect of s 35 on the will? Of course, the answer ought to be: None! In fact the position is considerably more complicated.

30.46 The principle was expressed by Farwell J in *Re Newman, Slater v Newman*:[1]

'If the testator uses language that can only be construed as a devise of real estate, and, notwithstanding the imposition of the statutory trusts, he dies without altering or confirming his will, the conversion effected by the statutory trusts adeems the devise, because there is nothing left for that devise to operate on. If, on the other hand, the testator uses language wide enough to carry any interest in the property, whether it be in law real or personal property, the conversion is immaterial.'

1 [1930] 2 Ch 409.

30.47 Four rules may be deduced from the cases.

(a) In general, a gift of an undivided share in realty in a pre-1926 will is converted into personalty, and passes as personalty. In *Re Kempthorne, Charles v Kempthorne*[1] the testator, who owned an undivided share in land, made a will in 1911 leaving a general gift of realty to R and a general gift of personalty to P. The share in land passed to P.

(b) This is so, even if there is a specific gift of the property. So, in *Re Newman, Slater v Newman*[2] the gift was not, as in *Re Kempthorne, Charles v Kempthorne*, a general gift of realty, but a gift of 'all my share in Blackacre'. This share was held to have been converted into personalty on 1 January 1926, and to pass as such. The words were 'not apt to pass anything but a moiety of real estate'.

(c) Ademption will not take place if the words of the gift are wide enough to pass personalty. So in *Re Mellish*[3] Eve J held that where the testator gave all his 'interest' in Blackacre, that was wide enough to pass personalty, so that the gift was not adeemed.

(d) Ademption will also take place if a post-1925 codicil confirms the will. If, by this means, the will can be treated as being post-1925, and the words used are applicable to realty, the words are treated as an example of misdescription, not of ademption.[4] In this case, even if the post-1925 codicil does not confirm the will, ademption will nevertheless be prevented.[5]

The result is, therefore, that if the words of the will are so narrow that they can apply only to realty, the courts regard themselves as bound. They will, however, strive to find some way round the difficulty.

1 [1930] 1 Ch 268.
2 [1930] 2 Ch 409.
3 Not reported, but see *Re Wheeler* [1929] 2 KB 81n; *Re Warren, Warren v Warren* [1932] 1 Ch 42 at 47.
4 *Re Warren, Warren v Warren*, above; *Re Lowman, Devenish v Pester* [1895] 2 Ch 348, as explained in *Re Newman, Slater v Newman*.
5 *Re Harvey, Public Trustee v Hosken* [1947] Ch 285.

Death of testator and destruction of asset

30.48 Where in the same calamity the testator dies and the asset which is the subject matter of the gift is destroyed, and the order of events is uncertain, the asset is deemed to have perished before the testator, so that the gift adeems.[1] This will be the case, for example, if the testator leaves a picture by a specific bequest, and there is a fire which destroys the picture and in which the testator dies. The question is of practical importance, because if the beneficiary can show that the testator died first, so that the gift did not adeem, he will be entitled to the proceeds of any insurance claim.[2]

1 *Durrant v Friend* (1852) 5 De G & Sm 343; *Re Gordis* (1930) 38 OWN 317; *Re Mercer, Tanner v Bulmer* [1944] 1 All ER 759; *Re Ross* [1976] 3 WWR 465 (British Columbia).
2 For an example, see *Re Hunter* (1975) 58 DLR (3d) 175 (Ontario).

Republication following ademption

30.49 It might be thought that if ademption occurs through operation of law, a subsequent codicil will be sufficient to prevent ademption. On the other hand, in *Re Viscount Galway's Wills Trusts*,[1] as has been seen, a codicil made after the coming into effect of the Coal Act 1938 was held by Harman J not to give the beneficiary named a right to compensation. *Re Viscount Galway's Wills Trusts* is quoted as authority for the proposition that republication by codicil cannot operate to make good a legacy once adeemed, but this does not seem to be entirely correct. It is necessary to distinguish between three situations.

(a) If the testator has ceased to own the asset before the date of republication, then republication will generally not confer a right to the compensation. This is the *Re Viscount Galway's Wills Trusts* position.

(b) Exceptionally, if the codicil not only republishes but also indicates an intention to pass the compensation, then it will be effective to do so.

(c) If the testator retains the asset, but it undergoes a change in its legal nature, and the will is republished after that legal change, ademption will be prevented. This is the *Re Harvey, Public Trustee v Hoskin*[2] situation.

1 [1950] Ch 1.
2 [1947] Ch 285.

Contrary intention

30.50 The courts will apply the doctrine of ademption subject to any indication of the testator's intention expressed in the will. Where the asset ceases to exist, the most that the testator can do is either to treat the gift as general and not specific, or perhaps to provide for the possibility that the asset may no longer be owned. If, therefore, the testator wishes to give his house to his wife, he may give her 'my house', The Nook, or such other house as may be my principal residence at the date of my death'. There is little that a testator can do in advance of nationalisation or statutory conversion, and he must remember to alter his will after such measure has come into force.

30.51 The account of the decisions arising from the 1925 legislation has been purposely simplified. Even so, the spectacle of intellectual gymnastics by the judges is hardly edifying. The primary fault is that of the legislature. It is regrettable that the various legislation which has caused ademption, by either nationalisation or confiscation, does not expressly provide against ademption. This is surely what would most accord with the wishes of the majority of testators.

Improper act

30.52 Where the testator makes a will leaving a specific bequest, and the asset which is the subject matter of the gift is disposed of, the gift will, generally, be adeemed. There is, however, Commonwealth authority to the effect that this may not be so where the disposal was improper. In *Re Jeffery*[1] the testator made a will leaving certain shares to be held upon trust for his wife during her lifetime, and thereafter for his children. During his lifetime, the testator granted a power of attorney under which the shares were improperly sold to the children. It was held that as the sale of the shares was wrongful, the gift was not adeemed.[2]

1 (1974) 53 DLR (3d) 650.
2 The court indicated that if the sale had been to a third party, the gift would have been adeemed, even if rights of action arose against the attorney.

Abatement

The principles

30.53 Where there is insufficient in the estate after the payment of debts and liabilities to pay all legacies in full, they will abate in the following order:
(a) residue;
(b) general legacies;
(c) specific and demonstrative legacies.
This is, however, subject to any contrary intention shown in the will, and to the discussion in chapter 32 on the effect of the First Schedule to the Administration of Estates Act 1925.

Categories of gift for abatement

30.54 *Residue* In strict principle, the residue can be ascertained only after all other legacies have been paid, and if there is insufficient to meet them, the residuary beneficiary will take no benefit.[1]

1 *Purse v Snaplin* (1738) 1 Atk 414; *Fonnereau v Poyntz* (1785) 1 Bro CC 472; *Harley v Moon* (1861) 1 Drew & Sm 623; *Baker v Farmer* (1868) 3 Ch App 537.

30.55 *General legacies* The classification of legacies is considered elsewhere,[1] but for present purposes a general legacy is any legacy other than a specific legacy, and other than a demonstrative legacy to the extent indicated below. General legacies abate entirely before the specific legacies are touched.[2]

1 Below, paras 31.1–31.10.
2 *Clifton v Burt* (1720) 1 P Wms 678.

30.56 *Specific and demonstrative legacies* The last category to abate is specific legacies.[1] A demonstrative legacy is treated as a specific legacy so long as the asset out of which it is to be paid remains in existence.[2] When, however, the asset out of which it was to be paid is exhausted, the legacy is then treated as a general legacy, and abates with the other general legacies.[3]

1 *Barton v Cooke* (1800) 5 Ves 461.
2 *Roberts v Pocock* (1798) 4 Ves 150; *Creed v Creed* (1844) 11 Cl & Fin 491; *Robinson v Geldard* (1851) 3 Mac & G 735.
3 *Paget v Huish* (1863) 1 Hem & M 663.

Contrary intention

30.57 These rules are all subject to the testator's intention. A good example is the old decision in *Sayer v Sayer*.[1] There was a gift of both pecuniary legacies and specific legacies, but a direction that the pecuniary legacies should be taken out of the whole personalty. The effect was that the pecuniary legacies were taken first, causing the specific legacies to abate.

1 (1714) Prec Ch 392.

Abatement within each category

30.58 The general principle is that all legacies within each category abate rateably.[1] Where the legacy is of an asset which has a fluctuating value, such as stock exchange securities, the asset is valued at the end of one year from the testator's death.[2] Again, however, the testator can indicate that legacies within each class shall abate in some other way. In *Marsh v Evans*[3] the testator gave legacies to his two sons and his daughter, but he provided that if the estate was not large enough for the three legacies to be paid in full, the legacy to his daughter should be fully satisfied, and the legacies to his sons should abate.[4] Unless such a contrary intention can be shown, a legacy given for a specific purpose will abate rateably with all other legacies in the same category. So, a legacy to the executor as a recompense for his trouble,[5] or a charging clause for a solicitor-executor,[6] which ranks as a legacy,[7] will abate rateably with legacies not given for a specific purpose.

1 *Clifton v Burt* (1720) 1 P Wms 678; *Duke of Devon v Atkins* (1726) 2 P Wms 381; *Sleech v Thorington* (1754) 2 Ves Sen 560; *Fielding v Preston* (1857) 1 De G & J 438; *Re Cohen, National Provincial Bank v Katz* [1960] Ch 179.
2 *Blackshaw v Rogers*, cited in *Simmons v Vallance* (1793) 4 Bro CC 349; *Auther v Auther* (1843) 13 Sim 422. See also *Re Hollins* [1918] 1 Ch 503.
3 (1720) 1 P Wms 668.
4 See also *A-G v Robins* (1722) 2 P Wms 24; *Lewin v Lewin* (1752) 2 Ves Sen 415; *Beeston v Booth* (1819) 4 Madd 161; *Brown v Brown* (1836) 1 Keen 275; *Pepper v Bloomfield* (1843) 3 Dr & War 499; *Haynes v Haynes* (1853) 3 De GM & G 590; *Gyett v Williams* (1862) 2 John & H 429.
5 *Re White, Pennell v Franklin* [1898] 2 Ch 217, CA.
6 *Re Brown, Wace v Smith* [1918] WN 118; *O'Higgins v Walsh* [1918] 1 IR 126.
7 See above, para 6.41.

Interest on legacies

30.59 Interest on legacies, where it is payable,[1] is payable in full. It is not treated as an additional legacy, and so does not abate with the legacy itself.[2]

1 See below, paras 31.29ff.
2 *Re Wyles, Foster v Wyles* [1938] Ch 313.

Tax on legacies

30.60 Inheritance tax payable by virtue of the death may be imposed on the general estate, or on the subject matter of a specific gift.[1] If the burden of the tax would normally fall on the specific gift,[2] but the testator provides in his will that the gift is to be free of tax, for the purpose of the rule governing abatement, the testator is treated as making to the beneficiary a separate pecuniary legacy equivalent to the amount of the tax. Thus, if the estate is insufficient to meet all the gifts in full, the gift of an amount equivalent to the tax will abate with the other pecuniary legacies.[3] Accordingly, if the main gift is a specific legacy, and there is no contrary intention, the gift of the amount equivalent to the tax will abate before the main gift.[4]

1 If there is no provision in the will, the gifts do not bear their own tax: Inheritance Tax Act 1984, s 211.
2 For example, foreign assets.
3 *Re Turnbull, Skipper v Wade* [1905] 1 Ch 726; *Re McClintock* (1976) 12 OR (2d) 741 (Ontario).
4 *Farrer v St Catherine's College Cambridge* (1873) LR 16 Eq 19.

Orders under the family provision legislation

30.61 The position where the value of the estate reduces after an order has been made in favour of an applicant under the Inheritance (Provision for Family and Dependants) Act 1975 has been considered previously.[1]

1 Above, para 14.85.

RULES OF STATUTE AND PUBLIC POLICY

30.62 This section deals with those rules of statute or public policy which prevent a gift in a will having the effect which it appears to have on its face. The rule which in many cases prevents an attesting witness from taking a benefit was considered earlier.[1]

1 Above, paras 6.35–6.41.

Slaying the testator

The rule

30.63 It is a rule of public policy that a person shall not be allowed to benefit from his crime. If, therefore, A makes a will in favour of B, and B shoots A dead, B is not allowed to claim the property to which he would otherwise be entitled under the will. Likewise, he is not entitled to claim under an intestacy. Although the reported cases are concerned with murder and manslaughter, the rule appears to apply to any case of unlawful killing, including, for example, causing death by dangerous driving.

30.64 Moral blame is irrelevant. In *Re Giles, Giles v Giles*[1] a wife killed her husband by hitting him with what is described as a 'bedroom utensil'. Under the terms of the will she would have taken the entire estate. She was found guilty of manslaughter by reason of diminished responsibility, and was ordered to be detained in Broadmoor Hospital. Pennycuick V-C held that she could not take either under the will or under the intestacy rules. The judge professed some sympathy for the woman, but he appears to have been influenced in his decision by the thought that the relaxation of the rule in other cases of diminished responsibility could be harmful and dangerous. The case is unsatisfactory. At the criminal trial, the court accepted medical evidence that the woman should be detained in Broadmoor without limit of time. On the other hand, if the medical illness was so great that the verdict was 'not guilty by reason of insanity' the rule would have had no application.[2] Pennycuick V-C followed the approach of Hamilton LJ in *Re Hall's Estate, Hall v Knight and Baxter*,[3] where he refused to consider degrees of guilt on the ground[4] that it would 'encourage what, I am sure, would be very noxious – a sentimental speculation as to the motives and degree of moral guilt of a person who has been justly convicted'.[5]

1 [1972] Ch 544.
2 *Re Houghton, Houghton v Houghton* [1915] 2 Ch 173; *Re Pitts, Cox by Kilsby* [1931] 1 Ch 546; *Re Batten's Will Trusts* (1961) 105 Sol Jo 529.
3 [1914] P 1, CA.
4 Ibid, at 9.
5 See also *McKinnon v Lundy* (1894) 21 AR 560 where the Australian court held that the degree of moral guilt is irrelevant.

30.65 The rule is of comparatively recent origin. Before the Forfeiture Act 1870, where a felon was a beneficiary under the will of the person whom he murdered, the murderer's interest was forfeit to the Crown. Since 1870 the basis of the rule appears to have altered. In its early formulation in *Cleaver v Mutual Reserve Fund Life Association*[1] Fry LJ said: 'It appears to me that no system of jurisprudence can with reason include among the rights which it enforces rights directly resulting to the person asserting them from the crime of that person. If no action can arise from fraud, it seems impossible to suppose that it can arise from felony or misdemeanour.' In other words, the rule is expressed in terms that the law will not lend its aid to assist a criminal to recover. It left open the question whether the executors could nevertheless pay.[2] However, in *Re Callaway, Callaway v Treasury Solicitor*[3] Vaisey J said: 'Now this rule, based on public policy, is that no person is allowed to take any benefit arising out of a death brought about by the agency of that person acting feloniously, whether it be a case of murder or manslaughter.' Accordingly, the personal representatives should not make the payment, even if they are minded to do so.

1 [1892] 1 QB 147, CA.
2 Cf *Pullan v Koe* [1913] 1 Ch 9.
3 [1956] Ch 559.

Effect on the slayer

30.66 Unless an order is made relieving the slayer from the effect of the rule,[1] he cannot take under the will, or on intestacy, and it seems that he cannot make a successful application under the family provision legislation.[2] The theoretical effect of the operation of the rule is, however, unclear. Three different approaches have been adopted. These are:

(a) the gift is to be construed as if the slayer had died immediately before the testator, so that the gift lapses;[3]

(b) the will is to be read as if the gift to the slayer is merely struck out;[4] and

(c) the gift initially vests in the slayer, but there is a personal bar which prevents him from taking, with the result that the gift is void.[5]

Whichever of these bases is correct, the slayer himself will be prevented from taking any benefit.

1 Under the Forfeiture Act 1982; see below, para 30.72.
2 Hence the reason for s 3 of the Forfeiture Act 1982; see below, para 30.74.
3 *Re Crippen's Estate* [1911] P 108. Even if this is correct so far as concerns the slayer, it will not enable others to take as if the slayer had in fact predeceased the deceased; see below, para 30.69.
4 *Cleaver v Mutual Reserve Fund Life Association* [1892] 1 QB 147; *Re Callaway, Callaway v Treasury Solicitor* [1956] Ch 559.
5 *Aplin v Stone* [1904] 1 Ch 543; *Re Peacock, Midland Bank Executor and Trustee Co Ltd v Peacock* [1957] Ch 310.

Effect on others taking under the will

Absolute gifts

30.67 Where the testator left an absolute specific or pecuniary legacy to the slayer, the subject matter of the gift will fall into residue; and where the testator left an absolute gift of residue to the slayer, the property subject to that gift will devolve as on intestacy. In *Re Callaway*[1] the testatrix made a will leaving all her property to her daughter. She died leaving a son and the daughter. The daughter was convicted of killing the testatrix, and so could not take under the will. The whole estate was therefore undisposed of, and fell to be dealt with under the total intestacy rules. Under these rules, the son and the daughter would have normally taken half of the estate each, but as the daughter was also precluded from benefiting under the intestacy rules, Vaisey J held that the son was entitled to the whole estate.[2] By adopting this approach, the normal rules for distribution are disturbed as little as possible.

1 [1956] Ch 559.
2 Vaisey J rejected contentions that the Crown should step into the shoes of the daughter and so take the total estate under the will; or take the daughter's half share under the intestacy rules.

Future interests

30.68 If the testator made a will leaving a life interest to Adrian with remainder to Bernard, and Adrian criminally slays the testator, the interest of Bernard is accelerated. Bernard takes directly under the will, and his title is not derived through Adrian. If the will left property to Adrian for life, with remainder to Bernard for life, with the remainder to Colin, Bernard would take an immediate life interest in possession.[1]

1 See the distinction drawn by Fry J in *Cleaver v Mutual Reserve Fund Life Association* [1892] 1 QB 147 between independent rights, as in these examples, and dependent rights.

Substitutory gifts

30.69 Where the testator included a substitutory provision in his will, it is necessary to consider whether, on the proper construction of the will, and in the events which have happened, the substitutory provision is to take effect. Where a beneficiary criminally slays the testator, he is not treated as having predeceased the testator. In *Re Robertson's Estate, Marsden v Marsden*[1] the testator had appointed M to be the sole executor and beneficiary. He also provided that if M should predecease him, A should be the sole executrix and beneficiary. M survived the testator, but was convicted of murdering him. The court held that as M had not in fact predeceased[2] the testator, the gift to A did not take effect.[3]

1 (1963) 107 Sol Jo 318.
2 The contingency for the substituted gift to take effect was not satisfied. On the other hand, the substituted gift would have taken effect if the testator had provided for it to take effect if the initial gift *failed*. A similar problem arises where a gift to a former spouse is deemed to lapse following dissolution of the marriage; see above, para 8.77.
3 See also *Davis v Worthington* [1978] WAR 144. In that case the testatrix left her property to a person, and appointed him to be the sole executor, provided he survived her for 14 days. She also provided that if he did not survive her for that period, then another person should be her executor and her property should go to charity. The man survived the testatrix by 14 days, but was convicted of her murder. The court held that:
   (a) the testatrix intended the charity to take only if the man did not survive her; and
   (b) as there was no provision as to what should happen if the man did survive her, but was debarred from taking, the property was undisposed of, and passed on intestacy.

Dependent gifts

30.70 Just as the criminal slayer cannot[1] benefit under the will or intestacy of the deceased, so no other person can benefit if his title is dependent on that of the slayer.[2] In *Re Crippen's Estate*[3] Dr Crippen murdered his wife, who died intestate. Under the intestacy rules, had the wife died from natural causes, Dr Crippen would have been entitled to her whole estate. Dr Crippen was subsequently executed for the murder of his wife, having made a will in favour of his mistress. The court held that the mistress could not take, through Dr Crippen's estate, the property which devolved on the intestacy of the wife.

1 Subject to the exceptions noted below, para 30.73.
2 *Cleaver v Mutual Reserve Fund Life Association* [1892] 1 QB 147.
3 [1911] P 108.

Effect on joint owners

30.71 Where the killer and the deceased owned property jointly, then even if the property was held on a beneficial joint tenancy, the equitable interest of the deceased will not accrue to the killer, although the bare legal title will do so. In *Re Dreger*[1] a husband and wife owned property jointly. The husband murdered the wife, and then committed suicide. The Ontario High Court held that while the legal estate passed upon the death of the wife to the husband alone, and upon the husband's death to his personal representatives, they held the property as constructive trustees as to one half for the estate of the husband and as to the other half for the estate[2] of the wife.

1 (1976) 69 DLR (3d) 47 (Ontario).
2 The husband's estate was precluded from benefiting under the wife's estate.

Relief from forfeiture

30.72 Where a person criminally slays the deceased, he may apply to the court under the Forfeiture Act 1982 to modify the rule of public policy in so far as it affects him.[1] Where the applicant has been convicted of a criminal offence which includes an element of unlawful killing, the court can make an order in his favour only if he commences the application within three months from his conviction.[2]

1 Forfeiture Act 1982, s 2(1).
2 Ibid, s 2(3).

30.73 The court has no power to modify the effect of the rule where the slayer has been convicted of murder,[1] but in all other cases, including where the deceased was murdered, but there is no conviction, the court may modify the effect of the rule in whatever respect it thinks just.[2] The order can enable the applicant, and any person claiming through him, to take:
(a)   under the will;[3]
(b)   on intestacy;[4]
(c)   under a nomination;[5]
(d)   under a donatio mortis causa;[6]
(e)   the deceased's share of jointly owned property; and
(f)   other property held in trust.[7]

1 Forfeiture Act 1982, s 5.
2 Ibid, s 2(2). For an example, see *Re Ireland* (1983) Times, 4 April (Home News section).
3 Ibid, s 2(4)(a).
4 Ibid.
5 Ibid.
6 Ibid.
7 Ibid, s 2(4)(b).

Applications under the family provision legislation
30.74 Except where a person has been convicted of the murder of the deceased,[1] there is now no rule of public policy which precludes him from making an application under the family provision legislation,[2] but in considering whether, and, if so, to what extent, the court should exercise its discretion under that legislation in favour of the applicant, it will consider the conduct of the applicant towards the deceased, including the fact that the applicant killed him.[3]

1 Forfeiture Act 1982, s 5.
2 Ibid, s 3(1).
3 Section 3(1)(g) of the 1975 Act is wide enough to cover this.

Benefit otherwise than by succession

30.75 It may be that even where the court cannot,[1] or will not, make an order in favour of a person under the Forfeiture Act 1982, that person can still benefit indirectly following the death of the deceased. In *De Rocco v Young*[2] the testatrix made a will appointing her husband to be her executor and leaving her whole estate to him. The husband was convicted of her manslaughter, but subsequently he took occupation of her house, and remained in occupation of it. The Ontario High Court held that while the husband could not derive title to the house under the will of the testatrix, or under the intestacy rules, he could acquire a title to the house by adverse possession.

1 Because the slayer has been convicted of the murder of the deceased.
2 (1981) 31 OR (2d) 757 (Ontario).

Witnessing

30.76 The circumstances in which an attesting witness is barred from taking a benefit under the will were considered earlier.[1]

1 See above, paras 6.35–6.41.

Fraud

30.77 Although there has been very little litigation on the point, it is clear that a person is not entitled to benefit under a will if it was induced by fraud.[1] It has been suggested[2] that if a person, being already married, goes through a bigamous ceremony of marriage with the testator, who then makes a gift to 'my wife', that gift might be void for fraud.

1 *Lord Donegal's Case* (1751) 2 Ves Sen 408.
2 Bailey *Law of Wills* (6th edn) p 202. See *Re Posner, Posner v Miller* [1953] P 277, where the testator had given his estate to 'my wife Rose Posner' – unaware that she was bigamously married to him. Nevertheless, the court considered that the will itself had not been induced by fraud and the testator had intended Rose Posner to benefit regardless of the 'marriage'.

Illegal and immoral purposes

30.78 If the object of the will, or of a part of it, is to advance an illegal purpose, or a purpose which is against public policy, then no effect will be given to that object. Whether a purpose is illegal or against public policy will be decided in the same way as in the case of trusts.[1]

1 examples are *Thrupp v Collett* (1858) 26 Beav 125 where there was a trust to apply money to discharge persons committed to prison for non-payment of fines under the game laws; *Brown v Burdett* (1882) 21 Ch D 667, which was a direction to board up property so that it could not be used for 20 years.

Perpetuity and accumulations

30.79 A gift in a will does not take effect if it contravenes the perpetuity and accumulations rules. These are not considered in this book, and readers are referred to the standard books on property and trusts.

Uncertainty

30.80 It is convenient to mention here that if a gift is to take effect, both the subject matter of the gift, and the objects, must be stated with sufficient certainty to enable the court to enforce its terms.

30.81 The courts go to great lengths in order to save gifts which appear to be too vague. Thus, in *Re Lewis, Goronwy v Richards*[1] a gift to X and/or Y was upheld as a gift to X and Y as joint tenants, and in *Makeown v Ardagh*[2] a bequest of '. . . hundred pounds' has been upheld as a gift of one hundred pounds. In some cases, however, the courts are unable to give any effect to the words used. A good example occurred in *Asten v Asten*.[3] In his will the testator included a gift of 'all that newly-built house being No. . . . Sudeley Place' to A, and gifts in identical terms to B, C and D. He clearly intended to complete these gifts himself, but did not do so. They were all held to be invalid, as the subject matter of the gifts had not been sufficiently identified. Other examples of gifts which have failed for uncertainty are 'some of my best linen';[4] 'a handsome gratuity to each of my executors';[5] a devise to 'one of my sons' (without naming him).[6]

1 [1942] Ch 424.
2 (1876) IR 10 Eq 445. See now s 21 of the Administration of Justice Act 1982.
3 [1894] 3 Ch 260.
4 *Peck v Halsey* (1726) 2 P Wms 387.
5 *Jubber v Jubber* (1839) 9 Sim 503.
6 *Strode v Lady Russel* (1707) 2 Vern 621.

30.82 Where beneficiaries have a right to select articles, but the order in which they are to select is not stated, then they are to select in the order in which their names appear in the will. If they are described as members of a class and if they cannot agree among themselves, their order of choice is by lot. Both of these rules were illustrated by *Re Knapton, Knapton v Hindle*,[1] where a testatrix had given 'one house to each of my nephews and nieces and one to N.H. One to F.K. One to my sister. One to my brother.' The nephews and nieces were held entitled to choose first, then N.H., F.K., and then the sister and the brother. The nephews and nieces chose by lot between themselves. In *Re Davison*[2] the testator, who owned 150 acres of land, left 75 acres to each of his two named sons, without specifying which land each should take. It was held that the personal representatives should divide the land into halves, and that the first named son could select which half he wished to take.[3]

1 [1941] Ch 428.
2 (1980) 36 NSR (2d) 152 (Nova Scotia).
3 See also *Duckmanton v Duckmanton* (1860) 5 H & N 219; *Asten v Asten* [1894] 3 Ch 260.

Failure of condition

30.83 A gift under a will may be conditional, in which case the condition will be either precedent or subsequent. Whether the gift is precedent or subsequent depends on the intention of the testator in so far as it can be deduced from the construction of the will.[1] If the intestator intended that there should be no gift until the condition is fulfilled, the condition is a condition precedent.[2] If the testator intended that there should be a gift which would come to an end if the condition is not fulfilled, the condition is a condition subsequent.[3] In essence, if the condition is precedent, and the condition is never satisfied, the beneficiary takes no benefit. If it is subsequent, and the condition fails, the beneficiary may have derived benefit between the vesting of the interest and the non-compliance with the condition. In the case of a void condition, if it is precedent the gift fails,[4] whereas if it is subsequent, the gift takes effect as an unconditional gift.[5]

1 *Edgeworth v Edgeworth* (1869) LR 4 HL 35; *Yates v University College, London* (1875) LR 7 HL 438.
2 *Egerton v Earl Brownlow* (1853) 4 HL Cas 1.
3 *Re Boulter, Capital and Counties Bank v Boulter* [1922] 1 Ch 75; *Sifton v Sifton* [1938] AC 656, [1938] 3 All ER 435.
4 *Egerton v Earl Brownlow*, above; *Re Turton, Whittington v Turton* [1926] Ch 96.
5 *Morley v Rennoldson* (1843) 2 Hare 570.

30.84 Special considerations apply where the gift is subject to the condition that the donee pays a sum of money to a third party. In this case, the gift is generally construed either as
(a) imposing a charge on the subject matter of the gift in favour of the third party; or as
(b) creating a trust of the subject matter for the benefit of the third party.[1]
The former will be the case if, at the date when the will is made, it appears that there will be a substantial surplus. In either case, the third party will have a proprietary interest, which will not be defeated if the beneficiary fails to act.[2] The third possibility is that a purely personal obligation is created in favour of the third party.[3] In this case, the third party may need to protect his position in order to prevent time running against him under the Limitation Acts.

1 *Wright v Wilkin* (1860) 2 B & S 232; *AG v Wax Chandlers' Co* (1873) LR 6 HL 1.
2 Although where there is only a charge, the third party may be defeated by the Limitation Act: *Jacquet v Jacquet* (1859) 27 Beav 332.
3 *Rees v Engelback* (1871) LR 12 Eq 225; *Re Hodge, Hodge v Griffiths* [1940] Ch 260.

30.85 In general, where the testator prescribed a period within which the condition must be satisfied, that requirement must be strictly observed.[1] If, however, it is possible to achieve substantially what the testator intended, the court may extend the period.[2]

1   *Re Glubb, Bamfield v Rogers* [1900] 1 Ch 354; *Re Jones, Williams v Rowlands* [1948] Ch 67, [1947] 2 All ER 716.
2   *Re Bragg* [1977] 2 NZLR 137.

EQUITABLE DOCTRINES

Satisfaction

30.86   Equity has established certain presumptions which apply to the situation where a person is under an obligation to do an act, and then does some other act which may be regarded as fulfilling that obligation. The presumption is that the latter act is to be taken as being done in substitution for, and not in addition to, the existing obligation. The doctrine of satisfaction applies in three situations:

(a)   Satisfaction of a debt by a legacy. Suppose A owes B £1,000 and then in his will A leaves B £1,000. Is B entitled to both the debt and the legacy?
(b)   Satisfaction of a legacy by another legacy. The situation envisaged here is a gift in a will of £10,000 to A and a further gift of £10,000 to A later in the same will. Does A receive £10,000 or £20,000?
(c)   Satisfaction of a portion debt by a legacy. A portion may at this stage be described as a substantial gift for a child or other person to whom the testator stands in loco parentis. Suppose that in a marriage settlement C covenants to pay £5,000 for his child, and subsequently makes a will leaving that child £5,000. Can the child claim both?
(d)   Satisfaction (otherwise called ademption) of a legacy by a portion or a portion debt. This is the converse of (c). C here makes a will leaving his child D a legacy of £5,000, and subsequently either pays D £5,000 or enters into a covenant to pay £5,000. Is D entitled to both?

Satisfaction of a debt by a legacy

The rule
30.87   There is a presumption that a debt is to be satisfied by a legacy if all the following factors are present:
(a)   the debt must precede the will;
(b)   the amount of the legacy must equal or exceed the amount of the debt;
(c)   the legacy must be as advantageous to the creditor as the debt;
(d)   the nature of the debt must be the same as that of the legacy;
(e)   there is no contrary intention in the will.

30.88   *The debt must precede the will*   Because the doctrine is based on the presumed intention of the testator, he can only be presumed to have intended to satisfy a debt if it was in existence at the date of the will.[1] The testator's presumed intention is considered as at the date of the will, so that the presumption still applies if the debt is paid off in the testator's lifetime, and the legacy will not take effect.

1   *Cranmer's Case* (1702) 2 Salk 508; *Thomas v Bennet* (1725) 2 P Wms 341; *Fowler v Fowler* (1735) 3 P Wms 353; *Crichton v Crichton* [1896] 1 Ch 870; *Horlock v Wiggins* (1888) 39 Ch D 142.

30.89   The legacy must equal or exceed the debt   Although there is a presumption of satisfaction if the legacy is equal to or exceeds the value of the debt, there is no presumption of even partial satisfaction if the legacy is less than the debt.[1] The only reported exception to this is *Hammond v Smith*,[2] where the testator informed the creditor that the legacy was to be taken in part payment of the debt, and he did not object.

1   *Minuel v Sarazine* (1730) Mos 295; *Eastwood v Vinke* (1731) 2 P Wms 613; *Gee v Liddell* (1866) 35 Beav 621.
2   (1864) 33 Beav 452.

30.90   The legacy must be as advantageous as the debt   It must be shown on the face of the will that the legacy will be as advantageous as the debt. The presumption does not therefore apply where the amount of the legacy, as in the case of a share of residue, does not appear from the will itself.[1] This is so even if the legacy does in fact turn out to be more beneficial. An example of a case where a legacy is not as advantageous as the debt is where the debt is secured, whereas the legacy is not.[2]

1   *Crompton v Sale* (1729) 2 P Wms 553; *Barret v Beckford* (1750) 1 Ves Sen 519; *Lady Thynne v Earl of Glengall* (1848) 2 HL Cas 131.
2   *Re Stibbe, Cleverley v Stibbe* (1946) 175 LT 198; cf *Re Haves, Haves v Haves* [1951] 2 All ER 928.

30.91   There is doubt as to the position where there is no special provision as to the date of payment. The general rule is that legacies are payable by the end of the executor's year,[1] and it is probably true that even if the will directs earlier payment, it cannot be enforced before the end of the executor's year.[2] In *Re Horlock, Calham v Smith*[3] the testator owed £300, payable within three months of death, and left the creditor £400, without expressing time for payment. Stirling J held that the legacy was not as advantageous, so that there was no satisfaction. The logic of this view was overcome by Swinfen Eady J in *Re Rattenberry, Ray v Grant*.[4] In general, a legacy does not carry interest until one year from the date of death[5] but Lord Hardwicke had held in *Clark v Sewell*[6] that a legacy in satisfaction of a debt carries interest from the date of death. This rule enabled Swinfen Eady J in *Re Rattenberry, Ray v Grant* to hold that the legacy was as advantageous as the debt, and that therefore the debt was satisfied. This decision is clearly to be preferred; to follow *Re Horlock, Calham v Smith* would, in effect, be virtually to destroy the rule.

1   See below, para 31.24.
2   *Pearson v Pearson* (1802) 1 Sch & Lef 10; *Wood v Penoyre* (1807) 13 Ves 325; *Benson v Maude* (1821) 6 Madd 15; *Brooke v Lewis* (1822) 6 Madd 358.
3   [1895] 1 Ch 516.
4   [1906] 1 Ch 667.
5   See below, para 31.24.
6   (1744) 3 Atk 96.

30.92   If the debt itself carries interest under the agreement by which it was created, there will usually be some arrears of interest at the date of death. Suppose a debt of £1,000 carries interest at 10 per cent payable half yearly in arrear on 1 January and 1 July in each year. Suppose also that the testator paid the interest due on 1 January and died on 1 April. He will then owe £25 interest. Does a legacy of £1,000 satisfy this debt? In *Fitzgerald v National Bank Ltd*[1] it was held that for the purposes of the rule the 'debt' was to be taken as the capital sum outstanding, so that provided the legacy was equal to the amount of the debt, the debt itself would be satisfied. A separate action would lie for the arrears of interest. The reasoning for this decision lacks conviction: it is based on the fact that at the time of the decision in *Talbott v Duke of Shrewsbury*,[2] which is often regarded, erroneously, as having established the doctrine, interest had to be sued for separately. But while the reasoning may not convince, the result is surely in accordance with common sense.

1   [1929] 1 KB 394.
2   (1714) Prec Ch 394.

30.93   *Nature of debt and legacy*   Where there is a substantial difference in the nature of the debt and the legacy, there will be no satisfaction. So in *Eastwood v Vinke*[1] a gift of land by will did not satisfy a debt of money. On somewhat similar reasoning it was held in *Carr v Eastabrooke*[2] that a legacy did not satisfy the amount outstanding on a negotiable instrument, for the latter may have come into the hands of a third party.

1   (1731) 2 P Wms 613.
2   (1797) 3 Ves 561.

30.94   *Contrary intention*   The rule will operate only in the absence of a contrary intention. Such a contrary intention may be expressed or implied. An example of the latter would be if the motive for making the gift could be construed, and that motive was other than to satisfy the debt. Further, a direction to pay debts, or to pay debts and legacies, will show a contrary intention sufficient to rebut the rule.[1]

1   *Chancey's Case* (1717) 1 P Wms 408; *Horlock v Wiggins* (1888) 39 Ch D 142; *Re Manners, Public Trustee v Manners* [1949] 2 All ER 201 at 204. In *Garnett v Armstrong* (1978) 83 DLR (3d) 717 (New Brunswick) such a direction enabled the legatee to claim a legacy under the will in addition to an amount due to him under a quantum meruit claim. See also *Re Trider* (1978) 84 DLR (3d) 336 (Nova Scotia).

Satisfaction of a legacy by another legacy

30.95   If a testator has given two or more general legacies of the same amount to the same legatee, it must be determined whether the legacies are cumulative, so that they are all paid, or substitutional, so that the legacy is paid once only. Certain presumptions have been established to determine the testator's intention. The rules are:
(a)   Where the testator says expressly or by implication that both legacies are to be payable, that intention prevails.[1]
(b)   Where the legacies are

     (i)   of unequal amounts;[2] *or*
     (ii) of a different nature, such as a pecuniary legacy and a share of residue;[3] *or*
     (iii) are expressed to be given for different reasons;[4] *or*
     (iv) are given by separate instruments, such as will and codicil,[5]
     both are payable.

(c)   The only cases in which there is a presumption that only one legacy is payable are:
     (i)   where they are of the same amount and are given by the same instrument; or
     (ii) where they are of the same amount and are given in different instruments but for the same motive.[6]

1 *Re Silverston, Westminster Bank Ltd v Kohler* [1949] Ch 270.
2 *Re Davies, Davies v Mackintosh* [1957] 1 WLR 922 at 925.
3 *Kirkpatrick v Bedford* (1878) 4 App Cas 96.
4 *Hurst v Beach* (1821) 5 Madd 351.
5 *Hurst v Beach*, above; *Re Davies*, above.
6 *Hurst v Beach*, above.

Satisfaction of a portion debt by a legacy

Nature of a portion

30.96 A 'portion' is a substantial provision for the child of the testator, or some other person to whom he stands in loco parentis made with the object of establishing the child in life. There are, therefore, two aspects:
(a)   relationship between donor and donee; and
(b)   object of the gift.
The donee must be either the child of the testator, or the testator must stand in loco parentis to him. For this purpose, it is not necessary for the testator to adopt the child, or even necessarily to undertake all the obligations of parenthood. If the object of the gift satisfied the rule, a gift from a father will be presumed to be a portion. A gift from a mother would not previously have carried that presumption, but it is possible that in view of the altered social conditions, this may not now be the case.[1]

1 See *Loades-Carter v Loades-Carter* (1966) 197 Estates Gazette 361, CA, discussed in article at (1966) 110 Sol Jo 683; the traditional view is stated in *Re Ashton, Ingram v Papillon* [1897] 2 Ch 574.

30.97 The object of the gift was described by Jessel MR in *Taylor v Taylor*[1] in these words:

'I have always understood that an advancement by way of portion is something given by the parent to establish the child in life, or to make what is called a provision for him . . . You may make the provision by way of marriage portion on the marriage of the child. You may make it on putting him into a profession or business in a variety of ways . . . or by a father giving a large sum to a child in one payment.'

The occasion of making the gift is also important. Unless it is made on marriage, prima facie an advancement must be made in early life.[2] The gift must be substantial, having regard to both the purpose for which it was intended and the size of the testator's estate.[3]

1 (1875) LR 20 Eq 155 at 157, 158.
2 Ibid, at 155.
3 *Re Scott, Langton v Scott* [1903] 1 Ch 1; *Re Hayward, Kerrod v Hayward* [1957] Ch 528.

30.98 A portion debt is an obligation created by the testator, as under a covenant, with the same object as giving a portion.

The rule

30.99 There is a presumption that a portion debt will be satisfied by a legacy if the following conditions are present:
(a) the portion debt precedes the will;
(b) there is no substantial difference between the nature of the debt and of the legacy; and
(c) there is no contrary intention in the will.
The operation of the doctrine, which applies only where there is the relationship of parent to child, could in principle work to the advantage of strangers. Suppose, therefore, that the testator leaves £120,000 to be divided between his two children A and B and his nephew N. Suppose also that he had incurred a portion debt to A of £30,000. The prima facie effect of the doctrine is to satisfy A's entitlement by £30,000, so that B and N would each receive £50,000 and A £20,000. It was held, however, in *Meinertzagen v Walters*[1] that where the residue is to be divided between children and strangers, the operation of the rule is not to increase the share of the stranger. Thus, on the same facts as in the example just given, the nephew N would receive his prima facie entitlement of £40,000, and the remaining £80,000 would be distributable as to £25,000 to A and £55,000 to B.

1 (1872) 7 Ch App 670.

30.100 In contradistinction to the satisfaction of ordinary debts by legacies, a portion debt can be satisfied pro tanto by a legacy of a smaller amount than the debt.[1] Where the will creates successive interests, the interest of the tenant for life can be satisfied, while the interest of the remaindermen is unaffected. Thus, in *Lord Chichester v Earl of Coventry* Lord Romilly said[2] that if a father covenanted to settle £10,000 on his daughter for her life, with remainder to the children of the marriage, this would be satisfied so far as the daughter was concerned by a legacy of £10,000, although the interests of the children would be unaffected.

1 *Warren v Warren* (1783) 1 Bro CC 305.
2 (1867) LR 2 HL 71 at 91.

30.101 The differences between the nature of the portion debt and of the legacy sufficient to exclude the presumption may be either as to the nature of the asset, or the nature of the interest. In *Grave v Earl of Salisbury*[1] it was held that where the portion debt is a covenant to pay money, and the will contains a devise of land, that will not give rise to the presumption, so that the child takes both.[2] Likewise, if one gift is absolute and the other contingent this difference will be sufficient to rebut the presumption, unless the contingency was so remote that the testator thought that it should not be taken into account.[3]

1 (1784) 1 Bro CC 425.
2 See also *Bellasis v Uthwatt* (1737) 1 Atk 426 at 428.
3 *Powys v Mansfield* (1837) 3 My & Cr 359 at 374, 375, per Lord Cottenham.

Effect of operation of rule

30.102   Where the portion debt is still outstanding at the date of death, the beneficiary has the option either to take what is due to him in respect of the debt, or to take the gift under the will. Unless the benefit given by the will is greater, the beneficiary will usually wish to rely on the debt, for this will rank as a liability of the estate, and so not be subject to abatement in the event of insufficiency of assets to pay the creditors in full[1] or to the diminution in the size of the legacy by virtue of an order made under the family provision legislation.[2]

1 See above, para 30.53.
2 See above, para 14.85.

Satisfaction of a legacy by a portion

30.103   This rule is the corollary of the previous one: in this case the legacy comes first, and it is followed by the portion. If a portion is given before the will, the child takes both, for this must have been the intention of the testator in making a will in favour of the child after making that gift. This is not so, however, where the testator merely incurs a portion debt before making the will. Although the general position is the same as has just been discussed, there are certain differences.

30.104   The general rule applies that if there is a substantial difference between the gift and the legacy, there is no satisfaction. An example of this difference occurs with subsequent marriage settlements. Suppose that a father gives a substantial benefit to his child by will, and that subsequently the child marries. If on the marriage of that child the father gives a portion to the child for life, with remainders over for his spouse or children, the legacy is adeemed. It was decided in *Earl of Durham v Wharton*,[1] however, that if the will contains not an absolute gift, but a life interest, and on the subsequent marriage, the portion is given to the child for life, with different remainders over, the differences between the two are too great to permit the rule to apply.

1 (1836) 10 Bli NS 526.

30.105   Likewise the rule is prevented from operating for the benefit of strangers. Under the rule in *Re Heather, Pumfrey v Fryer*,[1] the same type of calculation has to be made as was mentioned in connection with *Meinertzagen v Walters*.[2] Suppose, therefore, that the testator leaves his estate to be divided between his children A and B and X, a stranger. Suppose also that he gives a portion of £30,000 to A and dies leaving a residuary estate of £120,000. X receives his one third share of £40,000. The basis of the calculation as between A and B is:

Total apparent shares of A and B		£80,000
Portion of A, to be brought into account		£30,000
		£110,000
A's one half share	£55,000	
Less: portion	£30,000	£25,000
B's one half share		£55,000
		£80,000

1 [1906] 2 Ch 230.
2 (1872) 7 Ch App 670; above, para 30.99.

30.106 Although, therefore, the general position of the beneficiary is the same whether the will was made before or after the portion or portion debt, there is one important difference. Where the portion debt is incurred first, the beneficiary is, as has been said, entitled to exercise an option whether to rely on the debt, or to take under the will. Where the will comes first, and the portion or portion debt comes later, the beneficiary has no such option: the effect of giving the portion has been to extinguish the legacy. In this type of case, therefore, it is more appropriate to speak of ademption of legacies by portions.

The doctrine of election

The rule

30.107 Occasionally, either by accident[1] or design, a testator gives his own property to a beneficiary, and purports to give some of the beneficiary's property to a third party. In this case, the beneficiary becomes subject to a general principle that a person cannot take under a will without conforming to all its provisions.[2] If, therefore, he is to take the testator's property left to him, he must also hand over his property which the testator has purported to dispose of by will, or he must compensate the third party to the value of the property that that third party would have received. But the beneficiary named in the will cannot be compelled to take any action under it, and he may disclaim his legacy.

1 Not infrequently a testator wrongly believes he owns property absolutely and therefore thinks that he can dispose of it by will. He may, for example, be only a life tenant of the property in which he has lived so long that he has forgotten he does not own it. Alternatively, a property may be vested in the testator and another as beneficial joint tenants and the testator does not realise that he cannot dispose of his beneficial share by will.
2 *Codrington v Codrington* (1875) LR 7 HL 854. See especially Lord Cairns at 861, 862.

30.108 Suppose, therefore, that Edward makes a will leaving £20,000 to Frank, and Frank's car, worth £8,000, to Geraldine. In this case, three possibilities are open to Frank:

(a) he may *disclaim the legacy under the will*, in which case he derives no benefit whatever from that gift[1] and keeps his car;
(b) he may '*take under the will*', namely accept the legacy of £20,000 and transfer the car to Geraldine; or
(c) he may '*take against the will*', namely accept the legacy of £20,000, retain the car, but pay to Geraldine £8,000 to compensate her for not receiving the car.

In both the second and third cases Frank is a net sum of £12,000 better off, and Geraldine receives either the asset or cash to the value of £8,000.

1 With the result that it is usually only prudent to disclaim where the value of the gift under the will does not exceed the value of the property to be given to the third party.

30.109 Where the beneficiary elects to take against the will, and his entitlement is to an income interest, the income is withheld until a sufficient sum has been retained in order to pay the disappointed beneficiaries. If, however, the beneficiary who is put to his election was given a protective life interest,[1] the fact that the personal representatives must withhold income to satisfy the disappointed beneficiaries causes the life interest to come to an end, and the discretionary trusts to arise.[2]

1 Under Trustee Act 1925, s 33, or under an express trust to similar effect.
2 *McCarogher v Whieldon* (1867) LR 3 Eq 236; *Carter v Silber* [1891] 3 Ch 553; *Re Gordon's Will Trusts* [1977] Ch 27, [1976] 2 All ER 577.

Basis of the doctrine

There have been three suggestions as to the basis of the rule.

Implied condition
30.110 The earliest view was that the testator gave his property to the recipient on the implied condition that the recipient would give his property to the third party.[1] While this may be a satisfactory explanation of the situation where the recipient elects to take under the instrument, the inadequacy of this view is seen where he elects to take against it. If the testator expressly imposes a condition that the recipient must give his property to the third party, then if the recipient does not do so, he is entitled to no benefit under the will. The example just given, however, shows that the recipient can insist on keeping his own property, merely compensating the third party for the value which he would have received.

1 *Noys v Mordaunt* (1706) 2 Vern 581; *Streatfield v Streatfield* (1735) Cas *temp* Talb 176; *Ker v Wauchope* (1819) 1 Bligh 1.

Presumed intention of the testator
30.111 While in some cases the testator may actually intend to put the recipient to his election, the doctrine of election applies irrespective of the testator's actual intention, save that it will not apply where there is a clear contrary intention. In *Cooper v Cooper*[1] Lord Cairns expressly said that the rule was not based either on the testator's intention as expressed or on his

presumed intention. This view, that the doctrine is based on intention, cannot therefore stand.

1 (1874) LR 7 HL 53.

'Equity'
30.112 The most recent, and most satisfactory explanation is that it is a rule of equity imposed as a matter of conscience in order to achieve a just result in the circumstances of the case. It was expressed by Buckley J in *Re Mengel's Will Trusts*[1] as 'a doctrine by which equity fastens on the conscience of the person who is put to his election and refuses to allow him to take the benefit of a disposition contained in the will, the validity of which is not in question, except on certain conditions'.[2] This approach was affirmed by the Court of Appeal in *Re Gordon's Will Trusts, National Westminster Bank Ltd v Gordon*.[3]

1 [1962] Ch 791.
2 See also Lord Cairns in *Cooper v Cooper* (1874) LR 7 HL 53 at 67; *Brown v Gregson* [1920] AC 860.
3 [1978] Ch 145, [1978] 2 All ER 969, CA.

When the doctrine applies

In order for the doctrine to apply, it must be shown that all of the following five conditions are satisfied.

The donor must give his own property to the recipient
30.113 In *Bristow v Warde*[1] a father had a power to appoint stock in favour of his children, the trust instrument providing that in default of his appointment the children were entitled equally. By his will the father purported to appoint part of the fund to persons who were not objects of the power. As he had not given any of his own property to the children, there was no case for election, with the result that they took under the appointment the part of the fund that had been appointed to them, and they took in default of appointment that part of the fund which had been invalidly appointed to the non-objects. On the other hand, in *Whistler v Webster*,[2] where the facts were essentially the same except that the testator also gave his own property to the children, the children were put to their election, whether to take the father's own property under the will, and allow the appointment to the non-object to stand.[3]

1 (1794) 2 Ves 336; see also *Re Fowler's Trust* (1859) 27 Beav 362; *Fox v Charlton* (1862) 6 LT 743.
2 (1794) 2 Ves 367.
3 See also *Reid v Reid* (1858) 25 Beav 469; *Re Fletcher's Settlement Trusts* [1936] 2 All ER 236.

The recipient's property must be freely alienable
30.114 No case for election arises where the recipient is not able to dispose of his property which the testator has purported to leave. In *Re Lord Chesham, Cavendish v Dacre*[1] Lord Chesham was the tenant for life of certain chattels subject to a settlement. The testator left his own property to

Lord Chesham, his eldest son, and the chattels to his younger sons. Chitty J held that because Lord Chesham could not dispose of the chattels, he was entitled to take the benefit under the will and to keep the chattels. Where, however, the recipient does not own the whole of an asset, but does own absolutely a share in that asset, he can be made to elect to the extent of that share. Thus, in *Re Dicey, Julian v Dicey*[2] the defendant was entitled to a beneficial one half share in realty. The testatrix gave her own property to the defendant, and that realty to the plaintiff. The court held that the defendant had to elect, as she could assign to the plaintiff her one half share in the realty. If, however, the recipient has a protected life interest, he is not put to his election because that interest is effectively non-assignable.[3]

1   (1886) 31 Ch D 466.
2   [1957] Ch 145.
3   *Re Gordon's Will Trusts* [1978] Ch 145, [1978] 2 All ER 969, CA; cf *McCarogher v Whieldon* (1867) LR 3 Eq 236 and *Carter v Silber* [1891] 3 Ch 553.

Both gifts must be in the same instrument
30.115   The testator must give his own property to the recipient and the recipient's property to a third party in the same instrument. Otherwise, the recipient could take the benefit under one instrument, and ignore or disclaim under the other. For this purpose a will and any codicils are treated as one instrument.

The testator must intend to dispose of what he does not own
30.116   There is a strong presumption that a man has only intended to dispose of what he himself owns.[1] If, therefore, he owns an interest in property, and uses words which are capable of being construed either as leaving that interest only, or the whole property, they will carry the narrower meaning.[2] It will, then, rarely be possible to show that the doctrine should operate where the testator does in fact own some interest in the property given to the third party. An example of a case where the doctrine did apply, however, is *Padbury v Clark*.[3] In that case the testator owned a moiety[4] of a freehold house. In his will he gave some of his own property to the owner of the other moiety, and the whole house to a third person. The owner of the other moiety was put to his election.

1   See eg Turner LJ in *Evans v Evans* (1863) 2 New Rep 408 at 401. Also *Re Harris, Leacroft v Harris* [1909] 2 Ch 206; *Re Booker, Booker v Booker* (1886) 54 LT 239.
2   Lord Eldon in *Lord Rancliffe v Lady Parkyns* (1818) 6 Dow 149 at 185; Page Wood VC in *Howells v Jenkins* (1863) 2 John & H 706 at 713.
3   (1850) 2 Mac & G 298. See also *Miller v Thurgood* (1864) 33 Beav 496; *Wilkinson v Dent* (1871) 6 Ch App 339.
4   A half share.

30.117   Although the testator must intend to dispose of the property, it is not necessary for him to be aware that he does not own it.

Must the claim be outside the will?
30.118   In *Wollaston v King*[1] James V-C said that the rule of election 'is to be applied as between a gift under a will and a claim dehors the will, and adverse to it, and is not to be applied as between one clause in a will and another clause in the same will'. This is because where there are two gifts in

the same will, any inconsistency between them will usually be resolved by the principles of construction. The facts of *Wollaston v King* were that the testatrix had a power of appointment over property in favour of her children, who were also entitled in default of appointment. She appointed £5,000 to her son on certain trusts, and the remainder of the fund to her daughters. She also gave her own property to her daughters. The gift to the son was void for perpetuity, so that the whole fund passed to the daughters under the residuary appointment. James V-C said:

'It would seem a very strange thing that in construing the same instrument the Court, dealing with a clause in which a fund is expressed to be given partly to A and partly to B, should hold that the gift to A, being void, the testator's intention is that B should take the whole; and then coming to another clause in which another fund is given to B, and no mention of A at all, it should hold that there is an implied intention that he should take.'

1 (1869) LR 8 Eq 165 at 174.

30.119 Doubt as to the extent of the principle has been thrown by the difficult decision in *Re Macartney, MacFarlane v Macartney*.[1] The testator held 95 per cent of the issued shares in a company, Macartney McElroy Ltd. That company held 90 per cent of the issued shares in Malta Tramways Ltd. The only asset of Malta Tramways Ltd of any value was a holding of £3,000 colonial stock, which was registered in the name of the testator as nominee for Malta Tramways. By his will the testator bequeathed the holding of colonial stock to his daughter Maggie, and gave his shares in Macartney McElroy Ltd to his seven children, including Maggie. As the stock belonged to Malta Tramways she could not take it, and Maggie sought compensation from the other children. If the testator had left the shares in Macartney McElroy Ltd to Malta Tramways Ltd, and the stock to Maggie, Malta Tramways would clearly have been put to their election. Because of the similarity of shareholdings, Neville J appears to have ignored the existence of the companies, regarding the children as being in the same position as Malta Tramways. On this basis he required the children to elect, and, in the event, to compensate Maggie for the stock which she did not receive.

1 [1918] 1 Ch 300.

30.120 If the case is viewed in this way, there appears to be no conflict with *Wollaston v King*,[1] but the case can also be seen, and with less ingenuity, as a case where both claims arose under the will. Whichever way the case is regarded, its difficulties are apparent. It is difficult to justify the equation of the position of the children with Malta Tramways, both because of the separate existence of the companies, and because of the fact that the shareholders in Macartney McElroy Ltd held only 95 per cent of 90 per cent of the colonial stock. *Re Macartney, MacFarlane v Macartney*[2] has been criticised[3] but the result does seem to accord with what the testator intended, namely that Maggie should have the stock and that the children generally should have the shares less the value of the stock represented in them. The decision shows that the doctrine will be extended beyond its normal limits where it is necessary in order to achieve a just result.[4]

1 (1869) LR 8 Eq 165.
2 [1918] 1 Ch 300.
3 See eg Pettit *Equity and the Law of Trusts* (6th edn) p 652.
4 For a further example of its extension, see *Re Allen's Estate* [1945] 2 All ER 264.

Method and time of election

30.121 Election may be express or by implication. In order to be held to have elected by implication, however, it must be shown that the beneficiary was in possession of all the relevant facts.[1] Where he has knowledge of these facts, acts such as receiving the income, or dealing with the property given under the will, may show an implied intention to take under the will.[2] Where election is made against the will, the amount of compensation which has to be paid is ascertained according to the value of the asset at the date of death of the testator.[3] If the will prescribes the time by which the election must be made, and person does not elect within that time, he is deemed to have elected against the instrument.[4]

1 *Pusey v Desbouverie* (1734) 3 P Wms 315; *Kidney v Coussmaker* (1806) 12 Ves 136.
2 *Dewar v Maitland* (1886) LR 2 Eq 834; *Re Shepherd, Harris v Shepherd* [1943] Ch 8.
3 *Re Hancock, Hancock v Pawson* [1905] 1 Ch 16.
4 *Dillon v Parker* (1818) 1 Swan 359 at 381.

CHAPTER 31

Extent of benefit

Legacies and devises

Types of legacy

31.1 It is customary to divide legacies into five categories, and it is proposed first to explain these categories and then to indicate the importance of the distinctions between them. The categories of legacy are:
(a) specific;
(b) demonstrative;
(c) general;
(d) pecuniary;
(e) residuary.

Specific legacy
31.2 This type of legacy is a gift of an asset which forms part of the testator's estate at the date of death, and is distinguished from the totality of the testator's assets, or from the totality of the residue. The will must show an intention that it should pass in specie. The subject matter of the gift may be either of one or more specified assets, or such assets as come within a description sufficient to include fluctuating items.[1] Examples of specific legacies are 'my book to Andrew', 'the money in my bag to Basil',[2] 'my books to Clarence',[3] and 'my 3,000 ICI shares to Deborah'.[4]

1 *Castle v Fox* (1871) LR 11 Eq 542. See especially at 552.
2 *Lawson v Stitch* (1738) 1 Atk 507.
3 See *Castle v Fox*, above.
4 This is specific because of the inclusion of the word 'my'. See below, para 31, and *Re Tetsall, Foyster v Tetsall* [1961] 2 All ER 801.

Demonstrative legacy
31.3 This is a gift of a general, that is, non-specific, nature, directed to be paid from a particular fund.[1] Thus, a gift of '£1,000 out of my account with Coutts Bank'[2] is a demonstrative legacy. The essential distinction between a specific legacy and a demonstrative legacy is one of intention: in the case of a specific legacy the testator shows an intention that the beneficiary shall receive only the specified asset, so that if it ceases to exist at the date of death, he receives nothing.[3] In the case of a demonstrative legacy, the

testator indicates an intention that the gift shall be taken *primarily* from the specified fund, but that any balance can be taken from the residue in the event of deficiency. In *Re Webster, Goss v Webster*,[4] for example, there was a gift of £3,000 from a specified business. At the testator's death the business was worth less than £3,000. Had the gift been specific, the beneficiary would have received only the value of the business, but in this case, as it was held on a true construction to be a demonstrative legacy, the beneficiary received the value of the business, and the deficiency was then made good to him from the remainder of the estate.

1   *Kirby v Potter* (1799) 4 Ves 748; *Re Webster, Goss v Webster* [1937] 1 All ER 602.
2   *Fowler v Willoughby* (1825) 2 Sim & St 354.
3   See above, para 30.36.
4   [1937] 1 All ER 602.

General legacy
31.4   This is a gift of an item irrespective of whether the testator owned such an item at the date of his death, or at the date when the will is made. Thus, a gift of 'a Rolls-Royce Phantom motor car to Edwina' will be a general legacy. The testator may never have owned such a motor car, but the effect of the will is to require his executors to purchase a motor car of this description for the beneficiary. Gifts of stocks and shares are prima facie general and not specific gifts, although they may be specific if they are described as '*my* shares in ICI'.

Pecuniary legacy
31.5   This is basically a gift of money. A gift of money may alternatively be a specific legacy or a demonstrative legacy. Thus '£1,000 to Frederick' is an example of a pecuniary legacy; '£1,000 out of my National Savings Certificates to Georgina' is a demonstrative legacy; and 'the £1,000 which William owes to me to Harriet' is a specific legacy. It follows that where a gift of money is not specific or demonstrative, it is general.

31.6   For the purposes of the Administration of Estates Act 1925, however, the expression 'pecuniary legacy' has a much wider significance. It is defined[1] to include a general legacy, an annuity, and a demonstrative legacy in so far as the gift is not discharged out of the designated property.

1   Section 55(1)(ix).

Residuary gift
31.7   This is what remains after the payment of all debts, liabilities, expenses and other legacies.

Devises
31.8   With regard to devises, it used to be said that all devises are specific.[1] This is no longer the case and devises may now be specific 'my freehold cottage The Nest, Swaffham, Suffolk to Isobel'; or general 'all my freehold land to Julie'; or residuary 'all my houses not otherwise disposed of by this my will to Kenneth'.

1   *Giles v Melsom* (1873) LR 6 HL 24 at 30; *Re Ridley, Nicholson v Nicholson* [1950] Ch 415 at 421.

31.9 As is shown below, certain consequences ensue from the classification of legacies. In order to modify those results, the testator is able to adopt his own classification, so that if he shows expressly or impliedly in the will that he intends a legacy to be treated as coming within a particular category, effect will be given to his intention. Thus, in *Re Compton, Vaughan v Smith*[1] the testator gave a gift of shares in a form which was clearly specific. He then included that legacy in the expression 'as general and not as specific legacies'. It was held that the legacy was, by virtue of these words, to be treated as general.

1 [1914] 2 Ch 119.

Importance of classification

31.10 The difficulty with this topic is that different classifications are relevant for different purposes, and it may be useful to summarise the position here in general terms. It is stressed that this summary is only in general terms and in many cases the rules themselves admit of certain exceptions.

(a) *Ademption.* This doctrine, considered above,[1] applies only to specific legacies.

(b) *Abatement.* The order of abatement is:[2] residuary gifts abate first, followed by pecuniary gifts (in the wide sense[3]) and, finally, specific legacies. A demonstrative legacy is treated as a specific legacy to the extent to which the fund on which it is charged exists but, to the extent that it does not, is treated as a pecuniary legacy.

(c) *Interest* is generally payable from death on specific legacies, but not normally on pecuniary legacies.[4]

(d) *Right of beneficiary to demand payment in lieu.* In the case of a general gift, the personal representatives are, in the absence of a contrary direction in the will, under an obligation either to purchase such item as is included in the gift if there is no article of that description in the estate, or to pay to the beneficiary that amount in lieu. In this case, the beneficiary is also entitled to interest on that sum at the rate of 6 per cent[5] from the expiration of the executor's year.[6] Where there is a capital deficiency, an annuitant has the right to demand a capital payment in lieu.[7]

1 See para 30.36.
2 See above, para 30.53.
3 As defined by Administration of Estates Act 1925, s 55(1)(ix), and see above, para 31.6.
4 See below, paras 31.31–31.42.
5 RSC (Amendment No 2) 1983, SI 1983/1181.
6 See below, para 31.32.
7 See below, paras 31.55–31.57.

Quantum of interest

Generally

31.11 Difficult problems sometimes arise where a testator has given property by will, and then subsequently in the same will attempts to cut down the extent of the gift. When a problem of this nature arises, it is necessary first to construe the provisions of the will. Thereafter it may be necessary to give effect to the provision in a manner different from that intended by the testator.

31.12 Suppose that the testator gives his residue to Mary for life, but with a provision that she can use the capital. Or suppose that he gives his residue to Mary outright, but with a provision that what still remains is to devolve on his children on the death of Mary. In such cases it is necessary first to establish whether the testator is in fact conferring upon Mary a life interest only, or whether he is conferring an absolute interest subject to an actual or purported restriction. There is no objection in law to giving a life interest coupled with a power of disposition over capital.[1] There is also no objection in law to giving a person an absolute interest subject to a condition that he pays out of that sum an amount which that person considers appropriate. So, where a testator left his total estate to his widow 'to use and distribute to my relatives in a reasonable manner' it was held[2] that the widow was absolutely entitled subject only to the obligation to distribute such amounts, if any, that she considered necessary to her nephew and niece, who were her relatives for this purpose.[3]

1 *Bradly v Westcott* (1807) 13 Ves 445; *Reith v Seymour* (1828) 4 Russ 263; *Nannock v Horton* (1802) 7 Ves 391; *Archibald v Wright* (1838) 9 Sim 161; *Scott v Josselyn* (1859) 26 Beav 174; *Pennock v Pennock* (1871) LR 13 Eq 144; *Re Keighley, Keighley v Keighley* [1919] 2 Ch 388. See also *Re Thorpe Estate* (1974) 6 Nfld & PEIR 419 (Newfoundland).
2 *Re Gunnis-Wood* (1974) 49 DLR (3d) 199 (Ontario).
3 *Earl of Coventry v Coventry* (1742) 2 Atk 366.

31.13 If, however, upon a true construction of the will the testator has given an absolute gift, and has then attempted to cut down the gift, the subsequent provision is void, as being repugnant to the nature of the absolute gift, and the gift takes effect without restriction.[1] Likewise, if the testator grants an absolute interest, and then makes a gift over in case the beneficiary dies intestate[2] or mentally ill[3] the gift over is void.

1 *Re Wilcocks' Settlement* (1875) 1 Ch D 229; *Re Ashton, Ballard v Ashton* [1920] 2 Ch 481. See also *Re Sutherland, Sutherland and Watt v Nurgitz* [1974] 5 WWR 764 (Manitoba) (gift of residue equally among the testator's children for their own use absolutely, followed by direction that shares of two of the children to be held in trust until they attained the age of 28. Held: earlier words an absolute gift, and subsequent words could not cut them down).
2 *Holmes v Godson* (1856) 8 De GM & G 152; *Barton v Barton* (1857) 3 K & J 512; *Re Babcock* (1892) 9 Gr 427; *Re Gee* (1973) 41 DLR (3d) 317 (British Columbia).
3 *Re Ashton, Ballard v Ashton* [1920] 2 Ch 481.

Gifts to spouses and then to issue

31.14 A special statutory rule applies in the case of a gift by the testator to his spouse. If the testator gives property to his spouse in terms which, by themselves, would give the spouse an absolute interest, and he purports to give his issue an interest in the same property, the gift takes effect as an absolute interest to the spouse.[1] This is so only where the purported gift to the issue is in the same instrument as the gift to the spouse, and where there is no contrary intention.[2] This provision has been considered in more detail above.[3]

1 Administration of Justice Act 1982, s 22.
2 Ibid.
3 See para 11.53.

Acceleration

The general rule

31.15 The doctrine of acceleration applies to the case where interests are conferred in succession – such as to husband for life, with remainder to his brother – and for some reason the gift to the first person entitled determines before the time envisaged by the testator. This may be because the first person entitled dies, or because he disclaims his life interest, or because he witnessed the will, or because it was revoked by codicil, or for any other reason. The principle of acceleration regards the interest of the next person entitled as being the whole interest in the asset or property subject to the prior right of the first person entitled so that when it appears that the first person cannot take, the next person's interest is at once accelerated. So in *Re Davies, Davies v Mackintosh*[1] there was a gift to A for life with remainder to his issue. When A disclaimed, Vaisey J held that the gift to the issue was accelerated. Likewise, in *Jull v Jacobs*,[2] where there was a gift to A for life, with remainder to the children of A, and A could not take because she witnessed the will, Malins VC held that the children's interest was accelerated.

1 [1957] 3 All ER 52.
2 (1876) 3 Ch D 703.

31.16 In some circumstances the interest of the remaindermen may not be vested absolutely, but vested subject to divesting, eg to A for life, with remainder to B, but if C shall have a child, then to that child. If A is unable to take, the interest of B will be accelerated, and he will be entitled to the income, but distribution of the capital must be delayed until it is known whether C will have a child.[1]

1 *Re Taylor, Lloyds Bank Ltd v Jones* [1957] 3 All ER 56.

Acceleration prevented

31.17 The words of the will may suggest that the interest of the remainderman is to take effect at a specified time in the future. If, on a true construction, this is what the testator intended, acceleration will be prevented. Thus, if the testator makes a gift to A until 1999, and in 1999 to B, this will probably be construed as meaning that B can take no benefit until 1999. If A cannot take, the income of the property will belong to the residuary beneficiary until 1999.

31.18   The courts are, however, very reluctant to adopt a construction which prevents the acceleration of the remainderman's interest. If, therefore, there is a gift to A for life and after A's death to B, the words 'after A's death' will be treated, in the absence of a clear contrary expression, as meaning 'after the termination of A's interest'. So that if, for example, A disclaims, B's interest is accelerated.[1] This approach is an exception to the general rule of construction that words carry their natural meaning.

1   *Re Flower's Settlement Trusts* [1957] 1 All ER 462.

Acceleration and class gifts

31.19   Suppose the gift is to A for life with remainder to such of his children who attain the age of 21. If A enjoys the property until his death, the class will then close, to admit all children then alive who do in fact attain 21.[1] But now suppose that in his lifetime A disclaims and has children after the disclaimer: are those after-born children excluded from the class? In *Re Davies, Davies v Mackintosh*[2] Vaisey J held, on similar facts, that the interest of the class was accelerated, and that the closing rules should be applied as at the date of disclaimer to exclude after-born children.[3] However, in *Re Kebty-Fletcher's Will Trusts*[4] Stamp J doubted whether *Re Davies, Davies v Mackintosh* was correctly decided, and refused to follow it in the case of a disclaimer of the prior interest. Children born during the lifetime of A were held entitled to be members of the class.

1   See above, para 11.39(d).
2   [1957] 3 All ER 52.
3   See also *Jull v Jacobs* (1876) 3 Ch D 703; *Re Townsend's Estate* (1886) 34 Ch D 357.
4   [1969] 1 Ch 339.

31.20   The doubts expressed as to the correctness of *Re Davies* were reinforced when, in *Re Harker's Will Trusts, Kean v Harker*,[1] Goff J refused to follow *Re Davies*. A fund was held upon trust for a father for life, with remainder to the children who should attain 21. During his lifetime he surrendered his interest in the fund to his children. At that time, he had one son over 21 and two under that age. The eldest son claimed that the class-closing rule applied as soon as the father's interest was surrendered, so that his share of the fund could be distributed forthwith. Goff J rejected this, and held that the class remained open until the death of the father. The basis of his decision[2] is that it would be wrong to allow one person by his unilateral act to defeat the interest of others, or, as applied to these facts, that the father by the deed of release should be able to defeat the interest of children born after the execution of the deed.[3]

1   [1969] 3 All ER 1.
2   Ibid, at 4.
3   *Packham v Gregory* (1845) 4 Hare 396; *Re Jobson, Jobson v Richardson* (1889) 44 Ch D 154.

Future entitlement

31.21 A problem which is similar to that of acceleration sometimes arises where the will provides for a legacy to be paid at a future date. In *Re Cohn, National Westminster Bank Ltd v Cohn*[1] the testator made his will at a time when his son and his grandson were both living. By his will the testator gave a life interest to his son, and provided that if on the death of the son the grandson had attained the age of 25, a capital sum should be paid to him. The grandson reached the age of 25, but predeceased the son. In general, where a legacy is given with a direction for payment at a future date, and no immediate interest is given, the gift is treated as being contingent on the recipient being alive on the date for payment.[2] In this case, however, it was apparent from the will that the payment of the legacy was postponed only to enable the prior life interest to be given to the son. Accordingly, the grandson acquired a vested interest when he attained the age of 25, although enjoyment was postponed, and the grandson's estate therefore took on the death of the son.

1 [1974] 3 All ER 928, CA.
2 See also *Re Scott, Widdows v Friends of the Clergy Corpn* [1975] 2 All ER 1033; above, para 12.53.

Administrative powers affecting beneficial entitlement

31.22 In some circumstances, the acts of the personal representatives in the administration of the estate can affect beneficial entitlement. In these cases, the beneficiaries are entitled to insist that the result of the personal representatives' action is fair to all beneficiaries affected. This is illustrated by the decision in *Fenton v Whittier*.[1] In that case the testatrix left pecuniary legacies of $C3,000 'or stock to that amount'. She then left 'all the other shares to Helen Hopkins', and her residue to other beneficiaries. If the legacies were paid entirely in the form of stock, Helen Hopkins would suffer, but if they were paid entirely in cash, the residuary beneficiaries would suffer. The Nova Scotia court held that in order to treat Helen Hopkins on the one hand and the residuary beneficiaries on the other hand fairly, the executors should pay the legacies as to $C1,500 from cash and $C1,500 from stock.

1 (1977) 26 NSR (2d) 662 (Nova Scotia).

31.23 The position of the beneficiaries may also be affected by the speed with which the personal representatives administer the estate, particularly where the values of assets change after the date of death. Where assets are appropriated,[1] they are appropriated at their value at the date of appropriation, but in order to determine entitlement values are generally taken as at the date of death. However, in *Re Udd*[2] the general approach adopted in the case of appropriation was followed. In that case the testator left certain legacies, but only if his net estate was at least $C500,000. At the date of death it was under $C500,000, but the property appreciated in value during the course of the administration of the estate. It was held that the test to be applied was whether the net estate was worth more than $C500,000 at the date at which the executors could realise all the assets of the estate.

1 Either under the general power of appropriation (below, paras 31.1–33.5) or in the case of the appropriation of the matrimonial home to the surviving spouse under the intestacy rules (above, paras 12.16–12.22).
2 (1978) 84 DLR (3d) 606.

Time for payment

Legacies

31.24 The period of one year from the testator's death is known as the executor's year. During this year the executor must ascertain the assets and liabilities of the deceased, so that he can make arrangements for the discharge of liabilities and the distribution of the remainder of the estate.[1] Although this does not mean that the estate must be fully administered by the end of that year – this may be impossible because of complications affecting the assets, or difficulty in the construction of the will – the converse is true, namely that a beneficiary cannot compel the representative to make payment before the end of that year. Accordingly, any direction for payment at any time before the end of the year takes effect as if it were a direction to pay at the end of the year. So, in *Brooke v Lewis*[2] the testator directed certain legacies to be paid within six months from his death, and directed the residue to be divided among such of certain named persons who were living at the time of distribution. If the obligation to distribute arose at the expiration of six months from death, the persons living at that time would have taken the residue. It was held, however, that only those living at the end of the year from death were entitled, as that was the time when the obligation came into force.[3]

1 *Garthshore v Chalie* (1804) 10 Ves 1; *Re Tankard, Tankard v Midland Bank Executor and Trustee Co Ltd* [1942] Ch 69.
2 (1822) 6 Madd 358.
3 See also *Benson v Maude* (1821) 6 Madd 15.

31.25 This rule is expressed in the Administration of Estates Act 1925, s 44, which provides that 'a personal representative is not bound to distribute the estate of the deceased before the expiration of one year from the death'. This is, however, subject to sub-s 36(10). It is explained towards the end of this chapter that a personal representative may transfer to a beneficiary real and leasehold property by means of an assent, and that he may require the beneficiary to give security for outstanding liabilities before giving the assent. Sub-section 36(10), however, provides that a personal representative must not delay in giving an assent to the person entitled where reasonable arrangements have been made for discharging the liabilities. Subject to this exception, personal representatives cannot be compelled to make payment before the end of the executor's year, although they may do so if they so wish.[1] Where a claim may be made under the family provision legislation,[2] it may well be inadvisable to distribute much of the estate too early.[3]

1 *Pearson v Pearson* (1802) 1 Sch & Lef 10; *Angerstein v Martin* (1823) Turn & R 232; *Garthshore v Chalie* (1804) 10 Ves 1.
2 *Re Simson, Simson v National Provincial Bank Ltd* [1950] Ch 38.
3 See above, paras 14.95–14.98.

Potential applications

31.26 Personal representatives may be liable[1] if they distribute the assets in a manner which is proper at the time of distribution, but which becomes improper by virtue of a subsequent decision of the court. Personal representatives are, therefore, prudent, where the circumstances are appropriate, to wait until six months from the issue of a grant of representation in case there are applications:
(a) under the family provision legislation;[2] or
(b) to rectify the will;[3]
and where the death was caused by a criminal act on the part of a beneficiary, three months from the date of conviction in case the criminal-beneficiary applies to be relieved from the forfeiture of his interest.[4]

1 *Re Simson, Simson v National Provincial Bank Ltd* [1950] Ch 38.
2 See above, para 14.95.
3 Under s 20 of the Administration of Justice Act 1982; see above, para 5.59.
4 Under s 2 of the Forfeiture Act 1982; see above, para 30.72.

Annuities

31.27 The general rule applies to annuities left by will, so that the first sum becomes payable at the end of the executor's year.[1] Some problems can arise with regard to the calculation of the first payment. The rules are as follows.
(a) In the absence of a contrary direction in the will, annuities commence at death and are payable yearly in arrear. Accordingly, the first payment made at the end of the executor's year is in respect of the year from the testator's death.
(b) Accordingly, if without further direction there is a gift in the will of an annuity of £520 pa to Alfred, the first payment he receives is of £520 at the end of one year.
(c) If the annuity is directed to commence at some date within the executor's year, the calculation is made from the date directed, although payment need not be made until the end of the year. Thus, if there is a gift by will of a testator dying on 1 January of an annuity of £520 to Bertie, to be payable three-monthly to commence three months after death, the first payment which becomes due is in respect of the period 1 April to 30 June. The executors may pay then, or they may defer payment until 1 January in the following year, when a total of £390 will be due.[2]

1 *Re Friend, Friend v Young (No 2)* (1898) 78 LT 222.
2 *Houghton v Franklin* (1823) 1 Sim & St 390; *Byrne v Healy* (1828) 2 Mol 94; *Irvin v Ironmonger* (1831) 2 Russ & M 531; *Williams v Wilson* (1865) 5 New Rep 267.

Premature entitlement

31.28 Although the will may specify a future date at which a beneficiary will become entitled,[1] under the rule in *Saunders v Vautier*[2] beneficiaries can call for their legacies before the date specified in the will if (a) the beneficiaries are sui juris (and so are able to make an effective demand) and (b) no other person can take any beneficial interest in any circumstances. Under *Saunders v Vautier* itself, a trustee held a sum of money upon trust to accumulate the income until a specified date, and then to pay it to a beneficiary. The beneficiary reached the age of 21, and so became sui juris, before the date specified for distribution. He successfully claimed that the capital and accumulated income to date should be paid over to him.[3]

1 See below, para 31.37.
2 (1841) Cr & Ph 240.
3 See also *Josselyn v Josselyn* (1837) 9 Sim 63; *Gosling v Gosling* (1859) John 265; *Wharton v Masterman* [1895] AC 186; *Re Johnston, Mills v Johnston* [1894] 3 Ch 204; *Re Smith, Public Trustee v Aspinall* [1928] Ch 915; *Re Lord Nunburnholme, Wilson v Nunburnholme* [1911] 2 Ch 510; *Berry v Geen* [1938] AC 575.

Interest and income

Distinction

31.29 This section is concerned with the extent to which a beneficiary is entitled to receive income from an asset between the date of death and the date when it is actually transferred to him; and the extent to which a pecuniary legatee is entitled to receive interest on his legacy during that period. Interest is a calculation, usually at 6 per cent, on the amount of the legacy, and, where the legatee is entitled to interest, it is payable whether or not the estate actually receives any income. Income is the actual income produced by an asset, and is payable only to the extent that it is so earned. The rules are complicated, and it is necessary to consider each type of gift.

Gifts of realty

31.30 The testator can make a gift of the income produced by any asset, including realty, from the date of death to the date of transfer. He could, for example, give land to Angela, but direct that the income derived from it during the course of administration should belong to the residuary beneficiary. Subject to this, and to any other contrary direction in the will, the person entitled to realty is entitled also to the income which it produces from the date of death. This applies whether the gift is specific or residuary,[1] and whether the gift is vested or contingent.[2]

1 Law of Property Act 1925, s 175(1).
2 Ibid.

Specific gifts of personalty

31.31 A specific gift of personalty also carries with it the income which the asset produces, subject to any direction in the will to the contrary. This is so whether the gifts is vested[1] or contingent,[2] and whether it is a present or future gift.[3] The rule is not confined to income in the accounting sense, and includes any accretion derived from the asset. Thus, if there is a specific gift of shares, the beneficiary is entitled not only to the shares themselves, and to the dividends,[4] but also to any bonus and rights issues.[5]

1 *Barrington v Tristram* (1801) 6 Ves 345; *Bristow v Bristow* (1842) 5 Beav 289; *Re Marten, Shaw v Marten* [1901] 1 Ch 370; *Re Jacob, M'Coy v Jacob* [1919] 1 IR 134.
2 Law of Property Act 1925, s 175(1); *Sleech v Thorington* (1754) 2 Ves Sen 560; *Clive v Clive* (1854) Kay 600.
3 Ibid, s 175(1).
4 *Re Joel, Johnson v Joel* [1936] 2 All ER 962.
5 *Re Edwards, Newberry v Edwards* [1918] 1 Ch 142; *Re Bate, Public Trustee v Bate* [1938] 4 All ER 218.

General and demonstrative legacies

The principle
31.32 It is necessary to draw a distinction between two periods of time. The first is the period of one year from the date of death, when, generally, interest is not payable on general and demonstrative legacies.[1] The second period is that following the first year from the death, in which interest is generally payable. A legacy is normally payable at the end of the executor's year[2] and interest becomes due from the end of that year in order to compensate the beneficiary for failure to pay him the legacy by the due date. The right to interest is, therefore, not treated as an example of the testator's bounty, but as a question of fairness.[3] To this general principle there are numerous exceptions.

1 *Webster v Hale* (1803) 8 Ves 410; *Bourke v Ricketts* (1804) 10 Ves 330; *Wood v Penoyre* (1807) 13 Ves 325; *Marquis of Hertford v Lord Lowther* (1846) 9 Beav 266; *Re Lord's Estate, Lord v Lord* (1867) 2 Ch App 782.
2 See above, para 31.24.
3 *Re Wyles, Foster v Wyles* [1938] Ch 313; see below, para 31.48.

Exceptions
Interest is payable from death in the following cases.

31.33 *Legacy to child of testator.* Where the testator gives a legacy to his child, then, if certain conditions are satisfied, the law assumes that the legacy was intended for the maintenance of the child, and it will carry interest from the date of death. The conditions are:
(a) the legacy is given to the child of the testator, or to some other child to whom he stood in loco parentis;[1]
(b) the child is a minor;[2]
(c) the child is entitled to the legacy either upon attaining the age of 18, or marrying under that age;[3]
(d) the legacy is expressed to be payable to the child, and not to others, such as trustees, on his behalf;[4]
(e) the will contains no other provision for his maintenance.
Subject to these conditions being satisfied, the legacy will carry interest from death, even if it is contingent.

1 *Wilson v Maddison* (1843) 2 Y & C Ch Cas 372.

31.34 *Extent of benefit*

2 *Raven v Waite* (1818) 1 Swan 553; *Wall v Wall* (1847) 15 Sim 513.
3 *Re Pollock, Pugsley v Pollock* [1943] Ch 338.
4 *Re Medlock, Ruffle v Medlock* (1886) 55 LJ Ch 738; *Re Pollock, Pugsley v Pollock* [1943] Ch 338.

31.34 *Legacy for maintenance of other children.* Where the testator gives a legacy to a child not falling within paragraph 33, but he shows an intention that the legacy should be used for the maintenance of that child, the legacy will carry interest from the date of death.[1]

1 See *Re Hardgrave* [1978] Qd R 471 (Queensland). (The testator directed the executors to pay to his grand-daughter Robyn one sixth of his net estate if and when she should attain the age of 25. He also conferred on the executors power to pay or apply the income and up to one half of the capital for the maintenance, education, benefit or advancement in life of Robyn. The court held that by conferring a power to maintain, the testator had shown an intention that the legacy should carry interest until Robyn attained the age of 18; but that she was not entitled to interest between the ages of 18 and 25.)

31.35 *Legacy in satisfaction of debt.* It was said in *Clark v Sewell*[1] that where the legacy is in satisfaction of a debt, interest is always followed from death. While this is clearly fair if the debt was payable at death, the rule may not apply if the debt itself was interest free and not payable until some time after death.

1 (1744) 3 Atk 96.

31.36 *Legacy charged on realty.* This exception applies only where the legacy is charged on realty, and not merely on land which is regarded as converted into personalty under a trust for sale.[1] The legacy bears interest from death.

1 *Pearson v Pearson* (1802) 1 Sch & Lef 10; cf *Turner v Buck* (1874) LR 18 Eq 301.

Future legacies

31.37 A legacy might not be payable until some future date, either because the will is worded to that effect, or because the nature of the property makes it impracticable to make the payments earlier. Where the will expressly provides that the legacy is not to be payable until some future date, interest runs only from that date. This is so whether a particular date is specified,[1] or whether the legacy is to be payable only if an event occurs.[2] It is generally considered that if the will specifies that the legacy is to be payable only upon the happening of an event, and that event actually occurs before the death of the testator, then the legacy is treated as an ordinary legacy, and interest is payable from the end of the executor's year.[3]

1 *Thomas v A-G* (1837) 2 Y & C Ex 525; *Donovan v Needham* (1846) 9 Beav 164; *Re Gyles, Gibbon v Chaytor* [1907] 1 IR 65; *Re White, White v Shenton* (1909) 101 LT 780.
2 *Holmes v Crispe* (1849) 18 LJ Ch 439; *Re Lord's Estate, Lord v Lord* (1867) 2 Ch App 782.
3 *Re Palfreeman, Public Trustee v Palfreeman* [1914] 1 Ch 877; cf *Pickwick v Gibbes* (1839) 1 Beav 271; *Coventry v Higgins* (1844) 14 Sim 30.

31.38 Where payment is delayed because of the nature of the assets, different considerations apply. Suppose, for example, that the only asset out of which the legacy can be paid is a reversionary interest, and that it is not

practicable to realise the asset before it falls into possession. In general, the
ordinary rule applies, so that the interest is payable from the end of the
executor's year.[1] The beneficiary is not to suffer because of the form of the
assets. However, this is subject to the rule that the testator may show a
contrary intention, and if in fact he indicates that the legacy is not to be
payable until the asset falls in, interest runs only from that date.[2]

1   *Re Blachford, Blachford v Worsley* (1884) 27 Ch D 676.
2   *Holmes v Crispe* (1849) 18 LJ Ch 439; *Re Lord's Estate, Lord v Lord* (1867) 2 Ch App 782.

Contingent legacies

31.39   It has been shown[1] that in the case of *specific* bequests, the rules are
the same whether the gift is vested or contingent. This is not so with general
legacies. In general, a contingent general legacy does not carry interest until
the contingency has happened.[2] This is, however, subject to a contrary
intention on the part of the testator, and such a contrary intention will be
assumed if the testator directs the legacy to be set aside for the benefit of the
legatee. In that case, the general rule applies.[3]

1   See above, paras 31.30 and 31.31.
2   *Wyndham v Wyndham* (1789) 3 Bro CC 58; *Rawlins v Rawlins* (1796) 2 Cox Eq Cas 425; *Re
    George* (1877) 5 Ch D 837; *Re Dickson, Hill v Grant* (1885) 29 Ch D 331; *Re Inman, Inman
    v Rolls* [1893] 3 Ch 518.
3   *Kidman v Kidman* (1871) 40 LJ Ch 359; *Re Medlock, Ruffle v Medlock* (1886) 55 LJ Ch 738;
    Re Inman, Inman v Rolls [1893] 3 Ch 518; *Re Clements, Clements v Pearsall* [1894] 1 Ch 665;
    Re Snaith, Snaith v Snaith (1894) 71 LT 318; *Re Woodin, Woodin v Glass* [1895] 2 Ch 309.

Vested legacies subject to divesting

31.40   Where a legacy is vested, but is subject to divesting, the legatee is
entitled to interest in accordance with the ordinary rules until the defeasance
occurs.[1]

1   *Re Buckley's Trusts* (1883) 22 Ch D 583.

Contrary intention

31.41   The rules so far discussed are subject to contrary directions by the
testator. So, if the testator directs that a legacy shall be paid on a specific
date, even although it is in the executor's year, interest runs from that date.[1]
But very clear evidence of intention that interest should run from a date
earlier than the end of the executor's year is required. Thus, interest will run
only from the end of that year even if the legacy is directed to be paid 'as
soon as possible', and there are funds available to pay it.[2]

1   *Harrison v Rhodes* (1753) 1 Lee 197; *Lord Londesborough v Somerville* (1854) 19 Beav 295;
    Re Pollock, Pugsley v Pollock [1943] Ch 338.
2   *Webster v Hale* (1803) 8 Ves 410; *Benson v Maude* (1821) 6 Madd 15.

31.42   The testator may also indicate his intention that interest is not to be
paid on ordinary pecuniary legacies from the end of the executor's year. In
Re Robinson[1] the testator said in his will that the executors *need* not pay
interest. The court held that although, owing to a lack of funds in the estate,
the legacies were not paid for five years from the date of death, the legatees
were not entitled to interest.

1   (1975) 14 NSR (2d) 340 (Nova Scotia).

Residuary gifts of personalty

Vested gifts
31.43 A residuary beneficiary with a vested interest is not entitled to interest, but he is entitled to the actual income produced by the estate, to which no other legatee is entitled.

Contingent gifts
31.44 In general, a contingent gift of personalty, or of realty and personalty, carries the intermediate income,[1] and it has been shown that this is also the case where there is a contingent residuary gift of realty.[2] However, the residuary beneficiary is not entitled to the income arising after the expiration of a trust for accumulation.[3] In this case, the income is undisposed of, and devolves as on intestacy.

1 *Re Dumble, Williams v Murrell* (1883) 23 Ch D 360; *Re Burton's Will, Banks v Heaven* [1892] 2 Ch 38; *Re Taylor, Smart v Taylor* [1901] 2 Ch 134; *Re Mellor, Alvarez v Dodgson* [1922] 1 Ch 312.
2 See above, para 31.30.
3 *Re Ransome's Will Trusts, Moberly v Ransome* [1957] Ch 348.

Future gifts
31.45 A future gift of residue does not, in principle, carry the intermediate income,[1] so that, unless the income is disposed of by the will, it is undisposed of, and passes as on intestacy.[2]

1 *Bective v Hodgson* (1864) 10 HL Cas 656.
2 *Re Gillett's Will Trusts, Barclays Bank Ltd v Gillett* [1950] Ch 102; *Re Geering, Gulliver v Geering* [1964] Ch 136.

Annuities

31.46 In principle, an annuity is a series of legacies,[1] and as interest is paid on legacies which are overdue, it would appear that it ought to be paid on overdue annuity payments. However, in *Re Hiscoe, Hiscoe v Waite*[2] Kekewich J, after reviewing the authorities, held that interest on annuity payments was only to be paid in exceptional circumstances, and this was followed by the Court of Appeal in *Re Berkeley, Inglis v Countess of Berkeley*,[3] although at first instance Cross J observed[4] that whatever the reason may have been for preventing the payment of interest, 'it no longer obtains, and the rule is one that I at least would be glad to see swept away by the Law Commission in some tidying up operation'. An example of an exceptional circumstance in which interest is payable is where the non-payment of the annuity is due to the fault of the person entitled to the surplus income.[5]

1 Per Cross J in *Re Berkeley, Inglis v Countess of Berkeley* [1967] 3 All ER 170 at 176.
2 (1902) 71 LJ Ch 347; see at 349–351.
3 [1968] Ch 744, [1968] 3 All ER 364.
4 [1967] 3 All ER 170 at 177.
5 Ibid.

Ancillary aspects

Rate of interest

31.47 Where interest is payable, it is normally calculated at the rate of 6 per cent per annum.[1] Where, however, the testator is the parent of the beneficiary, or stands in loco parentis to him, the rate of interest, which is payable from the date of death, is 5 per cent per annum.[2] Only simple, not compound, interest is payable on legacies.

1 RSC Ord 44, r 10. The rate was increased from 5 per cent by RSC (Amendment No 2) 1983, SI 1983/1181, which became operative on 1 October 1983.
2 Trustee Act 1925, s 31(3): 5 per cent 'subject to any rules of the court to the contrary'. RSC Ord 44, r 10 – see preceding footnote – does not apply.

The nature of the right to interest

31.48 In *Re Wyles, Foster v Wyles*[1] Farwell J was concerned with the nature of the right to interest. In that case the testator gave various legacies, including legacies to two nephews, but he included in his will a provision that if the estate should not be sufficient, the legacies to the nephews should abate before the other legacies. The judge said[2] that interest 'is a sum given in the course of administration to the legatee because justice requires that owing to the failure to pay his legacy in due time he should be put in the position which he would have been had it been so paid'. He therefore held that while the legacies themselves abated, the interest did not. The result is, however, curious. Interest is intended to compensate the legatee for late payment. The effect of *Re Wyles* is that the legatee is compensated at a rate appropriate to a larger sum than that to which, in the circumstances, he is entitled.

1 [1938] Ch 313.
2 Ibid, at 316.

Treatment of payments on account

31.49 Subject to any direction in the will, where a payment is made to a beneficiary on account of his entitlement to a legacy and to interest on it, the beneficiary may treat the sum paid as interest, to the extent of his entitlement to interest, leaving the whole or part of the legacy itself outstanding.[1] Or, he may treat it, pro tanto, as satisfying the legacy, leaving the claim for interest outstanding. He will be guided largely by income tax considerations in making his choice, for he will be taxable in the interest, but not on the legacy itself.[2]

1 *Re Prince, Hardman v Willis* (1935) 51 TLR 526; *Re Morley's Estate, Hollenden v Morley* [1937] Ch 491 (the will gave 922 legacies).
2 See below, para 36.19.

Expenses of property specifically given

31.50 Just as a specific beneficiary is entitled, generally, to the actual income produced from the asset, so he must suffer the expenses in respect of it. This is considered later.[1]

1 See below, para 31.76.

Annuities

Nature

31.51 An annuity is a periodic payment. It may either be secured on land, in which case it is known as a rentcharge, or secured on other property or unsecured, in which case it is known as an annuity. The Administration of Estates Act 1925, s 55(1)(ix), defines 'pecuniary legacy' to include an annuity, so that the general rules previously mentioned with regard to pecuniary legacies apply also to annuities. Two special problems, however, arise with regard to annuities:

(a)   the circumstances in which the annuitant is entitled to payment of a capital sum in lieu of the annuity;

(b)   the extent to which annuities abate for the payment of debts.

Capital sum in lieu

31.52 In general, an annuitant is not entitled to a capital sum in lieu of his annuity.[1] The will may give the annuitant the right to take a capital sum in lieu of the annuity, but even if it does not, the annuitant has this right in two other circumstances:

(a)   where the will directs the personal representatives to purchase an annuity for him; and

(b)   where there is insufficient capital, after payment of other legacies, to secure his annuity.

1   This is because the testator intended that he should receive annual payments.

Direction in will to purchase

31.53 If the will sets aside a capital sum to be used for the purchase of an annuity, the beneficiary has the option either to take that sum[1] or to have it applied in the purchase of an annuity, usually from an insurance company.[2] Although in many cases annuities purchased from an insurance company have taxation advantages, in that part of the payment is regarded as capital, and so is received by the annuitant free of tax,[3] this advantage does not apply in the case of an annuity purchased pursuant to a direction in a will.[4] Accordingly, where a will is being prepared, it is preferable from the tax point of view to leave the annuitant a lump sum. If he chooses to purchase an annuity with it, he will then obtain the tax relief just described.

1   *Re Robbins, Robbins v Legge* [1907] 2 Ch 8; *Re Brunning, Gammon v Dale* [1909] 1 Ch 276.
2   Formerly where there was a direction to purchase an annuity, without giving the personal representatives power to purchase from a public company, they were compelled to purchase an annuity from the government. Since 1962 it has not been possible to purchase government annuities, but the tables are still used for the purposes of calculating the capital value of a spouse's life interest arising on an intestacy under Administration of Estates Act 1925, s 47A: see above, para 12.14.
3   *IRC v Lady Castlemaine* [1943] 2 All ER 471.
4   Income and Corporation Taxes Act 1988, s 656.

31.54 If the testator gives a sum for the purchase of an annuity, and then adds to it a direction that an annuity must be purchased, and the annuitant is not entitled to its value, it seems that notwithstanding that provision the annuitant is entitled to the capital sum.[1] The explanation given is that the subsequent restriction is inconsistent with the gift itself.[2] On the other hand, where another person is entitled to the annuity upon the happening of a particular event, the annuitant is not entitled to the capital sum. For example, if the will provides that the annuity shall go to another if the annuitant assigns or charges his annuity, that provision is effective to prevent him claiming the capital sum.[3] The distinction between these two situations is very fine. It has even been held that if the annuitant dies before the annuity has been purchased, then the capital sum forms part of the annuitant's estate.[4]

1 *Stokes v Cheek* (1860) 28 Beav 620; *Re Nunn's Trusts* (1875) LR 19 Eq 331; *Hunt-Foulston v Furber* (1876) 3 Ch D 285.
2 *Re Mabbett, Pitman v Holborrow* [1891] 1 Ch 707 at 713.
3 *Power v Hayne* (1869) LR 8 Eq 262; *Re Draper* (1888) 57 LJ Ch 942; *Roper v Roper* (1876) 3 Ch D 714; *Re Thomas, Public Trustee v Falconer* [1946] Ch 36.
4 *Re Draper* (1888) 57 LJ Ch 942.

Insufficient capital to secure

31.55 An annuitant is entitled to demand that his interest is protected.[1] This is done by setting aside a sufficient part of the capital of the estate to provide adequate income to meet the annuity. There can, of course, be no absolute assurance that the capital set aside will be sufficient and, if there is a deficiency, the annuitant would be entitled to have recourse to the remainder of the residue.[2] In general, therefore, the personal representatives should not distribute the whole of the remainder of the residue even where a fund has been set aside for the payment of the annuity. If they wish to distribute, the personal representatives must either rely upon a provision in the will that upon a sum being set aside the residue is exonerated,[3] a clause which many well-drawn wills contain, or alternatively make an application to the court.

1 *May v Bennett* (1826) 1 Russ 370; *Boyd v Buckle* (1840) 10 Sim 595.
2 *May v Bennett* (1826) 1 Russ 370; *Mills v Drewitt* (1855) 20 Beav 632; *Ingleman v Worthington* (1855) 25 LJ Ch 46; *Carmichael v Gee* (1880) 5 App Cas 588.
3 *Baker v Baker* (1858) 6 HL Cas 616; *Michell v Wilton* (1875) LR 20 Eq 269.

31.56 The rule that the annuitant may require part of the capital to be set aside is one of convenience only. It must be remembered that unless there is a direction in the will to the contrary, an annuitant is entitled to have any deficiency of income made up from capital, though this has taxation disadvantages.[1] The position was reviewed by the Court of Appeal in *Re Hill, Westminster Bank Ltd v Wilson*.[2] In that case a number of pecuniary legacies were given, together with several annuities. At the outset there was insufficient capital for all pecuniary legacies to be paid in full and for sums to be set aside for the annuities, although there was no commercial risk that the annuities would not be paid in full. As soon as even the smallest of the annuities ceased to be payable, the income of the residue would have been sufficient to meet all the annuities. In the meantime, it was possible to resort to capital to the small degree necessary. At first instance Uthwatt J thought that the annuitants had a right to the capital sum, the rule[3] being a rule of law. This was reversed on appeal. In the Court of Appeal Lord Greene MR said that the rule:

'has obviously no application to a case like the present where it is plain that the available estate is more than sufficient to provide for the payment in full of the annuities out of income and capital as directed by the testator unless a series of events should transpire entirely outside the scope of human expectation, namely, the joint survival of all the annuitants for a period of time of impossible length having regard to their respective ages at the time when the matter is to be considered'.

1 See below, para 31.59.
2 [1944] Ch 270.
3 The rule that the annuitant is entitled to have a capital sum set aside. See *Re Cox, Public Trustee v Eve* [1938] Ch 556; see also *Wroughton v Colquhoun* (1847) 1 De G & Sm 357; *Re Cottrell, Buckland v Bedingfield* [1910] 1 Ch 402.

31.57 Where it cannot be said that there is no commercial risk of any insufficiency, the rule applies. The valuation of the annuity is made actuarially, disregarding risks which attach to the annuitant's occupation.[1] The capital value of an annuity will always be less than the capital sum needed to pay the annuity out of income. (£1,000 invested at 5 per cent will produce £50 pa; but to purchase an annuity of £50 pa the amount will depend on the age of the annuitant. It may be possible to purchase for, say, £400 an annuity of £50 pa if the annuitant is elderly.) It may be, then, that the capitalised value of the annuity, taken with the amount of the legacies, does not exceed the total value of the estate. In this case, legatees and annuitants are paid in full by capital sums, unless the will attaches conditions to the annuity, such as for its payment to another upon the happening of certain events, in which case another annuity will have to be purchased with the capitalised value. If the capitalised value of the annuity, and the amount of the legacies, exceed the value of the estate, they abate rateably.

1 *Re Bradberry, National Provincial Bank Ltd v Bradberry* and *Re Fry, Tasker v Gulliford*, both reported at [1943] Ch 35.

Capital sum by agreement
31.58 It is possible for the annuitant to take a capital sum if he can reach agreement with the residuary beneficiaries under the rule in *Saunders v Vautier*.[1] If all the residuary beneficiaries are not ascertained or are not sui juris, and the amount at issue is large enough, an application can be made to the court under the Variation of Trusts Act 1958. A capital sum is not subject to income tax.

1 (1841) Cr & Ph 240.

Annuities paid from capital

31.59 Periodic payments of income are subject to special rules of income tax. The person making the payment is in all cases obliged to pay or suffer tax on the fund from which the payment is made, and to make the payment to the recipient out of that taxed fund.[1] Suppose that £1,000 is invested at 10 per cent pa interest. The personal representatives receive each year £100 interest. They will pay tax on that at the basic rate of income tax for the time being in force. If this is 25 per cent they are left with a net sum of £75. Now suppose that they have to pay an annuity of £100 pa. In all cases they must pay the annuity subject to deduction of tax. In this case they pay over £75 to the annuitant. As this has come from a taxed fund, there are no further tax complications. Suppose, however, that on the same basic facts the annuity is £400 pa. The net sum to be paid to the annuitant is £300, being the annuity of £400 less tax thereon – which must be paid to the Revenue.[2] The executors will therefore have utilised £300 of the capital to make up the deficiency, so effectively attracting tax of £75 on a payment of capital. Accordingly, the capital of the residue is used at higher rate than that needed to make up the deficiency in income for the annuitant. For this reason, testators should be reluctant to include in their wills provisions directing any deficiency of income for an annuitant to be made up from capital.[3] The taxation liability on payments from capital must be taken into account when deciding whether there is any commercial risk of insufficiency for the purposes of *Re Hill, Westminster Bank Ltd v Wilson*.[4]

1 See below, paras 36.8–36.11.
2 Income and Corporation Taxes Act 1988, s 657(2)(c).
3 In some cases it is possible to prevent hardship to the annuitant by using the power of advancement where there is an income deficiency.
4 [1944] Ch 270.

Retention to cover future insufficiency

31.60 Where the testator makes provision for an annuity, he will usually charge that income on a particular fund, or on the residuary estate, leaving the surplus income elsewhere. In this case a problem arises where the personal representatives wish to retain the surplus income, and hold it against future deficits of capital. The personal representatives are entitled to retain the surplus income where they foresee a future deficiency. In doing so they will be withholding the income, but not accumulating it. It is not within the legislation regulating accumulations, so that there is no limit to the time for which it may be retained.[1]

1 *Re Berkeley, Inglis v Countess of Berkeley* [1968] Ch 744, [1968] 3 All ER 364.

Annuities 'tax-free'

31.61 When considering leaving an annuity, the testator may approach the problem from the size of the income of his estate, or from the needs of the beneficiary. If he adopts the former approach, and leaves an annuity of, say, £1,000 pa, income tax will be deducted from that sum at the basic rate in force for each year for which the annuity is paid. As the basic rate of tax fluctuates, the annuitant does not know the actual net amount which he will receive year by year. To counter this, the testator may wish to leave an annuity of, say, £1,000 pa 'free of tax', so that however the basic rate of tax might fluctuate, the annuitant is left with the net sum of £1,000. Generally, one may not make an agreement to make payments free of tax[1] but there is no objection to directing in a will or settlement that they shall be free of tax. The result is the same as if the testator had directed his personal representatives to pay an annuity of such sum as after the deduction of tax will amount to the specified amount. In this case the annuitant receives the payment free of tax at the basic rate, and if he pays higher rate income tax, he is entitled to recover from the personal representatives the tax at the higher rate which he has paid on the annuity. This increases still further the burden on the estate. If, however, the beneficiary is entitled to a repayment of income tax, perhaps because his total income is low, he must pay back to the personal representatives so much of that repayment as relates to the annuity.[2]

1 Taxes Management Act 1970, s 106(2).
2 *Re Pettit, Le Fevre v Pettit* [1922] 2 Ch 765; *Re Kingcome, Hickley v Kingcome* [1936] Ch 566.

31.62 The result is different if the testator expressly says that the annuity shall be of such a sum as after the deduction of income tax at the basic rate for the time being in force shall leave the specified sum. In this case the annuitant cannot claim his higher rate income tax from the estate, but on the other hand is not obliged to account for any repayment of tax which he receives.[1]

1 *Re Bates, Selmes v Bates* [1925] Ch 157.

Advantages of capital sum

31.63 From the point of view of the annuitant, it will almost always be in his interest to take a capital sum. In the first place, the amount which he receives is free of income tax,[1] whereas, as has just been shown, if he receives an annuity, the whole of the payments will be subject to tax. Furthermore, provided the annuitant receives the actuarial value of his annuity, he may himself purchase an annuity of the equivalent amount mentioned in the will, but if he purchases it, as distinct from the personal representatives purchasing it for him, he will be entitled to the special tax advantage under the Income and Corporation Taxes Act 1988, s 656.[2]

1 *IRC v Lady Castlemaine* [1943] 2 All ER 471.
2 See above, para 31.53.

31.64 It will also often be in the interest of the residuary beneficiaries for the annuitant to be paid a capital sum. Suppose that the annuitant is entitled to an annuity of £1,000 pa, and that the actuarial valuation of the annuity is £6,000. If the annuity is to be met from capital, £20,000 will have to be set aside, and subject to what was said above[1] the residue will have to be retained to meet any income deficiency. If the annuitant is paid a capital sum, he will receive £6,000. The balance of £14,000 can be paid forthwith to the residuary beneficiaries, and the remainder of the residue distributed.

1 See above, para 31.60.

Options

31.65 The testator may during his lifetime have granted to another an option to purchase a particular asset which is exercisable after his death, or he may in his will grant an option to a person to purchase an asset at less than its true value. Different considerations arise in these cases.

Option granted during testator's lifetime

31.66 When a binding contract for the sale of an asset is made, in the view of equity the asset in the hands of the vendor is converted into money.[1] The same principle applies where a binding contract comes into force following the exercise of an option. For general purposes, the vendor becomes under a binding obligation to sell at the time when the option is exercised[2] but for the purpose of the administration of estates, the conversion is regarded, illogically, as being retroactive to the date of the grant of the option. Unless there is a provision to the contrary in the option agreement, the option is exercisable notwithstanding the death of the grantor.[3]

1   *Lady Foliamb's Case* (1651) cited in *Daire v Beversham* (1661) Nels 76.
2   *Edwards v West* (1878) 7 Ch D 858.
3   *Laybutt v Amoco Australia Pty Ltd* (1974) 4 ALR 482 (High Court of Australia) where an option was equated with a conditional contract.

31.67 Suppose, therefore, that the testator during his lifetime grants an option to Andrew to purchase his house for £100,000, and dies having made a will leaving his realty to Rita and his personalty to Paul. If the option is exercised in the lifetime of Andrew, the house will be converted into personalty at that time, and the proceeds of sale will accrue to Paul even if the sale is not completed until after death. Where the option is exercised after death one would expect that as the house was not converted at the date of death, it would belong to Rita, so that in the event of the exercise of the option, she would be entitled to the proceeds of sale. The rule is, however, firmly established that for the purpose of deciding between respective beneficiaries the option, once exercised, is deemed to have caused conversion at the date of the grant of the option, that is, in the testator's lifetime, so that the proceeds of sale belong to the beneficiary entitled to personalty.

31.68 The rule was established in the leading case of *Lawes v Bennett*.[1] In 1758 the testator granted to his lessee an option to purchase the freehold reversion at any time before 29 September 1765. The testator died in 1763, leaving his realty to Bennett, and his personalty to Bennett and Lawes in equal shares. The option was exercised in February 1765. Kenyon MR held that when exercised, the option related back to the original agreement so that Lawes was entitled to half the proceeds of sale. The rule applies even where the option cannot be exercised before the death of the testator.[2]

1   (1785) 1 Cox Eq Cas 167.
2   *Re Isaacs, Isaacs v Reginall* [1894] 3 Ch 506.

31.69 Until the option is exercised, the person prima facie entitled to the asset under the will is entitled to the rents and profits.[1] Thus, on the facts of *Lawes v Bennett*,[2] Bennett, being entitled to the realty, would have been entitled to the rent from the date of death to the date of the exercise of the option.[3] The illogical result is that for the purpose of determining devolution of capital, the asset is deemed to be converted at the date of grant of the option, whereas for the purpose of determining entitlement to income, the asset is converted at the date of exercise of the option.

1 *Re Adams and Kensington Vestry* (1884) 27 Ch D 394.
2 (1785) 1 Cox Eq Cas 167.
3 In fact this point was not decided in *Lawes v Bennett* itself.

31.70 The rule in *Lawes v Bennett*[1] operates only to carry into effect the presumed intention of the testator, so that it will be excluded by contrary evidence in the will.[2] Although the rule applies in principle whether the option is granted before or after the making of the will, if the option was granted before the will, and the will contains a specific devise, that will point to an intention on the part of the testator that the devisee shall take either the property itself or its proceeds.[3] The rule will also be excluded where the will precedes the option, but contains a specific devise and is republished after the grant of the option.[4]

1 (1785) 1 Cox Eq Cas 167.
2 *Re Pyle, Pyle v Pyle* [1895] 1 Ch 724.
3 *Drant v Vause* (1842) 1 Y & C Ch Cas 580.
4 *Emuss v Smith* (1848) 2 De G & Sm 722.

31.71 The operation of the rule is not restricted to contests between the person entitled to realty on the one hand and the person entitled to personalty on the other hand, but it extends to contests between persons entitled to different types of personalty. In *Re Carrington, Ralphs v Swithenbank*[1] the testator bequeathed a holding of preference shares to A, and left his residuary personalty to B. Subsequently he granted an option to C to purchase those shares, the option to be exercised within one month of his death. The Court of Appeal applied the rule in *Lawes v Bennett* to hold that when exercised, the option became retroactive to the date of grant, so that B was entitled to the proceeds of sale. The decision is unpopular because the illogicality of the rule in *Lawes v Bennett* led to a general feeling that it should be restricted to options for the purchase of freeholds, and because the equitable doctrine of conversion is properly concerned with conversion between realty and personalty, and not with conversion of one class of personalty into another.[2] The decision has, however, been followed.

1 [1932] 1 Ch 1.
2 Hanbury (1933) 49 LQR 173.

Options granted by will

31.72 Where the option is granted by the will itself, no problem arises as long as the size of the estate is sufficient to pay all debts and legacies. In this case, the person entitled to the asset under the will takes it subject to the option, and if the option is exercised, that person becomes entitled to the proceeds of sale.

31.73 A problem does arise where the estate is not sufficiently large for the payment of all debts and legacies. Where the option is to purchase at less than the market value, the difference between the market value and the option price can be regarded as a gift. Nevertheless it was held in *Re Eve*[1] that this gift was not a specific gift, and, indeed, that it did not come within any of the paragraphs 1 to 6 in the First Schedule to the Administration of Estates Act.[2] The asset itself is available for the payment of debts, but only after all classes of assets within the Schedule have been exhausted. It has not yet been decided how the various types of assets available for the payment of debts which are not within the Schedule rank between themselves. It follows that to ascertain whether the estate is solvent, it is necessary to consider whether the purchase price payable under the option, and not the value of the asset itself, together with the other assets, is capable of meeting all the debts.

1 [1956] Ch 479.
2 See below, para 32.19.

31.74 If the testator grants an option by will, he may, instead of fixing the price at which the option is to be exercised, prescribe that the beneficiary shall have the option of purchasing at a 'reasonable valuation', or some similar expression. In this case the valuation will be made as at death if no other time for valuation is specified in the will, but in making this valuation account may also be taken of subsequent events. So, in *Talbot v Talbot* Harman LJ said:[1] 'that does not mean . . . that the valuers are to draw blinkers over their eyes or to shut their eyes to the fact that . . . the lands have very much increased in value since [the date of death]: they are entitled to say what, today, knowing what they do, and discounting back for the three years [since death], is the proper market value'. In any case, the person who is given the option is entitled to have the property valued before deciding whether to exercise the option. Harman LJ expressed the memorable principle: 'before we buy the pig, take it out of the poke'.

1 [1968] Ch 1 at 13.

31.75 It also follows that because of the rules as to abatement, it can be more advantageous to have an option at a fairly low price than to have a legacy.

Administration expenses in respect of specific assets

31.76 It has been shown that where an asset is specifically bequeathed, and produces income, the beneficiary is entitled to the income produced from the date of death of the testator, unless there is a provision in the will to the contrary.[1] The corollary to this is that where expenditure is incurred on the preservation and upkeep of property specifically bequeathed, those expenses are payable by the beneficiary, and not out of the general residue.[2] This principle, which applies whether or not the property is income producing, would cover expenditure for items such as storage and insurance. If, however, the beneficiary becomes specifically entitled only at some time later than the death of the testator, he is responsible for bearing the expenses only from the date when he becomes specifically entitled.[3] So, if an asset is appropriated by way of a share of residue, the liability for expenses would commence at the date of appropriation. And if there is a power to select items from the estate, the liability arises at the time of selection.

1 See above, para 31.31.
2 *Re Rooke, Jeans v Gatehouse* [1933] Ch 970.
3 *Re Collins's Settlement Trusts, Donne v Hewetson* [1971] 1 All ER 283.

Refunding legacies

31.77 In certain circumstances, a legatee may be compelled to refund his legacy, or a part of it, if further liabilities of the estate appear. These circumstances are:
(a) where the payment was made by the executor under the threat of proceedings;[1] and
(b) where the payment was made voluntarily, and at the time of payment the personal representatives had no notice of the debt.[2]
If the personal representatives pay the legacy with clear notice of the debt, they cannot recover from the legatee, and will be required to make good the deficiency from their own pockets.[3] Personal representatives are not prevented from recovering, however, if the liability was at the date of payment only a remote possibility. Where the personal representatives honestly make an overpayment, and they subsequently become due to make further payments, the overpayment may be adjusted from those further payments.[4] Unsatisfied creditors, and non-paid or under-paid legatees or next of kin also have rights against the legatees, but these rights are not considered in this book.[5]

1 *Newman v Barton* (1690) 2 Vern 205.
2 *Jervis v Wolferstan* (1874) LR 18 Eq 18 at 25; *Whittaker v Kershaw* (1890) 45 Ch D 320 at 325.
3 *Jervis v Wolferstan* (1874) LR 18 Eq 18.
4 *Livesey v Livesey* (1827) 3 Russ 287; *Dibbs v Goren* (1849) 11 Beav 483; *Re Horne, Wilson v Cox Sinclair* [1905] 1 Ch 76; *Re Ainsworth, Finch v Smith* [1915] 2 Ch 96.
5 Reference should be made to the standard books on equity.

CHAPTER 32

The incidence of debts and legacies

Introduction

32.1 This chapter is concerned with problems which arise in the course of the administration of a solvent estate. Suppose that the deceased bought a house on mortgage, and that the mortgage was outstanding at the date of his death. Is the person who takes the house under the will entitled to have the mortgage discharged out of the general estate, or does he have to take the property subject to the mortgage? Suppose again that the testator gave various legacies and left his residuary personalty to Andrew and his realty to Bernard. Are the legacies to be paid from the personalty only; or from both realty and personalty; and if from both, in what proportions? These questions most frequently affect the size of the benefit which the persons entitled to residue, or entitled to property which is undisposed of, take under the intestacy rules. It is convenient first to consider the position with regard to the payment of debts, and then to consider problems with regard to legacies. The debts considered are those outstanding at the date of death.[1] Debts properly incurred during the administration of the estate are administration expenses. Special rules, which are not considered in this book, govern the incidence of inheritance tax.

1 The moment of time at which a debt or liability arises is important. The liability in respect of inheritance tax arises immediately prior to death: Inheritance Tax Act 1984, s 4(1); see below, para 35.17. However, estate duty arose immediately after death, with the result that a direction in a will as to the incidence of debts did not affect estate duty: *Chase v La Barrie* (1972) 18 WIR 415 (West Indies Associated States).

32.2 At the outset, however, the reader is warned. The relevant parts of the Administration of Estates Act are drafted extremely badly, and the problems are legion. To describe the position as 'tortuous'[1] or 'notoriously obscure'[2] is to express it mildly. No part of this branch of the law warrants more the use of the cold towel.

1 Per Harman J in *Re Midgley, Barclays Bank Ltd v Midgley* [1955] Ch 576, [1955] 2 All ER 625.
2 Per Salt QC in *Re Taylor's Estate and Will Trusts* [1969] 2 Ch 245.

Debts charged on property

When the charge arises

32.3 In certain circumstances debts can, prior to the death of the deceased, be charged on specific assets, and the general principle is that where this is so, the beneficiary takes the asset subject to the liability to discharge the debt. The debt may be charged on the property in one of three situations:
(a) where it was charged under the old law, and that law still prevails;
(b) where the liability is an incident of the property itself; and
(c) where s 35 of the Administration of Estates Act applies.

Provisions of the old law
32.4 Before Locke King's Acts of 1854, 1867 and 1877, a devisee of land could generally require a mortgage debt to be paid off out of the general personal estate. However, this right applied only to mortgage debts which the testator had himself created[1] or which, if created by others, he had adopted, as by paying the interest, or making repayments of capital. Where the testator had not created or adopted the debt the devisee took the property subject to that liability,[2] and the devisee still takes such property subject to the liabilities. He does so as a result of the old general principle, and not as a result of s 35 of the Administration of Estates Act, which is considered below, but the circumstances in which this arises in practice are rare indeed. In certain other unusual circumstances, the general personal estate was not liable for the debts, and in these cases also the beneficiary under the will takes the assets subject to the burden of the debts.[3]

1 *Ibbetson v Ibbetson* (1841) 12 Sim 206; *Jenkinson v Harcourt* (1854) Kay 688; *Field v Moore* (1855) 7 De GM & G 691; *Re Anthony, Anthony v Anthony* [1893] 3 Ch 498.
2 *Perkins v Baynton* (1784) 1 Bro CC 375; *Noel v Lord Henley* (1819) 7 Price 241; *Scott v Beecher* (1820) 5 Madd 96; *Swainson v Swainson* (1856) 6 De GM & G 648; *Re Leeming* (1861) 3 De GF & J 43; *Hepworth v Hill* (1862) 30 Beav 476.
3 *Edwards v Freeman* (1727) 2 P Wms 435; *Lanoy v Athol* (1742) 2 Atk 444; *Graves v Hicks* (1833) 6 Sim 391; *Loosemore v Knapman* (1853) Kay 123.

Incidents of the property
32.5 A legatee of leasehold property takes the property subject to the burdens of the lease itself, which includes the liability to pay the rent.[1] This applies to all liabilities which arise from the relationship of landlord and tenant. But the executors may themselves also be liable to the landlord,[2] and, as has been seen,[3] they are entitled to insist on indemnities before transferring the property to the beneficiary.

1 *Eccles v Mills* [1898] AC 360; *Re Hughes, Ellis v Hughes* [1913] 2 Ch 491; *Re Day's Will Trusts* [1962] 3 All ER 699.
2 See above, paras 26.49–26.53 and 28.22–28.23.
3 See above, para 26.54.

Under section 35 of the Administration of Estates Act 1925
32.6 Section 35 of the 1925 Act, which replaces Locke King's Acts, applies to all property which at the time of the death of the deceased is charged with the payment of money. It provides that so far as beneficiaries claiming through the deceased are concerned, the property charged is primarily liable

for the payment of the debt. The section affects only the ultimate burden of the debt and it does not affect the position of the creditors, who are entitled to payment in any event.[1] If the amount of the debt is greater than the value of the asset, the beneficiary will take no benefit under the will, and the creditor will have a right of recourse against uncharged assets of the estate. The section does not affect the position of any beneficiary who takes otherwise than through the deceased: it does not, for example, affect the beneficiary who takes the property on the death of the deceased under a pre-existing trust.[2] And even where it does affect the beneficiary, it does not impose upon him any personal liability to discharge the debt.[3]

1 Administration of Estates Act 1925, s 35(2).
2 *Re Anthony, Anthony v Anthony* [1893] 3 Ch 498; *Re Ritson, Ritson v Ritson* [1899] 1 Ch 128; *Re Fison's Will Trusts, Fison v Fison* [1950] Ch 394.
3 *Syer v Gladstone* (1885) 30 Ch D 614.

Extent of charge under section 35

32.7 The section applies to any form of specific charge, whether legal or equitable. As well as a charge by way of legal mortgage, it applies to a rentcharge,[1] a local land charge which is registered,[2] and a charge which is registered in order to secure the payment of duty or tax.[3] An equitable mortgage is included,[4] as is any other form of equitable charge or lien.[5] It is probable, however, that the charge must be specific, and that a general charge, such as a banker's lien, is outside the scope of the section.[6]

1 *Re Fraser, Lowther v Fraser* [1904] 1 Ch 726.
2 *Re Hesketh, Saunders v Bibby Hesketh* (1900) 45 Sol Jo 11 (decided prior to the Land Charges Acts 1925 and 1972).
3 *Re Bowerman, Porter v Bowerman* [1908] 2 Ch 340.
4 *Pembrooke v Friend* (1860) 1 John & H 132; *Coleby v Coleby* (1866) LR 2 Eq 803; *Davis v Davis* (1876) 24 WR 962; *Re Hawkes, Reeve v Hawks* [1912] 2 Ch 251.
5 *Re Cockcroft, Broadbent v Groves* (1883) 24 Ch D 94; *Re Kidd, Brooman v Withall* [1894] 3 Ch 558; *Re Turner, Tennant v Turner* [1938] Ch 593.
6 *Re Dunlop, Dunlop v Dunlop* (1882) 21 Ch D 583.

32.8 The section applies only to the extent that the debt is charged on the property, even if other debts have been incurred in respect of the asset. The distinction is illustrated by *Re Birmingham, Savage v Stannard*.[1] The testatrix had contracted to purchase a house, but died before completing the purchase, and before paying the balance of the purchase money. Her estate therefore owned the equitable interest in the property, subject to the vendor's lien for unpaid purchase money. Shortly before her death, the testatrix executed a codicil giving the house to one person, and the residue of her estate to others. The person claiming the house had to discharge the vendor's lien, but the legal costs in connection with the purchase, which were only a simple contract debt, and not a charge on the property, were payable out of residue.

1 [1959] Ch 523.

32.9 It is sometimes necessary to consider carefully whether a debt is in fact charged. Where the testator carried on business in unincorporated form, and bequeathed the business to a beneficiary, one might for general purposes regard the 'business' as an entity consisting of the goodwill, stock and other assets on the one hand, but subject to the debts on the other hand. However, the debts are not by their nature charged on the assets of the business, so that, unless there is an effective expression of contrary intention,[1] the beneficiary who becomes entitled to the assets of the business will take them free of the business debts.[2]

1   See below, paras 32.13–32.15.
2   *Knight v Davis* (1833) 3 My & K 358; *Re Grisor* (1980) 101 DLR (3d) 728, 26 OR (2d) 57 (Ontario).

Special circumstances

More than one beneficiary
32.10   If more than one person is entitled to the property subject to the charge, each is responsible for discharging the charge according to the value of his benefit.[1]

1   *Evans v Wyatt* (1862) 31 Beav 217; *Trestrail v Mason* (1878) 7 Ch D 665; *Re Newmarch, Newmarch v Storr* (1878) 9 Ch D 12; *Leonino v Leonino* (1879) 10 Ch D 460; *Re Major, Taylor v Major* [1914] 1 Ch 278.

More than one security
32.11   More than one asset may be charged to secure the same debt. Suppose, for example, that the deceased purchased a house with the aid of a mortgage, but that the lender required additional security in the form of a charge over, say, another property or a life policy. In such cases it is necessary to establish whether both assets charged together constitute the primary security, or whether only one is the primary security and the other is secondary. This is a question of fact, and is not resolved by the description which the parties give to the deed of charge.[1] If both properties are given to the same person, then, subject to what is said below, that person must discharge the total liability. If the properties are given to separate persons, those persons will bear the liability rateably if both properties were primary securities.[2] If, however, only one property is the primary security the beneficiary of that property bears the whole of the debt, to the extent of its value, and the beneficiary of the secondary security is responsible only to the extent that the primary security is insufficient.[3]

1   *Re Athill, Athill v Athill* (1880) 16 Ch D 211.
2   Ibid.
3   *Marquis of Bute v Cunynghame* (1826) 2 Russ 275; *Re Athill*, above; *Re Ritson, Ritson v Ritson* [1899] 1 Ch 128.

More than one property given to the same beneficiary
32.12   The testator may give to the same beneficiary two or more assets each subject to separate liabilities. If the assets are given separately, the beneficiary can treat them as being unrelated. Thus, if the debt on one asset exceeds its value, the undischarged balance is payable out of the general residue, and not out of the other properties.[1] If, however, the assets were given as one composite gift, the beneficiary takes subject to the obligation to

discharge the total liabilities attaching to them and he does not have recourse to the general estate.[2]

1 *Re Holt, Holt v Holt* (1916) 85 LJ Ch 779.
2 *Re Baron Kensington* [1902] 1 Ch 203.

'Contrary or other intention'

32.13 The operation of the section may be negatived by a contrary intention expressed in the will, or in any other deed or document.[1] While the expression of contrary intention need not be in the will itself, it is not effective if it is only oral. In *Perry v Hicknell*[2] the testator, who owned a house subject to a mortgage, devised the house without making any mention of the mortgage debt. Shortly before his death, he took out a policy of insurance on his life to provide a fund for the payment off of the mortgage debt on his death, so that the devisee would take the house free of the debt. The court[3] held that while an effective expression of contrary intention could have been included in the insurance policy document, on the facts this had not been done. Accordingly, as there was only an oral statement by the testator, there was no effective expression of contrary intention. The devisee therefore took the property subject to the mortgage, and the residuary beneficiaries were entitled to the proceeds of the insurance policy.

1 Administration of Estates Act 1925, s 35(1) expressly declares its operation to be subject to any contrary intention.
2 (1982) 34 OR (2d) 246 (Ontario).
3 The Ontario High Court.

32.14 Even where the expression of contrary intention is in writing, sub-s 35(2) provides that a contrary intention is not shown merely by:
(a) a general direction to pay debts out of the personal estate;[1]
(b) a direction to pay debts out of the residuary real and personal estate, or the residuary realty;[2] or
(c) a charge of debts upon any such property.[3]
It is not even sufficient to direct that all sums 'secured on mortgage' are to be paid.[4] But the contrary intention can be shown by implication. In *Re Valpy, Valpy v Valpy*[5] there was a direction to pay all debts, except a mortgage debt on a particular property, and this was held to show an intention that all other mortgage debts should be paid from residue. Generally it is necessary to show that the testator intended that a particular debt should be paid from residue.

1 Administration of Estates Act 1925, s 35(2)(a).
2 Ibid.
3 Ibid, s 35(2)(b).
4 *Re Beirnstein, Barnett v Beirnstein* [1925] Ch 12.
5 [1906] 1 Ch 531.

32.15 Although sub-s 35(2) provides that a *mere* general direction to pay debts does not constitute an effective expression of contrary intention, if there is such a general direction, together with some further indication of contrary intention, that can be effective. This is illustrated by the decision of the Supreme Court of New South Wales in *McPhie v Mackay*.[1] In that case, four days before he made his will, the testator had contracted to purchase real estate on terms that the greater part of the purchase price would be payable after five years, and secured by a mortgage over the property. By his will, the testator left his house to his daughter, and the newly purchased property to his stepson. He directed the trustees to pay all his debts, and left his residue thereafter to his daughter. The testator also provided that if the residue was not sufficient for the payment of debts, they were to be borne by the daughter and stepson in proportion to the values of their shares in the estate. The residue was not sufficient to pay the mortgage debt on the new property. The Court held that by providing that, in the event of insufficiency of residue, the debts were to be borne by the daughter and stepson proportionately, the testator had signified an expression of contrary intention which went beyond the statute;[2] that the statute did not therefore restrict the construction of the will; and that the expression of contrary intention should be applied according to its terms.

1   [1975] 2 NSWLR 369.
2   The New South Wales statute was the same in this respect as s 35(2).

Position where contrary intention shown

32.16   The section refers to a contrary 'or other' intention because the testator might intend that the debts should be dealt with in one of two ways. He might indicate that the debts should be paid from a particular fund. If he does so, s 35 is displaced only to the extent that the fund is adequate.[1] So, in *Re Fegan, Fegan v Fegan*[2] the testator left to his children insurance policies worth about £4,000, but which were subject to charges of £2,000. He left another fund to be used to pay his debts. It was held that the children were entitled to have the debts on the policies discharged from the other fund so far as was possible, but that they were responsible for discharging the balance of the policy debt which could not be discharged from the fund.

1   *Re Birch, Hunt v Thorn* [1909] 1 Ch 787; *Re Major, Taylor v Major* [1914] 1 Ch 278; *Re Fegan, Fegan v Fegan* [1928] 1 Ch 45.
2   [1928] 1 Ch 45.

32.17   On the other hand, the testator may merely displace s 35 without making provision for the payment from any other fund. In this event, the position is as if the section had not been enacted. Property in the first two categories specified at the beginning of this chapter, which bear their own charges independently of the statute, continue to do so, unless the will shows an intention that these debts also should be discharged from residue. Other debts are treated in the same manner as uncharged debts, shortly to be considered.

Acceptance of liability to pay debts

32.18   The testator may give a legacy to a beneficiary on condition that the beneficiary pays all the debts. The legatee can disclaim the legacy,[1] but, if he accepts it, he is responsible for paying all the debts, even if they exceed the value of the property given to him.[2] Where this occurs, there is no call for the application of any other principles as to the incidence of debts.

1   See above, para 30.1.
2   *Messenger v Andrews* (1828) 4 Russ 478; *Dover v Gregory* (1839) 10 Sim 393. Cf *Henvell v Whitaker* (1827) 3 Russ 343.

Incidence of uncharged debts: generally

The statutory schedule

32.19   The Administration of Estates Act 1925, s 34(3) provides that a deceased person's real and personal estate shall 'be applicable towards the discharge of the funeral, testamentary and administration expenses, debts and liabilities payable thereout in the order mentioned in Part II of the First Schedule' to the Act. The Schedule is as follows:

Order of Application of Assets where the Estate is Solvent:
1   Property of the deceased undisposed of by will, subject to the retention thereout of a fund sufficient to meet any pecuniary legacies.
2   Property of the deceased not specifically devised or bequeathed but included (either by a specific or general description) in a residuary gift, subject to the retention out of such property of a fund sufficient to meet any pecuniary legacies, so far as not provided for as aforesaid.
3   Property of the deceased specifically appropriated or devised or bequeathed (either by a specific or general description) for the payment of debts.
4   Property of the deceased charged with, or devised or bequeathed (either by a specific or general description) subject to a charge for the payment of debts.
5   The fund, if any, retained to meet pecuniary legacies.
6   Property specifically devised or bequeathed, rateably according to value.
7   Property appointed by will under a general power, including the statutory power to dispose of entailed interests, rateably according to value.
8   The order of application may be varied by the will of the deceased.

Assets outside the Schedule

32.20   It is curious that the seven classes of assets given in the Schedule are not comprehensive, and that other assets are available for the payment of creditors. They are:
(a)   funds payable to the estate upon the exercise of an option;[1]
(b)   property subject to a donatio mortis causa; and
(c)   property subject to a general power of appointment exercisable by deed if it had been exercised.[2]

With regard to the first category, in *Re Eve, National Provincial Bank v Eve*[3] a beneficiary was granted by will an option to purchase certain shares from the estate. Rowburgh J held that this did not amount to a specific gift of the shares, within category 6 of the Schedule, and that so long as the purchase price payable under the option, and the remainder of the assets were together sufficient for the payment of debts, the purchase price was to be used for creditors, and not the shares themselves.

1   *Re Eve, National Provincial Bank v Eve* [1956] Ch 479.
2   *Re Phillips, Lawrence v Huxtable* [1931] 1 Ch 347.
3   [1956] Ch 479.

32.21   The heading of Part II of the First Schedule to the 1925 Act refers to the order of application of 'assets'. It may be that there can exist various types of inchoate or other rights which so lack substance that they cannot properly be referred to as 'assets' and so cannot come within the Schedule. This was the approach adopted by the Saskatchewan court in *Re Sieben*[1] which held that a claim against a third party for causing the wrongful death of the deceased was not an 'asset' until judgment was obtained.[2] In *Re Eve, National Provincial Bank Ltd v Eve*[3] Roxburgh J held that the property which was the subject of the testamentary option was to be taken after all assets specified in the Schedule, and it may be that the same approach will be adopted to all types of property which are available for creditors, but which are not specified in the Schedule.

1   (1980) 102 DLR (3d) 571.
2   See also *Davenport v Chilver* [1983] Ch 293, [1983] STC 426, where the right was not an asset within the scope of the Schedule.
3   [1956] Ch 479, [1956] 2 All ER 321.

Secured debts

32.22   The Schedule has no application to secured debts to the extent to which the creditor relies on his security.[1] The Schedule is operated by deducting the amount of the secured debt, to that extent, from the asset upon which it is secured. If, however, the beneficiary is not to suffer the debt,[2] it seems that the debt will be treated as an unsecured debt for the purposes of the Schedule. However, in this case the testator will have often expressed a particular intention as to the manner in which the debt is to be borne, and that intention must be followed.

1   See above, para 32.7.
2   See above, paras 32.13–32.15.

Applying the Schedule

32.23   In order to apply the Schedule, it is necessary:
(a)   to place the assets of the testator in the categories specified in the Schedule;
(b)   to discharge the debts from assets in one category before resorting to assets in a subsequent category; and
(c)   where the debts will be paid from some, but not all, of the assets in a category, to determine the manner in which the debts are to be borne between the beneficiaries interested in assets in that category.
It is proposed to consider first the position where there is no expression of contrary intention, and thereafter to consider the main ways in which the testator might vary the statutory rules.

Incidence of uncharged debts: no contrary intention

The example (1)

32.24 The assets of the deceased are placed into categories having regard both to whether they are the subject matter of an effective gift under the will, and to the nature of the gift according to the terms of the will. The position will be illustrated by the following example. Suppose that the deceased died owning:

A house, worth	£100,000	
subject to a mortgage debt of	£60,000	
giving a net value of		£40,000
A motor car, worth		£6,000
Other personal chattels, worth		£30,000
Cash, and investments, worth		£60,000
Total estate net of secured debts		£136,000

Suppose also that, by his will, the testator left

The house to Andrew
The motor car to Brian
£10,000 to Colin
The residue to be divided as to:
(a)   two thirds to Desmond; and
(b)   one third to Edward.
Suppose, finally, that both Brian and Edward predecease the testator, and that the gifts to them lapse. The application of the rules to these facts is considered in later pages,[1] but it is necessary to deal first with two rules of general application.

1   Below, paras 32.37ff.

Assets and values

32.25 Section 34 and the Schedule refer to 'assets' or 'property' of the deceased. It is necessary to determine the nature of the gift, to see, for example, whether it is specific, and it may[1] be necessary to determine the nature of the property, to see whether it is realty or personalty. However, except where it is necessary to do so, it will be more convenient to apply the rules by reference to the values of the assets, than to do so by reference to the nature of the gift, or to the property.

1   See below, paras 32.35–32.37 and 32.48.

Overlap

32.26 In various circumstances, property might appear to fall within more than one category. Suppose, for example, that the will directs the residue to be divided into two equal parts, and that the gift of one part lapses. That part will appear to fall both within category 1, as property undisposed of, and within category 2, as residue. Or suppose that the testator gives his motor car worth £10,000 to Peter, subject to the payment thereout of debts amounting to £2,000. The motor car might appear to fall both within category 4, as property charged with the payment of debts, and within category 6 as property specifically bequeathed. Although there is no statutory provision which deals with these circumstances, it was decided in *Re Kempthorne, Charles v Kempthorne*[1] that where property falls within more than one category, it is to be treated as falling within the higher category only. Thus, in the two examples just considered, the property will fall within categories 1 and 4 respectively.

1 [1930] 1 Ch 268.

Provisional categorisation of residue

Generally

32.27 The starting point in the process of categorisation is to make a provisional categorisation of the residuary property. In order to do this, depending on the circumstances, it may be necessary to make the calculation in three stages, the products of which may be conveniently called:[1]
(a) provisional residue;
(b) adjusted provisional residue; and
(c) final residue.
The provisional residue is the total of the gross asset value of the testator's estate other than:
(a) the amount of secured debts; and
(b) the value of property which is the subject of effective specific bequests or devises, taking that value as being net of the secured debts.
In the example, the provisional residue is:

Total estate net of secured debts	£136,000
less: net value of the gift of the house	£40,000
Provisional residue	£96,000

No account is taken of the motor car, because, although this was intended to be the subject of the specific gift to Brian, as Brian predeceased the testator, the gift was not effective.

1 The expressions are not statutory.

32.28 It will be appreciated that, for this purpose, the expression 'residuary property' does not have its ordinary meaning. In general, the residue is what is left over after the payment of all funeral, testamentary and administration expenses, debts and liabilities and after the payment of or provision for all specific and pecuniary gifts. However, this does not apply for the purposes of the Schedule. In the first place, the Schedule requires the assets of the estate to be placed into certain categories, with the intention that the debts are to be borne by the properties in those categories. The residuary property must, therefore, logically be identified *before* the debts are dealt with. In the second place, the Schedule itself requires that a fund is to be set aside out of the residue, once ascertained, to meet pecuniary legacies, so that, again logically, those pecuniary legacies cannot be deducted before the residue is ascertained.

Realty
32.29 Special conditions arise where the gift is of realty. Before 1926 all gifts of freehold land were treated as specific, even though residuary in form.[1] Now, it is clear that a gift of realty can be residuary. The apparent result of the cases is that a gift of realty will be residuary if it is so either objectively, or was intended to be residuary by the testator. Thus, if there is a gift of my house in London to Margaret, and all my other freehold land to Rose, the latter is a gift of residue, just as is a gift of all my freehold land to Rose, even if there is no prior specific gift of realty to Margaret.[2] In *Re Ridley, Nicholson v Nicholson*,[3] however, there was, in effect, a gift of all my land to Margaret, and the residue of my property to Rose. Harman J held that the gift of the land was specific, because the wording used in the will showed that the testatrix regarded all her property together, with the land taken out first. It was only her personalty that she thought of as residue.

1 *Hensman v Fryer* (1867) 3 Ch App 420; *Lancefield v Iggulden* (1874) 10 Ch App 136.
2 *Re Rowe, Bennetts v Eddy* [1941] Ch 343 at 348.
3 [1950] Ch 415, [1950] 2 All ER 1.

Undisposed of residue
32.30 The expression 'adjusted provisional residue' is used in this chapter to denote the value of the provisional residue, less such part of it as is undisposed of. If there is no effective gift of residue, there will be no need to make this adjustment. Where there is more than one gift of residue, the provisional residue is divided in the proportions specified in the will. In the example, the adjusted provisional residue is:

Provisional residue	£96,000
Less: the proportion thereof which is undisposed of, namely[1]	
£96,000 × ⅓	£32,000
Adjusted residue	£64,000

1 On the facts of the example, Edward's lapsed one third share.

Final residue
32.31 It will be seen that the amount of the residuary property, in category 2, is the amount of the provisional residue, adjusted where necessary, after the setting thereout of any sum required for pecuniary legacies. This is considered later.[1]

1 Below, paras 32.33–32.37.

Category 1: Property undisposed of

32.32 Category 1 is the property undisposed of by will, subject to the retention thereout of a fund sufficient to meet any effective pecuniary legacies. As applied to the example, the property in category 1 is:

The proportion of provisional residue not effectively disposed of[1]	£32,000
less: the amount required for the pecuniary legacy	£10,000
Category 1	£22,000

1 That is, Edward's lapsed one third share of the residue.

Category 2: Residuary property

Generally
32.33 Category 2 is the residuary property of the deceased, subject to the retention thereout of a fund sufficient to meet any effective pecuniary legacies, except to the extent that the fund has been constituted from property undisposed of. On the facts of the example, the pecuniary legacies fund has been fully constituted from property undisposed of, and no further provision is needed from the residuary property. In this case, therefore, the property in category 2 is the same as the adjusted provisional residue. If, however, the testator had left a pecuniary legacy of £50,000 to Colin, this would have been constituted as to £32,000 from the property undisposed of, and as to the balance of £18,000 from the adjusted provisional residue.

Burden of the pecuniary legacies fund
32.34 Where there is more than one residuary beneficiary, the pecuniary legacy fund is borne by them rateably. Suppose that a testator died leaving a gross estate of £30,000, and debts of £3,000. Suppose also that apart from a pecuniary legacy of £9,000, he left his residue as to two thirds to Mary and one third to Norma. The residuary property, calculated in the usual way for the purposes of the Schedule, that is, without taking into account debts or pecuniary legacies, is £30,000. The pecuniary legacy fund is £9,000, reducing the residuary property to £21,000. Of this Mary is entitled to £14,000 and Norma to £7,000.

Separate gifts of realty and personalty
32.35 It is uncertain whether the same principle applies where the separate residuary gifts are of realty and personalty. On one view realty and personalty should be dealt with without distinction. This view is based on the Schedule itself, which uses the word 'property' and appears to treat all property alike.[1] Section 32 of the Act provides that 'the real and personal estate . . . of a deceased person . . . are assets for the payment of his debts'. This view was supported by Luxmoore LJ in *Re Harland-Peck, Hercy v Mayglothing*.[2]

494

1 See definition of 'property' in s 55(1)(xvii), which 'includes a thing in action and any interest in real or personal property'.
2 [1941] Ch 182.

32.36 The other view is based on the fact that before 1926 legacies were taken from personalty before realty, and that the Schedule does not alter the rules as to incidence within a class. This approach was followed in *Re Anstead, Gurney v Anstead*.[1] In that case the testator's estate consisted of realty worth about £15,000 and personalty worth about £95,000. The testator left various pecuniary legacies as well as gifts of residue. Uthwatt J directed the executors to set aside a fund sufficient to satisfy the pecuniary legacies entirely from that part of the residue which consisted of personalty, leaving the realty and the remainder of the personalty to answer the debts.

1 [1943] Ch 161.

32.37 The decision in *Re Anstead, Gurney v Anstead*[1] has been followed in *Re Wilson, Wilson v Mackay*.[2] The testatrix died leaving personalty of about £16,500, and realty of about £7,000. She gave pecuniary legacies totalling £27,000, and 'all my real estate and the residue of my personal estate' to my daughter. There was a clear indication that all the realty was to go to the daughter, and, if necessary, that indication was sufficient under paragraph 8 to displace the statutory order. Pennycuick J held that a fund was to be set aside from the personalty to meet the legacies. As the amount of the legacies exceeded the value of the personalty, the whole of the personalty was earmarked for them. However, as the testatrix had shown a clear intention that none of the realty was available for the legacies, no part of them was charged on the realty. The decision depends on the particular working of the will, but Pennycuick J observed[3] that 'it may well be that if the incidence of legacies were not covered by express provision in the will the result would be the same under paragraph 2 of Part 2 of Schedule 1'. The judge then held that the realty came within paragraph 2 of the Schedule, and the debts were taken from that.

1 [1943] Ch 161.
2 [1967] Ch 53.
3 Ibid, at 67.

Categories 3 and 4: Property appropriated for or charged with the payment of debts

32.38 Property falls within category 3 if the testator in his will specifically set it aside for the payment of debts and does not leave it to any person. This would be the case, for example, if a testator directed his executors to pay his debts from the funds standing to the credit of a particular bank account, and the debts exceeded the balance on that account. Property falls within category 4 if the testator by his will gives it to a named beneficiary, subject to that beneficiary discharging either all the debts, or some specified debts. An example would be where the testator gives his stamp collection to Peter subject to Peter paying his debts.

Category 5: The pecuniary legacies fund

32.39   The pecuniary legacies fund is the fund which was constituted from any property undisposed of, or from residue. On the facts of the example, it amounts to £10,000.

Category 6: Property specifically devised or bequeathed

32.40   The property in category 6 is that property which is the subject of an effective specific devise or bequest. Where the property was charged prior to the death of the testator, it is brought into account at its value after deducting the amount of that charged debt. If, however, the testator has displaced the general rule prescribed by s 35 of the Administration of Estates Act 1925,[1] and has expressed a contrary intention, the property will be brought into account at its gross value. On the facts of the example, the property in category 5 is the house, which is brought into account at its net value of £40,000.

1   See above, paras 32.16 and 32.17.

Category 7: Property appointed by a general power

32.41   Category 7 consists of property of which the deceased was not the outright owner, but of which he attempted to dispose by a general power exercised by the will. The property which most commonly falls in this category is that subject to a general power of appointment.

The categories: a summary

32.42   All the steps which have been taken so far have consisted of taking the gross assets of the deceased,[1] and putting them into groups. At this stage, that of categorisation, no debt is paid. Accordingly, in every case the aggregate of the values of the property in each category will equal the gross asset value of the deceased, subject only, in general, to the secured liabilities. On the facts of the example, the categorisation is:

Category			
1			£22,000
2			£64,000
3			nil
4			nil
5			£10,000
6	House	£100,000	
	Mortgage debt	£60,000	£40,000
Total estate net of secured liabilities			£136,000

1   Subject only to secured debts.

Discharge of debts from categorised property

Generally
32.43 The debts are discharged from property in one category before resorting to property in any subsequent category. Accordingly, one category will be used in its entirety, before there is any encroachment on a subsequent category.

Incidence within the same category
32.44 The Schedule provides that where it is necessary to discharge debts and liabilities from property in category 6, the debts are taken from the assets within that category rateably according to the gross values of those assets, but the principle is almost certainly intended to apply to property in all categories. Suppose, therefore, that after setting aside a pecuniary legacies fund, there is £40,000 left in category 2. Suppose also that the will provides that Frank is entitled to 75 per cent of the residue, and Gordon to 25 per cent. Suppose further that there are unsecured liabilities totalling £10,000, and no property undisposed of. Frank will bear debts to the value of £7,500, and Gordon will bear debts to the value of £2,500.

Separate gifts of realty and personalty
32.45 It has been seen[1] that where there are separate gifts of residuary realty and residuary personalty, and a pecuniary legacies fund is to be constituted, it is unclear whether that fund is to be constituted so far as possible from residuary personalty, or rateably from residuary personalty and residuary realty. That problem arises at the stage of categorisation, but a similar problem arises when the debts are being discharged from the property in the statutory categories. This problem is whether the debts are to be discharged primarily or exclusively from personalty, or rateably from personalty and realty. The problem arises because the Act is silent as to the extent to which realty is liable for the payment of debts, and in order to appreciate the position it is necessary first to consider the pre-1926 rules, and then to see whether they have been modified.

1 Above, paras 32.35–32.37.

32.46 *Pre-1926 rules.* Before 1926 the extent to which realty could be taken for the payment of debts was clear. The rules were:
(a) debts were payable primarily out of general personalty;[1]
(b) liability for debts could be shifted from the general personalty to a specific fund of personalty by charging them on the specific fund;[2]
(c) liability for debts could be shifted from personalty to realty, but in order to do so, it was necessary not only to charge the debts on the realty, but also to show an intention to exonerate the personalty.[3] A charge of the debts on realty, unaccompanied by an intention to exonerate the personalty, merely made the realty liable after the personalty had been exhausted.[4]

1 *Manning v Spooner* (1796) 3 Ves 114; *Harmood v Oglander* (1803) 8 Ves 106.
2 *Webb v De Beauvoisin* (1862) 31 Beav 573; *Vernon v Earl Manvers* (1862) 31 Beav 623; *Coventry v Coventry* (1865) 2 Drew & Sm 470; *Trott v Buchanan* (1885) 28 Ch D 446.

3   *Bootle v Blundell* (1815) 1 Mer 193; *Bickham v Cruttwell* (1838) 3 My & Cr 763; *Collis v Robins* (1847) 1 De G & Sm 131; *Trott v Buchanan* (1885) 28 Ch D 446.
4   *Rhodes v Rudge* (1826) 1 Sim 79; *Walker v Hardwick* (1833) 1 My & K 396; *Forrest v Prescott* (1870) LR 10 Eq 545; *Poole v Heron* (1873) 42 LJCh 348; *Re Ovey* (1885) 31 Ch D 113.

32.47   *Post-1925 position: realty in prior class.*   Two situations are to be considered. The first is where there is realty in one category, and personalty in a later category. The second is where there is both realty and personalty in the same category. It is clear beyond doubt that realty in one category can be taken before personalty in a subsequent category. The Schedule uses the word 'property', and the definition section[1] shows that 'property' includes any interest in real or personal property. Thus, debts should be paid from undisposed of property, even if it is all realty, before residuary property, even if it is all personalty.

1   Administration of Estates Act 1925, s 55(1)(xvii).

32.48   *Post-1925 position: realty and personalty in same class.*   Where realty and personalty are in the same class, the position is not clear. On the one hand, it has been said that the personalty must be used in its entirety before any part of the realty can be taken. On the other hand, it has been said that the realty and personalty should be taken rateably. It has been seen[1] that in setting aside the pecuniary legacies fund, it is probably correct to set aside this fund from personalty before realty, unless there is a contrary intention in the will. It is possible that this approach, which is in accord with the pre-1926 position, also applies to the incidence of debts within the same category. However, as the Schedule is concerned primarily with debts, and as the legislation treats realty and personalty alike, it may well be that realty and personalty bear the liability rateably.[2]

1   Above, paras 32.35–32.37.
2   See *Re Anstead, Gurney v Anstead* [1943] Ch 161; above, para 32.36.

32.49   *Calculation of apportionment.*   It was pointed out above[1] that where the pecuniary legacy fund is taken out of residue, the individual gifts of residue are reduced. At the stage when the burden of the debts is apportioned, the apportionment is made according to the values of the individual gifts of residue as so reduced.

1   See para 32.34.

32.50   *Property specifically devised or bequeathed.*   The statute provides that the property in this category shall be subject to the payment of debts 'rateably according to value', so that there is no question of personalty being taken before realty.

The example (2)

32.51   The effect of some of these rules can be seen by taking the facts of the example, and by assuming that the unsecured liabilities amounted to (a) £10,000 or (b) £50,000 or (c) £90,000.

	Unsecured debts amount to		
	£10,000	£50,000	£90,000
Debts are discharged from			
Property undisposed of	£10,000	£22,000	£22,000
Residue	nil	£28,000	£64,000
Pecuniary legacies fund	nil	nil	£4,000
Specific property	nil	nil	nil
Total	£10,000	£50,000	£90,000
Leaving a net sum of	£126,000	£86,000	£46,000
which			
devolves on intestacy	£12,000	nil	nil
is paid to residuary beneficiary Desmond	£64,000	£36,000	nil
is paid to pecuniary legatee Colin	£10,000	£10,000	£6,000
is paid to specific legatee Andrew	£40,000	£40,000	£40,000
Total	£126,000	£86,000	£46,000

The result of applying the Schedule is to give effect to what it might be expected the ordinary testator would wish to happen were the point to be put to him. In making his will, a testator generally puts the greatest importance on specific gifts, and then on pecuniary gifts. The residuary property is generally thought of as being what is left over, with no great importance being placed on any one item. And those who might benefit on intestacy are generally not thought of at all, at least in that capacity.

Incidence of uncharged debts: contrary intention

Generally

32.52 Creditors are unaffected by the rules governing the incidence of debts: they will be paid in any event. The rules as to incidence merely affect how the testator's bounty is distributed among the beneficiaries. As the creditors will be paid in full, the testator can[1] distribute his bounty as he wishes, and he can, therefore, vary the statutory order in whatever way he likes. While the testator is able to alter the statutory rules as he wishes, the variations are usually one or more of the following:
(a) alteration of the order in which debts are taken from the categories;
(b) alteration of the composition of the categories; and
(c) alteration of the rules for some, but not all, purposes.

1 By showing a contrary intention.

Alteration of the order of categories

32.53 The testator can alter the order of the categories as he wishes, but most commonly this arises in relation to category 3 (dealing with property appropriated for the payment of debts) and category 4 (property charged with the payment of debts). The difficulty is that property can be brought within categories 3 or 4 only by some provision in the will – but does not any such provision automatically indicate an intention that the debts should be paid from that property before any other? Suppose, for example, that the testator leaves £10,000 to Harry, subject to the payment of debts, and the residue to Iolanthe. By charging the debts on the legacy, has not the testator shown that Iolanthe is to take the residue free from the debts? If so, the statutory order has been altered.

32.54 In order to determine whether, in such a case, the statutory order has been altered, the courts have accepted that there are two possible types of provision in a will:
(a) a mere appropriation or charging of property, which does not displace the statutory order; and
(b) a direction to pay debts from specified property, coupled with an intention to exonerate property. This has the effect that the specified property does become liable before any other.
An example of the first type of provision is *Re Gordon, Watts v Rationalist Press Association Ltd.*[1] In that case a testatrix gave by her will a specific legacy, and a legacy of £50, with a direction to pay from it her debts, and to pay over the balance to another. Her residue was undisposed of. It was held that the statutory order was not displaced, with the result that the debts were paid from the undisposed of residue, rather than from the legacy set aside for this purpose. It could not be said that there was any intention to exonerate the residue.[2]

1 [1940] Ch 769.
2 See also *Re Kempthorne, Charles v Kempthorne* [1930] 1 Ch 268.

32.55 There are several cases where the intention to exonerate has been shown. For example, in *Re James, Lloyds Bank v Atkins*[1] the testator directed payment of his debts from a particular fund, and left the residue to his wife. Roxburgh J said: 'I should hold that the direction to pay debts out of a particular fund necessarily involved an intention to exonerate some other fund which the testator disposed of in some other part of his will – in other words, necessarily involved an intention to exonerate the residue of his estate which he devised and bequeathed to his wife absolutely.' The judge was asking himself not in general terms whether there was a contrary intention, but whether there was an intention to exonerate other property. This intention appeared to come automatically from the gift of residue. This was followed in *Re Meldrum.*[2] The testator bequeathed to his daughter the money in a bank account after the payment of legacies and debts, and left the residue of his property between his son and daughter. Upjohn J expressly approved the dictum of Roxburgh J quoted above, and held that the direction to pay debts from the bank account showed an intention to exonerate the residue.

1 [1947] Ch 256.
2 [1952] Ch 208.

32.56 Whether or not the courts will hold that the statutory order has been displaced has in these cases been influenced very largely by the existence or otherwise of a gift of the residue to another person, but in all cases it is a question of construction.

Alteration of the composition of categories

32.57 It is possible for the testator to keep the statutory order, but to prescribe that the categories are to be differently constituted. For example, the testator could provide that category 6 (property specifically devised or bequeathed) should include only realty. However, the most frequent alteration to the manner in which a category is to be constituted is with regard to residue.

32.58 It has been seen that if a share of residue lapses, it is necessary first to identify, provisionally, the residuary property as just described and *then* to identify the share which is undisposed of. Suppose that the testator leaves all his property, worth £50,000, to be divided between his two brothers, Frank and George, and that Frank predeceases him. Suppose also that the debts amount to £10,000. The residuary property is provisionally identified as the full £50,000,[1] and the property undisposed of is provisionally identified as £25,000. If there are no other adjustments to be made, the debts of £10,000 are discharged in full from the property undisposed of, so that £25,000 would go to George, and £15,000 would devolve as on intestacy. Thus, in *Re Sanger, Taylor v North*[2] there was a direction to pay debts, followed by a gift of residue. The debts were not charged on the residue, and Simonds J held that, in the usual way, the division should be made before the debts were discharged, and that the debts should be discharged from the undisposed of share. This is a reversal of the 1926 position, but it has the advantage of benefiting those who are the conscious objects of the testator's bounty, rather than those entitled on intestacy, whoever they may be.

1 Ie the gross estate. The only deductions would be of property specifically devised or bequeathed: see above, para 32.27.
2 [1939] Ch 238.

32.59 Although the general rule is that just described, the testator may indicate a contrary intention. The testator may direct that the debts are to be paid before the residue is ascertained, in which case the testator, in effect, directs that the residue is to be ascertained in a different manner from that described above. Alternatively, the testator may charge the debts on the whole of the residue. In this case, the residue itself can be ascertained in the usual way, but the property undisposed of can be identified only after the debts have been deducted.

32.60   *Debts paid before residue ascertained.*   An example of this situation is *Re Kempthorne, Charles v Kempthorne.*[1] In that case the testator left all his property, after payment of debts and legacies, to be divided among his brothers and sisters. Two predeceased him. At first instance Maugham J held that the mere fact that the testator had directed debts to be paid did not vary the statutory order. Accordingly, he made his division first, and then directed the debts to be paid from the undisposed of share. This was reversed on appeal: in the opinion of the Court of Appeal the wording of the will, which left the residue 'after' payment of expenses, debts and legacies, showed that the testator intended that the debts should be paid before the residue could be ascertained, and so before it could be divided.[2]

1   [1930] 1 Ch 268.
2   See also *Re Petty, Holliday v Petty* [1929] 1 Ch 726; *Re Atkinson, Webster v Walter* [1930] 1 Ch 47.

32.61   *Debts charged on whole of residue.   Re Harland-Peck, Hercy v Mayglothing*[1] is an example of the other situation in which a contrary intention can be shown, namely where the debts are charged on the whole of the residue. In that case the testator left his property 'subject to the payment of funeral and testamentary expenses and debts' to two persons. The Court of Appeal held that these words charged the debts on the whole residue, and that they had to be discharged before the division was made. The court drew a distinction between a gift which is made subject to the payment of debts; and a direction to pay debts followed by a gift of residue. In the first case, but not in the second, there is a charge on the property given.

1   [1941] Ch 182.

32.62   The distinction between these types of case is easy to state in principle, but very difficult to decide in practice in the absence of clarity of drafting.[1] Yet there seems to be no satisfactory solution. In most cases, it is more convenient to divide first, so that the debts can be paid from property undisposed of, but, on the other hand, the testator must retain his right to vary the order if he wishes.

1   In most professionally drawn wills the testator will have varied the statutory order. This is commonly done by placing the residue on trust for sale and directing the executors to pay debts out of the proceeds of sale. Alternatively, it may be done by making the gift to the residuary beneficiaries 'subject to' or 'after payment of' the debts. In both cases it will be a direction to pay debts from residuary estate before division into shares, including any lapsed share.

Variation for some purposes only

32.63   The testator can alter the ordinary rules for some, but not all, purposes. He can, therefore, in effect direct that the statutory order is to be followed for some types of debt, but not for others. An example is *Re McDevitt, Brown v Prior.*[1] In that case the testatrix:
(a)   gave certain specific legacies and devises;

(b)   directed that they should be paid free of death duties; and
(c)   made a gift of residue.
The residue was insufficient to meet the death duties as well as the other debts and liabilities. The court held that the direction to pay the specific legacies free of death duties was a variation of the statutory order so far as death duties[2] were concerned, but that there was no variation so far as concerned other debts and liabilities. The categorisation of the estate, and the order in which it was resorted to, was, therefore:

Category
1   None.
2   Residue, after setting aside the pecuniary legacies fund.
3,4   None.
5(a)   Prima facie, the pecuniary legacies fund; but
  (b)   by virtue of the direction, the pecuniary legacies fund was not to be resorted to for the payment of death duties; so that
  (c)   the pecuniary legacies fund could only be resorted to for other debts and liabilities.
6(a)   Prima facie, the property specifically devised and bequeathed; but
  (b)   there was no source left from which the death duties should be paid; so that
  (c)   by invoking the general principle of pro rata abatement, the specific legacies and devises suffered the burden of the death duties proportionately according to value.

The final result was that:
(a)   residue was available for all liabilities;
(b)   testamentary expenses were taken next, from the pecuniary legacies fund, the pecuniary legacies abating rateably according to value;
(c)   the death duties were paid from the balance of the pecuniary legacies, and the specific bequests and devises, all abating rateably according to value.

1   [1976] Tas SR 1 (Tasmania).
2   At that time devises bore their own duty in the absence of contrary provision.

The incidence of legacies: the problems

32.64   It has been seen that the position with regard to the incidence of debts has been altered substantially by the 1925 Act: it has been the subject of much discussion whether the pre-1926 rules as to legacies were also changed by the same legislation, so that the present rules as to the incidence of debts also apply to the incidence of legacies.[1] On this fundamental point there are irreconcilable differences of judicial approach. As an example of one view, in *Re Worthington, Nichols v Hart*[2] Lord Hanworth MR said: 'The provisions of the statute indicate that unless there is some provision in the will which negatives the prescribed order of administration, that order of administration must apply both to legacies and to debts.' The statement would have been more convincing if Lord Hanworth had indicated which provisions he had in mind, or, more importantly, if there were in fact any provisions which gave that indication. In fact, Lord Hanworth was inventing a new rule, although, as will be seen, he has been followed in so doing.[3] On the other hand, *Re Thompson, Public Trustee v Husband*[4] is an example of the other view. In that case, Clauson J said:

'It is suggested that the effect of that provision [s 34(3)] is to alter the law [to equate the incidence of debts and legacies] . . . The provision does not say so, and the provision is not concerned with any such matter. The provision is concerned with the way in which funeral, testamentary and administration expenses, debts and liabilities are to be met. There is no indication that there is any intention of altering the law in respect of the rights of the legatees as against those interested in the residuary personalty and residuary real estate, or in respect of the rights inter se of those interested in the residuary realty and personalty respectively, as regards bearing the charge of legacies, and I can see no foundation for the suggestion that that provision has in any way altered "the law" as previously laid down.'

1   See Ryder 'The Incidence of General Pecuniary Legacies' [1956] CLJ 80.
2   [1933] Ch 771.
4   Eg *Re Lamb, Vipond v Lamb* [1929] 1 Ch 722; *Re Gillett's Will Trusts* [1950] Ch 102.
4   [1936] Ch 676.

32.65   As a result of this complete conflict of judicial approach it is too dangerous to ask the simple question whether the post-1925 rules as to the incidence of debts apply also to legacies. Rather, it is necessary to identify three subsidiary questions which are concealed by the broad simple one, and to ask:

(a)   Do the pre-1926 rules still operate to identify what property has lapsed, and what forms part of residue?
(b)   Does the statutory order apply where no point arises as to the nature of the property, such as where it is all personalty?
(c)   Where the property consists of both realty and personalty, to what extent is realty available for legacies?

In order to answer these questions it is necessary to state the pre-1926 position; and the post-1925 position as to debts; and then to consider the post-1925 position as to legacies.

Legacies from lapsed share of residue

The problem

32.66   The problem is the same as that considered in paras 32.59 to 32.61 for debts. Suppose that a testator makes a will leaving £1,000 to his secretary, and directing that his residue is to be divided between his three nephews. Suppose also that one of his nephews predeceases him so that a third share of the residue lapses. Is the estate divided into three parts, and the legacy taken from the lapsed share? Or is the legacy taken from the estate first, and the residue then divided into three parts?

32.67   In essence, the problem consists not in applying the statutory schedule, but in deciding how to ascertain the size of the lapsed share. If the estate in the example just considered is £10,000, and the former solution is adopted the lapsed share is £3,333, and the legacy is taken from that. If the latter solution is adopted, the lapsed share is £3,000.

Pre-1926 position

32.68 Before 1926 the legacies were paid from the entire estate, and the residue was ascertained only when that had been done. Consequently, legacies were not taken from the lapsed share.

Post-1925 position as to debts

32.69 It has been suggested above[1] that the general rule after 1925 in respect of debts is that the estate is divided into shares first, and that debts are to be taken so far as is possible from the lapsed share; but that this is subject to a contrary intention shown either by an expression that the debts are to be paid before division; or a charging of the debts on the whole of the residue.

1 See para 32.30.

Post-1925 position as to legacies

Statutory trust for sale

32.70 The decisions in the various cases seem often to have depended on the nature of the trust for sale which arises in respect of the lapsed property, although, at least in some of the cases, this factor does not appear to have been in the forefront of the judges' minds. It will be appreciated that usually there will be either an express or a statutory trust for sale.[1] If the will does not contain an express trust for sale, the statutory trust for sale applicable to a total or partial intestacy under s 33 will apply. This section does not indicate how the undisposed of property is to be calculated, but s 33(2) appears to envisage that debts and legacies will be treated in the same way. In the case of a statutory trust for sale, then, it may be expected that the rules as to debts and legacies will be the same, and this does indeed appear to be the case.

1 There cannot be both an express and a statutory trust for conversion: *Re McKee, Public Trustee v McKee* [1931] 2 Ch 145 (per Maughan J at 149); *Re Taylor's Estate and Will Trusts* [1969] 1 All ER 113 at 117.

32.71 Thus, in *Re Worthington, Nichols v Hart*[1] the testatrix left certain legacies and her residue to be divided between two persons, one of whom predeceased her, and the question was whether the legacies should be taken before or after the division of the residue into shares. At first instance, Bennett J held that the old law applied, and that the legacies were payable out of the general estate before the residue was ascertained, although he applied the new law to the payment of debts, which were taken from the lapsed share. In so far as it related to legacies, the decision was reversed in the Court of Appeal, and it was held that the residue should be divided first, and the legacies taken from the lapsed share after division.

1 [1933] Ch 771.

32.72 *Re Worthington* was followed in *Re Gillett's Will Trusts, Barclays Bank Ltd v Gillett.*[1] In that case, the testator had given certain legacies, and then left his residue to provide annuities for four people. On the death of the last of the annuitants, the balance of the fund was then to be held on trust for others. The testator made no provision for the income from the fund which would arise between the deaths of the first and fourth annuitants, and this surplus income was therefore property undisposed of. Roxburgh J held that the legacies were to be paid from the property undisposed of, rather than from the residue of the general estate.

1 [1950] Ch 102.

Express trust for sale
32.73 Different considerations apply where there is an express trust for sale, for the testator may give his own answer to the problem. It may be clear from the words which he uses that the legacies are to be paid before the residue can be ascertained, and so before the division into shares can be made. Where this is so, it is not a question whether the old law or the new law applies, but merely what the testator intended. Where, however, no indication is given, the authorities leave the question open. In *Re Midgley, Barclays Bank Ltd v Midgley*[1] the testatrix left certain legacies, and then gave her residue upon an express trust for sale for the benefit of six people. She revoked the gift to one of the six, without making any substitutory provision, so that it was undisposed of. Harman J held that the division should take place first, and the legacies should be taken primarily from the undisposed of share of residue. On the other hand, the opposite result was reached in *Re Beaumont's Will Trusts, Walker v Lawson*[2] and in the more recent decision in *Re Taylor's Estate and Will Trusts.*[3] In the latter case the testatrix left five pecuniary legacies of £100 each, and subject thereto her residuary estate upon trust for sale, and thereafter for division among certain persons, one of whom predeceased the testatrix. The judge found that there was no indication of how the legacies should be borne, and then held that the old law continued to apply.

1 [1955] Ch 576.
2 [1950] Ch 462.
3 [1969] 2 Ch 245.

The solution

32.74 Quite apart from the inconsistency among the express trust for sale cases themselves, it is absurd that the result should depend on whether or not there is an express, as contrasted with a statutory, trust for sale. For the reasoning given in respect of debts,[1] it is suggested that the decisions in *Re Beaumont* and *Re Taylor* are wrong[2] and that the position should be the same as that for debts, whether the trust for sale is statutory or express. It is suggested, therefore, that the rule *should* be that the residue should be divided first, and the legacies taken from the lapsed share, unless there is some provision to the contrary in the will.

1 See above, paras 32.57ff.
2 See Albery (1969) 85 LQR 464.

Does the statutory schedule apply to legacies?

The problem

32.75 The problem just considered involves the application of the statutory schedule, but it is really a preliminary to it: the rules just considered identify the size of the property undisposed of, and the Schedule can then apply, unless in the very process of the ascertainment of the property undisposed of, the legacies have been paid. The true nature of the problem is seen by taking situations where there is no property undisposed of. Suppose, for example, that a testator gives a fund of £5,000 to Vanessa, subject to the payment thereout of a legacy of £300 to her grandson, and the residue to Matilda. Is the legacy to be taken from the property charged with the payment of the legacy which would be the position under the pre-1926 law; or are they to be taken from residue applying paragraph 2 of the Schedule, in priority to the legacy to Vanessa (paragraph 4)?

Post-1925 rules as to legacies

32.76 There is a good deal of superficial attraction in suggesting that the Schedule does not apply. The Schedule is governed by s 34(3), which provides that 'debts and liabilites' shall be payable in the order mentioned in the Schedule. It would not normally even be suggested that the word 'liabilities' includes legacies. There is no express provision that the Schedule shall apply to legacies. Further, the wording of the Schedule itself contains surprising omissions if it is to govern legacies. For example, it would be expected that paragraphs 3 and 4 would also deal with legacies. It seems, therefore, fairly likely that the legislature did not intend legacies to be affected by the Schedule.

32.77 But the position is open. There is, as yet, no authority to determine the solution to the problem posed above affecting Vanessa and Matilda. And the inconsistency of judicial approach mentioned earlier shows that the basis for the solution has not been established in any way.

The solution

32.78 In these circumstances one is free to suggest the solution. Again, it is suggested that the rules as to debts and legacies should be equated, as in the case of the suggestion made above[1] as to the incidence of legacies where there is a lapsed share. But it is stressed that this is only a suggestion: the actual position is open.

1   See paras 32.57ff.

Availability of realty to satisfy legacies

The problem

32.79   The problem here does not specifically involve the Schedule. Suppose that the testator leaves a legacy of £50,000 to his wife, and the residue of his property between his brothers Peter and Paul. Suppose also that the estate consists of personalty worth £40,000 and realty worth £60,000. Is the legacy to be paid as to £20,000 from personalty and as to £30,000 from realty? Or is it to be paid so far as possible from personalty, so that the whole of the personalty is taken, and only £10,000 from realty? Or, even, is it to be paid only to the extent that personalty is available, so that while the whole of the personalty is taken, no part of the realty is available, and the legacy therefore abates to £40,000? The problem is important from three points of view. The legatee is concerned to know whether the legacy will be paid in full. The position of the residuary beneficiaries is affected if there is a gift of realty to one person and personalty to another. And the incidence of inheritance tax might also be affected.[1]

1   Although in respect of deaths after 25 July 1983, in the absence of contrary provision in the will, inheritance tax is borne out of the residue of the estate: Inheritance Tax Act 1984, s 211. To the extent the residue is insufficient to meet the tax, there will be an abatement.

Pre-1926 position

32.80   The position before 1926 was as follows.
(a)   In the absence of a contrary intention in the will, pecuniary legacies were payable only out of residuary personalty. If that was not sufficient, the legacies abated proportionately.[1]
(b)   Where there was a gift of residuary realty and personalty together, the testator was presumed to have intended that the residuary realty could be taken after the personalty was exhausted.[2] Thus, all the residuary personalty would be taken first, and then resort could be made to the realty.
(c)   Where there was a gift of personalty and realty together, and the testator expressly directed that the legacies were to be paid from it, the realty and personalty were proportionately liable to satisfy the legacies.[3]
(d)   Legacies could be paid from realty in priority to personalty if, and only if, the testator both charged the realty with payment of legacies and also showed an intention to exonerate the personalty.[4]

1   *Robertson v Broadbent* (1883) 8 App Cas 812.
2   *Greville v Browne* (1859) 7 HL Cas 689.
3   *Roberts v Walker* (1830) 1 Russ & M 752.
4   *Elliot v Dearsley* (1880) 16 Ch D 322.

Post-1925 position as to debts

32.81 It was suggested above[1] that realty and personalty should be treated without distinction, but that the authorities, particularly *Re Anstead*[2] and *Re Wilson*,[3] show that personalty is to be used first.

1 See above, paras 32.35–32.37.
2 [1943] Ch 161.
3 [1967] Ch 53.

Post-1925 position as to legacies

32.82 There is a strong indication that the pre-1926 rules still apply. *Re Thompson, Public Trustee v Husband*[1] has already been mentioned.[2] The testator's estate consisted of, in very general figures, personalty worth about £2,000 and net realty worth about £10,000. He left legacies of £3,000, and gifts of residue. Clauson J rejected a suggestion that about £500 should be taken from personalty, and £2,500 from realty. He directed that the £2,000 personalty should be taken in full, and the balance made up from realty. *Re Wilson*[3] strongly suggests that this approach will be followed. It is against this general approach that two specific situations can be considered.

1 [1936] Ch 676.
2 See above, para 32.64.
3 [1967] Ch 53.

Realty and personalty in same class
32.83 The pre-1926 law has been applied to show that where realty and personalty are in the same class, generally legacies can only be paid from personalty, and that they will abate to the extent that the personalty is not sufficient.[1] Realty can, however, be used to make up a shortfall where there is insufficient personalty if both are given in one mass;[2] and, presumably, realty and personalty will be taken rateably where there is a direction to pay the legacies from a fund of realty and personalty given in one mass.[3]

1 *Re Rowe, Bennetts v Eddy* [1941] Ch 343.
2 *Re Anstead, Gurney v Anstead* [1943] Ch 161; *Re Timson, Harper v Timson* [1953] 2 All ER 1252.
3 See, on the pre-1926 law, *Re Boards, Knight v Knight* [1895] 1 Ch 499.

Realty and personalty in different classes
32.84 It seems clear that where there is a statutory trust for sale, the realty ceases to exist as such, and what was realty is available for legacies. Thus, in *Re Martin, Midland Bank Executor and Trustee Co Ltd v Marfleet*[1] a gift of realty which lapsed, and was undisposed of, but which was subject to the statutory trust for sale, was held to be available for the payment of legacies in priority to residuary personalty.[2] In the absence of authority, the same would appear to be the approach in the case of an express trust for sale.

1 [1955] Ch 698.
2 See also *Re Berrey's Will Trusts, Greening v Walters* [1959] 1 WLR 30; and (1959) 23 Conv (NS) 139.

The solution

32.85 The general approach of preserving the pre-1926 law, and thus giving priority to personalty, accords with the general position in respect of debts, and thus is consistent with the view maintained here that the rules as to debts ought to be equated with those governing legacies. On the other hand, it is now distinctly archaic to treat land in this special way, and the ideal solution will be to treat land in the same way as personalty both as regards debts and as regards legacies.

The pecuniary legacies fund

32.86 A final problem affects the incidence of both debts and legacies. It will be recalled that paragraph 1 of the Schedule deals with property undisposed of 'subject to the retention thereout of a fund sufficient to meet any pecuniary legacies'. Paragraph 2 deals with residuary property 'subject to the retention out of such a property of a fund sufficient to meet any pecuniary legacies, so far as not provided for [under paragraph 1]'. It is suggested that these words mean what they say, and that personal representatives are under an obligation to set aside a pecuniary legacies fund from undisposed of property, and, if necessary, from residue.[1] In *Re Taylor's Estate and Will Trusts*,[2] however, Salt QC came to the opposite conclusion, and held that the words did not impose a mandatory obligation, but were to be read subject to words such as 'if appropriate' or 'at the discretion of the personal representatives'. The judge gave four reasons in support of his view.

1 See above, paras 32.35–32.37.
2 [1969] 1 All ER 113.

32.87 First, in respect of property undisposed of, an inconsistency arises with s 33(2). This sub-section, which imposes a statutory trust to convert property which devolves on a total or partial intestacy in accordance with the intestacy rules, provides that the personal representatives must pay the debts, and that out of the residue of the converted property they must set aside a fund to provide for pecuniary legacies. Thus, s 33 envisages that the pecuniary legacies fund is not to be established until after the debts have been paid: and this would be inconsistent with an obligation in paragraphs 1 and 2 to establish a pecuniary legacies fund before the debts have been paid. The judge maintained that the clearly mandatory provisions of s 33(2) are not to be modified by the less strong words of the Schedule. Yet the expressions in paragraphs 1 and 2 must be intended to have the same meaning whenever they apply; and there can be no inconsistency with s 33 in the case of property undisposed of where there is an express trust for sale[1] or where the gift is of residue. The inconsistency is, therefore, confined to the case of a total or partial intestacy where there is no express trust for sale. In order to preserve consistency within the Schedule, it seems better to modify the apparent effect of s 33. The apparent effect of one or the other must be modified.

1 Because there cannot be both a subsisting express trust for sale and a statutory trust for sale:

Re McKee, Public Trustee v McKee [1931] 2 Ch 145, per Maugham J at 149. In *Re Taylor's Estate and Will Trusts*, Salt QC Ch accepted this principle (at 117).

32.88 Secondly, paragraph 5 of the Schedule deals with 'The fund, if any, retained to meet pecuniary legacies'. The judge considered that this wording indicated that there may be a gift of pecuniary legacies, where no fund has been set aside to answer them. Had this not been so, he suggested that the Schedule would have been worded 'The fund retained to meet pecuniary legacies, if any'. To this it may be answered that in a Schedule where there has been so much imprecision in other respects – which has occupied most of this chapter – such precision would be surprising. Surely the more obvious meaning of the paragraph is any fund which has been retained in accordance with the previous provisions, without indicating whether or not there was an obligation under those previous to set such a fund aside.

32.89 Thirdly, the words 'subject to the retention . . .' are a curious formula if the legislature had intended to impose (as in s 33(2)) a clear obligation on the personal representatives to retain a fund to meet pecuniary legacies.[1] This may be so, but it is hardly a sufficient ground for going in the face of what is suggested to be their obvious meaning.

1 [1969] 1 All ER 113 at 118.

32.90 Finally, if the words were read in a mandatory sense, they would, as has been seen,[1] reverse the pre-1926 rules. It is here that one comes back to the basic problem: was this the intention?

1 See above, paras 32.76 and 32.77.

32.91 The judge's reasons are hardly convincing – even though, individually, they may not be capable of convincing reply.[1] But the words 'subject to the retention . . .' must be intended to have some meaning, if Parliament has made a solemn act, and not a solemn farce. It would lead to an absurd result to read the words, as the judge suggested, as being subject to the personal representatives' discretion: clearly beneficial entitlement cannot be allowed to depend on the personal representatives' discretion without the very clearest words. It is suggested that the decision is wrong, and that the words do impose a statutory duty.

1 But see Albery (1969) 85 LQR 464.

CHAPTER 33

Distribution among beneficiaries

Power of appropriation

33.1 It is realised that a beneficiary who is left, say, a pecuniary legacy might prefer to take articles of similar value belonging to the estate. Section 41 of the Administration of Estates Act 1925, which applies to both testate and intestate estates,[1] accordingly confers a power of appropriation on the personal representatives. The power may be exercised in favour of legatees, or in favour of persons entitled to a share in residue.[2] It may not be exercised in respect of property which is subject to a specific devise or bequest[3] without the consent of the specific beneficiary but, subject to that, the power applies in respect of all property of any description forming part of the estate. Property which is appropriated is taken in the actual condition or state of investment which it has at the time of appropriation[4] and it is likewise valued at that time.[5]

1 Administration of Estates Act 1925, s 41(9).
2 Ibid, s 41(1).
3 Ibid, s 41(1) proviso (i).
4 Ibid, s 41(1).
5 *Re Lepine, Dowsett v Culver* [1892] 1 Ch 210; *Re Brooks, Coles v Davis* (1897) 76 LT 771; *Re Nickels, Nickels v Nickels* [1898] 1 Ch 630; *Re Charteris, Charteris v Biddulph* [1917] 2 Ch 379.

33.2 The statutory power can be exercised only subject to certain consents. If the beneficiary is absolutely entitled, he must consent, or, if he is not sui juris, his parent or person having control over his property may consent on his behalf.[1] Where an appropriation is being made in respect of an interest under the will which is settled, the consent required is that of the tenant for life,[2] or of the trustee if he is a person different from the personal representative.[3]

1 Administration of Estates Act 1925, s 41(1) proviso (ii)(b).
2 Ibid.
3 Ibid, s 41(9).

33.3 Section 41 expressly authorises[1] the setting apart of a fund to answer an annuity by means of the income of that fund, or in some other way, but it is unclear whether, following such an appropriation, the annuitant loses his right of recourse to other parts of residue in the event of deficiency.[2]

1 Sub-s (8).
2 But on principle he should lose it: *Baker v Farmer* (1867) LR 4 Eq 382; *Ballard v Marsden* (1880) 14 Ch D 374; *Fraser v Murdoch* (1881) 6 App Cas 855.

33.4 Once an appropriation has been made it binds all persons who have consented, by virtue of their consent, and all persons who are interested in the property but whose consent is not required by virtue of the section.[1]

1 Administration of Estates Act 1925, s 41(4).

33.5 The statutory power is important. Once made, the beneficiary to whom property is appropriated suffers any subsequent loss of the property, and obtains the benefit of any accretions. Wills, too, frequently contain an express power of appropriation, incorporating the statutory power but declaring it to be exercisable without any of the consents required by s 41.[1]

1 This was often standard practice in professionally drawn wills, to avoid ad valorem stamp duty which was payable on the value of the assets appropriated by agreement. As stamp duty is no longer payable on appropriations, that particular reason for an express provision no longer applies, but such a power may still provide useful flexibility.

Transfer subject to existing liabilities

33.6 Items of property may automatically be subject to two types of liability. Where during the lifetime of the deceased incumbrances were charged on them, then the personal representatives may transfer the property to the beneficiary entitled subject to that charge. Where there is no danger that the creditor will not be paid there is no objection to this course. Thus, if a house worth £50,000 is subject to a mortgage of £30,000, then, as was pointed out earlier,[1] in the absence of contrary intention in the will, the devisee takes subject to that mortgage. The personal representatives will, however, be liable if the creditor is not paid, perhaps because of the subsequent diminution in value of the asset transferred. They must, therefore, require payment to be made prior to transfer to the beneficiary if there is any doubt.

1 See above, para 32.6.

33.7 Secondly, property may be transferred to a beneficiary subject to inheritance tax. Inheritance tax is dealt with in two ways. The general principle is that the tax payable by virtue of the death of the deceased is to be discharged out of the residue.[1] In this case, the personal representatives transfer to the beneficiary entitled assets which are specifically devised or bequeathed free from any liability to tax. However, the testator may provide that the tax should be borne by the beneficiary of the gift, when it becomes a charge on the property[2] and the personal representatives may safely transfer it to the beneficiary entitled, subject to that charge.[3] In the absence of a contrary provision a gift of property situate outside the United

Kingdom will bear its own tax.[4] The personal representatives are not themselves liable for payment of the tax on such property,[5] although an Inland Revenue charge is imposed on it.[6]

1 Inheritance Tax Act 1984, s 211(1).
2 Ibid, s 237(1).
3 Ibid, s 211(2), enables a contrary intention to oust s 211(1), which imposes the liability for tax on the personal representatives.
4 Ibid, s 211(1), (2).
5 Ibid, s 200(1)(a), imposing the liability, applies only to the deceased's free estate in the UK.
6 Ibid, s 237(1), although in practice the charge may not be enforceable unless the funds are remitted back to the UK: s 237(2).

Mode of transfer

Assent

Nature

33.8 In essence, an assent is an act by a personal representative in favour of a beneficiary indicating that the personal representative does not require an asset for the purposes of the administration of the deceased's estate, and that the asset can, therefore, pass to the beneficiary in accordance with the will. The assent confers upon the beneficiary the right to possession of the asset in respect of which it is made. If a beneficiary takes possession of an asset which is specifically given to him before an assent is made, the personal representative can recover the asset, even if the personal representative can discharge the debts and liabilities without recourse to it.[1]

1 *Mead v Lord Orrery* (1745) 3 Atk 235 at 239.

Assets other than land

33.9 In the case of assets other than land, an assent can be in any form which shows that the personal representative intended the beneficiary to take possession of the asset, or it can be oral.[1] It will also be presumed where the beneficiary takes possession, and retains possession for a considerable time without the personal representative objecting or seeking to recover it.[2]

1 *Doe d Sturges v Tatchell* (1832) 3 B & Ad 675; *Barnard v Pumfrett* (1841) 5 My & Cr 63 at 70.
2 *Cole v Miles* (1852) 10 Hare 179; *Richardson v Gifford* (1834) 1 Ad & El 52.

Land

33.10 Both executors and administrators[1] may transfer an estate or interest in realty and in leaseholds[2] by means of an assent.[3] Assents differ from the general rule that a document transferring a legal estate must be by deed in that by virtue of the Administration of Estates Act 1925, s 6(4), they need only be in writing. That sub-section also requires an assent to be signed by the personal representatives, and to name the person in whose favour it is given. The power to make an assent is restricted to personal representatives, and cannot be used by trustees.

1 Administration of Estates Act 1925, s 36(1).
2 Ibid.
3 Ibid.

33.11 There is some doubt as to the circumstances in which an assent may be used. Section 36(1) confers upon personal representatives the power to use an assent to vest a legal estate in 'any person who (whether by devise, bequest, devolution, appropriation or otherwise) may be entitled thereto'. The doubt relates to whether an assent may be used in favour of a purchaser. The nearest decision appears to be *GHR Co Ltd v IRC*.[1] In his lifetime the testator had sold his property, and had received the purchase money for it, but he had not executed a conveyance in favour of the purchaser. His executor had to make title, and did so by means of an assent. This was upheld. There is no decision where the purchase price is payable upon the handing over of the sale deed, as is the normal case, although there is little advantage in using an assent.[2] Where a personal representative is expressed to assent 'as personal representative' he will thereby give the same covenants for title as if he were executing a conveyance.[3]

1 [1943] KB 303.
2 It would still attract stamp duty if the consideration exceeds £60,000.
3 Administration of Estates Act 1925, s 36(3).

Informal assents in relation to land
33.12 In the case of land, a written assent is necessary to pass the legal title.[1] However, an informal act may constitute an effective assent for other purposes.[2] In *Re Edwards' Will Trusts, Edwards v Edwards*[3] a wife died intestate owning two plots of land. Her husband, who was beneficially entitled to the whole of her estate under the intestacy rules, obtained a grant of letters of administration to her estate. He did not execute any written assent in his favour, but took possession of the land, and retained it until his death. The Court of Appeal held that while the legal title remained in the estate of the wife, the act of taking possession by the husband, with his concurrence (in his capacity as his wife's personal representative) caused the equitable interest to pass to the husband, so that, on the death of the husband, it became subject to the trusts of his will.

1 *Re King's Will Trusts* [1964] Ch 542.
2 *Re Hodge, Hodge v Griffiths* [1940] Ch 260.
3 [1982] Ch 30, [1981] 2 All ER 941.

Effect
33.13 When an assent is made, it is that document which vests the legal estate in the person in whose favour it is made.[1] Under the will, or the intestacy rules, he acquires only an equitable interest.[2] However, when the assent is made, it relates back to the death of the deceased unless it contains an expression of intention to the contrary.[3]

1 Administration of Estates Act 1925, s 36(2).
2 See above, Chapter 30.
3 Administration of Estates Act 1925, s 36(2).

33.14 It has already been pointed out that the personal representative will not wish to distribute the estate until provision has been made for all outstanding liabilities. He is given power to require a beneficiary to give security for outstanding liabilities as a condition of giving an assent, and an assent may be subject to any legal mortgage.[1] The personal representative may not, however, delay giving an assent because of outstanding liabilities if reasonable arrangements have been made for them.[2]

1 Administration of Estates Act 1925, s 26(10).
2 Ibid.

33.15 Where he wishes to defer giving an assent, the personal representative may take advantage of the Administration of Estates Act, s 43. Under that section, he may allow a person who appears to be entitled to an assent to enter into possession of the property prior to giving the assent. That permission does not prevent him subsequently retaking possession, and disposing of the property if this is necessary in the course of the administration of the estate. By using s 43 the beneficiary can be given possession at an early date, leaving the assent to follow when all liabilities have been dealt with.

Protection of purchasers and others

33.16 A beneficiary in whose favour an assent is made is entitled to insist that a notice of the assent is endorsed on the probate or letters of administration at the cost of the estate. He may also require the personal representatives at any future time to produce the grant to prove that the notice has been endorsed.[1] As will now be shown, the endorsement of this notice protects the beneficiary against a disposition in favour of a purchaser.

1 Administration of Estates Act 1925, s 36(5).

33.17 A purchaser will normally insist that the conveyance to him contains a statement by the personal representatives that they have not previously given or made any assent or conveyance in respect of the legal estate.[1] If this statement is correct, it does not prejudice the title of any previous purchaser, but if the personal representatives have previously made an assent in favour of a beneficiary, the execution of the conveyance with this statement operates to shift the legal estate from that beneficiary to the purchaser.[2] The conveyance only has this effect, however, if the purchaser accepted the conveyance on the faith of this statement, and if there was no notice of a previous assent endorsed on the grant of representation. There is little advantage in including in an assent to a beneficiary a statement that the personal representative has not previously given any assent or made any conveyance because the statutory protection applies only in favour of purchasers. Conversely, although purchasers are entitled to have a notice of their conveyance endorsed on the grant[3] they will not be prejudiced if they fail to do so.

1 Administration of Estates Act 1925, s 36(6).
2 Ibid (second para).
3 Ibid, s 36(5).

33.18 It is a principle of the 1925 legislation that equitable interests are kept off the title, and a will can since 1925 affect only the equitable interests. Accordingly, a purchaser is never concerned to look at the will when investigating title from personal representatives.[1] As a result he does not know that the assent or conveyance is made in favour of the person properly entitled. Section 36(7) confers a large measure of protection. It provides that in favour of a purchaser, the fact that an assent or conveyance is made by a personal representative is 'sufficient evidence that the person in whose favour [it] is given is the person entitled to have the legal estate conveyed to him'. This will usually be adequate protection for the purchaser, but it should be noted that 'sufficient evidence' is not 'conclusive evidence'. Almost certainly a purchaser is not required to examine the will to ensure that the assent is made in favour of the correct person, but he will be affected by notice received during the proper investigation of title of the fact that the assent or conveyance should have been made in favour of another. Thus, in *Re Duce and Boots Cash Chemists (Southern) Ltd's Contract*[2] a recital in the assent showed that the land was prior to the death of the deceased settled, and that it remained settled notwithstanding his death. Accordingly it should have been vested in the next tenant for life. In fact the assent was in favour of the remainderman, and the purchaser's objection to the title was upheld.

1 The date of a will is often recited in a conveyance from personal representatives. Many standard forms of conveyance contain such a recital. This is unnecessary as the will is irrelevant to the devolution of title. In an assent such a recital is dangerous – as is shown in *Re Duce*, below.
2 [1937] Ch 642.

Other instruments

33.19 Apart from assents, the formalities normally observed for the transfer to beneficiaries of the legal title of other assets will depend on the nature of the assets to be transferred, as illustrated in the summary below.

33.20 *Summary of formalities for transfer of assets*

ASSET	METHOD OF TRANSFER
1 Unregistered land.	
(a) transfer to beneficiary absolutely entitled.	Assent.
(b) transfer to purchaser.	Conveyance (or perhaps assent).
(c) transfer to tenant for life in case of settlement.	Vesting assent.
2 Registered land.	
(a) transfer to beneficiary.	Land Registry form of assent, to be accompanied by Land Certificate.*
(b) transfer to purchaser.	Transfer.*
(c) transfer to tenant for life in case of settlement.	Land Registry form of vesting assent, to be accompanied by Land Certificate.*
3 Stock exchange securities.	Transfer accompanied by stock or share certificate.*

ASSET	METHOD OF TRANSFER
4 Choses in action; choses in equity.	Assignment, with notice to debtor.
5 Mortgage of land. (a) unregistered title. (b) registered title.	 Transfer of mortgage. Land Registry form of transfer of mortgage, accompanied by Charge Certificate.*
6 Bank account.	Written instructions to transfer from personal representatives, accompanied by copy of grant of representation. If already registered, by cheque.
7 Building society account.	The appropriate form of transfer prescribed by the society.
8 National Savings account, Trustee Savings Bank account, National Savings Certificates, etc.	Withdrawal or transfer forms, following registration of grant of representation.
9 Chattels.	(a) Manual delivery; or (b) assent, which may be by deed or only under hand.

* Note: if the personal representatives are not themselves registered as proprietors of the land, mortgage or shares (which they may have been following production of their grant to the Land Registry, or to the company registrar with a letter of request), a copy of the grant of representation is also required.

Currency of pecuniary legacies

33.21 In general, it is presumed that where the testator was domiciled in one country, and a beneficiary is resident elsewhere, legacies are to be paid in the currency of the country in which the testator died domiciled.[1] This is subject to any contrary intention on the part of the testator, and a contrary intention will be presumed where:

(a) the legacy is expressed in a foreign currency, such as a gift of $US100;[2] or

(b) a specific, immovable property abroad is charged with the payment of a legacy, in which case the legacy is payable in the currency of the country of the property.[3] If, however, all the testator's immovable property abroad, in several countries, is charged generally with the payment of legacies, they are payable in the currency of the country of the testator's domicile.[4]

Subject to any direction in the will to the contrary, where a legacy is payable to a beneficiary in another country, the rate of exchange is that prevailing on the first anniversary of the testator's death.[5] No deduction is made for the cost of remitting.[6] If, however, payment is made to a beneficiary from assets situated in the country of the beneficiary, the value of the legacy is calculated according to the official exchange rate, and not according to the sum which would actually be required to purchase that currency.[7]

1   *Saunders v Drake* (1742) 2 Atk 465; *Pierson v Garnet* (1786) 2 Bro CC 38; *Malcolm v Martin* (1790) 3 Bro CC 50; *Marchioness of Lansdowne v Marquis Lansdowne* (1820) 2 Bligh 60; *Yates v Maddan* (1849) 16 Sim 613.
2   *Raymond v Brodbelt* (1800) 5 Ves 199.
3   *Saunders v Drake* (1742) 2 Atk 465; *Pierson v Garnet* (1786) 2 Bro CC 38.
4   *Phipps v Earl of Anglesea* (1721) 5 Vin Abr 209 pl 8; *Wallis v Brightwell* (1722) 2 PWms 88; *Marchioness of Lansdowne v Marquis of Lansdowne* (1820) 2 Bligh 60.
5   *Re Eighmie, Colbourne v Wilks* [1935] Ch 524.
6   *Cockerell v Barber* (1810) 16 Ves 461; *Re Schnapper, Westminster Bank Ltd v Schnapper* [1936] 1 All ER 322.
7   *Campbell v Graham* (1831) 1 Russ & M 453.

Allocation of assets

33.22   Before the transfer of an asset to the beneficiary entitled, the personal representatives may set aside that asset for him, and, unless the asset is land,[1] they will thenceforth hold the asset as bare trustees for the beneficiary. This will be so even although the general administration of the estate has not been completed. The decision in *Re Berry*[2] illustrates the danger of setting assets aside before the liabilities of the estate have been finally ascertained. In that case, the executor thought that the estate would be sufficient to meet a pecuniary legacy, and he set aside the money to meet it, but retained that money under his control. It subsequently transpired that the estate was insolvent. It was held that the beneficiary was entitled to the legacy, and the executor was forced to make good the loss from his own funds.

1   *Re Cockburn's Will Trusts* [1957] Ch 438, [1957] 2 All ER 522.
2   (1981) 34 OR (2d) 56 (Ontario).

Costs of transfer

33.23   It has been shown[1] that a beneficiary is responsible for the cost of upkeep of an asset from the time when he becomes specifically entitled to it. He is also responsible for all costs incurred in connection with the transfer of the asset from the executors to him.[2] Thus, in *Re Fitzpatrick, Bennett v Bennett*[3] the testator left assets in Monaco to a beneficiary living in England. It was held that the beneficiary had to pay the cost of carriage and insurance. This rule is often contrary to what the testator would intend, and some well-drawn wills include express provisions for the costs of transfer to be paid from residue.

1   See above, para 31.76.
2   For earlier decisions against this principle, see *Perry v Meddowcroft* (1841) 4 Beav 197; *Re De Sommery, Coelenbier v De Sommery* [1912] 2 Ch 622; *Re Scott, Scott v Scott* [1915] 1 Ch 592, CA; *Re Hewett, Eldridge v Hewett* [1920] WN 366.
3   [1952] Ch 86.

CHAPTER 34

Donatio mortis causa

34.1 A donatio mortis causa is a type of gift which is midway between a lifetime and a testamentary gift. It has some of the characteristics of a lifetime gift, in particular delivery of the subject matter of the gift in the donor's lifetime, and some characteristics of a legacy, in particular that it does not become fully effective until death. The origin of donationes mortis causa is in Roman law, where they were used to avoid the technicalities of testamentary law. Although Brackden reproduced the Roman text, there was little need for them in English law until the Statute of Frauds 1677 virtually abolished nuncupative wills. The doctrine was introduced into English law through the Church courts. The first reported case is *Hedges v Hedges*,[1] in which Lord Cowper justified its recognition in the following terms:

'Where a man lies in extremity, or being surprised with sickness, and not having an opportunity of making his will; but lest he should die before he could make it, he gives with his own hands his goods to his friends about him: this, if he dies, shall operate as a legacy; but if he recovers, then does the property thereof revert to him.'

1   (1708) Prec Ch 269.

34.2 In *Re Beaumont*[1] Buckley LJ described a donatio mortis causa as:

'a singular form of gift. It may be said to be of an amphibious nature, being a gift which is neither entirely inter vivos nor testamentary. It is an act inter vivos by which the donee is to have the absolute title to the subject of the gift not at once but if the donor dies. If the donor dies the title becomes absolute and not under but as against his executor. In order to make the gift valid it must be made so as to take effect on the donor's death.'

1   [1902] 1 Ch 889 at 892.

34.3 A donatio mortis causa may therefore be defined as a gift made by a person in his lifetime with the intention that it should take effect only on his death. The gift is therefore conditional upon death, but once the condition is satisfied it takes effect retrospectively, from the date the gift was made.[1] It therefore follows that the donor must have intended that the gift should be absolute on the condition being fulfilled.[2]

1 *Rigden v Vallier* (1751) 2 Ves Sen 252.
2 *Re Beaumont* [1902] 1 Ch 889.

Requirements for establishing donatio mortis causa

34.4 The requirements for establishing a valid donatio mortis causa were set out by Lord Russell of Killowen CJ in *Cain v Moon*,[1] where he stated that three things must combine:

(a) the gift must have been made in contemplation, although not necessarily in expectation, of death;

(b) there must have been a delivery to the donee of the subject matter of the gift; and

(c) the gift was intended to be conditional on the donor's death and intended to revert if the donor recovered.

1 [1896] 2 QB 283.

Contemplation of death

34.5 The first requirement for establishing a donatio mortis causa is that it must have been made in contemplation, but not necessarily in expectation, of death. To satisfy this condition, the donor must not simply be considering the possibility of death at some time in the future, but the probability of his death within the near future, and from some reason which he believes to be impending.[1] The contemplation of death may be express or inferred from the circumstances. A donor may expressly indicate that he feels he is 'done for'[2]. The courts are, however, willing to infer the contemplation of death from the circumstances, particularly if it is during the donor's last illness, which is frequently the case. So in *Gardner v Parker*[3] the donor, who was seriously ill, gave a bond to the donee two days before the date of his death with the words: 'There, take that and keep it.' The gift was held to be made in contemplation of death.

1 *Re Craven's Estate (No 1)* [1937] Ch 423 at 426; see also *Wilkes v Allington* [1931] 2 Ch 104 at 110.
2 As in *Re Lillingston* [1952] 2 All ER 184, below, para 34.17.
3 (1818) 3 Madd 184.

34.6 It is immaterial that death supervenes from some cause other than that originally contemplated, provided the danger from which the death was originally apprehended continues to threaten until the donor's death. In *Wilkes v Allington*[1] the donor knew he was suffering from cancer and was aware that he did not have long to live. With this knowledge, he handed to his two nieces an envelope containing a mortgage which he wished to give them. He subsequently caught a chill and developed double pneumonia, from which he died nearly six weeks after making the gift. This was held to be a valid donatio mortis causa as the contemplation of death in his mind had continued up to the time of actual death even though, in fact, he died from another cause.

1 [1931] 2 Ch 104.

Contemplation of death from suicide
34.7 Is the requirement of contemplation of death met if that contemplation is death by suicide? This had to be considered by the Irish court in *Agnew v Belfast Banking Co.*[1] In that case the donor handed a bank deposit receipt to the plaintiff with the words: 'That is yours if anything should happen to me.' Nine days later the donor died having poisoned herself, and leaving a note dated the day on which she had handed the bank deposit receipt to the plaintiff clearly showing her intention to commit suicide. Fitzgibbon LJ declared:[2]

'But while I think that a danger of death may found a donation, whether it arises from natural causes or is incurred in the discharge of some duty, possibly including the duty of self sacrifice, I hold that a donation cannot be supported on a danger which is so purely voluntary as to be criminal in its origin . . . This brings in the dilemma. The delivery of this deposit receipt did not take effect as a gift until the death of the donor. Part of her condition of mind was that it was not to cease to be her property till her death: if she was insane at her death, she had then no capacity to complete the gift; if she was sane, we must attribute to her the intention of giving effect to the gift by a crime. . . . I hold that it is against public policy to uphold a gift which is intended to take effect by means of self-destruction.'

1 [1896] 2 IR 204.
2 Ibid, at 221, 223.

34.8 It fell to Russell LJ in *Re Dudman*[1] to determine whether contemplation of death by suicide would be accepted in the English courts as establishing a donatio mortis causa. A few days before her death, the deceased had given her brother three envelopes, each of which contained other envelopes with money and letters. One of the letters, written to an aunt, clearly indicated suicide:

'A line to wish you goodbye. I do not want to live any longer, there is no one that cares, and my ill health; if I was well I should not care. But I cannot fight any longer. It has been one long fight for me, and I am so tired of everything. It won't make much difference just a year or two more or less. Goodbye once more, you were very kind to me in days gone by. I hope you will find the enclosed fifty pounds useful.'

Russell LJ simply referred to the dictum of Fitzgibbon LJ in *Agnew v Belfast Banking Co*[2] and, without analysing it any further, concluded that 'the Irish case does not bind me, but it is the decision of the court for which I have the greatest respect and I intend to follow it'. Accordingly, he found that there had been no valid donatio mortis causa.

1 [1925] 1 Ch 553.
2 [1896] 2 IR 204.

34.9 If, however, one looks at the judgment of Fitzgibbon LJ, as supported by Russell LJ, two reasons were given for the decision: first, that the donor must remain sane up to the moment of her death; second, that if the donor remained sane she would be giving effect to the gift by a crime. If the first reason were strictly applied, probably the majority of gifts would fail as frequently a person goes into a coma or enters into a vegetative state before death. The second reason, that it would be contrary to public policy to allow a person to give effect to a gift by a crime, may have been pertinent at the date of the decision. However, this second ground ceased to be valid in 1961, when the crime of suicide was abolished.[1] Even if contemplation of suicide were to invalidate a donatio mortis causa, the contemplation of death by suicide must have been formed at the time the delivery is made. If the donor contemplated involuntary death when he made the delivery, a subsequent decision to commit suicide does not invalidate the gift. This is illustrated by another Irish case, *Mills v Shields*.[2] Mills suffered from neurosis and he was considering going to Dublin for what he knew could prove dangerous treatment. Accordingly, he deposited with his priest a parcel containing £600 worth of stocks and shares. Mills told the priest that if anything should happen to him while he was away, the priest was to give the parcel to Mills's brothers in South Africa. Before receiving treatment, Mills hanged himself. A verdict was entered of suicide while temporarily insane. Medical evidence was provided to show that Mills had seemed quite sane before he had left for treatment and that he was merely worried. It was held that the donatio mortis causa was not defeated merely because the donor may have contemplated being visited with a suicidal urge at the time of delivery rather than having formed an intention to commit suicide.

1 Suicide Act 1961. No one was ever convicted of suicide! However, the attempt to commit the offence carried the criminal sanction.
2 [1948] IR 367.

Does the contemplation of death have to be reasonable?
34.10 All the cases in English law where a donatio mortis causa has been established have arisen in situations where the donor reasonably contemplated death (and generally died from the cause feared). What, however, is the position if the fear was unreasonable or the donor mistakenly believed that he would die in the near future? Suppose a donor has a superstitious terror of spiders and believes that if he sees three in one day his death is imminent, and in this state of mind he makes a donatio. Or suppose the donor has been wrongly diagnosed as having terminal cancer and in those circumstances also makes a donatio but is killed in a car accident shortly afterwards. A passing mention was made in *Agnew v Belfast Banking*[1] that death should be contemplated from 'natural causes or incurred in the discharge of some duty, possibly including the duty of self sacrifice'. These words suggest that the contemplation of death should be reasonable. However, none of the English cases appears to support such an objective test but, rather, suggests that the test is subjective: the requirement of contemplation of death is one of belief in the mind of the donor rather than of its reasonableness. In *Re Miller*[2] it was not disputed that a woman about to fly from London to Geneva was capable of making a donatio mortis causa, even though flying is statistically safer than driving a motor car. However, in *Thompson v Mechan*[3] the Ontario Court of Appeal

adopted an objective assessment of the requirement of contemplation of death. In that case too, the donor had a fear of air travel.

1 [1896] 2 IR 204, per Fitzgibbon LJ at 221; see above, para 34.7.
2 (1961) 105 Sol Jo 207.
3 [1958] OR 357 (Ontario).

Delivery to the donee of the subject matter of the gift

34.11 To constitute a valid donatio mortis causa, the donor must have handed over the subject matter of the gift. It is this delivery which distinguishes a donatio mortis causa from a legacy and is an overt act made by the donor to give effect to the gift. If mere words were required, the whole object of the Wills Act 1837 would be defeated. There must therefore be:
(a) a parting with dominion of the subject matter of the gift,
(b) to the donee himself or to the donee's agent, and
(c) a delivery of the subject matter of the gift or a means of access to it.

Delivery with intention of parting with dominion
34.12 The donor must intend to part with dominion or control over the asset rather than deliver it for some other purpose, such as safe custody. Accordingly, delivering a locked cashbox, but keeping control of the key and reserving a right of dealing with the contents, would be construed as a delivery for the purpose of safe custody and not of parting with dominion.[1] The delivery must also be for the purpose of giving the donee exclusive dominion or control over the subject matter of the gift. Accordingly, if the donor delivers to the donee one of two keys to a box containing the subject matter of the gift, this may be construed as failure to give full dominion to the donee.[2] However, the mere fact that the donor retains a key will not automatically be construed as a failure if the surrounding circumstances indicate otherwise. In *Woodard v Woodard*[3] the donor was gravely ill in hospital when he handed the keys of his car to his son by way of a donatio mortis causa. Although the donor had retained a duplicate set of keys this did not invalidate the gift as, in practical terms, only the son had access to the car.

1 *Reddel v Dobree* (1839) 10 Sim 244; *Re Johnson* (1905) 92 LT 357; see too *Wildish v Fowler* (1892) 8 TLR 457 where an item was handed by a sick lodger to his landlady with instructions to 'take care of this'.
2 *Re Craven's Estate (No 1)* [1937] Ch 423 at 428. In *Sen v Headley* [1991] 2 All ER 636, CA, which established that there could be a donatio of land by delivery of title deeds, no claim was made for a donatio of the contents of the house as the donor had retained his own set of keys to the house.
3 [1992] RTR 35, CA.

34.13 If there has been a delivery to the donee with the intention of parting with dominion, a redelivery to the donor for the purpose of safe custody will not necessarily restore dominion to the donor. In *Re Hawkins*,[1] on his death-bed the donor placed cash for the intended donees in two envelopes which were placed in turn in a third and yet fourth envelope, and were then handed to his niece. The niece suggested that the envelope be kept in the deed box in the donor's room. This redelivery did not restore dominion to the donor as the envelope was handed back merely for the purpose of safe custody: effectively, the donor became bailee for the donee.

1 [1924] 2 Ch 47.

34.14 A delivery antecedent to the intention to give will be sufficient. Accordingly, if an asset is delivered for the purpose of safe custody, but subsequently the bailee is told to hold it in a different capacity, this will amount to a constructive delivery of the gift to the donee in that new capacity. In *Cain v Moon*[1] Mrs Cain had delivered a deposit note to her mother for safe custody. Later, when Mrs Cain fell ill and did not expect to recover, she referred to the deposit note held by her mother and declared: 'Everything I possess and the bank note is yours if I die.' This was held to be an effective delivery.

1 [1896] 2 QB 283.

Delivery to the donee or to the donee's agent
34.15 Delivery to the donee's agent will constitute sufficient delivery for the purpose of parting with dominion. Delivery to the donor's agent is not, however, adequate as the donor is in a position to demand it back from his agent. If the holder is a servant or employee of the donor there is a presumption that that person is an agent of the donor. Accordingly, a key given to the donor's housekeeper does not constitute a sufficient delivery.[1] A delivery to a fiduciary agent or trustee may, however, be a sufficient parting with dominion to put it outside the control of the donor. In *Mills v Shields*[2] the donor, before undergoing dangerous treatment, had handed his priest a parcel of stocks and shares to give to his brothers in South Africa if he did not recover. This was held to be an adequate delivery: the priest could be regarded as a fiduciary agent.

1 *Trimmer v Danby* (1856) 25 LJ Ch 424.
2 [1948] IR 367.

34.16 This may be contrasted with *Re Miller*.[1] While at London airport awaiting a flight to Italy, Mrs Miller put four shillings in a slot machine for which she was issued with a coupon for insurance. The terms of the coupon provided that the insurance company would pay to a bona fide holder of the coupon or his personal representatives the sum of £2,000 if he suffered death by violent accidental means within 24 hours of issue of the coupon. Mrs Miller folded the coupon, put a stamp on it and posted it to her sister. She then set off on her flight, during the course of which she wrote a letter to her sister, saying she hoped that her sister would not have to make a claim. The plane crashed in Italy later that day. Mrs Miller's sister did not receive the coupon until the following day. It was held that the claim that Mrs Miller had made a donatio mortis causa to her sister failed on two grounds. First, the court came to the conclusion that the coupon was posted to the sister not with the intention of making a donatio but for the purpose of safe custody; had the deceased taken the coupon with her, evidence of the insurance may have been destroyed. It was natural to send it to someone for safe custody. The second ground was that the subject matter had not been delivered to the addressee at the date of the deceased's death. It is considered that this objection is flawed: once a letter has been posted, the post office is in the position of a fiduciary agent and is obliged to make delivery to the addressee. The donor has put the delivery of the letter outside his control and has therefore parted with dominion of it.

1 (1961) 105 Sol Jo 207.

Delivery of the subject matter of the gift

34.17 The requirements for delivery of the subject matter of a donatio mortis causa are generally more lax than those required to establish a lifetime gift. Assets that may constitute the subject matter of a donatio mortis causa are considered in greater detail below.[1] Essentially, however, there must be a delivery of the subject matter of the gift: in the case of a chattel, the asset itself; in respect of a chose in action, delivery of one or more essential indicia of title. Delivery of a means of access to the subject matter will suffice, even though this may not have constituted sufficient delivery to establish a lifetime gift. Accordingly, delivery of the only set of keys to a box containing the subject matter of the donatio will be sufficient.[2] However, the donor must hand over the very means by which possession can be obtained, not merely a symbol of possession.[3] In *Re Lillingston*[4] the court even allowed a 'treasure hunt'. Mrs Lillingston, who had been in poor health and confined to bed for some months, told the intended donee that she felt she was 'done for'. She declared that: 'I am going to give you all my jewellery. I am giving you my key to the safe deposit at Harrods and when I am gone you can go and get the jewellery.' With that, she handed over the keys of the trunk in her room, continuing: 'here is the key to the trunk over there. You will find the key to the Harrods safe deposit on the right-hand side of the finger of a glove. The key to my city safe is at Harrods. I want you to have all my jewellery except my diamond necklace which is for my goddaughter. That is in my city safe.' She then took a packet from under her pillow, stating: 'This is also for you.' She then proceeded to open the packet, containing more jewellery, which she then put back into the packet and then into the trunk. She then locked the trunk and handed the key to the donee with the words: 'Keep the key, it is now yours.' The court held that there had been a valid donatio mortis causa of all the jewellery, including that found in the trunk and in the Harrods and city safes.

1 See paras 34.27–34.39.
2 *Re Craven's Estate (No 1)* [1937] Ch 423, in respect of delivery of access to a chattel. *Sen v Headley* [1991] Ch 425, CA, in respect of access to title deeds.
3 *Ward v Turner* (1752) 2 Ves Sen 431; *Bunn v Markham* (1816) 7 Taunt 224.
4 [1952] 2 All ER 184.

The gift is intended to be conditional on the donor's death and to revert if the donor recovers

34.18 The gift must be intended to be conditional on the donor's death. An intention that the gift is to be immediate and absolute is inconsistent with the conditional nature of a donatio mortis causa. Accordingly, an imperfect lifetime gift cannot be saved by attempting to construe it as a donatio mortis causa if it was not intended as such.[1] The circumstances in which the gift is made have to be considered. The donor may express the gift in terms that appear absolute, such as 'Keep the key, it is now yours',[2] whereas in their context the words can be construed as being conditional on death. The courts are particularly inclined to infer the conditional nature of a gift where it is made during the donor's last illness.[3]

1 *Edwards v Jones* (1836) 1 My & Cr 226; *Agnew v Belfast Banking Co* [1896] 2 IR 204.
2 *Re Lillingston* [1952] 2 All ER 184.
3 Ibid; *Gardner v Parker* (1818) 3 Madd 184: 'There, take that and keep it', where a bond was handed to the donee two days before the donor's death and when he was on his death-bed.

34.19 An intended donatio mortis causa is normally expressed orally. To incorporate it in writing raises a presumption that it was not intended as a donatio mortis causa but as an attempted lifetime gift or an attempt at making a testamentary disposition.[1] However, the mere existence of writing will not invalidate a donatio mortis causa if it can be explained as fulfilling for some other purpose. In *Wilkes v Allington*[2] the donor had delivered a mortgage deed as an intended donatio mortis causa and had written on the envelope containing the deeds: 'Deeds relating to Astwood. To be given up at death.' This endorsement on the deed was not construed as an abortive lifetime gift as the court did not regard it as having any reference at all to the circumstances in which the donor had handed over the envelope but, rather, as a method of identifying the subject matter of the gift.

1 *Edwards v Jones* (1836) 1 My & Cr 226.
2 [1931] 2 Ch 104.

Conditional nature of the gift

34.20 The conditional nature of the gift and the fact that it will revert to the donor if he recovers do not have to be specified in its making but may be readily inferred from the circumstances in which it is made. In *Staniland v Willott*[1] the donor, when he was very ill, declared that he did not think he would get better. With that he had handed the donee his watch and morning rings; three days later he executed a share transfer in favour of the donee. A month later, the donor recovered and went abroad to recuperate, but there became insane. The donee had handed back the watch and rings and the action, brought on the donor's behalf, successfully recovered the shares, which were held to revert to the donor as he no longer contemplated death.

1 (1850) 3 Mac & G 664.

The time of recovery

34.21 In some cases it may be difficult to determine at what stage the donor does recover. It would appear to be when the donor ceases to contemplate the risk of death within a reasonably short time. So where a donor with a dread of flying makes a donatio mortis causa in contemplation of his death during an imminent flight, the gift would revert when the aircraft lands safely at its destination airport. Accordingly, if after landing the donor were killed by a luggage transporter in the airport terminal, the donatio would be ineffective. On the other hand, if the donor continued to fear death from a return journey, the gift would not revert until his eventual safe return.

Charge on the gift
34.22 There must be an intention to make a present gift conditional on the donor's death, not merely to make a gift in the future. However, a request to pay expenses out of the asset does not make its delivery a future gift. In *Re Ward*,[1] on the day before his death, the donor handed his post office savings book to the donee, telling him that the balance was his, subject to him paying the donor's funeral expenses out of the account. This was a valid donatio mortis causa, even though the precise amount of the gift was not ascertainable at that time as there was a charge on it. On the other hand, if the court is of the opinion that the deceased was really attempting to make the donee an executor to administer the assets on the donor's death, it will fail as a donatio mortis causa. In *Re Harrison*[2] the deceased had made up four parcels of Treasury Notes, writing the names of intended donees on each. He then put the parcels in a deeds box beside his bed and gave his daughter the key. The daughter took the box to the bank and kept the key until her father died. The court came to the conclusion that the testator was effectively endeavouring to make his daughter the executrix by directing her to take possession of the parcels after his death and to distribute them in a particular way.

1 [1946] 2 All ER 206.
2 [1934] WN 25, 78 Sol Jo 135.

Suppose death is certain?
34.23 As a donatio mortis causa is conditional upon death, the donor is able to revoke the gift at any time before his death. An essential attribute therefore of a donatio mortis causa is that the delivery is conditional on death but with the possibility that it will be revoked by the donor's recovery. It has therefore been suggested that if death is certain, so that the possibility of the donor's recovery is removed, there is no scope for a donatio mortis causa: the purported gift must either be treated as an attempted lifetime gift or fail as a testamentary disposition. This argument was raised in *Lord Advocate v M'Court*.[1] The deceased gave his brother a written receipt for £100 for the deceased's interest in their pawnbroking business. This was merely a nominal sum and therefore involved a substantial element of gift. Some three months later the deceased died and death duties were claimed on the share in the partnership as being a donatio mortis causa.[2] The Court of Session determined that this constituted a lifetime gift and not a donatio mortis causa. The donor was suffering from a disease from which he could not recover. Accordingly, there was no room to read into the gift a condition that it was to operate only on his death as, equally, there was no occasion for the implied condition that if he recovered it would revert to him. Lord M'Larn considered that while in many cases the condition of death can be presumed, yet in the present case[3] 'the nature of the disease was such that he could not possibly recover . . . and knew that he had only a few weeks or months to live. That being so, there was no occasion for any implied condition about recovery, and I am not going to read such a condition where the circumstances are not such as would give rise to it.' Consequently, the gift took immediate effect.

1   (1893) 20 R 488.
2   At that time a lifetime gift did not attract duty, but a donatio mortis causa did as being property passing on death.
3   (1893) 20 R 488 at 500.

34.24   However, it is submitted that the statement is not an authority for saying that if death is certain, the possibility of a donatio mortis causa is excluded: all the court was refusing to do was to infer that the gift was conditional. It is no authority for saying that a person cannot make an express condition under such circumstances, such as by stating: 'if I die' or words to that effect. Two further factors reduce the authority of this case. First, a consideration, although nominal, was paid, so it was not entirely a gift. Secondly, the transfer was in writing which made no mention of the condition of the death of the donor: the writing left out an essential term of the bargain if that term had been intended as such. It may be said that the condition can be implied unless it is excluded, either expressly or by implication from the fact that it is not mentioned in a document which appears to represent the entire agreement.

34.25   The argument was again raised in *Re Lillingston*.[1] It was claimed that as the deceased was certain to die she was incapable of making a donatio mortis causa. Death being certain, the gift either constituted an invalid oral will or was an abortive lifetime gift in respect of all the jewellery apart from the packet actually handed to the donee (delivery of access by a key being insufficient to constitute a lifetime gift). Wyn Parry J considered that if the donor knew she was certain to die in the immediate future, it might be possible to adopt the view that there could be no donatio mortis causa. However, he found on the facts that such an argument did not apply to the instant case: there was insufficient evidence that the donor was bound to die in the immediate, or even near, future as she had suffered heart attacks before. Further, from the words 'when I am gone', he construed an implied condition that if the donor were to survive she would expect the jewellery and the key to be returned. The argument, apart from the Scottish case, has not really been raised before and is perhaps an unhelpful and unfortunate point.

1   [1952] 2 All ER 184.

The condition of death

34.26   It may be necessary to determine whether death is a condition subsequent or a condition precedent. Lord Russell CJ in *Cain v Moon*[1] initially suggests that death is a condition subsequent so that 'the gift must be made under such circumstances as to show that the thing is to revert to the donor in case he should recover'. In other words, the gift is to make immediate effect, but is to revert to the donor if he recovers. He then continues: 'this . . . is sometimes put somewhat differently, and it is said that the gift must be made under circumstances showing that it is to take effect only if the death of the donor follows'. This alternative would make death a condition precedent and so the gift would not take effect until death. Lord Russell CJ then concluded that 'it is not necessary to say which way of putting it is better'. However, the distinction may be critical. If death is a condition precedent, the donee has no title to pass until death. Suppose the donor makes a donatio mortis causa of his car, which is sold by the donee before the donor's death. If the donor recovers, so that the gift reverts to him, can the donor reclaim the car from the purchaser?

1 [1896] 2 QB 283.

Assets which may constitute the subject matter of a donatio mortis causa

34.27 As we have seen, the formalities required for delivery of the subject matter of a donatio mortis causa are more lax than those required to establish a lifetime gift. Since delivery is essential, as for a lifetime gift, only tangible personal property should strictly be capable of forming the subject matter of a donatio. The courts have, however, relaxed this strict requirement of delivery in the case of a donatio mortis causa, to embrace anomalous classes of assets that are not really capable of delivery. The general rule that equity will not perfect an imperfect gift is thus often relaxed in the case of a donatio mortis causa. Accordingly, a delivery of some document which is the 'essential indicia or evidence of title, possession or production of which entitles the possessor to the money or property purported to be given'[1] will be sufficient. While in such cases the donee obtains only the equitable title, equity will nevertheless perfect an imperfect gift on the donor's death by compelling the personal representatives to transfer the legal or other title in the appropriate way, except where this is not necessary such as in the case of bearer securities.

1 Per Evershed, MR, in the Court of Appeal in *Birch v Treasury Solicitor* [1951] Ch 298 at 311.

34.28 Adopting this broad principle, it may be useful to consider what assets may constitute the subject matter of a donatio mortis causa. The list that follows is not intended to be exhaustive and may change from time to time as practice alters or develops.

34.29 *Bearer securities.* These include banknotes or other securities payable to bearer, where title is simply transferred by delivery.

34.30 *Negotiable instruments, cheques and promissory notes drawn in favour of the donor.* To constitute a valid lifetime gift, these documents would require endorsement by the donor. As these assets represent an enforceable right of action against the drawer, however, they are capable of forming the subject matter of a donatio.

34.31 *The donor's own cheque or promissory note.* Such documents given by the donor are, in the absence of consideration, unenforceable as they do not constitute property. The donor's own cheque is not property, it is only a revocable order to his banker. However, it will form the subject matter of a donatio if:

(a)   the donee negotiates the cheque for value to a bona fide holder in the donor's lifetime. The holder can then enforce it against the donor's personal representative after the donor's death. However, in view of the conditional nature of a donatio, pending death, it would appear that the donee would have to hold the cash or goods received for the cheque as trustee or bailee for the donor.

(b)   the donee cashes the cheque or credits it to his account before the donor dies, and probably even after the donor's death provided the donor's bank had not at the time of encashment received notice of the donor's death. The transfer of the funds from the account constitutes delivery. However, it would appear that the donee will have to hold the proceeds on the donor's behalf pending the donor's death as the gift does not become absolute until death.

34.32   *Bank deposit books.*   If the deposit book must be produced to withdraw money, then its delivery can form the subject matter of a donatio mortis causa. In *Birch v Treasury Solicitor*[1] the donor in contemplation of death handed to two intended donees a post office savings bank book, a London Trustee Savings Bank book, a Barclays Bank deposit passbook and Westminster Bank deposit account passbook. The Court of Appeal held that all of these documents constituted essential indicia of title. Each of them had to be produced to obtain withdrawal of the funds from the respective accounts. On the other hand, a passbook does not constitute an essential indicia of title if its production is not required for the withdrawal of funds.[2] Passbooks for high street bank deposit accounts are now relatively rare. Where there are no passbooks but the accounts are simply held on computer, they are treated like any other bank account and not capable of delivery.

1   [1951] Ch 298; see also *Re Dillon* (1890) 44 Ch D 76 (banker's deposit note); *Moore v Darton* (1851) 4 De G & Sm 517.
2   *Delgoffe v Fader* [1939] Ch 922.

34.33   *Bank accounts.*   If money is held in a bank account – whether current or deposit or in any other form – it cannot form the subject matter of a donatio mortis causa. Such accounts are held on computer and the statement is merely evidence thereof. Simply to hand over a bank statement would therefore be insufficient to establish a donatio: the statement does not have to be produced to obtain payment from the account.

34.34   *Building society passbooks.*   It is normal for funds held in a building society to be entered in a passbook. If the passbook must be produced to withdraw funds from the account, it can form the subject matter of a donatio mortis causa.[1] If the account is represented in another form, such as a statement of the balance held, that statement will not constitute an essential indicium of title.

1   *Griffiths and the Abbey National Building Society* (1947) [1938–1949] Registrar's Reports of Selected Disputes 14: the Registrar of Friendly Societies held that the delivery of a building society share account passbook constituted a valid donatio.

34.35   *National Savings Certificates.*   Where, in the case of National

Savings products – such as National Savings Certificates – the certificates must be produced to obtain payment, they can form the subject matter of a donatio.

34.36 *Life assurance policies.* Before payment is made under a policy it normally has to be produced to the insurance company when the claim is made. It is the policy document that incorporates the obligation to pay imposed on the insurance company, and it may therefore constitute the subject matter of a donatio.

34.37 *Company shares.* It has been suggested that registered shares in a company cannot constitute the subject matter of a donatio mortis causa.[1] However, in *Staniland v Willott*[2] it was accepted without debate that company shares could. Similarly, in *Re Craven's Estate (No 1)*[3] there was a valid donatio of shares that had been transferred to the donee. Accordingly, company shares and building society shares represented by certificates are capable of passing by donatio mortis causa provided the donor makes a valid transfer of them to the donee. It may also be sufficient if he simply delivers the certificates with a document that amounts to a transfer, even if the transfer is not registered with the company registrar before the date of death. Bearer shares, like other bearer securities, may simply be delivered to the donee without further formality to effect a donatio.

1 *Moore v Moore* (1874) LR 18 Eq 474; *Re Weston* [1902] 1 Ch 680, decided on a misinterpretation of *Ward v Turner* (1752) 2 Ves Sen 431, which held merely that receipts for the purchase of shares were insufficient but did not preclude delivery of the stock certificate itself with a transfer.
2 (1852) 3 Mac & G 664.
3 [1937] Ch 423.

34.38 *Mortgage debts.* The delivery of a mortgage deed which contains a covenant to pay can form the subject matter of a donatio mortis causa.[1] In *Wilkes v Allington*[2] the delivery of the mortgage deed constituted a donatio notwithstanding that the deed did not contain such a covenant.

1 *Duffield v Elwes* (1827) 1 Bli NS 497.
2 [1931] 2 Ch 104.

34.39 *Land.* The House of Lords in *Duffield v Elwes*[1] considered obiter that land could not form the subject matter of a donatio even though a mortgage deed in that case was held capable of being so delivered. This view remained unchallenged until *Sen v Headley*,[2] when the Court of Appeal resolved that the title deeds to unregistered freehold property could form the subject matter of a donatio. The plaintiff and the deceased had lived together as husband and wife for a number of years and thereafter had remained close friends up to the date of the deceased's death in 1986. The deceased had been admitted into hospital with terminal cancer and was aware of his imminent, inevitable death. Three days before his death, when the deceased and the plaintiff were alone together in the hospital, the plaintiff had asked the deceased what she should do about the house if anything should happen to him. The deceased had replied: 'The house is yours, Margaret. You have the keys. They are in your bag. The deeds are in the steel box.' When the plaintiff then asked about the contents of the house, the deceased replied: 'Do what you like. It's all yours.' No further discussion took place about the subject of the house and contents. Following the deceased's death, the plaintiff found a bunch of keys that the deceased had slipped unnoticed into her handbag. One of these keys, which appears to have been an only key, was to a locked box containing the title deeds to the house. The deceased died intestate. The plaintiff claimed a donatio mortis causa of the house by constructive delivery of the title deeds to the house by handing over the only key to the locked box containing the title deeds, accompanied by the words of gift. The first two criteria for establishing a donatio mortis causa were not in dispute: the gift was made in contemplation, if not necessarily in expectation, of impending death; and was made upon the condition that it was to be absolute and perfected only on the donor's death, being revocable until that event. The issue in contention arose on the third requirement, that there should be a delivery of the subject matter of the gift, or the essential indicia of title thereto. Nourse LJ, delivering the judgment of the Court of Appeal in favour of the plaintiff, accepted that the doctrine of donatio mortis causa is anomalous and concluded:[3]

> 'Anomalies do not justify anomalous exceptions. If due account is taken of the present state of the law in regard to mortgages and choses in action, it is apparent that to make a distinction in the case of land would be to make just such an exception. A donatio mortis causa of land is neither more nor less anomalous than any other. Every such gift is a circumvention of the Wills Act 1837. Why should the additional statutory formalities for the creation and transmission of interests in land be regarded as some larger obstacle? The only step which has to be taken is to extend the application of the implied or constructive trust arising on the donor's death from the conditional to the absolute estate. Admittedly this is a step which the House of Lords would not have taken in *Duffield v Elwes* and, if the point had been the subject of decision, we would have loyally followed it in this court. But we cannot decide a case in 1991 as the House of Lords would have decided it, but did not decide it, in 1827.'

Accordingly, delivery of title deeds to unregistered property is capable of forming the subject matter of a donatio mortis causa. The Court of Appeal did not express an opinion as to whether delivery of a land certificate in respect of a registered title would suffice. The question is whether the land certificate is an essential indicium of title – whether it must be produced to enable the property to be sold. There are practical difficulties in completing a sale speedily if the land certificate cannot be produced, but the problem can be overcome by implementing the prescribed procedures for dealing with a lost certificate.[4] However, an essential indicium of title does not cease to be such merely because with certain formalities the problems of its loss can be overcome. It is undoubtedly accepted that a life policy is an indicium of title, but if it is lost payment can still be made by the claimant signing an appropriate declaration and indemnity in respect of the loss. Likewise, if a building society passbook is lost, although there will be difficulty in dealing with the account, a society will allow payment thereunder on the making of a suitable declaration and indemnity as to its loss.

1   (1827) 1 Bli NS 497.

2   [1991] Ch 425, [1991] 2 All ER 636, CA.
3   2 All ER at 647.
4   Where a land certificate or charge certificate has been lost or destroyed, a replacement may be issued on such terms as to advertisement, notice or delay as may be prescribed: Land Registration Act 1925, s 67(2). Land Registration Rules 1925, r 271 prescribes that a replacement certificate may be issued after taking such indemnities as the Chief Land Registrar considers necessary and the insertion of notices in the *Gazette* and a local newspaper.

The effect of death

Devolution of property

34.40   It has already been stated that once the gift has become unconditional by virtue of the donor's death, it takes effect retroactively to the date of delivery. The ownership therefore passes by the gift, and does not devolve on the personal representatives.[1] This was so before 1926, and there is no provision in the Administration of Estates Act 1925 to alter the position.

1   *Rigden v Vallier* (1751) 2 Ves Sen 252; *Kelly v O'Connor* [1917] 1 IR 312.

34.41   Accordingly, in the case of a chose in possession, on the donor's death the donee has nothing else to do as his title becomes absolute as against the donor's personal representatives. If the asset is in the hands of the personal representatives, for example if the donor has by delivery of a key made a donatio of the contents of a safe in a house of which the personal representatives took possession on death, the donee will have to take action to recover the asset. In the case of a chose in action, unless the subject matter of the donatio is a bearer security, on the donor's death the title in the asset will pass to his personal representatives who can be compelled to perfect the gift.[1]

1   *Duffield v Elwes* (1827) 1 Bli NS 497; *Re Wasserberg, Union of London and Smiths Bank v Wasserberg* [1915] 1 Ch 195 at 202.

Lapse

34.42   If after the donor has made a delivery to the donee of the subject matter of the gift the donee dies, the question that may then arise is whether the donatio has lapsed. On the footing that the donatio does not become absolute until the donor's death, it is arguable that the gift should lapse. On the other hand, if the condition of death is a condition subsequent, it is arguable that the donatio took immediate effect subject only to being divested if the donor recovers but not if the donee predeceases the donor, and accordingly the gift should not lapse. If, however, the gift would lapse, the further question then arises as to whether it would be saved from lapse under one of the general principles outlined above.[1] Certainly it would not be saved from lapse under s 33 of the Wills Act 1837, as that section applies only where 'a *will* contains a devise or bequest'[2] to the testator's issue.

1   See above, para 30.17.
2   Emphasis supplied.

The effect of a subsequent will

34.43 A question may also arise if the donor, after delivery of the subject matter of the gift, makes a will disposing of the same asset to a different beneficiary. It is arguable that the donatio should prevail on the basis that it becomes complete and irrevocable at the moment of death, before the will has time to operate: it is analogous to a beneficial share in a joint tenancy which on death passes by survivorship independently of the will and which cannot be disposed of by the will. There is, however, a contrary argument that the will should prevail: as a donatio may be revoked at any time before death, the making of a will could be construed as showing an intention to revoke. Against this contrary argument, however, it could be contended that the will is ambulatory and has no effect until death, by which time the donatio has become absolute.

Availability for debts

34.44 Although the property in the gift passes to the donee in the donor's lifetime, it has been held that where the deceased's estate is not sufficient for the payment of all his debts and liabilities, then property given by a donatio may be used for this purpose, but only after all the assets of the estate have been exhausted completely.[1]

1 *Smith v Casen*, not reported, but mentioned in *Drury v Smith* (1717) 1 P Wms 404; *Re Korvine's Trust* [1921] 1 Ch 343. See, however, S. Warnock Smith ' "Donationes Mortis Causa" and the Payment of Debts' [1978] Conv 130.

Inheritance tax

34.45 As a donatio mortis causa does not become absolute until the death of the donor it will be treated as having been transferred by the deceased immediately before his death.[1] The value of the gift at the date of death will therefore be aggregated with the free estate of the donor and the gift bears a proportionate part of the inheritance tax accordingly.[2] The donee, not the personal representatives, is liable to pay the tax.[3] If the personal representatives do pay the tax, they automatically obtain a charge over the property comprised in the gift for reimbursement.[4]

1 Inheritance Tax Act 1984, ss 4(1), 5(1).
2 See below, Chapter 35.
3 Inheritance Tax Act 1984, s 200(1)(c).
4 Ibid, s 211(3).

34.46 Cases involving a donatio mortis causa usually involve a dispute between the personal representatives and the donee as to whether the subject matter of the gift passes to the donee or forms part of the donor's estate. However, there is one situation where the personal representatives may themselves endeavour to establish a donatio to reduce the tax burden on the estate. Assume that a donor, who has already exhausted her inheritance tax nil-rate band by making lifetime gifts,[1] makes a donatio of all her jewellery, worth £500,000. Suppose also that in her will the deceased gave the donee the same jewellery. If the donee receives the jewellery by virtue of the donatio mortis causa, the donee will be liable for the tax thereon: at the current rate of 40 per cent, £200,000. On the other hand, if the donatio were ineffective and the legacy took effect instead, in the absence of any contrary provision the tax is borne out of the residue of the estate.[2] As legatee, the donee would receive the jewellery free of tax, throwing the burden of that tax on the residuary beneficiaries. It would therefore be in the interest of the residuary beneficiary to establish that the donatio was valid.

1 See below, para 35.3.
2 Inheritance Tax Act 1984, s 211; see below, para 35.58.

Defective donationes mortis causa

34.47 Where the deceased has attempted to make a donatio mortis causa, but has done so ineffectively, the personal representatives will not be compelled to complete the gift. It is an illustration of the rule that equity will not assist a volunteer.[1] Nevertheless, it may be possible for the gift to be saved under the rule in *Strong v Bird*.[2] The principle in this case is that where the deceased intended to make a gift to the donee, but attempted to do so ineffectively, then if the donee subsequently acquires the legal title to that property, the gift will be completed. This is because there are two elements in a complete gift: an intention to make the gift, and the transfer of the legal title. Accordingly, where the intention continued to the date of death,[3] and the legal title is then transferred to the donee, the two elements are present, albeit perhaps not concurrently. The legal title is usually acquired by a grant of probate[4] or letters of administration,[5] but it may be acquired in any other way.[6]

1 Per Lord Eldon LC in *Duffield v Elwes* (1827) 1 Bli NS 497.
2 (1874) LR 18 Eq 315; *Re Stewart, Stewart v McLaughlin* [1908] 2 Ch 251.
3 *Re Freeland, Jackson v Rodgers* [1952] Ch 110; see also *Re Innes, Innes v Innes* [1910] 1 Ch 188.
4 As in *Strong v Bird* itself. See further above, para 17.62.
5 *Re James, James v James* [1935] Ch 449.
6 *Re Ralli's Will Trust* [1964] Ch 288.

34.48 In theory, there is a difference between the element of intention required for the rule in *Strong v Bird*[1] to operate, on the one hand, and for there to be a valid donatio mortis causa on the other. The intention in the former case is to make a lifetime gift, whereas in the latter case it is to make a gift conditional on death. Despite this theoretical difference, however, it may well be possible in practice to establish sufficient evidence for *Strong v Bird* to apply where it is not possible to establish a valid donatio mortis causa.

1 (1874) LR 18 Eq 315.

PART VIII

Taxation

CHAPTER 35

Inheritance tax

Introduction

35.1 Death has always provided an excellent opportunity for taxing wealth.[1] It is a relatively easy tax to collect as all assets tend to be assembled together on death, vulnerable to attack. The beneficiaries are receiving their inheritance for nothing, so should hardly be expected to complain. Further, if the deceased has decided to postpone his charity until he is dead[2] rather than be generous in his lifetime to avoid the tax,[3] he should not complain either. The power of inherited wealth makes its taxation politically sensitive and so highly volatile to change.[4] Tax on death is accordingly often presented as a social rather than a revenue-raising measure,[5] with a social objective: that the ability to rule from the grave should be restricted.[6] The law of succession is inevitably entwined with inheritance tax in respect of those estates that fall within its ambit.[7] The way an estate is distributed among the beneficiaries may itself affect the amount of tax payable.[8] Further, the amount beneficiaries receive from an estate liable to tax will be directly affected by the way the burden of the tax is distributed between them.[9]

1 Many of the feudal duties arose on death, in particular Relief, Escheat and Wardship. One of the earliest forms of tax avoidance, the 'use' was largely devised to avoid Wardship.
2 'He who defers his charity until he is dead is generous of another's, not his own': Samuel Johnson.
3 As will be seen, if a donor survives for seven years tax will normally be avoided, unless the donor has retained a benefit in the gift.
4 In 1975 a socialist government replaced estate duty with capital transfer tax, but estate duty, in a mutated form, was effectively reintroduced in 1986 as inheritance tax, although by that time many of its teeth had been drawn.
5 The total revenue raised from inheritance tax in 1991/92 was about £1.3 billion, or only about 1.5% of total tax revenue.
6 'Nature gives man no power over his earthly goods beyond the term of his life. What power he possesses to prolong his will after his death – the right of a dead hand to dispose of property – is a pure creation of the law, and the State has the right to prescribe the conditions and limitations under which that power shall be exercised.' Statement by Sir William Harcourt during his budget speech of 1894, introducing estate duty in that year by the then Liberal government.
7 The 1993/94 threshold for inheritance tax is £150,000, although, as will be seen, this may be affected by lifetime gifts deducted from that threshold or be extended by exemptions and reliefs.

8   For example, gifts to spouses and charities are normally exempt.
9   This involves the subject of incidence of tax, considered below, para 35.54.

35.2   This chapter is intended to give only an introduction to the law relating to inheritance tax, as a glimpse of its relevance and importance to the law of succession and to will drafting and estate planning.[1] The principal statute governing the present law is the consolidating Inheritance Tax Act 1984, and statutory references in this chapter are to that Act unless otherwise indicated. The Finance Act 1986 introduced the potentially exempt transfer[2] and governs the provisions relating to gifts with reservation.[3]

1   For more detailed consideration refer to the standard books on the subject, including the author's Inheritance Tax Division of the regularly updated *Butterworths Wills, Probate and Administration Service.*
2   Considered below, para 35.8.
3   Considered below, para 35.17.

Concept

35.3   The broad concept of inheritance tax is that it is payable on gifts made by the deceased within seven years of the date of his death. These are progressively cumulated, or added together, in determining the tax on the estate. If the cumulated gifts and the estate exceed the tax threshold of, currently,[1] £150,000, the balance over that figure is taxed at 40 per cent. However, the gifts are treated as having been made in the order in which they are actually made, the earlier gifts therefore having the benefit of being able to utilise the nil-rate tax band first. Accordingly, the earlier gifts may not pay tax but, because of the principle of cumulation, the tax threshold will be progressively eroded by lifetime gifts, thereby throwing the burden of tax on the later gifts and ultimately on the estate. This is an important factor to bear in mind when will drafting.

1   1993/94.

35.4   Gifts to spouses, charities, political parties and certain other bodies are exempt from tax[1] and therefore effectively ignored for the purpose of these calculations. Other assets may be reduced in value for the purpose of calculating tax only, in some cases to the extent of the whole of the asset. These reliefs apply principally to business and agricultural property.[2]

1   See below, paras 35.20ff.
2   See below, paras 35.26ff.

35.5   As will be seen,[1] provisions have been included to prevent a person giving away his assets and surviving seven years but nevertheless effectively enjoying them. The legislation also contains detailed provisions concerning the taxation of trusts.[2]

1   Below, paras 35.13–35.16.
2   See below, paras 35.40ff.

The charge of inheritance tax

Terminology

35.6 Although conventionally a person making a gift is referred to as the donor and the recipient as the donee, the transaction itself being a gift, new terminology was introduced by the Finance Act 1975 in so far as it affected inheritance tax (then capital transfer tax). A person who makes a gratuitous disposition is known as the transferor, and he makes a transfer of value to a transferee. Strangely, this terminology was not used in the gift with reservation provisions in the Finance Act 1986.[1] The word 'gift' is also used in the definition of a potentially exempt transfer, also introduced by the Finance Act 1986.[2]

1 These still refer to donor, donee and gift. These provisions were reintroduced from the estate duty legislation, which had used only the conventional terminology. See below, paras 35.13–35.16.
2 See below, para 35.11.

Transfer of value

35.7 Inheritance tax is charged on the value transferred by a chargeable transfer of value made by an individual but which is not an exempt transfer.[1] A transfer of value is in turn defined as any disposition made by an individual as a result of which the value of his estate immediately after the disposition is less than it would have been but for the disposition.[2] It is therefore the net loss to the estate which is the value transferred. On death, a person is deemed to have made a transfer of value equal to the value of his estate immediately before his death.[3]

1 Inheritance Tax Act 1984, s 2.
2 Ibid, s 3(1).
3 Ibid, s 4(1).

The loss to the estate
35.8 As the value transferred is the net loss to the estate of the transferor, it does not necessarily bear a direct relationship to the benefit received by the transferee. To calculate the loss to the estate, the value of the transferor's estate is assessed before and after the disposition and it is the net difference which represents the loss to the estate. For example, if a father has a pair of fine paintings individually worth £5,000, but as a pair worth £20,000, and he gives one of the paintings to his son, the loss to his estate is £15,000 as after the disposition he is left with only a picture worth £5,000.

Persons domiciled outside the United Kingdom
35.9 Inheritance tax does not apply to assets situated outside the United Kingdom belonging to an individual who is also domiciled outside the United Kingdom.[1] However, to avoid a person transferring all his assets abroad and becoming domiciled outside the United Kingdom shortly before his death, an extended meaning is given to domicile for inheritance tax purposes.[2]

1 Inheritance Tax Act 1984, s 23(2). The UK includes the mainland of Northern Ireland but excludes the Channel Islands and the Isle of Man.
2 Ibid, s 267 provides that a person is deemed to be domiciled in the UK if *either* he was domiciled in the UK at any time within three years immediately preceding the transfer *or* he was resident in the UK for not less than 17 of the 20 years of assessment ending with the year of assessment in which the transfer took place.

Dispositions by associated operations

35.10 One of the reasons for the complexity of tax law generally is the ingenuity taxpayers display in arranging their affairs to reduce the tax burden. Accordingly, anti-avoidance provisions are introduced. As one illustration of this, Inheritance Tax Act 1984, s 268 provides that where more than one step is taken to achieve a desired result, but each of the steps taken does not itself constitute a transfer of value, if the overall effect results in a loss to the transferor's estate, it is taxed accordingly. In other words, the individual steps are not treated in isolation, but judged by their overall effect.

Lifetime transfers

There are two types of transfers of value which may be made by a transferor in his lifetime.

Potentially exempt transfers

35.11 The Finance Act 1986 introduced a new category of transfers of value which do not attract a charge to tax on their making, or a charge on death if the transferor survives the gift by seven years and has not reserved any benefit from the gift. In practice, most forms of gift will constitute a potentially exempt transfer. Such a transfer is a gift made by an individual to an individual after 17 March 1986 and which would otherwise be a chargeable transfer.[1] It is also possible to make such gifts to certain specified benign forms of trust[2] and gifts into or termination of interest in possession trusts. It is assumed that a potentially exempt transfer will prove to be exempt,[3] and it becomes exempt as soon as the transferor has survived the gift by seven years.[4] If, however, the transferor dies within the seven years, the gift becomes a chargeable transfer.[5] Whether any tax is payable thereon, however, will depend on whether, taking into account any prior chargeable transfers, the tax threshold[6] is exceeded. If tax is payable, the rate will be at 40 per cent, but the amount of tax payable (not the value of the transfer) is reduced after the third year by 20 per cent for every year the transferor has survived thereafter.[7]

1 Inheritance Tax Act 1984, s 3A.
2 Provided it was effected after 16 March 1987.
3 Inheritance Tax Act 1984, s 3A(5).
4 Ibid, s 3A(4).
5 Ibid.
6 For 1993/94, £150,000.
7 Inheritance Tax Act 1984, s 7(4).

Lifetime chargeable transfers

35.12 Any lifetime transfer of value which does not qualify as a potentially exempt transfer will constitute a lifetime chargeable transfer. For example, a transfer into a discretionary trust, not being a gift to an individual or into an interest in possession trust, would constitute a lifetime chargeable transfer. Tax on a lifetime chargeable transfer is payable at the time it is made, unless it falls within the tax threshold. Tax is charged at 20 per cent, but if the transferor dies within three years tax will be paid at the death rate of 40 per cent. After three years, however, the amount of tax payable (not the value of the transfer) is reduced by 20 per cent for every year (after the third) the transferor has survived.[1] Effectively, in most cases no further tax becomes payable after the transferor has survived five years. Nevertheless, the transfer does not fall out of account in the cumulative total until the transferor has survived the full seven years.

1 Inheritance Tax Act 1984, s 7(4).

Gifts with reservation

35.13 A donor who gives away assets and survives seven years will avoid tax. However, if he gives away assets but continues to enjoy the benefit from them as though he still owned them, it is only a gift of the formal title to the assets, not of their enjoyment. Accordingly, when inheritance tax was introduced by the Finance Act 1986, provisions modelled on the old estate duty ones were incorporated to prevent a donor from escaping tax by simply surviving a gift for seven years while effectively continuing to derive a benefit from it in one way or another.

Definition

35.14 It is therefore provided[1] that where an individual disposes of any property by way of gift and, in the seven years before his death:
(a) possession and enjoyment of the property are not bona fide assumed by the donee, *or*
(b) the donor is not excluded, or virtually excluded, from any benefit, whether directly or indirectly,
for inheritance tax purposes the gift is effectively treated as though it had never been made. The subject matter of such a gift is then described as property subject to a reservation. The critical period is the seven years before the date of death. So if a donor makes a gift ten years before his death, without deriving any benefit from it, but later derives some such benefit within the seven years before his death, the gift then becomes property subject to a reservation.[2]

1 Finance Act 1986, s 102.
2 Ibid, s 102(1). *Stamp Duties Comr of New South Wales v Permanent Trustee Co of New South Wales* [1956] AC 512, [1956] 2 All ER 512, PC.

Consequences

35.15 If the property ceases to be property subject to a reservation before the donor's death, at that time the donor is deemed to have disposed of the property by making a potentially exempt transfer.[1] On the other hand, if the donor continues to enjoy the benefit from the property up to the date of his death, then for tax purposes he is treated as having owned it at the date of his death and is taxed on it accordingly as part of his estate.[2] Suppose a father gives his house to his son, but continues to live there up to the date of his death. On his death the house will be taxed as though the father had owned it at the date of his death. The value of the house will be added to the value of the estate to arrive at the total tax liability,[3] and the tax apportioned between that house and the estate according to their respective values.

1 Finance Act 1986, s 102(4).
2 Ibid, s 102(3). However, there are complex provisions to avoid a double charge to tax on both the original gift if made within seven years of death and again on death under these provisions.
3 This is the principle of aggregation whereby all assets passing or deemed to pass on death are added together to ascertain the total tax payable, which is then apportioned between the assets.

Relaxations of the rule

35.16 If the donor only enjoys the property for a full consideration in money or money's worth, he will not be treated as having reserved a benefit in it.[1] In the last example, this relaxation of the rule would apply if the father had paid a full market rent for the house up to the date of his death. There is a further statutory concession,[2] providing that where the donor has given away his property to a relative, but since then circumstances have changed, the donor's subsequent occupation will not be treated as a gift with reservation if he occupies it by reason of being unable to maintain himself through old age, infirmity or otherwise. So, again referring to the earlier example, if father should become infirm and return to the house he gave to his son to be cared for by his son and family, it would fall within this relaxation.[3]

1 Finance Act 1986, Sch 20, para 6(1)(a).
2 Ibid, para 6(1)(b), which sets out the detailed requirements for this relaxation only briefly mentioned here.
3 This relaxation applies only to an interest in *land*, so would not cover, for example, valuable antiques that may have been given to the donee.

Inheritance tax on death

35.17 Death is deemed to be the final transfer of value. When a person dies tax is charged as if immediately before his death he had made a transfer of value equal to the value of his estate immediately before his death.[1]

1 Inheritance Tax Act 1984, s 4(1).

35.18 With the exception of gifts subject to a reservation, any lifetime transfers are not treated as having taken place on death. However, the subsequent death of the transferor may still affect such transfers. If a death has occurred within seven years of the transfer, tax may become payable on potentially exempt transfers[1] or a higher rate of tax on any lifetime chargeable transfers.[2] Further, the estate will be directly affected by any chargeable transfers made within the seven years before the date of death as their value will be cumulated and the total cumulation of value deducted from the tax threshhold available to the estate. This can be best illustrated with an example. Suppose a father, who has fully utilised his annual gift exemption,[3] makes the following additional gifts:

(a) in June 1986, £100,000 to his son, Sidney;
(b) in June 1990, £50,000 to his daughter, Doris;
(c) in June 1992, £20,000 to his grandson, Graham.

If father died in May 1993, within seven years of making the three gifts, Sidney will pay no tax on his gift as it falls within the tax threshhold. Neither will Doris as her gift also just falls within the threshhold. On father's death, therefore, the whole of the nil-rate tax band of £150,00 will have been utilised, so the gift to Graham will bear tax at 40 per cent, as will the entirety of the estate. If, however, father should die in 1994, by that time the gift to Sidney will have dropped out of account. The gift to Doris will be cumulated, as will the gift to Graham. As the total cumulation of chargeable gifts within the seven years before the date of death is now only £70,000, the balance of the nil-rate band – £80,000 – is available for the benefit of the estate. As will be realised from this example, lifetime gifts have the advantage of utilising the nil-rate tax band first, thereby throwing the burden of the tax on the estate. This is an important factor to bear in mind when considering the net estate that will be available for distribution among the beneficiaries.

1 Considered above, para 35.11.
2 Considered above, para 35.12.
3 See below, para 35.25.

Assets aggregated with the estate

35.19 In addition to the deceased's free estate, a number of other assets pass or are deemed to pass on death. The following must be added together for the purpose of ascertaining the tax payable. That tax is then apportioned rateably between the assets.

(a) The deceased's free estate: assets owned beneficially by the deceased.[1]
(b) The deceased's beneficial share in any property passing by survivorship. This extends to any beneficial joint tenancy, whether of land, a bank account, etc.[2]
(c) Interests in possession in settlements. A person beneficially entitled to an interest in possession, such as a life interest, is treated as being beneficially entitled to the property in which the interest subsists.[3]
(d) Assets over which the deceased had a *general* power of appointment are treated as his assets for inheritance tax purposes.[4]
(e) Gifted property which is still subject to a reservation in favour of the donor at the date of his death.[5]
(f) Donationes mortis causa. Such gifts do not become absolute until death.[6] They will therefore be treated as having been transferred by

the deceased immediately before his death and will be aggregated with the free estate.[7]

1   Inheritance Tax Act 1984, s 5(1), other than excluded property.
2   Ibid, s 17(1).
3   Ibid, s 49(1); see below, para 35.41.
4   Ibid, s 5(2); other than a power of appointment over settled property.
5   Finance Act 1986, s 102(3); see above, paras 35.13–35.16.
6   See above, para 34.40.
7   Inheritance Tax Act 1984, s 4(1).

Exemptions

35.20   There are two types of exemption from inheritance tax:
(a)   exemption based on the character of the transferee;
(b)   exemption based on limited lifetime gifts.

Exempt transferees

Spouses
35.21   Gifts between spouses are normally[1] totally exempt whether the transfer is made during lifetime or on death. The exemption also applies where an interest in possession passes between spouses. The exemption therefore applies regardless of whether the gift is outright or settled. Two conditions have to be satisfied to qualify for this exemption.[2]
(a)   in effect the spouse must take an immediate interest in possession, except that a contingency clause not exceeding twelve months does not invalidate this condition; and
(b)   the disposition must not depend on a condition which is not satisfied within twelve months after the transfer.

1   Unless the transferor is domiciled in the UK and the transferee spouse outside the UK, when the exemption is limited to £55,000: Inheritance Tax Act 1984, s 18(2).
2   Ibid, s 18(3).

Charities
35.22   Gifts to charities are totally exempt whether made during the donor's lifetime or on death.[1] However, these are subject to the same conditions imposed in respect of transfers between spouses, together with some additional conditions imposed to avoid abuse of the exemption.[2]

1   Inheritance Tax Act 1984, s 23.
2   Ibid, s 23(3)–(5).

Gifts for national purposes and/or the public benefit
35.23   Such gifts are exempt without limit, provided they fall within the requisite description[1] and comply with the same conditions imposed on charities.

1   Under Inheritance Tax Act 1984, ss 25 and 26 respectively.

Political parties
35.24 Politicians have also taken care to protect themselves, as any gifts to political parties made in one's lifetime or on death are totally exempt, subject to the same conditions that apply to charities.[1] The relief extends only to a qualifying political party, defined as one where at the general election preceding the transfer either two members of that party were elected to the House of Commons or one member was elected and no less than 150,000 votes were given to candidates who were members of that party.[2]

1 Inheritance Tax Act 1984, s 24.
2 Ibid, s 24(2).

Exempt lifetime transfers

35.25 There are a number of exemptions consisting of lifetime gifts which are not made to exempt transferees and would therefore normally constitute chargeable transfers, but nevertheless are exempt within the limits of exemption given. These include:

(a) an annual exemption of £3,000 in any tax year (with a carry forward for one year only);[1]

(b) small gifts exemption of not more than £250 each to an unlimited number of persons (other than one to which the annual exemption applies);[2]

(c) gifts in consideration of marriage, within certain limits:[3] £5,000 from each of the parents of either party to the marriage, £2,500 from any remoter ancestors and £1,000 from any other person;

(d) normal expenditure out of income. Such gifts are exempt to the extent it it shown that the payments were made by the transferor as part of his normal expenditure and, taking one year with another, such payments were made out of income and did not affect the transferor's style of living.[4]

1 Inheritance Tax Act 1984, s 19.
2 Ibid, s 20.
3 Ibid, s 22.
4 Ibid, s 21.

Reliefs

35.26 There are two categories of assets – business property and agricultural property – which receive favourable treatment by reducing the chargeable value of the transfer, whether made in a person's lifetime or on death. This may have the advantage of reducing the tax burden on other lifetime chargeable transfers and on death as the relief operates by reducing the value of the transfer, not merely the tax on it. To avoid abuse of these substantial reliefs, strict requirements have to be complied with which are dealt with here only briefly.

Business property relief

35.27 Two aspects of this relief must be considered:[1]
(a) the qualification for the relief; and
(b) the relief given.

1 The detailed provisions are contained in Inheritance Tax Act 1984, ss 104–114.

To qualify for the relief
35.28 The transferor must have owned the business throughout the period of two years immediately preceding its transfer.[1]

1 Inheritance Tax Act 1984, s 106.

The relief given
35.29 This is effected by reducing the value of the business for tax purposes by 100 or 50 per cent.[1] Relief will be given at 100 per cent in respect of a business of which the transferor was the sole proprietor or a partner; unquoted shares of a trading company controlled by the transferor immediately before transfer; and unquoted shares in any other company giving the transferor more than 25 per cent of the votes. The 50 per cent relief is available in other cases such as a minority holding in unquoted shares; quoted shares in a trading company controlled by the transferor immediately before the transfer; land, buildings and machinery, etc, used for the purpose of a business or its being carried on by a company of which the transferor had control or of which he was a partner (this also extends to assets held in a settlement to which the transferor was beneficially entitled).

1 Inheritance Tax Act 1984, s 106.

Successions
35.30 There is a further provision[1] that if a beneficiary inherits business property on a death, he is deemed to have owned it from the date of death. Further, if the beneficiary was the transferor's spouse, then that spouse can also utilise any period of ownership by the deceased and add it to his or her own if he or she should then make a gift of the property.[2]

1 Inheritance Tax Act 1984, s 108.
2 This provision applies only to a spouse (and not any other beneficiary) who succeeds on death, but does not apply to a lifetime gift. It is a useful provision where, for example, the deceased does not fully satisfy the requisite period of ownership before his death but it can then be completed by the surviving spouse before in turn making a transfer of the property.

Ownership qualification
35.31 To prevent the transferor using the relief to make an effective cash gift by first transferring the business to a beneficiary to sell the property, there is a retention of ownership qualification.[1] Accordingly, if the transferor dies within seven years of any lifetime transfer the relief will be lost unless the business property:
(a) continues to be owned by the transferee up to the date of the transferor's death (or earlier death of the transferee); *and*

(b)   continues to qualify as business property up to the death of the transferor (or earlier death of the transferee).

1   Inheritance Tax Act 1984, ss 113A, 113B.

Sale prior to transfer
35.32   The relief is wholly lost if the property has been sold prior to the transfer, a sale for this purpose being made at the date of the contract and not the date of completion.

Agricultural property relief

35.33   Two aspects of this important relief have to be considered separately:[1]
(a)   the requisite conditions for establishing the relief; and
(b)   the relief given if these conditions are satisfied.

1   The detailed provisions are contained in Inheritance Tax Act 1984, ss 115–124.

Occupation or ownership qualifications
35.34   To qualify for agricultural property relief, the transferor must establish one of two requirements.[1] Either that he, or a company controlled by him,[2] must have:
(a)   occupied the property for the purpose of agriculture throughout the period of two years ending with the date of transfer (regardless of whether he is owner or tenant); *or*
(b)   owned the property throughout the period of seven years ending with the date of transfer and it has been occupied by himself or another throughout that period for agricultural purposes.

1   Inheritance Tax Act 1984, s 117(1).
2   Ibid, s 119.

The relief given
35.35   The relief given is to reduce the chargeable value of the agricultural value[1] of the property by 100 per cent if the transferor has vacant possession of the property or the right to obtain it within twelve months of the transfer. The reduction is 50 per cent in all other cases.[2]

1   The relief applies only to the agricultural value of agricultural property and not, for example, to any development value. Agricultural value is defined as being the value of the property if it were subject to a perpetual covenant prohibiting its use other than for agriculture: Inheritance Tax Act 1984, s 115(3).
2   Ibid, s 116(2).

Successions
35.36   There is a further provision[1] that if a beneficiary inherits agricultural property on a death, he is deemed to have owned it (or if he subsequently occupies it, to have occupied it) from the date of death. Further, if the beneficiary is the transferor's spouse, then that spouse can also utilise any period of ownership or occupation by the deceased and add it to his or her own if he or she should then make a gift of the property.[2]

1   Inheritance Tax Act 1984, s 120. This provision is similar to that applying to business
    property relief – see above, para 35.30.
2   This provision applies only to a spouse (and not to any other beneficiary) who succeeds on
    death, but does not apply to a lifetime gift. It is useful where, for example, the deceased
    does not fully satisfy the requisite period of ownership or occupation before his death but it
    can then be completed by the surviving spouse before in turn making a gift of the property.

Retention of ownership by the transferee qualification

35.37   As in the case of business property relief, restrictions are imposed to
prevent the transferor using the relief to make an effective cash gift by first
transferring the agricultural property to an intended beneficiary to sell it.
Accordingly, if the transferor dies within seven years of any lifetime
transfer, the relief will be lost unless:[1]

(a)   the agricultural property continues to be owned by the transferee up to
      the date of the transferor's death (or earlier death of the transferee);
      and

(b)   the property must not only be agricultural property immediately before
      the death but must have been occupied for the purpose of agriculture
      (by the transferee or another) since the date of transfer to the date of
      death of the transferor (or earlier death of the transferee).

Relief would therefore be lost if, for example, the transferee disposes of the
property by way of sale or gift in the event of the transferor dying within the
seven years. There are, however, provisions whereby a replacement
property acquired by the transferee may continue to qualify, provided a
number of conditions are satisfied.[2]

1   Inheritance Tax Act 1984, s 124A.
2   Ibid, s 124B.

Sale

35.38   Relief is lost if at the time of the transfer there is a binding contract
for the sale of the agricultural property.[1]

1   Inheritance Tax Act 1984, s 124.

Charged debts

35.39   A charged debt is deducted from the value of the asset on which it is
charged before applying the relief, so that it is only the net value which will
attract valuation relief.[1] Accordingly, if the charge on a property can be
removed in advance before making the transfer, the relief will be available
on the whole of that value. How this may be achieved is illustrated in
chapter 37.[2]

1   Inheritance Tax Act 1984, s 162(4).
2   See para 37.8.

Settled property

35.40   The inheritance tax legislation makes a distinction between two
types of settlement:

(a)   interest in possession settlements; and
(b)   settlements without interests in possession.

Interest in possession settlements

35.41   Broadly speaking, a person has an interest in possession in property if he has the immediate right to receive any income arising from it or the use and enjoyment of the property.[1] A person beneficially entitled to an interest in possession in property is treated as being beneficially entitled to the underlying property in which his interest subsists.[2] If he is entitled to part only of the income from the property, he will be treated as being beneficially entitled to a proportionate part.[3] Where a person beneficially entitled to an interest in possession in settled property disposes of that interest or that interest comes to an end during his lifetime or on his death, while such a disposition is not itself a transfer of value, tax is charged as if at that time he had made a transfer of value equal to the value of the property in which his interest subsists.[4]

1   *Pearson v IRC* [1981] AC 753, [1980] 2 All ER 479, HL.
2   Inheritance Tax Act 1984, s 49(1).
3   Ibid, s 50(1).
4   Ibid, ss 51(1), 52(1).

35.42   It will therefore be seen that a charge to tax arises on the underlying assets passing whenever there is a change of interest in possession in the trust fund, whether this is during a lifetime (when it constitutes a potentially exempt transfer)[1] or on death. Adopting this principle, there will be no charge to tax where there is no change of interest in possession, even though there may have been a change in the ownership of the underlying trust funds. Accordingly, if a settlor settles property in himself for life, no charge to tax arises on the creation of the settlement. Likewise, there is no change of interest in possession and consequently no charge to tax if a remainderman surrenders his interest to the life tenant so that the life tenant becomes the absolute owner.[2] For this reason, reversionary interests do not attract a charge to tax. For example, if property is settled on A for life with remainder to B absolutely and B disposes of his interest in remainder in his lifetime, that disposal will not itself attract a charge to tax as A has been in possession throughout. On A's death, of course, tax will be chargeable when the property passes to the assignee, unless that assignee is an exempt transferee.

1   See above, para 35.11.
2   Inheritance Tax Act 1984, s 55(1).

Settlements without interests in possession

35.43   Where under a settlement there is no person entitled to an interest in possession, under the rules outlined above, a charge to tax could be avoided by ensuring that no person ever became entitled to an interest in possession. Such settlements without interests in possession commonly arise where the income is to be accumulated, or where there is a discretionary settlement whereby the income is paid to beneficiaries not as of right but only at the discretion of the trustees. Although at one time a discretionary trust was an effective method of avoiding estate duty by ensuring that there were always at least two beneficiaries, special rules now apply to such trusts.

35.44 With a traditional interest in possession settlement, tax would normally be payable each time the trust fund passed from one generation to another. Under the provisions relating to trusts without an interest in possession, if such a trust continues for thirty-three and a third years, effectively tax is paid once on the whole trust, but only at the lifetime rate of 20 per cent. This is achieved by taxing the trust fund every ten years at 30 per cent of the lifetime rate. Basically – and subject to detailed rules[1] concerning the calculation of the amount in the trust fund, and assets leaving and being added to the trust fund between the ten-year anniversaries – every ten years the trust fund is taxed at 6 per cent of its value after first deducting the nil-rate tax band prevailing at the date of the anniversary.

1   The provisions relating to settlements without an interest in possession are contained in Inheritance Tax Act 1984, ss 58–85.

35.45 There are special provisions relating to accumulation and main-tenance trusts,[1] where income is to be accumulated until a person attains an age not exceeding 25 years. No charge to tax arises when that person becomes entitled in possession at the specified age. There is a similar favourable treatment of protective trusts[2] and trusts for disabled persons.[3]

1   Inheritance Tax Act 1984, s 71.
2   Ibid, s 88.
3   Ibid, s 89.

Summary

35.46 Where a person has an interest in possession, tax will be charged on the underlying trust fund when that interest in possession changes, whether it be to another person absolutely or in possession or it shifts to become settled without an interest in possession. Once a trust fund is held on trust without an interest in possession, it will then be governed by the special rules applicable to such trusts. So, to give a final example: S settles property on his son A for life and on A's death it is to be held on a discretionary trust. Fifteen years after A's death the discretionary trust fund is vested by the trustees in B absolutely. The following charges to tax will arise.

(a)   The creation of the settlement constitutes a potentially exempt transfer and therefore attracts no charge to tax if S survives for seven years.

(b)   On A's death the whole trust fund will be charged to tax and be aggregated with A's estate to ascertain the rate payable.

(c)   Ten years from the date of A's death there will be a periodic charge on the ten-year anniversary of the creation of the discretionary trust. Tax will be charged at 6 per cent of the value of the trust fund at that time, after first deducting the then prevailing nil-rate band.

(d)   When the appointment is made in favour of B there will be an exit charge to tax, at 3 per cent of the value of the trust fund at that time, again after first deducting the then prevailing nil-rate band.[1]

1   When an appointment is made out of the trust fund between the ten-year periods, tax is charged pro rata from the date of the preceding periodic charge. Thus in this case the fund is appointed after five years, so the rate will be five tenths of 6 per cent.

Accountability

35.47   The subject of accountability determines who is liable to account to the Crown for the inheritance tax that falls due: the person or persons to whom the Inland Revenue may look for payment. In many instances there will be more than one person liable to account for the tax, when the liability will be joint and several.

Lifetime chargeable transfers
35.48   The initial tax payable on lifetime chargeable transfers[1] is the primary liability of the transferor or, failing him, the transferee. The Revenue may also look to the beneficiaries of a settlement for payment. Further, the Revenue may also have recourse to the property itself, unless sold at a time when no Inland Revenue charge had been registered. If additional tax becomes payable because of the death of the transferor within seven years, the primary liability for this tax falls on the transferee, although if he does not pay it the Revenue may then have recourse to the personal representatives of the transferor.[2]

1   Inheritance Tax Act 1984, s 199(1).
2   Ibid, s 199(2).

Potentially exempt transfers
35.49   The primary liability for any tax which becomes payable by reason of the death of the transferor within seven years of the transfer falls on the transferee. If the tax is not paid within twelve months, however, the Inland Revenue may have recourse to the transferor's personal representatives.[1]

1   Inheritance Tax Act 1984, s 199(2).

Gifts with reservation
35.50   The primary liability for the tax payable on gifts with reservation falls on the donee,[1] although again the Revenue may have recourse to the personal representatives, who have a statutory right to recover the tax from the donee.[2]

1   Finance Act 1986, Sch 19, paras 28(3), 29.
2   Inheritance Tax Act 1984, s 204(9).

The deceased's free estate
35.51   On death, the personal representatives will be liable for the tax on the deceased's free estate in the United Kingdom which vests in them.[1]

1   Inheritance Tax Act 1984, s 200.

Settled property

35.52 The persons liable for the tax are the trustees of the settlement, although the Revenue may also have recourse to anyone entitled under the settlement.[1]

1 Inheritance Tax Act 1984, s 201.

Joint tenancy

35.53 The surviving joint tenant or tenants are both trustees and beneficiaries and as such liable to account for the tax payable on the death of a joint tenant whose share passes to them by survivorship.

Incidence of tax

35.54 The subject of incidence determines on whom the ultimate burden of tax will fall: how the tax is to be borne between the various beneficiaries, regardless of who accounts for the tax to the Revenue.

Lifetime transfers

35.55 The transferee is liable for any initial tax and any subsequent tax arising by reason of the death of the donor within seven years.

Settled property

35.56 The tax will be paid out of the capital of the trust fund regardless whether it is a settlement with or without an interest in possession. For the purpose of calculating the tax the settled property is aggregated with the deceased's free estate to calculate the total tax payable and then rateably apportioned between them.

Joint tenancy

35.57 The surviving joint tenant or tenants will bear the tax. The deceased's beneficial share passing by survivorship is aggregated with the free estate in the same way as settled property.

Deceased's free estate in the United Kingdom

35.58 In the absence of any contrary provision in the will, tax on a deceased's free estate situate in the United Kingdom and passing to his personal representatives will be treated as part of the general and testamentary expenses of the estate.[1] Accordingly, in the absence of any contrary provision in the will, the tax is borne out of the residue of the estate so far as this is sufficient and to the extent it is not there will be an abatement.

1 Inheritance Tax Act 1984, s 211 in respect of deaths after 25 July 1983. Prior to that date there had been uncertainty as to whether a devise should bear its own tax.

CHAPTER 36

Taxation during the administration period

36.1 At appropriate places in the preceding chapters references have been made to some of the tax implications of transactions, and it may now be useful to give a general statement[1] of the position during the administration of the estate in relation to income tax and capital gains tax.

1 For more detailed consideration see the standard books in this area, including the author's divisions of the regularly updated *Butterworths Wills, Probate and Administration Service*.

The administration period

36.2 Certain special provisions apply for income tax purposes to the 'administration period', which is defined in Income and Corporation Taxes Act 1988, s 695(1), as the period from the date of death to the completion of the administration of the estate. There is, however, no legislative rule to determine when the administration of an estate is complete although, curiously, s 702, which applies only to Scotland, provides that any reference to the completion of the administration of an estate is to be construed as a reference to the date at which 'after discharge of, or provision for, liabilities falling to be met out of the deceased's estate (including, without prejudice to the generality of the foregoing, debts, legacies immediately payable, prior rights of surviving spouse on intestacy and legal rights of surviving spouse or children),[1] the free balance held in trust for behoof of the residuary legatees has been ascertained'. By using this section as an analogy, and by applying the general principles of law, it appears that the administration is complete when the residue is ascertained, and is available for distribution or appropriation to the residuary beneficiaries.[2] This chapter is confined to the administration period. Thereafter the rules applicable to private individuals or trustees, according to whether the residuary estate was distributed or continues to be held in trust, will operate.

1 These are rights under Scottish law to a fixed proportion of the deceased's assets, and the reference here is not to legacies.
2 See above, para 22.2. See also *Lilley v Public Trustee of the dominion of New Zealand* [1981] AC 839, [1981] 2 WLR 661, PC.

General principles of income taxation

There are four general principles which govern income taxation during the administration period.

Taxable receipts

36.3 The fundamental principle is that only the same type of receipt is taxable in the hands of personal representatives as would be taxable in the hands of a private individual taxpayer. Accordingly, if it can be shown that a receipt would not normally be taxable, it will not be taxable in the hands of the personal representatives. The types of taxable income with which personal representatives will be concerned most frequently are interest on bank and building society accounts, dividends and interest from stock exchange and similar securities, the profits of any business which they carry on prior to disposal and profits from any land which is let.

A separate and continuing body

36.4 The law, in effect, constitutes the personal representatives together as a single continuing body of persons,[1] separate from the individuals themselves. Assessments are therefore made on the personal representatives as such. Any changes in their number are irrelevant for taxation purposes, and any assessment made on them as personal representatives has no effect whatever on their personal tax position. The only circumstance in which their representative capacity overlaps with their private one is that if, having had funds to meet an assessment raised on them as personal representatives, they distribute all the assets of the estate, they can be made personally liable for the amount of that assessment.

1 Income and Corporation Taxes Act 1988, s 701(4), defines them by reference to the Administration of Estates Act 1925, s 55. For capital gains tax they are defined by Taxation of Chargeable Gains Act 1992, s 62(3), as 'a single and continuing body of persons (distinct from the persons who may from time to time be personal representatives)' with the same residence, ordinary residence and domicile as the deceased at the date of his death.

All income taxable at basic rate

36.5 The normal income tax structure is for tax to be payable on a sliding scale. A private individual is entitled to a personal allowance, with the result that the first part of his income is tax free. Thereafter the first £2,500 is taxed at 20 per cent, the next £21,200 at 25 per cent and the remainder at 40 per cent. In the case of personal representatives, however, all income is taxable at the basic rate of 25%. There are no personal allowances or personal reliefs, and no higher or lower rates of tax are payable.

36.6 With regard to reliefs, a distinction must be drawn between personal allowances and other allowances or reliefs. Although the personal representatives cannot claim in respect of the income of the estate any personal allowance and although where they carry on the deceased's business any profits are not treated as earned income, they may claim non-personal reliefs. These are loss relief, in which case a loss may be set off against other profits,[1] and a limited relief for loan interest paid.[2]

1 Either by carrying it forward against future profits from the same source under Income and Corporation Taxes Act 1988, s 385, or carrying back profits under s 380.
2 Under the provisions of ibid, ss 358, 364.

36.7 It was established in *IRC v Countess of Longford*[1] that personal representatives are not liable for higher rates of income tax however high the income of the estate may be. It is, therefore, sometimes wise to disclaim interest on a legacy or on a statutory entitlement, if the recipient would personally be liable to tax at the higher rate.[2]

1 [1928] AC 252.
2 See below, para 36.19.

Net income paid to beneficiaries

36.8 Personal representatives must make payments of an income nature other than interest to the beneficiaries subject to deduction of tax. These payments will include the income from a fund in which the beneficiary has a life interest; payments of an annuity from the estate; and the actual income from assets specifically devised or bequeathed. At the same time the personal representative issues to the beneficiary a certificate that the payment has been made subject to deduction of tax. On the other hand, interest on legacies, where payable, is paid gross.

36.9 The income received by the personal representatives will itself either have been taxed at source or have been received by them gross. Other types of income will have been received subject to deduction of tax at the basic rate, so that the personal representatives will be under no further liability for that. If they let property, or carry on a business, the profits made will be gross. The personal representatives must, therefore, make a return showing all income received by them, and the amount of the tax suffered by them in respect of sums received subject to deduction of tax. The balance of tax due, being the tax at the basic rate on the income received by them gross, is payable by the personal representatives to the Revenue, so that in the result all the income in their hands will have been taxed, and they are left with a net sum. It is this net sum, less expenses attributable to income, which is paid to the beneficiaries.[1]

1 Income and Corporation Taxes Act 1988, s 349(2).

36.10 The procedure whereby payments are made to the beneficiaries subject to deduction of tax cannot work to their overall disadvantage. If they are liable to pay tax at the basic rate, they will have no further tax to pay on the amounts received from the estate. If, on the other hand, their total income is sufficiently low for them not to have to pay at the basic rate, they can obtain a refund of tax by production of the certificate of deduction of tax issued by the personal representatives when making the payment.

36.11 In order to ascertain whether a payment to be made to a beneficiary is to be made subject to deduction of tax, it is necessary to consider the character of the receipt in his hands. If in his hands the receipt is taxable, it is necessary for the personal representatives to deduct tax when paying, and this is so even if the total income of the estate is not large enough to support the payment. The serious effects of this were considered earlier[1] in respect of annuity payments, and the same principle applies wherever the income payments due from the estate exceed its actual income. It will be seen from that discussion that where a payment has to be made good from capital, a much larger sum – the actual sum depending on the basic rate at the time when payment is made – must be taken from capital. The loser is the estate, with the Revenue being the only party to gain. Accordingly, it is now unwise to include in a will a provision that a deficiency of income should be made good from capital.[2]

1 At para 31.59.
2 The disadvantage can sometimes be overcome by giving the personal representatives power to advance a capital sum.

Distribution of residuary income

36.12 Payments of interest on legacies, annuities, and the actual income from assets specifically devised or bequeathed follow the principles just discussed, and present no other problems. The position is different where a distribution is made of residuary income, the difference arising from the fact that in general payments are made to residuary beneficiaries during the course of the administration of the estate generally on account of the amount due to them, so that as each interim payment is made, it may not be possible to show how much represents income, and how much capital, or, where it clearly does represent income, in respect of what period it accrued.

36.13 Accordingly, a distinction is drawn between a residuary beneficiary who has a 'limited' interest, that is, a right only to income from the property,[1] and a beneficiary who has an 'absolute' interest, which is a right to the residuary capital when ascertained, together with the right to income from it until ascertainment.[2]

1 Income and Corporation Taxes Act 1988, s 695.
2 Ibid, s 696.

Residuary beneficiary with a 'limited' interest

36.14 The rules are as follows.
(a) All sums paid to the beneficiary during the administration period are treated at first as part of his total income for the year of assessment in

which they are actually paid. These sums will have been paid subject to deduction of tax at source, so that their grossed up equivalent will form part of the beneficiary's total income.
(b) On completion of the administration, the sums actually paid are added to those which remain due to the beneficiary. The total is then deemed to have accrued from day to day.
(c) A final computation is made, and revised assessments, if necessary, are issued to cover each of the years of assessment during the administration period.
The total income paid to the residuary beneficiary will therefore be the total income of the estate, less income paid to others, and less management expenses, but spread out equally over the whole period of the administration.

36.15 An example may illustrate these rules. Harriet died on 5 January 1990, having left her residuary estate to Rupert for life, with remainder to Lavinia. The executors make to Rupert the following payments:

1 January 1991	£2,000
1 January 1992	£8,000
1 January 1993	£1,600

On completion of the administration of the estate, on 5 October 1993, they are holding a further £7,900 for Rupert. Provisional assessments are raised on Rupert as follows:

1989/90[1]	nil
1990/91	£2,000
1991/92	£8,000
1992/93	£1,600

In this case no provisional assessment is made for 1993/94, as it will then be possible to calculate the amended assessments. In 1993/94 it is possible to make the recalculation. The total income produced and available for Rupert is £19,500, and the administration period has lasted three and three-quarter years. On an even day-to-day basis, therefore, income has accrued at the rate of £5,200 pa. It is now possible to make the revised assessments as follows:

	PROVISIONAL ASSESSMENT	INCOME AS FINALLY APPORTIONED	ADJUSTMENT TO PROVISIONAL ASSESSMENT
1989/90 (administration period only occupied three months: ¼ × £5,200)	nil	£1,300	+£1,300
1990/91	£2,000	£5,200	+£3,300
1991/92	£8,000	£5,200	−£2,800
1992/93	£1,600	£5,200	+£3,600
1994/95 (administration period only occupied six months: ½ × £5,200)	nil	£2,600	+£2,600

1 A year of assessment runs from 6 April to the following 5 April.

Residuary beneficiaries with an absolute interest

36.16 The rules are different. During the administration of the estate, various sums might be paid to the residuary beneficiary generally on account of the amount due to him and without distinguishing between capital and income. In order to distinguish between capital and income, the following process is adopted.

(a) The 'residuary income' of the estate is calculated for each year of assessment or part of a year of assessment during the administration period. 'Residuary income' for a period is the total income received by the personal representatives during that period, less interest paid on legacies, annuity payments and management expenses relating to income.

(b) The payments actually made to the residuary beneficiary in each of the years of assessment are then regarded as having been payments of income up to the total of the residuary income for that year, the balance being treated as capital.

(c) On completion of the administration of the estate, the whole of the residuary income is deemed to have been paid to the beneficiary, and any necessary revised assessment will be made.

36.17 Again an example may help. Martin dies on 6 April 1990, leaving a legacy of £4,000 to his son, and the remainder to his widow absolutely. The total net estate is about £84,000. On 5 April 1991 the executors pay the legacy to the son, together with interest at 6 per cent from the date of death, and they also pay to the widow £2,000 generally on account. They pay the widow a further £40,000 generally on account on 5 April 1992, and complete the administration of the estate and pay her the balance in July 1992. The expenses of the administration attributable to income amount to £200 pa. The residuary income for the various years of assessment is:

1990/91	Actual gross income from estate	£5,040
	Less	
	Management expenses attributable to income	200
		£4,840
	Interest on legacy paid to son	240
		£4,600
1991/92	Actual gross income from balance of estate	£4,480
	Less:	
	Management expenses attributable to income	200
		£4,280
1992/93	Actual gross income to completion of administration of estate	£1,200
	Less:	
	Management expenses attributable to income	120
		£1,180

For 1990/91, because the amount of the residuary income is greater than the amount paid to the residuary beneficiary, the residuary beneficiary is treated as having received the whole £2,000 as income subject to deduction of tax. For 1991/92, she is treated as having received the whole of the residuary income, subject to deduction of tax, and the balance of £35,720 would be regarded as capital. For 1992/93 she would be treated as having received income of £1,180, and the balance of whatever was paid to her is regarded as capital. On completion of the administration of the estate, it would then appear that although the whole of the residuary income for the years 1991/92 and 1992/93 would have been deemed to have been paid to the widow, only £2,000 gross of the £4,600 gross available for distribution would have been paid to her for 1990/91. A revised assessment for that balance of £2,600 would then be raised on her for 1990/91.[1]

1 Income and Corporation Taxes Act 1988, ss 696, 697.

Subsidiary rules

Tax on apportionments

36.18 The rule in *Re Earl of Chesterfield's Trusts*[1] requires an apportionment to be made between life tenant and remainderman when a reversionary interest falls into possession. Suppose that a reversionary interest of £30,000 is received two years after the inception of a trust. The rule of apportionment directs the personal representatives to ascertain what sum would, if invested at the date of death at 4 per cent compound interest with yearly rests, less income tax for the time being in force, have produced £30,000 at the time when it was in fact received. Assuming a basic rate of income tax throughout at 25 per cent, the net income earned at 4 per cent on each £100 of capital is £3. Working backwards, the sum needed to produce the £30,000 after one year of investment would be calculated as follows:

$$\frac{30,000 \times 100}{103} = £29,126.22$$

and the sum needed to produce £30,000 after two years of investment would be:

$$\frac{29,126.22 \times 100}{103} = £28,277.88$$

The sum of £28,277.88 would be added to the capital, and the remaining £1,722.12 paid to the life tenant as compensation for the loss of income from the asset over the previous two years. The object of the rule is to compensate the life tenant for loss of income, and income tax is deducted when making the calculations because if the asset had been in hand at the date of death, the life tenant would have suffered tax on the income. The apportionment rules require tax to be taken into account, but this is solely for the purpose of determining the exact loss to the life tenant. The apportionment itself is of a capital sum, and by applying the rule, no part of the sum is actually converted into income. Accordingly, it is not necessary for the executors or beneficiary to include the figures in their tax returns.

1 (1883) 24 Ch D 643.

Tax on disclaimed interest

36.19 The general rule is[1] that although tax is usually charged on the amount to which a person is entitled, in the case of interest on legacies tax is charged only on what is received, so that where interest is disclaimed, no tax will, in principle, be chargeable on it. This principle was established in *Dewar v IRC*.[2] This only applies, however, so long as the interest to which the legatee is entitled is not set aside for him. *Spens v IRC*[3] was concerned with the liability of a life tenant to surtax on income from the trust to which he was entitled but which he did not receive. Megarry J drew the distinction between the two situations in these words:

> 'In *Dewar*'s case the true point was that no identifiable income had come into existence. No income had been segregated by the executors as being the interest which the legatee could claim. On the other hand, where a trustee who receives income from investments holds those investments on trust for a life tenant, each sum received by the trustee is for surtax purposes the income of the life tenant as soon as it is received, for it is forthwith under the life tenant's control.'

1 See above, para 30.10.
2 [1935] 2 KB 351.
3 [1970] 3 All ER 295.

Capital gains tax

Basic principles

36.20 Capital gains tax imposes a charge to tax on the difference between the price at which an asset is acquired, plus indexation thereon, and the value at which it is disposed of. A person is deemed to dispose of all his assets on death, and, where they devolve upon the personal representatives, they acquire the assets at their value at the date of death.[1] Although the deceased is treated as having disposed of his assets on death, no charge to tax arises as a result of that disposal.[2] If the assets devolve on someone other than the personal representatives, that person is deemed to have acquired them on the death of the deceased for their market value at that time. Where personal representatives are assessable to capital gains tax, the rate of charge is 25 per cent of the gain.[3] The liability for capital gains tax following the death of the deceased depends on whether the personal representatives sell the asset, or transfer it to a beneficiary.

1 Taxation of Chargeable Gains Act 1992, s 62(1)(a).

2 Ibid, s 62(1)(b).
3 Ibid, s 4(1); sub-ss (2)–(4) apply only to individuals.

Assets sold by personal representatives

36.21 Where the personal representatives sell the assets in order to pay the inheritance tax or administration expenses, or to provide a fund for the payment of legacies, and they sell for a figure in excess of that at which they are deemed to have acquired the asset at the date of death, the estate will be liable to tax. There are certain exceptions from the charge to capital gains tax, and for the year of assessment in which the death occurs and in each of the next two years of assessment, personal representatives are entitled to the same annual exemption as is granted to an individual.[1] At present[2] this is £5,800 a year.

1 Taxation of Chargeable Gains Act 1992, s 3(7).
2 1993/94.

Assets transferred to beneficiaries

36.22 Where an asset is transferred to a beneficiary in accordance with the terms of the will, or in accordance with the provisions relating to total or partial intestacy, that beneficiary is treated, retrospectively, as having acquired the asset at the date of death of the deceased. This provision applies whether the transferee takes beneficially or as a trustee. As a result, the personal representatives are not themselves liable for capital gains tax on any of the assets transferred to the beneficiaries in respect of any increase in the value of those assets between the date of death and the date of transfer.[1] The transferee is deemed to acquire the assets at their market value at the date of death.

1 Taxation of Chargeable Gains Act 1992, s 62(4).

36.23 Section 60 of the Taxation of Chargeable Gains Act 1992 provides that in relation to assets held by a person as nominee or trustee for another person 'absolutely entitled as against the trustee, or for any person who would be so entitled but for being an infant or other person under disability', the property in the hands of the trustee or nominee is regarded as being in the hands of the beneficiary. Accordingly, no charge to capital gains tax can arise when the trustee or nominee in fact transfers the asset to the beneficiary. Therefore, when the personal representatives hold an asset absolutely for a beneficiary, and transfer it to him, no charge to tax can arise.[1]

1 Taxation of Chargeable Gains Act 1992, s 60(1).

Deeds of variation

36.24 The terms of a will may be varied or the intestacy provisions altered by the beneficiaries entitled. Provided the deed of variation is executed within two years of the date of death and written notice is given to the Inland Revenue within six months thereof, the variation is treated for capital gains tax purposes as having been effected by the deceased and not by the beneficiaries redirecting their interests.[1] These provisions are considered in the next chapter.

1 Taxation of Chargeable Gains Act 1992, s 62(6)–(10).

Expenses of sale or transfer

36.25 Where an asset is sold, and the personal representatives are liable for capital gains tax, they may deduct from the gain accruing on disposal the expenses of putting themselves in a position to sell and also the expenses of sale. So, a proportion of the solicitor's costs of obtaining probate, and of making a valuation for probate may be deducted.[1] Where an asset is transferred to a beneficiary entitled under the will or under the intestacy rules. In this case, the beneficiary can add the expense of transfer to the market value at which he is deemed to acquire the asset, and by thus increasing his acquisition value, he reduces the gain which he will ultimately make when he disposes.[2] The expenses which can be treated in this way include the actual cost of transfer, together with the costs reasonably incurred in making any valuation or apportionment for capital gains tax purposes, including particularly the expenses of ascertaining the market value of the asset.[3]

1 *IRC v Richards' Executors* [1971] 1 All ER 785, HL.
2 Taxation of Chargeable Gains Act 1992, s 39.
3 Ibid, s 38.

CHAPTER 37

Tax and estate planning

Pre-death planning

37.1 The processes of tax planning and will making are inextricably interactive. Planning for death should be an ongoing process, to be reviewed at regular intervals having regard to changing financial circumstances, the tax regime, and the state of the testator's family, including the maturity or otherwise of the intended beneficiaries. From the inheritance tax point of view, the ideal strategy would be for a donor, just over seven years before his death, to give away all his assets, retaining just £150,000 capital. Before doing this he could also buy an annuity to provide him with an income that would die with him. The obvious flaw with such a strategy is that although death is certain, the date of death is not. Even if it were, other uncertainties remain. A changed government might remove[1] or at least extend[2] the current seven-year cut-off period for lifetime gifts. There is the possibility that a donee will predecease his donor, be a Lloyd's name, become bankrupt or divorced, join the Moonies – or simply himself give away all his assets. Quite apart from these and the other uncertainties of life, it is natural for a testator who has worked and accumulated wealth during his lifetime to wish to retain adequate reserves to provide for his old age, even though perhaps the most tax-efficient way of making such provision would be to purchase an index-linked pension. There is thus an inevitable reluctance to give away one's hard-earned cash, particularly if there is a possibility of seeing it dissipated by the donee or being swallowed up in the donee's divorce settlement.

1 When capital transfer tax was introduced by the Finance Act 1975, there was a lifetime cumulation of gifts.
2 The cumulation period was reduced to ten years by the Finance Act 1985. The present seven-year cut-off was introduced by the Finance Act 1986.

37.2 For these and many other reasons, a testator may wish to retain many of his assets until death. However, even where a testator is reluctant to part with his assets in his lifetime and wishes to dispose of them entirely on his death, there are many ways to achieve this and still reduce or eliminate inheritance tax on death. The purpose of this brief chapter is not to deal comprehensively with tax mitigation, which itself could form the subject matter of an entire book, but to give the reader a glimpse into what may be achieved and, hopefully, stimulate his or her interest in the field of estate planning.

37.3 Estate planning should not be entirely dominated by taxation considerations. If a testator wishes to avoid tax, he may simply give everything to charity.[1] However, this is hardly likely to achieve his objective of providing for his family or any other persons whom he may wish to benefit. The first objective of estate planning is to ascertain the testator's wishes regardless of tax considerations. Having determined those objectives, it is then the responsibility of the professional adviser to recommend the best method of attaining the objectives with the minimum of tax. As will be seen, this can sometimes be achieved very simply; in other cases more complex devices may have to be employed. In some cases, a compromise will have to be made between fulfilling the testator's objectives and accepting the inevitability of paying some tax. A tax system breathes on its exemptions and reliefs. It is therefore for the testator to ensure that these aspects of the tax system are fully utilised to the extent that they are available to him. These two routes for tax mitigation – the exemptions and the reliefs – are now considered in turn.

1   Gifts to charities are wholly exempt: Inheritance Tax Act 1984, s 23; see above, para 35.22.

Use of exemptions

37.4 One of the simplest illustrations of taking advantage of an exemption is to ensure that each individual utilises the nil-rate tax band; this is available to each spouse. Suppose spouses have £150,000 each, which they give to each other: no tax is payable on the first death. If the survivor holds the same assets, which are then left to the children, tax of £60,000 will be paid on the total estate of £300,000.[1] From the tax point of view, it is therefore advisable that both spouses should not leave their estates to each other but, rather, direct to the children, who would then end up with the combined estates without paying tax. This tax saving may, however, be in conflict with the testator's objective of providing for the surviving spouse. Simply to leave the survivor with £150,000 (the whole or a substantial part of which may comprise the matrimonial home) may not make sufficient provision. One way of achieving these contradictory objectives may be to create a discretionary trust of the estate of the first to die, with the survivor included among the potential beneficiaries. The use of this type of trust is considered later.[2]

1   Based on the current (1993/94) threshold of £150,000 and tax rate of 40%.
2   See below, para 37.24ff. This particular use of a discretionary trust is considered at para 37.28.

Use of reliefs

37.5 As we have seen,[1] the business and agricultural property reliefs are generous. However, they can be utilised only by a beneficiary who would otherwise pay tax. If an asset which qualifies for relief is given to an exempt beneficiary, the relief is wasted as it duplicates the exemption. Take a simple illustration of this principle. Suppose a testator has a farm which is worth £1 million and which qualifies for 100 per cent agricultural relief. He also has other assets worth £1 million which do not qualify for any relief. If the testator gives his farm to his wife and the residue of his estate to his son, tax on the estate will amount to £340,000. On the other hand, if these gifts were transposed so that the son received the farm and the widow the other assets, there would be no tax on the estate. This is, of course, somewhat simplistic as the widow would still be left with £1 million in her estate to dispose of to the son and which potentially could attract tax on her death. To avoid this secondary danger, however, the widow could buy the farm from her son at its market value of £1 million.[2] This would realise the testator's original objective of giving the farm to his wife and the other assets to his son. The tax objective would also have been fulfilled. The widow could give the farm to her son by will without any inheritance tax being payable. To achieve this the widow must have farmed the property in the two years before her death.[3] However, the estate planner should anticipate this and have made the wife a partner with the testator before his death; she would then have been farming the property for two years at the testator's death and the scheme would be immediately effective even if the widow died shortly after the testator.[4]

1 Above, paras 35.29 and 35.35.
2 This would not constitute a transfer of value as there has been no loss to the value of the widow's estate: see above, para 35.7.
3 See above, para 35.34.
4 Another permutation of this scheme would be to put the farm into a discretionary trust, which utilises the relief, and for the widow to buy the farm from the trust.

37.6 As a further illustration of maximising the reliefs, if a testator does not qualify for relief, it may be possible to utilise some other statutory provisions. Suppose in the last example the testator had owned and occupied the farm for only one year and was making his will on his death-bed. If he were to leave the farm to his son and die before he had occupied it for two years, the relief would be lost. If instead the father gave the whole of his estate to his wife (other, perhaps, than the nil-rate tax band, which he could give to his son), no tax would be payable on the testator's death. However, by virtue of the provisions relating to successions[1] the widow could add her husband's period of occupation to her own to establish the two-year qualification. She could then promptly make a lifetime gift of the farm to her son and no tax would then be payable thereon even if she were not to survive seven years.

1 Inheritance Tax Act 1984, s 120. See above, para 35.36.

Charged debts

37.7 As we have seen,[1] a charged debt is deducted from the value of the asset on which it is charged before applying the relief: it is only the net value that attracts the relief.[2] This is of particular significance in the case of agricultural property relief, where the charge is on an asset that qualifies for the relief. If the charge on the property can be removed before making the transfer, the relief will be available on the whole of the agricultural value.

1 Above, para 35.39.
2 Inheritance Tax Act 1984, s 162(4).

37.8 Suppose a widower owns a farm worth £1 million, which qualifies for 100 per cent agricultural property relief, on which there is a mortgage of £500,000. In addition, he has life policies and other assets not qualifying for relief amounting to £650,000. If he dies leaving his entire estate to his son in that form, the chargeable estate will be assessed in accordance with Scenario A below.[1] If, however, the charge on the farm can be removed and converted into an overdraft secured by a guarantee and/or solely on assets which do not attract relief, the tax may be eliminated, as shown in Scenario B below.

	Scenario A	*Scenario B*
Value of farm	£1,000,000	£1,000,000
Less charge	500,000	—
Value on which relief available	500,000	1,000,000
Relief at 100%	500,000	1,000,000
Net relieved value	0	0
Add unrelieved assets	650,000	650,000
	650,000	650,000
Deduct other liabilities (overdraft)	—	500,000
Chargeable estate	650,000	150,000
Tax (assuming no lifetime transfers)	200,000	0

Consequently, if the charge is removed in advance of making the transfer, relief will be obtained on the whole value of the asset rather than the net value after deduction of the charged debt. A temporary arrangement could be made for this purpose shortly before making a lifetime transfer or in a death-bed situation.[2]

1 Based on the current (1993/94) threshold of £150,000 and a tax rate of 40%.
2 In a death-bed situation life policies may provide adequate security. In addition, an overdraft could, for example, be guaranteed by the prospective beneficiary.

Post-death planning

37.9 Pre-death planning is inevitably shrouded with uncertainty: as to when the testator will die, whether he will be survived by the intended beneficiaries, the circumstances of the beneficiaries who do survive, the size and nature of his estate at that time and the tax regime then prevailing. With these and many other factors unquantifiable at the time the testator makes his will, how wonderful it would be if he could plan his estate with the benefit of hindsight; could draft his will as he was being lowered into his grave or being consumed by the cremation furnace. The current tax legislation provides just such an opportunity. Indeed, it goes further and provides a period of two years from the date of death to arrange matters in the most tax-efficient way – provided, however, that all the beneficiaries who wish to vary their interests sui iuris and able to agree.

Variations and disclaimers effective for inheritance tax purposes

37.10 Section 142 of the Inheritance Tax Act 1984 enables a beneficiary entitled under a will or on intestacy to vary or disclaim his entitlement in such a way that it is treated as having been effected by the deceased. To be effective for inheritance tax purposes, such variation or disclaimer must be:
(a) made in writing,
(b) within two years of the date of death, and
(c) in the case of a variation (but not a disclaimer) there must be an election that it is to be effective for inheritance tax purposes and notice of that election must be given to the Inland Revenue within six months of its date.

37.11 These provisions apply only to property comprised in a person's estate for inheritance tax purposes immediately before his death.[1] Accordingly, they extend only to the deceased's free estate or property passing by survivorship.[2] The section does not therefore extend to lifetime gifts; or to gifts with reservation.[3] The distribution of settled property cannot be varied,[4] but a person may disclaim an interest in settled property.

1 Inheritance Tax Act 1984, s 142(1)(a).
2 The deceased's severable share of a joint tenancy may therefore be severed by a deed of variation and redirected accordingly.
3 Inheritance Tax Act 1984, s 142(5).
4 Ibid expressly excludes settled property unless the deceased by will exercised a *general* power of appointment over the property.

Variations and disclaimers effective for capital gains tax purposes

37.12 Similar provisions apply in respect of capital gains tax. These are contained in s 62(6)–(10) of the Taxation of Chargeable Gains Act 1992 and mirror the provisions relating to inheritance tax contained in s 142. Accordingly, where within two years of a person's death a beneficiary's entitlement under a will or on intestacy is varied or the benefit disclaimed in writing, such variation or disclaimer does not constitute a disposal for capital gains tax purposes and the variation takes effect as if it had been made by the deceased or, in the case of a disclaimer, had never been conferred.[1] In the case of a variation, however, written notice to that effect is to be given to the Inland Revenue by the person or persons making the instrument within six months after the date thereof.[2] No such election, however, has to be made in the case of a disclaimer.

1 Taxation of Chargeable Gains Act 1992, s 62(6).
2 Ibid, s 62(7).

37.13 A separate election can be made in respect of inheritance tax and capital gains tax.

The use of these provisions

37.14 Accordingly, any beneficiary entitled under the will or on intestacy who is sui iuris can vary or disclaim his interest in the deceased's estate and redirect it in any way they wish for personal purposes or to achieve a tax saving. The permutations to which such variations and disclaimers may be put are virtually limitless, but a few illustrations of circumstances in which they are used are summarised below.

Taking advantage of the nil-rate tax band
37.15 As we have seen,[1] if spouses leave their estates to each other either outright or for life, on the first death the nil-rate tax band is wasted. Accordingly, with the consent of the surviving spouse, the will can be redrawn to provide, for example, that the nil-rate tax band amount should pass direct to the children (or into a discretionary trust), and for the balance of the estate to go to the surviving spouse. This may be achieved after the death of the second spouse with the consent of the beneficiaries of the second spouse's estate. Suppose spouses have both made wills leaving their entire estates to each other or to their children in the event of the other dying first. Suppose also that the husband dies one year before his wife. On the wife's death, the children, as beneficiaries of her estate, can redirect the nil-rate tax band amount in the husband's estate to themselves, thereby reducing their mother's taxable estate and saving £60,000 in tax.[2]

1 Above, para 37.4.
2 At the current (1993/94) threshold of £150,000 and a tax rate of 40%.

Subsequent death of beneficiary
37.16 The last example has illustrated that if a beneficiary of an estate has died within two years of the deceased, it may be advantageous to bypass the estate of the beneficiary if his estate will consequently pay tax or more tax. A further illustration would be where a father leaves his estate to his son and the son survives his father but dies within two years of his father's death: it may be advantageous to redirect the son's share direct to the son's children rather than for it to fall into the son's estate and possibly attract tax on his death.

Use of reliefs
37.17 As has been illustrated above,[1] if an asset qualifying for business or agricultural property relief is left to an exempt transferee, the relief is effectively wasted. Where this occurs the will can be redrawn to ensure that the asset passes to a non-exempt transferee who is capable of benefiting. So, if a father has left his business to his wife and the balance of his estate to his son, a deed of variation can transpose these gifts.

1 See para 37.5.

To take advantage of a technicality
37.18 There are a number of technicalities of which a testator may not have been aware but which, in the events that have occurred, may be utilised to reduce tax. One of these is where spouses have died in circumstances rendering the order of their deaths uncertain, leaving wills in each other's favour. By virtue of Law of Property Act 1925, s 184, they are deemed to have died in order of seniority.[1] However, by virtue of Inheritance Tax Act 1984, s 4(2), they are deemed to have died at the same instance for inheritance tax purposes so that the estate of the elder spouse passes direct to the contingent beneficiaries. Nevertheless, for the purpose of Inheritance Tax Act 1984, s 18, the spouse exemption is utilised as the estate of the elder spouse passes momentarily into the estate of the surviving spouse by virtue of s 184. The consequence of the interaction of these provisions is that the estate of the elder spouse passes direct to the contingent beneficiaries free of inheritance tax, regardless of the size of the estate, even if it should be many millions of pounds. The benefit of this interaction is lost, however, if a survival clause is incorporated in the will of the elder spouse as the terms of the will remove the possibility of the momentary vesting of the elder spouse's estate in the estate of the younger spouse. However, by a deed of variation it is possible to remove the offending survival clause to avoid wasting this anomalous but potentially enormous benefit in inheritance tax saving.[2]

1 See above, para 30.28.
2 The same principle can be applied where spouses have died intestate in commorientes circumstances. The Intestates' Estates Act 1952, s 1(4), provides that the intestate is deemed not to have left a surviving spouse (see above, para 30.33), therefore preventing the momentary vesting of the elder spouse's estate in the survivor. This statutory provision can be reversed to take advantage of the anomaly.

Two-year power of appointment

37.19 A testator will sometimes be conscious that the tax and personal circumstances prevailing at the date of his death may be substantially different from those prevailing at the date he makes his will. Even if a testator regularly reviews his will, he may wish the flexibility to vary his will to be incorporated in the will itself in case he should fail or be unable (such as through mental disability) to review his will according to changing tax and personal circumstances. A testator may also wish his estate to be distributed by his trustees in such a way that he would not want his detailed wishes to be public knowledge. While the beneficiaries under a will may themselves vary the distribution of the estate under s 142, this does require their agreement, which may not be forthcoming, and their capacity to do so, which is not possible in the case of beneficiaries who are not sui iuris.

Inheritance tax implications

37.20 Accordingly, a method of satisfying such a testator's wishes is provided in s 144 of the Inheritance Tax Act 1984. This section enables a testator to incorporate a provision whereby a specific asset, a legacy, the residue or the whole of his estate is given to trustees on discretionary trusts with the widest possible powers of appointment among a class comprising all persons whom the testator may possibly wish to benefit. If a distribution is made from such a trust within two years of the date of death, it will not attract a charge to inheritance tax. Normally there would be an exit charge when an appointment is made out of a trust without an interest in possession.[1] For inheritance tax purposes therefore, the distribution will be treated as having been made by the testator.

1 Under Inheritance Tax Act 1984, s 65(1); see above, para 35.46. However, the distribution must not be made within three months of the date of death: s 144 only operates where there would otherwise be a charge to tax, and s 65(1) provides that there is no charge to tax in the first quarter of the trust.

37.21 It is therefore possible for a testator to provide for his estate to be distributed in accordance with his wishes but with flexibility in doing so if circumstances change subsequent to the date of his will or indeed subsequent to the date of his death, and in the most tax-efficient way. The testator leaves the ultimate decision with his trustees, who should for that reason be selected with extreme care. For the same reason, the trustees should be provided with written guidance about the testator's wishes and the criteria to be used by them in the exercise of their discretion. These instructions are not proved under the will and are therefore not public information.

37.22 If the distribution is made outside the initial two-year period, the appointment will be subject to the normal inheritance tax exit charge.[1] However, during the first ten years of such a trust, the tax is calculated on the basis of the value of the trust when it was created, at the testator's death. Accordingly, if the discretionary trust did not exceed the tax threshold at the date of death, appointments out of the trust can be made free of inheritance tax for up to ten years less one day from the date of death. If it is left until the ten-year anniversary there will be a periodic charge to tax based on the value of the trust fund at that time.[2] As an exception to this general rule, if an appointment is made outside the initial two-year period but before the first ten-year anniversary in respect of assets qualifying for business or agricultural property relief, the whole of that relief will be lost.[3]

1 Inheritance Tax Act 1984, s 65(1).
2 Ibid, s 64. See above, para 35.44.
3 Ibid, s 68(5).

Capital gains tax implications

37.23 Section 144 applies only to inheritance tax. Unlike variations, there is no corresponding provision in the capital gains tax legislation. Accordingly, if a gain is made during the period between the date of death and the date of distribution, the normal capital gains tax rules will apply. However, if the appointment is left until after the two years have elapsed, it is possible to 'hold over' any capital gain when transferring assets to a beneficiary, who will be deemed to acquire them at their original value but without paying any capital gains tax at that point.[1]

1 This arises by virtue of Taxation of Chargeable Gains Act 1992, s 260, which provides that where a disposal attracts an immediate charge to inheritance tax, the gain may be held over. If an appointment is made within the two years, as s 144 provides that there is no charge to inheritance tax, s 260 is ousted.

Discretionary trusts

37.24 The use of discretionary trusts has been touched upon when considering the application of s 144 of the Inheritance Tax Act 1984 in respect of appointments out of such trusts within two years of the date of death of the testator. Their use is not, however, restricted to tax saving. Indeed, tax mitigation may sometimes be the least important objective in establishing a discretionary trust. It may therefore be useful to summarise some of the wider purposes for using a discretionary trust. The following summary is not intended to be exhaustive, but merely illustrations of the enormous flexibility which can be provided to a testator to meet changing and unexpected circumstances by the use of such trusts.

Ease of changing instructions
37.25 The instructions to the trustees can be changed from time to time informally, even orally, and without having to make a new will. The instructions are not binding on the trustees but, as already mentioned, a testator should appoint trustees in whom he has confidence, so that he can rest secure in the knowledge that they will carry out his wishes.

Loss of testamentary capacity
37.26 The trustees are able to take into account any factors arising before the testator's death where perhaps the testator no longer has testamentary capacity to change his will.

Post-death factors
37.27 The trustees will also be able to take into account factors that may arise following the date of death. These may include:
(a) the death of a potential beneficiary;
(b) the divorce or other matrimonial difficulty of a beneficiary;
(c) the discovery that a beneficiary is a spendthrift or has joined the Moonies, or other indications that the inheritance will be dissipated;
(d) the bankruptcy of the beneficiary. This may sometimes be unexpected, as in the case of a Lloyd's 'name' who was once a person of substance but because of claims may find himself bankrupt.

In these circumstances the trustees can distribute the trust fund to other beneficiaries or hold it back until the intended beneficiary's problem has been resolved. In the case of the bankruptcy of the intended beneficiary, for example, distribution can be withheld until a discharge from bankruptcy has been secured. There will then be a fund waiting to enable him to start afresh.

Use of the nil-rate band
37.28 As we have seen,[1] if spouses simply leave their estates to each other, on the death of the survivor the nil-rate tax band of the first spouse to die will have been wasted. Often a testator is prepared to accept this tax disadvantage to achieve his paramount wish: that the surviving spouse

should be provided with adequate funds. However, by using a discretionary trust it is possible to 'eat one's cake and keep it'. If spouses leave life interests to each other, as these are interests in possession, on the death of the survivor the whole of the trust fund in which the survivor had a life interest will be charged to tax.[2] In the case of a discretionary trust, however, if the surviving spouse benefits from it, he or she is not entitled to such benefit as of right but only at the discretion of the trustees; thus the survivor does not have an interest in possession. For this reason, it is common practice to incorporate in each will a discretionary trust comprising the maximum sum possible without paying inheritance tax, with the balance of the estate being paid to the surviving spouse. In this way no tax is payable on the death of the first spouse, but a trust fund is created which has utilised the whole of the tax threshold of the first spouse to die. The surviving spouse can be made one of the potential beneficiaries of that discretionary trust so that, at the discretion of the trustees, income and capital can be advanced to him or her as required. On the death of the surviving spouse any balance held in the discretionary trust can be held for the ultimate beneficiaries and will attract no tax if distributed within ten years.[3] If the trust fund is distributed after that time, there may be a relatively small exit charge.[4]

1 Above, para 37.4.
2 Inheritance Tax Act 1984, s 52(1). See above, para 35.41.
3 Ibid, s 68(5). See above, para 37.22.
4 Ibid, s 69. See above, para 35.46.

37.29 Such a device is particularly useful if the principal asset of the spouses is the matrimonial home, which the survivor wishes to continue to occupy. If the property is vested in the spouses as beneficial tenants in common in equal shares, on the first death a half share in the house may be held in a discretionary trust with the surviving spouse continuing to occupy the whole of the property. If the surviving spouse owns his or her own share in the property, he or she is then occupying it as of right by virtue of joint ownership and not simply at the discretion of the trustees. If the whole of the property is held in the discretionary trust, the Revenue will treat the surviving spouse's possession as a de facto right of occupation, thereby potentially attracting a charge to tax on the survivor's death.

APPENDICES

Contents

APPENDIX A

Statutes

Contents

WILLS ACT 1837

(Will 4 & 1 Vict, c 26)

Meaning of certain words in this Act
1. The words and expressions hereinafter mentioned, which in their ordinary signification have a more confined or a different meaning, shall in this Act, except where the nature of the provision or the context of the Act shall exclude such construction, be interpreted as follows: (that is to say), the word 'will' shall extend to a testament, and to a codicil, and to an appointment by will or by writing in the nature of a will in exercise of a power, and also to a disposition by will and testament or devise of the custody and tuition of any child, by virtue of an Act passed in the Twelfth year of the reign of King Charles the Second, intituled *An Act for taking away the courts of wards and liveries, and tenures in capite and by Knights service, and purveyance, and for settling a Revenue upon His Majesty in lieu thereof* (*Tenures Abolition Act 1660*), or by virtue of an Act passed in Parliament of Ireland in the fourteenth and fifteenth years of the reign of King Charles the Second, intituled *An Act for taking away the court of ward and Liveries, and Tenures in capite and by Knight's Service* (*Tenures Abolition Act* (*Ireland*) *1662*) and to any other testamentary disposition; and the words 'real estate' shall extend to manors, advowsons, messuages, lands, tithes, rents, and hereditaments, whether freehold, customary freehold, tenant right, customary or copyhold, or of any other tenure, and whether corporeal, incorporeal, or personal, and to any undivided share thereof, and to any estate, right, or interest (other than a chattel interest) therein; and the words 'personal estate' shall extend to leasehold estates and other chattels real, and also to monies, shares of government and other funds, securities for money (not being real estates), debts, choses in action, rights, credits, goods, and all other property whatsoever, which by law devolves upon the executor or administrator, and to any share or interest therein; and every word importing the singular number only shall extend and be applied to several persons or things as well as one person or thing; and every word importing the masculine gender only shall extend and be applied to a female as well as a male.

2. [Repealed by Statute Law Revision Act 1874, s 45.]

All property may be disposed of by will
3. It shall be lawful for every person to devise, bequeath, or dispose of, by his will executed in manner hereinafter required, all real estate, and all personal estate which he shall be entitled to, either at law or in equity, at the time of his death, and which, if not so devised, bequeathed or disposed of would devolve upon the heir at law, or customary heir of him, or if he became entitled by descent, of his ancestor, or upon his executor or administrator; and the power hereby given shall extend to all real estate of the nature of customary freehold or tenant right, or customary or copyhold, notwithstanding that the testator may not have surrendered the same to the use of his will, or notwithstanding that, being entitled as heir, devisee, or otherwise to be admitted thereto, he shall not have been admitted thereto; or notwithstanding that the same, in consequence of the want of a custom to devise or surrender to the use of a will or otherwise, could not at law have

been disposed of by will if this Act had not been made, or notwithstanding that the same, in consequence of there being a custom that a will or a surrender to the use of a will should continue in force for a limited time only, or any other special custom, could not have been disposed of by will according to the power contained in this Act, if this Act had not been made: and also to estates pur autre vie, whether there shall or shall not be any special occupant thereof, and whether the same shall be freehold, customary freehold, tenant right, customary or copyhold, or of any other tenure, and whether the same shall be a corporeal or an incorporeal hereditament; and also to all contingent, executory, or other future interests in any real or personal estate, whether the tesator may or may not be ascertained as the person or one of the persons in whom the same respectively may become vested, and whether he may be entitled thereto under the instrument by which the same respectively were created, or under any disposition thereof by deed or will; and also to all rights of entry for conditions broken, and other rights of entry; and also to such of the same estates, interests, and rights respectively, and other real and personal estate, as the testator may be entitled to the same subsequently to the execution of his will.

[See also Law of Property Act 1925, s 178:

'Section three of the Wills Act 1837 shall (without prejudice to the rights and interests of a personal representative) authorise and be deemed always to have authorised any person to dispose of real property or chattels real by will notwithstanding that by reason of illegitimacy or otherwise he did not leave an heir or next of kin surviving him.'

See also Law of Property Act 1925, s 176 in respect of estates tail.]

4–6. [Repealed by Statute Law (Repeals) Act 1969.]

No will of a minor valid
7. No will made by any person under the age of eighteen years shall be valid.

[As amended by Family Law Reform Act 1969, s 3(1)(a).]

8. [Repealed by Statute Law (Repeals) Act 1969.]

Signing and attestation of wills
9. No will shall be valid unless:

(a) it is in writing, and signed by the testator, or by some other person in his presence and by his direction; and

(b) it appears that the testator intended by his signature to give effect to the will; and

(c) the signature is made or acknowledged by the testator in the presence of two or more witnesses present at the same time; and

(d) each witness either—

   (i) attests and signs the will; or
   (ii) acknowledges his signature,

in the presence of the testator (but not necessarily in the presence of any other witness),

but no form of attestation shall be necessary.

[As substituted by Administration of Justice Act 1982, s 17.]

Appointments by will to be executed like other wills
10. No appointment made by will, in exercise of any power, shall be valid, unless the same be executed in manner hereinbefore required; and every will executed in manner hereinbefore required shall, so far as respects the execution and attestation thereof, be a valid execution of a power of appointment by will, notwithstanding it shall have been expressly required that a will made in exercise of such power should be executed with some additional or other form of execution or solemnity.

Soldiers and mariners wills excepted
11. Provided always . . . that any soldier being in actual military service, or any mariner or seaman being at sea, may dispose of his personal estate as he might have done before the making of this Act.

12. [Repealed by the Admiralty Powers Act 1865, s 1.]

Publication not to be requisite
13. Every will executed in manner hereinbefore required shall be valid without any other publication thereof.

Will not void by incompetency of witnesses
14. If any person who shall attest the execution of a will shall at the time of the execution thereof or at any time afterwards be incompetent to be admitted a witness to prove the execution thereof, such will shall not on that account be invalid.

Gifts to an attesting witness to be void
15. If any person shall attest the execution of any will to whom or to whose wife or husband any beneficial devise, legacy, estate, interest, gift or appointment, of or affecting and real or personal estate (other than and except charges and directions for the payment of any debt or debts), shall be thereby given or made, such devise, legacy, estate, interest, gift, or appointment, shall, so far only as concerns such person attesting the execution of such will, or the wife or husband of such person, or any person claiming under such person or wife, or husband, be utterly null and void, and such person so attesting shall be admitted as witness to prove the execution of such will, or to prove the validity or invalidity thereof, notwithstanding such devise, legacy, estate, interest, gift, or appointment mentioned in such will.
[See now Wills Act 1968:
1. (1) For the purpose of section 15 of the Wills Act 1837 (avoidance of gifts to attesting witnesses and their spouses) the attestation of a will by a person to whom or to whose spouse there is given or made any such disposition as is described in that section shall be disregarded if the will is duly executed without his attestation and without that of any other such person.
(2) This section applies to the will of any person dying after the passing of this Act, whether executed before or after the passing of this Act.
2. (1) This Act may be cited as the Wills Act 1968.
(2) This Act does not extend to Scotland or Northern Ireland.]

Creditor attesting to be admitted a witness
16. In case by any will any real or personal estate shall be charged with any debt or debts, and any creditor, or the wife or husband, of any such creditor whose debt is so charged, shall attest the execution of such will, such creditor notwithstanding such charge shall be admitted a witness to prove the execution of such will, or to prove the validity or invalidity thereof.

Executor to be admitted a witness
17. No person shall, on account of his being an executor of a will, be incompetent to be admitted a witness to prove the execution of such will, or a witness to prove the validity or invalidity thereof.

Wills to be revoked by marriage, except in certain cases
18. (1) Subject to subsections (2) to (4) below, a will shall be revoked by the testator's marriage.
(2) A disposition in a will in exercise of a power of appointment shall take effect notwithstanding the testator's subsequent marriage unless the property so appointed would in default of appointment pass to his personal representatives.
(3) Where it appears from a will that at the time it was made the testator was expecting to be married to a particular person and that he intended that the will should not be revoked by the marriage, the will shall not be revoked by his marriage to that person.
(4) Where it appears from a will that at the time it was made the testator was expecting to be married to a particular person and that he intended that a disposition in the will should not be revoked by his marriage to that person—

(a)   that disposition shall take effect notwithstanding the marriage; and
(b)   any other disposition in the will shall take effect also, unless it appears from the will that the testator intended the disposition to be revoked by the marriage.

[As substituted by Administration of Justice Act 1982, s 18(1).]

Effect of dissolution or annulment of marriage on wills
18A. (1) Where, after a testator has made a will, a decree of a court dissolves or annuls his marriage or declares it void—

(a)   the will shall take effect as if any appointment of the former spouse as an executor or as the executor and trustee of the will were omitted; and
(b)   any devise or bequest to the former spouse shall lapse.

except in so far as a contrary intention appears by the will.
(2) Subsection (1)(b) above is without prejudice to any right of the former spouse to apply for financial provision under the Inheritance (Provision for Family and Dependants) Act 1975.
(3) Where—

(a)   by the terms of a will an interest in remainder to a life interest; and
(b)   the life interest lapses by virtue of subsection (1)(b) above,

the interest in remainder shall be treated as if it had not been subject to the

life interest and, if it was contingent upon the termination of the life interest, as if it had not been so contingent.
[Added by Administration of Justice Act 1982, s 18(2).]

No will to be revoked by presumption
19. No will shall be revoked by any presumption of an intention on the ground of an alteration in circumstances.

In what cases wills may be revoked
20. No will or codicil, or any part thereof, shall be revoked otherwise than as aforesaid, or by another will or codicil executed in manner hereinbefore required, or by some writing declaring an intention to revoke the same, and executed in the manner in which a will is hereinbefore required to be executed, or by the burning, tearing, or otherwise destroying the same by the testator, or by some person in his presence and by his direction, with the intention of revoking the same.

No alteration in a will shall have any effect unless executed as a will
21. No obliteration, interlineation, or other alteration made in any will after the execution thereof shall be valid or have any effect, except so far as the words or effect of the will before such alteration shall not be apparent, unless such alteration shall be executed in like manner as hereinbefore is required for the execution of the will; but the will, with such alteration as part thereof, shall be deemed to be duly executed if the signature of the testator and the subscription of the witnesses be made in the margin or on some other part of the will opposite or near to such alteration, or at the foot or end of or opposite to a memorandum referring to such alteration, and written at the end or some other part of the will.

How revoked will shall be revived
22. No will or codicil, or any part thereof, which shall be in any manner revoked, shall be revived otherwise than by the re-execution thereof, or by a codicil executed in manner hereinbefore required, and showing an intention to revive the same; and when any will or codicil which shall be partly revoked, and afterwards wholly revoked, shall be revived, such revival shall not extend to so much thereof as shall have been revoked before the revocation of the whole thereof, unless an intention to the contrary shall be shown.

When a devise not to be rendered inoperative
23. No conveyance or other act made or done subsequently to the execution of a will of or relating to any real or personal estate therein comprised, except an act by which such will shall be revoked as aforesaid, shall prevent the operation of the will with respect to such estate or interest in such real or personal estate as the testator shall have power to dispose of by will at the time of his death.

A will to speak from the death of the testator
24. Every will shall be construed, with reference to the real estate and personal estate comprised in it, to speak and take effect as if it has been executed immediately before the death of the testator, unless a contrary intention shall appear by the will.

What a residuary devise shall include
25. Unless the contrary intention shall appear by the will, such real estate or interest therein shall be comprised or intended to be comprised in any devise in such will contained, which shall fail or be void by reason of the death of the devisee in the lifetime of the testator, or by reason of such devise being contrary to law or otherwise incapable of taking effect, shall be included in the residuary devise (if any) contained in such will.

What a general devise shall include
26. A devise of the land of the testator, or of the land of the testator in any place or in the occupation of any person mentioned in his will, or otherwise described in a general manner and any other general devise which would describe a customary, copyhold, or leasehold estate if the testator had no freehold estate which could be described by it, shall be construed to include the customary, copyhold and leasehold estates of the testator, or his customary, copyhold and leasehold estates, or any of them, to which such description shall extend, as the case may be, as well as freehold estates, unless a contrary intention shall appear by the will.

What a general gift shall include
27. A general devise of the real estate of the testator, or of the real estate of the testator in any place or in the occupation of any person mentioned in his will, or otherwise described in a general manner, shall be construed to include any real estate, or any real estate to which such descriptions shall extend (as the case may be), which he may have power to appoint in any manner he may think proper, and shall operate as an execution of such power, unless a contrary intention shall appear by the will; and in like manner a bequest of the personal estate of the testator, or any bequest of personal property described in a general manner, shall be construed to include any personal estate, or any personal estate to which such description shall extend (as the case may be), which he may have power to appoint in any manner he may think proper, and shall operate as an execution of such power, unless a contrary intention shall appear by the will.

How a devise without words of limitation shall be construed
28. Where any real estate shall be devised to any person without any words of limitation, such devise shall be construed to pass the fee simple, or other the whole estate or interest which the testator had power to dispose of by will in such real estate, unless a contrary intention shall appear by the will.

How the words 'die without issue' shall be construed
29. In any devise or bequest of real or personal estate the words 'die without issue' or 'die without leaving issue', or 'have no issue', or any other words which may import either a want or failure of issue of any person in his lifetime, or at the time of his death, or an indefinite failure of his issue, shall be construed to mean a want or failure of issue in the lifetime or at the time of the death of such person, and not an indefinite failure of his issue, unless a contrary intention shall appear by the will, by reason of such person having a prior estate tail or of a preceding gift, being, without any implication arising from such words, a limitation of an estate tail to such person or issue, or otherwise; Provided that this Act shall not extend to cases where such words as aforesaid import if no issue described in a

preceding gift shall be born, or if there shall be no issue who shall live to attain the age or otherwise answer the description required for obtaining a vested estate by a preceding gift to such issue.

No devise to trustees or executors, except in certain cases, shall pass a chattel interest
30. Where any real estate (other than or not being a presentation to a church) shall be devised to any trustee or executor, such devise shall be construed to pass the fee simple or other the whole estate or interest which the testator had power to dispose of by will in such real estate, unless a definite term of years, absolute or determinable or an estate of freehold, shall thereby be given to him expressly or by implication.

Trustees under an unlimited devise, etc to take the fee
31. Where any real estate shall be devised to a trustee, without any express limitation of the estate to be taken by such trustee, and the beneficial interest in such real estate, or in the surplus rents and profits thereof, shall not be given to any person for life, but the purposes of the trust may continue beyond the life of such person, such devise shall be construed to vest in such trustee the fee simple or other the whole legal estate which the testator had power to dispose of by will in such real estate, and not an estate determinable when the purposes of the trust shall be satisfied.

Devises of estates tail shall not lapse
32. Where any person to whom any real estate shall be devised for an estate tail or an estate in quasi entail shall die in the lifetime of the testator leaving issue who would be inheritable under such entail, and any such issue shall be living at the time of the death of the testator, such devise or bequest shall not lapse, but shall take effect as if the death of such person had happened immediately after the death of the testator, unless a contrary intention shall appear by the will.

Gifts to children or other issue who leave issue living at the testator's death shall not lapse
33. (1) Where—

(a)   a will contains a devise or bequest to a child or remoter descendant of the testator; and
(b)   the intended beneficiary dies before the testator, leaving issue; and
(c)   issue of the intended beneficiary are living at the testator's death.

then, unless a contrary intention appears by the will, the devise or bequest shall take effect as a devise or bequest to the issue living at the testator's death.
(2) Where—

(a)   a will contains a devise or bequest to a class of persons consisting of children or remoter descendants of the testator; and
(b)   a member of the class dies before the testator, leaving issue; and
(c)   issue of that member are living at the testator's death.

then, unless a contrary intention appears by the will, the devise or bequest shall take effect as if the class included the issue of its deceased member living at the testator's death.

[Substituted by Administration of Justice Act 1982, s 19.]

To what wills and estates this Act shall extend
34. This Act shall not extend to any will made before the first day of January, one thousand eight hundred and thirty-eight, and every will re-executed or republished, or revived by any codicil, shall for the purposes of this Act be deemed to have been made at the time at which the same shall be so re-executed, republished, or revived; and this Act shall not extend to any estate pur autre vie of any person who shall die before the first day of January, one thousand eight hundred and thirty-eight.

Extent
35. This Act shall not extend to Scotland.

36. [Repealed by Statute Law Revision Act 1874.]

ADMINISTRATION OF ESTATES ACT 1925

(1925 Chapter 23)

An Act to consolidate Enactments relating to the Administration of the Estates of Deceased Persons   [9th April 1925]

PART I

DEVOLUTION OF REAL ESTATE

Devolution of real estate on personal representative
1. (1) Real estate to which a deceased person was entitled for an interest not ceasing on his death shall on his death, and notwithstanding any testamentary disposition thereof, devolve from time to time on the personal representative of the deceased, in like manner as before the commencement of this Act chattels real devolved on the personal representative from time to time of a deceased person.
(2) The personal representatives for the time being of a deceased person are deemed in law his heirs and assigns within the meaning of all trusts and powers.
(3) The personal representatives shall be the representative of the deceased in regard to his real estate to which he was entitled for an interest not ceasing on his death as well as in regard to his personal estate.

Application to real estate of law affecting chattels real
2. (1) Subject to the provisions of this Act, all enactments and rules of law, and all jurisdiction of any court with respect to the appointment of administrators or to probate or letters of administration, or to dealings before probate in the case of chattels real, and with respect to costs and

other matters in the administration of personal estate, in force before the commencement of this Act, and all powers, duties, rights, equities, obligations, and liabilities of a personal representative in force at the commencement of this Act with respect to chattels real, shall apply and attach to the personal representative and shall have effect with respect to real estate vested in him, and in particular all such powers of disposition and dealing as were before the commencement of this Act exercisable as respects chattels real by the survivor or survivors of two or more personal representatives, as well as by a single personal representative, or by all the personal representatives together, shall be exercisable by the personal representatives or representative of the deceased with respect to his real estate.

(2) Where as respects real estate there are two or more personal representatives, a conveyance of real estate devolving under this Part of this Act shall not, save as otherwise provided as respects trust estates including settled land, be made without the concurrence therein of all such representatives or an order of the court, but where probate is granted to one or some of two or more persons named as executors, whether or not power is reserved to the other or others to prove, any conveyance of the real estate may be made by the proving executor or executors for the time being, without an order of the court, and shall be as effectual as if all the persons named as executors had concurred therein.

(3) Without prejudice to the rights and powers of a personal representative, the appointment of a personal representative in regard to real estate shall not, save as hereinafter provided, affect—

(a) any rule as to marshalling or as to administration of assets;
(b) the beneficial interest in real estate under any testamentary disposition;
(c) any mode of dealing with any beneficial interest in real estate, or the proceeds of sale thereof;
(d) the right of any person claiming to be interested in the real estate to take proceedings for the protection or recovery thereof against any person other than the personal representative.

PART II

EXECUTORS AND ADMINISTRATORS

Interpretation of Part I
3. (1) In this Part of this Act *real estate* includes—

(i)   Chattels real, and land in possession, remainder, or reversion, and every interest in or over land to which a deceased person was entitled at the time of his death; and
(ii) Real estate held on trust (including settled land) or by way of mortgage or security, but not money to arise under a trust for sale of land, nor money secured or charged on land.

(2) A testator shall be deemed to have been entitled at his death to any

interest in real estate passing under any gift contained in his will which operates as an appointment under a general power to appoint by will, or operates under the testamentary power conferred by statute to dispose of an entailed interest.

(3) An entailed interest of a deceased person shall (unless disposed of under the testamentary power conferred by statute) be deemed an interest ceasing on his death, but any further or other interest of the deceased in the same property in remainder or reversion which is capable of being disposed of by his will shall not be deemed to be an interest so ceasing.

(4) The interest of a deceased person under a joint tenancy where another tenant survives the deceased is an interest ceasing on his death.

(5) On the death of a corporator sole his interest in the corporation's real and personal estate shall be deemed to be an interest ceasing on his death and shall devolve to his successor.

This subsection applies on the demise of the Crown as respects all property, real and personal, vested in the Crown as a corporation sole.

General Provisions

Cesser of right of executor to prove
5. Where a person appointed executor by a will—

(i) survives the testator but dies without having taken out probate of the will; or
(ii) is cited to take out probate of the will and does not appear to the citation; or
(iii) renounces probate of the will;

his rights in respect of the executorship shall wholly cease, and the representation to the testator and the administration of his real and personal estate shall devolve and be committed in like manner as if that person had not been appointed executor.

Withdrawal of renunciation
6. (1) Where an executor who has renounced probate has been permitted, whether before or after the commencement of this Act, to withdraw the renunciation and prove the will, the probate shall take effect and be deemed always to have taken effect without prejudice to the previous acts and dealings of and notices to any other personal representative who has previously proved the will or taken out letters of administration, and a memorandum of the subsequent probate shall be endorsed on the original probate or letters of administration.

(2) This section applies whether the testator died before or after the commencement of this Act.

Executor of executor represents original testator
7. (1) An executor of a sole or last surviving executor of a testator is the executor of that testator.

This provision shall not apply to an executor who does not prove the will of his testator, and, in the case of an executor who on his death leaves surviving him some other executor of his testator who afterwards proves the will of that testator, it shall cease to apply on such probate being granted.

(2) So long as the chain of such representation is unbroken, the last executor in the chain is the executor of every preceding testator.

(3) The chain of such representation is broken by—

(a)   an intestacy; or
(b)   the failure of a testator to appoint an executor; or
(c)   the failure to obtain probate of a will;
    but is not broken by a temporary grant of administration if probate is subsequently granted.

(4) Every person in the chain of representation to a testator—

(a)   has the same rights in respect of the real and personal estate of that testator as the original executor would have had if living; and
(b)   is, to the extent to which the estate whether real or personal of that testator has come to his hands, answerable as if he were an original executor.

Right of proving executors to exercise powers
8. (1) Where probate is granted to one or some of two or more persons named as executors, whether or not power is reserved to the others or other to prove, all the powers which are by law conferred on the personal representative may be exercised by the proving executor or executors for the time being and shall be as effectual as if all the persons named as executors had concurred therein.

(2) This section applies whether the testator died before or after the commencement of this Act.

Vesting of estate of intestate between death and grant of administration
9. Where a person dies intestate, his real and personal estate, until administration is granted in respect thereof, shall vest in the Probate Judge in the same manner and to the same extent as formerly in the case of personal estate it vested in the ordinary.

Executor not to act while administration is in force
15. Where administration has been granted in respect of any real or personal estate of a deceased person, no person shall have power to bring any action or otherwise act as executor of the deceased person in respect of the estate comprised in or affected by the grant until the grant has been recalled or revoked.

Continuance of legal proceedings after revocation of temporary administration
17. [(1)] If, while any legal proceeding is pending in any court by or against an administrator to whom a temporary administration has been granted, that administration is revoked, that court may order that the proceeding be continued by or against the new personal representative in like manner as if the same had been originally commenced by or against him, but subject to such conditions and variations, if any, as that court directs.

[(2) The county court has jurisdiction under this section where the proceedings are pending in that court.]

Appendix A

Annotations
Amended by the County Courts Act 1984, s 148(1), Sch 2, para 11.

Rights and liabilities of administrator
21. Every person to whom administration of the real and personal estate of a deceased person is granted, shall, subject to the limitations contained in the grant, have the same rights and liabilities and be accountable in like manner as if he were the executor of the deceased.

A Debtor who becomes creditor's executor by representation or administrator to account for debt to estate
21A. [(1) Subject to subsection (2) of this section, where a debtor becomes his deceased creditor's executor by representation or administrator—

(a) his debt shall thereupon be extinguished; but
(b) he shall be accountable for the amount of the debt as part of the creditor's estate in any case where he would be so accountable if he had been appointed as an executor by the creditor's will.

(2) Subsection (1) of this section does not apply where the debtor's authority to act as executor or administrator is limited to part only of the creditor's estate which does not include the debt; and a debtor whose debt is extinguished by virtue of paragraph (a) shall not be accountable for its amount by virtue of paragraph (b) of that subsection in any case where the debt was barred by the Limitation Act 1939 before he became the creditor's executor or administrator.

(3) In this section *debt* includes any liability, and *debtor* and *creditor* shall be construed accordingly.]

Annotations
Added by the Limitation Amendment Act 1980, s 10.

SPECIAL PROVISIONS AS TO SETTLED LAND

Special executors as respects settled land
22. (1) A testator may appoint, and in default of such express appointment shall be deemed to have appointed, as his special executors in regard to settled land, the persons, if any, who are at his death the trustees of the settlement thereof, and probate may be granted to such trustees specially limited to the settled land.

In this subsection *settled land* means land vested in the testator which was settled previously to his death and not by his will.

(2) A testator may appoint other persons either with or without such trustees as aforesaid or any of them to be his general executors in regard to his other property and assets.

Provisions where, as respects settled land, representation is not granted to the trustees of the settlement
23. (1) Where settled land becomes vested in a personal representative, not being a trustee of the settlement, upon trust to convey the land to or assent to the vesting thereof in the tenant for life or statutory owner in order to give effect to a settlement created before the death of the deceased and not by his will, or would on the grant of representation to him, have become so vested, such representative may—

(a) before representation has been granted, renounce his office in regard only to such settled land without renouncing it in regard to other property;

(b) after representation has been granted, apply to the court for revocation of the grant in regard to the settled land without applying in regard to other property.

(2) Whether such renunciation or revocation is made or not, the trustees of the settlement, or any person beneficially interested thereunder, may apply to the High Court for an order appointing a special or additional personal representative in respect of the settled land, and a special or additional personal representative, if and when appointed under the order, shall be in the same position as if representation had originally been granted to him alone in place of the original personal representative, if any, or to him jointly with the original personal representative, as the case may be, limited to the settled land, but without prejudice to the previous acts and dealings, if any, of the personal representative originally constituted or the effect of notices given to such personal representative.

(3) The court may make such order as aforesaid subject to such security, if any, being given by or on behalf of the special or additional personal representative, as the court may direct, and shall, unless the court considers that special considerations apply, appoint such persons as may be necessary to secure that the persons to act as representatives in respect of the settled land shall, if willing to act, be the same persons as are the trustees of the settlement, and an office copy of the order when made shall be furnished to the [principal registry of the Family Division of the High Court] for entry, and a memorandum of the order shall be endorsed on the probate or administration.

(4) The person applying for the appointment of a special or additional personal representative shall give notice of the application to the [principal registry of the Family Division of the High Court] in the manner prescribed.

(5) Rules of court may be made for prescribing for all matters required for giving effect to the provisions of this section, and in particular—

(a) for notice of any application being given to the proper officer;

(b) for production of orders, probates, and administration to the registry;

(c) for the endorsement on a probate or administration of a memorandum of an order, subject or not to any exceptions;

(d) for the manner in which the costs are to be borne;

(e) for protecting purchasers and trustees and other persons in a fiduciary position, dealing in good faith with or giving notices to a personal representative before notice of any order has been endorsed on the probate or administration or a pending action has been registered in respect of the proceedings.

Annotations
Sub-ss (3), (4): amended by the Administration of Justice Act 1970, s 1(6), Sch 2, para 3.

Power for special personal representatives to dispose of settled land
24. (1) The special personal representatives may dispose of the settled land without the concurrence of the general personal representatives, who may likewise dispose of the other property and assets of the deceased without the concurrence of the special personal representatives.

(2) In this section the expression *special personal representatives* means

the representatives appointed to act for the purposes of settled land and includes any original personal representative who is to act with an additional personal representative for those purposes.

DUTIES, RIGHTS AND OBLIGATIONS

Duty of personal representatives
25. [The personal representative of a deceased person shall be under a duty to—

(a) collect and get in the real and personal estate of the deceased and administer it according to law;
(b) when required to do so by the court, exhibit on oath in the court a full inventory of the estate and when so required render an account of the administration of the estate to the court;
(c) when required to do so by the High Court, deliver up the grant of probate or administration to that court.]

Annotations
Substituted by the Administration of Estates Act 1971, s 9

Rights of action by and against personal representative
26. (1), (2) . . .
   (3) A personal representative may distrain for arrears of a rentcharge due or accruing to the deceased in his lifetime on the land affected or charged therewith, so long as the land remains in the possession of the person liable to pay the rentcharge or of the persons deriving title under him, and in like manner as the deceased might have done had he been living.
   (4) A personal representative may distrain upon land for arrears of rent due or accruing to the deceased in like manner as the deceased might have done had he been living.
Such arrears may be distrained for after the termination of the lease or tenancy as if the term or interest had not determined, if the distress is made—

(a) within six months after the termination of the lease or tenancy;
(b) during the continuance of the possession of the lessee or tenant from whom the arrears were due.

   The statutory enactments relating to distress for rent apply to any distress made pursuant to this subsection,
(5), (6) . . .

Annotations
Sub-ss (1), (2), (5), (6): repealed by the Law Reform (Miscellaneous Provisions) Act 1934, s 1(7).

Protection of persons on probate or administration
27. (1) Every person making or permitting to be made any payment or disposition in good faith under a representation shall be indemnified and protected in so doing, notwithstanding any defect or circumstance whatsoever affecting the validity of the representation.
   (2) Where a representation is revoked, all payments and dispositions made in good faith to a personal representative under the representation

before the revocation thereof are a valid discharge to the person making the same; and the personal representative who acted under the revoked representation may retain and reimburse himself in respect of any payments or dispositions made by him which the person to whom representation is afterwards granted might have properly made.

Liability of person fraudulently obtaining or retaining estate of deceased
28. If any person, to the defrauding of creditors or without full valuable consideration, obtains, receives or holds any real or personal estate of a deceased person or effects the release of any debt or liability due to the estate of the deceased, he shall be charged as executor in his own wrong to the extent of the real and personal estate received or coming to his hands, or the debt or liability released, after deducting—

(a) any debt for valuable consideration and without fraud due to him from the deceased person at the time of his death; and

(b) any payment made by him which might properly be made by a personal representative.

Liability of estate of personal representative
29. Where a person as personal representative of a deceased person (including an executor in his own wrong) wastes or converts to his own use any part of the real or personal estate of the deceased, and dies, his personal representative shall to the extent of the available assets of the defaulter be liable and chargeable in respect of such waste or conversion in the same manner as the defaulter would have been if living.

Provisions applicable where administration granted to nominee of the Crown
30. (1) Where the administration of the real and personal estate of any deceased person is granted to a nominee of the Crown (whether the Treasury Solicitor, or a person nominated by the Treasury Solicitor, or any other person), any legal proceeding by or against that nominee for the recovery of the real or personal estate, or any part or share thereof, shall be of the same character, and be instituted and carried on in the same manner, and be subject to the same rules of law and equity (including, except as otherwise provided by this Act, the rules of limitation under the statutes of limitation or otherwise), in all respects as if the administration had been granted to such nominee as one of the persons interested under this Act in the estate of the deceased.

(2) An information or other proceeding on the part of His Majesty shall not be filed or instituted, and a petition of right shall not be presented, in respect of the real or personal estate of any deceased person or any part or share thereof, or any claim thereon, except . . . subject to the same rules of law and equity within and subject to which a proceeding for the like purposes might be instituted by or against a subject.

(3) The Treasury Solicitor shall not be required, when applying for or obtaining administration of the estate of a deceased person for the use or benefit of His Majesty, to deliver, nor shall . . . the High Court or the Commissioners of Inland Revenue be entitled to receive in connexion with any such application or grant of administration, any affidavit, statutory declaration, account, certificate, or other statement verified on oath; but the Treasury Solicitor shall deliver and the said Division and Commissioners

respectively shall accept, in lieu thereof, an account or particulars of the estate of the deceased signed by or on behalf of the Treasury Solicitor.

(4) References in sections two, four . . . and seven of the Treasury Solicitor Act, 1876, and in subsection (3) of section three of the Duchy of Lancaster Act, 1920, to *personal estate* shall include real estate.

Annotations

Sub-s (3): words omitted repealed by the Administration of Justice Act 1970, s 54, Sch 11.

Sub-s (4): words omitted repealed by the Statute Law (Repeals) Act 1981.

Power to make rules

31. Provision may be made by rules of court for giving effect to the provisions of this Part of this Act so far as relates to real estate and in particular for adapting the procedure and practice on the grant of letters of administration to the case of real estate.

PART III

ADMINISTRATION OF ASSETS

Real and personal estate of deceased are assets for payment of debts

32. (1) The real and personal estate, whether legal or equitable, of a deceased person, to the extent of his beneficial interest therein, and the real and personal estate of which a deceased person in pursuance of any general power (including the statutory power to dispose of entailed interests) disposes by his will, are assets for payment of his debts (whether by specialty or simple contract) and liabilities, and any disposition by will inconsistent with this enactment is void as against the creditors, and the court shall if necessary, administer the property for the purpose of the payment of the debts and liabilities.

This subsection takes effect without prejudice to the rights of incumbrancers.

(2) If any person to whom any such beneficial interest devolves, or is given, or in whom any such interest vests, disposes thereof in good faith before an action is brought or process is sued out against him, he shall be personally liable for the value of the interest so disposed of by him, but that interest shall not be liable to be taken in execution in the action or under the process.

Trust for sale

33. (1) On the death of a person intestate as to any real or personal estate, such estate shall be held by his personal representatives—

(a)   as to the real estate upon trust to sell the same; and
(b)   as to the personal estate upon trust to call in sell and convert into money such part thereof as may not consist of money,

with power to postpone such sale and conversion for such a period as the personal representatives, without being liable to account, may think proper, and so that any reversionary interest be not sold until it falls into possession, unless the personal representatives see special reason for sale, and so also that, unless required for purposes of administration owing to want of other assets, personal chattels be not sold except for special reason.

(2) Out of the net money to arise from the sale and conversion of such real and personal estate (after payment of costs), and out of the ready money of the deceased (so far as not disposed of by his will, if any), the personal representative shall pay all such funeral, testamentary and administration expenses, debts and other liabilities as are properly payable thereout having regard to the rules of administration contained in this Part of this Act, and out of the residue of the said money the personal representative shall set aside a fund sufficient to provide for any pecuniary legacies bequeathed by the will (if any) of the deceased.

(3) During the minority of any beneficiary or the subsistence of any life interest and pending the distribution of the whole or any part of the estate of the deceased, the personal representatives may invest the residue of the said money, or so much thereof as may not have been distributed, in any investments for the time being authorised by statute for the investment of trust money, with power, at the discretion of the personal representatives, to change such investments for others of a like nature.

(4) The residue of the said money and any investments for the time being representing the same, including (but without prejudice to the trust for sale) any part of the estate of the deceased which may be retained unsold and is not required for the administration purposes aforesaid, is in this Act referred to as *the residuary estate of the intestate.*

(5) The income (including net rents and profits of real estate and chattels real after payment of rates, taxes, rent, costs of insurance, repairs and other outgoings properly attributable to income) of so much of the real and personal estate of the deceased as may not be disposed of by his will, if any, or may not be required for the administration purposes aforesaid, may, however such estate is invested, as from the death of the deceased, be treated and applied as income, and for that purpose any necessary apportionment may be made between tenant for life and remainderman.

(6) Nothing in this section affects the rights of any creditor of the deceased or the rights of the Crown in respect of death duties.

(7) Where the deceased leaves a will, this section has effect subject to the provisions contained in the will.

Administration of assets
34. (1), (2) . . .

(3) Where the estate of a deceased person is solvent his real and personal estate shall, subject to rules of court and the provisions hereinafter contained as to charges on property of the deceased, and to the provisions, if any, contained in his will, be applicable towards the discharge of the funeral, testamentary and administration expenses, debts and liabilities payable thereout in the order mentioned in Part II of the First Schedule to this Act.

Annotations
Sub-s (1): repealed by the Insolvency Act 1985, s 235, Sch 10, Part III, and the Insolvency Act 1986, s 437, Sch 11.
  Sub-s (2): repealed by the Administration of Estates Act 1971, s 12(2), (4), (6), Sch 2, Part II.

Charges on property of deceased to be paid primarily out of the property charged
35. (1) Where a person dies possessed of, or entitled to, or, under a general power of appointment (including the statutory power to dispose of entailed interests) by his will disposes of, an interest in property, which at the time of his death is charged with the payment of money, whether by way of legal mortgage, equitable charge or otherwise (including a lien for unpaid purchase money), and the deceased has not by will deed or other document signified a contrary or other intention, the interest so charged, shall as between the different persons claiming through the deceased, be primarily liable for the payment of the charge; and every part of the said interest, according to its value, shall bear a proportionate part of the charge on the whole thereof.

(2) Such contrary or other intention shall not be deemed to be signified—

(a) by a general direction for the payment of debts or of all the debts of the testator out of his personal estate, or his residuary real and personal estate, or his residuary real estate; or
(b) by a charge of debts upon any such estate;
unless such intention is further signified by words expressly or by necessary implication referring to all or some part of the charge.

(3) Nothing in this section affects the right of a person entitled to the charge to obtain payment or satisfaction thereof either out of the other assets of the deceased or otherwise.

Effect of assent or conveyance by personal representative
36. (1) A personal representative may assent to the vesting, in any person who (whether by devise, bequest, devolution, appropriation or otherwise) may be entitled thereto, either beneficially or as a trustee or personal representative, of any estate or interest in real estate to which the testator or intestate was entitled or over which he exercised a general power of appointment by his will, including the statutory power to dispose of entailed interests, and which devolved upon the personal representative.

(2) The assent shall operate to vest in that person the estate or interest to which the assent relates, and, unless a contrary intention appears, the assent shall relate back to the death of the deceased.

(3) The statutory covenants implied by a person being expressed to convey as personal representative, may be implied in an assent in like manner as in a conveyance by deed.

(4) An assent to the vesting of a legal estate shall be in writing, signed by the personal representative, and shall name the person in whose favour it is given and shall operate to vest in that person the legal estate to which it relates; and an assent not in writing or not in favour of a named person shall not be effectual to pass a legal estate.

(5) Any person in whose favour an assent or conveyance of a legal estate is made by a personal representative may require that notice of the assent or conveyance be written or endorsed on or permanently annexed to the probate or letters of administration, at the cost of the estate of the deceased, and that the probate or letters of administration be produced, at the like cost, to prove that the notice has been placed thereon or annexed thereto.

(6) A statement in writing by a personal representative that he has not

given or made an assent or conveyance in respect of a legal estate, shall, in favour of a purchaser, but without prejudice to any previous disposition made in favour of another purchaser deriving title mediately or immediately under the personal representative, be sufficient evidence that an assent or conveyance has not been given or made in respect of the legal estate to which the statement relates, unless notice of a previous assent or conveyance affecting that estate has been placed on or annexed to the probate or administration.

A conveyance by a personal representative of a legal estate to a purchaser accepted on the faith of such a statement shall (without prejudice as aforesaid and unless notice of a previous assent or conveyance affecting that estate has been placed on or annexed to the probate or administration) operate to transfer or create the legal estate expressed to be conveyed in like manner as if no previous assent or conveyance had been made by the personal representative.

A personal representative making a false statement, in regard to any such matter, shall be liable in like manner as if the statement had been contained in a statutory declaration.

(7) An assent or conveyance by a personal representative in respect of a legal estate shall, in favour of a purchaser, unless notice of a previous assent or conveyance affecting that legal estate has been placed on or annexed to the probate or administration, be taken as sufficient evidence that the person in whose favour the assent or conveyance is given or made is the person entitled to have the legal estate conveyed to him, and upon the proper trusts, if any, but shall not otherwise prejudicially affect the claim of any person rightfully entitled to the estate vested or conveyed or any charge thereon.

(8) A conveyance of a legal estate by a personal representative to a purchaser shall not be invalidated by reason only that the purchaser may have notice that all the debts, liabilities, funeral, and testamentary or administration expenses, duties, and legacies of the deceased have been discharged or provided for.

(9) An assent or conveyance given or made by a personal representative shall not, except in favour of a purchaser of a legal estate, prejudice the right of the personal representative or any other person to recover the estate or interest to which the assent or conveyance relates, or to be indemnified out of such estate or interest against any duties, debts, or liability to which such estate or interest would have been subject if there had not been any assent or conveyance.

(10) A personal representative may, as a condition of giving an assent or making a conveyance, require security for the discharge of any such duties, debt, or liability, but shall not be entitled to postpone the giving of an assent merely by reason of the subsistence of any such duties, debt or liability if reasonable arrangements have been made for discharging the same; and an assent may be given subject to any legal estate or charge by way of legal mortgage.

(11) This section shall not operate to impose any stamp duty in respect of an assent, and in this section *purchaser* means a purchaser for money or money's worth.

(12) This section applies to assents and conveyances made after the commencement of this Act, whether the testator or intestate died before or after such commencement.

597

Validity of conveyance not affected by revocation of representation
37. (1) All conveyances of any interest in real or personal estate made to a purchaser either before or after the commencement of this Act by a person to whom probate or letters of administration have been granted are valid, notwithstanding any subsequent revocation or variation, either before or after the commencement of this Act, of the probate or administration.

(2) This section takes effect without prejudice to any order of the court made before the commencement of this Act, and applies whether the testator or intestate died before or after such commencement.

Right to follow property and powers of the court in relation thereto
38. (1) An assent or conveyance by a personal representative to a person other than a purchaser does not prejudice the rights of any person to follow the property to which the assent or conveyance relates, or any property representing the same, into the hands of the person in whom it is vested by the assent or conveyance, or of any other person (not being a purchaser) who may have received the same or in whom it may be vested.

(2) Notwithstanding any such assent or conveyance the court may, on the application of any creditor or other person interested—

(a) order a sale, exchange, mortgage, charge, lease, payment, transfer or other transaction to be carried out which the court considers requisite for the purpose of giving effect to the rights of the persons interested;
(b) declare that the person, not being a purchaser, in whom the property is vested is a trustee for those purposes;
(c) give directions respecting the preparation and execution of any conveyance or other instrument or as to any other matter required for giving effect to the order;
(d) make any vesting order, or appoint a person to convey in accordance with the provisions of the Trustee Act 1925.

(3) This section does not prejudice the rights of a purchaser or a person deriving title under him, but applies whether the testator or intestate died before or after the commencement of this Act.

[(4) The county court has jurisdiction under this section where the estate in respect of which the application is made does not exceed in amount or value the county court limit.]

Annotations
Sub-s (4): added by the County Courts Act 1984, s 148(1), Sch 2, para 12.

Powers of management
39. (1) In dealing with the real and personal estate of the deceased his personal representatives shall, for purposes of administration, or during a minority of any beneficiary or the subsistence of any life interest, or until the period of distribution arrives, have—

(i) the same powers and discretions, including power to raise money by mortgage or charge (whether or not by deposit of documents), as a personal representative had before the commencement of this Act, with respect to personal estate vested in him, and such power of raising money by mortgage may in the case of land be exercised by way of legal mortgage; and

(ii) all the powers, discretions and duties conferred or imposed by law on trustees holding land upon an effectual trust for sale (including power to overreach equitable interests and powers as if the same affected the proceeds of sale); and

(iii) all the powers conferred by statute on trustees for sale, and so that every contract entered into by a personal representative shall be binding on and be enforceable against and by the personal representative for the time being of the deceased, and may be carried into effect, or be varied or rescinded by him, and, in the case of a contract entered into by a predecessor, as if it had been entered into by himself.

(2) Nothing in this section shall affect the right of any person to require an assent or conveyance to be made.

(3) This section applies whether the testator or intestate died before or after the commencement of this Act.

Powers of personal representative for raising money, etc
40. (1) For giving effect to beneficial interests the personal representative may limit or demise land for a term of years absolute, with or without impeachment for waste, to trustees on usual trusts for raising or securing any principal sum and the interest thereon for which the land, or any part thereof, is liable, and may limit or grant a rentcharge for giving effect to any annual or periodical sum for which the land or the income thereof or any part thereof is liable.

(2) This section applies whether the testator or intestate died before or after the commencement of this Act.

Powers of personal representative as to appropriation
41. (1) The personal representative may appropriate any part of the real or personal estate, including things in action, of the deceased in the actual condition or state of investment thereof at the time of appropriation in or towards satisfaction of any legacy bequeathed by the deceased, or of any other interest or share in his property, whether settled or not, as to the personal representative may seem just and reasonable, according to the respective rights of the persons interested in the property of the deceased:
Provided that—

(i) an appropriation shall not be made under this section so as to affect prejudicially any specific devise or bequest;

(ii) an appropriation of property, whether or not being an investment authorised by law or by the will, if any, of the deceased for the investment of money subject to the trust, shall not (save as hereinafter mentioned) be made under this section except with the following consents—

(a) when made for the benefit of a person absolutely and beneficially entitled in possession, the consent of that person;

(b) when made in respect of any settled legacy share or interest, the consent of either the trustee thereof, if any (not being also the personal representative), or the person who may for the time being be entitled to the income:

If the person whose consent is so required as aforesaid is an infant or [is incapable by reason of mental disorder within the meaning of [the

Mental Health Act 1983], of managing and administering his property and affairs] the consent shall be given on his behalf by his parents or parent, testamentary or other guardian . . . or receiver, or if, in the case of an infant, there is no such parent or guardian, by the court on the application of his next friend;

(iii) no consent (save of such trustee as aforesaid) shall be required on behalf of a person who may come into existence after the time of appropriation, or who cannot be found or ascertained at that time;

(iv) if no [receiver is acting for a person suffering from mental disorder] then, if the appropriation is of an investment authorised by law or by the will, if any, of the deceased for the investment of money subject to the trust, no consent shall be required on behalf of the [said person];

(v) if, independently of the personal representative, there is no trustee of a settled legacy share or interest, and no person of full age and capacity entitled to the income thereof, no consent shall be required to an appropriation in respect of such legacy share or interest, provided that the appropriation is of an investment authorised as aforesaid.

[(1A) The county court has jurisdiction under proviso (ii) to subsection (1) of this section where the estate in respect of which the application is made does not exceed in amount or value the county court limit.]

(2) Any property duly appropriated under the powers conferred by this section shall thereafter be treated as an authorised investment, and may be retained or dealt with accordingly.

(3) For the purposes of such appropriation, the personal representative may ascertain and fix the value of the respective parts of the real and personal estate and the liabilities of the deceased as he may think fit, and shall for that purpose employ a duly qualified valuer in any case where such employment may be necessary; and may make any conveyance (including an assent) which may be requisite for giving effect to the appropriation.

(4) An appropriation made pursuant to this section shall bind all persons interested in the property of the deceased whose consent is not hereby made requisite.

(5) The personal representative shall, in making the appropriation, have regard to the rights of any person who may thereafter come into existence, or who cannot be found or ascertained at the time of appropriation, and of any other person whose consent is not required by this section.

(6) This section does not prejudice any other power of appropriation conferred by law or by the will (if any) of the deceased, and takes effect with any extended powers conferred by the will (if any) of the deceased, and where an appropriation is made under this section, in respect of a settled legacy, share or interest, the property appropriated shall remain subject to all trusts for sale and powers of leasing, disposition, and management or varying investments which would have been applicable thereto or to the legacy, share or interest in respect of which the appropriation is made, if no such appropriation had been made.

(7) If after any real estate has been appropriated in purported exercise of the powers conferred by this section, the person to whom it was conveyed disposes of it or any interest therein, then, in favour of a purchaser, the appropriation shall be deemed to have been made in accordance with the requirements of this section and after all requisite consents, if any, had been given.

(8) In this section, a settled legacy, share or interest includes any legacy, share or interest to which a person is not absolutely entitled in possession at the date of the appropriation, also an annuity, and *purchaser* means a purchaser for money or money's worth.

(9) This section applies whether the deceased died intestate or not, and whether before or after the commencement of this Act, and extends to property over which a testator exercises a general power of appointment, including the statutory power to dispose of entailed interests, and authorises the setting apart of a fund to answer an annuity by means of the income of that fund or otherwise.

Annotations
Sub-s (1): amended by the Mental Health Act 1959, s 149(1), Sch 7, Part I and the Mental Health Act 1983, s 148, Sch 4, para 7.
Sub-s (1A): added by the County Courts Act 1984, s 148(1), Sch 2, para 13.

Power to appoint trustees of infants· property
42. (1) Where an infant is absolutely entitled under the will or on the intestacy of a person dying before or after the commencement of this Act (in this subsection called *the deceased*) to a devise or legacy, or to the residue of the estate of the deceased, or any share therein, and such devise, legacy, residue or share is not under the will, if any, of the deceased, devised or bequeathed to trustees for the infant, the personal representatives of the deceased may appoint a trust corporation or two or more individuals not exceeding four (whether or not including the personal representatives or one or more of the personal representatives), to be the trustee or trustees of such devise, legacy, residue or share for the infant, and to be trustees of any land devised or any land being or forming part of such residue or share for the purposes of the Settled Land Act 1925, and of the statutory provisions relating to the management of land during a minority, and may execute or do any assurance or thing requisite for vesting such devise, legacy, residue or share in the trustee or trustees so appointed.

On such appointment the personal representatives, as such, shall be discharged from all further liability in respect of such devise, legacy, residue, or share, and the same may be retained in its existing condition or state of investment, or may be converted into money, and such money may be invested in any authorised investment.

(2) Where a personal representative has before the commencement of this Act retained or sold any such devise, legacy, residue or share, and invested the same or the proceeds thereof in any investments in which he was authorised to invest money subject to the trust, then, subject to any order of the court made before such commencement, he shall not be deemed to have incurred any liability on that account, or by reason of not having paid or transferred the money or property into court.

Obligations of personal representative as to giving possession of land and powers of the court
43. (1) A personal representative, before giving an assent or making a conveyance in favour of any person entitled, may permit that person to take possession of the land, and such possession shall not prejudicially affect the right of the personal representative to take or resume possession nor his power to convey the land as if he were in possession thereof, but subject to

the interest of any lessee, tenant or occupier in possession or in actual occupation of the land.

(2) Any person who as against the personal representative claims possession of real estate, or the appointment of a receiver thereof, or a conveyance thereof, or an assent to the vesting thereof, or to be registered as proprietor thereof under the Land Registration Act 1925, may apply to the court for directions with reference thereto, and the court may make such vesting or other order as may be deemed proper, and the provisions of the Trustee Act 1925, relating to vesting orders and to the appointment of a person to convey, shall apply.

(3) This section applies whether the testator or intestate died before or after the commencement of this Act.

[(4) The county court has jurisdiction under this section where the estate in respect of which the application is made does not exceed in amount or value the county court limit.]

Annotations

Sub-s (4): added by the County Courts Act 1984, s 148(1), Sch 2, para 14.

Power to postpone distribution
44. Subject to the foregoing provisions of this Act, a personal representative is not bound to distribute the estate of the deceased before the expiration of one year from the death.

PART IV

DISTRIBUTION OF RESIDUARY ESTATE

Abolition of descent to heir, curtesy, dower and escheat
45. (1) With regard to the real estate and personal inheritance of every person dying after the commencement of this Act, there shall be abolished—

(a) All existing modes rules and canons of descent, and of devolution by special occupancy or otherwise, of real estate, or of a personal inheritance, whether operating by the general law or by the custom of gavelkind or borough english or by any other custom of any county, locality, or manor, or otherwise howsoever; and

(b) Tenancy by the curtesy and every other estate and interest of a husband in real estate as to which his wife dies intestate, whether arising under the general law or by custom or otherwise; and

(c) Dower and freebench and every other estate and interest of a wife in real estate as to which her husband dies intestate, whether arising under the general law or by custom or otherwise: Provided that where a right (if any) to freebench or other like right has attached before the commencement of this Act which cannot be barred by a testamentary or other disposition made by the husband, such right shall, unless released, remain in force as an equitable interest; and

(d) Escheat to the Crown or the Duchy of Lancaster or the Duke of Cornwall or to a mesne lord for want of heirs.

(2) Nothing in this section affects the descent or devolution of an entailed interest.

Succession to real and personal estate on intestacy

46. (1) The residuary estate of an intestate shall be distributed in the manner or be held on the trusts mentioned in this section, namely:—

[(i) If the intestate leaves a husband or wife, then in accordance with the following Table:

TABLE

If the intestate—

(1) leaves—

    (a) no issue, and

    (b) no parent, or brother or sister of the whole blood, or issue of a brother or sister of the whole blood

the residuary estate shall be held in trust for the surviving husband or wife absolutely.

(2) leaves issue (whether or not persons mentioned in subparagraph (b) above also survive)

the surviving husband or wife shall take the personal chattels absolutely and, in addition, the residuary estate of the intestate (other than the personal chattels) shall stand charged with the payment of a [fixed net sum], free of death duties and costs, to the surviving husband or wife with interest thereon from the date of the death [at such rate as the Lord Chancellor may specify by order] until paid or appropriated, and, subject to providing for that sum and the interest thereon, the residuary estate (other than the personal chattels) shall be held—

    (a) as to one half upon trust for the surviving husband or wife during his or her life, and, subject to such life interest, on the statutory trusts for the issue of the intestate, and

    (b) as to the other half, on the statutory trusts for the issue of the intestate.

(3) leaves one or more of the following, that is to say, a parent, a brother or sister of the whole blood, or issue of a brother or sister of the whole blood, but leaves no issue

the surviving husband or wife shall take the personal chattels absolutely and, in addition, the residuary estate of the intestate (other than the personal chattels) shall stand charged with the payment of a [fixed net sum], free of death duties and costs, to the surviving husband or wife with interest thereon from the date of the death [at such rate as the Lord Chancellor may specify by order] until paid or appropriated, and, subject to providing for that sum and the interest thereon, the residuary estate (other than the personal chattels) shall be held—

    (a) as to one half in trust for the surviving husband or wife absolutely, and (*b*) as to the other half—

                (i) where the intestate leaves one parent or both parents (whether or not brothers or sisters of the intestate or their issue also survive) in trust for the parent absolutely or, as the case may be, for the two parents in equal shares absolutely

                (ii) where the intestate leaves no parent, on the statutory trusts for the brothers and sisters of the whole blood of the intestate.

[The fixed net sums referred to in paragraphs (2) and (3) of this Table shall be of the amounts provided by or under section 1 of the Family Provision Act 1966]

    (ii) If the intestate leaves issue but no husband or wife, the residuary estate of the intestate shall be held on the statutory trusts for the issue of the intestate;

    (iii) If the intestate leaves [no husband or wife and] no issue but both parents, then . . . the residuary estate of the intestate shall be held in trust for the father and mother in equal shares absolutely;

    (iv) If the intestate leaves [no husband or wife and] no issue but one parent, then . . . the residuary estate of the intestate shall be held in trust for the surviving father or mother absolutely;

    (v) If the intestate leaves no [husband or wife and no issue and no] parent, then . . . the residuary estate of the intestate shall be held in trust for the following persons living at the death of the intestate, and in the following order and manner, namely:—

        First, on the statutory trusts for the brothers and sisters of the whole blood of the intestate; but if no person takes an absolutely vested interest under such trusts; then

        Secondly, on the statutory trusts for the brothers and sisters of the half blood of the intestate; but if no person takes an absolutely vested interest under such trusts; then

        Thirdly, for the grandparents of the intestate and, if more than one survive the intestate, in equal shares; but if there is no member of this class; then

        Fourthly, on the statutory trusts for the uncles and aunts of the intestate (being brothers or sisters of the whole blood of a parent of the intestate); but if no person takes an absolutely vested interest under such trusts; then

        Fifthly, on the statutory trusts for the uncles and aunts of the intestate (being brothers or sisters of the half blood of a parent of the intestate) . . .

    (vi) In default of any person taking an absolute interest under the foregoing provisions, the residuary estate of the intestate shall belong to the Crown or to the Duchy of Lancaster or to the Duke of Cornwall for the time being, as the case may be, as bona vacantia, and in lieu of any right to escheat.

The Crown or the said Duchy or the said Duke may (without prejudice to the powers reserved by section nine of the Civil List Act 1910, or any other powers), out of the whole or any part of the property devolving on them respectively, provide, in accordance with the existing practice, for dependents, whether kindred or not, of the intestate, and other persons for whom the intestate might reasonably have been expected to make provision.

[(1A) The power to make orders under subsection (1) above shall be exercisable by statutory instrument subject to annulment in pursuance of a resolution of either House of Parliament; and any such order may be varied or revoked by a subsequent order made under the power.]

(2) A husband and wife shall for all purposes of distribution or division under the foregoing provisions of this section be treated as two persons.

[(3) Where the intestate and the intestate's husband or wife have died in circumstances rendering it uncertain which of them survived the other and the intestate's husband or wife is by virtue of section one hundred and eighty-four of the Law of Property Act 1925, deemed to have survived the intestate, this section shall, nevertheless, have effect as respects the intestate as if the husband or wife had not survived the intestate.

(4) The interest payable on [the fixed net sum] payable to a surviving husband or wife shall be primarily payable out of income.]

Annotations

Sub-s (1): para (i) substituted by the Intestates' Estates Act 1952, s 1, and amended by the Family Provision Act 1966, s 1, and the Administration of Justice Act 1977, s 28(1)(a); words omitted from paras (iii), (iv), (v) repealed and amendments in square brackets made by the Intestates' Estates Act 1952.
  Sub-s (1A): added by the Administration of Justice Act 1977, s 28(1).
  Sub-ss (3), (4): added by the Intestates' Estates Act 1952, s 1(4).
  Sub-s (4): amended by the Family Provision Act 1966, s 1.

Statutory trusts in favour of issue and other classes of relatives of intestate
47. (1) Where under this Part of this Act the residuary estate of an intestate, or any part thereof, is directed to be held on the statutory trusts for the issue of the intestate, the same shall be held upon the following trusts, namely:—

 (i) In trust, in equal shares if more than one, for all or any the children or child of the intestate, living at the death of the intestate, who attain the age of [eighteen] years or marry under that age, and for all or any of the issue living at the death of the intestate who attain the age of [eighteen] years or marry under that age of any child of the intestate who predeceases the intestate, such issue to take through all degrees, according to their stocks, in equal shares if more than one, the share which their parent would have taken if living at the death of the intestate, and so that no issue shall take whose parent is living at the death of the intestate and so capable of taking;

 (ii) The statutory power of advancement, and the statutory provisions which relate to maintenance and accumulation of surplus income, shall apply, but when an infant marries such infant shall be entitled to give valid receipts for the income of the infant's share or interest;

 (iii) Where the property held on the statutory trusts for issue is divisible into shares, then any money or property which, by way of advancement or on the marriage of a child of the intestate, has been paid to such child by the intestate or settled by the intestate for the benefit of such child (including any life or less interest and including property covenanted to be paid or settled) shall, subject to any contrary intention expressed or appearing from the circumstances of the case, be taken as being so paid or settled in or towards satisfaction of the share of such child or the share which such child would have taken if living at the death of the intestate, and shall be brought into account, at a valuation (the value to be reckoned as at the death of the intestate), in accordance with the requirements of the personal representatives;

(iv) The personal representatives may permit any infant contingently interested to have the use and enjoyment of any personal chattels in such manner and subject to such conditions (if any) as the personal representatives may consider reasonable, and without being liable to account for any consequential loss.

(2) If the trusts in favour of the issue of the intestate fail by reason of no child or other issue attaining an absolutely vested interest—

(a) the residuary estate of the intestate and the income thereof and all statutory accumulations, if any, of the income thereof, or so much thereof as may not have been paid or applied under any power affecting the same, shall go, devolve and be held under the provisions of this Part of this Act as if the intestate had died without leaving issue living at the death of the intestate;

(b) references in this Part of this Act to the intestate *leaving no issue* shall be construed as *leaving no issue who attain an absolutely vested interest*;

(c) references in this Part of this Act to the intestate *leaving issue* or *leaving a child or other issue* shall be construed as *leaving issue who attain an absolutely vested interest.*

(3) Where under this Part of this Act the residuary estate of an intestate or any part thereof is directed to be held on the statutory trusts for any class of relatives of the intestate, other than issue of the intestate, the same shall be held on trusts corresponding to the statutory trusts for the issue of the intestate (other than the provision for bringing any money or property into account) as if such trusts (other than as aforesaid) were repeated with the substitution of references to the members or member of that class for references to the children or child of the intestate.

[(4) References in paragraph (i) of subsection (1) of the last foregoing section to the intestate leaving, or not leaving, a member of the class consisting of brothers or sisters of the whole blood of the intestate and issue of brothers or sisters of the whole blood of the intestate shall be construed as references to the intestate leaving, or not leaving, a member of that class who attains an absolutely vested interest.]

(5) . . .

Annotations

Sub-s (1): amended, where it applies to the estate of an intestate dying after 1 January 1970, by the Family Law Reform Act 1969, s 3(2).

Sub-s (4): added by the Intestates' Estates Act 1952, s 1(3)(c).

Sub-s (5): repealed by the Family Provision Act 1966, ss 9, 10, Sch 2.

A Right of surviving spouse to have his own life interest redeemed
47A. [(1) Where a surviving husband or wife is entitled to the interest in part of the residuary estate, and so elects, the personal representative shall purchase or redeem the life interest by paying the capital value thereof to the tenant for life, or the persons deriving title under the tenant for life, and the costs of the transaction; and thereupon the residuary estate of the intestate may be dealt with and distributed free from the life interest.

(2) . . .

(3) An election under this section shall only be exercisable if at the time of the election the whole of the said part of the residuary estate consists of property in possession, but, for the purposes of this section, a life interest in property partly in possession and partly not in possession shall be treated as consisting of two separate life interests in those respective parts of the property.

[(3A) The capital value shall be reckoned in such manner as the Lord Chancellor may by order direct, and an order under this subsection may include transitional provisions.

(3B) The power to make orders under subsection (3A) above shall be exercisable by statutory instrument subject to annulment in pursuance of a resolution of either House of Parliament; and any such order may be varied or revoked by a subsequent order made under the power.]

(4) . . .

(5) An election under this section shall be exercisable only within the period of twelve months from the date on which representation with respect to the estate of the intestate is first taken out:

Provided that if the surviving husband or wife satisfies the court that the limitation to the said period of twelve months will operate unfairly—

(a)   in consequence of the representation first taken out being probate of a will subsequently revoked on the ground that the will was invalid, or

(b)   in consequence of a question whether a person had an interest in the estate, or as to the nature of an interest in the estate, not having been determined at the time when representation was first taken out, or

(c)   in consequence of some other circumstances affecting the administration or distribution of the estate,
      the court may extend the said period.

(6) An election under this section shall be exercisable, except where the tenant for life is the sole personal representative, by notifying the personal representative (or, where there are two or more personal representatives of whom one is the tenant for life, all of them except the tenant for life) in writing; and a notification in writing under this subsection shall not be revocable except with the consent of the personal representative.

(7) Where the tenant for life is the sole personal representative an election under this section shall not be effective unless written notice thereof is given to the [[Senior Registrar] of the Family Division of the High Court] within the period within which it must be made; and provision may be made by probate rules for keeping a record of such notices and making that record available to the public.

In this subsection the expression *probate rules* means rules [of court made under section 127 of the Supreme Court Act 1981].

(8) An election under this section by a tenant for life who is an infant shall be as valid and binding as it would be if the tenant for life were of age; but the personal representative shall, instead of paying the capital value of the life interest to the tenant for life, deal with it in the same manner as with any other part of the residuary estate to which the tenant for life is absolutely entitled.

(9) In considering for the purposes of the foregoing provisions of this section the question when representation was first taken out, a grant limited to settled land or to trust property shall be left out of account and a grant limited to real estate or to personal estate shall be left out of account unless a grant limited to the remainder of the estate has previously been made or is made at the same time.]

Annotations

Added by the Intestates' Estates Act 1952, s 2.

Sub-ss (2), (4): repealed by the Administration of Justice Act 1977, ss 28(2), 32(4), Sch 5, Part VI.

Sub-ss (3A), (3B): added by the Administration of Justice Act 1977, s 28(3).

Sub-s (7): first amendment made by the Administration of Justice Act 1970, s 1(6), Sch 2, para 4, further amended by the Supreme Court Act 1981, s 152(1), Sch 5; final amendment made by the Supreme Court Act 1981, s 152(1), Sch 5.

Powers of personal representative in respect of interests of surviving spouse
48. (1) . . .

(2) The personal representatives may raise—

(a)   [the fixed net sum] or any part thereof and the interest thereon payable to the surviving husband or wife of the intestate on the security of the whole or any part of the residuary estate of the intestate (other than the personal chattels), so far as that estate may be sufficient for the purpose of the said sum and interest may not have been satisfied by an appropriation under the statutory power available in that behalf; and

(b)   in like manner the capital sum, if any, required for the purchase or redemption of the life interest of the surviving husband or wife of the intestate, or any part thereof not satisfied by the application for that purpose of any part of the residuary estate of the intestate;

and in either case the amount, if any, properly required for the payment of the costs of the transaction.

Annotations

Sub-s (1): repealed by the Intestates' Estates Act 1952, s 2.
Sub-s (2): amended by the Family Provision Act 1966, s 1.

Application to cases of partial intestacy
49. [(1)] Where any person dies leaving a will effectively disposing of part of his property, this Part of this Act shall have effect as respects the part of his property not so disposed of subject to the provisions contained in the will and subject to the following modifications:—

[(*aa*) where the deceased leaves a husband or wife who acquires any beneficial interests under the will of the deceased (other than personal chattels specifically bequeathed) the references in this Part of this Act to [the fixed net sum] payable to a surviving husband or wife, and to interest on that sum, shall be taken as references to the said sum diminished by the value at the date of death of the said beneficial interests, and to interest on that sum as so diminished, and accordingly, where the said value exceeds the said sum, this Part of this Act shall have effect as if references to the said sum, and interest thereon, were omitted;]

(a)   The requirements [of section forty-seven of this Act] as to bringing property into account shall apply to any beneficial interests acquired by any issue of the deceased under the will of the deceased, but not to beneficial interests so acquired by any other persons;

(b)   The personal representative shall, subject to his rights and powers for the purposes of administration, be a trustee for the persons entitled under this Part of this Act in respect of the part of the estate not expressly disposed of unless it appears by the will that the personal representative is intended to take such part beneficially.

[(2) References in the foregoing provisions of this section to beneficial interests acquired under a will shall be construed as including a reference to a beneficial interest acquired by virtue of the exercise by the will of a general power of appointment (including the statutory power to dispose of entailed interests), but not of a special power of appointment.

(3) For the purposes of paragraph (*aa*) in the foregoing provisions of this section the personal representative shall employ a duly qualified valuer in any case where such employment may be necessary.

(4) The references in subsection (3) of section forty-seven A of this Act to property are references to property comprised in the residuary estate and, accordingly, where a will of the deceased creates a life interest in property in possession, and the remaining interest in that property forms part of the residuary estate, the said references are references to that remaining interest (which, until the life interest determines, is property not in possession).]

Annotations

Sub-s (1): para (*aa*) added by the Intestates' Estates Act 1952, s 3, amended by the Family Provision Act 1966, s 1; para (*a*) amended by the Intestates' Estates Act 1952, s 3.

Sub-ss (2) (4): added by the Intestates' Estates Act 1952, s 3.

Construction of documents

50. (1) References to any Statutes of Distribution in an instrument inter vivos made or in a will coming into operation after the commencement of this Act, shall be construed as references to this Part of this Act; and references in such an instrument or will to statutory next of kin shall be construed, unless the context otherwise requires, as referring to the persons who would take beneficially on an intestacy under the foregoing provisions of this Part of this Act.

(2) Trusts declared in an instrument inter vivos made, or in a will coming into operation, before the commencement of this Act by reference to the Statutes of Distribution, shall, unless the contrary thereby appears, be construed as referring to the enactments (other than the Intestates' Estates Act 1890) relating to the distribution of effects of intestates which were in force immediately before the commencement of this Act.

[(3) In subsection (1) of this section the reference to this Part of this Act, or the foregoing provisions of this Part of this Act, shall in relation to an instrument inter vivos made, or a will or codicil coming into operation, after the coming into force of section 18 of the Family Law Reform Act 1987 (but not in relation to instruments inter vivos made or wills or codicils coming into operation earlier) be construed as including references to that section.]

Annotations

Sub-s (3): added with savings by the Family Law Reform Act 1987, s 33(1), Sch 2, para 3, Sch 3, para 1; for savings see also SI 1989 No 382, art 3, Sch 2.

Savings
51. (1) Nothing in this Part of this Act affects the right of any person to take beneficially, by purchase, as heir either general or special.

(2) The foregoing provisions of this Part of this Act do not apply to any beneficial interest in real estate (not including chattels real) to which a [person of unsound mind] or defective living and of full age at the commencement of this Act, and unable, by reason of his incapacity, to make a will, who thereafter dies intestate in respect of such interest without having recovered his testamentary capacity, was entitled at his death, and any such beneficial interest (not being an interest ceasing on his death) shall, without prejudice to any will of the deceased, devolve in accordance with the general law in force before the commencement of this Act applicable to freehold land, and that law shall, notwithstanding any repeal, apply to the case.

For the purposes of this subsection, a [person of unsound mind] or defective who dies intestate as respects any beneficial interest in real estate shall not be deemed to have recovered his testamentary capacity unless his . . . receiver has been discharged.

(3) Where an infant dies after the commencement of this Act without having been married, and independently of this subsection he would, at his death, have been equitably entitled under a settlement (including a will) to a vested estate in fee simple or absolute interest in freehold land, or in any property settled to devolve therewith or as freehold land, such infant shall be deemed to have had an entailed interest, and the settlement shall be construed accordingly.

(4) This Part of this Act does not affect the devolution of an entailed interest as an equitable interest.

Annotations

Sub-s (2): amendment in square brackets made by the Mental Treatment Act 1930, s 20(5); words omitted repealed by the Mental Health Act 1959, s 149(2), Sch 8.

Interpretation of Part IV
52. In this Part of this Act *real and personal estate* means every beneficial interest (including rights of entry and reverter) of the intestate in real and personal estate which (otherwise than in right of a power of appointment or of the testamentary power conferred by statute to dispose of entailed interests) he could, if of full age and capacity, have disposed of by his will [and references (however expressed) to any relationship between two

persons shall be construed in accordance with section 1 of the Family Law Reform Act 1987].

Annotations

Words in square brackets added by the Family Law Reform Act 1987, s 33(1), Sch 2, para 4.

PART V

SUPPLEMENTAL

General savings
53. (1) Nothing in this Act shall derogate from the powers of the High Court which exist independently of this Act or alter the distribution of business between the several divisions of the High Court, or operate to transfer any jurisdiction from the High Court to any other court.
(2) Nothing in this Act shall affect any unrepealed enactment in a public general Act dispensing with probate or administration as respects personal estate not including chattels real.
(3) . . .

Annotations

Sub-s (3): repealed by the Finance Act 1975, ss 52(2), 59(5), Sch 13, Part I.

Application of Act
54. Save as otherwise expressly provided, this Act does not apply in any case where the death occurred before the commencement of this Act.

Definitions
55. In this Act, unless the context otherwise requires, the following expressions have the meanings hereby assigned to them respectively, that is to say:—

(1) (i) *Administration* means, with reference to the real and personal estate of a deceased person, letters of administration whether general or limited, or with the will annexed or otherwise:
     (ii) *Administrator* means a person to whom administration is granted:
     (iii) *Conveyance* includes a mortgage, charge by way of legal mortgage, lease, assent, vesting, declaration, vesting instrument, disclaimer, release and every other assurance of property or of an interest therein by any instrument, except a will, and *convey* has a corresponding meaning, and *disposition* includes a *conveyance* also a devise bequest and an appointment of property contained in a will, and *dispose of* has a corresponding meaning:
     [(iiiA) *the County Court limit*, in relation to any enactment contained in this Act, means the amount for the time being specified by an Order in Council under section 145 of the County Courts Act 1984 as the county court limit for the purposes of that

611

enactment (or, where no such Order in Council has been made, the corresponding limit specified by Order in Council under section 192 of the County Courts Act 1959);]

(iv) *the Court* means the High Court and also the county court, where that court has jurisdiction . . .

(v) *Income* includes rents and profits:

(vi) *Intestate* includes a person who leaves a will but dies intestate as to some beneficial interest in his real or personal estate:

(vii) *Legal estates* mean the estates charges and interests in or over land (subsisting or created at law) which are by statute authorised to subsist or to be created at law; and *equitable interests* mean all other interests and charges in or over land or in the proceeds of sale thereof:

(viii) *[Person of unsound mind]* includes a [person of unsound mind] whether so found or not, and in relation to a [person of unsound mind] not so found; . . . and *defective* includes every person affected by the provisions of section one hundred and sixteen of the Lunacy Act 1890, as extended by section sixty-four of the Mental Deficiency Act 1913, and for whose benefit a receiver has been appointed:

(ix) *Pecuniary legacy* includes an annuity, a general legacy, a demonstrative legacy so far as it is not discharged out of the designated property, and any other general direction by a testator for the payment of money, including all death duties free from which any devise, bequest, or payment is made to take effect:

(x) *Personal chattels* mean carriages, horses, stable furniture and effects (not used for business purposes), motor cars and accessories (not used for business purposes), garden effects, domestic animals, plate, plated articles, linen, china, glass, books, pictures, prints, furniture, jewellery, articles of household or personal use or ornament, musical and scientific instruments and apparatus, wines, liquors and consumable stores, but do not include any chattels used at the death of the intestate for business purposes nor money or securities for money:

(xi) *Personal representative* means the executor, original or by representation, or administrator for the time being of a deceased person, and as regards any liability for the payment of death duties includes any person who takes possession of or intermeddles with the property of a deceased person without the authority of the personal representatives or the court, and *executor* includes a person deemed to be appointed executor as respects settled land:

(xii) *Possession* includes the receipt of rents and profits or the right to receive the same, if any:

(xiii) *Prescribed* means prescribed by rules of court . . . :

(xiv) *Probate* means the probate of a will:

[(xv) *Probate judge* means the President of the Family Division of the High Court:]

(xvi) . . .

(xvii) *Property* includes a thing in action and any interest in real or personal property:

(xviii) *Purchaser* means a lessee, mortgagee, or other person who in good faith acquires an interest in property for valuable consideration, also an intending purchaser and *valuable consideration* includes marriage, but does not include a nominal consideration in money:

(xix) *Real estate* save as provided in Part IV of this Act means real estate, including chattels real, which by virtue of Part I of this Act devolves on the personal representative of a deceased person:

(xx) *Representation* means the probate of a will and administration, and the expression *taking out representation* refers to the obtaining of the probate of a will or of the grant of administration:

(xxi) *Rent* includes a rent service or a rentcharge, or other rent, toll, duty, or annual or periodical payment in money or money's worth, issuing out of or charged upon land, but does not include mortgage interest; and *rentcharge* includes a fee farm rent:

(xxii) . . .

(xxiii) *Securities* include stocks, funds, or shares:

(xxiv) *Tenant for life, statutory owner,, land, settled land, settlement, trustees of the settlement, term of years absolute, death duties,* and *legal mortgage,* have the same meanings as in the Settled Land Act 1925, and *entailed interest* and *charge by way of legal mortgage* have the same meanings as in the Law of Property Act 1925:

(xxv) *Treasury solicitor* means the solicitor for the affairs of His Majesty's Treasury, and includes the solicitor for the affairs of the Duchy of Lancaster:

(xxvi) *Trust corporation* means the public trustee or a corporation either appointed by the court in any particular case to be a trustee or entitled by rules made under subsection (3) of section four of the Public Trustee Act 1906, to act as custodian trustee:

(xxvii) *Trust for sale,* in relation to land, means an immediate binding trust for sale, whether or not exercisable at the request or with the consent of any person, and with or without a power at discretion to postpone the sale; and *power to postpone a sale* means power to postpone in the exercise of a discretion:

(xxviii) *Will* includes codicil.

(2) References to a child or issue living at the death of any person include child or issue en ventre sa mere at the death.

(3) References to the estate of a deceased person include property over which the deceased exercises a general power of appointment (including the statutory power to dispose of entailed interests) by his will.

Annotations

Sub-s (1): para (iiiA) added by the County Courts Act 1984, s 148(1), Sch 2, para 15; words omitted from para (iv) repealed by the Courts Act 1971, s 56(4), Sch 11, Part II; words omitted from para (viii) repealed by the Mental Health Act 1959, s 149(2), Sch 8, Part I, and amendments in square brackets made by the Mental Treatment Act 1930, s 20(5); words omitted from para (xiii) repealed by the Supreme Court Act 1981, s 152(4), Sch 7; para (xv) substituted by the Administration of Justice Act 1970, s 1(6), Sch 2, para 5; paras (xvi), (xxii) repealed by the Supreme Court Act 1980, s 152(4), Sch 7.

Modification: definition *Trust corporation* modified in relation to Charities, by the Charities Act 1993, s 35.

Application to Crown
57. (1) The provisions of this Act bind the Crown and the Duchy of Lancaster, and the Duke of Cornwall for the time being as respects the estates of persons dying after the commencement of this Act, but not so as to affect the time within which proceedings for the recovery of real or personal estate vesting in or devolving on His Majesty in right of His Crown, or His Duchy of Lancaster, or on the Duke of Cornwall, may be instituted.
(2) Nothing in this Act in any manner affects or alters the descent or devolution of any property for the time being vested in His Majesty either in right of the Crown or of the Duchy of Lancaster or of any property for the time being belonging to the Duchy of Cornwall.

Short title, commencement and extent
58. (1) This Act may be cited as the Administration of Estates Act 1925.
(2) . . .
(3) This Act extends to England and Wales only:

Annotations

Sub-s (2): repealed by the Statute Law Revision Act: 1950.

SCHEDULE 1

Section 34

Part II

Order of Application of Assets where the Estate is Solvent

1. Property of the deceased undisposed of by will, subject to the retention thereout of a fund sufficient to meet any pecuniary legacies.

2. Property of the deceased not specifically devised or bequeathed but included (either by a specific or general description) in a residuary gift, subject to the retention out of such property of a fund sufficient to meet any pecuniary legacies, so far as not provided for as aforesaid.

3. Property of the deceased specifically appropriated or devised or bequeathed (either by a specific or general description) for the payment of debts.

4. Property of the deceased charged with, or devised or bequeathed (either by a specific or general description) subject to a charge for the payment of debts.

5. The fund, if any, retained to meet pecuniary legacies.

6. Property specifically devised or bequeathed, rateably according to value,

7. Property appointed by will under a general power, including the statutory power to dispose of entailed interests, rateably according to value.

8. The following provisions shall also apply—
(a) The order of application may be varied by the will of the deceased.
(b) . . .

Annotations

Para 8: words omitted repealed by the Finance (No 2) Act 1983, s 16(4), Sch 2, Part II.

WILLS ACT 1963

(1963 Chapter 44)

An Act to repeal the Wills Act 1861 and make new provision in lieu thereof; and to provide that certain testamentary instruments shall be probative for the purpose of the conveyance of heritable property in Scotland [31st July 1963]

General rule as to formal validity
1. A will shall be treated as properly executed if its execution conformed to the internal law in force in the territory where it was executed, or in the territory where, at the time of its execution or of the testator's death, he was domiciled or had his habitual residence, or in a state of which, at either of those times, he was a national.

Additional rules
2. (1) Without prejudice to the preceding section, the following shall be treated as properly executed—

(a) a will executed on board a vessel or aircraft of any description, if the execution of the will conformed to the internal law in force in the territory with which, having regard to its registration (if any) and other relevant circumstances, the vessel or aircraft may be taken to have been most closely connected;

(b) a will so far as it disposes of immovable property, if its execution conformed to the internal law in force in the territory where the property was situated;

(c) a will so far as it revokes a will which under this Act would be treated as properly executed or revokes a provision which under this Act would be treated as comprised in a properly executed will, if the execution of the later will conformed to any law by reference to which the revoked will or provision would be so treated;

(d) a will so far as it exercises a power of appointment, if the execution of the will conformed to the law governing the essential validity of the power.

(2) A will so far as it exercises a power of appointment shall not be treated as improperly executed by reason only that its execution was not in accordance with any formal requirements contained in the instrument creating the power.

Certain requirements to be treated as formal
3. Where (whether in pursuance of this Act or not) a law in force outside the United Kingdom falls to be applied in relation to a will, any requirement of that law whereby special formalities are to be observed by testators answering a particular description, or witnesses to the execution of a will are

to possess certain qualifications, shall be treated, notwithstanding any rule of that law to the contrary, as a formal requirement only.

Construction of wills
4. The construction of a will shall not be altered by reason of any change in the testator's domicile after the execution of the will.

Interpretation
6. (1) In this Act—
internal law in relation to any territory or state means the law which would apply in a case where no question of the law in force in any other territory or state arose;
state means a territory or group of territories having its own law of nationality;
will includes any testamentary instrument or act, and *testator* shall be construed accordingly.

(2) Where under this Act the internal law in force in any territory or state is to be applied in the case of a will, but there are in force in that territory or state two or more systems of internal law relating to the formal validity of wills, the system to be applied shall be ascertained as follows—

(a) if there is in force throughout the territory or state a rule indicating which of those systems can properly be applied in the case in question, that rule shall be followed; or
(b) if there is no such rule, the system shall be that with which the testator was most closely connected at the relevant time, and for this purpose the relevant time is the time of the testator's death where the matter is to be determined by reference to circumstances prevailing at his death, and the time of execution of the will in any other case.

(3) In determining for the purposes of this Act whether or not the execution of a will conformed to a particular law, regard shall be had to the formal requirements of that law at the time of execution, but this shall not prevent account being taken of an alteration of law affecting wills executed at that time if the alteration enables the will to be treated as properly executed.

Short title, commencement, repeal and extent
7. (1) This Act may be cited as the Wills Act 1963.
(2) This Act shall come into operation on 1st January 1964.
(3) . . .
(4) This Act shall not apply to a will of a testator who died before the time of the commencement of this Act and shall apply to a will of a testator who dies after that time whether the will was executed before or after that time, but so that the repeal of the Wills Act 1861 shall not invalidate a will executed before that time.
(5) It is hereby declared that this Act extends to Northern Ireland . . . .

Annotations
Sub-s (3): repeals the Wills Act 1861.
Sub-s (5): words omitted repealed by the Northern Ireland Constitution Act 1973, Sch 6, Part I.

FAMILY LAW REFORM ACT 1969

(1969 Chapter 46)

PART IV

MISCELLANEOUS AND GENERAL

Right of illegitimate child to succeed on intestacy of parents, and of parents to succeed on intestacy of illegitimate child
14. (1) Where either parent of an illegitimate child dies intestate as respects all or any of his or her real or personal property, the illegitimate child or, if he is dead, his issue, shall be entitled to take any interest therein to which he or such issue would have been entitled if he had been born legitimate.

(2) Where an illegitimate child dies intestate in respect of all or any of his real or personal property, each of his parents, if surviving, shall be entitled to take any interest therein to which that parent would have been entitled if the child had been born legitimate.

(3) In accordance with the foregoing provisions of this section, Part IV of the Administration of Estates Act 1925 (which deals with the distribution of the estate of an intestate) shall have effect as if—

(a) any reference to the issue of the intestate included a reference to any illegitimate child of his and to the issue of any such child;
(b) any reference to the child or children of the intestate included a reference to any illegitimate child or children of his; and
(c) in relation to an intestate who is an illegitimate child, any reference to the parent, parents, father or mother of the intestate were a reference to his natural parent, parents, father or mother.

(4) For the purposes of subsection (2) of this section and of the provisions amended by subsection (3)(c) thereof, an illegitimate child shall be presumed not to have been survived by his father unless the contrary is shown.

(5) This section does not apply to or affect the right of any person to take any entailed interest in real or personal property.

(6) The reference in section 50(1) of the said Act of 1925 (which relates to the construction of documents) to Part IV of that Act, or to the foregoing provisions of that Part, shall in relation to an instrument inter vivos made, or a will or codicil coming into operation, after the coming into force of this section (but not in relation to instruments inter vivos made or wills or codicils coming into operation earlier) be construed as including references to this section.

(7) Section 9 of the Legitimacy Act 1926 (under which an illegitimate child and his issue are entitled to succeed on the intestacy of his mother if she leaves no legitimate issue, and the mother of an illegitimate child is entitled to succeed on his intestacy as if she were the only surviving parent) is hereby repealed.

(8) In this section 'illegitimate child' does not include an illegitimate child who is—

(a) a legitimated person within the meaning of the said Act of 1926 or a person recognised by virtue of that Act or at common law as having been legitimated; or

(b)   an adopted person under an adoption order made in any part of the United Kingdom, the Isle of Man or the Channel Islands or under an overseas adoption as defined in section 4(3) of the Adoption Act 1968.

(9) This section does not affect any rights under the intestacy of a person dying before the coming into force of this section.

Presumption that in dispositions of property references to children and other relatives include references to, and to persons related through, illegitimate children

15. (1) In any disposition made after the coming into force of this section—

(a)   any reference (whether express or implied) to the child or children of any person shall, unless the contrary intention appears, be construed as, or as including, a reference to any illegitimate child of that person; and

(b)   any reference (whether express or implied) to a person or persons related in some other manner to any person shall, unless the contrary intention appears, be construed as, or as including, a reference to anyone who would be so related if he, or some other person through whom the relationship is deduced, had been born legitimate.

(2) The foregoing subsection applies only where the reference in question is to a person who is to benefit or to be capable of benefiting under the disposition or, for the purpose of designating such a person, to someone else to or through whom that person is related; but that subsection does not affect the construction of the word 'heir' or 'heirs' or of any expression which is used to create an entailed interest in real or personal property.

(3) In relation to any disposition made after the coming into force of this section, section 33 of the Trustee Act 1925 (which specifies the trusts implied by a direction that income is to be held on protective trusts for the benefit of any person) shall have effect as if—

(a)   the reference to the children or more remote issue of the principal beneficiary included a reference to any illegitimate child of the principal beneficiary and to anyone who would rank as such issue if he, or some other person through whom he is descended from the principal beneficiary, had been born legitimate; and

(b)   the reference to the issue of the principal beneficiary included a reference to anyone who would rank as such issue if he, or some other person through whom he is descended from the principal beneficiary, had been born legitimate.

[Subsection 15(4) repealed by the Children Act 1975.]

(5) Where under any disposition any real or personal property or any interest in such property is limited (whether subject to any preceding limitation or charge or not) in such a way that it would, apart from this section, devolve (as nearly as the law permits) along with a dignity or title of honour, then, whether or not the disposition contains an express reference to the dignity or title of honour, and whether or not the property or some interest in the property may in some event become severed therefrom, nothing in this section shall operate to sever the property or any interest therein from the dignity or title, but the property or interest shall devolve in all respects as if this section had not been enacted.

[Subsection 15(6) repealed by the Children Act 1975.]

(7) There is hereby abolished, as respects dispositions made after the coming into force of this section, any rule of law that a disposition in favour of illegitimate children not in being when the disposition takes effect is void as contrary to public policy.

(8) In this section 'disposition' means a disposition, including an oral disposition, of real or personal property whether inter vivos or by will or codicil; and, notwithstanding any rule of law, a disposition made by will or codicil executed before the date on which this section comes into force shall not be treated for the purposes of this section as made on or after that date by reason only that the will or codicil is confirmed by a codicil executed on or after that date.

Annotations
Sections 14 and 15 will only be relevant to the estate of persons dying intestate after 1970 but before 4 April 1988 (see para 12.45) and to the construction of wills and other dispositions *made* between these dates (see para 11.15).

Rebuttal of presumption as to legitimacy and illegitimacy
26. Any presumption of law as to the legitimacy or illegitimacy of any person may in any civil proceedings be rebutted by evidence which shows that it is more probable than not that that person is illegitimate or legitimate, as the case may be, and it shall not be necessary to prove that fact beyond reasonable doubt in order to rebut the presumption.

Annotations
Commencement order: SI 1969 No 1140.

INHERITANCE (PROVISION FOR FAMILY AND DEPENDANTS) ACT 1975

(1975 Chapter 63)

An Act to make fresh provisions for empowering the court to make orders for the making out of the estate of a deceased person of provision for the spouse, former spouse, child, child of the family or dependant of that person; and for matters connected therewith [12th November 1975]

POWERS OF COURT TO ORDER FINANCIAL PROVISION FROM DECEASED'S ESTATE

Application for financial provision from deceased's estate
1. (1) Where after the commencement of this Act a person dies domiciled in England and Wales and is survived by any of the following persons—

(a) the wife or husband of the deceased;
(b) a former wife or former husband of the deceased who has not remarried;
(c) a child of the deceased;
(d) any person (not being a child of the deceased) who, in the case of any marriage to which the deceased was at any time a party, was treated by the deceased as a child of the family in relation to that marriage;

(e)   any person (not being a person included in the foregoing paragraphs of
this subsection) who immediately before the death of the deceased was
being maintained, either wholly or partly, by the deceased;

that person may apply to the court for an order under section 2 of this Act
on the ground that the disposition of the deceased's estate effected by his
will or the law relating to intestacy, or the combination of his will and that
law, is not such as to make reasonable financial provision for the applicant.

(2) In this Act *reasonable financial provision*—

(a)   in the case of an application made by virtue of subsection (1) (*a*) above
by the husband or wife of the deceased (except where the marriage
with the deceased was the subject of a decree of judicial separation
and at the date of death the decree was in force and the separation was
continuing), means such financial provision as it would be reasonable
in all the circumstances of the case for a husband or wife to receive,
whether or not that provision is required for his or her maintenance;
(b)   in the case of any other application made by virtue of subsection (1)
above, means such financial provision as it would be reasonable in all
the circumstances of the case for the applicant to receive for his
maintenance.

(3) For the purposes of subsection (1) (*e*) above, a person shall be treated
as being maintained by the deceased, either wholly or partly, as the case
may be, if the deceased, otherwise than for full valuable consideration, was
making a substantial contribution in money or money's worth towards the
reasonable needs of that person.

Powers of court to make orders
2. (1) Subject to the provisions of this Act, where an application is made
for an order under this section, the court may, if it is satisfied that the
disposition of the deceased's estate effected by his will or the law relating to
intestacy, or the combination of his will and that law, is not such as to make
reasonable financial provision for the applicant, make any one or more of
the following orders—

(a)   an order for the making to the applicant out of the net estate of the
deceased of such periodical payments and for such term as may be
specified in the order;
(b)   an order for the payment to the applicant out of that estate of a lump
sum of such amount as may be so specified;
(c)   an order for the transfer to the applicant of such property comprised in
that estate as may be so specified;
(d)   an order for the settlement for the benefit of the applicant of such
property comprised in that estate as may be so specified;
(e)   an order for the acquisition out of property comprised in that estate of
such property as may be so specified and for the transfer of the
property so acquired to the applicant or for the settlement thereof for
his benefit;
(f)   an order varying any ante-nuptial or post-nuptial settlement (including
such a settlement made by will) made on the parties to a marriage to
which the deceased was one of the parties, the variation being for the
benefit of the surviving party to that marriage, or any child of that

marriage, or any person who was treated by the deceased as a child of the family in relation to that marriage.

(2) An order under subsection (1) (*a*) above providing for the making out of the net estate of the deceased of periodical payments may provide for—

(a) payments of such amount as may be specified in the order,
(b) payments equal to the whole of the income of the net estate or of such portion thereof as may be so specified,
(c) payments equal to the whole of the income of such part of the net estate as the court may direct to be set aside or appropriated for the making out of the income thereof of payments under this section,

or may provide for the amount of the payments or any of them to be determined in any other way the court thinks fit.

(3) Where an order under subsection (1) (*a*) above provides for the making of payments of an amount specified in the order, the order may direct that such part of the net estate as may be so specified shall be set aside or appropriated for the making out of the income thereof of those payments; but no larger part of the net estate shall be so set aside or appropriated than is sufficient, at the date of the order, to produce by the income thereof the amount required for the making of those payments.

(4) An order under this section may contain such consequential and supplemental provisions as the court thinks necessary or expedient for the purpose of giving effect to the order or for the purpose of securing that the order operates fairly as between one beneficiary of the estate of the deceased and another and may, in particular, but without prejudice to the generality of this subsection—

(a) order any person who holds any property which forms part of the net estate of the deceased to make such payment or transfer such property as may be specified in the order;
(b) varying the disposition of the deceased's estate effected by the will or the law relating to intestacy, or by both the will and the law relating to intestacy, in such manner as the court thinks fair and reasonable having regard to the provisions of the order and all the circumstances of the case;
(c) confer on the trustees of any property which is the subject of an order under this section such powers as appear to the court to be necessary or expedient.

Matters to which court is to have regard in exercising powers under s 2
3. (1) Where an application is made for an order under section 2 of this Act, the court shall, in determining whether the disposition of the deceased's estate effected by his will or the law relating to intestacy, or the combination of his will and that law, is such as to make reasonable financial provision for the applicant and, if the court considers that reasonable financial provision has not been made, in determining whether and in what manner it shall exercise its powers under that section, have regard to the following matters, that is to say—

(a) the financial resources and financial needs which the applicant has or is likely to have in the forseeable future;
(b) the financial resources and financial needs which any other applicant

for an order under section 2 of this Act has or is likely to have in the foreseeable future;

(c)   the financial resources and financial needs which any beneficiary of the estate of the deceased has or is likely to have in the foreseeable future;

(d)   any obligations and responsibilities which the deceased had towards any applicant for an order under the said section 2 or towards any beneficiary of the estate of the deceased;

(e)   the size and nature of the net estate of the deceased;

(f)   any physical or mental disability of any applicant for an order under the said section 2 or any beneficiary of the estate of the deceased;

(g)   any other matter, including the conduct of the applicant or any other person, which in the circumstances of the case the court may consider relevant.

(2) Without prejudice to the generality of paragraph (g) of subsection (1) above, where an application for an order under section 2 of this Act is made by virtue of section 1 (1) (a) or 1 (1) (b) of this Act, the court shall, in addition to the matters specifically mentioned in paragraphs (a) to (f) of that subsection, have regard to—

(a)   the age of the applicant and the duration of the marriage;

(b)   the contribution made by the applicant to the welfare of the family of the deceased, including any contribution made by looking after the home or caring for the family;

and, in the case of an application by the wife or husband of the deceased, the court shall also, unless at the date of death a decree of judicial separation was in force and the separation was continuing, have regard to the provision which the applicant might reasonably have expected to receive if on the day on which the deceased died the marriage, instead of being terminated by death, had been terminated by a decree of divorce.

(3) Without prejudice to the generality of paragraph (g) of subsection (1) above, where an application for an order under section 2 of this Act is made by virtue of section 1 (1) (c) or 1 (1) (d) of this Act, the court shall, in addition to the matters specifically mentioned in paragraphs (a) to (f) of that subsection, have regard to the manner in which the applicant was being or in which he might expect to be educated or trained, and where the application is made by virtue of section 1 (1) (d) the court shall also have regard—

(a)   to whether the deceased had assumed any responsibility for the applicant's maintenance and, if so, to the extent to which and the basis upon which the deceased assumed that responsibility and to the length of time for which the deceased discharged that responsibility;

(b)   to whether in assuming and discharging that responsibility the deceased did so knowing that the applicant was not his own child;

(c)   to the liability of any other person to maintain the applicant.

(4) Without prejudice to the generality of paragraph (g) of subsection (1) above, where an application for an order under section 2 of this Act is made by virtue of section 1 (1) (e) of this Act, the court shall, in addition to the matters specifically mentioned in paragraphs (a) to (f) of that subsection, have regard to the extent to which and the basis upon which the deceased assumed responsibility for the maintenance of the applicant, and to the length of time for which the deceased discharged that responsibility.

(5) In considering the matters to which the court is required to have

regard under this section, the court shall take into account the facts as known to the court at the date of the hearing.

(6) In considering the financial resources of any person for the purposes of this section the court shall take into account his earning capacity and in considering the financial needs of any person for the purposes of this section the court shall take into account his financial obligations and responsibilities.

Time-limit for applications
4. An application for an order under section 2 of this Act shall not, except with the permission of the court, be made after the end of the period of six months from the date on which representation with respect to the estate of the deceased is first taken out.

Interim orders
5. (1) Where an application for an order under section 3 of this Act it appears to the court-

(a) that the applicant is in immediate need of financial assistance, but it is not yet possible to determine what order (if any) should be made under that section; and

(b) that property forming part of the net estate of the deceased is or can be made available to meet the need of the applicant;

the court may order that, subject to such conditions or restrictions, if any, as the court may impose and to any further order of the court, there shall be paid to the applicant out of the net estate of the deceased such sum or sums and (if more than one) at such intervals as the court thinks reasonable; and the court may order that, subject to the provisions of this Act, such payments are to be made until such date as the court may specify, not being later than the date on which the court either makes an order under the said section 2 or decides not to exercise its powers under that section.

(2) Subsections (2), (3) and (4) of section 2 of this Act shall apply in relation to an order under this section as they apply in relation to an order under that section.

(3) In determining what order, if any, should be made under this section the court shall, so far as the urgency of the case admits, have regard to the same matters as those to which the court is required to have regard under section 3 of this Act.

(4) An order made under section 2 of this Act may provide that any sum paid to the applicant by virtue of this section shall be treated to such an extent and in such manner as may be provided by that order as having been paid on account of any payment provided for by that order.

Variation, discharge, etc of orders for periodical payments
6. (1) Subject to the provisions of this Act, where the court has made an order under section 2 (1) (*a*) of this Act (in this section referred to as *the original order*) for the making of periodical payments to any person (in this section referred to as *the original recipient*), the court, on an application under this section, shall have power by order to vary or discharge the original order or to suspend any provision of it temporarily and to revive the operation of any provision so suspended.

(2) Without prejudice to the generality of subsection (1) above, an order made on an application for the variation of the original order may—

(a)   provide for the making out of any relevant property of such periodical
      payments and for such term as may be specified in the order to any
      person who has applied, or would but for section 4 of this Act be
      entitled to apply, for an order under section 2 of this Act (whether or
      not, in the case of any application, an order was made in favour of the
      applicant);
(b)   provide for the payment out of any relevant property of a lump sum of
      such amount as may be so specified to the original recipient or to any
      such person as is mentioned in paragraph (*a*) above;
(c)   provide for the transfer of the relevant property, or such part thereof
      as may be so specified, to the original recipient or to any such person
      as is so mentioned.

(3) Where the original order provides that any periodical payments
payable thereunder to the original recipient are to cease on the occurrence
of an event specified in the order (other than the remarriage of a former
wife or former husband) or on the expiration of a period so specified, then,
if, before the end of the period of six months from the date of the
occurrence of that event or of the expiration of that period, an application is
made for an order under this section, the court shall have power to make
any order which it would have had power to make if the application had
been made before the date (whether in favour of the original recipient or
any such person as is mentioned in subsection (2) (*a*) above and whether
having effect from that date or from such later date as the court may
specify).

(4) Any reference in this section to the original order shall include a
reference to an order made under this section and any reference in this
section to the original recipient shall include a reference to any person to
whom periodical payments are required to be made by virtue of an order
under this section.

(5) An application under this section may be made by any of the
following persons, that is to say—
(a)   any person who by virtue of section 1 (1) of this Act has applied, or
      would but for section 4 of this Act be entitled to apply, for an order
      under section 2 of this Act,
(b)   the personal representatives of the deceased,
(c)   the trustees of any relevant property, and
(d)   any beneficiary of the estate of the deceased.

(6) An order under this section may only affect—

(a)   property the income of which is at the date of the order applicable
      wholly or in part for the making of periodical payments to any person
      who has applied for an order under this Act, or
(b)   in the case of an application under subsection (3) above in respect of
      payments which have ceased to be payable on the occurrence of an
      event or the expiration of a period, property the income of which was
      so applicable immediately before the occurrence of that event or the
      expiration of that period, as the case may be,

and any such property as is mentioned in paragraph (*a*) or (*b*) above is in
subsections (2) and (5) above referred to as *relevant property*.

(7) In exercising the powers conferred by this section the court shall have

regard to all circumstances of the case, including any change in any of the matters to which the court was required to have regard when making the order to which the application relates.

(8) Where the court makes an order under this section, it may give such consequential directions as it thinks necessary or expedient having regard to the provisions of the order.

(9) No such order as is mentioned in section 2 (1) (*d*), (*e*) or (*f*), 9, 10 or 11 of this Act shall be made on an application under this section.

(10) For the avoidance of doubt it is hereby declared that, in relation to an order which provides for the making of periodical payments which are to cease on the occurrence of an event specified in the order (other than the remarriage of a former wife or former husband) or on the expiration of a period so specified, the power to vary an order includes power to provide for the making of periodical payments after the expiration of that period or the occurrence of that event.

Payment of lump sums by instalments
7. (1) An order under section 2 (1) (*b*) or 6 (2) (*b*) of this Act for the payment of a lump sum may provide for the payment of that sum by instalments of such amount as may be specified in the order.

(2) Where an order is made by virtue of subsection (1) above, the court shall have power, on an application made by the person to whom the lump sum is payable, by the personal representatives of the deceased or by the trustees of the property out of which the lump sum is payable, to vary that order by varying the number of instalments payable, the amount of any instalment and the date on which any instalment becomes payable.
Property available for financial provision

Property treated as part of 'net estate'
8. (1) Where a deceased person has in accordance with the provisions of any enactment nominated any person to receive any sum of money or other property on his death and that nomination is in force at the time of his death, that sum of money, after deducting therefrom any inheritance tax payable in respect thereof, or that other property, to the extent of the value thereof at the date of the death of the deceased after deducting therefrom any inheritance tax so payable, shall be treated for the purposes of this Act as part of the net estate of the deceased; but this subsection shall not render any person liable for having paid that sum or transferred that other property to the person named in the nomination in accordance with the directions given in the nomination.

(2) Where any sum of money or other property is received by any person as a donatio mortis causa made by a deceased person, that sum of money, after deducting therefrom any inheritance tax payable thereon, or that other property, to the extent of the value thereof at the date of the death of the deceased after deducting therefrom any inheritance tax so payable, shall be treated for the purposes of this Act as part of the net estate of the deceased; but this subsection shall not render any person liable for having paid that sum or transferred that other property in order to give effect to that donatio mortis causa.

(3) The amount of inheritance tax to be deducted for the purposes of this section shall not exceed the amount of that tax which has been borne by the

person nominated by the deceased or, as the case may be, the person who has received a sum of money or other property as a donatio mortis causa.

Annotations
Capital Transfer Tax: except in relation to a liability to tax arising before 25 July 1986 capital transfer tax shall be known as inheritance tax and the Capital Transfer Tax Act 1984 may be cited as the Inheritance Tax Act 1984, by virtue of the Finance Act 1986, s 100.

Property held on a joint tenancy
9. (1) Where a deceased person was immediately before his death beneficially entitled to a joint tenancy of any property, then, if, before the end of the period of six months from the date on which representation with respect to the estate of the deceased was first taken out, an application is made for an order under section 2 of this Act, the court for the purpose of facilitating the making of financial provision for the applicant under this Act may order that the deceased's severable share of that property, at the value thereof immediately before his death, shall, to such extent as appears to the court to be just in all the circumstances of the case, be treated for the purposes of this Act as part of the net estate of the deceased.

(2) In determining the extent to which any severable share is to be treated as part of the net estate of the deceased by virtue of an order under subsection (1) above, the court shall have regard to any inheritance tax payable in respect of that severable share.

(3) Where an order is made under subsection (1) above, the provisions of this section shall not render any person liable for anything done by him before the order was made.

(4) For the avoidance of doubt it is hereby declared that for the purposes of this section there may be a joint tenancy of a chose in action.

Annotations
Capital Transfer Tax: except in relation to a liability to tax arising before 25 July 1986 capital transfer tax shall be known as inheritance tax and the Capital Transfer Tax Act 1984 may be cited as the Inheritance Tax Act 1984, by virtue of the Finance Act 1986, s 100.

POWERS OF COURT IN RELATION TO TRANSACTIONS INTENDED TO DEFEAT APPLICATIONS FOR FINANCIAL PROVISION

Dispositions intended to defeat applications for financial provision
10. (1) Where an application is made to the court for an order under section 2 of this Act, the applicant may, in the proceedings on that application, apply to the court for an order under subsection (2) below.

(2) Where on an application under subsection (1) above the court is satisfied—

(a) that, less than six years before the date of the death of the deceased, the deceased with the intention of defeating an application for financial provision under this Act made a disposition, and
(b) that full valuable consideration for that disposition was not given by the person to whom or for the benefit of whom the disposition was made (in this section referred to as *the donee*) or by any other person, and

(c)   that the exercise of the powers conferred by this section would facilitate the making of financial provision for the applicant under this Act,

then, subject to the provisions of this section and of sections 12 and 13 of this Act, the court may order the donee (whether or not at the date of the order he holds any interest in the property disposed of to him or for his benefit by the deceased) to provide, for the purpose of the making of that financial provision, such sum of money or other property as may be specified in the order.

(3) Where an order is made under subsection (2) above as respects any disposition made by the deceased which consisted of the payment of money to or for the benefit of the donee, the amount of any sum of money or the value of any property ordered to be provided under that subsection shall not exceed the amount of the payment made by the deceased after deducting therefrom any inheritance tax borne by the donee in respect of that payment.

(4) Where an order is made under subsection (2) above as respects any disposition made by the deceased which consisted of the transfer of property (other than a sum of money) to or for the benefit of the donee, the amount of any sum of money or the value of any property ordered to be provided under that subsection shall not exceed the value at the date of the death of the deceased of the property disposed of by him to or for the benefit of the donee (or if that property has been disposed of by the person to whom it was transferred by the deceased, the value at the date of that disposal thereof) after deducting therefrom any inheritance tax borne by the donee in respect of the transfer of that property by the deceased.

(5) Where an application (in this subsection referred to as *the original application*) is made for an order under subsection (2) above in relation to any disposition, then, if on an application under this subsection by the donee or by any applicant for an order under section 2 of this Act the court is satisfied—

(a)   that, less than six years before the date of the death of the deceased, the deceased with the intention of defeating an application for financial provision under this Act made a disposition other than the disposition which is the subject of the original application, and

(b)   that full valuable consideration for that other disposition was not given by the person to whom or for the benefit of whom that other disposition was made or by any other person,

the court may exercise in relation to the person to whom or for the benefit of whom that other disposition was made the powers which the court would have had under subsection (2) above if the original application had been made in respect of that other disposition and the court had been satisifed as to the matters set out in paragraphs (*a*), (*b*) and (*c*) of that subsection; and where any application is made under this subsection, any reference in this section (except in subsection (2) (*b*)) to the donee shall include a reference to the person to whom or for the benefit of whom that other disposition was made.

(6) In determining whether and in what manner to exercise its powers under this section, the court shall have regard to the circumstances in which any disposition was made and any valuable consideration which was given

therefor, the relationship, if any, of the donee to the deceased, the conduct and financial resources of the donee and all the other circumstances of the case.

(7) In this section *disposition* does not include—

(a) any provision in a will, any such nomination as is mentioned in section 8 (1) of this Act or any donatio mortis causa, or
(b) any appointment of property made, otherwise than by will, in the exercise of a special power of appointment,

but, subject to these exceptions, includes any payment of money (including the payment of a premium under a policy of assurance) and any conveyance, assurance, appointment or gift of property of any description, whether made by an instrument or otherwise.

(8) The provisions of this section do not apply to any disposition made before the commencement of this Act.

Annotations
Capital Transfer Tax: except in relation to a liability to tax arising before 25 July 1986 capital transfer tax shall be known as inheritance tax and the Capital Transfer Tax Act 1984 may be cited as the Inheritance Tax Act 1984, by virtue of the Finance Act 1986, s 100.

Contracts to leave property by will
11. (1) Where an application is made to a court for an order under section 2 of this Act, the applicant may, in the proceedings on that application, apply to the court for an order under this section.

(2) Where on an application under subsection (1) above the court is satisfied—

(a) that the deceased made a contract by which he agreed to leave by his will a sum of money or other property to any person or by which he agreed that a sum of money or other property would be paid or transferred to any person out of his estate, and
(b) that the deceased made that contract with the intention of defeating an application for financial provision under this Act, and
(c) that when the contract was made full valuable consideration for that contract was not given or promised by the person with whom or for the benefit of whom the contract was made (in this section referred to as *the donee*) or by any other person, and
(d) that the exercise of the powers conferred by this section would facilitate the making of financial provision for the applicant under this Act,

then, subject to the provisions of this section and of sections 12 and 13 of this Act, the court may make any one or more of the following orders, that is to say—

(i) if any money has been paid or any other property has been transferred to or for the benefit of the donee in accordance with the contract, an order directing the donee to provide, for the purpose of the making of that financial provision, such sum of money or other property as may be specified in the order;

(ii)   if the money or all the money has not been paid or the property or all the property has not been transferred in accordance with the contract, an order directing the personal representatives not to make any payment or transfer any property, or not to make any further payment or transfer any further property, as the case may be, in accordance therewith or directing the personal representatives only to make such payment or transfer such property as may be specified in the order.

(3)   Notwithstanding anything in subsection (2) above, the court may exercise its powers thereunder in relation to any contract made by the deceased only to the extent that the court considers that the amount of any sum of money paid or to be paid or the value of any property transferred or to be transferred in accordance with the contract exceeds the value of any valuable consideration given or to be given for that contract, and for this purpose the court shall have regard to the value of property at the date of the hearing.

(4) In determining whether and in what manner to exercise its powers under this section, the court shall have regard to the circumstances in which the contract was made, the relationship, if any, of the donee to the deceased, the conduct and financial resources of the donee and all the other circumstances of the case.

(5) Where an order has been made under subsection (2) above in relation to any contract the rights of any person to enforce that contract or to recover damages or to obtain other relief for the breach thereof shall be subject to any adjustment made by the court under section 12(3) of this Act and shall survive to such extent only as is consistent with giving effect to the terms of that order.

(6) The provisions of this section do not apply to a contract made before the commencement of this Act.

Provisions supplementary to ss 10 and 11
12. (1) Where the exercise of any of the powers conferred by section 10 or 11 of this Act is conditional on the court being satisfied that a disposition or contract was made by a deceased person with the intention of defeating an application for financial provision under this Act, that condition shall be fulfilled if the court is of the opinion that, on a balance of probabilities, the intention of the deceased (though not necessarily his sole intention) in making the disposition or contract was to prevent an order for financial provision being made under this Act or to reduce the amount of the provision which might otherwise be granted by an order thereunder.

(2) Where an application is made under section 11 of this Act with respect to any contract made by the deceased and no valuable consideration was given or promised by any person for that contract then, notwithstanding anything in subsection (1) above, it shall be presumed, unless the contrary is shown, that the deceased made that contract with the intention of defeating an application for financial provision under this Act.

(3) Where the court makes an order under section 10 or 11 of this Act it may give such consequential directions as it thinks fit (including directions requiring the making of any payment or the transfer of any property) for giving effect to the order or for securing a fair adjustment of the rights of the persons affected thereby.

(4) Any power conferred on the court by the said section 10 or 11 to

order the donee, in relation to any disposition or contract, to provide any sum of money or other property shall be exercisable in like manner in relation to the personal representative of the donee, and—

(a) any reference in section 10(4) to the disposal of property by the donee shall include a reference to disposal by the personal representative of the donee, and

(b) any reference in section 10(5) to an application by the donee under that subsection shall include a reference to an application by the personal representative of the donee;

but the court shall not have power under the said section 10 or 11 to make an order in respect of any property forming part of the estate of the donee which has been distributed by the personal representative; and the personal representative shall not be liable for having distributed any such property before he has notice of the making of an application under the said section 10 or 11 on the ground that he ought to have taken into account the possibility that such an application would be made.

Provisions as to trustees in relation to ss 10 and 11
13. (1) Where an application is made for—

(a) an order under section 10 of this Act in respect of a disposition made by the deceased to any person as a trustee, or

(b) an order under section 11 of this Act in respect of any payment made or property transferred, in accordance with a contract made by the deceased, to any person as a trustee,

the powers of the court under the said section 10 or 11 to order that trustee to provide a sum of money or other property shall be subject to the following limitation (in addition, in a case of an application under section 10, to any provision regarding the deduction of inheritance tax) namely, that the amount of any sum of money or the value of any property ordered to be provided—

(i) in the case of an application in respect of a disposition which consisted of the payment of money or an application in respect of the payment of money in accordance with a contract, shall not exceed the aggregate of so much of that money as is at the date of the order in the hands of the trustee and the value at that date of any property which represents that money or is derived therefrom and is at that date in the hands of the trustee;

(ii) in the case of an application in respect of a disposition which consisted of the transfer of property (other than a sum of money) or an application in respect of the transfer of property (other than a sum of money) in accordance with a contract, shall not exceed the aggregate of the value at the date of the order of so much of that property as is at that date in the hands of the trustee and the value at that date of any property which represents the first mentioned property or is derived therefrom and is at that date in the hands of the trustee.

(2) Where any such application is made in respect of a disposition made to any person as a trustee or in respect of any payment made or property transferred in pursuance of a contract to any person as a trustee, the trustee shall not be liable for having distributed any money or other property on the

ground that he ought to have taken into account the possibility that such an application would be made.

(3) Where any such application is made in respect of a disposition made to any person as a trustee or in respect of any payment made or property transferred in accordance with a contract to any person as a trustee, any reference in the said section 10 or 11 to the donee shall be construed as including a reference to the trustee or trustees for the time being of the trust in question and any reference in subsection (1) or (2) above to a trustee shall be construed in the same way.

Annotations
Capital Transfer Tax: except in relation to a liability to tax arising before 25 July 1986 capital transfer tax shall be known as inheritance tax and the Capital Transfer Tax Act 1984 may be cited as the Inheritance Tax Act 1984, by virtue of the Finance Act 1986, s 100.

SPECIAL PROVISIONS RELATING TO CASES OF DIVORCE, SEPARATION, ETC

Provision as to cases where no financial relief was granted in divorce proceedings, etc
14. (1) Where, within twelve months from the date on which a decree of divorce or nullity of marriage has been made absolute or a decree of judicial separation has been granted, a party to the marriage dies and—

(a) an application for a financial provision order under section 23 of the Matrimonial Causes Act 1973 or a property adjustment order under section 24 of that Act has not been made by the other party to that marriage, or
(b) such an application has been made but the proceedings thereon have not been determined at the time of the death of the deceased,

then, if an application for an order under section 2 of this Act is made by that other party, the court shall, notwithstanding anything in section 1 or section 3 of this Act, have power, if it thinks it just to do so, to treat that party for the purposes of that application as if the decree of divorce or nullity of marriage had not been made absolute or the decree of judicial separation had not been granted, as the case may be.

(2) This section shall not apply in relation to a decree of judicial separation unless at the date of the death of the deceased the decree was in force and the separation was continuing.

Restriction imposed in divorce proceedings, etc on application under this Act
15. [(1) On the grant of a decree of divorce, a decree of nullity of marriage or a decree of judicial separation or at any time thereafter the court, if it considers it just to do so, may, on the application of either party to the marriage, order that the other party to the marriage shall not on the death of the applicant be entitled to apply for an order under section 2 of this Act. In this subsection *the court* means the High Court or, where a county court has jurisdiction by virtue of Part V of the Matrimonial and Family Proceedings Act 1984, a county court.]

(2) In the case of a decree of divorce or nullity of marriage an order may be made under subsection (1) above before or after the decree is made absolute, but if it is made before the decree is made absolute it shall not take effect unless the decree is made absolute.

(3) Where an order made under subsection (1) above on the grant of a decree of divorce or nullity of marriage has come into force with respect to a party to a marriage, then, on the death of the other party to that marriage, the court shall not entertain any application for an order under section 2 of this Act made by the first-mentioned party.

(4) Where an order made under subsection (1) above on the grant of a decree of judicial separation has come into force with respect to any party to a marriage, then, if the other party to that marriage dies while the decree is in force and the separation is continuing, the court shall not entertain any application for an order under section 2 of this Act made by the first-mentioned party.

Annotations
Sub-s (1): substituted by the Matrimonial and Family Proceedings Act 1984, s 8.

A Restriction imposed in proceedings under Matrimonial and Family Proceedings Act 1984 on application under this Act
15. [(1) On making an order under section 17 of the Matrimonial and Family Proceedings Act 1984 (orders for financial provision and property adjustment following overseas divorces, etc.) the court, if it considers it just to do so, may, on the application of either party to the marriage, order that the other party to the marriage shall not on the death of the applicant be entitled to apply for an order under section 2 of this Act.
In this subsection *the court* means the High Court or, where a county court has jurisdiction by virtue of Part V of the Matrimonial and Family Proceedings Act 1984, a county court.

(2) Where an order under subsection (1) above has been made with respect to a party to a marriage which has been dissolved or annulled, then, on the death of the other party to that marriage, the court shall not entertain an application under section 2 of this Act made by the first-mentioned party.

(3) Where an order under subsection (1) above has been made with respect to a party to a marriage the parties to which have been legally separated, then, if the other party to the marriage dies while the legal separation is in force, the court shall not entertain an application under section 2 of this Act made by the first-mentioned party.]

Annotations
Commencement order: SI 1985 No 1316.
   Added by the Matrimonial and Family Proceedings Act 1984, s 25.

Variation and discharge of secured periodical payments orders made under Matrimonial Causes Act 1973
16. (1) Where an application for an order under section 2 of this Act is made to the court by any person who was at the time of the death of the deceased entitled to payments from the deceased under a secured periodical payments order made under the Matrimonial Causes Act 1973, then, in the proceedings on that application, the court shall have power, if an application is made under this section by that person or by the personal representative of the deceased, to vary or discharge that periodical payments order or to revive the operation of any provision thereof which has been suspended under section 31 of that Act.

(2) In exercising the powers conferred by this section the court shall have regard to all the circumstances of the case, including any order which the court proposes to make under section 2 or section 5 of this Act and any change (whether resulting from the death of the deceased or otherwise) in any of the matters to which the court was required to have regard when making the secured periodical payments order.

(3) The powers exercisable by the court under this section in relation to an order shall be exercisable also in relation to any instrument executed in pursuance of the order.

Variation and revocation of maintenance agreements
17. (1) Where an application for an order under section 2 of this Act is made to the court by any person who was at the time of the death of the deceased entitled to payments from the deceased under a maintenance agreement which provided for the continuation of payments under the agreement after the death of the deceased, then, in the proceedings on that application, the court shall have power, if an application is made under this section by that person or by the personal representative of the deceased, to vary or revoke that agreement.

(2) In exercising the powers conferred by this section the court shall have regard to all the circumstances of the case, including any order which the court proposes to make under section 2 or section 5 of this Act and any change (whether resulting from the death of the deceased or otherwise) in any of the circumstances in the light of which the agreement was made.

(3) If a maintenance agreement is varied by the court under this section the like consequences shall ensue as if the variation had been made immediately before the death of the deceased by agreement between the parties and for valuable consideration.

(4) In this section *maintenance agreement*, in relation to a deceased person, means any agreement made, whether in writing or not and whether before or after the commencement of this Act, by the deceased with any person with whom he entered into a marriage, being an agreement which contained provisions governing the rights and liabilities towards one another when living separately of the parties to that marriage (whether or not the marriage has been dissolved or annulled) in respect of the making or securing of payments or the disposition or use of any property, including such rights and liabilities with respect to the maintenance or education of any child, whether or not a child of the deceased or a person who was treated by the deceased as a child of the family in relation to that marriage.

Availability of court's powers under this Act in applications under ss 31 and 36 of the Matrimonial Causes Act 1973
18. (1) Where—

(a) a person against whom a secured periodical payments order was made under the Matrimonial Causes Act 1973 has died and an application is made under section 31(6) of that Act for the variation or discharge of that order or for the revival of the operation of any provision thereof which has been suspended, or

(b) a party to a maintenance agreement within the meaning of section 34 of that Act has died, the agreement being one which provides for the continuation of payments thereunder after the death of one of the parties, and an application is made under section 36(1) of that Act for the alteration of the agreement under section 35 thereof.

the court shall have power to direct that the application made under the said section 31(6) or 36(1) shall be deemed to have been accompanied by an application for an order under section 2 of this Act.

(2) Where the court gives a direction under subsection (1) above it shall have power, in the proceedings on the application under the said section 31(6) or 36(1), to make any order which the court would have had power to make under the provisions of this Act if the application under the said section 31(6) or 36(1), as the case may be, had been made jointly with an application for an order under the said section 2; and the court shall have power to give such consequential directions as may be necessary for enabling the court to exercise any of the powers available to the court under this Act in the case of an application for an order under section 2.

(3) Where an order made under section 15(1) of this Act is in force with respect to a party to a marriage, the court shall not give a direction under subsection (1) above with respect to any application made under the said section 31(6) or 36(1) by that party on the death of the other party.
Miscellaneous and supplementary provisions

Effect, duration and form of orders

19. (1) Where an order is made under section 2 of this Act then for all purposes, including the purposes of the enactments relating to inheritance tax, the will or the law relating to intestacy, or both the will and the law relating to intestacy, as the case may be, shall have effect and be deemed to have had effect as from the deceased's death subject to the provisions of the order.

(2) Any order made under section 2 or 5 of this Act in favour of—

(a)   an applicant who was the former husband or former wife of the deceased, or

(b)   an applicant who was the husband or wife of the deceased in a case where the marriage with the deceased was the subject of a decree of judicial separation and at the date of death the decree was in force and the separation was continuing,

shall, in so far as it provides for the making of periodical payments, cease to have effect on the remarriage of the applicant, except in relation to any arrears due under the order on the date of the remarriage.

(3) A copy of every order made under this Act [other than an order made under section 15(1) of this Act] shall be sent to the principal registry of the Family Division for entry and filing, and a memorandum of the order shall be endorsed on, or permanently annexed to, the probate or letters of administration under which the estate is being administered.

Annotations

Sub-s (3): amended by the Administration of Justice Act 1982, s 52.
Capital Transfer Tax: except in relation to a liability to tax arising before 25 July 1986 capital transfer tax shall be known as inheritance tax and the Capital Transfer Tax Act 1984 may be cited as the Inheritance Tax Act 1984, by virtue of the Finance Act 1986, s 100.

Provisions as to personal representatives
20. (1) The provisions of this Act shall not render the personal representative of a deceased person liable for having distributed any part of the estate of the deceased, after the end of the period of six months from the date on which representation with respect to the estate of the deceased is first taken out, on the ground that he ought to have taken into account the possibility—

(a)   that the court might permit the making of an application for an order under section 2 of this Act after the end of that period, or

(b)   that, where an order has been made under the said section 2, the court might exercise in relation thereto the powers conferred on it by section 6 of this Act,

but this subsection shall not prejudice any power to recover, by reason of the making of an order under this Act, any part of the estate so distributed.

(2) Where the personal representative of a deceased person pays any sum directed by an order under section 5 of this Act to be paid out of the deceased's net estate, he shall not be under any liability by reason of that estate not being sufficient to make the payment, unless at the time of making the payment he has reasonable cause to believe that the estate is not sufficient.

(3) Where a deceased person entered into a contract by which he agreed to leave by his will any sum of money or other property to any person or by which he agreed that a sum of money or other property would be paid or transferred to any person out of his estate, then, if the personal representative of the deceased has reason to believe that the deceased entered into the contract with the intention of defeating an application for financial provision under this Act, he may, notwithstanding anything in that contract, postpone the payment of that sum of money or the transfer of that property until the expiration of the period of six months from the date on which representation with respect to the estate of the deceased is first taken out or, if during that period an application is made for an order under section 2 of this Act, until the determination of the proceedings on that application.

Admissibility as evidence of statements made by deceased
21. In any proceedings under this Act a statement made by the deceased, whether orally or in a document or otherwise, shall be admissible under section 2 of the Civil Evidence Act 1968 as evidence of any fact stated therein in like manner as if the statement were a statement falling within section 2(1) of that Act; and any reference in that Act to a statement admissible, or given or proposed to be given, in evidence under section 2 thereof or to the admissibility or the giving in evidence of a statement by virtue of that section or to any statement falling within section 2(1) of that Act shall be construed accordingly.

Determination of date on which representation was first taken out
23. In considering for the purposes of this Act when representation with respect to the estate of a deceased person was first taken out, a grant limited to settled land or to trust property shall be left out of account, and a grant limited to real estate or to personal estate shall be left out of account unless

a grant limited to the remainder of the estate has previously been made or is made at the same time.

Effect of this Act on s 46(1)(vi) of Administration of Estates Act 1925
24. Section 46(1)(vi) of the Administration of Estates Act 1925, in so far as it provides for the devolution of property on the Crown, the Duchy of Lancaster or the Duke of Cornwall as bona vacantia, shall have effect subject to the provisions of this Act.

Interpretation
25. (1) In this Act—
beneficiary, in relation to the estate of a deceased person, means—

(a)   a person who under the will of the deceased or under the law relating to intestacy is beneficially interested in the estate or would be so interested if an order had not been made under this Act, and

(b)   a person who has received any sum of money or other property which by virtue of section 8(1) or 8(2) of this Act is treated as part of the net estate of the deceased or would have received that sum or other property if an order had not been made under this Act;

child includes an illegitimate child and a child en ventre sa mere at the death of the deceased;
the court [unless the context otherwise requires] means the High Court, or where a county court has jurisdiction by virtue of section 22 of this Act, a county court;
[*former wife* or *former husband* means a person whose marriage with the deceased was during the lifetime of the deceased either—

(a)   dissolved or annulled by a decree of divorce or a decree of nullity of marriage granted under the law of any part of the British Islands, or

(b)   dissolved or annulled in any country or territory outside the British Islands by a divorce or annulment which is entitled to be recognised as valid by the law of England and Wales;]

net estate, in relation to a deceased person, means—

(a)   all property of which the deceased had power to dispose by his will (otherwise than by virtue of a special power of appointment) less the amount of his funeral, testamentary and administration expenses, debts and liabilities, including any inheritance tax payable out of his estate on his death;

(b)   any property in respect of which the deceased held a general power of appointment (not being a power exercisable by will) which has not been exercised;

(c)   any sum of money or other property which is treated for the purposes of this Act as part of the net estate of the deceased by virtue of section 8(1) or (2) of this Act;

(d)   any property which is treated for the purposes of this Act as part of the net estate of the deceased by virtue of an order made under section 9 of the Act;

(e)   any sum of money or other property which is, by reason of a disposition or contract made by the deceased, ordered under section 10 or 11 of this Act to be provided for the purpose of the making of financial provision under this Act;

property includes any chose in action;

reasonable financial provision has the meaning assigned to it by section 1 of this Act;

valuable consideration does not include marriage or a promise of marriage;

will includes codicil.

(2) For the purposes of paragraph (*a*) of the definition of *net estate* in subsection (1) above a person who is not of full age and capacity shall be treated as having power to dispose by will of all property of which he would have had power to dispose by will if he had been of full age and capacity.

(3) Any reference in this Act to provision out of the net estate of a deceased person includes a reference to provision extending to the whole of that estate.

(4) For the purposes of this Act any reference to a wife or husband shall be treated as including a reference to a person who in good faith entered into a void marriage with the deceased unless either—

(a) the marriage of the deceased and that person was dissolved or annulled during the lifetime of the deceased and the dissolution or annulment is recognised by the law of England and Wales, or

(b) that person has during the lifetime of the deceased entered into a later marriage.

(5) Any reference in this Act to remarriage or to a person who has remarried includes a reference to a marriage which is by law void or voidable or to a person who has entered into such a marriage, as the case may be, and a marriage shall be treated for the purposes of this Act as a remarriage, in relation to any party thereto, notwithstanding that the previous marriage of that party was void or voidable.

(6) Any reference in this Act to an order or decree made under the Matrimonial Causes Act 1973 or under any section of that Act shall be construed as including a reference to an order or decree which is deemed to have been made under that Act or under that section thereof, as the case may be.

(7) Any reference in this Act to any enactment is a reference to that enactment as amended by or under any subsequent enactment.

Annotations

Sub-s (1): amended by the Matrimonial and Family Proceedings Act 1984, ss 8, 25. Capital Transfer Tax: except in relation to a liability to tax arising before 25 July 1986 capital transfer tax shall be known as inheritance tax and the Capital Transfer Tax Act 1984 may be cited as the Inheritance Tax Act 1984, by virtue of the Finance Act 1986, s 100.

Consequential amendments, repeals and transitional provisions
26. (1) . . .

(2) Subject to the provisions of this section, the enactments specified in the Schedule to this Act are hereby repealed to the extent specified in the third column of the Schedule; . . .

(3) The repeal of the said enactment shall not affect their operation in relation to any application made thereunder (whether before or after the

commencement of this Act) with reference to the death of any person who died before the commencement of this Act.

(4) Without prejudice to the provisions of section 38 of the Interpretation Act 1889 (which relates to the effect of repeals) nothing in any repeal made by this Act shall affect any order made or direction given under any enactment repealed by this Act, and, subject to the provisions of this Act, every such order or direction (other than an order made under section 4A of the Inheritance (Family Provision) Act 1938 or section 28A of the Matrimonial Causes Act 1965) shall, if it is in force at the commencement of this Act or is made by virtue of subsection (2) above, continue in force as if it had been made under section 2(1)(*a*) of this Act, and for the purposes of section 6(7) of this Act the court in exercising its powers under that section in relation to an order continued in force by this subsection shall be required to have regard to any change in any of the circumstances to which the court would have been required to have regard when making that order if the order had been made with reference to the death of any person who died after the commencement of this Act.

Annotations

Sub-ss (1), (2): words omitted amend the Matrimonial Causes Act 1973, s 36, Sch 2, para 5(2).

MISCELLANEOUS AND SUPPLEMENTARY PROVISIONS

Short title, commencement and extent
27. (1) This Act may be cited as the Inheritance (Provision for Family and Dependants) Act 1975.
(2) This Act does not extend to Scotland or Northern Ireland.
(3) This Act shall come into force on 1st April 1976.

SUPREME COURT ACT 1981

(1981 Chapter 54)

PART V

PROBATE CAUSES AND MATTERS

PROCEDURE IN PROBATE REGISTRIES IN RELATION TO GRANTS OF REPRESENTATION

Applications
105. Applications for grants of probate or administration and for the revocation of grants may be made to—

(a) the Principal Registry of the Family Division (in this Part referred to as *the Principal Registry*); or
(b) a district probate registry.

Annotations

This section derived from the Supreme Court of Judicature (Consolidation) Act 1925, ss 150, 151(1).

PROCEDURE IN PROBATE REGISTRATRIES IN RELATION TO GRANTS OF REPRESENTATION

Grants by district probate registrars
106. (1) Any grant made by a district probate registrar shall be made in the name of the High Court under the seal used in the registry.
  (2)-(4) . . .

Annotations

This section derived from the Supreme Court of Judicature (Consolidation) Act 1925, s 151.
Sub-ss (2)-(4): repealed by the Administration of Justice Act 1985, ss 51, 67(2), Sch 8, Pt III.

PROCEDURE IN PROBATE REGISTRIES IN RELATION TO GRANTS OF REPRESENTATION

No grant where conflicting applications
107. Subject to probate rules, no grant in respect of the estate, or part of the estate, of a deceased person shall be made out of the Principal Registry or any district probate registry on any application if, at any time before the making of a grant, it appears to the registrar concerned that some other application has been made in respect of that estate or, as the case may be, that part of it and has not been either refused or withdrawn.

Annotations

This section derived from the Supreme Court of Judicature (Consolidation) Act 1925, s 152(1).

Caveats
108. (1) A caveat against a grant of probate or administration may be entered in the Principal Registry or in any district probate registry.
  (2) On a caveat being entered in a district probate registry, the district probate registrar shall immediately send a copy of it to the Principal Registry to be entered among the caveats in that Registry.

Annotations

This section derived from the Supreme Court of Judicature (Consolidation) Act 1925, s 154.

Refusal of grant where inheritance tax unpaid
109. (1) Subject to subsections (2) and (3), no grant shall be made, and no grant made outside the United Kingdom shall be resealed, except on the production of an account prepared in pursuance of [the Inheritance Tax Act 1984] showing by means of such receipt or certification as may be prescribed

by the Commissioners of Inland Revenue (in this and the following section referred to as *the Commissioners*) either—

(a) that the inheritance tax payable on the delivery of the account has been paid; or

(b) that no such tax is so payable.

(2) Arrangements may be made between the President of the Family Division and the Commissioners providing for the purposes of this section in such cases as may be specified in the arrangements that the receipt or certification of an account may be dispensed with or that some other document may be substituted for the account required by [the Inheritance Tax Act 1984].

(3) Nothing in subsection (1) applies in relation to a case where the delivery of the account required by that Part of that Act has for the time being been dispensed with by any regulations under [section 256(1)(*a*) of the Inheritance Tax Act 1984].

Annotations

Sub-ss (1), (2) derived from the Supreme Court of Judicature (Consolidation) Act 1925, s 156A; sub-s (3) derived from the Finance Act 1980, s 94(1)(*a*).

Words in square brackets substituted by the Inheritance Tax Act 1984, ss 274, 276, Sch 8, para 20.

Capital Transfer Tax: except in relation to a liability to tax arising before 25 July 1986 capital transfer tax shall be known as inheritance tax and the Capital Transfer Tax Act 1984 may be cited as the Inheritance Tax Act 1984, by virtue of the Finance Act 1986, s 100.

Documents to be delivered to Commissioners of Inland Revenue
110. Subject to any arrangements which may from time to time be made between the President of the Family Division and the Commissioners, the Principal Registry and every district probate registry shall, within such period after a grant as the President may direct, deliver to the Commissioners or their proper officer the following documents—

(a) in the case of a grant of probate or of administration with the will annexed, a copy of the will;

(b) in every case, such certificate or note of the grant as the Commissioners may require.

Annotations

This section derived from the Supreme Court of Judicature (Consolidation) Act 1925, s 157.

Records of grants
111. (1) There shall continue to be kept records of all grants which are made in the Principal Registry or in any district probate registry.

(2) Those records shall be in such form, and shall contain such particulars, as the President of the Family Division may direct.

Annotations

This section derived from the Supreme Court of Judicature (Consolidation) Act 1925, s 156.

POWERS OF COURT IN RELATION TO PERSONAL REPRESENTATIVES

Summons to executor to prove or renounce
112. The High Court may summon any person named as executor in a will to prove, or renounce probate of, the will, and to do such other things concerning the will as the court had power to order such a person to do immediately before the commencement of this Act.

Annotations

This section derived from the Supreme Court of Judicature (Consolidation) Act 1925, s 159.

Power of court to sever grant
113. (1) Subject to subsection (2), the High Court may grant probate or administration in respect of any part of the estate of a deceased person, limited in any way the court thinks fit.

(2) Where the estate of a deceased person is known to be insolvent, the grant of representation to it shall not be severed under subsection (1) except as regards a trust estate in which he had no beneficial interest.

Annotations

This section derived from the Supreme Court of Judicature (Consolidation) Act 1925, s 155(1).

Number of personal representatives
114. (1) Probate or administration shall not be granted by the High Court to more than four persons in respect of the same part of the estate of a deceased person.

(2) Where under a will or intestacy any beneficiary is a minor or a life interest arises, any grant of administration by the High Court shall be made either to a trust corporation (with or without an individual) or to not less than two individuals, unless it appears to the court to be expedient in all the circumstances to appoint an individual as sole administrator.

(3) For the purpose of determining whether a minority or life interest arises in any particular case, the court may act on such evidence as may be prescribed.

(4) If at any time during the minority of a beneficiary or the subsistence of a life interest under a will or intestacy there is only one personal representative (not being a trust corporation), the High Court may, on the application of any person interested or the guardian or receiver of any such person, and in accordance with probate rules, appoint one or more additional personal representatives to act while the minority or life interest subsists and until the estate is fully administered.

(5) An appointment of an additional personal representative under subsection (4) to act with an executor shall not have the effect of including him in any chain of representation.

Annotations

This section derived from the Supreme Court of Judicature (Consolidation) Act 1925, s 160.

Appendix A

POWERS OF COURT IN RELATION TO PERSONAL REPRESENTATIVES

Grants to trust corporations
115. (1) The High Court may—

(a) where a trust corporation is named in a will as executor, grant probate to the corporation either solely or jointly with any other person named in the will as executor, as the case may require; or
(b) grant administration to a trust corporation, either solely or jointly with another person;

and the corporation may act accordingly as executor or administrator, as the case may be.

(2) Probate or administration shall not be granted to any person as nominee of a trust corporation.

(3) Any officer authorised for the purpose by a trust corporation or its directors or governing body may, on behalf of the corporation, swear affidavits, give security and do any other act which the court may require with a view to the grant to the corporation of probate or administration; and the acts of an officer so authorised shall be binding on the corporation.

[(4) Subsections (1) to (3) shall also apply in relation to any body which is exempt from the provisions of section 23(1) of the Solicitors Act 1974 (unqualified persons not to prepare papers for probate etc.) by virtue of any of paragraphs (*e*) to (*h*) of subsection (2) of that section.]

Annotations

This section derived from the Supreme Court of Judicature (Consolidation) Act 1925, s 161(1)ù(3).
    Sub-s (4): prospectively added by the Courts and Legal Services Act 1990, s 54(2), as from a day to be appointed.

Power of court to pass over prior claims to grant
116. (1) If by reason of any special circumstances it appears to the High Court to be necessary or expedient to appoint as administrator some person other than the person who, but for this section, would in accordance with probate rules have been entitled to the grant, the court may in its discretion appoint as administrator such person as it thinks expedient.

(2) Any grant of administration under this section may be limited in any way the court thinks fit.

Annotations

This section derived from the Supreme Court of Judicature (Consolidation) Act 1925, s 162(1), proviso (*b*).

Administration pending suit
117. (1) Where any legal proceedings concerning the validity of the will of a deceased person, or for obtaining, recalling or revoking any grant, are pending, the High Court may grant administration of the estate of the deceased person in question to an administrator pending suit, who shall, subject to subsection (2), have all the rights, duties and powers of a general administrator.

(2) An administrator pending suit shall be subject to the immediate

control of the court and act under its direction; and, except in such circumstances as may be prescribed, no distribution of the estate, or any part of the estate, of the deceased person in question shall be made by such an administrator without the leave of the court.

(3) The court may, out of the estate of the deceased, assign an administrator pending suit such reasonable remuneration as it thinks fit.

Annotations

This section derived from the Supreme Court of Judicature (Consolidation) Act 1925, s 163.

Effect of appointment of minor as executor
118. Where a testator by his will appoints a minor to be an executor, the appointment shall not operate to vest in the minor the estate, or any part of the estate, of the testator, or to constitute him a personal representative for any purpose, unless and until probate is granted to him in accordance with probate rules.

Annotations

This section derived from the Supreme Court of Judicature (Consolidation) Act 1925, s 165(2).

Administration with will annexed
119. (1) Administration with the will annexed shall be granted, subject to and in accordance with probate rules, in every class of case in which the High Court had power to make such a grant immediately before the commencement of this Act.

(2) Where administration with the will annexed is granted, the will of the deceased shall be performed and observed in the same manner as if probate of it had been granted to an executor.

Annotations

This section derived from the Supreme Court of Judicature (Consolidation) Act 1925, s 166.

Power to require administrators to produce sureties
120. (1) As a condition of granting administration to any person the High Court may, subject to the following provisions of this section and subject to and in accordance with probate rules, require one or more sureties to guarantee that they will make good, within any limit imposed by the court on the total liability of the surety or sureties, any loss which any person interested in the administration of the estate of the deceased may suffer in consequence of a breach by the administrator of his duties as such.

(2) A guarantee given in pursuance of any such requirement shall enure for the benefit of every person interested in the administration of the estate of the deceased as if contained in a contract under seal made by the surety or sureties with every such person and, where there are two or more sureties, as if they had bound themselves jointly and severally.

(3) No action shall be brought on any such guarantee without the leave of the High Court.

(4) Stamp duty shall not be chargeable on any such guarantee.

(5) This section does not apply where administration is granted to the Treasury Solicitor, the Official Solicitor, the Public Trustee, the Solicitor for the affairs of the Duchy of Lancaster or the Duchy of Cornwall or the Crown Solicitor for Northern Ireland, or to the consular officer of a foreign state to which section 1 of the Consular Conventions Act 1949 applies, or in such other cases as may be prescribed.

Annotations

This section derived from the Supreme Court of Judicature (Consolidation) Act 1925, s 167.

Revocation of grants and cancellation of resealing at instance of court
121. (1) Where it appears to the High Court that a grant either ought not to have been made or contains an error, the court may call in the grant and, if satisfied that it would be revoked at the instance of a party interested, may revoke it.

(2) A grant may be revoked under subsection (1) without being called in, if it cannot be called in.

(3) Where it appears to the High Court that a grant resealed under the Colonial Probates Acts 1892 and 1927 ought not to have been resealed, the court may call in the relevant document and, if satisfied that the resealing would be cancelled at the instance of a party interested, may cancel the resealing.

In this and the following subsection *the relevant document* means the original grant or, where some other document was sealed by the court under those Acts, that document.

(4) A resealing may be cancelled under subsection (3) without the relevant document being called in, if it cannot be called in.

Annotations

Sub-ss (1), (2) derived from the Administration of Justice Act 1956, s 17.

ANCILLARY POWERS OF COURT

Examination of person with knowledge of testamentary document
122. (1) Where it appears that there are reasonable grounds for believing that any person has knowledge of any document which is or purports to be a testamentary document, the High Court may, whether or not any legal proceedings are pending, order him to attend for the purpose of being examined in open court.

(2) The court may—

(a) require any person who is before it in compliance with an order under subsection (1) to answer any question relating to the document concerned; and

(b) if appropriate, order him to bring in the document in such manner as the court may direct.

(3) Any person who, having been required by the court to do so under this section, fails to attend for examination, answer any question or bring in any document shall be guilty of contempt of court.

Supreme Court Act 1981

Annotations

Sub-ss (1), (2) derived from the Court of Probate Act 1857, s 26.

Subpoena to bring in testamentary document
123. Where it appears that any person has in his possession, custody or power any document which is or purports to be a testamentary document, the High Court may, whether or not any legal proceedings are pending, issue a subpoena requiring him to bring in the document in such manner as the court may in the subpoena direct.

Annotations

This section derived from the Court of Probate Act 1858, s 23.

PROVISIONS AS TO DOCUMENTS

Place for deposit of original wills and other documents
124. All original wills and other documents which are under the control of the High Court in the Principal Registry or in any district probate registry shall be deposited and preserved in such places as the Lord Chancellor may direct; and any wills or other documents so deposited shall, subject to the control of the High Court and to probate rules, be open to inspection.

Annotations

This section derived from the Supreme Court of Judicature (Consolidation) Act 1925, s 170.

Copies of wills and grants
125. An office copy, or a sealed and certified copy, of any will or part of a will open to inspection under section 124 or of any grant may, on payment of the prescribed fee, be obtained—

(a) from the registry in which in accordance with section 124 the will or documents relating to the grant are preserved; or
(b) where in accordance with that section the will or such documents are preserved in some place other than a registry, from the Principal Registry; or
(c) subject to the approval of the Senior Registrar of the family Division, from the Principal Registry in any case where the will was proved in or the grant was issued from a district probate registry.

Annotations

This section derived from the Supreme Court of Judicature (Consolidation) Act 1925, s 171.

Depositories for wills of living persons
126. (1) There shall be provided, under the control and direction of the High Court, safe and convenient depositories for the custody of the wills of living persons; and any person may deposit his will in such a depository on payment of the prescribed fee and subject to such conditions as may be

prescribed by regulations made by the President of the Family Division with the concurrence of the Lord Chancellor.

(2) Any regulations made under this section shall be made by statutory instrument which shall be laid before Parliament after being made; and the Statutory Instruments Act 1946 shall apply to a statutory instrument containing regulations under this section in like manner as if they had been made by a Minister of the Crown.

Annotations

Sub-s (1) derived from the Supreme Court of Judicature (Consolidation) Act 1925, s 172.

Prospectively repealed by the Administration of Justice Act 1982, s 75, Sch 9, Part I, as from a day to be appointed.

PROBATE RULES

Probate rules
127. (1) The President of the Family Division may, with the concurrence of the Lord Chancellor, make rules of court (in this Part referred to as *probate rules*) for regulating and prescribing the practice and procedure of the High Court with respect to non-contentious or common form probate business.

(2) Without prejudice to the generality of subsection (1), probate rules may make provision for regulating the classes of persons entitled to grants of probate or administration in particular circumstances and the relative priorities of their claims thereto.

(3) Probate rules shall be made by statutory instrument subject to annulment in pursuance of a resolution of either House of Parliament; and the Statutory Instruments Act 1946 shall apply to a statutory instrument containing probate rules in like manner as if they had been made by a Minister of the Crown.

Annotations

Sub-ss (1), (3) derived from the Supreme Court of Judicature (Consolidation) Act 1925, s 100.

INTERPRETATION OF PART V AND OTHER PROBATE PROVISIONS

Interpretation of Part V and other probate provisions
128. In this Part, and in the other provisions of this Act relating to probate causes and matters, unless the context otherwise requires—
administration includes all letters of administration of the effects of deceased persons, whether with or without a will annexed, and whether granted for general, special or limited purposes;
estate means real and personal estate, and *real estate* includes—

(a)   chattels real and land in possession, remainder or reversion and every interest in or over land to which the deceased person was entitled at the time of his death, and
(b)   real estate held on trust or by way of mortgage or security, but not money to arise under a trust for sale of land, nor money secured or charged on land;

grant means a grant of probate or administration;

non-contentious or common form probate business means the business of obtaining probate and administration where there is no contention as to the right thereto, including—

(a)   the passing of probates and administrations through the High Court in contentious cases where the contest has been terminated,

(b)   all business of a non-contentious nature in matters of testacy and intestacy not being proceedings in any action, and

(c)   the business of lodging caveats against the grant of probate or administration;

Principal Registry means the Principal Registry of the Family Division;

probate rules means rules of court made under section 127;

trust corporation means the Public Trustee or a corporation either appointed by the court in any particular case to be a trustee or authorised by rules made under section 4(3) of the Public Trustee Act 1906 to act as a custodian trustee;

will includes a nuncupative will and any testamentary document of which probate may be granted.

Annotations

This section derived from the Supreme Court of Judicature (Consolidation) Act 1925, s 175.

Modification: definition *Trust corporation* modified in relation to Charities, by the Charities Act 1993, s 35.

FORFEITURE ACT 1982

(1982 Chapter 34)

An Act to provide for relief for persons guilty of unlawful killing from forfeiture of inheritance and other rights; to enable such persons to apply for financial provision out of the deceased's estate; to provide for the question whether pension and social security benefits have been forfeited to be determined by the Social Security commissioners; and for connected purposes. [13th July 1982]

The 'forfeiture rule'

1. (1) In this Act, the *forfeiture rule* means the rule of public policy which in certain circumstances precludes a person who has unlawfully killed another from acquiring a benefit in consequence of the killing.

(2) References in this Act to a person who has unlawfully killed another include a reference to a person who has unlawfully aided, abetted, counselled or procured the death of that other and references in this Act to unlawful killing shall be interpreted accordingly.

Power to modify the rule

2. (1) Where a court determines that the forfeiture rule has precluded a person (in this section referred to as *the offender*) who has unlawfully killed another from acquiring any interest in property mentioned in subsection (4) below, the court may make an order under this section modifying the effect of that rule.

(2) The court shall not make an order under this section modifying the effect of the forfeiture rule in any case unless it is satisfied that, having regard to the conduct of the offender and of the deceased and to such other circumstances as appear to the court to be material, the justice of the case requires the effect of the rule to be so modified in that case.

(3) In any case where a person stands convicted of an offence of which unlawful killing is an element, the court shall not make an order under this section modifying the effect of the forfeiture rule in that case unless proceedings for the purpose are brought before the expiry of the period of three months beginning with his conviction.

(4) The interests in property referred to in subsection (1) above are—

(a) any beneficial interest in property which (apart from the forfeiture rule) the offender would have acquired—

(i) under the deceased's will (including, as respects Scotland, any writing having testamentary effect) or the law relating to intestacy or by way of ius relicti, ius relictae or legitim;
(ii) on the nomination of the deceased in accordance with the provisions of any enactment;
(iii) as a donatio mortis causa made by the deceased; or
(iv) under a special destination (whether relating to heritable or moveable property); or

(b) any beneficial interest in property which (apart from the forfeiture rule) the offender would have acquired in consequence of the death of the deceased, being property which, before the death, was held on trust for any person.

(5) An order under this section may modify the effect of the forfeiture rule in respect of any interest in property to which the determination referred to in subsection (1) above relates and may do so in either or both of the following ways, that is—

(a) where there is more than one such interest, by excluding the application of the rule in respect of any (but not all) of those interests; and
(b) in the case of any such interest in property, by excluding the application of the rule in respect of part of the property.

(6) On the making of an order under this section, the forfeiture rule shall have effect for all purposes (including purposes relating to anything done before the order is made) subject to the modifications made by the order.

(7) The court shall not make an order under this section modifying the effect of the forfeiture rule in respect of any interest in property which, in consequence of the rule, has been acquired before the coming into force of this section by a person other than the offender or a person claiming through him.

(8) In this section—
property includes any chose in action or incorporeal moveable property; and
will includes codicil.

Application for financial provision not affected by the rule
3. (1) The forfeiture rule shall not be taken to preclude any person from making any application under a provision mentioned in subsection (2) below or the making of any order on the application.

(2) The provisions referred to in subsection (1) above are—

(a) any provision of the Inheritance (Provision for Family and Dependants) Act 1975; and
(b) sections 31(6) (variation etc. of periodical payments orders) and 36(1) (variation of maintenance agreements) of the Matrimonial Causes Act 1973 and section 5(4) of the Divorce (Scotland) Act 1976 (variation etc. of periodical allowances).

Commissioner to decide whether rule applies to social security benefits
4. (1) Where a question arises as to whether, if a person were otherwise entitled to or eligible for any benefit or advantage under a relevant enactment, he would be precluded by virtue of the forfeiture rule from receiving the whole or part of the benefit or advantage, that question shall (notwithstanding anything in any relevant enactment) be determined by a Commissioner.

[(1A) Where a Commissioner determines that the forfeiture rule has precluded a person (in this section referred to as *the offender*) who has unlawfully killed another from receiving the whole or part of any such benefit or advantage, the Commissioner may make a decision under this subsection modifying the effect of that rule and may do so whether the unlawful killing occurred before or after the coming into force of this subsection.

(1B) The Commission shall not make a decision under subsection (1A) above modifying the effect of the forfeiture rule in any case unless he is satisfied that, having regard to the conduct of the offender and of the deceased and to such other circumstances as appear to the Commissioner to be material, the justice of the case requires the effect of the rule to be so modified in that case.

(1C) Subject to subsection (1D) below, a decision under subsection (1A) above may modify the effect of the forfeiture rule in either or both of the following ways—

(a) so that it applies only in respect of a specified proportion of the benefit or advantage;
(b) so that it applies in respect of the benefit or advantage only for a specified period of time.

(1D) Such a decision may not modify the effect of the forfeiture rule so as to allow any person to receive the whole or any part of a benefit or advantage in respect of any period before the commencement of this subsection.

(1E) If the Commissioner thinks it expedient to do so, he may direct that his decision shall apply to any future claim for a benefit or advantage under a relevant enactment, on which a question such as is mentioned in subsection (1) above arises by reason of the same unlawful killing.

(1F) It is immaterial for the purposes of subsection (1E) above whether the claim is in respect of the same or a different benefit or advantage.

(1G) For the purpose of obtaining a decision whether the forfeiture rule should be modified the Secretary of State may refer to a Commissioner for review any determination of a question such as is mentioned in subsection (1) above that was made before the commencement of subsections (1A) to (1F) above (whether by a Commissioner or not) and shall do so if the offender requests him to refer such a determination.

(1H) Subsections (1A) to (1F) above shall have effect on a reference under subsection (1G) above as if in subsection (1A) the words *it has been determined* were substituted for the words *a Commissioner determines*.]

(2) Regulations under this section may make such provision as appears to [the Lord Chancellor] to be necessary or expedient for carrying this section into effect; and (without prejudice to the generality of that) the regulations may, in relation to the question mentioned in subsection (1) above or any determination under that subsection [or any decision under subsection (1A) above]—

(a) apply any provision of any relevant enactment, with or without modifications, or exclude or contain provision corresponding to any such provision; and

(b) make provision for purposes corresponding to those for which provision may be made by regulations under [section 59 of the Social Security Administration Act 1992] (matters relating to adjudication).

(3) The power to make regulations under this section shall be exercisable by statutory instrument which shall be subject to annulment in pursuance of a resolution of either House of Parliament.

(4) [Section 175(3) to (5) of the Social Security Contributions and Benefits Act 1992] (provision about extent of power to make regulations) shall apply to the power to make regulations conferred by this section as it applies to the power to make regulations conferred by that Act, but as if for references to that Act there were substituted references to this section.

(5) In this section—

Commissioner has the same meaning as in the [Social Security Administration Act 1992]; and

relevant enactment means any provision of the following and any instrument made by virtue of such a provision:

the Personal Injuries (Emergency Provisions) Act 1939,
the Pensions (Navy, Army, Air Force and Mercantile Marine) Act 1939,
the Polish Resettlement Act 1947,
[the Child Benefit Act 1975,
[the Social Security Acts 1975 to 1991]]
[the Social Security Contributions and Benefits Act 1992,]
and any other enactment relating to pensions or social security prescribed by regulations under this section.

Annotations

Commencement order: SI 1982 No 1731.

Sub-ss (1A)-(1H): added by the Social Security Act 1986, s 76(2).

Sub-s (2): first amendment made by SI 1984 No 1818, art 3; second amendment made by the Social Security Act 1986, s 76(3); final words in square brackets substituted by the Social Security (Consequential Provisions) Act 1992, s 4, Sch 2, para 63(1).

Sub-s (4): words in square brackets substituted by the Social Security (Consequential Provisions) Act 1992, s 4, Sch 2, para 63(2).

Sub-s (5): words in square brackets in definition *Commissioner* substituted by the Social Security (Consequential Provisions) Act 1992, s 4, Sch 2, para 63(3); in definition *relevant enactment*, first words in square brackets substituted by the Social Security Act 1986, s 86, Sch 10, Part VI, para 108(*b*), words in square brackets therein substituted by the Statutory Sick Pay Act 1991, s 3(1), final words in square brackets added by the Social Security (Consequential Provisions) Act 1992, s 4, Sch 2, para 63(3).

Functions of Secretary of State transferred to the Lord Chancellor for certain purposes by SI 1984 No 1818, art 2, Schedule; functions of the Secretary of State for Social Services transferred to the Secretary of State for Social Security by the Transfer of Functions (Health and Social Security) Order 1988 (SI 1988 No 1843), art 1(2), Sch 1.

Exclusion of murderers
5. Nothing in this Act or in any order made under section 2 or referred to in section 3(1) of this Act [or in any decision made under section 4(1A) of this Act] shall affect the application of the forfeiture rule in the case of a person who stands convicted of murder.

Annotations

Amended by the Social Security Act 1986, s 76(4).

Corresponding provision for Northern Ireland
6. An Order in Council under paragraph 1(1)(*b*) of Schedule 1 to the Northern Ireland Act 1974 (legislation for Northern Ireland in the interim period) which contains a statement that it is made only for purposes corresponding to the purposes of this Act—

(a) shall not be subject to paragraph 1(4) and (5) of that Schedule (affirmative resolution of both Houses of Parliament); but

(b) shall be subject to annulment in pursuance of a resolution of either House.

Short title, etc.
7. (1) This Act may be cited as the Forfeiture Act 1982.

(2) Section 4 of this Act shall come into force on such day as the Secretary of State may appoint by order made by statutory instrument; and sections 1 to 3 and 5 of this Act shall come into force on the expiry of the period of three months beginning with the day on which it is passed.

(3) This Act, except section 6, does not extend to Northern Ireland.

(4) Subject to section 2(7) of this Act, an order under section 2 of this Act or an order referred to in section 3(1) of this Act and made in respect of a person who has unlawfully killed another may be made whether the unlawful killing occurred before or after the coming into force of those sections.

Annotations

Functions of the Secretary of State for Social Services transferred to the Secretary of State for Social Security, by the Transfer of Functions (Health and Social Security) Order 1988 (SI 1988 No 1843), art 1(2), Sch 1.

ADMINISTRATION OF JUSTICE ACT 1982

(1982 Chapter 53)

PART IV

WILLS

RECTIFICATION AND INTERPRETATION OF WILLS

Rectification
20. (1) If a court is satisfied that a will is so expressed that it fails to carry out the testator's intentions, in consequence—

(a) of a clerical error; or
(b) of a failure to understand his instructions,
     it may order that the will shall be rectified so as to carry out his intentions.

(2) An application for an order under this section shall not, except with the permission of the court, be made after the end of the period of six months from the date on which representation with respect to the estate of the deceased is first taken out.

(3) The provisions of this section shall not render the personal representatives of a deceased person liable for having distributed any part of the estate of the deceased, after the end of the period of six months from the date on which representation with respect to the estate of the deceased is first taken out, on the ground that they ought to have taken into account the possibility that the court might permit the making of an application for an order under this section after the end of that period; but this subsection shall not prejudice any power to recover, by reason of the making of an order under this section, any part of the estate so distributed.

(4) In considering for the purposes of this section when representation with respect to the estate of a deceased person was first taken out, a grant limited to settled land or to trust property shall be left out of account, and a grant limited to real estate or to personal estate shall be left out of account unless a grant limited to the remainder of the estate has previously been made or is made at the same time.

Interpretation of wills – general rules as to evidence
21. (1) This section applies to a will—

(a) in so far as any part of it is meaningless;
(b) in so far as the language used in any part of it is ambiguous on the face of it;
(c) in so far as evidence, other than evidence of the testator's intention, shows that the language used in any part of it is ambiguous in the light of surrounding circumstances.

(2) In so far as this section applies to a will extrinsic evidence, including evidence of the testator's intention, may be admitted to assist in its interpretation.

RECTIFICATION AND INTERPRETATION OF WILLS

Presumption as to effect of gifts to spouses
22. Except where a contrary intention is shown it shall be presumed that if a

testator devises or bequeaths property to his spouse in terms which in themselves would give an absolute interest to the spouse, but by the same instrument purports to give his issue an interest in the same property, the gift to the spouse is absolute notwithstanding the purported gift to the issue.

FAMILY LAW REFORM ACT 1987

(1987 Chapter 42)

Part I

General Principle

General principle
1. (1) In this Act and enactments passed and instruments made after the coming into force of this section, references (however expressed) to any relationship between two persons shall, unless the contrary intention appears, be construed without regard to whether or not the father and mother of either of them, or the father and mother of any person through whom the relationship is deduced, have or had been married to each other at any time.

(2) In this Act and enactments passed after the coming into force of this section, unless the contrary intention appears—

(a) references to a person whose father and mother were married to each other at the time of his birth include; and

(b) references to a person whose father and mother were not married to each other at the time of his birth do not include,

references to any person whom subsection (3) below applies, and cognate references shall be construed accordingly.

(3) This subsection applies to any person who—

(a) is treated as legitimate by virtue of section 1 of the Legitimacy Act 1976;

(b) is a legitimated person within the meaning of section 10 of that Act;

(c) is an adopted child within the meaning of Part IV of that Act 1976; or

(d) is otherwise treated in law as legitimate.

(4) For the purpose of construing references falling within subsection (2) above, the time of a person's birth shall be taken to include any time during the period beginning with—

(a) the insemination resulting in his birth; or

(b) where there was no such insemination, his conception,

and (in either case) ending with his birth.

Annotations

Commencement order: SI 1988 No 425.

PART III

PROPERTY RIGHTS

Succession on intestacy
18. (1) In Part IV of the Administration of Estates Act 1925 (which deals with the distribution of the estate of an intestate), references (however expressed) to any relationship between two persons shall be construed in accordance with section 1 above.

(2) For the purposes of subsection (1) above and that Part of that Act, a person whose father and mother were not married to each other at the time of his birth shall be presumed not to have been survived by his father, or by any person related to him only through his father, unless the contrary is shown.

(3) In section 50(1) of that Act (which relates to the construction of documents), the reference to Part IV of that Act, or to the foregoing provisions of that Part, shall in relation to an instrument inter vivos made, or a will or codicil coming into operation, after the coming into force of this section (but not in relation to instruments inter vivos made or wills or codicils coming into operation earlier) be construed as including references to this section.

(4) This section does not affect any rights under the intestacy of a person dying before the coming into force of this section.

Annotations

Commencement order: SI 1988 No 425.

Dispositions of property
19. (1) In the following dispositions, namely—

(a) dispositions inter vivos made on or after the date on which this section comes into force; and

(b) dispositions by will or codicil where the will or codicil is made on or after that date,

references (whether express or implied) to any relationship between two persons shall be construed in accordance with section 1 above.

(2) It is hereby declared that the use, without more, of the word *heir* or *heirs* or any expression which is used to create an entailed interest in real or personal property does not show a contrary intention for the purposes of section 1 as applied by subsection (1) above.

(3) In relation to the dispositions mentioned in subsection (1) above, section 33 of the Trustee Act 1925 (which specifies the trust implied by a direction that income is to be held on protective trusts for the benefit of any person) shall have effect as if any reference (however expressed) to any relationship between two persons were constructed in accordance with section 1 above.

(4) Where under any disposition of real or personal property, any interest in such property is limited (whether subject to any preceding limitation or charge or not) in such a way that it would, apart from this section, devolve (as nearly as the law permits) along with a dignity or title of honour, then—

(a)   whether or not the disposition contains an express reference to the dignity or title of honour; and

(b)   whether or not the property or some interest in the property may in some event become severed from it,

nothing in this section shall operate to sever the property or any interest in it from the dignity or title, but the property or interest shall devolve in all respects as if this section had not been enacted.

(5) This section is without prejudice to section 42 of the Adoption Act 1976 (construction of dispositions in cases of adoption).

(6) In this section *disposition* means a disposition, including an oral disposition, of real or personal property whether inter vivos or by will or codicil.

(7) Notwithstanding any rule of law, a disposition made by will or codicil executed before the date on which this section comes into force shall not be treated for the purposes of this section as made on or after that date by reason only that the will or codicil is confirmed by a codicil executed on or after that date.

Annotations

Commencement order: SI 1988 No 425.

No special protection for trustees and personal representatives
20. . .

Annotations

Commencement order: SI 1988 No 425.
This section repeals the Family Law Reform Act 1969, s 17.

Entitlement to grant of probate etc
21. (1) For the purpose of determining the person or persons who would in accordance with probate rules be entitled to a grant of probate or administration in respect of the estate of a deceased person, the deceased shall be presumed, unless the contrary is shown, not to have been survived—

(a)   by any person related to him whose father and mother were not married to each other at the time of his birth; or

(b)   by any person whose relationship with him is deduced through such a person as is mentioned in paragraph (*a*) above.

(2) In this section *probate rules* means rules of court made under section 127 of the Supreme Court Act 1981.

(3) This section does not apply in relation to the estate of a person dying before the coming into force of this section.

Annotations

Commencement order: SI 1988 No 425.

PART VI

MISCELLANEOUS AND SUPPLEMENTAL

MISCELLANEOUS

Artificial insemination
27. (1) Where after the coming into force of this section a child is born in England and Wales as the result of the artificial insemination of a woman who—

(a) was at the time of the insemination a party to a marriage (being a marriage which had not at that time been dissolved or annulled); and
(b) was artificially inseminated with the semen of some person other than the other party to that marriage,

then, unless it is proved to the satisfaction of any court by which the matter has to be determined that the other party to that marriage did not consent to the insemination, the child shall be treated in law as the child of the parties to that marriage and shall not be treated as the child of any person other than the parties to that marriage.

(2) Any reference in this section to a marriage includes a reference to a void marriage if at the time of the insemination resulting in the birth of the child both or either of the parties reasonably believed that the marriage was valid; and for the purposes of this section it shall be presumed, unless the contrary is shown, that one of the parties so believed at that time that the marriage was valid.

(3) Nothing in this section shall affect the succession to any dignity or title of honour or render any person capable of succeeding to or transmitting a right to succeed to any such dignity or title.

Annotations

Commencement order: SI 1988 No 425.
   See further: the Human Fertilisation and Embryology Act 1990, s 49.

Children of void marriages
28. . . .

Annotations

Commencement order: SI 1988 No 425.
This section amends the Legitimacy Act 1976; s 1(1) and adds sub-ss (3), (4).

APPENDIX B

Statutory Instruments

Contents

NON-CONTENTIOUS PROBATE RULES 1987

(1987 No. 2024)

Made – - – 24th November 1987

Citation and commencement
1. These Rules may be cited as the Non-Contentious Probate Rules 1987 and shall come into force on 1st January 1988.

Interpretation
2. (1) In these Rules, unless the context otherwise requires—
the Act means the Supreme Court Act 1981;
authorised officer means any officer of a registry who is for the time being authorised by the President to administer any oath or to take any affidavit required for any purpose connected with his duties;
the Crown includes the Crown in right of the Duchy of Lancaster and the Duke of Cornwall for the time being;
[*district judge* means a district judge of the Principal Registry;]
grant means a grant of probate or administration and includes, where the context so admits, the resealing of such a grant under the Colonial Probates Acts 1892 and 1927;
gross value in relation to any estate means the value of the estate without deduction for debts, incumbrances, funeral expenses or inheritance tax (or other capital tax payable out of the estate);
[*judge* means a judge of the High Court;]
oath means the oath required by rule 8 to be sworn by every applicant for a grant;
personal applicant means a person other than a trust corporation who seeks to obtain a grant without employing a solicitor, and *personal application* has a corresponding meaning;
[*registrar* means the district probate registrar of the district probate registry—

  (i)   to which an application for a grant is made or is proposed to be made,
 (ii)   in rules 26,40,41 and 61(2), from which the grant issued, and
(iii)   in rules 46,47 and 48, from which the citation has issued or is proposed to be issued;]

registry means the Principal Registry or a district probate registry;
[*the senior district judge* means the Senior District Judge of the Family Division or, in his absence, the senior of the district judges in attendance at the Principal Registry;]
. . .
. . .
the Treasury Solicitor means the solicitor for the affairs of Her Majesty's Treasury and includes the solicitor for the affairs of the Duchy of Lancaster and the solicitor of the Duchy of Cornwall;
trust corporation means a corporation within the meaning of section 128 of the Act as extended by section 3 of the Law of Property (Amendment) Act 1926.
  (2) A form referred to by number means the form so numbered in the

First Schedule; and such forms shall be used wherever applicable, with such variation as a [district judge or] registrar may in any particular case direct or approve.

Annotations

Para (1): definitions *district judge* and *judge* added, definitions *statutory guardian* and *testamentary guardian* revoked, definition *registrar* substituted, and definition *the senior district judge* substituted for original definition *the Senior Registrar*, by SI 1991 No 1876, rr 2, 6.

Para (2): words in square brackets substituted by SI 1991 No 1876, r 7(1).

Modifications: any reference to Solicitors etc modified to include references to Recognised Bodies, by the Solicitors' Incorporated Practices Order 1991, SI 1991 No 2684, arts 4, 5, Sch 1.

Application of other rules
3. Subject to the provisions of these Rules and to any enactment, the Rules of the Supreme Court 1965 shall apply, with the necessary modifications, to non-contentious probate matters, save that nothing in Order 3 shall prevent time from running in the Long Vacation.

Applications for grants through solicitors
4. (1) A person applying for a grant through a solicitor may apply at any registry or sub-registry.

(2) Every solicitor through whom an application for a grant is made shall give the address of his place of business within England and Wales.

Annotations

Modifications: any reference to Solicitors etc modified to include references to Recognised Bodies, by the Solicitors' Incorporated Practices Order 1991, SI 1991 No 2684, arts 4, 5, Sch 1.

Personal applications
5. (1) A personal applicant may apply for a grant at any registry or sub-registry.

(2) Save as provided for by rule 39 a personal applicant may not apply through an agent, whether paid or unpaid, and may not be attended by any person acting or appearing to act as his adviser.

(3) No personal application shall be proceeded with if—

(a) it becomes necessary to bring the matter before the court by action or summons;
(b) an application has already been made by a solicitor on behalf of the applicant and has not been withdrawn; or
(c) the [district judge or] registrar so directs.

(4) After a will has been deposited in a registry by a personal applicant, it may not be delivered to the applicant or to any other person unless in special circumstances the [district judge or] registrar so directs.

(5) A personal applicant shall produce a certificate of the death of the deceased or such other evidence of the death as the [district judge or] registrar may approve.

(6) A personal applicant shall supply all information necessary to enable the papers leading to the grant to be prepared in the registry.

(7) Unless the [district judge or] registrar otherwise directs, every oath or affidavit required on a personal application shall be sworn or executed by all the deponents before an authorised officer.

(8) No legal advice shall be given to a personal applicant by an officer of a registry and every such officer shall be responsible only for embodying in proper form the applicant's instructions for the grant.

Annotations

Paras (3)–(5), (7): words in square brackets added by SI 1991 No 1876, r 7(1).

Modifications: any reference to Solicitors etc modified to include references to Recognised Bodies, by the Solicitors' Incorporated Practices Order 1991, SI 1991 No 2684, arts 4, 5, Sch 1.

Duty of [district judge or] registrar on receiving application for grant
6. (1) A [district judge or] registrar shall not allow any grant to issue until all inquiries which he may see fit to make have been answered to his satisfaction.

(2) Except with the leave of a [district judge or] registrar, no grant of probate or of administration with the will annexed shall issue within seven days of the death of the deceased and no grant of administration shall issue within fourteen days thereof.

Annotations

Words in square brackets added by SI 1991 No 1876, r 7(1).

Grants by district probate registrars
7. (1) No grant shall be made by a . . . registrar—

(a) in any case in which there is contention, until the contention is disposed of; or

(b) in any case in which it appears to him that a grant ought not to be made without the directions of a judge or a [district judge].

(2) In any case in which paragraph (1)(b) applies, the . . . registrar shall send a statement of the matter in question to the Principal Registry for directions.

(3) A [district judge] may either confirm that the matter be referred to a judge and give directions accordingly or may direct the . . . registrar to proceed with the matter in accordance with such instructions as are deemed necessary, which may include a direction to take no further action in relation to the matter.

Annotations

Paras (1), (3): words omitted revoked, and words in square brackets substituted, by SI 1991 No 1876, r 7(2), (3).

Para (2): words omitted revoked by SI 1991 No 1876, r 7(2).

Oath in support of grant
8. (1) Every application for a grant other than one to which rule 39 applies shall be supported by an oath by the applicant in the form applicable to the circumstances of the case, and by such other papers as the [district judge or] registrar may require.

(2) Unless otherwise directed by a [district judge or] registrar, the oath shall state where the deceased died domiciled.

(3) Where the deceased died on or after 1st January 1926, the oath shall state whether or not, to the best of the applicant's knowledge, information and belief, there was land vested in the deceased which was settled previously to his death and not by his will and which remained settled land notwithstanding his death.

(4) On an application for a grant of administration the oath shall state in what manner all persons having a prior right to a grant have been cleared off and whether any minority or life interest arises under the will or intestacy.

Annotations

Paras (1), (2): words in square brackets added by SI 1991 No 1876, r 7(1).

Grant in additional name
9. Where it is sought to describe the deceased in a grant by some name in addition to his true name, the applicant shall depose to the true name of the deceased and shall specify some part of the estate which was held in the other name, or give any other reason for the inclusion of the other name in the grant.

Marking of wills
10. (1) Subject to paragraph (2) below, every will in respect of which an application for a grant is made—

(a) shall be marked by the signatures of the applicant and the person before whom the oath is sworn; and
(b) shall be exhibited to any affidavit which may be required under these Rules as to the validity, terms, condition or date of execution of the will.

(2) The [district judge or] registrar may allow a facsimile copy of a will to be marked or exhibited in lieu of the original document.

Annotations

Para (2): words in square brackets added by SI 1991 No 1876, r 7(1).

Engrossments for purposes of record
11. (1) Where the [district judge or] registrar considers that in any particular case a facsimile copy of the original will would not be satisfactory for purposes of record, he may require an engrossment suitable for facsimile reproduction to be lodged.

(2) Where a will—

(a) contains alterations which are not to be admitted to proof; or
(b) has been ordered to be rectified by virtue of section 20(1) of the Administration of Justice Act 1982,

there shall be lodged an engrossment of the will in the form in which it is to be proved.

(3) Any engrossment lodged under this rule shall reproduce the punctuation, spacing and division into paragraphs of the will and shall follow continuously from page to page on both sides of the paper.

Annotations

Para (1): words in square brackets added by SI 1991 No 1876, r 7(1).

Evidence as to due execution of will
12. (1) Subject to paragraphs (2) and (3) below, where a will contains no attestation clause or the attestation clause is insufficient, or where it appears to the [district judge or] registrar that there is doubt about the due execution of the will, he shall before admitting it to proof require an affidavit as to due execution from one or more of the attesting witnesses or, if no attesting witness is conveniently available, from any other person who was present when the will was executed; and if the [district judge or] registrar, after considering the evidence, is satisfied the will was not duly executed, he shall refuse probate and mark the will accordingly.

(2) If no affidavit can be obtained in accordance with paragraph (1) above, the [district judge or] registrar may accept evidence on affidavit from any person he may think fit to show that the signature on the will is in the handwriting of the deceased, or of any other matter which may raise a presumption in favour of due execution of the will, and may if he thinks fit require that notice of the application be given to any person who may be prejudiced by the will.

(3) A [district judge or] registrar may accept a will for proof without evidence as aforesaid if he is satisfied that the distribution of the estate is not thereby affected.

Annotations

Words in square brackets added by SI 1991 No 1876, r 7(1).

Execution of will of blind or illiterate testator
13. Before admitting to proof a will which appears to have been signed by a blind or illiterate testator or by another person by direction of the testator, or which for any other reason raises doubt as to the testator having had knowledge of the contents of the will at the time of its execution, the [district judge or] registrar shall satisfy himself that the testator had such knowledge.

Annotations

Words in square brackets added by SI 1991 No 1876, r 7(1).

Evidence as to terms, condition and date of execution of will
14. (1) Subject to paragraph (2) below, where there appears in a will any obliteration, interlineation, or other alteration which is not authenticated in the manner prescribed by section 21 of the Wills Act 1837, or by the re-execution of the will or by the execution of a codicil, the [district judge or] registrar shall require evidence to show whether the alteration was present at the time the will was executed and shall give directions as to the form in which the will is to be proved.

(2) The provisions of paragraph (1) above shall not apply to any alteration which appears to the [district judge or] registrar to be of no practical importance.

(3) If a will contains any reference to another document in such terms as

to suggest that it ought to be incorporated in the will, the [district judge or] registrar shall require the document to be produced and may call for such evidence in regard to the incorporation of the document as he may think fit.

(4) Where there is a doubt as to the date on which a will was executed, the [district judge or] registrar may require such evidence as he thinks necessary to establish the date.

Annotations

Words in square brackets added by SI 1991 No 1876, r 7(1).

Attempted revocation of will
15. Any appearance of attempted revocation of a will by burning, tearing, or otherwise destroying and every other circumstance leading to a presumption of revocation by the testator, shall be accounted for to the [district judge's or] registrar's satisfaction.

Annotations

Words in square brackets added by SI 1991 No 1876, r 7(5).

Affidavit as to due execution, terms etc, of will
16. A [district judge or] registrar may require an affidavit from any person he may think fit for the purpose of satisfying himself as to any of the matters referred to in rules 13, 14 and 15, and in any such affidavit sworn by an attesting witness or other person present at the time of the execution of a will the deponent shall depose to the manner in which the will was executed.

Annotations

Words in square brackets added by SI 1991 No 1876, r 7(1).

Wills proved otherwise than under section 9 of the Wills Act 1837
17. (1) Rules 12 to 15 shall apply only to a will that is to be established by reference to section 9 of the Wills Act 1837 (signing and attestation of wills).

(2) A will that is to be established otherwise than as described in paragraph (1) of this rule may be so established upon the [district judge or] registrar being satisfied as to its terms and validity, and includes (without prejudice to the generality of the foregoing)—

(a) any will to which rule 18 applies; and
(b) any will which, by virtue of the Wills Act 1963, is to be treated as properly executed if executed according to the internal law of the territory or state referred to in section 1 of that Act.

Annotations

Para (2): words in square brackets added by SI 1991 No 1876, r 7(1).

Wills of persons on military service and seamen
18. Where the deceased died domiciled in England and Wales and it appears to the [district judge or] registrar that there is prima facie evidence that a will is one to which section 11 of the Wills Act 1837 applies, the will

may be admitted to proof if the registrar is satisfied that it was signed by the testator or, if unsigned, that it is in the testator's handwriting.

Annotations

Words in square brackets added by SI 1991 No 1876, r 7(1).

Evidence of foreign law
19. Where evidence as to the law of any country or territory outside England and Wales is required on any application for a grant, the [district judge or] registrar may accept—

(a)   an affidavit from any person whom, having regard to the particulars of his knowledge or experience given in the affidavit, he regards as suitably qualified to give expert evidence of the law in question; or
(b)   a certificate by, or an act before, a notary practising in the country or territory concerned.

Annotations

Words in square brackets added by SI 1991 No 1876, r 7(1).

Order of priority for grant where deceased left a will
20. Where the deceased died on or after 1 January 1926 the person or persons entitled to a grant in respect of a will shall be determined in accordance with the following order of priority, namely—

(a)   the executor (but subject to rule 36(4)(*d*) below);
(b)   any residuary legatee or devisee holding in trust for any other person;
(c)   any other residuary legatee or devisee (including one for life) or where the residue is not wholly disposed of by the will, any person entitled to share in the undisposed of residue (including the Treasury Solicitor when claiming bona vacantia on behalf of the Crown), provided that—

   (i)   unless a [district judge or] registrar otherwise directs, a residuary legatee or devisee whose legacy or devise is vested in interest shall be preferred to one entitled on the happening of a contingency, and
   (ii)   where the residue is not in terms wholly disposed of, the [district judge or] registrar may, if he is satisfied that the testator has nevertheless disposed of the whole or substantially the whole of the known estate, allow a grant to be made to any legatee or devisee entitled to, or to share in, the estate so disposed of, without regard to the persons entitled to share in any residue not disposed of by the will;

(d)   the personal representative of any residuary legatee or devisee (but not one for life, or one holding in trust for any other person), or of any person entitled to share in any residue not disposed of by the will;
(e)   any other legatee or devisee (including one for life or one holding in trust for any other person) or any creditor of the deceased, provided that, unless a [district judge or] registrar otherwise directs, a legatee or devisee whose legacy or devise is vested in interest shall be preferred to one entitled on the happening of a contingency;

(f) the personal representative of any other legatee or devisee (but not one for life or one holding in trust for any other person) or of any creditor of the deceased.

Annotations

Paras (c), (e): words in square brackets added by SI 1991 No 1876, r 7(1).

Grants to attesting witnesses, etc
21. Where a gift to any person fails by reason of section 15 of the Wills Act 1837, such person shall not have any right to a grant as a beneficiary named in the will, without prejudice to his right to a grant in any other capacity.

Order of priority for grant in case of intestacy
22. (1) Where the deceased died on or after 1 January 1926, wholly intestate, the person or persons having a beneficial interest in the estate shall be entitled to a grant of administration in the following classes in order of priority, namely—

(a) the surviving husband or wife;
(b) the children of the deceased and the issue of any deceased child who died before the deceased;
(c) the father and mother of the deceased;
(d) brothers and sisters of the whole blood and the issue of any deceased brother or sister of the whole blood who died before the deceased;
(e) brothers and sisters of the half blood and the issue of any deceased brother or sister of the half blood who died before the deceased;
(f) grandparents;
(g) uncles and aunts of the whole blood and the issue of any deceased uncle or aunt of the whole blood who died before the deceased;
(h) uncles and aunts of the half blood and the issue of any deceased uncle or aunt of the half blood who died before the deceased.

(2) In default of any person having a beneficial interest in the estate, the Treasury Solicitor shall be entitled to a grant if he claims bona vacantia on behalf of the Crown.

(3) If all persons entitled to a grant under the foregoing provisions of this rule have been cleared off, a grant may be made to a creditor of the deceased or to any person who, notwithstanding that he has no immediate beneficial interest in the estate, may have a beneficial interest in the event of an accretion thereto.

(4) Subject to paragraph (5) of rule 27, the personal representative of a person in any of the classes mentioned in paragraph (1) of this rule or the personal representative of a creditor of the deceased shall have the same right to a grant as the person whom he represents provided that the persons mentioned in sub-paragraphs (*b*) to (*h*) of paragraph (1) above shall be preferred to the personal representative of a spouse who has died without taking a beneficial interest in the whole estate of the deceased as ascertained at the time of the application for the grant.

Order of priority for grant in pre-1926 cases
23. Where the deceased died before 1st January 1926, the person or persons entitled to a grant shall, subject to the provisions of any enactment, be

determined in accordance with the principles and rules under which the court would have acted at the date of death.

Right of assignee to a grant
24. (1) Where all the persons entitled to the estate of the deceased (whether under a will or on intestacy) have assigned their whole interest in the estate to one or more persons, the assignee or assignees shall replace, in the order of priority for a grant of administration, the assignor or, if there are two or more assignors, the assignor with the highest priority.

(2) Where there are two or more assignees, administration may be granted with the consent of the others to any one or more (not exceeding four) of them.

(3) In any case where administration is applied for by an assignee the original instrument of assignment shall be produced and a copy of the same lodged in the registry.

Joinder of administrator
25. (1) A person entitled in priority to a grant of administration may, without leave, apply for a grant with a person entitled in a lower degree, provided that there is no other person entitled in a higher degree to the person to be joined, unless every other such person has renounced.

(2) Subject to paragraph (3) below, an application for leave to join with a person entitled in priority to a grant of administration a person having no right or no immediate right thereto shall be made to a [district judge or] registrar, and shall be supported by an affidavit by the person entitled in priority, the consent of the person proposed to be joined as administrator and such other evidence as the [district judge or] registrar may direct.

(3) Unless a [district judge or] registrar otherwise directs, there may without any such application be joined with a person entitled in priority to administration—

(a) any person who is nominated under paragraph (3) of rule 32 or paragraph (3) of rule 35;
(b) a trust corporation.

Annotations

Paras (2), (3): words in square brackets added by SI 1991 No 1876, r 7(1).

Additional personal representatives
26. (1) An application under section 114(4) of the Act to add a personal representative shall be made to a [district judge or] registrar and shall be supported by an affidavit by the applicant, the consent of the person proposed to be added as personal representative and such other evidence as the [district judge or] registrar may require.

(2) On any such application the [district judge or] registrar may direct that a note shall be made on the original grant of the addition of a further personal representative, or he may impound or revoke the grant or make such other order as the circumstances of the case may require.

Annotations

Words in square brackets added by SI 1991 No 1876, r 7(1).
The Act: Supreme Court Act 1981.

Grants where two or more persons entitled in same degree

27. [(1) Subject to paragraphs (1A), (2) and (3) below, where, on an application for probate, power to apply for a like grant is to be reserved to such other of the executors as have not renounced probate, notice of the application shall be given to the executor or executors to whom power is to be reserved; and, unless the district judge or registrar otherwise directs, the oath shall state that such notice has been given.

(1A) Where power is to be reserved to executors who are appointed by reference to their being partners in a firm, and not by their names, notice need not be given to them under paragraph (1) above if probate is applied for by another partner in that firm.]

(2) Where power is to be reserved to partners of a firm, notice for the purposes of paragraph (1) above may be given to the partners by sending it to the firm at its principal or last known place of business.

(3) A [district judge or] registrar may dispense with the giving of notice under paragraph (1) above if he is satisfied that the giving of such a notice is impracticable or would result in unreasonable delay or expense.

(4) A grant of administration may be made to any person entitled thereto without notice to other persons entitled in the same degree.

(5) Unless a [district judge or] registrar otherwise directs, administration shall be granted to a person of full age entitled thereto in preference to a guardian of a minor, and to a living person entitled thereto in preference to the personal representative of a deceased person.

(6) A dispute between persons entitled to a grant in the same degree shall be brought by summons before a [district judge or] registrar.

(7) The issue of a summons under this rule in [the Principal Registry or] a district probate registry shall be notified forthwith to the registry in which the index of pending grant applications is maintained.

(8) If the issue of a summons under this rule is known to the [district judge or] registrar, he shall not allow any grant to be sealed until such summons is finally disposed of.

Annotations

Paras (1), (1A): substituted for original para (1) by SI 1991 No 1876, r 8(1).
Paras (3), (5), (6), (8): words in square brackets added by SI 1991 No 1876, r 7(1).
Para (7): words in square brackets added by SI 1991 No 1876, r 8(2).

Exceptions to rules as to priority

28. (1) Any person to whom a grant may or is required to be made under any enactment shall not be prevented from obtaining such a grant notwithstanding the operation of rules 20, 22, 25 or 27.

(2) Where the deceased died domiciled outside England and Wales rules 20, 22, 25 or 27 shall not apply except in a case to which paragraph (3) of rule 30 applies.

Grants in respect of settled land

29. [(1) In this rule *settled land* means land vested in the deceased which was settled prior to his death and not by his will, and which remained settled land notwithstanding his death.

(2) The person or persons entitled to a grant of administration limited to

settled land shall be determined in accordance with the following order of priority:

  (i) the special executors in regard to settled land constituted by section 22 of the Administration of Estates Act 1925;

 (ii) the trustees of the settlement at the time of the application for the grant; and

(iii) the personal representatives of the deceased.

(3) Where there is settled land and a grant is made in respect of the free estate only, the grant shall expressly exclude the settled land.]

Annotations

Substituted by SI 1991 No 1876, r 9.

Grants where deceased died domiciled outside England and Wales
30. (1) Subject to paragraph (3) below, where the deceased died domiciled outside England and Wales, [a district judge or registrar may order that a grant, limited in such way as the district judge or registrar may direct,] do issue to any of the following persons—

(a)   to the person entrusted with the administration of the estate by the court having jurisdiction at the place where the deceased died domiciled; or

(b)   where there is no person so entrusted, to the person beneficially entitled to the estate by the law of the place where the deceased died domiciled or, if there is more than one person so entitled, to such of them as the [district judge or] registrar may direct; or

(c)   if in the opinion of the [district judge or] registrar the circumstances so require, to such person as the [district judge or] registrar may direct.

(2) A grant made under paragraph (1)(*a*) or (*b*) above may be issued jointly with such person as the [district judge or] registrar may direct if the grant is required to be made to not less than two administrators.

(3) Without any order made under paragraph (1) above—

(a)   probate of any will which is admissible to proof may be granted—

     (i)   if the will is in the English or Welsh language, to the executor named therein; or

    (ii)   if the will describes the duties of a named person in terms sufficient to constitute him executor according to the tenor of the will, to that person; or

(b)   where the whole or substantially the whole of the estate in England and Wales consists of immovable property, a grant in respect of the whole estate may be made in accordance with the law which would have been applicable if the deceased had died domiciled in England and Wales.

Annotations

Para (1): first words in square brackets substituted and other words in square brackets added by SI 1991 No 1876, rr 7(1), 10.
   Para (2): words in square brackets added by SI 1991 No 1876, r 7(1).

Grants to attorneys
31. (1) Subject to paragraphs (2) and (3) below, the lawfully constituted attorney of a person entitled to a grant may apply for administration for the use and benefit of the donor, and such grant shall be limited until further representation be granted, or in such other way as the [district judge or] registrar may direct.

(2) Where the donor referred to in paragraph (1) above is an executor, notice of the application shall be given to any other executor unless such notice is dispensed with by the [district judge or] registrar.

(3) Where the donor referred to in paragraph (1) above is mentally incapable and the attorney is acting under an enduring power of attorney, the application shall be made in accordance with rule 35.

Annotations

Paras (1), (2): words in square brackets added by SI 1991 No 1876, r 7(1).

Grants on behalf of minors
32. (1) Where a person to whom a grant would otherwise be made is a minor, administration for his use and benefit, limited until he attains the age of eighteen years, shall, unless otherwise directed, and subject to paragraph (2) of this rule, be granted to

[(a) a parent of the minor who has, or is deemed to have, parental responsibility for him in accordance with—

    (i) section 2(1), 2(2) or 4 of the Children Act 1989,
    (ii) paragraph 4 or 6 of Schedule 14 to that Act, or
    (iii) an adoption order within the meaning of section 12(1) of the Adoption Act 1976, or

(b) a guardian of the minor who is appointed, or deemed to have been appointed, in accordance with section 5 of the Children Act 1989 or in accordance with paragraph 12, 13 or 14 of Schedule 14 to that Act];

provided that where the minor is sole executor and has no interest in the residuary estate of the deceased, administration for the use and benefit of the minor limited as aforesaid, shall, unless a [district judge or] registrar otherwise directs, be granted to the person entitled to the residuary estate.

[(2) A district judge or registrar may by order appoint a person to obtain administration for the use and benefit of the minor, limited as aforesaid, in default of, or jointly with, or to the exclusion of, any person mentioned in paragraph (1) of this rule; and the person intended shall file an affidavit in support of his application to be appointed.]

(3) Where there is only one person competent and willing to take a grant under the foregoing provisions of this rule, such person may, unless a [district judge or] registrar otherwise directs, nominate any fit and proper person to act jointly with him in taking the grant.

Annotations

Para (1): first words in square brackets substituted and final words in square brackets added by SI 1991 No 1876, rr 3, 7(1).
    Para (2): substituted by SI 1991 No 1876, r 4.
    Para (3): words in square brackets added by SI 1991 No 1876, r 7(1).

Grants where a minor is a co-executor
33. (1) Where a minor is appointed executor jointly with one or more other executors, probate may be granted to the executor or executors not under disability with power reserved to the minor executor, and the minor executor shall be entitled to apply for probate on attaining the age of eighteen years.

(2) Administration for the use and benefit of a minor executor until he attains the age of eighteen years may be granted under rule 32 if, and only if, the executors who are not under disability renounce or, on being cited to accept or refuse a grant, fail to make an effective application therefor.

Renunciation of the right of a minor to a grant
34. (1) The right of a minor executor to probate on attaining the age of eighteen years may not be renounced by any person on his behalf.

(2) The right of a minor to administration may be renounced only by a person [appointed] under paragraph (2) of rule 32, and authorised by the [district judge or] registrar to renounce on behalf of the minor.

Annotations

Para (2): words in square brackets substituted or added by SI 1991 No 1876, rr 5, 7(1).

Grants in case of mental incapacity
35. (1) Unless a [district judge or] registrar otherwise directs, no grant shall be made under this rule unless all persons entitled in the same degree as the incapable person referred to in paragraph (2) below have been cleared off.

(2) Where a [district judge or] registrar is satisfied that a person entitled to a grant is by reason of mental incapacity incapable of managing his affairs, administration for his use and benefit, limited until further representation be granted or in such other way as the [district judge or] registrar may direct, may be granted in the following order of priority—

(a) to the person authorised by the Court of Protection to apply for a grant;
(b) where there is no person so authorised, to the lawful attorney of the incapable person acting under a registered enduring power of attorney;
(c) where there is no such attorney entitled to act, or if the attorney shall renounce administration for the use and benefit of the incapable person, to the person entitled to the residuary estate of the deceased.

(3) Where a grant is required to be made to not less than two administrators, and there is only one person competent and willing to take a grant under the foregoing provisions of this rule, administration may, unless a [district judge or] registrar otherwise directs, be granted to such person jointly with any other person nominated by him.

(4) Notwithstanding the foregoing provisions of this rule, administration for the use and benefit of the incapable person may be granted to such two or more other persons as the [district judge or] registrar may by order direct.

(5) Notice of an intended application under this rule shall be given to the Court of Protection.

Annotations

Paras (1)-(4): words in square brackets added by SI 1991 No 1876, r 7(1).

Grants to trust corporations and other corporate bodies

36. (1) An application for a grant to a trust corporation shall be made through one of its officers, and such officer shall depose in the oath that the corporation is a trust corporation as defined by these Rules and that it has power to accept a grant.

(2)

(a) Where the trust corporation is the holder of an official position, any officer whose name is included on a list filed with the [senior district judge] of persons authorised to make affidavits and sign documents on behalf of the office holder may act as the officer through whom the holder of that official position applies for the grant.

(b) In all other cases a certified copy of the resolution of the trust corporation authorising the officer to make the application shall be lodged, or it shall be deposed in the oath that such certified copy has been filed with the [senior district judge], that the officer is therein identified by the position he holds, and that such resolution is still in force.

(3) A trust corporation may apply for administration otherwise than as a beneficiary or the attorney of some person, and on any such application there shall be lodged the consents of all persons entitled to a grant and of all persons interested in the residuary estate of the deceased save that the [district judge or] registrar may dispense with any such consents as aforesaid on such terms, if any, as he may think fit.

(4)

(a) Subject to sub-paragraph (d) below, where a corporate body would, if an individual, be entitled to a grant but is not a trust corporation as defined by these Rules, administration for its use and benefit, limited until further representation be granted, may be made to its nominee or to its lawfully constituted attorney.

(b) A copy of the resolution appointing the nominee or the power of attorney (whichever is appropriate) shall be lodged, and such resolution or power of attorney shall be sealed by the corporate body, or be otherwise authenticated to the [district judge's or] registrar's satisfaction.

(c) The nominee or attorney shall depose in the oath that the corporate body is not a trust corporation as defined by these Rules.

(d) The provisions of paragraph (4)(*a*) above shall not apply where a corporate body is appointed executor jointly with an individual unless the right of the individual has been cleared off.

Annotations

Para (2): words in square brackets substituted by SI 1991 No 1876, r 7(4).
   Paras (3), (4): words in square brackets added by SI 1991 No 1876, r 7(1), (5).

Renunciation of probate and administration

37. (1) Renunciation of probate by an executor shall not operate as renunciation of any right which he may have to a grant of administration in some other capacity unless he expressly renounces such right.

(2) Unless a [district judge or] registrar otherwise directs, no person who has renounced administration in one capacity may obtain a grant thereof in some other capacity.

(3) A renunciation of probate or administration may be retracted at any time with the leave of a [district judge or] registrar; provided that only in exceptional circumstances may leave be given to an executor to retract a renunciation of probate after a grant has been made to some other person entitled in a lower degree.

(4) A direction or order giving leave under this rule may be made either by the registrar of a district probate registry where the renunciation is filed or by a [district judge].

Annotations

Paras (2), (3): words in square brackets added by SI 1991 No 1876, r 7(1).
  Para (4): words in square brackets substituted by SI 1991 No 1876, r 7(3).

Notice to Crown of intended application for grant
38. In any case in which it appears that the Crown is or may be beneficially interested in the estate of a deceased person, notice of intended application for a grant shall be given by the applicant to the Treasury Solicitor, and the [district judge or] registrar may direct that no grant shall issue within 28 days after the notice has been given.

Annotations

Words in square brackets added by SI 1991 No 1876, r 7(1).

Resealing under Colonial Probates Acts 1892 and 1927
39. (1) An application under the Colonial Probates Acts 1892 and 1927 for the resealing of probate or administration granted by the court of a country to which those Acts apply may be made by the person to whom the grant was made or by any person authorised in writing to apply on his behalf.

(2) On any such application an Inland Revenue affidavit or account shall be lodged.

(3) Except by leave of a [district judge or] registrar, no grant shall be resealed unless it was made to such a person as is mentioned in sub-paragraph (*a*) or (*b*) of paragraph (1) of rule 30 or to a person to whom a grant could be made under sub-paragraph (*a*) of paragraph (3) of that rule.

(4) No limited or temporary grant shall be resealed except by leave of a [district judge or] registrar.

(5) Every grant lodged for resealing shall include a copy of any will to which the grant relates or shall be accompanied by a copy thereof certified as correct by or under the authority of the court by which the grant was made, and where the copy of the grant required to be deposited under subsection (1) of section 2 of the Colonial Probates Act 1892 does not include a copy of the will, a copy thereof shall be deposited in the registry before the grant is resealed.

(6) The [district judge or] registrar shall send notice of the resealing to the court which made the grant.

(7) Where notice is received in the Principal Registry of the resealing of a grant issued in England and Wales, notice of any amendment or revocation of the grant shall be sent to the court by which it was resealed.

Annotations

Paras (3), (4), (6): words in square brackets added by SI 1991 No 1876, r 7(1).

Application for leave to sue on guarantee
40. An application for leave under section 120(3) of the Act or under section 11(5) of the Administration of Estates Act 1971 to sue a surety on a guarantee given for the purposes of either of those sections shall, unless the [district judge or] registrar otherwise directs under rule 61, be made by summons to a [district judge or] registrar and notice of the application shall be served on the administrator, the surety and any co-surety.

Annotations

Words in square brackets added by SI 1991 No 1876, r 7(1).
    The Act: Supreme Court Act 1981.

Amendment and revocation of grant
41. (1) Subject to paragraph (2) below, if a [district judge or] registrar is satisfied that a grant should be amended or revoked he may make an order accordingly.
    (2) Except on the application or with the consent of the person to whom the grant was made, the power conferred in paragraph (1) above shall be exercised only in exceptional circumstances.

Annotations

Para (1): words in square brackets added by SI 1991 No 1876, r 7(1).

Certificate of delivery of Inland Revenue affidavit
42. Where the deceased died before 13th March 1975 the certificate of delivery of an Inland Revenue affidavit required by section 30 of the Customs and Inland Revenue Act 1881 to be borne by every grant shall be in Form 1.

Standing searches
43. [(1) Any person who wishes to be notified of the issue of a grant may enter a standing search for the grant by lodging at, or sending by post to any registry or sub-registry, a notice in Form 2.]
    (2) A person who has entered a standing search will be sent an office copy of any grant which corresponds with the particulars given on the completed Form 2 and which—

(a) issued not more than twelve months before the entry of the standing search; or
(b) issues within a period of six months after the entry of the standing search.

    (3)

    (a) Where an applicant wishes to extend the said period of six months, he or his solicitor may lodge at, or send by post to, [the registry or sub-registry at which the standing search was entered] written application for extension.

(b)   An application for extension as aforesaid must be lodged, or received by post, within the last month of the said period of six months, and the standing search shall thereupon be effective for an additional period of six months from the date on which it was due to expire.

(c)   A standing search which has been extended as above may be further extended by the filing of a further application for extension subject to the same conditions as set out in sub-paragraph (*b*) above.

Annotations

Para (1): substituted by SI 1991 No 1876, r 11(1).
   Para (3): words in square brackets substituted by SI 1991 No 1876, r 11(2).
   Modifications: any reference to Solicitors etc modified to include references to Recognised Bodies, by the Solicitors' Incorporated Practices Order 1991, SI 1991 No 2684, arts 4, 5, Sch 1.

Caveats
44. (1) Any person who wishes to show cause against the sealing of a grant may enter a caveat in any registry or sub-registry, and the [district judge or] registrar shall not allow any grant to be sealed (other than a grant ad colligenda bona or a grant under section 117 of the Act) if he has knowledge of an effective caveat; provided that no caveat shall prevent the sealing of a grant on the day on which the caveat is entered.

(2) Any person wishing to enter a caveat (in these Rules called *the caveator*), or a solicitor on his behalf, may effect entry of a caveat—

(a)   by completing Form 3 in the appropriate book at any registry or sub-registry; or

(b)   by sending by post at his own risk a notice in Form 3 to any registry or sub-registry and the proper officer shall provide an acknowledgement of the entry of the caveat.

(3)

(a)   Except as otherwise provided by this rule or by rules 45 or 46, a caveat shall be effective for a period of six months from the date of entry thereof, and where a caveator wishes to extend the said period of six months, he or his solicitor may lodge at, or send by post to, the registry or sub-registry at which the caveat was entered a written application for extension.

(b)   An application for extension as aforesaid must be lodged, or received by post, within the last month of the said period of six months, and the caveat shall thereupon (save as otherwise provided by this rule) be effective for an additional period of six months from the date on which it was due to expire.

(c)   A caveat which has been extended as above may be further extended by the filing of a further application for extension subject to the same conditions as set out in sub-paragraph (*b*) above.

(4) An index of caveats entered in any registry or sub-registry shall be maintained at the same registry in which the index of pending grant applications is maintained, and a search of the caveat index shall be made—

(a)   on receipt of an application for a grant at that registry; and

(b)   on receipt of a notice of an application for a grant made in any other registry,

and the appropriate [district judge or] registrar shall be notified of the entry of a caveat against the sealing of a grant for which application has been made in that other registry.

(5) Any person claiming to have an interest in the estate may cause to be issued from the registry in which the caveat index is maintained a warning in Form 4 against the caveat, and the person warning shall state his interest in the estate of the deceased and shall require the caveator to give particulars of any contrary interest in the estate; and the warning or a copy thereof shall be served on the caveator forthwith.

(6) A caveator who has no interest contrary to that of the person warning, but who wishes to show cause against the sealing of a grant to that person, may within eight days of service of the warning upon him (inclusive of the day of such service), or at any time thereafter if no affidavit has been filed under paragraph (12) below, issue and serve a summons for directions.

(7) On the hearing of any summons for directions under paragraph (6) above the [district judge or] registrar may give a direction for the caveat to cease to have effect.

(8) Any caveat in force when a summons for directions is issued shall remain in force until the summons has been disposed of unless a direction has been given under paragraph (7) above [or until it is withdrawn under paragraph (11) below].

(9) The issue of a summons under this rule shall be notified forthwith to the registry in which the caveat index is maintained.

(10) A caveator having an interest contrary to that of the person warning may within eight days of service of the warning upon him (inclusive of the day of such service) or at any time thereafter if no affidavit has been filed under paragraph (12) below, enter an appearance in the registry in which the caveat index is maintained by filing Form 5 . . . ; and he shall serve forthwith on the person warning a copy of Form 5 sealed with the seal of the court.

(11) A caveator who has not entered an appearance to a warning may at any time withdraw his caveat by giving notice at the registry or sub-registry at which it was entered, and the caveat shall thereupon cease to have effect; and, where the caveat has been so withdrawn, the caveator shall forthwith give notice of withdrawal to the person warning.

(12) If no appearance has been entered by the caveator or no summons has been issued by him under paragraph (6) of this rule, the person warning may at any time after eight days of service of the warning upon the caveator (inclusive of the day of such service) file an affidavit in the registry in which the caveat index is maintained as to such service and the caveat shall thereupon cease to have effect provided that there is no pending summons under paragraph (6) of this rule.

(13) Unless a [district judge or, where application to discontinue a caveat is made by consent, a registrar] by order made on summons otherwise directs, any caveat in respect of which an appearance to a warning has been entered shall remain in force until the commencement of a probate action.

(14) Except with the leave of a [district judge], no further caveat may be entered by or on behalf of any caveator whose caveat is either in force or has ceased to have effect under paragraphs (7) or (12) of this rule or under rule 45(4) or rule 46(3).

Annotations

Paras (1), (4), (7): words in square brackets added by SI 1991 No 1876, r 7(1).
  Para (8): words in square brackets added by SI 1991 No 1876, r 12(1).
  Para (10): words omitted revoked by SI 1991 No 1876, r 12(2).
  Para (13): words in square brackets substituted by SI 1991 No 1876, rr 7(3), 12(3).
  Para (14): words in square brackets substituted by SI 1991 No 1876, r 7(3).
  Modifications: any reference to Solicitors etc modified to include references to Recognised Bodies, by the Solicitors' Incorporated Practices Order 1991, SI 1991 No 2684, arts 4, 5, Sch 1.
  The Act: Supreme Court Act 1981.

Probate actions
45. (1) Upon being advised by the court concerned of the commencement of a probate action the [senior district judge] shall give notice of the action to every caveator other than the plaintiff in the action in respect of each caveat that is in force.

(2) In respect of any caveat entered subsequent to the commencement of a probate action the [senior district judge] shall give notice to that caveator of the existence of the action.

(3) Unless a [district judge] by order made on summons otherwise directs, the commencement of a probate action shall operate to prevent the sealing of a grant (other than a grant under section 117 of the Act) until application for a grant is made by the person shown to be entitled thereto by the decision of the court in such action.

(4) Upon such application for a grant, any caveat entered by the plaintiff in the action, and any caveat in respect of which notice of the action has been given, shall cease to have effect.

Annotations

Paras (1), (2): words in square brackets substituted by SI 1991 No 1876, r 7(4).
  Para (3): words in square brackets substituted by SI 1991 No 1876, r 7(3).
  The Act: Supreme Court Act 1981.

Citations
46. (1) Any citation may issue from the Principal Registry or a district probate registry and shall be settled by a [district judge or] registrar before being issued.

(2) Every averment in a citation, and such other information as the registrar may require, shall be verified by an affidavit sworn by the person issuing the citation (in these Rules called the *citor*), provided that the [district judge or] registrar may in special circumstances accept an affidavit sworn by the citor's solicitor.

(3) The citor shall enter a caveat before issuing a citation and, unless a [district judge] by order made on summons otherwise directs, any caveat in force at the commencement of the citation proceedings shall, unless withdrawn pursuant to paragraph (11) of rule 44, remain in force until application for a grant is made by the person shown to be entitled thereto by the decision of the court in such proceedings, and upon such application any caveat entered by a party who had notice of the proceedings shall cease to have effect.

(4) Every citation shall be served personally on the person cited unless

the [district judge or] registrar, on cause shown by affidavit, directs some other mode of service, which may include notice by advertisement.

(5) Every will referred to in a citation shall be lodged in a registry before the citation is issued, except where the will is not in the citor's possession and the [district judge or] registrar is satisfied that it is impracticable to require it to be lodged.

(6) A person who has been cited to appear may, within eight days of service of the citation upon him (inclusive of the day of such service), or at any time thereafter if no application has been made by the citor under paragraph (5) of rule 47 or paragraph (2) of rule 48, enter an appearance in the registry from which the citation issued by filing Form 5 and shall forthwith thereafter serve on the citor a copy of Form 5 sealed with the seal of the registry.

Annotations

Paras (1), (2), (4), (5): words in square brackets added by SI 1991 No 1876, r 7(1).
  Para (3): words in square brackets substituted by SI 1991 No 1876, r 7(3).

Citation to accept or refuse or to take a grant
47. (1) A citation to accept or refuse a grant may be issued at the instance of any person who would himself be entitled to a grant in the event of the person cited renouncing his right thereto.

(2) Where power to make a grant to an executor has been reserved, a citation calling on him to accept or refuse a grant may be issued at the instance of the executors who have proved the will or the survivor of them or of the executors of the last survivor of deceased executors who have proved.

(3) A citation calling on an executor who has intermeddled in the estate of the deceased to show cause why he should not be ordered to take a grant may be issued at the instance of any person interested in the estate at any time after the expiration of six months from the death of the deceased, provided that no citation to take a grant shall issue while proceedings as to the validity of the will are pending.

(4) A person cited who is willing to accept or take a grant may, after entering an appearance, apply ex parte by affidavit to a [district judge or] registrar for an order for a grant to himself.

(5) If the time limited for appearance has expired and the person cited has not entered an appearance, the citor may—

(a) in the case of a citation under paragraph (1) of this rule, apply to a [district judge or] registrar for an order for a grant to himself;

(b) in the case of a citation under paragraph (2) of this rule, apply to a [district judge or] registrar for an order that a note be made on the grant that the executor in respect of whom power was reserved has been duly cited and has not appeared and that all his rights in respect of the executorship have wholly ceased; or

(c) in the case of a citation under paragraph (3) of this rule, apply to a [district judge or] registrar by summons (which shall be served on the person cited) for an order requiring such person to take a grant within a specified time or for a grant to himself or to some other person specified in the summons.

(6) An application under the last foregoing paragraph shall be supported by an affidavit showing that the citation was duly served.

(7) If the person cited has entered an appearance but has not applied for a grant under paragraph (4) of this rule, or has failed to prosecute his application with reasonable diligence, the citor may—

(a)　in the case of a citation under paragraph (1) of this rule, apply by summons to a [district judge or] registrar for an order for a grant to himself;

(b)　in the case of a citation under paragraph (2) of this rule, apply by summons to a [district judge or] registrar for an order striking out the appearance and for the endorsement on the grant of such a note as is mentioned in sub-paragraph (*b*) of paragraph (5) of this rule; or

(c)　in the case of a citation under paragraph (3) of this rule, apply by summons to a [district judge or] registrar for an order requiring the person cited to take a grant within a specified time or for a grant to himself or to some other person specified in the summons;

and the summons shall be served on the person cited.

Annotations

Paras (4), (5), (7): words in square brackets added by SI 1991 No 1876, r 7(1).

Citation to propound a will
48. (1) A citation to propound a will shall be directed to the executors named in the will and to all persons interested thereunder, and may be issued at the instance of any citor having an interest contrary to that of the executors or such other persons.

(2) If the time limited for appearance has expired, the citor may—

(a)　in the case where no person has entered an appearance, apply to a [district judge or] registrar for an order for a grant as if the will were invalid and such application shall be supported by an affidavit showing that the citation was duly served; or

(b)　in the case where no person who has entered an appearance proceeds with reasonable diligence to propound the will, apply to a [district judge or] registrar by summons, which shall be served on every person cited who has entered an appearance, for such an order as is mentioned in paragraph (*a*) above.

Annotations

Para (2): words in square brackets added by SI 1991 No 1876, r 7(1).

Address for service
49. All caveats, citations, warnings and appearances shall contain an address for service in England and Wales.

Application for order to attend for examination or for subpoena to bring in a will
50. (1) An application under section 122 of the Act for an order requiring a person to attend for examination may, unless a probate action has been commenced, be made to a [district judge or] registrar by summons which shall be served on every such person as aforesaid.

(2) An application under section 123 of the Act for the issue by a [district judge or] registrar of a subpoena to bring in a will shall be supported by an affidavit setting out the grounds of the application, and if any person served with the subpoena denies that the will is in his possession or control he may file an affidavit to that effect in the registry from which the subpoena issued.

Annotations

Words in square brackets added by SI 1991 No 1876, r 7(1).
The Act: Supreme Court Act 1981.

Grants to part of an estate under section 113 of the Act
51. An application for an order for a grant under section 113 of the Act to part of an estate may be made to a [district judge or] registrar, and shall be supported by an affidavit setting out the grounds of the application, and

(a)   stating whether the estate of the deceased is known to be insolvent; and
(b)   showing how any person entitled to a grant in respect of the whole estate in priority to the applicant has been cleared off.

Annotations

Words in square brackets added by SI 1991 No 1876, r 7(1).
  The Act: Supreme Court Act 1981.

Grants of administration under discretionary powers of court, and grants ad colligenda bona
52. An application for an order for—

(a)   a grant of administration under section 116 of the Act; or
(b)   a grant of administration ad colligenda bona,

may be made to a [district judge or] registrar and shall be supported by an affidavit setting out the grounds of the application.

Annotations

Words in square brackets added by SI 1991 No 1876, r 7(1).
  The Act: Supreme Court Act 1981.

Applications for leave to swear to death
53. An application for leave to swear to the death of a person in whose estate a grant is sought may be made to a [district judge or] registrar, and shall be supported by an affidavit setting out the grounds of the application and containing particulars of any policies of insurance effected on the life of the presumed deceased together with such further evidence as the [district judge or] registrar may require.

Annotations

Words in square brackets added by SI 1991 No 1876, r 7(1).

Grants in respect of nuncupative wills and copies of wills
54. (1) Subject to paragraph (2) below, an application for an order

admitting to proof a nuncupative will, or a will contained in a copy or reconstruction thereof where the original is not available, shall be made to a [district judge or] registrar.

(2) In any case where a will is not available owing to its being retained in the custody of a foreign court or official, a duly authenticated copy of the will may be admitted to proof without the order referred to in paragraph (1) above.

(3) An application under paragraph (1) above shall be supported by an affidavit setting out the grounds of the application, and by such evidence on affidavit as the applicant can adduce as to—

(a) the will's existence after the death of the testator or, where there is no such evidence, the facts on which the applicant relies to rebut the presumption that the will has been revoked by destruction;
(b) in respect of a nuncupative will, the contents of that will; and
(c) in respect of a reconstruction of a will, the accuracy of that reconstruction.

(4) The [district judge or] registrar may require additional evidence in the circumstances of a particular case as to due execution of the will or as to the accuracy of the copy will, and may direct that notice be given to persons who would be prejudiced by the application.

Annotations

Paras (1), (4): words in square brackets added by SI 1991 No 1876, r 7(1).

Application for certification of a will
55. (1) An application for an order that a will be rectified by virtue of section 20(1) of the Administration of Justice Act 1982 may be made to a [district judge or] registrar, unless a probate action has been commenced.

(2) The application shall be supported by an affidavit, setting out the grounds of the application, together with such evidence as can be adduced as to the testator's intentions and as to whichever of the following matters as are in issue:—

(a) in what respects the testator's intentions were not understood; or
(b) the nature of any alleged clerical error.

(3) Unless otherwise directed, notice of the application shall be given to every person having an interest under the will whose interest might be prejudiced by the rectification applied for and any comments in writing by any such person shall be exhibited to the affidavit in support of the application.

(4) If the [district judge or] registrar is satisfied that, subject to any direction to the contrary, notice has been given to every person mentioned in paragraph (3) above, and that the application is unopposed, he may order that the will be rectified accordingly.

Annotations

Paras (1), (4): words in square brackets added by SI 1991 No 1876, r 7(1).

Notice of election by surviving spouse to redeem life interest
56. (1) Where a surviving spouse who is the sole or sole surviving personal

representative of the deceased is entitled to a life interest in part of the residuary estate and elects under section 47A of the Administration of Estates Act 1925 to have the life interest redeemed, he may give written notice of the election to the [senior district judge] in pursuance of subsection (7) of that section by filing a notice in Form 6 in the Principal Registry or in the district probate registry from which the grant issued.

(2) Where the grant issued from a district probate registry, the notice shall be filed in duplicate.

(3) A notice filed under this rule shall be noted on the grant and the record and shall be open to inspection.

Annotations

Para (1): words in square brackets substituted by SI 1991 No 1876, r 7(4).

Index of grant application
57. (1) The [senior district judge] shall maintain an index of every pending application for a grant made in any registry.

(2) Notice of every application for a grant shall be sent by the registry in which the application is made to the registry in which the index is maintained and shall be in the form of a document stating the full name of the deceased and the date of his death.

(3) On receipt of the notice referred to in paragraph (2) above, the registry shall search its current index and shall give a certificate as to the result of that search to the registry which sent the notice.

(4) The requirements of paragraph (2) above shall not apply in any case in which the application for a grant is made in the registry in which the index is maintained.

(5) In this rule *registry* includes a sub-registry.

Annotations

Para (1): words in square brackets substituted by SI 1991 No 1876, r 7(4).

Inspection of copies of original wills and other documents
58. An original will or other document referred to in section 124 of the Act shall not be open to inspection if, in the opinion of a [district judge or] registrar, such inspection would be undesirable or otherwise inappropriate.

Annotations

Words in square brackets added by SI 1991 No 1876, r 7(1).
   The Act: Supreme Court Act 1981.

Issue of copies of original wills and other documents
59. Where copies are required of original wills or other documents deposited under section 124 of the Act, such copies may be facsimile copies sealed with the seal of the court and issued either as office copies or certified under the hand of a [district judge or] registrar to be true copies.

Annotations

Words in square brackets added by SI 1991 No 1876, r 7(1).
   The Act: Supreme Court Act 1981.

Taxation of costs

60. [Every bill of costs, other than a bill delivered by a solicitor to his client which falls to be taxed under the Solicitors Act 1974, shall be referred for taxation—

(a) where the order for taxation was made by a district judge, to a district judge, or to a taxing officer of the Principal Registry authorised to tax costs in accordance with Order 62, rule 19 of the Rules of the Supreme Court 1965;

(b) where the order for taxation was made by a registrar, to that registrar.]

Annotations

Substituted by SI 1991 No 1876, r 13.

Modifications: any reference to Solicitors etc modified to include references to Recognised Bodies, by the Solicitors' Incorporated Practices Order 1991, SI 1991 No 2684, arts 4, 5, Sch 1.

Power to require applications to be made by summons

61. (1) [Subject to rule 7(2),] a [district judge or] registrar may require any application to be made by summons to a [district judge or] registrar in chambers or a judge in chambers or open court.

(2) An application for an inventory and account shall be made by summons to a [district judge or] registrar.

(3) A summons for hearing by a [district judge or] registrar shall be issued out of the registry in which it is to be heard.

(4) A summons to be heard by a judge shall be issued out of the Principal Registry.

Annotations

Para (1): words in square brackets added by SI 1991 No 1876, rr 7(1), 14.

Paras (2), (3): words in square brackets added by SI 1991 No 1876, r 7(1).

Transfer of applications

62. A registrar to whom any application is made under these Rules may order the transfer of the application to another [district judge or] registrar having jurisdiction.

Annotations

Words in square brackets added by SI 1991 No 1876, r 7(1).

Power to make orders for costs

63. On any application dealt with by him on summons, the < ... > registrar shall have full power to determine by whom and to what extent the costs are to be paid.

Annotations

Words omitted revoked by SI 1991 No 1876, r 7(2).

Exercise of powers of judge during Long Vacation

64. All powers exercisable under these Rules by a judge in chambers may be exercised during the Long Vacation by a [district judge].

Annotations

Words in square brackets substituted by SI 1991 No 1876, r 7(3).

Appeals from [district judges or] registrars
65. (1) An appeal against a decision or requirement of a [district judge or] registrar shall be made by summons to a judge.

(2) If, in the case of an appeal under the last foregoing paragraph, any person besides the appellant appeared or was represented before the [district judge or] registrar from whose decision or requirement the appeal is brought, the summons shall be issued within seven days thereof for hearing on the first available day and shall be served on every such person as aforesaid.

Annotations

Words in square brackets added by SI 1991 No 1876, r 7(1), (6).

Service of summons
66. (1) A judge or [district judge] or, where the application is to be made to a district probate registrar, that registrar, may direct that a summons for the service of which no other provision is made by these Rules shall be served on such person or persons as the judge [or district judge may direct].

(2) Where by these Rules or by any direction given under the last foregoing paragraph a summons is required to be served on any person, it shall be served not less than two clear days before the day appointed for the hearing, unless a judge or [district judge or] registrar at or before the hearing dispenses with service on such terms, if any, as he may think fit.

Annotations

Para (1): words in square brackets substituted by SI 1991 No 1876, r 7(3), (7).
  Para (2): words in square brackets added by SI 1991 No 1876, r 7(1).

Notices, etc
67. Unless a [district judge or] registrar otherwise directs or these Rules otherwise provide, any notice or other document required to be given to or served on any person may be given or served in the manner prescribed by Order 65 Rule 5 of the Rules of the Supreme Court 1965.

Annotations

Words in square brackets added by SI 1991 No 1876, r 7(1).

Application to pending proceedings
68. Subject in any particular case to any direction given by a judge or [district judge or] registrar, these Rules shall apply to any proceedings which are pending on the date on which they come into force as well as to any proceedings commenced on or after that date.

Annotations

Words in square brackets added by SI 1991 No 1876, r 7(1).

APPENDIX C

Wills, Oaths and Grants

Contents

Specimen Will

THIS IS THE LAST WILL AND TESTAMENT of me **CHERRY BLOSSOM** of The Lodge Lime Grove Surbiton Surrey whereby I revoke all former wills and testamentary dispositions made by me.

1. I APPOINT my husband William David Blossom to be the sole executor of this my will but if the appointment fails (because he dies before me or before proving my Will or is unable or unwilling to act for any other reason) I appoint the partners at the date of my death in the firm of Trustalls Temple Chambers Stable Street Oxford or the firm which at that date carries on its practice to be my executors and trustees and in this Will the expression "my Executors" shall where the context admits mean and include the executor or executors trustee or trustees for the time being thereof whether original additional or substituted. I declare that any of my Executors who is engaged in a profession shall be entitled to be paid fees for work done by him or his firm on the same basis as if he were not one of my Executors but employed to act on behalf of my Executors.

2. IF my husband dies before me I appoint my sister Susan Wilson and her husband Gerald Wilson or the survivor of them and any person or persons authorised by them or the survivor of them to act after death or incapacity to be the guardians of any of my children who are under the age of eighteen years.

3. MY EXECUTORS shall hold the residue of my estate on trust either to retain or sell it and:

(a) to pay debts inheritance tax and executorship expenses and subject thereto;
(b) to pay or transfer the residue to my husband if he shall survive me but if he does not or if for any other reason this gift to him shall fail;
(c) to divide the residue of my estate equally among such of my children who shall survive me and attain the age of eighteen years but if any of them shall die before me or before attaining a vested interest leaving children then those children shall on reaching eighteen take equally the share which their parent would otherwise have taken.

4. MY EXECUTORS shall have the following powers:

(a)   to apply for the benefit of any beneficiary as my Executors think fit the whole or any part of the income from that part of my estate to which he is entitled or may in future be entitled;

(b)   to apply for the benefit of any beneficiary as my Executors think fit the whole or any part of the capital to which that beneficiary is entitled or may in future be entitled and on becoming absolutely entitled he shall bring into account any payments received under this subclause;

(c)   to invest or retain trust money and transpose investments with the same unrestricted freedom in their choice of investment as if they were absolute owners beneficially entitled and to purchase retain or improve a freehold or leasehold house or other dwelling of any nature or any share or interest therein on trust for sale (with power to postpone the sale) to be used as a residence by a beneficiary or contingent beneficiary on such terms as my Executors shall in their absolute discretion deem fit and without being liable for loss;

(e)   to exercise the power of appropriation under section 41 of the Administration of Estates Act 1925 without obtaining any of the required consents;

(f)   to insure against the loss or damage by fire or from any other risk any asset for the time being comprised in my estate to any amount and on such terms as they think fit and even though a person may be absolutely entitled to the property and to pay the premiums for such insurance out of the income or capital of my estate or the property itself and any money received by my Executors under such a policy shall be treated as if it were the proceeds of sale of the property insured.

5. I DESIRE that my body be cremated.

AS WITNESS my hand this   day of   1993.

SIGNED by the Testatrix in our ⎫
presence and attested by us in the ⎬
presence of her and of each other: ⎭

APPENDIX C2

Oath for executor

IN THE HIGH COURT OF JUSTICE

FAMILY DIVISION [PROBATE]

THE DISTRICT REGISTRY AT OXFORD

Extracted by: TRUSTALLS
Temple Chambers
Stable Street
Oxford OX1 1YL
DX:234550 OXFORD

Reference for Grant: C/B7000

IN THE ESTATE OF CHERRY BLOSSOM DECEASED

I, **WILLIAM DAVID BLOSSOM**, of The Lodge Lime Grove Oxford, chartered surveyor, make Oath and say that I believe the paper writing now produced and marked by me to contain the true and original last Will and Testament of **Cherry Blossom** of The Lodge Lime Grove Oxford deceased, who died on the 1st day of August 1993, aged 43 years, domiciled in England and Wales and that to the best of my knowledge, information and belief there was no land vested in the said deceased which was settled previously to her death (and not by her Will) and which remained settled land notwithstanding her death.

And I further make Oath and say that I am the husband of the said deceased and the sole Executor named in the said Will and that I will (i) collect, get in and administer according to the law the real and personal Estate of the said deceased; (ii) when required to do so by the Court exhibit on oath in the Court a full inventory of the said Estate to the Court; and (iii) when required to do so by the Court, deliver up the grant of probate to that Court; and that to the best of my knowledge, information and belief the gross estate passing under the grant amounts to £556,979 and the net estate amounts to £502,297.

SWORN by the above named
Deponent at Oxford

this   day of   1993

Before me,

A Commissioner for Oaths.

Oath for administrators

IN THE HIGH COURT OF JUSTICE

FAMILY DIVISION [PROBATE]

THE DISTRICT REGISTRY AT OXFORD

Extracted by: TRUSTALLS
Temple Chambers
Stable Street
Oxford OX1 1YL
DX:234550 OXFORD

Reference for Grant: C/B6800

IN THE ESTATE OF FLORENCE LLOYD DECEASED

We, Emily Lloyd of 90 Spring Road Worcester, spinster, and Elsie Eleanor Edwards of 63 Wicker Lane Hereford, married woman, make Oath and say that **Florence Lloyd** of The Gables Stone Street Hereford deceased, died on the 20th day of June 1993, aged 86 years, domiciled in England and Wales, INTESTATE, a spinster without issue or parent or any other person entitled in priority to share in the estate by virtue of any enactment; that no minority nor life interest arises under the intestacy; and that to the best of our knowledge, information and belief there was no land vested in the said deceased which was settled previously to her death and which remained settled land notwithstanding her death.

And we further make Oath and say that we are the lawful sisters of the whole blood and two of the persons entitled to share in the estate of the said Intestate and that we will (i) collect, get in and administer according to the law the real and personal Estate of the said deceased; (ii) when required to do so by the Court exhibit on oath in the Court a full inventory of the said Estate to the Court; and (iii) when required to do so by the Court, deliver up the grant of letters of administration to that Court; and that to the best of our knowledge, information and belief the gross estate passing under the grant amounts to £318,928 and the net estate amounts to £317,928.

SWORN by the above named
Deponents at Hereford

this   day of   1993

Before me,

A Commissioner for Oaths.

APPENDIX C4

Grant of probate

IN THE HIGH COURT OF JUSTICE
The District Probate Registry at Oxford

BE IT KNOWN that **CHERRY BLOSSOM**

of **The Lodge Lime Grove Oxford**

died on the **1st** day of **August 1993**
domiciled in **England and Wales**

AND BE IT FURTHER KNOWN that the last Will and Testament of the said deceased (a copy of which is annexed) was proved and registered in the Administration of all the estate which by law devolves to and vests in the personal representative of the said deceased was granted by the High Court of Justice on this date

to the Executor
> **WILLIAM DAVID BLOSSOM** of **The Lodge Lime Grove Oxford**

It is hereby certified that it appears from information supplied on the application for this grant that the gross value of the said estate in the United Kingdom amounts to £556,979 and the net value of such estate amounts to £502,297

Dated the **30th** day of **August 1993**

Probate Officer

Extracted by   **TRUSTALLS (Ref. C/B7000) Temple Chambers Stable Street Oxford OX1 2YL**

PROBATE

APPENDIX C5

Grant of administration

IN THE HIGH COURT OF JUSTICE
The District Probate Registry at Oxford

BE IT KNOWN that **FLORENCE LLOYD**

of **The Gables Stone Street Hereford**

died on the **20th** day of **June 1993**
domiciled in **England and Wales INTESTATE**

AND BE IT FURTHER KNOWN that Administration of all the estate which by law devolves to and vests in the personal representative of the said deceased was granted by the High Court of Justice on this date

to

EMILY LLOYD of **90 Spring Road Worcester**
and   **ELSIE ELEANOR EDWARDS** of **63 Wicker Lane Hereford**

It is hereby certified that it appears from information supplied on the application for this grant that the gross value of the said estate in the United Kingdom amounts to £318,928 and the net value of such estate amounts to £317,928

695

Appendix C

Dated the **21st** day of **July 1993**

District Registrar/Probate Officer

Extracted by   **TRUSTALLS (Ref. C/B6800) Temple Chambers Stable Street Oxford OX1 2YL**

ADMINISTRATION

Family Relationship Chart

As can be seen from the chart, the right to inherit on intestacy extends to persons having a grandparent in common with the deceased – subject to the detailed rules discussed in chapter 12. Those descended only from a common great-grandparent or remoter ancestor (for example, great aunts and uncles, second, third and remoter cousins) are excluded.

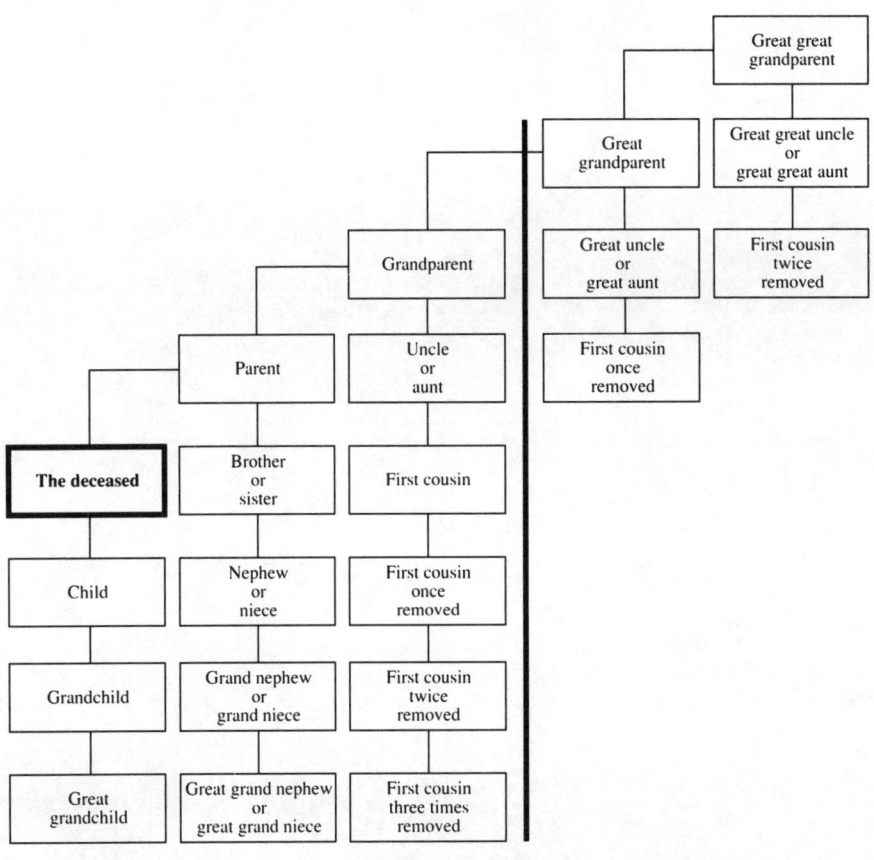

Reproduced by kind permission of Payton & Tate, international probate genealogists.

Index

Beneficiaries–*continued*
debts–*continued*
uncharged, incidence of,
application of Schedule, 32.23
assets outside Schedule, 32.20–32.21
contrary intention,
composition of categories, alteration
of, 32.57–32.62
generally, 32.52
order of categories, alteration of,
32.53–32.56
variation for some purposes only,
32.63
generally, 32.19–32.23
no contrary intention,
assets and values, 32.25
categories, 32.32–32.42
discharge of debts, 32.43–32.50
example, 32.24, 32.51
overlap, 32.26
payment of debts, property
appropriated for or charged
with, 32.38
pecuniary legacies fund, 32.39
property appointed by general
power, 32.41
property specifically devised or
bequeathed, 32.40
property undisposed of, 32.32
residuary property, 32.33–32.37
residue, provisional categorisation
of, 32.27–32.31
secured debts, 32.22
statutory schedule, 32.19
deed of variation, 30.14
disclaimer,
reasons for disclaiming,
capital gains tax saving, 30.12
generally, 30.4
income tax saving, 30.10
inheritance tax saving, 30.12
intestacy, taking of, 30.11
moral inhibitions, effect of, 30.13
onerous property, 30.6–30.9
part, disclaimer of, 30.6–30.9
unacceptable conditions, 30.5
retraction of, 30.3
right to disclaim, 30.1–30.2
distribution among,
allocation of assets, 33.22
appropriation, power of, 33.1–33.5
costs of transfer, 33.23
existing liabilities, transfer subject to,
33.6–33.7
mode of transfer,
assent,
assets other than land, 33.9
effect, 33.13–33.15
informal, in relation to land, 33.12
land, 33.10–33.11
nature, 33.8
purchaser, protection of,
33.16–33.18
other instruments, 33.19–33.20
pecuniary legacies, currency of, 33.21

Beneficiaries–*continued*
donatio mortis causa. *See* DONATIO MORTIS
CAUSA
election, doctrine of,
application of, 30.113–30.120
basis of,
equity, 30.112
implied condition, 30.110
presumed intention of testator, 30.111
method of, 30.121
rule, 30.107–30.109
time of, 30.121
extent of benefit,
acceleration,
class gifts, and, 31.19–31.20
general rule, 31.15–31.16
prevention of, 31.17–31.18
administration expenses in respect of
specific assets, 31.76
administrative powers, 31.22–31.23
annuities,
capital sum , advantages of,
31.63–31.64
capital sum in lieu, 31.52–31.58
future insufficiency, retention to cover,
31.60
interest and income, 31.46
nature, 31.51
paid from capital, 31.59
tax-free, 31.61–31.62
time for payment, 31.27
classification, importance of, 31.10
devises, 31.8
future entitlement, 31.21
income. *See* interest and income *below*
interest and income,
ancillary aspects, 31.47–31.50
annuities, 31.46
demonstrative legacy, 31.32–31.42
distinction, 31.29
general legacy, 31.32–31.42
gifts of realty, 31.30
personalty,
residuary gifts of, 31.43–31.45
specific gifts of, 31.31
legacy, types of, 31.1–31.9
options,
generally, 31.65
testator's lifetime, granted during,
31.66–31.71
will, granted by, 31.72–31.75
premature entitlement, 31.28
quantum of interest,
generally, 31.11–31.13
gift to spouses and then to issue, 31.14
refunding legacies, 31.77
time for payment,
annuities, 31.27
legacy, 31.24–31.25
potential applications, 31.26
failure of benefit,
abatement. *See* abatement *above*
accumulations, 30.79

Index

Beneficiaries–*continued*
failure of benefit–*continued*
ademption. *See* ademption *above*
commorientes. *See* commorientes *above*
condition, failure of, 30.83–30.85
death, presumption of, 30.34–30.35
deed of variation, 30.14
disclaimer. *See* disclaimer *above*
election. *See* election, doctrine of *above*
equitable doctrines, 30.86–30.121
fraud, 30.77
illegal purposes, 30.78
immoral purposes, 30.78
lapse. *See* lapse *below*
perpetuity, 30.79
public policy, rules of, 30.62–30.85
slaying testator,
benefit otherwise than by succession, 30.75
dependent gifts, 30.70
effect on slayer, 30.66
forfeiture, relief from, 30.72–30.74
joint owners, effect on, 30.71
others taking under will, effect on,
absolute gift, 30.67
future interests, 30.68
substitutory gifts, 30.69
rule, 30.63–30.65
statute, rules of, 30.62–30.85
uncertainty, 30.80–30.82
witnessing, 30.76
financial position of, 14.53–14.54
lapse,
children and issue, gift to, 30.17–30.22
corporation, gift to, 30.25
entail, gift of, 30.16
general charitable gifts, 30.24
general principle, 30.15
gift,
children and issue, to, 30.17–30.22
corporation, to, 30.25
entail, of, 30.16
general charitable, 30.24
moral obligation, in satisfaction of, 30.23
moral obligation, gift in satisfaction of, 30.23
substitutory provisions, 30.26
legacies,
availability of realty to satisfy,
post-1925 position, 32.82–32.84
pre-1926 position, 32.80
problem, 32.79
solution, 32.85
incidence of, 32.1–32.2, 32.64–32.65
lapsed share of residue, from,
post-1925 position, 32.70–32.73
pre-1926 position, 32.68
problem, 32.66–32.67
solution, 32.74
pecuniary , currency of, 33.21
pecuniary legacies fund, 32.39, 32.86–32.91
refunding, 31.77

Beneficiaries–*continued*
legacies–*continued*
satisfaction. *See* satisfaction *below*
statutory schedule, application of,
post-1925 rules, 32.76–32.77
problem, 32.75
solution, 32.78
types of, 31.1–31.9
limitation of action, 28.56–28.57
net income paid to, 36.8–36.11
presumption of death, 30.34–30.35
satisfaction,
doctrine of, 30.86
legacy,
another legacy, satisfaction by, 30.95
portion , satisfaction by, 30.103–30.106
portion debt, satisfaction of,
nature of portion, 30.96–30.98
operation of rule, effect of, 30.102
rule, 30.99–30.101
satisfaction of debt by, 30.87–30.94
slaying testator. *See* failure of benefit *above*
subsequent death of, post-death planning, 37.16
trading contract, position relating to,
authority in will, 28.16
generally, 28.15
indemnity, 28.18–28.19
intestacy, 28.17
subrogation, 28.18–28.19
will prepared by, suspicious circumstances
relating to, 5.35–5.40
witness benefiting,
professional charging clause, 6.41
prohibition of benefit, 6.35–6.39
solicitor's duty to, 6.42–6.43
supernumerary witnesses, 6.40
Bequest
meaning, 2.19
Bereavement
fatal accident, claim relating to, 23.44
Blindness
testamentary capacity, effect on, 5.25
Blood
relationship by, 11.23–11.25
Breach of trust. *See* TRUST
Brothers
whole blood, of, rights on intestacy, 12.37
Burden of proof. *See* PROOF
Burial
directions as to, 2.3
Business property
capital gains tax, 1.4
IHT. *See* INHERITANCE TAX
Capacity
mental, test of, 5.5–5.8
testamentary. *See* TESTAMENTARY CAPACITY
Capital gains tax
agricultural property, 1.4
assets,
beneficiaries, transferred to, 36.22–36.23
personal representative, sold by, 36.21
basic principles, 36.20

702

Disposition
inter vivos, power of personal
representative, 22.31
lifetime. *See* FAMILY PROVISION
meaning, 15.5–15.6
Distress
personal representative's power to levy,
23.48
Distribution of estate
beneficiaries, among. *See* BENEFICIARIES
intestacy, governed by inflexible rules
relating to, 1.1
Divorce
imaginary guideline, 14.36–14.39
Document
existence of will without, 6.56
mistake, execution by, 5.53
probate, admissible to. *See* PROBATE
revival of will, existence of document
necessary for, 9.15
revocation of will by. *See* REVOCATION OF
WILL
Domicile
deceased, of, 14.11–14.13
foreign, acquisition of, 15.2
person domiciled abroad, position of
personal representative without grant,
25.9
Donatio mortis causa
assets which may constitute subject matter
of, 34.27–34.39
death,
contemplation of, 34.5–34.10
effect of,
availability for debts, 34.44
devolution of property, 34.40–34.41
inheritance tax, 34.45–34.46
lapse, 34.42
subsequent will, effect of, 34.43
debts and liabilities, discharge of, 26.10
defective, 34.47–34.48
nature of, 34.1–34.3
net estate and, 14.80
requirements for establishing,
conditional gift on donor's death,
34.18–34.26
death, contemplation of, 34.5–34.10
generally, 34.4
subject matter of gift, delivery to donee
of, 34.11–34.17
will distinguished from, 2.13
Drink
testamentary capacity, effect on, 5.24
Drugs
testamentary capacity, effect on, 5.24
Ejusdem generis
construction of will, 10.34–10.36
Employee
remuneration of, as preferred debt, 26.35
Estate planning
discretionary trust, 37.24–37.29
intending testator, clarification of ideas of,
1.7–1.12

Estate planning–*continued*
net estate. *See* NET ESTATE
post-death,
capital gains tax, variations and
disclaimers effective for, 37.12–37.13
discretionary trust, 37.27
generally, 37.9
inheritance tax, variations and
disclaimers effective for, 37.10–37.11
nil-rate band, taking advantage of, 37.15
reliefs, use of, 37.17
subsequent death of beneficiary, 37.16
technicality, taking advantage of, 37.18
use of provisions, 37.14–37.18
pre-death,
charged debts, 37.7–37.8
exemptions, use of, 37.4
generally, 37.1–37.3
reliefs, use of, 37.5–37.6
succession as integral part of, 1.3
two-year power of appointment,
capital gains tax implications, 37.23
generally, 37.19
inheritance tax implications, 37.20–37.22
will in context of, 1.1–1.12
Estoppel
proprietary, doctrine of, 3.21–3.23
Evidence
extrinsic, use in construction of will,
admissible evidence, nature of,
generally, 10.58
persons dying after 1982, 10.62
persons dying before 1983, 10.59–10.61
ambiguity,
circumstances, in light of, 10.52–10.54
face of will, on, 10.51
meaningless provisions, 10.55–10.56
armchair rule, 10.47–10.50
equitable presumptions, evidence to
rebut, 10.57
general rule, 10.46
lost will, reconstruction of, 18.50–18.51
probate action, in,
attesting witness, 20.11–20.14
declaration by testator,
destroyed will, 20.21–20.24
generally, 20.16–20.20
lost will, 20.21–20.24
other evidence, 20.15
Exclusion order
family provision, relating to, 14.22
Executor
acceptance, 17.30–17.32
appointment of,
acceptance, 17.30–17.32
chain of representation, 17.6–17.13
conditional, 17.25
executor de son tort, 17.28
express, 17.21
generally, 2.3
implied, 17.22–17.24
ineffective, 17.29
life interest, during, 17.4

Land–*continued*
  settled. *See* SETTLED LAND
Lapse
  beneficiaries, position of. *See*
    BENEFICIARIES
Law Society
  solicitor, will confers substantial benefit on,
    5.40n
Lease
  contingent liabilities,
    assignee, liability as, 26.50–26.52
    entry into possession, liability after,
      26.53
    generally, 26.49
  personal representative, liability of,
    28.22–28.23
Leasehold
  personal representative, devolution on,
    23.18
Leasehold property
  personal representative, devolution on,
    23.31
Legacy
  beneficiaries, position of. *See*
    BENEFICIARIES
Legitimate relations. *See* RELATIONSHIPS
Legitimated children. *See* CHILDREN
Legitio portio
  principle of, 14.1n
Liabilities
  contingent,
    generally, 26.46–26.48
    lease,
      assignee, liability as, 26.50–26.52
      entry into possession, liability after,
        26.53
      generally, 26.49
  discharge of. *See* PERSONAL
    REPRESENTATIVE
Life interest
  appointment of executor during, 17.4
  capital payment in lieu of, right to require,
    12.14–12.15
  intestacy after,
    partial intestacy rules, application of,
      13.17–13.20
    valuation of life interest, 13.21
  valuation of, 13.21
Life tenant
  death of, land ceasing to be settled land
    following, 24.3–24.5
Lifetime disposition
  family provision and. *See* FAMILY
    PROVISION
Lifetime gift. *See* GIFT INTER VIVOS
Lifetime transfer. *See* INHERITANCE TAX
Limitation of action
  beneficiary, claim by, 28.56–28.57
  creditor, claim by, 28.53–28.55
Lost will
  formalities of execution, 18.52–18.53
  non-contentious probate, 18.47–18.54
  probate action, evidence in, 20.21–20.24

Lost will–*continued*
  rebuttal of presumption of revocation,
    18.54
  reconstruction,
    evidence of, 18.50–18.51
    generally, 18.48–18.49
Lucid interval
  meaning, 5.11
  will made during, 5.10–5.11
Lunatic
  lucid interval, will made during, 5.11
Maintenance. *See* FAMILY PROVISION
Making will
  acknowledgment,
    attestation, of, 6.31
    signature, of, 6.22–6.24
  attestation,
    acknowledgment, 6.31
    attest and sign, 6.28–6.30
    clause, 6.34
    presence of testator, in, 6.32–6.33
    requirements, 6.27
  contract to make will, 3.3–3.4
  foreign formalities, will executed in
    accordance with, 6.47–6.50
  formal requirements,
    attestation,
      acknowledgment, 6.31
      attest and sign, 6.28–6.30
      clause, 6.34
      requirements, 6.27
      testator, in presence of, 6.32–6.33
    beneficiary witness,
      professional charging clause, 6.41
      prohibition of benefit, 6.35–6.39
      solicitor's duty to, 6.42–6.43
      supernumerary witnesses, 6.40
    existence without document, 6.56
    foreign, will executed in accordance with,
      6.47–6.50
    generally, 6.1–6.2
    incorporation by reference,
      effect of, 6.63–6.64
      existence of document,
        generally, 6.58
        reference to, 6.59–6.61
      identification of document, 6.62
      requirements,
        existence of document, 6.58
        generally, 6.57
        identification of document, 6.62
        reference to existence of document,
          6.59–6.61
      statutory will forms, 6.67
      use of doctrine, 6.65–6.66
    international will, 6.51–6.54
    mental patient, execution of will of,
      6.44–6.45
    need for, 6.3–6.9
    overcoming formal defects, 6.55
    presence,
      concept of, 6.25–6.26
      testator, of, attestation in, 6.32–6.33

Index